THE MEMOIRS
OF FIELD-MARSHAL MONTGOMERY

The author when Chief of the Imperial General Staff, 1947

THE
MEMOIRS

OF

FIELD-MARSHAL THE VISCOUNT

MONTGOMERY

OF ALAMEIN, K.G.

COLLINS
ST JAMES'S PLACE, LONDON
1958

Yet man is born unto trouble, as
the sparks fly upward

JOB 5, 7

Contents

CONTENTS

List of Plates

9

LIST OF PLATES

List of Maps

Foreword

THIS BOOK does not owe its inception to any personal inclination to authorship, or to any wish to achieve further publicity. I write it because of many suggestions that such a book of memoirs is needed. I aim to give to future generations the impressions I have gained in a life that has been full of interest, and to define the principles under which I have considered it my duty to think and act.

Every word of the book was written in the first instance in pencil in my own handwriting. That being done, and the chapters typed in turn, they were read by three trusted friends whose opinions I value. The chapters were re-drafted by me in the light of their comments and suggestions. Finally, the complete book was read through by the same three, for balance and accuracy.

Chief among the three was Brigadier E. T. Williams, Warden of Rhodes House, Oxford—frequently referred to in the book as Bill Williams. I owe him a great debt of gratitude for the time he gave to reading and comment.

Next was Sir James Grigg, also referred to in the book; his comments and suggestions were invaluable. And last was Sir Arthur Bryant; this great historian gave much of his time to reading the chapters.

To these three I extend my grateful thanks.

I am grateful to those who typed the chapters and helped in organising the maps and photographs. Again, I extend my gratitude for permission to publish extracts from letters and books, and I apologise in any case where such permission has been overlooked.

I recognise—by the quotation which is at the beginning of

this book—that I have often been a controversial figure. But my thoughts, actions, mistakes have been but human. Throughout my life and conduct my criterion has been not the approval of others nor of the world; it has been my inward convictions, my duty and my conscience. I have never been afraid to say what I believed to be right and to stand firm in that belief. This has often got me into trouble. I have not attempted to answer my critics but rather to tell the story of my long and enjoyable military life as I see it, and as simply as possible. Some of my comrades-in-arms of the Second World War have told their story about those days; this is mine.

I have tried to explain what seems to me important and to confine the story to matters about which my knowledge is first-hand. Whatever the book may lack in literary style, it will therefore have, it is my hope, the merit of truth.

Montgomery of Alamein

F.M.

Isington Mill,
Alton, Hampshire
September 1958

CHAPTER I

BOYHOOD DAYS

I was born in London, in St. Mark's Vicarage, Kennington Oval, on 17th November 1887.

Sir Winston Churchill in the first volume of *Marlborough, His Life and Times* wrote thus about the unhappy childhood of some men: "The stern compression of circumstances, the twinges of adversity, the spur of slights and taunts in early years, are needed to evoke that ruthless fixity of purpose and tenacious mother-wit without which great actions are seldom accomplished."

Certainly I can say that my own childhood was unhappy. This was due to a clash of wills between my mother and myself. My early life was a series of fierce battles, from which my mother invariably emerged the victor. If I could not be seen anywhere, she would say— "Go and find out what Bernard is doing and tell him to stop it." But the constant defeats and the beatings with a cane, and these were frequent, in no way deterred me. I got no sympathy from my two elder brothers; they were more pliable, more flexible in disposition, and they easily accepted the inevitable. From my eldest sister, who was next in the family after myself, I received considerable help and sympathy; but, in the main, the trouble had to be suffered by myself alone. I never lied about my misdeeds; I took my punishment. There were obvious faults on both sides. For myself, although I began to know fear early in life, much too early, the net result of the treatment was probably beneficial. If my strong will and indiscipline had gone unchecked, the result might have been even more intolerable than some people have found me. But I have often wondered whether my mother's treatment for me was not a bit too much of a good thing: whether, in fact, it was a good thing at all. I rather doubt it.

I suppose we were an average Victorian family. My mother was engaged at the age of fourteen and married my father in July 1881, when she was scarcely out of the schoolroom. Her seventeenth birthday was on the 23rd August 1881, one month after her wedding day. My father was then Vicar of St. Mark's, Kennington Oval, and my mother was plunged at once into the activities of the wife of a busy London vicar.

Children soon appeared. Five were born between 1881 and 1889, in which year my father was appointed Bishop of Tasmania—five children before my mother had reached the age of twenty-five. I was the fourth. There was then a gap of seven years, when two more were born in Tasmania; then another gap of five years still in Tasmania, when another boy arrived. The last, my youngest brother Brian, was born after we had left Tasmania and were back in London.

So my mother bore nine children in all. The eldest, a girl, died just after we arrived in Tasmania, and one of my younger brothers died in 1909 when I was serving with my regiment in India. That left seven, and all seven are alive today.

As if this large family was not enough, we always had other children living with us. In St. Mark's Vicarage in Kennington were three small boys, distant cousins, whose parents were in India. In Tasmania, cousins arrived from England who were delicate and needed Tasmanian air. In London after our return from Tasmania, there was always someone other than ourselves.

It was really impossible for my mother to cope with her work as the wife of a London vicar or as a Bishop's wife, and also devote her time to her children, and to the others who lived with us. Her method of dealing with the problem was to impose rigid discipline on the family and thus have time for her duties in the parish or diocese, duties which took first place. There were definite rules for us children; these had to be obeyed; disobedience brought swift punishment. A less rigid discipline, and more affectionate understanding, might have wrought better, certainly different, results in me. My brothers and sisters were not so difficult; they were more amenable to the régime and gave no trouble. I was the bad boy of the family, the rebellious one, and as a result I learnt early to stand or fall on my own. We elder ones certainly never became a united family. Possibly the younger ones did, because my mother mellowed with age.

Against this curious background must be set certain rewarding facts. We have all kept on the rails. There have been no scandals in the family; none of us have appeared in the police courts or gone to prison; none of us have been in the divorce courts. An uninteresting family, some might say. Maybe, and if that was my mother's object she certainly achieved it. But there was an absence of affectionate understanding of the problems facing the young, certainly as far as the five elder children were concerned. For the younger ones things always seemed to me to be easier; it may have been that my mother was exhausted with dealing with her elder children, especially with myself. But when all is said and done, my mother was a most remarkable woman, with a strong and sterling character. She brought her family up in her own way; she taught us to speak the truth, come what may, and so far as my knowledge goes none of her children have ever done anything which would have caused her shame. She made me afraid of her when I was a child and a young boy. Then the time came when her authority could no longer be exercised. Fear then disappeared, and respect took its place. From the time I joined the Army until my mother died, I had an immense and growing respect for her wonderful character. And it became clear to me that my early troubles were mostly my own fault.

However, it is not surprising that under such conditions all my childish affection and love was given to my father. I worshipped him. He was always a friend. If ever there was a saint on this earth, it was my father. He got bullied a good deal by my mother and she could always make him do what she wanted. She ran all the family finances and gave my father ten shillings a week; this sum had to include his daily lunch at the Athenaeum, and he was severely cross-examined if he meekly asked for another shilling or two before the end of the week. Poor dear man, I never thought his last few years were very happy; he was never allowed to do as he liked and he was not given the care and nursing which might have prolonged his life. My mother nursed him herself when he could not move, but she was not a good nurse. He died in 1932 when I was commanding the 1st Battalion The Royal Warwickshire Regiment in Egypt. It was a tremendous loss for me. The three outstanding human beings in my life have been my father, my wife, and my son. When my father died in 1932, I little thought that five years later I would be left alone with my son.

We came home from Tasmania late in 1901, and in January 1902 my brother Donald and myself were sent to St. Paul's School in London. My age was now fourteen and I had received no preparation for school life; my education in Tasmania had been in the hands of tutors imported from England. I had little learning and practically

19

no culture. We were " Colonials," with all that that meant in England in those days. I could swim like a fish and was strong, tough, and very fit; but cricket and football, the chief games of all English schools, were unknown to me.

I hurled myself into sport and in little over three years became Captain of the Rugby XV, and in the Cricket XI. The same results were not apparent on the scholastic side.

In English I was described as follows:

1902   essays very weak.
1903   feeble.
1904   very weak; can't write essays.
1905   tolerable; his essays are sensible but he has no notion of style.
1906   pretty fair.

Today I should say that my English is at least clear; people may not agree with what I say but at least they know what I am saying. I may be wrong; but I claim that I am clear. People may misunderstand what I am doing but I am willing to bet that they do not misunderstand what I am saying. At least they know quite well what they are disagreeing with.

After I had been three years at St. Paul's my school report described me as backward for my age, and added: " To have a serious chance for Sandhurst, he must give more time for work."

This report was rather a shock and it was clear I must get down to work if I was going to get a commission in the Army. This I did, and passed into Sandhurst half-way up the list without any difficulty. St. Paul's is a very good school for work so long as you want to learn; in my case, once the intention and the urge was clear the masters did the rest and for this I shall always be grateful. I was very happy at St. Paul's School. For the first time in my life leadership and authority came my way; both were eagerly seized and both were exercised in accordance with my own limited ideas, and possibly badly. For the first time I could plan my own battles (on the football field) and there were some fierce contests. Some of my contemporaries have stated that my tactics were unusual and the following article appeared in the School magazine in November 1906. I should explain that my nickname at St. Paul's was Monkey.

OUR UNNATURAL HISTORY COLUMN

No. 1—*The Monkey*

"This intelligent animal makes its nest in football fields, football vests, and other such accessible resorts. It is vicious, of unflagging energy, and much feared by the neighbouring animals owing to its unfortunate tendency to pull out the top hair of the head. This it calls 'tackling.' It may sometimes be seen in the company of some of them, taking a short run, and, in sheer exuberance of animal spirits, tossing a cocoanut from hand to hand! To foreign fauna it shows no mercy, stamping on their heads and twisting their necks, and doing many other inconceivable atrocities with a view, no doubt, to proving its patriotism.

To hunt this animal is a dangerous undertaking. It runs strongly and hard, straight at you, and never falters, holding a cocoanut in its hand and accompanied by one of its companions. But just as the unlucky sportsman is expecting a blow, the cocoanut is transferred to the companion, and the two run past the bewildered would-be Nimrod.

So it is advisable that none hunt the monkey. Even if caught he is not good eating. He lives on doughnuts. If it is decided to neglect this advice, the sportsman should first be scalped, so as to avoid being collared."

I had little pocket money in those days; my parents were poor; we were a large family; and there was little spare cash for us boys. But we had enough and we all certainly learnt the value of money when young.

I was nineteen when I left St. Paul's School. My time there was most valuable as my first experience of life in a larger community than was possible in the home. The imprint of a school should be on a boy's character, his habits and qualities, rather than on his capabilities whether they be intellectual or athletic. In a public school there is more freedom than is experienced in a preparatory or private school; the danger is that a boy should equate freedom with laxity. This is what happened to me, until I was brought up with a jerk by a bad report. St. Paul's left its imprint on my character; I was sorry to leave, but not so sorry as to lose my sense of proportion. For pleasant as school is, it is only a stepping stone. Life lies ahead, and for me the next step was Sandhurst. "When I became a man, I put away childish things"—some of them, anyway.

And so I went to Sandhurst in January 1907.

Looking back on their boyhood, some people would no doubt be able to suggest where things might have been changed for the better. Briefly, in my own case, two matters cannot have been right: both due to the fact that my mother ran the family and my father stood back. First, I began to know fear when very young and gradually withdrew into my own shell and battled on alone. This without doubt had a tremendous effect on the subsequent development of my character. Secondly, I was thrown into a large public school without having had certain facts of life explained to me; I began to learn them for myself in the rough and tumble of school life, and not finally until I went to Sandhurst at the age of nineteen. This neglect might have had bad results; but luckily, I don't think it did. Even so, I wouldn't let it happen to others.

When I went to school in London I had learnt to play a lone hand, and to stand or fall alone. One had become self-sufficient, intolerant of authority and steeled to take punishment.

By the time I left school a very important principle had just begun to penetrate my brain. That was that life is a stern struggle, and a boy has to be able to stand up to the buffeting and set-backs. There are many attributes which he must acquire if he is to succeed: two are vital, hard work and absolute integrity. The need for a religious background had not yet begun to become apparent to me. My father had always hoped that I would become a clergyman. That did not happen and I well recall his disappointment when I told him that I wanted to be a soldier. He never attempted to dissuade me; he accepted what he must have thought was the inevitable; and if he could speak to me today I think he would say that it was better that way. If I had my life over again I would not choose differently. I would be a soldier.

CHAPTER 2

MY EARLY LIFE IN THE ARMY

IN 1907 entrance to the Royal Military College, Sandhurst, was by competitive examination. There was first a qualifying examination in which it was necessary to show a certain minimum standard of mental ability; the competitive examination followed a year or so later. These two hurdles were negotiated without difficulty, and in the competitive examination my place was 72 out of some 170 vacancies. I was astonished to find later that a large number of my fellow cadets had found it necessary to leave school early and go to a crammer in order to ensure success in the competitive entrance examination.

In those days the Army did not attract the best brains in the country. Army life was expensive and it was not possible to live on one's pay. It was generally considered that a private income or allowance of at least £100 a year was necessary, even in one of the so-called less fashionable County regiments. In the cavalry, and in the more fashionable infantry regiments, an income of up to £300 or £400 was demanded before one was accepted. These financial matters were not known to me when I decided on the Army as my career; nobody had explained them to me or to my parents. I learned them at Sandhurst when it became necessary to consider the regiment of one's choice, and this was not until about halfway through the course at the college.

The fees at Sandhurst were £150 a year for the son of a civilian and this included board and lodging, and all necessary expenses. But additional pocket money was essential and after some discussion my parents agreed to allow me £2 a month; this was also to continue in the holidays, making my personal income £24 a year.

It is doubtful if many cadets were as poor as myself; but I managed. Those were the days when the wrist watch was beginning to appear and they could be bought in the College canteen; most cadets acquired

23

one. I used to look with envy at those watches, but they were not for me; I did not possess a wrist watch till just before the beginning of the war in 1914. Now I suppose every boy has one at the age of seven or eight.

Outside attractions being denied to me for want of money, I plunged into games and work. On going to St. Paul's in 1902, I had concentrated on games; now work was added, and this was due to the sharp jolt I had received on being told the truth about my idleness at school. I very soon became a member of the Rugby XV, and played against the R.M.A., Woolwich, in December 1907 when we inflicted a severe defeat on that establishment.

In the realm of work, to begin with things went well. The custom then was to select some of the outstanding juniors, or first term cadets, and to promote them to lance-corporal after six weeks at the College. This was considered a great distinction; the cadets thus selected were reckoned to be better than their fellows and to have shown early the essential qualities necessary for a first class officer in the Army. These lance-corporals always became sergeants in their second term, wearing a red sash, and one or two became colour-sergeants carrying a sword; colour-sergeant was the highest rank for a cadet.

I was selected to be a lance-corporal. I suppose this must have gone to my head; at any rate my downfall began from that moment. The Junior Division of " B " Company, my company at the College, contained a pretty tough and rowdy crowd and my authority as a lance-corporal caused me to take a lead in their activities. We began a war with the juniors of " A " Company who lived in the storey above us; we carried the war into the areas of other companies living farther away down the passages. Our company became known as " Bloody B," which was probably a very good name for it. Fierce battles were fought in the passages after dark; pokers and similar weapons were used and cadets often retired to hospital for repairs. This state of affairs obviously could not continue, even at Sandhurst in 1907 when the officers kept well clear of the activities of the cadets when off duty.

Attention began to concentrate on " Bloody B " and on myself. The climax came when during the ragging of an unpopular cadet I set fire to the tail of his shirt as he was undressing; he got badly burnt behind, retired to hospital, and was unable to sit down with any comfort for some time. He behaved in an exemplary manner in refusing to disclose the author of his ill-treatment, but it was no good; one's sins are always found out in the end and I was reduced to the ranks.

A paragraph appeared in College Orders to the effect that Lance-Corporal Montgomery reverted to the rank of gentleman-cadet, no reason being given. My mother came down to Sandhurst and discussed my future with the Commandant. She learnt that it had been decided at one time to make me the next colour-sergeant of "B" Company. But this was all now finished; I had fallen from favour and would be lucky to pass out of the College at all. My Company Commander turned against me; no wonder. But there was one staunch friend among the Company Officers, a major in the Royal Scots Fusiliers called Forbes. He was my friend and adviser and it is probably due to his protection and advice that I remained at Sandhurst, turned over a new leaf, and survived to make good. If he is alive today and reads these lines he will learn of my debt to him and of my gratitude. I have often wondered what the future would have held for me if I had been made colour-sergeant of "B" Company at Sandhurst. I personally know of no case of a cadet who became the head of his company rising later to the highest rank in the Army. Possibly they developed too soon and then fizzled out.

That was the second jolt I had received and this time it was clear to me that the repercussions could be serious. A number of selected cadets of my batch were to be passed out in December 1907, after one year at the College; my name was not included in the lucky number and I remained on for another six months. But now I had learnt my lesson, and this time for good. I worked really hard during those six months and was determined to pass out high.

It had for some time been clear to me that I could not serve in England for financial reasons. My parents could give me no allowance once I was commissioned into the Army, and it would be necessary to live entirely on my pay. This would be 5s. 3d. a day as a second lieutenant and 6s. 6d. a day when promoted lieutenant; a young officer could not possibly live on this income as his monthly mess bill alone could not be less than £10.

Promotion was not by length of service as it is now, but depended on vacancies, and I had heard of lieutenants in the Army of nineteen years' service. In India it was different; the pay in the Indian Army was good, and one could even live on one's pay in a British battalion stationed in that country. I therefore put down my name for the Indian Army. There was very keen competition because of the financial reasons I have already outlined, and it was necessary to pass out within the first 30 to be sure of a vacancy; on very rare occasions No. 35 had been known to get the Indian Army.

When the results were announced, my name was No. 36. I had failed to get the Indian Army. I was bitterly disappointed. All cadets were required to put down a second choice. I had no military background and no County connection; but it was essential to get to India where I could live on my pay in a British battalion, so I put my name down for the Royal Warwickshire Regiment which had one of its two regular battalions in that country. I have often been asked why I chose this regiment. The first reason was that it had an attractive cap badge which I admired; the second was that enquiries I then made gave me to understand that it was a good, sound English County Regiment and not one of the more expensive ones. My placing in the final list at Sandhurst was such that once the Indian Army candidates had been taken, I was certain of the regiment of my choice, provided it would accept me. Accept me it did; and I joined the Royal Warwickshire, the senior of a batch of three cadets from Sandhurst. I have never regretted my choice. I learnt the foundations of the military art in my regiment; I was encouraged to work hard by the Adjutant and my first Company Commander. The former, Colonel C. R. Macdonald, is now retired, being well over eighty, and he has always been one of my greatest friends; I hope that I have been able to repay in later life some of the interest and kindness received from him in my early days in the regiment. The future of a young officer in the Army depends largely on the influences he comes under when he joins from Sandhurst. I have always counted myself lucky that among a somewhat curious collection of officers there were some who loved soldiering for its own sake and were prepared to help anyone else who thought the same.

And now I am the Colonel of my regiment, a tremendous honour which I never thought would come my way when I joined the 1st Battalion at Peshawar, on the North-West Frontier of India, in December 1908. I was then just twenty-one, older than most newly joined subalterns. The reason was that I had stayed on longer than most at school because of idleness, and did not go to Sandhurst till I was over nineteen; and I had stayed on an extra six months at Sandhurst, also because of idleness. Twice I had nearly crashed and twice I had been saved by good luck and good friends.

Possibly at this stage of my life I did not realise how lucky I was. I had come from a good home and my parents had given me the best education they could afford; there had never been very much spare money for luxuries and that taught us children the value of money when young. I had no complaint when my parents could not give me an allowance after I had left Sandhurst and joined the Army; it is very good for a boy when launched in life to earn his own living. My own son was educated at a first class Preparatory School, at Winchester, and at Trinity, Cambridge; it had always been agreed between us that on leaving Cambridge he would earn his own living, and he has done so without any further allowance from me.

From the time I joined the Army in 1908 until the present day, I have never had any money except what I earned. This I have never regretted. Later on when I was Chief of the Imperial General Staff under the Socialist Government and worked closely with my political masters in Whitehall, I sometimes reminded Labour Ministers of this fact when they seemed to imagine that I was one of the " idle rich." They knew I wasn't idle; but I had to assure them that I wasn't rich either.

Life in the British Army in the days before World War I was very different from what it is now. Certain things one had to do because tradition demanded it. When I first entered the ante-room of the Officers' Mess of my regiment in Peshawar, there was one other officer in the room. He immediately said " Have a drink " and rang the bell for the waiter. It was mid-winter on the frontier of India, and intensely cold; I was not thirsty. But two whiskies and sodas arrived and there was no escape; I drank one, and tasted alcohol for the first time in my life.

All the newly joined officers had to call on all the other units in the garrison and leave cards at the Officers' Messes. You were offered a drink in each mess and it was explained to me that these must never be declined; it was also explained that you must never ask for a lemon squash or a soft drink. An afternoon spent in calling on regimental officers' messes resulted in a considerable consumption of alcohol, and a young officer was soon taught to drink. I have always disliked alcohol since.

I remember well my first interview with the senior subaltern of the battalion. In those days the senior subaltern was a powerful figure but has nowadays lost his power and prestige.

One of the main points he impressed on us newly joined subalterns was that at dinner in the mess at night we must never ask a waiter for a drink till the fish had been served. I had never before attended a dinner where there was a fish course in addition to a main meat course, so I wondered what was going to happen. Dinner in the mess at night was an imposing ceremony. The President and Vice-President for the week sat at opposite ends of the long table which was laden with the regimental silver, all the officers being in scarlet mess jackets. These two officials could not get up and leave the table until every officer had left, and I often sat as a lonely figure in the Vice-President's chair while two old majors at the President's end of the table exchanged stories over their port far into the night. Sometimes a kindly President would tell the young Vice-President he need not wait, but this seldom happened; it was considered that young officers must be disciplined in these matters and taught to observe the traditions. Perhaps it was good for me, but I did not think so at the time.

At breakfast in the mess nobody spoke. Some of the senior officers were not feeling very well at that hour of the day. One very senior major refused to sit at the main table; he sat instead at a small table in a corner of the room by himself, facing the wall and with his back to the other officers. Then there was the senior officer who wanted to get married. When he had located a suitable lady he would spend what he considered was a reasonable sum in her entertainment. His limit was £100; that sum spent, if the lady's resistance was not broken down, he transferred his amorous activities elsewhere.

The transport of the battalion was mule carts and mule pack animals, and as I knew nothing about mules I was sent on a course to learn. At the end of the course there was an oral examination which was conducted by an outside examiner. Since there appeared to be no suitable officer in the Peshawar garrison, an outside examiner came up from central India; he had obviously been very many years in the country and had a face like a bottle of port. He looked as if he lived almost entirely on suction; nevertheless he was considered to be the greatest living expert on mules and their habits.

I appeared before this amazing man for my oral examination. He looked at me with one bloodshot eye and said: " Question No. 1: How many times in each 24 hours are the bowels of a mule moved? "

This question was not one which I had expected, nor did it seem to me at the time that it was a problem which need receive any great attention by an ambitious young officer who was keen to get to grips with his profession. But I was wrong; it did matter. There was an awkward silence. My whole future was at stake; I had hoped that one day I might be a major with a similar crown to his on my shoulder; I saw my army career ending in disaster. In desperation I cast my mind back to the mule lines, with the animals patiently standing in the hot sun. How many times? Would it be three times in the morning, and three in the afternoon? And at night possibly the bladder but not the bowels?

The examiner said: " Are you ready? " I said: " Yes; six times."
He said: " No; Question No. 1 failed; no marks."
I said: " What is the right answer? " He told me it was eight times.

I then said: " It doesn't seem to me, Sir, to matter very much whether it is six or eight."

He replied: " Don't be impertinent, Question No. 2."

I passed the examination in the end, and returned to my regiment with that crown seeming after all to be just possible but also with the firm hope that there would be no more hurdles of that sort to be jumped.

Soldiering in India seemed to me at that time to lack something. I saw a good deal of the Indian Army. The men were splendid; they were natural soldiers and as good material as anyone could want. The British officers were not all so good. The basic trouble was a beastly climate and the absence of contact with Europe; they tended to age rapidly after about forty-five. An expression heard frequently was that so-and-so was a " good mixer." A good mixer of drinks, I came to believe, for it soon appeared to me that a good mixer was a man who had never been known to refuse a drink. My observations led me to think that a British officer would need to be a man of strong character to spend, say, thirty years in the hot climate of India and yet retain his energy and vitality. Some did so and emerged as fit for the highest commands in peace and war; such a one was Slim.

Overall, by the time I left India in 1913 I was glad that fate had decided against my passing high enough out of Sandhurst to be elected for the Indian Army.

It was true that those who passed the highest out of Sandhurst were taken for the Indian Army; but all of those were not necessarily the best cadets. The good ones had to be supremely good to survive the conditions of life in India, and the climate, and few did so; I feel certain that I should not have done so myself.

The battalion left Peshawar at the end of 1910 and moved to Bombay for the last two years of its foreign service tour. I had now begun to work hard and seriously. Looking back, I would put this period as the time when it was becoming apparent to me that to succeed one must master one's profession. It was clear that the senior regimental officers were not able to give any help in the matter since their knowledge was confined almost entirely to what went on at battalion level; they had little or no knowledge of other matters. When the battalion arrived at a new station the first question the C.O. would ask was: "How does the General like the attack done?"

And the attack was carried out in that way; whatever might be the conditions of ground, enemy, or any other factor. At this time there did seem to me to be something lacking in the whole business, but I was not able to analyse the problem and decide what exactly was wrong; nor did I bother unduly about it. I was happy in the battalion and I had become devoted to the British soldier. As for the officers, it was not fashionable to study war and we were not allowed to talk about our profession in the Officers' Mess.

While in Bombay I got mixed up in a row at the Royal Bombay Yacht Club. An officer in the battalion, Captain R. Wood, a bachelor, gave a dinner party at the Club to three young subalterns, of whom I was one. Wood, being an old and staid captain, went home early and left us three subalterns to it. The next morning the senior of our party received the following letter from the Secretary of the Club:

"It has been reported to me by several members of the Club that last evening after dinner you and your friends behaved in a most ungentlemanly and uproarious way in the bar of the Royal Bombay Yacht Club between the hours of 10.30 p.m. and 2 a.m., shouting loudly, beating the brass topped bar tables and drumming on them. This conduct caused great annoyance and disgust to members who were playing billiards and to other members playing cards upstairs. I am informed that your shouts and cries and drummings could be heard all over the club building. When the Hall Porter of the Club went to you, pointing out the rule which prohibits such disgraceful and unseemly proceedings in the Club, you apparently paid no attention to him but continued as before. The Hall Porter then reported to me. When I arrived I found that the officers concerned had left and the disturbance had, for the time, ceased.

"I have to refer you to By-Law VII which you have broken. The occurrence will be reported to the Committee of the Club and will be dealt with. The officer chiefly concerned in the uproarious proceedings, in addition to yourself, was Lieut. B. L. Montgomery."

The battalion returned to England in 1913 and an officer of our 2nd Battalion was posted to it who had just completed the two-year course at the Staff College at Camberley. His name was Captain Lefroy. He was a bachelor and I used to have long talks with him about the Army and what was wrong with it, and especially how one could get to real grips with the military art. He was interested at once, and helped me tremendously with advice about what books to read and how to study. I think it was Lefroy who first showed me the path to tread and encouraged my youthful ambition. He was killed later in the 1914-18 war and was a great loss to me and to the Army.

All this goes to show how important it is for a young officer to come in contact with the best type of officer and the right influences early in his military career. In the conditions which existed in the British Army between the South African war and the 1914-18 war, it was entirely a matter of luck whether this would happen. In my case the ambition was there, and the urge to master my profession. But it required advice and encouragement from the right people to set me on the road, and once that was forthcoming it was plainer sailing.

In August 1914, I was a full lieutenant of twenty-six. It was to take the experiences of the 1914-18 war to show me what was wrong in the Army. My battalion mobilised at Shorncliffe. The mobilisation scheme provided, amongst other things, that all officers' swords were to go to the armourers' shop on the third day of mobilisation to be sharpened. It was not clear to me why, since I had never used my sword except for saluting. But of course I obeyed the order and my sword was made sharp for war. The C.O. said that in war it was advisable to have short hair since it was then easier to keep it clean; he had all his hair removed with the clippers by the regimental barber and looked an amazing sight; personally I had mine cut decently by a barber in Folkestone. Being totally ignorant about war, I asked the C.O. if it was necessary to take any money with me; he said money was useless in war as everything was provided for you. I was somewhat uncertain about this and decided to take ten pounds with me in gold. Later I was to find this invaluable, and was glad I had not followed his advice about either hair or money.

We crossed over to France as part of the 4th Division. We missed the battle of Mons by a few days, and moved forward by march route up towards Le Cateau. On the early morning of the 26th August 1914, the 10th Brigade to which my battalion belonged was bivouacked in the cornfields near the village of Haucourt after a long night march. One battalion was forward on a hill, covering the remainder of the brigade in the valley behind; we could see the soldiers having breakfast, their rifles being piled. That battalion was suddenly surprised by the Germans and fire opened on it at short range; it withdrew rapidly down the hill towards us, in great disorder.

Our battalion was deployed in two lines; my company and one other were forward, with the remaining two companies out of sight some hundred yards to the rear. The C.O. galloped up to us forward companies and shouted to us to attack the enemy on the forward hill at once. This was the only order; there was no reconnaissance, no plan, no covering fire. We rushed up the hill, came under heavy fire, my Company Commander was wounded and there were many casualties. Nobody knew what to do, so we returned to the original position from which we had begun to attack. If this was real war it struck me as most curious and did not seem to make any sense against the background of what I had been reading.

The subsequent days were very unpleasant and the story of them is contained in what is known as the " Retreat from Mons." For my part, the two forward companies which had made the attack I have just mentioned received no further orders; we were left behind when the retreat began and for three days we marched between the German cavalry screen and their main columns following behind, moving mostly by night and hiding by day. In command of our party was a first class regimental officer, Major A. J. Poole, and it was due entirely to him that we finally got back to the British Expeditionary Force and joined up with our battalion. We then heard that our C.O. had been cashiered, as also had another C.O. in the Brigade, and Poole took command. Our C.O. was Lieut.-Colonel Elkington; on being cashiered he joined the French Foreign Legion, where he made good in a magnificent manner.

Such was the beginning of my experience of war. But it was not yet the end of the beginning. After some minor engagements on the Aisne front, the battalion was transferred with the remainder of the B.E.F. to the northern flank of the Allied front in the West. Some grim fighting then began and on the 13th October the battalion was launched to the attack for the second time; but now Poole was in command, and there was a plan and there were proper orders. Two companies were forward, my company on the left being directed on a group of buildings on the outskirts of the village of Meteren. When zero hour arrived I drew my recently sharpened sword and shouted to my platoon to follow me, which it did. We charged forward towards the village; there was considerable fire directed at us and some of my men became casualties, but we continued on our way. As we neared the objective I suddenly saw in front of me a trench full of Germans, one of whom was aiming his rifle at me.

In my training as a young officer I had received much instruction in how to kill my enemy with a bayonet fixed to a rifle. I knew all about the various movements—right parry, left parry, forward lunge. I had been taught how to put the left foot on the corpse and extract the bayonet, giving at the same time a loud grunt. Indeed, I had been considered good on the bayonet-fighting course against sacks filled with straw, and had won prizes in man-to-man contests in the gymnasium. But now I had no rifle and bayonet; I had only a sharp sword, and I was confronted by a large German who was about to shoot me. In all my short career in the Army no one had taught me how to kill a German with a sword. The only sword exercise I knew was saluting drill, learnt under the sergeant-major on the barrack square.

An immediate decision was clearly vital. I hurled myself through the air at the German and kicked him as hard as I could in the lower part of the stomach; the blow was well aimed at a tender spot. I had read much about the value of surprise in war. There is no doubt that the German was surprised and it must have seemed to him a new form of war; he fell to the ground in great pain and I took my first prisoner! A lot of fighting went on during the remainder of the day, our task being to clear the Germans from the village. During these encounters amongst the houses I got wounded, being shot through the chest. But we did the job and turned the Germans out of the village. It was for this action at Meteren that I was awarded the D.S.O. I was still only a lieutenant. My life was saved that day by a soldier of my platoon. I had fallen in the open and lay still hoping to avoid further attention from the Germans. But a soldier ran to me and began to put a field dressing on my wound; he was shot through the head by a sniper and collapsed on top of me. The sniper continued to fire at us and I got a second wound in the knee; the soldier received many bullets intended for me. No further attempt was made by my platoon to rescue us; indeed, it was presumed we were both dead. When it got dark the stretcher-bearers came to carry us in; the soldier was dead and I was in a bad way. I was taken back to the Advanced Dressing Station; the doctors reckoned I could not live and, as the station was shortly to move, a grave was dug for me. But when the time came to move I was still alive; so I was put in a motor ambulance and sent back to a hospital. I survived the journey and recovered, I think because I was very fit and healthy after two months of active service in the field. I was evacuated to hospital in England and for some months I took no further part in the war. I had time for reflection in hospital and came to the conclusion that the old adage was probably correct: the pen was mightier than the sword. I joined the staff.

I returned to the Western Front in France early in 1916, this time as a brigade-major. During the Somme battle that summer an infantry brigade, which had better remain nameless, was to be the leading brigade in a divisional attack. It was important that the Brigade Commander should receive early information of the progress of his forward troops since this would affect the movement of reserves in the rear. The problem then arose how to ensure the early arrival of the required information, and intense interest was aroused at Brigade H.Q. when it was disclosed that a pigeon would be used to convey the news. In due course the bird arrived and was kept for some days in a special pigeon loft. When the day of the attack arrived the pigeon was given to a soldier to carry. He was to go with the leading sub-units and was told that at a certain moment an officer would write a message to be fastened to the pigeon's leg; he would then release the pigeon which would fly back to its loft at Brigade H.Q. The attack was launched and the Brigade Commander waited anxiously for the arrival of the pigeon. Time was slipping by and no pigeon arrived; the Brigadier walked feverishly about outside his H.Q. dug-out. The soldiers anxiously searched the skies; but there was no sign of any pigeon.

At last the cry went up: " The pigeon," and sure enough back it came and alighted safely in the loft.

Soldiers rushed to get the news and the Brigade Commander roared out: " Give me the message."

It was handed to him, and this is what he read:

" I am absolutely fed up with carrying this bloody bird about France."

When the war broke out I was a platoon commander. When it ended I was Chief of Staff (GSO 1) of a Division and rising thirty-one, well able to think clearly, although my mind was still untrained. To an ambitious young officer with an enquiring mind, many things seemed wrong.

There was little contact between the generals and the soldiers. I went through the whole war on the Western Front, except during the period I was in England after being wounded; I never once saw the British Commander-in-Chief, neither French nor Haig, and only twice did I see an Army Commander.

The higher staffs were out of touch with the regimental officers and with the troops. The former lived in comfort, which became greater as the distance of their headquarters behind the lines increased. There was no harm in this provided there was touch and sympathy between the staff and the troops. This was often lacking. At most large headquarters in back areas the doctrine seemed to me to be that the troops existed for the benefit of the staff. My war experience led me to believe that the staff must be the servants of the troops, and that a good staff officer must serve his commander and the troops but himself be anonymous.

The frightful casualties appalled me. The so-called " good fighting generals " of the war appeared to me to be those who had a complete disregard for human life. There were of course exceptions and I suppose one such was Plumer; I had only once seen him and had never spoken to him. There is the story of Sir Douglas Haig's Chief of Staff who was to return to England after the heavy fighting during the winter of 1917-18 on the Passchendaele front. Before leaving he said he would like to visit the Passchendaele Ridge and see the country.

When he saw the mud and the ghastly conditions under which the soldiers had fought and died, he was horrified and said: " Do you mean to tell me that the soldiers had to fight under such conditions?" And when he was told that it was so, he said: " Why was I never told about this before? "

The fact that the Chief of Staff of the British Armies in Europe had no idea of the conditions under which the troops had to live, fight, and die, will be sufficient to explain the uncertainties that were passing through my mind when the war ended.

I remember a leave period spent in London. I went to a music hall one night and the big joke of the evening was when a comedian asked the question: " If bread is the staff of life, what is the life of the staff? "

He then gave the answer: " One big loaf."

There was tremendous applause, in which I joined. In fact, the staff worked hard. But the incident made me think seriously, and from my own experiences I knew something was wrong.

One further matter should be mentioned before leaving the First War period. For the last six months of the war I was GSO 1 of the 47th (London) Division. I devoted much thought to the problem of how to get to Divisional Headquarters quickly the accurate information of the progress of the battle which is so vital, and which enables a general to adjust his dispositions to the tactical situation as it develops. We finally devised a system of sending officers with wireless sets up to the headquarters of the leading battalions and they sent messages back by wireless. The difficulty in those days was to get reliable sets which could be carried by a man and would give the required range. Our system was very much a make-shift and often broke down; but it also often worked, and overall it produced useful results. This was the germ of the system I developed in the 1939-45 war, and which finally produced the team of liaison officers in jeeps operating from my Advanced Tactical Headquarters, a technique which Sir Winston Churchill describes in his Triumph and Tragedy, Book Two, Chapter 5. In 1918 in the 47th Division we were groping in the dark and trying to evolve ideas which would give increased efficiency to our operations.

I have said enough to make it clear that by the time the 1914-18 war was over it had become very clear to me that the profession of arms was a life-study, and that few officers seemed to realise this fact.

It was at this stage in my life that I decided to dedicate myself to my profession, to master its details, and to put all else aside.

It was not clear to me how all this would be done and I knew none of the top leaders in the Army. I was certain that the first step was to get to the Staff College; this was re-opened when the war ended and the first course was a short one in 1919, for which I was not selected. I fastened my hopes on the second course which was to assemble in January 1920, and to last for one year. When the names were announced for this course I was not selected. But all was not yet lost.

The Commander-in-Chief of the British Army of Occupation in Germany at the time was Sir William Robertson. I did not know him. He was fond of tennis and I was invited one day to play at his house in Cologne; I decided to risk all and tell him my trouble. He had struggled a good deal himself in his youth and had a kind heart for the young; this I knew and I hoped for the best.

Shortly after that tennis party I heard that my name had been added to the list and I was ordered to report at the Staff College, Camberley, in January 1920. The C.-in-C. had done what was required. The way now seemed clear. But it was not to be so easy as all that. The story of my further progress in the Army, as subsequent chapters of this book will reveal, is one of constant struggle linked to many set-backs and disappointments. I think that I can say now that the story has a happy ending, for me, anyhow.

CHAPTER 3

BETWEEN THE WARS

UP TO this point in my career I had received no training in the theory of my profession; I had behind me the practical experience of four years of active service in the field, but no theoretical study as a background to that experience. I had read somewhere the remarks of Frederick the Great when speaking about officers who relied only on their practical experience and who neglected to study; he is supposed to have said that he had in his Army two mules who had been through forty campaigns, but they were still mules.

I had also heard of a German general who delivered himself of the following all-embracing classification about officers, presumably those of the German Army. I understand that he said this: "I divide my officers into four classes: the clever, the stupid, the industrious and the lazy. Every officer possesses at least two of these qualities. Those who are clever and industrious are fitted for high staff appointments; use can be made of those who are stupid and lazy. The man who is clever and lazy is fitted for the highest command; he has the temperament and the requisite nerve to deal with all situations. But whoever is stupid and industrious is a danger and must be removed immediately."

I went to the Staff College at Camberley in January 1920 with no claim to cleverness. I thought I had a certain amount of common sense, but it was untrained; it seemed to me that it was *trained* common sense which mattered.

I must admit that I was critical and intolerant; I had yet to learn that uninformed criticism is valueless.

My fellow students at Camberley were all supposed to be the pick of the Army, men who were destined for the highest commands; very few of them ever reached there. The instructors also were picked men; but only one reached the top and that was Dill, who was a very fine character. Among my fellow students I was greatly impressed by one who had a first class brain and was immensely able, and that was

the late George Lindsay in the Rifle Brigade; he was eventually retired as a Major-General and I never understood why such an able
officer was allowed to leave the Army.

The " good fighting generals " of the war were in all the high
commands. They remained in office far too long, playing musical
chairs with the top jobs but never taking a chair away when the
music stopped. Milne was C.I.G.S. for seven years, from 1926 to
1933. After him the Army was unlucky in its professional chiefs.
Milne was succeeded by Montgomery-Massingberd, who was in
office at a most vital time in Army affairs, 1933 to 1936; his appointment was in my judgment a great mistake and under him the Army
drifted about like a ship without a rudder. The right man for the job
at that time was Jock Burnett-Stuart, the most brilliant general in the
Army. It has always been a mystery to me why this outstanding
soldier, with a quick and clear brain, was not made C.I.G.S. in 1933
instead of Montgomery-Massingberd. The Army would have been
better prepared for war in 1939 if he had been.

Deverell succeeded Montgomery-Massingberd in 1936 but he had
a very raw deal from the Secretary of State for War, Hore-Belisha,
and was turned out after 18 months in office; he would have achieved
something if he had been allowed to stay there. But Hore-Belisha
preferred Gort. He was entirely unsuited for the job but he remained
C.I.G.S. until the outbreak of war in September 1939.

The result of all this was that the Army entered the Second World
War in 1939 admirably organised and equipped to fight the 1914 war,
and with the wrong officers at the top.

Truly the ways of the British politicians in the days between the
wars were amazing. It always seems to me that a political leader must
be a good judge of men; he must choose the right men for the top
Service jobs. In peace time he has to judge by character, ability, the
drive to get things done, and so on. Between the wars they chose
badly by any standard, if indeed they understood at all what standards
were required.

I passed out of the Staff College in December 1920. I believe I got
a good report, but do not know as nobody ever told me if I had done
well or badly: which seemed curious. However, I was sent as brigade-
major to the 17th Infantry Brigade in Cork and went straight into
another war—the struggle against the Sinn Fein in Southern Ireland.
In many ways this war was far worse than the Great War which had

39

ended in 1918. It developed into a murder campaign in which, in the end, the soldiers became very skilful and more than held their own. But such a war is thoroughly bad for officers and men; it tends to lower their standards of decency and chivalry, and I was glad when it was over.

It was during this period that the Geddes axe began to operate in the Army, and every officer had to be reported on as to his fitness to remain. Opportunity was taken to get rid of a great deal of inefficient material in the lower ranks, but in the higher ranks much dead wood was left untouched. My own feeling now, after having been through two world wars, is that an extensive use of weedkiller is needed in the *senior* ranks after a war; this will enable the first class younger officers who have emerged during the war to be moved up. This did not happen after the 1914-18 war. I was in a position to see that it did happen after the 1939-45 war.

After the Sinn Fein war was over in 1922, I held various staff appointments in England until January 1926, when I was sent as an instructor at the Staff College.

The preceding five years had been for me years of hard work and intense study. I had served under some good and sympathetic generals who had encouraged the development of my ideas and had given me a free hand in carrying them out; these included General Sir Charles Harington, and Brigadier Tom Hollond, both good trainers. In this I was lucky, for it could so easily have been otherwise. Under them I was taught a high sense of duty; I also learnt that the discipline demanded from the soldier must become loyalty in the officer. I imagine that it was during this period that I began to become known as an officer who was studying his profession seriously, and this led to my appointment to the Staff College. I was glad as I felt the Camberley appointment put a hallmark on my Army career and my foot was now at last a little up the ladder. I doubt if I was right, but that is how it seemed to me at the time.

At certain moments in life an opportunity is presented to each one of us; some of us are not aware of the full significance of what has happened, and the moment is lost. Others, alert and enthusiastic, seize the opportunity with both hands and turn it to good advantage; these have ambition, as every man who is worth his salt should have—not too much, but rather the determination to succeed by his own efforts and not merely by stamping on other people who get in the way.

My father at Cape Barren Island, on a missionary tour in 1895, and my mother, in the 1930's

What I looked like when aged nine

Three Old Paulines in Arras in 1916. Left, my brother Donald, in the 29th Bn. Canadian Expeditionary Force. Centre, Major B. M. Arnold in the Artillery. Right, the author who was Brigade-Major 104 Inf. Bde. in the 35th (Bantam) Division

The author and his Brigadier, back from a tour of the trenches on the Arras front, 1916

In my case it seemed that here was an opportunity for three years of hard study; I knew enough by then to realise that the teacher learns much more than his students. And these three years would be spent working closely with certain other instructors already there, ones who were known to me as some of the best officers in the Army: Brooke (now Lord Alanbrooke), Paget, Franklyn, and others. And by teaching I would myself learn; I was conscious that I needed that learning, as a solid background which would enable me to handle bigger jobs later on with confidence.

I must pass quickly over the next few years of my military life since they have no significant place in this book of memoirs. As the sparks flew upwards I was often in trouble, due to my habit of saying what I thought in no uncertain voice. But in 1930 I was selected by the War Office to re-write the manual of Infantry Training. This was a considerable compliment and I decided to make the book a comprehensive treatise on war for the infantry officer. All my work had to be approved by a committee in the War Office and some heated arguments took place; I could not accept many of their amendments to my doctrine of infantry war. We went through the manual, chapter by chapter. I then recommended that the committee should disband and that I should complete the book in my own time; this was agreed. I produced the final draft, omitting all the amendments the committee had put forward. The book when published was considered excellent, especially by its author.

Here I must turn aside to deal with something much more important than my military career, the ten short years of my married life.

During the time I was an instructor at the Staff College, Camberley, I fell in love. We were married on the 27th July 1927. My son David was born on the 18th August 1928. My wife died on the 19th October 1937. I would like to tell the full story.

In January 1926 I went to Switzerland for a holiday before beginning work at the Staff College at the end of the month. I was then thirty-eight years old and a confirmed bachelor. Women had never interested me and I knew very few; I disliked social life and dinner parties. My life was devoted almost entirely to my profession and I worked at it from morning to night, sometimes taking exercise in the afternoon. I believe some ribald officer once said that the Army was my wife and I had no need for another! However that might be, I was intent on mastering my profession and was determined to do so. I was very certain that my country would be involved in another war and I had seen what had happened the first time. I was determined that whatever else might happen next time, at least I myself would be prepared, and trained, and ready when the call came. I had at times a kind of inward feeling that the call *would* come, to me personally, and in my prayers morning and evening I used to ask that I might be given help and strength so that I might not fail when put to the test.

In Switzerland, at Lenk in the Bernese Oberland, I met Mrs. Carver and her two boys aged eleven and twelve. I have always been devoted to young people and I like helping them: possibly because of my own unhappy childhood. I soon made friends with the boys and with their mother, and the holiday passed pleasantly. Another friend I made that winter was Sir Edward Crowe; this acquaintance developed and he is now one of my most valued friends, though considerably older than I am.

I decided to visit Lenk again in January 1927, with Sir Edward Crowe and his family and their friends. Mrs. Carver was there again with her two boys. Her husband had been killed in Gallipoli in 1915 and the boys were taught to hate war and anything to do with soldiers. This time I saw a great deal of Betty Carver and by the time the holiday was over I had fallen in love: for the first and only time in my life. My love was returned in full measure, although I was a soldier, and we were married in Chiswick Parish Church on the 27th July 1927. A time of great happiness then began; it had never before seemed possible that such love and affection could exist. We went everywhere, and did everything, together. We were parted only twice, the first time when I took my battalion to Palestine in January 1931 and she followed later, and the second time when I had to send her and David home from Quetta after the earthquake in May 1935. On both occasions the parting was only for a short time. My wife was forty when David was born and she was never very strong afterwards; but she was always energetic and happy, and was never ill.

She was a very good " Colonel's lady " when I was commanding the 1st Battalion of my regiment in Palestine and Egypt. I always remember how amused she was at one incident. In order to keep the soldiers happy and contented in the hot weather in Egypt I encouraged hobbies of every kind, and one of these was the keeping of pigeons; this was very popular and we kept some ourselves. One day the quartermaster accused a corporal of having stolen one of his pigeons; the corporal denied the accusation and said the pigeon was his. I had to give judgment. I asked both parties, the quartermaster and the corporal, if a pigeon when released would always fly direct to its own loft; they both agreed this was so. I then ordered the pigeon to be kept for 24 hours in the Battalion Orderly Room. The next day at 10 a.m. I released the pigeon; the whole battalion had heard of the incident and some 800 men watched from vantage points to see what would happen. The pigeon, when released, circled the barracks for a few minutes and then went direct to my own pigeon loft and remained there! This result was accepted by both parties, and the quartermaster withdrew his accusation.

In the spring of 1934 the battalion was stationed at Poona in southern India and while there I was ordered to hand over command and go as Chief Instructor at the Staff College, Quetta, being promoted colonel. We spent three happy years in Quetta, except for the earthquake in May 1935, and I was then given command of the 9th Infantry Brigade at Portsmouth. On arrival in England we had two months' leave. David was at his preparatory school at Hindhead and my wife and I went on a motor tour in the Lake District and visited our friends in the north of England. She seemed to be weaker than formerly and easily got tired; but she was always cheerful and happy. On return from the north I had to go into camp on Salisbury Plain with my brigade towards the end of August, and I sent Betty and David to a hotel at Burnham-on-Sea for the remainder of his school holidays.

One afternoon when they were both together on the sands, Betty was stung on the foot by some insect; she could not say what sort of insect it was, and this was never known. That night her leg began to swell and became painful; a doctor was called in and he put her at once into the local Cottage Hospital, and sent for me. She got worse and the pain increased; at last came the time when the pain became too great and she had to have constant injections and was seldom conscious. By then I had moved into our house at Portsmouth; David had gone back to his school at Hindhead. I spent all the time that was possible at the Cottage Hospital; there were times when Betty was better and other times when there was cause for serious alarm. I was summoned frequently in the middle of the night and made many motor journeys to Burnham-on-Sea; the road became very familiar.

The poison spread slowly up the leg. Then came the day when the doctors decided that the only hope was to amputate the leg; I agreed, and gained hope. But it was no good; nothing could stop the onward move of the poison; we could only wait. The doctors did everything that was possible; the nurses were splendid; but the septicaemia had got a firm hold. Betty died on the 19th October 1937, in my arms. During her illness I had often read to her, mostly from the Bible. The last reading, a few minutes before she died, was the 23rd Psalm.

I buried her in the cemetery at Burnham-on-Sea. I would not let David attend the funeral and, indeed, would never let him come and see his mother at any time when she was in great pain and slowly dying. I could not bring myself to let him see her suffering. He was only nine years old and was happy at school; after the funeral I went to his school and told him myself. Perhaps I was wrong, but I did what I thought was right.

After staying with David for a while I went back to my house in Portsmouth, which was to have been our home; I remained there alone for many days and would see no one. I was utterly defeated. I began to search my mind for anything I had done wrong, that I should have been dealt such a shattering blow. I could not understand it; my soul cried out in anguish against this apparent injustice. I seemed to be surrounded by utter darkness; all the spirit was knocked out of me. I had no one to love except David and he was away at school.

After a time I began to understand that God works out all these things in His own way, and it must be His will; there must therefore be no complaint, however hard it may seem at the time. I had duties to others, to my brigade and as the Commander of the Portsmouth Garrison. I realised that I must get on with my work. There was also David to be considered; we were now alone in the world, just the two of us, and he must be visited regularly at his school and well cared for in his holidays.

And so after a few weeks I began to live again. I was much helped all this time by my brigade-major, an officer called Major F. W. Simpson; he was a tower of strength and took from my shoulders everything he could. " Simbo " was my Chief of Staff when I was a Corps Commander after Dunkirk, and he became my Vice-Chief when I was C.I.G.S. He developed into one of the most able and efficient staff officers in the Army. He is now General Sir Frank

Simpson, and is retired. Helped by Simpson and others like him, I recovered.

David had been handled in his early years almost entirely by his mother and he had at times somewhat resented any interference on my part in this procedure. He had a strong will and his mother was always defeated by him. Remembering my own boyhood, it was our plan that I should become the predominant partner in his upbringing when he went to his preparatory school. We had just started on this plan and the sparks used to fly when I insisted on obedience; then suddenly his mother died. He and I now had to make a new life together; the old troubles ceased very soon and he transferred his love and affection to me. We had some happy holidays together and became close friends; he was nine when his mother died and I was fifty.

My friends were delighted that I began a normal life again and some even said that I would marry again. They little knew what they were saying. I do not believe a man can love twice, not really, in the way I had loved.

I was now alone, except in the school holidays when David was with me, and I plunged into my work again with renewed vigour. I made the 9th Infantry Brigade as good as any in England and none other could compete with us in battle on the training area. We were selected to carry out the special exercises and trials needed by the War Office in 1937 and 1938, and generally were in the public eye a good deal.

During the years since the war ended in 1918, I had worked under, and with, very able officers at the Staff Colleges at Camberley and Quetta. By hard and continuous work, and by the experience gained in command, I had acquired a certain mastery of my profession; this gave me confidence in my ability to be able to handle most situations which might come my way. Maybe I was too confident, and showed it. But I had received many rebuffs and there is no doubt they were good for me; they kept me from kicking over the traces too often and saved me from becoming too overbearing. I have a feeling that by the time I took over command of the brigade at Portsmouth in 1937 the worst was over; I had learnt my lesson and was sailing along with a fair wind.

I had always lived a great deal by myself and had acquired the habit of concentration. This ability to concentrate, and to sort out the essentials from a mass of detail, was now made easier for me than formerly because of the intense loneliness that descended on me after my wife's death. I became completely dedicated to my profession.

During my time at Portsmouth I got into severe trouble with the War Office and at one moment things began to look awkward for me. It occurred in this way. My Garrison funds were in need of a substantial increase because of certain improvements which were needed in the welfare services for the married families. I therefore decided to let the Clarence Football Field on Southsea Common to a Fair promoter for August Bank Holiday week; he offered me £1000 and I finally closed with him for £1500. The Portsmouth City Council heard of my plan and refused to agree to a Fair on Southsea Common. I then went privately to the Lord Mayor of Portsmouth and offered to give him £500 of the money for a pet project which he was promoting if he would get my project through the Council; he agreed. I concluded the deal, collected the £1500, gave £500 to the Lord Mayor and spent the £1000 quickly on the Garrison welfare services. Then the War Office heard about it and pointed out that I had broken an Army Regulation in letting War Department land; they were prepared to overlook this provided I handed over the £1500 at once. I replied that the £1500 had been spent; £500 had been paid to the Lord Mayor, and £1000 had been spent on the welfare of the married families. I produced all the receipts. The fur then began to fly. The Major-General i/c Administration Southern Command, Salisbury, came to see me and said that this incident had ruined my chances of promotion in the Army. But General Wavell, G.O.C.-in-C. Southern Command, took a different view; he was really rather amused that I had improved the Garrison amenities, at the expense of the War Office, all square and above board. He backed me and kept the file on the move between the War Office and Salisbury. The file was growing rather large. Then I was suddenly promoted, and I have never heard any more about that file since. But I was " dicky on the perch " for a while.

In October 1938, after little more than a year at Portsmouth, I was ordered to Palestine to take command of the Army units in northern Palestine engaged in quelling the Arab rebellion; I was to form them into a new division, the 8th Division with headquarters at Haifa. This was a task greatly to my liking. I was now a major-general, in spite of my misdeeds at Portsmouth. But the journey to Palestine meant leaving David, and some kind friends at Portsmouth took charge of him for me. My son had an unsatisfactory life from then onwards, since war broke out in 1939 very soon after I had left Palestine. I was never able to make a home for him again until 1948. Two main factors play the major part in the moulding of personality and character: heredity and environment. David had the first one without any doubt; he came from a long line of ancestors who served either the Church or State and did their duty. In environment he was unlucky after his mother died. For a few years he often had to spend his holidays in " holiday homes for children." It was not until I went to Africa in August 1942 that he was finally placed with Major and Mrs. Reynolds at Hindhead, and those two noble people brought him up and helped to mould his character while I was away fighting. Major Reynolds was headmaster of David's preparatory school at Hindhead; he was an old and valued friend of many years' standing and from 1942 to 1948 that school building became David's home and mine. Major Reynolds died in 1953; he and his wife were responsible for developing the character of many boys on the right lines, and the nation lost in him a man of sterling character. I owe them much. And so does David; they developed his character in the difficult formative years and cared for him as if he was their own son.

During the winter of 1938-39 while fighting in Palestine, I was informed that I had been selected to command the 3rd Division in England. This was a regular division, with headquarters on Salisbury Plain, and it contained the 9th Infantry Brigade which I had commanded at Portsmouth before going to Palestine. I was delighted. The 3rd Division was part of the British Expeditionary Force to go to Continental Europe in the event of war. The war clouds were banking up and it looked as if it might begin to rain; it was necessary to ensure that our military umbrella was in good condition and that was a task I would enjoy. I was to take command of the 3rd Division in August 1939.

But now a crisis arose and in May 1939 I suddenly became very ill; I was taken on a stretcher to the military hospital in Haifa and, since a patch was found on my lung, it was commonly supposed I had contracted tuberculosis. I got no better and finally demanded to be sent home to England; I was confident that once I got away from the hot and humid climate of Haifa, I should recover. I was sent to

England in the charge of two nursing sisters and two men nursing orderlies, as I was judged to be desperately ill. I was.

The sea voyage put me right and I walked off the ship at Tilbury in good health. I went direct to Millbank Hospital in London and asked for a thorough medical overhaul; this took three days and the verdict was that nothing was wrong with me. I asked about the patch on my lung; it had disappeared.

After a period of leave, I went to the War Office and asked if I could now go and take over command of the 3rd Division. The war clouds had indeed banked up and the Army was about to mobilise. I was told that on mobilisation all appointments made previously automatically lapsed, and those actually in the jobs remained there. The commander of the 3rd Division at the time had been selected as a Colonial Governor, and was even to go off to his Colony very shortly; he was now to remain in command of the division.

I then said I would return to Palestine and resume command of the 8th Division; but the answer was "No," as a new commander had taken over that division. I was told I was to go into the pool of Major-Generals waiting for employment. This did not suit me at all; Britain was mobilising for war and I was in a pool of officers waiting for employment. I pestered the War Office. Eventually the general was sent off to take up his Colonial Governorship, a job for which he was well fitted and in which he rendered good service. I took over the 3rd Division a few days before war was declared.

CHAPTER 4

BRITAIN GOES TO WAR IN 1939

I HAD taken over command of the 3rd Division on the 28th August. Partial mobilisation was then in process and full mobilisation was ordered on the 1st September, the day on which the Germans invaded Poland and an ultimatum was sent to Germany.

In this chapter I shall confine myself solely to the actions of the British Expeditionary Force which went to France soon after the war began, and in which I was a Divisional Commander. I know nothing about what happened in other theatres during this period, e.g. Norway, except what I have heard or read.

The full story of the transfer of the B.E.F. across the Channel to France in September and October, of the first winter of the war, and of the operations that began on the 10th May 1940 and ended in June, has been told in the book entitled *The War in France and Flanders 1939-1940*, by Major L. F. Ellis, and published by the Stationery Office in 1953. It is a very good publication and the story is well told. But it is a large volume and contains a great deal of detail which will not be read by the general public. Furthermore, of necessity it omits certain fundamental factors affecting the final issue; to raise them will be to place the responsibility for much of what happened squarely on the shoulders of the political and military chiefs in the years before the war.

In September 1939 the British Army was totally unfit to fight a first class war on the continent of Europe. It had for long been considered that in the event of another war with Germany the British contribution to the defence of the West should consist mainly of the naval and air forces. How any politician could imagine that, in a world war, Britain could avoid sending her Army to fight alongside the French passes all understanding.

In the years preceding the outbreak of war no large-scale exercises with troops had been held in England for some time. Indeed, the

Regular Army was unfit to take part in a realistic exercise. The Field Army had an inadequate signals system, no administrative backing, and no organisation for high command; all these had to be improvised on mobilisation. The transport was inadequate and was completed on mobilisation by vehicles requisitioned from civilian firms. Much of the transport of my division consisted of civilian vans and lorries from the towns of England; they were in bad repair and, when my division moved from the ports up to its concentration area near the French frontier, the countryside of France was strewn with broken-down vehicles.

The anti-tank equipment of my division consisted of 2-pounder guns. The infantry armament against tanks was the ·8-inch rifle. Some small one-pounder guns on little hand-carts were hurriedly bought from the French and a few were given to each infantry battalion. Apart from these, a proportion of the 25-pounders of my Divisional Artillery was supposed to be used in an anti-tank role, firing solid shot.

There was somewhere in France, under G.H.Q., one Army Tank Brigade. For myself, I never saw any of its tanks during the winter or during the active operations in May. And we were the nation which had invented the tank and were the first to use it in battle, in 1916.

It must be said to our shame that we sent our Army into that most modern war with weapons and equipment which were quite inadequate, and we had only ourselves to blame for the disasters which early overtook us in the field when fighting began in 1940.

Who was to blame? In my view, successive British Governments between the wars and especially those from 1932 onwards, in which year the need for rearmament on a modern scale began to be discussed. Until 1938 it never got much beyond the range of discussion, and by the spring of 1939 it was still proceeding only on a small scale. Knowing the precise situation regarding the British Field Army in France in general, and in particular in my division, I was amazed to read in a newspaper one day in France in October 1939 the speech of the Secretary of State for War (Hore-Belisha) in Parliament when he was announcing the arrival of the B.E.F. in France. He gave Parliament and the British people to understand that the Army we had just sent to France was equipped " in the finest possible manner which could not be excelled. Our Army is as well if not better equipped than any similar Army."

Now we must turn to the organisation for command and control in the field; in the last resort it is on this that everything depends, given adequate equipment and a good standard of training. Owing to the speed of operations, with a faulty command set-up all may well be lost in modern war.

Probably three of the most important officers in the War Office at the outbreak of the war were the following. The Chief of the Imperial General Staff (Lord Gort), the professional head of the British Army. The word " Imperial " was added to the title in 1909; it now has no significance. The Director of Military Operations and Intelligence (Major-General Henry Pownall), who was responsible for all war plans, and for the Intelligence on which they were based. In those days one major-general was in charge of both branches, Operations and Intelligence; now they have been separated, each under a general officer. The Director-General of the Territorial Army (Major-General Douglas Brownrigg). This Army had been doubled in March 1939 by a Cabinet decision taken without the advice or knowledge of the C.I.G.S. Gort, who was C.I.G.S. at the time, told me that he knew nothing about it until he saw it announced one morning in the Press.

All of these three officers left the War Office on the day war was declared.

> Gort to become Commander-in-Chief
> Pownall to become Chief of the General Staff } of the B.E.F.
> Brownrigg to become Adjutant-General

It is almost unbelievable that such a thing should have been allowed to happen. But it did. I understand that the War Office emptied in a similar way in 1914.

It had always been understood in the Army that the G.O.C.-in-C. Aldershot Command was the C.-in-C. Designate of any British Army to be sent out of the country in war-time, and he was selected accordingly. General Dill was at Aldershot in September 1939, and we all thought, and hoped, that he would get the top command. But rumour had it General Ironside had been promised the command in the event of war, as some recompense for being passed over by Gort as C.I.G.S.; he was at that time Inspector-General of the Overseas Forces, a post that does not now exist. I heard a vague rumour that he had actually gone to Camberley and had begun to form his G.H.Q. in the buildings of Sandhurst a few days before war was declared. These two candidates, Dill and Ironside, must have been astonished when a third candidate got the job: Gort, who was C.I.G.S. The Army was certainly amazed. And it was even more amazed when Ironside was made C.I.G.S., in place of Gort; in May 1940 he was removed from his appointment.

Now let us look at the C.-in-C. and his General Headquarters. Gort was a most delightful person, a warm-hearted friend, sincere in his dealings, and incapable of anything mean or underhand. He was the perfect example of the best type of regimental officer; he knew everything there was to know about the soldier, his clothing and boots, and the minor tactics of his battlefield. The highest command he had ever held before had been an infantry brigade. He was not clever and he did not bother about administration; his whole soul was in the battle and especially in the actions of fighting patrols in no-man's-land.

Gort established his G.H.Q. in and around Habarcq, the head-quarters of the various Branches and Services occupying thirteen villages covering an area of some fifty square miles. This dispersed system called for a cumbersome network of communications. It was difficult to know where anyone was and command from the top suffered from the very beginning. It was an amazing layout.

I have always held the opinion that Gort's appointment to command the B.E.F. in September 1939 was a mistake; the job was above his ceiling. One only has to read his instructions signed by Hore-Belisha, and dated 3rd September 1939, to see what he was in for; that directive is a pretty fair commentary on the command set-up and it would have taxed a much better brain than Gort's to deal with such a complicated problem. Furthermore, he was asked to attempt the impossible: his Headquarters had to act as a G.H.Q., and at the same time had to exercise direct command over the fighting and administrative forces allotted to him. The instructions to the C.-in-C. are given below.

INSTRUCTIONS FOR THE COMMANDER-IN-CHIEF,
BRITISH FIELD FORCE

"*Role*
   1. The role of the force under your command is to co-operate with our Allies in the defeat of our common enemy.
   2. You will be under the command of the French Commander-in-

Chief 'North-East Theatre of Operations.' In the pursuit of the common object you will carry out loyally any instructions issued by him. At the same time, if any order given by him appears to you to imperil the British Field Force, it is agreed between the British and French Governments that you should be at liberty to appeal to the British Government before executing that order. While it is hoped that the need for such an appeal will seldom, if ever, arise you will not hesitate to avail yourself of your right to make it, if you think fit.

3. Initially the force under your command will be limited to two corps of two divisions with G.H.Q., Corps and L. of C. Troops together with a Royal Air Force Component of two bomber, four fighter and six Army co-operation squadrons.

4. It is the desire of His Majesty's Government to keep the British Forces under your command, as far as possible, together. If at any time the French Commander-in-Chief 'North-East Theatre of Operations' finds it essential for any reason to transfer any portion of the British troops to an area other than that in which your main force is operating, it should be distinctly understood that this is only a temporary arrangement, and that as soon as practicable the troops thus detached should be reunited to the main body of the British forces.

5. Whilst the Royal Air Force Component of the Field Force is included under your command, the Advanced Air Striking Force, which will also operate from French territory, is an independent Force under the direct control of the Air Officer Commanding-in-Chief, Bomber Command, in the United Kingdom. The War Office has nevertheless undertaken the maintenance of this Force from the common bases up to rail-head and for this you, as Commander-in-Chief of the Field Force, will be responsible. You are not, however, responsible for the protection of the aerodromes or railheads of the Advanced Air Striking Force. This has been undertaken by the French. But should a situation arise which would make it necessary for you to assume responsibility for the protection of this Force, you will receive instructions from the War Office.

6. It is realised that you may require air co-operation beyond the resources of the Royal Air Force Component of the Field Force. Additional assistance may be necessary for the general protection

of your Force against hostile air attack, for offensive air action in furtherance of military operations, or to establish local air superiority at certain times. You should apply for such assistance when you require it to the Air Officer Commanding Advanced Air Striking Force.

(Signed) Leslie Hore-Belisha "

3/9/39

Having read these instructions we should look at the command set-up in France, given *on the opposite page.*

General Gamelin was the Supreme Commander. The B.E.F. is shown as in Army Group No. 1, under General Billotte. But the instructions to Gort placed him under the *direct* command of General Georges. Here were possibilities of trouble, and they descended on the North-Eastern front in full measure.

Active operations began on the 10th May 1940 and on the next day the line-up on the front from Longwy to the sea was as follows from south to north:

General Billotte's Army Group No. 1
    Second French Army
    Ninth French Army
    First French Army
    These armies held the front from Longwy northwards through Sedan to Wavre. The Ardennes-Meuse part of this front was held by the Second and Ninth Armies consisting mostly of second-grade divisions. The First Army was next to the B.E.F., and consisted mostly of first-grade divisions.

The B.E.F.
    Not under General Billotte, but taking orders direct from General Georges. My 3rd Division was the left division of the B.E.F., with the Belgian Army on our left.

The Belgian Army
    Independent, and commanded by the King of the Belgians.

Seventh French Army (Giraud)
    Included in Army Group No. 1 and intended by General Georges to be held in reserve under him behind the left flank;

CHAIN OF COMMAND ALLIED FORCES

COMMANDER-IN-CHIEF ALLIED FORCES

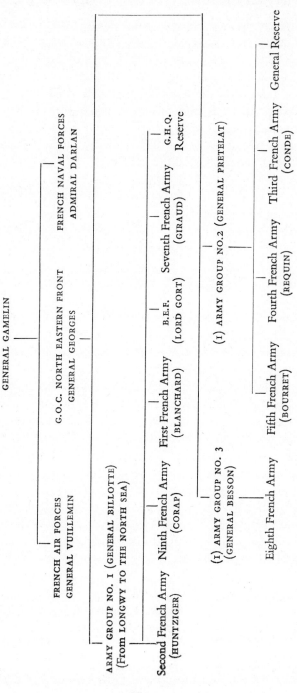

GENERAL GAMELIN

FRENCH AIR FORCES
GENERAL VUILLEMIN

G.O.C. NORTH EASTERN FRONT
GENERAL GEORGES

FRENCH NAVAL FORCES
ADMIRAL DARLAN

ARMY GROUP NO. 1 (GENERAL BILLOTTE)
(From LONGWY TO THE NORTH SEA)

Second French Army
(HUNTZIGER)

Ninth French Army
(CORAP)

First French Army
(BLANCHARD)

B.E.F.
(LORD GORT)

Seventh French Army
(GIRAUD)

G.H.Q.
Reserve

(I) ARMY GROUP NO. 3
(GENERAL BESSON)

Eighth French Army

Fifth French Army
(BOURRET)

(I) ARMY GROUP NO.2 (GENERAL PRETELAT)

Fourth French Army
(REQUIN)

Third French Army
(CONDE)

General Reserve

NOTES: (i) Army Groups Nos. 2 and 3 extended from Swiss frontier to Longwy.
        (ii) On the 10th May the Belgian Forces, approximately 22 Divisions, operated independently.
        (iii) On the 10th May the Dutch Forces, approximately 10 Divisions, operated independently and capitulated on 15th May.

55

this decision of Georges was correct. But Gamelin decided otherwise; he directed that this Army of seven divisions should operate forward across Belgium towards Antwerp in order to support the Belgian and Dutch forces. It suffered heavy losses and ran out of ammunition; it achieved nothing nor could it have done so. Its forward move was one of Gamelin's greatest mistakes since it unbalanced the whole North-East front. Things might have been not so bad as they were had this Army been kept in reserve behind the left flank.

Quite apart from this faulty command set-up, the state of the signal communications did not tend to make things easier or to facilitate command. From the day war was declared the French had insisted on such a high degree of wireless silence that little or no practice of operators was possible, certainly not with the higher-powered sets. The result was that wireless communication within the B.E.F. was never efficient; outside the B.E.F. it hardly existed. Because of this, inter-communication within the Allied forces was almost entirely by civil telephone and this was always "insecure."

Moreover, G.H.Q. of the B.E.F. had never conducted any exercises, either with or without troops, from the time we landed in France in 1939 up to the day active operations began in May 1940. The need for wireless silence was given as an excuse; but an indoor exercise on the model could easily have been held. The result was a total lack of any common policy or tactical doctrine throughout the B.E.F.; when differences arose these differences remained, and there was no firm grip from the top.

On the 12th May it was agreed that the operations of the B.E.F. and of the Belgian Army would be "co-ordinated" by General Billotte on behalf of General Georges. This co-ordination never amounted to effective command of all the forces involved. In battle this is vital. General Billotte disappeared on the 21st May, seriously injured in a motor accident, and died two days later. There was then nobody to co-ordinate French, British and Belgian operations. After three days' delay General Blanchard of the First French Army was finally appointed to succeed Billotte; but it was then too late.

The civil telephone was still the main channel of communication, supplemented by liaison officers and visits by Commanders and their

My wife and her three sons, April 1930. Left to right: Dick Carver, David, John Carver

My wife and David in Switzerland, January 1936

The author and David in Switzerland, January 1937

1st Bn., The Royal Warwickshire Regiment, in camp near the pyramids outside Cairo in 1933. The author, the C.O., mounted in front of the battalion

Lord Gort and Mr. Hore-Belisha visit the 3rd Division area in France. General Brooke can be seen behind and to the left of Hore-Belisha. The author is on the right in battle dress—the first General Officer ever to wear that dress. Date—19th November 1939

staffs. From the 16th May onwards the German advance began to cut the land lines, and telephone communications ceased on that day between Supreme H.Q. (Gamelin) and H.Q. North-East Front (Georges). From the same date all direct communication ceased between General Georges and Army Group No. 1 (Billotte). Also, from the 17th May Gort had no land telephone lines to the Belgian H.Q. on his left, the First French Army on his right, and H.Q. North-East Front (Georges) behind.

In fact, it may be said that there was no co-ordination between the operations of the Belgians, the B.E.F., and the First French Army; the commanders of these armies had no means of direct communication except by personal visits.

Gort's plan was to go forward with a small Advanced H.Q. when active operations began, leaving his Main H.Q. at Arras. As time went on, more and more officers said it was essential that they should be at the Advanced H.Q.; this soon became so big that the project was dropped. The final plan was to have a small Command Post well forward. Since signal communications were so inadequate, the Command Post could be set up only at places—few and far between—where the international buried cable system came to the surface. There was also, naturally, a lack of security. The traffic consequently thrown on the wireless was too great for the few available sets to handle. And the size of the Command Post grew and grew.

Finally, there was a breakdown in the Intelligence organisation. On the 15th May the French began to be in difficulties on the right of the B.E.F. The break-through by the Germans had occurred on the front of the Ninth French Army, and G.H.Q. had no liaison officer at that H.Q. such as they had with the First French Army immediately on the right of the B.E.F. Anyhow, G.H.Q. was not given details about the break-through at once. It was clear that G.H.Q. (Intelligence) was not getting proper information from the French about the situation of either their own troops or of the enemy. An amazing decision was now taken. On the 16th May Gort took the head of his Intelligence Staff (Major-General Mason-MacFarlane) and put him in command of a small force to protect the right rear of the B.E.F., and the general took with him a senior staff officer of his department as his GSO 1 for the force (Lieut.-Colonel Gerald Templer). There-after Gort was often without adequate information of the enemy. Overall, the distribution of staff duties between G.H.Q. and the

Command Post was badly organised from the very beginning; the staff plan was amateur and lacked the professional touch.

Enough has been said to show that from the point of view of command and control of the forces available in France in May 1940, the battle was really almost lost before it began. The whole business was a complete " dog's breakfast."

Who must bear the chief blame? Obviously General Gamelin. He was Supreme Commander and, as such, was responsible. He did nothing to put it right. But I would also blame the British Chiefs of Staff. They should never have allowed the British Army to go into battle with such a faulty command set-up. It is clear that Gort and his Chief of Staff were also greatly to blame; knowing the hopeless organisation of the high command, they should have organised G.H.Q. in a more professional way. I never myself thought very much of the staff at G.H.Q. Nobody in a subordinate command ever does!

My own divisional area was south of Lille. My operational task was to work on defences which were being undertaken in order to prolong the Maginot Line behind the Belgian frontier. Until the 10th May Belgium was a strictly neutral country. Apart from the defensive tasks, I concentrated on training the division for the active operations which I was certain must come. My soul revolted at what was happening. France and Britain stood still while Germany swallowed Poland; we stood still while the German armies moved over to the West, obviously to attack *us* later on; we waited patiently to be attacked; and during all this time we occasionally bombed Germany *with leaflets*. If this was war, I did not understand it.

I well remember the visit of Neville Chamberlain to my division; it was on the 16th December 1939. He took me aside after lunch and said in a low tone so that no one could hear: "I don't think the Germans have any intention of attacking us. Do you?"

I made it quite clear that in my view the attack would come at the time of their own choosing; it was now winter and we must get ready for trouble to begin when the cold weather was over.

The 3rd Division certainly put that first winter to good use and trained hard. If the Belgians were attacked, we were to move forward and occupy a sector astride Louvain behind the River Dyle. I trained the division for this task over a similar distance moving westwards, i.e. backwards into France. We became expert at a long night move, and then occupying a defensive position in the dark, and by dawn being fully deployed and in all respects ready to receive attack. This is what I felt we might have to do; and it was.

My Corps Commander was General Brooke (now Lord Alan-brooke). We had been instructors together at the Staff College and I knew him well. I had, and retain, a great liking and an enormous admiration and respect for him. I consider he is the best soldier that *any* nation has produced for very many years. I never worried him about things that didn't matter, and so far as I can remember I never asked him a question after he had given his orders even in the middle of the most frightful operational situations; there was never any need to ask questions since all his orders and instructions were very clear. He handled me very well in that he gave me a completely free hand as regards carrying out his orders. He saved me from getting into trouble on several occasions before the war ended, and always backed me when others wanted to " down " me. At times he would get angry and I received quite a few " backhanders " from him; but I would take anything from him and I have no doubt I deserved all I got.

During the winter G.H.Q. arranged for divisions to send infantry brigades in turn down to the active front in the Saar, holding positions in front of the Maginot Line in contact with the German positions in the Siegfried Line. I went down there in January 1940 to visit one of my brigades and spent a few days having a look round. That was my first experience in the war of the French Army in action; I was seriously alarmed and on my return I went to see my Corps Commander, and told him of my fears about the French Army and what we might have to expect from that quarter in the future. Brooke had been down there himself and had formed the same opinion.

The popular cries in the Maginot Line were: *Ils ne passeront pas* and *On les aura.*

But the general attitude did not give me any confidence that either of these two things would happen. Brooke and I agreed not to talk about it to our subordinates; I believe he discussed the matter with Gort.

I got into serious trouble during that first winter of the war. It happened in this way. After a few months in France the incidence of venereal disease in the 3rd Division gave me cause for alarm. To stop it I enlisted the aid of the doctors and even the padres; but all efforts were unsuccessful and the figures increased. Finally I decided to write a confidential letter to all subordinate commanders in which I analysed the problem very frankly and gave my ideas about how to solve it. Unfortunately a copy of the letter got into the hands of the senior chaplains at G.H.Q., and the Commander-in-Chief (Gort) was told of my action. My views on how to tackle the problem were not considered right and proper and there was the father-and-mother of a row. They were all after my blood at G.H.Q. But my Corps Commander (Brooke) saved me by insisting on being allowed to handle the matter himself. This he did in no uncertain manner and I received from him a proper backhander. He said, amongst other things, that he didn't think much of my literary effort. Anyhow it achieved what I wanted, since the venereal disease ceased.

I do not propose to describe in any detail the operations of the 3rd Division in the campaign which began on the 10th May 1940. But certain episodes are of interest. The first task we had to perform was exactly what I had expected; it was to move forward and occupy a sector on the River Dyle astride Louvain. The division executed the movement perfectly. The sector on the Dyle was occupied by a Belgian division, which was not at that moment in contact with the Germans. When the Belgian soldiers woke up on the morning of the 11th May they found a British division doubled-up with them in the sector; we had arrived quietly and efficiently during the night, the Belgians being mostly asleep—presumably because there were no Germans about. I went to see the Belgian general, asked him to withdraw his division, and allow me to hold the front; he refused and said he had received no orders to that effect; furthermore, only Belgian troops could hold the ancient city of Louvain. The Germans were approaching and the Belgian Army on the line of the Albert Canal in front was falling back fast; there were too many troops in the sector and I therefore withdrew my division into reserve behind the Belgian division. I decided that the best way to get the Belgians *out* and my division *in* was to use a little flattery. So I told the Belgian General that it was essential to have one responsible commander in the sector and it must be the general whose division was holding the front; I would therefore place myself under his orders. He was delighted! The news got to G.H.Q. and there was terrific consternation; my Corps Commander came to see me. But I told him not to worry as I was about to get the Belgians *out*, and I would then be in front and be the responsible commander. When the Germans came within artillery range and shelling began I had no difficulty in taking over the front from the Belgian division; it moved into reserve and then went northwards and joined up with the main body of the Belgian Army.

It was during this campaign that I developed the habit of going to bed early, soon after dinner. I was out and about on the front all day long, saw all my subordinate commanders, and heard their problems and gave decisions and verbal orders. I was always back at my Divisional H.Q. about tea-time, and would see my staff and give orders for the night and next day. I would then have dinner and go to bed, and was never to be disturbed except in a crisis. I well remember how angry I was when I was woken up one night and told the Germans had got into Louvain. The staff officer was amazed when I said: " Go away and don't bother me. Tell the brigadier in Louvain to turn them out." I then went to sleep again.

The story of the withdrawal of the B.E.F., the desperate fighting that took place, and the final evacuation from Dunkirk and its beaches, has been told many times. My division did everything that was demanded of it; it was like a ship with all sails set in a rough sea, which rides the storm easily and answers to the slightest touch on the helm. Such was my 3rd Division. There were no weak links; all the doubtful commanders had been eliminated during the previous six months of training. The division was like a piece of fine steel. I was intensely proud of it.

I think the most difficult operation we had to do was on the 27th May when I was ordered to side-step the division to the left of the British front and fill a gap which had opened between the 50th Division and the Belgians. It involved a night move of the whole division within a couple of thousand yards of the 5th Division front, where a fierce battle had been raging all day and was still going on. If this move had been suggested by a student at the Staff College in a scheme, he would have been considered mad. But curious things have to be done in a crisis in war. The movement was carried out without a hitch and the gap was filled by daylight on the 28th May. Imagine my astonishment to learn at dawn on the 28th May that the King of the Belgians had surrendered the Belgian Army to the Germans at midnight on the 27th May, i.e. while I was moving my division into the gap! Here was a pretty pickle! Instead of having a Belgian Army on my left I now had nothing, and had to do some rapid thinking.

During the operations the food situation became difficult and the whole B.E.F. was put on half-rations. It made little difference. The civil population were mostly moving out, leaving their farms; we lived on the country, giving requisition forms to mayors of villages when they could be found. We never were short of meat as my R.A.S.C. used to requisition beef cattle and take it along with the division; " beef ration on the hoof."

The last headquarters of the 3rd Division before it moved into the final Dunkirk bridgehead was in a portion of the Abbaye de S. Sixte, at Westvleteren in Belgium. I still had all my kit with me, and some interesting papers which were not secret but which I did not want to lose; I also had a very good lunch basket. So I asked the Abbot, Fr. M. Rafael Hoedt, if he could look after a few things for me; possibly they could be buried in the garden. He agreed to take a small box, and my lunch basket, and he had them bricked up into a wall of the abbey in a very clever manner. I told him we would return to Belgium in due course, and then I would come for my possessions. When we liberated Belgium in September 1944, the Abbot wrote to me and said he had my belongings ready for me; they had remained safely in their hiding-place and had never been discovered by the Germans. I will always be grateful to the Abbot and his brave band of monks for their kindness in those days. They little knew the risks they were running; nor did I at that time. It is clear to me now that I should not have asked them to hide my belongings, which, in point of fact, were only of sentimental value to myself.

THE FINAL SCENE AT LA PANNE

G.H.Q. went to La Panne on the 28th May and remained there till the end. That place was chosen because the submarine cable to the U.K. entered the sea there; in consequence good telephone conversation was possible to Dover and London to the last. My 3rd Division moved into its position on the left of the Dunkirk bridgehead on the night 29th-30th May. We held the line of the canal between Furnes and Nieuport. My H.Q. were in the sand-dunes on the outskirts of La Panne. G.H.Q., or what was left of it, was in a house on the seafront; it now consisted only of Gort himself and a few staff officers. On the morning of the 30th May, Brooke came to see me at my

H.Q. in the sand-dunes. He told me he had been ordered to get back to England; he was terribly upset. We were great friends and I did my best to comfort him, saying it was clearly essential to get our best generals out of it as quickly as possible since there were many years of war ahead; if we were all to be lost, at least *he* must be saved. He then told me that I was to take command of his corps, the 2nd Corps. This surprised me as I was the junior major-general in the corps. Brooke left for England that evening.

Lord Gort held a final conference at his H.Q. on the sea-front that afternoon, the 30th May, to give his orders. Since I was now commanding the 2nd Corps, I attended. This was the first time I had seen him since the fighting began on the 10th May. My H.Q. were quite near and I went along and had a talk with him before the conference assembled; he was alone in the dining-room of the house and looked a pathetic sight, though outwardly cheerful as always. His first remark to me was typical of the man: " Be sure to have your front well covered with fighting patrols tonight."

At the conference he read us the telegram containing the final instructions of the Government. The instructions were as follows:

" Continue to defend the present perimeter to the utmost in order to cover maximum evacuation now proceeding well. Report every three hours through La Panne. If we can still communicate we shall send you an order to return to England with such officers as you may choose at the moment when we deem your command so reduced that it can be handed over to a Corps Commander. You should now nominate this Commander. If communications are broken you are to hand over and return as specified when your effective fighting force does not exceed the equivalent of three divisions. This is in accordance with correct military procedure and no personal discretion is left you in the matter. On political grounds it would be a needless triumph to the enemy to capture you when only a small force remained under your orders. The Corps Commander chosen by you should be ordered to carry on the defence in conjunction with the French and evacuation whether from Dunkirk or the beaches, but when in his judgment no further proportionate damage can be inflicted on the enemy he is authorised in consultation with the senior French Commander to capitulate formally to avoid useless slaughter."

It is commonly supposed that at this final conference Gort " nominated " Major-General H. R. L. G. Alexander to command after he himself had left. This is not so; moreover, Alexander himself was not even present at the conference. I will describe what actually happened.

The two Corps Commanders at the conference were Lieut.-General M. G. H. Barker, 1st Corps, and myself, who had just taken over command of 2nd Corps. Barker had been given command of 1st Corps when Dill returned to England in April to become Vice-Chief of the Imperial General Staff.

Gort's plan was based on the War Office telegram, and he ordered that I was to withdraw 2nd Corps the next night, 31st May/1st June, and that the 1st Corps would then be left in final command. He informed Barker that as a last resort he would surrender himself, and what remained of his corps, to the Germans. The conference then broke up. I stayed behind when the others had left and asked Gort if I could have a word with him in private. I then said it was my view that Barker was in an unfit state to be left in final command; what was needed was a calm and clear brain, and that given reasonable luck such a man might well get 1st Corps away, with no need for *anyone* to surrender. He had such a man in Alexander, who was commanding the 1st Division in Barker's corps. He should send Barker back to England at once and put Alexander in command of the 1st Corps. I knew Gort very well; so I spoke very plainly and insisted that this was the right course to take.

Gort acted promptly. Barker was sent off to England and I never saw him again. Alexander took over the 1st Corps. The two corps were now commanded by two major-generals and we met the next day in La Panne to discuss the situation; we were both confident that all would be well in the end. And it was; " Alex " got everyone away in his own calm and confident manner.

On the evening of the 30th May I held a conference of the divisional commanders of the 2nd Corps and gave out my orders for the withdrawal and evacuation from the beaches on the next night, the 31st May. It was very unpleasant in La Panne that evening and shells were bursting all round the house in which I held the conference. I ordered that any men who could not be embarked from the beaches were to move along the beach to Dunkirk and get on board ships in the harbour.

The next night I withdrew the 2nd Corps. The situation on the beaches was not good, for some of the improvised piers we had made began to break up; many had to walk to Dunkirk. While standing on the beach, my A.D.C. was wounded in the head by a splinter of shell. I cursed him soundly for not wearing his steel helmet, quite forgetting that I was not wearing one myself—as he pointed out! He was Charles Sweeny, in the Ulster Rifles; he was with me for much of the war and was killed right at the end, in Germany. He was a delightful Irish boy and I loved him dearly. In the end we ourselves walked along the beach to Dunkirk, some five or six miles away, together with Brigadier Ritchie (now General Sir Neil Ritchie) and my batman. We got there at dawn and embarked on a destroyer, landing in Dover on the morning of the 1st June.

LORD GORT

I have already said that the appointment of Gort to command the B.E.F. was a mistake. I have never departed from that view, and am still of the same opinion today.

The first point to understand is that the campaign in France and Flanders in 1940 was lost in Whitehall in the years before it ever began, and this cannot be stated too clearly or too often. One might add after Whitehall the words " and in Paris." Therefore the situation called for two almost super-men from the British Army: one as C.I.G.S., and one to command the B.E.F. The two actually selected were Ironside and Gort, and in my opinion both appointments were unsuitable. Furthermore, these two appointments were not made till war was declared; this, of course, was monstrous.

Gort then was faced with an almost impossible task. He faced it bravely and did his best; but, as we have seen, much that should have been done was not done. I would say myself that he did not choose his staff wisely; they were not good enough. He was a man who did not see very far, but as far as he did see he saw very clearly. When the crisis burst on the French and British armies, and developed in ever-increasing fury, he was quick to see that there was only one end to it: the French would crack and he must get as much of the British Army as he could back to England. Planning for the evacuation via Dunkirk was begun at G.H.Q., so far as I am aware, about the 21st May. Thereafter, Gort never wavered; he remained steady as a rock, and refused to be diverted from what he knew was the only right and proper course. When General Billotte disappeared on the 21st May and co-ordination broke down, Gort acted not on any definite orders but on what he considered to be his proper action in the spirit of the co-ordination agreement. His action, as time went on, was more and more tempered by another consideration: his duty to H.M. Government at home as being responsible for the safety of the B.E.F. And at the last moment he threw out Barker and put in Alexander to command the 1st Corps and take charge of the final evacuation.

It was *because* he saw very clearly, if only for a limited distance, that we all got away at Dunkirk. A cleverer man might have done something different and perhaps tried to swing back to the Somme, keeping touch with the French. If he had done this, the men of the B.E.F. might have found themselves eventually in French North Africa—without weapons and equipment.

Gort saw clearly that he must, *at the least*, get the men of the B.E.F. back to England with their personal weapons. For this I give him full marks and I hope history will do the same. He saved the men of the B.E.F. And being saved, they were able to fight again another day: which they did to some purpose, as the Germans found out.

CHAPTER 5

THE ARMY IN ENGLAND AFTER

DUNKIRK

I ARRIVED in London on the evening of the 1st June and went the next morning to the War Office to report myself to the C.I.G.S.: Jack Dill, an old friend.

He was despondent and said: "Do you realise that for the first time for a thousand years this country is now in danger of invasion?"

I had had a good night's sleep in a hotel and was feeling very full of beans. I laughed. This made Dill angry and he asked what there was to laugh about. I said that the people of England would never believe we were in danger of being invaded when they saw useless generals in charge of some of the Home Commands, and I gave him some examples. He could not but agree, but he ticked me off for speaking in such a way at such a time in our misfortunes, and said that remarks of that kind could only cause a loss of confidence. My answer was that plain speaking between the two of us, alone in his office, could do no harm. Again he agreed. But the next day I received a letter telling me to stop saying such things, which of course I obeyed; but one by one the useless generals disappeared.

Although I had been a Corps Commander at Dunkirk, I asked to be allowed, and was permitted, to go back to my 3rd Division, to reform it and get it ready for what lay ahead.

The officers and men of the B.E.F. were now back in England, less many brave men who sacrificed themselves that the majority should get away. Except for personal weapons our armament and equipment was mostly left behind in France.

There was in England sufficient transport and armament to re-equip one division completely, and no more. It was decided to give it to the 3rd Division and to get that division ready to go back across the Channel and join up with the small British forces which were still fighting with the French Army. This was a great compliment, although

I don't think any of us had any delusion about what we might be in for a second time. However, Brooke was to be the new C.-in-C. and we of the 3rd Division were prepared to go anywhere under his command.

We reformed in Somerset, received our new equipment, and were all ready to start back across the Channel by the middle of June. Then France capitulated, on the 17th June.

My division was then ordered to move to the south coast; we were to occupy a sector of the coast which included Brighton and the country to the west of it, and to prepare that area for defence against invasion which was considered imminent. So we moved to the south coast and descended like an avalanche on the inhabitants of that area; we dug in the gardens of the seaside villas, we sited machine-gun posts in the best places, and we generally set about our job in the way we were accustomed to do things in an emergency. The protests were tremendous. Mayors, County Councillors, private owners, came to see me and demanded that we should cease our work; I refused, and explained the urgency of the need and that we were preparing to defend the south coast against the Germans.

The real trouble in England in the early days after the fall of France was that the people did not yet understand the full significance of what *had* happened, and what *could* happen in the future. The fact that the B.E.F. had escaped through Dunkirk was considered by many to be a great victory for British arms. I remember the disgust of many like myself when we saw British soldiers walking about in London and elsewhere with a coloured embroidered flash on their sleeve with the title " Dunkirk." They thought they were heroes, and the civilian public thought so too. It was not understood that the British Army had suffered a crushing defeat at Dunkirk and that our island home was now in grave danger. There was no sense of urgency. Churchill was to bring it home to the nation in words that rang and thundered like the Psalms. The spirit was there all right but it needed a Winston Churchill to call it forth.

It was in that summer of 1940 on the south coast, near Brighton, that I first met Winston Churchill and his wife. We were to become great friends as the war went on, and today I regard him as chief among all my friends. Before proceeding with my story I would like to describe that first meeting, as my thoughts often return to it and he and I have often recalled it.

My Divisional Headquarters were near Steyning, in a house lying to the north of the downs. I was told the Prime Minister wished to spend the afternoon of the 2nd July with my division; he would arrive by car and I was to finish the tour in Brighton, so that he could return to London by train in the evening. I was not impressed by politicians in those days; I considered that they were largely responsible for our troubles. But I was keen to see this politician who had for many years before the war been telling a series of Governments what would happen; they had not listened, and now it had happened.

He arrived with Mrs. Churchill, as she then was, and some others, one of whom was Duncan Sandys. I have never discovered what Churchill thought of me that day; I know I was immensely impressed by him. I showed him all that was possible in the time. I took him to Lancing College, inhabited by the Royal Ulster Rifles, and showed him a counter-attack on the small airfield on the coast below which was assumed to have been captured by the Germans; he was delighted, especially by the action of the Bren-gun carrier platoon of the battalion. We then worked our way along the coast, finishing up in Brighton at about 7.30 p.m. He suggested I should have dinner with him and his party at the Royal Albion Hotel, and we talked much during the meal. He asked me what I would drink at dinner and I replied—water. This astonished him. I added that I neither drank nor smoked and was 100 per cent fit; he replied in a flash, that he both drank and smoked and was 200 per cent fit. This story is often told with embellishments, but the above is the true version. From the window of the dining-room we could see a platoon of guardsmen preparing a machine-gun post in a kiosk on Brighton pier, and he remarked that when at school near there he used to go and see the performing fleas in the kiosk. Then we talked about my problems. The main thing which seemed curious to me was that my division was immobile. It was the only fully equipped division in England, the only division fit to fight any enemy anywhere. And here we were in a static role, ordered to dig in on the south coast. Some other troops should take on my task; my division should be given buses, and be held in mobile reserve with a counter-attack role. Why was I left immobile? There were thousands of buses in England; let them give me some, and release me from this static role so that I could practise a mobile counter-attack role. The Prime Minister thought this was the cat's whiskers. I do not know what the War Office thought; but I got my buses.

The planners were now getting busy in Whitehall and various schemes were being considered. When it came to deciding which troops would carry out these wild-cat schemes, the answer was always the same: it must be the 3rd Division since there was no other formation yet ready for active operations. And so the planners decided as a first step that I must be ready to take my division overseas to seize the Azores; this was duly worked out, models of the islands were prepared, and detailed plans worked out for the operation.

Then I was told it was not to be the Azores, but the Cape Verde Islands. Then after much work, I was told to prepare plans for the seizure of Cork and Queenstown in Southern Ireland, so that the harbour could be used as a naval base for the anti-submarine war in the Atlantic. I had already fought the Southern Irish once, in 1921 and 1922, and it looked as if this renewed contest might be quite a party—with only one division.

None of these plans came to anything and I imagine that any work we did on them is tucked away in a cupboard in the War Office which is labelled "war babies." I have seen that cupboard. It seemed curious to me that anyone in his senses could imagine that, at a time when England was almost defenceless, the Prime Minister would allow to leave England the only division he had which was fully equipped and fit to fight in battle.

In July 1940 I was promoted to command the 5th Corps and from that time begins my real influence on the training of the Army then in England. By this I mean that the 5th Corps gave a lead in these matters which had repercussions far beyond the corps area of Hampshire and Dorset. In April 1941 I was transferred to command the 12th Corps in Kent, which was the expected invasion corner of England; and in December 1941 I was promoted to command the South-Eastern Army which included the counties of Kent, Surrey and Sussex. So the ideas and the doctrine of war, and training for war, which began as far west as Dorset, gradually spread along the south of England to the mouth of the Thames.

Let us examine those ideas; this is important for understanding, since it was the same doctrine which I carried with me to Africa in 1942, to Sicily and Italy in 1943 and to Normandy in 1944. In fact, what happened in the various commands I held in England during the two years after Dunkirk was the basis of success in all that happened in the long journey from Alamein to Berlin.

As time went on and my experience in command increased, so I was able to practise and confirm my ideas and to be ready when the call came to command the Eighth Army in August 1942. And I had served during those two years under some splendid officers, who had taught me much. In the 5th Corps I first served under Auchinleck, who had the Southern Command; I cannot recall that we ever agreed on anything. However, he soon went off as C.-in-C. in India and I then served in turn under Alexander and Paget; and Brooke was either C.-in-C. Home Forces or C.I.G.S. All these three were great friends and I held them all in high regard: as men and as soldiers.

The first point I tackled was the question of fitness: physical and mental. The Army in England was not fit and it must be made so. I often used to recall the lines of Kipling in his preface to *Land and Sea Tales*:

> " Nations have passed away and left no traces,
>   And history gives the naked cause of it—
>   One single, simple reason in all cases;
>   They fell because their peoples were not fit."

Training in the 5th Corps was ordered to be hard and tough; it must be carried out in all conditions of weather and climate; in rain, snow, ice, mud, fair weather or foul, at any hour of the day or night— we must be able to do our stuff better than the Germans. If they could only fight well in fine weather and in daylight, and we could fight with the maximum efficiency in any weather and at any time of the day or night, then we would beat them. All training was to be organised to lead up to exercises at the higher level, and all exercises were to be staged in an imaginative way. The large-scale exercises from the divisional level upwards must be designed to ensure that commanders, staffs and troops were capable of continuous and sustained operations over prolonged periods, and that all responsible echelons understood how to organise the twenty-four hours so that this would be possible.

Commanders and staff officers at any level who couldn't stand the strain, or who got tired, were to be weeded out and replaced— ruthlessly.

Total war demanded total fitness from the highest to the lowest.

As always happens, once active operations finished the paper work increased and staff officers and clerks became tied to offices. I ordered that at every headquarters the whole staff, officers and men, would turn out on one afternoon each week and do a seven-mile run. This applied to everyone under forty, and there would be no exception; those who didn't want to run the whole course could walk and trot, but they must go round the course even if they walked the whole way. There were many protests; but they all did it, even those over forty, and they enjoyed it in the end—some of them. I remember the case of a somewhat stout old colonel who went to the doctor and said if he did the run it would kill him; the doctor brought him to see me with a recommendation that he should be excused. I asked him if he truly thought he would die if he did the run; he said yes, and I saw a hopeful look in his eye. I then said that if he was thinking of dying it would be better to do it now, as he could be replaced easily and smoothly; it is always a nuisance if officers die when the battle starts and things are inclined to be hectic. His state of health was clearly not very good, and I preferred him to do the run and die. He did the run and so far as I know he is still alive today.

There was an urgent need to get rid of the " dead wood " which was hampering the initiative of keen and efficient young officers. There were old retired officers called up from the reserve; there were many inefficient regular officers from majors upwards who had never seen a shot fired in action and didn't want to. All these had to be weeded out and I made it my business to do so. I visited every unit and got to know all the senior officers and many of the junior ones; one by one the inefficient and lazy departed.

A struggle took place over wives. It was the custom for wives and families of officers to accompany units, and live in the towns and villages on the coast where invasion was expected at any time. I ordered that all wives and families were to leave at once; they were not allowed to live in the area of divisions that had an operational role in repelling invasion. I gave my reasons, which were as follows.

Invasion by the Germans was considered to be probable and we were all preparing to meet and defeat it. If an officer's wife and family were present with him in or near his unit area, and the attack came, an officer would at once be tempted to see to their safety first and to neglect his operational task; he would be fearful for their safety, amid all the shelling and bombing of the battle, and his thoughts would be with them rather than on the priority task of defeating the Germans. I was told that a good officer would never give a single thought to his wife and family in such conditions; his whole mind would be on the battle. I said that I did not believe it. Anyhow, human nature was weak and I was not prepared to let an officer be tempted to fail in his duty. The whole future of England, and indeed civilisation, was at stake; I would remove temptation and then there would be no doubt. Moreover, since the men could not have their families with them, the officers shouldn't either. The wives must go. And they did.

The command level was particularly important. A sense of urgency had to be instilled into officers and men and that precluded second-raters in command at any level. The unfit and incompetent had to be eliminated.

On the staff it was essential to ensure a standard of absolute service and technical efficiency. In fact, throughout the whole Army there was the definite necessity for physical and mental fitness, and for technical efficiency in the business of the conduct of battle.

The first prerequisite at all levels were commanders who knew their stuff and who were determined in spite of all the difficulties to get their own way in the conditions which obtained in those very difficult days. So far as I was concerned, encouragement of the young at any level played a big part.

There were certain dangers against which we had to guard. There was some danger that the staff might once again find themselves in the same position *vis-à-vis* the regimental officer as in the 1914-1918 war. There was a danger that the administrative echelons and units might accept the position of being the weaker vessels and decide that fighting was not their business. Fighting was the business of everyone and all must be trained to fight; that was my philosophy and I preached it unceasingly.

There was a danger that the few fighting units we had in the Army in England might think that the country and the British Army had "had it" (to use an expression dating I believe from this period) and that the Germans were invincible.

Lastly, there was a real danger that after the comparative rigours of the Dunkirk campaign, the survivors would sink back into the bosoms of their families and pay too much attention to the question of personal comfort and amenities. On this subject I laid down that while officers and men were not allowed to have their wives and families with them, they were to have leave in the normal way so that they could visit their families as often as possible. Also that while training was to be hard and tough, when it was over the troops were to return to good billets and good food, with good facilities for hot baths.

And so slowly but gradually a sense of urgency was instilled into the Army in England, and officers and men began to understand what it was all about and to see the need for all these things. We gradually got everyone on their toes after Dunkirk.

Some of the training exercises I organised and staged were harder and tougher than anything previously known in England. They were held in conditions of intense cold in the middle of winter, or in the heat of summer. When officers and men were exhausted, and commanders and staffs tired out, operational problems would flare up again with new situations developing in unexpected quarters. I remember one particular exercise very well, carried out in South-East England, in the spring of 1942. It was called "Exercise TIGER" and was the last exercise I directed before I went to Africa later that year. It was during that exercise that I first met Eisenhower; he was a major-general and had been sent over from the U.S.A. with some other generals to see what was going on. He wrote his name in my autograph book; the date was the 27th May 1942.

I found myself in disagreement with the general approach to the problem of the defence of Britain and refused to apply it in my corps area, and later in the South-Eastern Army. The accepted doctrine was that every inch of the coastline must be defended strongly, the defence being based on concrete pill-boxes and entrenchments on a linear basis all along the coastline.

There was no depth in the defensive layout and few troops available for counter-attack. Inland, "stop lines" were being dug all over England; when I asked what troops were available to man the stop lines I could get no clear answer. There were no troops.

My approach was different. I pulled the troops back from the beaches and held them ready in compact bodies in rear, poised for counter-attack and for offensive action against the invaders. After a sea crossing, troops would not feel too well and would be suffering from reaction; that is the time to attack and throw the invader back into the sea.

On the beaches themselves all I would allow was a screen of lightly equipped troops, with good communications and sufficient firepower to upset any landing and cause it to pause.

My whole soul revolted against allowing troops to get into trenches and become " Maginot-minded "; any offensive action would then be out of the question, and once the linear defensive system was pierced it would all disintegrate. My idea of the defence was that it must be like a spider's web; wherever the Germans went they must encounter fresh troops who would first subject them to heavy fire and would then attack them.

I rebelled against the " scorched earth " policy which had advocates in Whitehall; their reasoning was that as the Germans advanced inland towards London, so we would burn and destroy the countryside as we retreated. I said we would *not* retreat, nor would the Germans advance inland. Thus confidence in our ability to defeat the Germans was built up, at any rate in the area under my command.

In fact I set out to produce troops who were imbued with that offensive eagerness and infectious optimism which comes from physical well-being. And whenever I inspected any unit I used to make the men remove their steel helmets: not, as many imagined, to see if they had their hair properly cut, but to see if they had the light of battle in their eyes.

In 1942 the organisation of raiding operations on enemy coasts was one of the functions of Combined Operations Headquarters, the head of which was Admiral Mountbatten. In April 1942 the staff of that headquarters began work on a plan to raid Dieppe; I was made responsible for the Army side of the planning since I was then commanding the South-Eastern Army, from which the troops for the raid were to come. It was decided that the 2nd Canadian Division would carry out the raid, and intensive training was begun. The troops were embarked on the 2nd and 3rd July, and the raid was to take place on the 4th or one of the following days. Once embarked the troops were fully briefed, and were then " sealed " in their ships. The weather was unsuitable for launching the enterprise on the night of the 3rd July, and remained unsuitable till the 8th July—the last day on which conditions would permit it. The troops were then disembarked and dispersed to their camps and billets. All the troops had been fully informed of the objective of the raid and of the details connected with it; it was reasonable to expect that it was now a common subject of conversation in billets and pubs in the south of England, since nearly 5000 Canadian soldiers were involved as well as considerable numbers of sailors and airmen. Once all this force was "unsealed" and dispersed, I considered the operation was cancelled and I turned my attention to other matters.

But Combined Operations Headquarters thought otherwise; they decided to revive it and got the scheme approved by the British Chiefs of Staff towards the end of July. When I heard of this I was very upset; I considered that it would no longer be possible to maintain secrecy. Accordingly I wrote to General Paget, C.-in-C. Home Forces, telling him of my anxiety, and recommending that the raid on Dieppe should be considered cancelled "for all time." If it was considered desirable to raid the Continent, then the objective should not be Dieppe. This advice was disregarded. On the 10th August I left England to take command of the Eighth Army in the desert.

The raid was carried out on the 19th August and we received the news about it that night, when the Prime Minister was staying with me at Eighth Army H.Q.

The Canadians, and the Commandos working with them, fought magnificently, so did the Navy. But the Canadians lost heavily. The official history of the Canadian Army has the following remarks:

> "At Dieppe, from a force of fewer than 5000 men engaged for only nine hours, the Canadian Army lost more prisoners than in the whole eleven months of the later campaign in North-West Europe, or the twenty months during which Canadians fought in Italy. Sadder still was the loss in killed; the total of fatal casualties was 56 officers and 851 other ranks. Canadian casualties of all categories aggregated 3369."

Nearly 2000 of the total casualties were prisoners of war.
Certain modifications had been introduced into the revived plan. The most important were—first, the elimination of the paratroops and their replacement by commando units; secondly, the elimination of any preliminary bombing of the defences from the air. I should not myself have agreed to either of these changes. Commando units, if thought necessary, should have been an addition to, and not a replacement of, the paratroops; the demoralisation of the enemy defence by preliminary bombing was essential (as was done in Normandy in 1944) just before the troops touched down on the beaches.

My own feeling about the Dieppe raid is that there were far too many authorities with a hand in it; there was no one single operational commander who was solely responsible for the operation from start to finish, a Task Force Commander in fact. Without doubt the lessons learnt there were an important contribution to the eventual landing in Normandy on the 6th June 1944. But the price was heavy in killed and prisoners. I believe that we could have got the information and experience we needed without losing so many magnificent Canadian soldiers.

Early in August 1942 a large-scale exercise was to be held in Scotland and General Paget, then C.-in-C. Home Forces, suggested I should go up with him to see it. I was delighted to have an opportunity to see what other troops were doing and travelled north with Paget in "Rapier," the C.-in-C.'s special train (which I was myself to use in 1944). Then things began to happen: one after another, and fast. On the second day of the exercise the War Office telephoned me to return to London at once; I was to take over command of the First Army from Alexander, and begin work under Eisenhower on the plans for the landing in North Africa which was to take place in November 1942, under the code name TORCH. It was explained to me that Alexander had already gone to Egypt to become C.-in-C. Middle East; a brigadier would meet me in London and explain the situation. I returned to London at once, met the brigadier, who did not impress me, and then went to the War Office. I was there given more details and was told that the first thing I must do was to get Eisenhower to make a plan for the operation; time was getting on and the Chiefs of Staff could not get Eisenhower to produce his plan. The whole thing did not sound very good to me; a big invasion operation in North Africa in three months' time, and no plan yet made. Eisenhower I had barely met; I knew very few American soldiers and did not know how my methods would appeal to him. The crisis of the war was approaching and great events were to unfold. I was confident of being able to handle any job successfully if I was allowed to put into practice the ideas and methods that had become my military creed, and which by now I was convinced would bring us success in battle against the Germans. I returned to my Headquarters at Reigate hoping for the best; anyhow, I had now been two years in England—and it was time to move on.

The next morning (the 8th August) as I was shaving at about

7 a.m., the War Office telephoned and said the orders given me the previous day about the First Army and Operation TORCH were cancelled; I was to hold myself ready to proceed to Egypt at once to take command of the Eighth Army in the desert.

Alexander was already in Egypt and I would be serving under him. I was told later in the morning that Gott had been selected to command the Eighth Army but he had been killed, and I was to take his place.

Instead of carrying out an invasion of North Africa under a C.-in-C. whom I barely knew, I was now to serve under a C.-in-C. I knew well and to take command of an Army which was at grips with a German and Italian Army under the command of Rommel—of whom I had heard great things. This was much more to my liking and I felt I could handle that business, and Rommel.

It was true that I had never fought in the desert and I would have under me some very experienced generals who had been out there a long time. However, Rommel seemed to have defeated them all, and I would like to have a crack at him myself.

I was particularly glad that Alexander was to be my C.-in-C., as I knew that we would get on well together.

So it was with a light heart and great confidence that I made preparations for going to Africa. I was disturbed about my son David. When he was born I had entered him for Harrow, my father's school. But when the time came to send him to a public school in 1942 I decided against it; Harrow was too near London and the boys often had to sleep in the shelters. Instead I had sent him to Winchester. Some friends had suggested he should go to Canada with their boys; I declined the invitation; I wanted him in England. At the moment he was staying with friends for his summer holidays. I took a very quick decision and wrote to Major Reynolds, the headmaster of his former preparatory school, and asked if he and his wife would take charge of David for me, receive him into their family, and look after him till I returned from the war. I left for Africa before I received their reply but I had no fears; they took David in and treated him as their own son. I never saw him to say goodbye.

Since I had few belongings, my preparations for leaving England had been very simple. Everything I possessed had been destroyed by enemy bombing in Portsmouth in January 1941. I was now going to be given the opportunity to get my own back on the Germans.

A story is told by Sir Winston Churchill in *The Hinge of Fate* (Book Two, Chapter 3) about my departure:

" Montgomery started for the airfield with Ismay, who thus had an hour or more to give him the background of these sudden changes. A story—alas, not authenticated—has been told of this conversation. Montgomery spoke of the trials and hazards of a soldier's career. He gave his whole life to his profession, and lived long years of study and self-restraint. Presently fortune smiled, there came a gleam of success, he gained advancement, opportunity presented itself, he had a great command. He won a victory, he became world-famous, his name was on every lip. Then the luck changed. At one stroke all his life's work flashed away, perhaps through no fault of his own, and he was flung into the endless catalogue of military failures. ' But,' expostulated Ismay, ' you ought not to take it so badly as all that. A very fine Army is gathering in the Middle East. It may well be that you are not going to disaster.' ' What! ' cried Montgomery, sitting up in the car. ' What do you mean? I was talking about Rommel! ' "

Alas, not authenticated! I had not seen Ismay for many weeks when I left for Africa, and he did not go with me to the airfield.

I left England by air on the night of the 10th August and reached Gibraltar at dawn the next morning. We stayed at Gibraltar all that day and left in the evening of the 11th August for Cairo. During the journey I pondered over the problems which lay ahead and reached some idea, at least in outline, of how I would set about the business.

CHAPTER 6

MY DOCTRINE OF COMMAND

I was leaving England to exercise high command in the field. The work and experience of many years were about to be put to the test. But I have not yet explained the general principles of command which had gradually evolved in my mind during the past years and which I had preached as far back as 1934 when Chief Instructor at the Quetta Staff College. It is my firm belief that these principles of command and leadership were the biggest factor in achieving such success as came.

Although there is much to explain about my doctrine of command it can be summed up in one word: leadership.

In his *Memoirs*, Harry Truman says he learned from a study of history that " a leader is a man who has the ability to get other people to do what they don't want to do, and like it."

Leadership may be too complex for such a brief definition. On the other hand the word is often used somewhat loosely without its full meaning being understood. My own definition of leadership is this: " The capacity and the will to rally men and women to a common purpose, and the character which inspires confidence."

Merely to have the capacity is not enough; the leader must be willing to use it. His leadership is then based on truth and character; there must be truth in the purpose and will-power in the character.

The need for truth is not always realised. A leader must speak the truth to those under him; if he does *not* they will soon find it out and then their confidence in him will decline. I did not always tell *all* the truth to the soldiers in the war; it would have compromised secrecy, and it was not necessary.

I told them all they must know for the efficient carrying out of their tasks. But what I did tell them was always true and they knew it; that produced a mutual confidence between us. The good military leader will dominate the events which surround him; once he lets events get the better of him he will lose the confidence of his men, and when that happens he ceases to be of value as a leader.

When all is said and done the leader must exercise an effective influence, and the degree to which he can do this will depend on the personality of the man—the " incandescence " of which he is capable, the flame which burns within him, the magnetism which will draw the hearts of men towards him. What I personally would want to know about a leader is:

Where is he going?
Will he go all out?
Has he the talents and equipment, including knowledge, experience and courage? Will he take decisions, accepting full responsibility for them, and take risks where necessary?
Will he then delegate and decentralise, having first created an organisation in which there are definite focal points of decision so that the master plan can be implemented smoothly and quickly?

The matter of " decision " is vital. The modern tendency is to avoid taking decisions, and to procrastinate in the hope that things will come out all right in the wash. The only policy for the military leader is decision in action and calmness in the crisis: no bad doctrine for the political leader either.

I hold the view that the leader must know what he himself wants. He must see his objective clearly and then strive to attain it; he must let everyone else know what he wants and what are the basic fundamentals of his policy. He must, in fact, give firm guidance and a clear lead. It is necessary for him to create what I would call " atmosphere," and in that atmosphere his subordinate commanders will live and work.

I have known commanders who considered that once their plan was made and orders issued, they need take no further part in the proceedings, except to influence the battle by means of their reserves. Never was there a greater mistake. The modern battle can very quickly go off the rails. To succeed, a C.-in-C. must ensure from the beginning a very firm grip on his military machine; only in this way will his force maintain balance and cohesion and thus develop its full fighting potential. This firm grip does not mean interference, or cramping the initiative of subordinates; indeed, it is by the initiative of subordinates that the battle is finally won. The firm grip is essential in order that the master plan will not be undermined by the independent ideas of individual subordinate commanders at particular moments in the battle. Operations must develop within a predetermined pattern of action. If this is not done the result will be a compromise between the individual conceptions of subordinates about how operations should develop; alternatively, operations will develop as a result of situations created by subordinate action and in a way which does not suit the master plan. A third alternative is that the initiative might pass to the enemy. The master plan must never be so rigid that the C.-in-C. cannot vary it to suit the changing tactical situation; but nobody else may be allowed to change it at will—and, especially, not the enemy.

It is essential to understand the place of the " conference " when engaged on active operations in the field. By previous thought, by discussion with his staff, and by keeping in close touch with his subordinates by means of visits, a commander should know what he wants to do and whether it is possible to do it. If a conference of his subordinates is then necessary, it will be for the purpose of giving orders. He should never bring them back to him for such a conference; he must go forward to them. Then nobody looks over his shoulder. A conference of subordinates *to collect ideas* is the resort of a weak commander.

It is a mistake to think that once an order is given there is nothing more to be done; you have got to see that it is carried out in the spirit which you intended. Once he has decided on his outline plan and how he will carry it out, the commander should himself draft the initial operational order or directive, and not allow his staff to do so. His staff and subordinates then begin their more detailed work, and this is based on the written word of the commander himself. Mistakes are thus reduced to a minimum. This was my method, beginning from the days when I commanded a battalion.

No leader, however great, can long continue unless he wins victories. The battle decides all. How does one achieve success in battle?

In Sir Winston Churchill's study of Marlborough we note that:

" The success of a commander does not arise from following rules or models. It consists in an absolutely new comprehension of the dominant facts of the situation at the time, and all the forces at work. Every great operation of war is unique. What is wanted is a profound appreciation of the actual event. There is no surer road to disaster than to imitate the plans of bygone heroes and fit them to novel situations."

In battle, the art of command lies in understanding that no two situations are ever the same; each must be tackled as a wholly new problem to which there will be a wholly new answer.

I have always held the view that an army is not merely a collection of individuals, with so many tanks, guns, machine-guns, etc., and that the strength of the army is not just the total of all these things added together. The real strength of an army is, and must be, far greater than the sum total of its parts; that extra strength is provided by morale, fighting spirit, mutual confidence between the leaders and the led and especially with the high command, the quality of comradeship, and many other intangible spiritual qualities.

The raw material with which the general has to deal is men. The same is true in civil life. Managers of large industrial concerns have not always seemed to me to have understood this point; they think their raw material is iron ore, or cotton, or rubber—not men but commodities. In conversation with them I have disagreed and insisted that their basic raw material is *men*. Many generals have also not fully grasped this vital matter, nor understood its full implications, and that is one reason why some have failed.

An army must be as hard as steel in battle and can be made so; but, like steel, it reaches its finest quality only after much preparation and only provided the ingredients are properly constituted and handled. Unlike steel, an army is a most sensitive instrument and can easily become damaged; its basic ingredient is men and, to handle an army well, it is essential to understand human nature. Bottled up in men are great emotional forces which have got to be given an outlet in a way which is positive and constructive, and which warms the heart and excites the imagination. If the approach to the human factor is cold and impersonal, then you achieve nothing. But if you can gain the confidence and trust of your men, and they feel their best interests are safe in your hands, then you have in your possession a priceless asset and the greatest achievements become possible.

The morale of the soldier is the greatest single factor in war and the best way to achieve a high morale in war-time is by success in battle. The good general is the one who wins his battles with the fewest possible casualties; but morale will remain high even after considerable casualties, provided the battle has been won and the men know it was not wastefully conducted, and that every care has been taken of the wounded, and the killed have been collected and reverently buried.

Some think that morale is best sustained when the British soldier is surrounded by N.A.A.F.I.s, clubs, canteens, and so on. I disagree. My experience with soldiers is that they are at their best when they are asked to face up to hard conditions. Men dumped in some out-of-the-way spot in the desert will complain less of boredom, because they have to shift for themselves, than those surrounded by a wide choice of amenities. The creation of the Welfare State in Britain after the Second World War led too many to think that social security and individual prosperity were the only things worth while. But this is not so. If man wants prosperity he must work for it or else go without it. He won't get it merely by voting for it. The British soldier when properly led responds to a challenge and not to welfare benefits. Man does not live by bread alone. The soldier has to be kept active, alert, and purposeful all the time. He will do anything you ask of him so long as you arrange he gets his mail from home, the newspapers, and, curiously enough, plenty of tea. He then likes to know what is going on in the battle area and what you require him to do. He gets anxious if his home town is bombed and he cannot get any news about his girl, or his wife and children; that is one reason why letters and papers are so important. He leads a most unpleasant life in war. He will put up with this so long as he knows that you are living in relatively much the same way; and he likes to see the C.-in-C. regularly in the forward area, and be spoken to and noticed. He must know that you really care for him and will look after his interests, and that you will give him all the pleasures you can in the midst of his discomforts.

It is essential to understand that all men are different. The miners from Durham and Newcastle, the men from the Midlands, the Cockneys, the farmers from the West Country, the Scot, the Welshman—all are different. Some men are good at night; others prefer to fight in daylight. Some are best at the fluid and mobile battle; others are more temperamentally adapted to the solid killing match in close country. Therefore all *divisions* are different. In the 1914-18 war if ten divisions were needed for an offensive, the staff would take the ten most easily assembled. But a division develops an individuality of its own, which the higher commander must study and thus learn the type of battle each is best at. Once I had grasped this essential fact of difference, I used to match the troops to the job; having studied the conditions of any particular battle which was impending, I would employ in it divisions whose men were best suited to *those* conditions, and preferred them.

It is exactly the same with generals; all are different. Some will handle well a mobile battle; others are best at the set-piece. Generals must also be matched to the job. In fact, I spent a great deal of time in consideration of this human problem; I always used for each job in the master plan the general and the troops best fitted for that particular task. As a result each battle was already half-won before it ever began, because of the quality of my weapon *vis-à-vis* that of the enemy—who, as far as I could discover, did not work on the same philosophy.

The next point, still a human one, is the selection of commanders. Probably a third of my working hours were spent in the consideration of personalities. In dealing with subordinates, justice and a keen sense of fairness are essential—as also is a full measure of human consideration. I kept command appointments in my own hand, right down to and including the battalion or regimental level. Merit, leadership, and ability to do the job, were the sole criteria; I made it my business to know all commanders, and to insist on a high standard. Good senior commanders once chosen must be trusted and " backed " to the limit. Any commander is entitled to help and support from his immediate superior; sometimes he does not get it, a factor to be taken into account if the man fails. If, having received the help he might normally expect, a man fails—then he must go. It is sometimes thought that when an officer is promoted to the next higher command, he needs no teaching in how to handle it. This is a great mistake. There is a tremendous difference between a brigade and a division, between a division and a corps; when an officer got promotion, he needed help and advice in his new job and it was up to me to see that he got it.

Every officer has his " ceiling " in rank, beyond which he should not be allowed to rise—particularly in war-time. An officer may do well when serving under a first class superior. But how will he shape when he finds himself the boss ? It is one thing to be merely an adviser, with no real responsibility; it is quite another thing when you are the top man, responsible for the final decision. A good battalion commander does not necessarily make a good brigadier, nor a good divisional general a good corps commander. The judging of a man's ceiling in the higher ranks is one of the great problems which a commander must solve, and it occupied much of my time. The same problem must arise in civil life.

It is clear that my whole working creed was based on the fact that in war it is " the man " that matters. Commanders in all grades must have qualities of leadership; they must have initiative; they must have the " drive " to get things done; and they must have the character and ability which will inspire confidence in their subordinates. Above all, they must have that moral courage, that resolution, and that determination which will enable them to stand firm when the issue hangs in the balance. Probably one of the greatest assets a commander can have is the ability to radiate confidence in the plan and operations even (perhaps especially) when inwardly he is not too sure about the outcome. A C.-in-C. or Army Commander must therefore be a good judge of men, and be able to have the right men in the right places at the right times.

To work on this philosophy as regards all those under your command, you must watch your own morale carefully. A battle is, in effect, a contest between two wills—your own and that of the enemy general. If your heart begins to fail you when the issue hangs in the balance, your opponent will probably win.

It is absolutely vital that a senior commander should keep himself from becoming immersed in details, and I always did so. I would spend many hours in quiet thought and reflection in thinking out the major problems. In battle a commander has got to think how he will defeat the enemy. If he gets involved in details he cannot do this since he will lose sight of the essentials which really matter; he will then be led off on side issues which will have little influence on the battle, and he will fail to be that solid rock on which his staff can lean. Details are their province. No commander whose daily life is spent in the consideration of details, and who has not time for quiet thought and reflection, can make a sound plan of battle on a high level or conduct large-scale operations efficiently.

This principle applies equally in civil life and especially in Governmental affairs. I often think that the principle is not understood and applied by Cabinet Ministers, and by others who work in the Governmental machine. Many politicians holding high Governmental posts might well have the following inscribed on their tombstones when they die:

" Here lies a man who died of exhaustion brought about by preoccupation with detail. He never had time to think because he was always reading papers. He saw every tree, but never the whole wood."

On the operational side a C.-in-C. must draw up a master plan for the campaign he envisages and he must always think and plan two battles ahead—the one he is preparing to fight *and* the next one— so that success gained in one battle can be used as a spring board for the next. He has got to strive to read the mind of his opponent, to anticipate enemy reactions to his own moves, and to take quick steps to prevent enemy interference with his own plans. He has got to be a very clear thinker and able to sort out the essentials from the mass of factors which bear on every problem. If he is to do these things he must be abstemious and not be a heavy smoker, or drink much, or sit up late at night. He must have an ice-clear brain at all times. For myself, I do not smoke and I drink no alcohol of any sort; this is purely because I dislike both tobacco and alcohol, and therein I am lucky because I believe one is in far better health without them. In general, I consider that excessive smoking and drinking tend to cloud the brain; when men's lives are at stake this must never be allowed to happen, and it does happen too often. You cannot win battles unless you are feeling well and full of energy.

The plan of operations must always be made by the commander and must not be forced on him by his staff, or by circumstances, or by the enemy. He has got to relate what is strategically desirable with that which is tactically possible with the forces at his disposal; if this is not done he is unlikely to win. What is possible, given a bit of luck? And what is definitely not possible? That is always the problem. The plan having been made, there will be much detailed work to be done before the operation is launched; this detailed work must be done by the staff. The commander himself must stand back and have time to think; his attention must be directed to ensuring that the basic foundations and corner-stones of the master plan are not broken down by the mass of detail which will necessarily occupy the attention of the staff. If all these things are to be done successfully, a good Chief of Staff is essential. Fifty years ago a general could co-ordinate himself the work of his staff; today he cannot do so and must not try. The first piece of advice I would give any senior commander is to have a good Chief of Staff; I always did.

The commander must decide how he will fight the battle *before it begins*. He must then decide how he will use the military effort at his disposal to force the battle to swing the way he wishes it to go; he must make the enemy dance to his tune from the beginning, and never vice versa. To be able to do this, his own dispositions must be so balanced that he can utilise but need not react to the enemy's move but can continue relentlessly with his own plan. The question of "balance" was a definite feature of my military creed. Another feature was "grouping," i.e. seeing that each corps, which has to fight the tactical battle, is suitably composed for its task. Skill in grouping before the battle begins, and in re-grouping to meet the changing tactical situation, is one of the hall-marks of generalship.

A commander must be very thorough in making his tactical plan; once made, he must be utterly ruthless in carrying it out and forcing it through to success.

Before the battle begins an Army Commander should assemble all commanders down to the lieutenant-colonel level and explain to them the problem, his intention, his plan, and generally how he is going to fight the battle and make it go the way he wants. This practice is very necessary; if every unit commander in the army knows what is wanted, then all will fight the more intelligently and cohesion will be gained. Unit commanders must, at the right moment and having due regard to secrecy, pass on all relevant information to the regimental officers and men. Every single soldier must know, before he goes into battle, how the little battle he is to fight fits into the larger picture, and how the success of *his* fighting will influence the battle as a whole.

The whole army then goes into battle knowing what is wanted and how it is to be achieved. And when the troops see that the battle has gone exactly as they were told it would go, the increase in morale and the confidence in the higher command is immense—and this is a most important factor for the battles still to come.

The troops must be brought to a state of wild enthusiasm before the operation begins. They must have that offensive eagerness and that infectious optimism which comes from physical well-being. They must enter the fight with the light of battle in their eyes and definitely wanting to kill the enemy. In achieving this end, it is the spoken word which counts, from the commander to his troops; plain speech is far more effective than any written word.

Operational command in the battle must be direct and personal, by means of visits to subordinate H.Q. where orders are given verbally. A commander must train his subordinate commanders, and his own staff, to work and act on verbal orders. Those who cannot be trusted to act on clear and concise verbal orders, but want everything in writing, are useless. There is far too much paper in circulation in the Army, and no one can read even half of it intelligently.

Of course a commander must know in what way to give verbal orders to his subordinates. No two will be the same; each will require different treatment. Some will react differently from others; some will be happy with a general directive whilst others will like more detail. Eventually a mutual confidence on the subject will grow up between the commander and his subordinates; once this has been achieved there will never be any more difficulties or misunderstandings.

Command must be direct and personal. To this end a system of liaison officers is valuable during the battle; I have always used such a system from the days when I was commanding an infantry brigade.

It is essential to understand that battles are won primarily in the hearts of men. When Britain goes to war the ranks of her armed forces are filled with men from civil life who are not soldiers, sailors, or airmen by profession: and who never wanted to be. It must be realised that these men are very different from the soldiers and sailors of the Boer War era, or even of the 1914 period. The young man today reads the newspapers. He goes to the cinema and sees how people live and behave in other countries; he has the radio and television; his visual world is therefore extensive and he can now measure his everyday environment in a way which was impossible in the Victorian era. He is daily taking in information and relating it to himself.

He can think, he can appreciate, and he is definitely prepared to criticise. He wants to know what is going on, and what you want him to do—and why, and when. He wants to know that in the doing of it his best interests will be absolutely secure in your hands.

If all these things are understood by the military leader, and he acts accordingly, he will find it is not difficult to gain the trust and confidence of such men. The British soldier responds to leadership in a most remarkable way; and once you have won his heart he will follow you anywhere.

Finally, I do not believe that today a commander can inspire great armies, or single units, or even individual men, and lead them to achieve great victories, unless he has a proper sense of religious truth; he must be prepared to acknowledge it, and to lead his troops in the light of that truth. He must always keep his finger on the spiritual pulse of his armies; he must be sure that the spiritual purpose which inspires them is right and true, and is clearly expounded to one and all. Unless he does this, he can expect no lasting success. For all leadership, I believe, is based on the spiritual quality, the power to inspire others to follow; this spiritual quality may be for good, or evil. In many cases in the past this quality has been devoted towards personal ends, and was partly or wholly evil; whenever this was so, in the end it failed. Leadership which is evil, while it may temporarily succeed, always carries within itself the seeds of its own destruction.

This is only a short explanation of a very big subject. And I realise, of course, that it is very dogmatic. I have tried to state briefly, to boil down, what I believe to be the essence of the matter. But it may be enough to enable the reader to appreciate better what lay at the back of my mind when I arrived in Cairo on the morning of the 12th August 1942.

CHAPTER 7

EIGHTH ARMY

My thoughts during the flight to Egypt

I WAS taking with me the military creed which I have just outlined. But how to apply it?

The topography of North Africa was different from that to which I had been used. I had always been interested in the relationship between geography and strategy; this of course has to be carried a stage lower, and a relationship established between topography and the actual conduct of operations. As I understood it the objective was Tripoli, the next large port westwards from Alexandria. There were several small ports in between such as Tobruk, Benghazi, and other smaller ones. The country generally between Alamein and Tripoli was flat desert but three points of interest concerning it were uppermost in my mind.

First—The one metalled or tarmac road, which hugged the coast the whole way to Tripoli. This road was clearly a main supply axis, from port to port; but it was also an axis of main movement for forces.

Second—The Jebel Akhdar (The Green Mountains), a hilly area lying roughly between Tobruk and Benghazi which was sometimes referred to as the Cyrenaica " bulge " or more usually as simply " the Jebel."

This was clearly an important area but in previous campaigns it had usually been outflanked. If held strongly, with forces trained to attack southwards from it, it would be a valuable feature to possess and could not be by-passed.

Third—The Agheila position, usually referred to by the Germans as Mersa Brega. This was an area of soft sand and salt pans at the southernmost point of the Gulf of Sirte, and stretching inland to the south for many miles. There were only a few tracks through this sand sea, and so long as Rommel held the area he could hold up our advance, or alternatively could debouch at will against us. Our advance had taken us up to the Agheila position in February 1941 and again in early 1942; but on neither occasion had we been able to capture and to occupy the position in strength, and since March 1941 it had remained in Rommel's possession.

My thinking on topography left me with the conviction that the four main features that I must work into my plans were: the coast road to Tripoli, the ports along the coast, the Jebel between Tobruk and Benghazi, and the Agheila position. In my flight from Gibraltar to Cairo I was circling this very territory; the direct route was not safe for an aircraft flying alone and we took a detour to the south by night, to hit the Nile well south of Cairo in the early dawn.

The next point in my thinking concerned the forces which would be available to me, and how best to relate them to this topography.

From what I read and heard, Rommel's forces consisted of holding troops who manned static defence positions and held vital areas of ground, and mobile troops for counter-attack and to form the spearhead of offensives. The holding forces consisted largely of Italians and were mostly unarmoured; the mobile forces were German and for the greater part armoured. The *corps d'élite* was the Panzer Army consisting of 15th Panzer Division, 21st Panzer Division, and 90th Light Division.

I came to the conclusion that the Eighth Army must have its own Panzer Army—a corps strong in armour, well equipped, and well trained. It must never hold static fronts; it would be the spearhead of our offensives. Because of the lack of such a corps we had never done any lasting good. The formation of this corps of three or four divisions must be a priority task.

Then there was the question of morale. From what I had learnt the troops had their tails down and there was no confidence in the higher command. This would have to be put right at once, but until I had actually got the feel of things myself I could not decide how to set about it.

These thoughts, and many others, passed through my mind on the journey and when I landed in Egypt the problem was beginning to clarify in my mind. I was confident that the answers to the problems would come to me once I got to real grips with them.

I was not looking forward to my meeting with Auchinleck. I had heard certain things about his methods of command and knew that I could never serve happily under him. I also considered that he was a poor picker of men. A good judge of men would never have selected General Corbett to be his Chief of Staff in the Middle East. And to suggest that Corbett should take command of the Eighth Army, as Auchinleck did, passed all comprehension.

Again, nobody in his senses would have sent Ritchie to succeed Cunningham in command of the Eighth Army; Ritchie had not the experience or qualifications for the job and in the end he had to be removed too. Later, after he had gained experience in command of a division and a corps, Ritchie did very well in the campaign in North-West Europe; he was put into an impossible position when he was sent to command the Eighth Army.

On the 5th August 1942 the Prime Minister (Mr. Churchill) had visited General Auchinleck at H.Q. Eighth Army in the desert. Churchill was on his way to Moscow. Auchinleck had assumed direct command of the Eighth Army after he had relieved Ritchie of this command, and was also C.-in-C. Middle East. The Prime Minister was accompanied by the C.I.G.S. (Brooke). The general situation was investigated and it was pointed out to Auchinleck that he could not go on commanding the Middle East and also Eighth Army; he himself must return to G.H.Q. in Cairo and someone else must command the Eighth Army. Auchinleck agreed with Brooke's proposal that I should come to Egypt and command the Eighth Army.

Field-Marshal Smuts was in Cairo at the time and the matter was discussed with him later that day. The Prime Minister and Smuts both favoured Gott, who had made a great name for himself in the desert and who was strongly backed by general opinion in the Middle East.

On the 6th August the Prime Minister sent a telegram to the War Cabinet regarding the changes he proposed to make. These included the splitting-off of Persia and Irak from the Middle East Command, the replacement of Auchinleck by Alexander, and the assignment of the command of the Eighth Army to Gott. But Gott was shot down in an aircraft and killed on the 7th August and next day I was ordered to take command. On the same day Brigadier Jacob (now Sir Ian Jacob of the B.B.C.) took a letter from the Prime Minister to General Auchinleck at H.Q. Eighth Army in the desert telling him he was to be relieved of his command. On the 9th August, Alexander arrived

THE MEMOIRS OF FIELD-MARSHAL MONTGOMERY

in Cairo and met Auchinleck, who had by then come in from the desert, having handed over acting command of the Eighth Army to General Ramsden, the commander of 30 Corps.

It is now clear to me that the appointment of Gott to command the Eighth Army *at that moment* would have been a mistake. I had never met him; he was clearly a fine soldier and had done splendid work in the desert. But from all accounts he was completely worn out and needed a rest. He himself knew this. He said to a mutual friend: " I am very tired. Also we have tried every club in the bag and have failed. A new brain is wanted out here on this job; it's an old job but it needs a new brain. If they want me to do it I will try. But they ought to get someone else, a new man from England."

I arrived at an airfield outside Cairo early on the 12th August. I was met and taken to the Mena House Hotel near the Great Pyramid, where General Auchinleck had a room; there I had a bath and breakfast, and was then driven to Middle East H.Q. in Cairo. I arrived there soon after 10 a.m. and was taken straight to see Auchinleck. It was very hot and I was wearing service dress as in England; I had sent my A.D.C. off to buy some desert kit.

Auchinleck took me into his map-room and shut the door; we were alone. He asked me if I knew he was to go. I said that I did. He then explained to me his plan of operations; this was based on the fact that at all costs the Eighth Army was to be preserved " in being " and must not be destroyed in battle. If Rommel attacked in strength, as was expected soon, the Eighth Army would fall back on the Delta; if Cairo and the Delta could not be held, the army would retreat southwards up the Nile, and another possibility was a withdrawal to Palestine. Plans were being made to move the Eighth Army H.Q. back up the Nile.

I listened in amazement to this exposition of his plans. I asked one or two questions, but I quickly saw that he resented any question directed to immediate changes of policy about which he had already made up his mind. So I remained silent.

He then said I was to go down to the desert the next day and spend two days at Eighth Army H.Q., getting into the picture and learning the game. He was himself still commanding the Eighth Army, and he had ordered Ramsden to act for him. I was not to take over command till the 15th August, the day on which he would himself hand over to Alexander; he wished these two events to be simultaneous. In the event of an enemy attack, or of some crisis occurring, he himself would at once come to Eighth Army H.Q. and take direct command again from Ramsden. It all seemed most peculiar and I got out of the room as soon as I decently could.

I then went in search of Alexander; I soon found him in the headquarters, calm, confident and charming—as always.

I would like to make the point now, categorically, how lucky I was to have " Alex " as my C.-in-C. I could not have served under a better Chief; we were utterly different, but I liked him and respected him as a man. I will enlarge on this as my tale develops.

I at once put to him my plan for creating a reserve corps for the Eighth Army, strong in armour, similar to Rommel's. He agreed; but he was not yet C.-in-C. It was obviously useless to discuss the matter with Auchinleck or his Chief of Staff; they were both to go. So I went off to find the Deputy Chief of the General Staff, Major-General (now Field-Marshal Sir John) Harding. He had been a student under me at the Camberley Staff College and I had the highest opinion of his ability. He did not know what Alexander and myself were doing in Cairo; so I told him. I then put the whole plan to him and asked if he could form the corps which I wanted from the bits and pieces scattered around Egypt; 300 new Sherman tanks were due at Suez from America on the 3rd September and these would provide the equipment for the armoured divisions. He said he would go into it and I arranged to come back and see him again at 6 p.m. that evening to get the answer, and said I would ask Alexander to come with me. Alexander and I then went off to lunch at Shepheard's Hotel, where we discussed the whole affair. I outlined to him my ideas and got his general agreement to the course of action I would pursue in the Eighth Army. I spent the afternoon buying clothes suitable for the desert in August; these were badly needed, as having spent a busy day in Cairo in August in English serge uniform I was more than hot! I had been asked to stay that night at the British Embassy in Cairo, and had arranged that the Brigadier General Staff, Eighth Army, was to meet me the next morning at the cross-roads west of Alexandria at 9 a.m. and take me to Eighth Army H.Q.

At 6 p.m. Alexander and I went back to G.H.Q. to see Harding; he said he could produce the corps we wanted. It would be 10 Corps and would consist of:

1st Armoured Division		One armoured brigade
8th Armoured Division	Each of	One infantry brigade
10th Armoured Division		Divisional troops

New Zealand Div.—Two infantry brigades and one armoured brigade

This was splendid and we told him to go ahead.

One more thing had to be done that day and that was to collect a second A.D.C. I had brought one with me from England, Captain Spooner in the Royal Norfolk Regiment; neither he nor myself had campaigned in Egypt and I needed a second one who knew well the ways of life in the desert. I was told that Gott had recently taken on a young officer in the 11th Hussars; he had not been in the aircraft when Gott was shot down, and was now in Cairo, and he might be what I wanted. He came to see me. His name was John Poston; he was a Harrow boy, and had hardly left school when the war began. He could see I was a lieut.-general and he knew I wanted an A.D.C.; but he had never heard of me before and he did not know what I was doing in Egypt. I said to him: " My name is Montgomery. I arrived this morning from England and I am going down to the desert tomorrow to take command of the Eighth Army. I have not been in the desert before and I want an A.D.C. who will go about with me and generally help me. Will you come to me as my A.D.C. ? "

He was clearly somewhat startled; this was highly secret news, known to very few.

He didn't answer at once; he just looked at me, straight in the face. He looked sad; he had just been with Gott, who was known all over the Middle East and was obviously a hero to all young officers. And now his master was dead. I said nothing, but just waited for his answer: looking into a pair of steady grey eyes.

At last he said: " Yes, sir; I would like to come with you."

I could not have made a better choice. We trod the path together from Alamein to the Elbe, fighting our way through ten countries. I was completely devoted to him. He was killed in Germany in the last week of the war. The Promised Land by then was not so very far away and he, who had travelled so far and fought so hard, gave his young life that others might enjoy it.

At 5 a.m. on the 13th August I left the British Embassy by car to go down to the desert.

The B.G.S. of the Eighth Army was Brigadier (now Major-General Sir Francis) de Guingand. "Freddie" de Guingand and I were old friends; we had first met in York when I was a major and he was a newly-joined second-lieutenant; we had met again in Egypt in 1932 and 1933, in Quetta in 1935, and in 1939 when he was a sort of military assistant to Hore-Belisha, who was Secretary of State for War. He had a quick and fertile brain and I had in the past regarded him as an outstanding young officer. There he was again, waiting for me as had been arranged at the cross-roads outside Alexandria, where the road from Cairo turned westwards along the coast. He looked thin and worried; he was obviously carrying a heavy burden. I realised at once it was essential to re-establish the former close friendship before tackling the main problem; so I made him get into my car and I talked about our past days together, and we had a good laugh over several episodes I recalled. He quickly became less tense and after a while I said: "Well, Freddie my lad, you chaps seem to have got things into a bit of a mess here. Tell me all about it."

He then produced a document which he had written for me, giving the situation and all the relevant facts. I said: "Now, Freddie, don't be silly. You know I never read any papers when I can get the person concerned to tell me himself. Put that bumf away and unburden your soul."

He laughed and I saw at once I would now get a first class review of the present situation and the causes of it—with nothing held back. We sat close together with a map on our knees and he told me the story; the operational situation, the latest intelligence about the enemy, the generals commanding in the various sectors, the existing orders of Auchinleck about future action, his own views about things. I let him talk on. Occasionally I asked a question but only to clarify some point. When he had done, there was silence for a moment or two: then I asked about the morale of the officers and men. He said it wasn't good; the Eighth Army wanted a clear lead and a firm grip from the top; there was too much uncertainty and he thought the "feel of the thing" was wrong. I did not press him on this point; I knew he was trying to be loyal to his past chief.

The time passed quickly and in due course we left the coast road and turned south along a track into the open desert. We were quiet now and I was thinking: chiefly about de Guingand, and I have no doubt he was thinking about me and his own future.

The magnitude of the task in front of me was beginning to be apparent. I knew I could not tackle it alone; I must have someone to help me, a man with a quick and clear brain, who would accept responsibility, and who would work out the details and leave me free to concentrate on the major issues—in fact, a Chief of Staff who would handle all the detailed and intricate staff side of the business and leave me free to command. I knew that if I once got immersed in the details of the "dog's breakfast" that was being set in front of me, I would fail as others had failed before me.

Was Freddie de Guingand this man?

We were complete opposites; he lived on his nerves and was highly strung; in ordinary life he liked wine, gambling, and good food. Did these differences matter? I quickly decided they did not; indeed, differences were assets.

I have always considered that two people who are exactly the same do not make the best team. He was about 14 years younger than I but we had been great friends in the past and as I looked at him, thin and worried as he was, the old affection returned. And he had a first class brain, which was capable of working at high speed. Furthermore he knew me and my ways, and that was important. If he was to be the man he must be given the necessary power; he must be Chief of Staff, not just Chief of the General Staff.

But the British Army did not work on the Chief of Staff principle; a commander had a number of principal staff officers under him and he was supposed to co-ordinate their activities himself. This was impossible in the situation now confronting me. How could I co-ordinate all the staff work of the desert campaign? That is what all the others had done and it had led them to lose sight of the essentials; they had become immersed in details and had failed.

Before we arrived at Eighth Army H.Q. I had decided that de Guingand was the man; I would make him my Chief of Staff with full powers and together we would do the job. But I did not tell him then; I thought I would wait and announce it in front of the whole staff, so as to build him up in their eyes and make clear the difference the new appointment represented.

I have never regretted that decision. Freddie de Guingand and I went through the rest of the war together. Wherever I went, he came as my Chief of Staff; we journeyed side by side from Alamein to Berlin. And as we went, he grew in stature and I realised how lucky I was. He was a brilliant Chief of Staff and I doubt if such a one has ever before existed in the British Army or will ever do so again: although of course here I am prejudiced.

As we bumped over the desert track I came to the conclusion that I now had two tremendous assets. Behind me was Alexander, a firm friend and ally, who could be relied on to support me and do all that I asked of him—so long as it was sound, and I was successful. And by my side would be de Guingand, my trusted Chief of Staff. What was necessary next was to get good and reliable subordinate commanders below me.

With these thoughts in my mind I was quite cheerful when we arrived at the desert headquarters of the Eighth Army at about 11 a.m. The sight that met me was enough to lower anyone's morale. It was a desolate scene; a few trucks, no mess tents, work done mostly in trucks or in the open air in the hot sun, flies everywhere. I asked where Auchinleck used to sleep; I was told that he slept on the ground outside his caravan. Tents were forbidden in the Eighth Army; everyone was to be as uncomfortable as possible, so that they wouldn't be more comfortable than the men. All officers' messes were in the open air where, of course, they attracted the flies of Egypt. In the case of the mess of senior officers which I was inheriting, a mosquito net had been erected round the table; but it didn't shade one from the sun and the flies, once inside, could not get out. I asked where was the Air Force H.Q. I was told they were many miles back on the sea-shore, near Burg-el-Arab; the Army and the Air Forces appeared to be fighting two separate battles, without that close personal relationship which is so essential. The whole atmosphere of the Army Headquarters was dismal and dreary.

The acting Army Commander, Lt.-Gen. Ramsden, met me. I knew him of old since he had commanded the Hampshire Regiment in my 8th Division in Palestine in 1938-39; he was a very good battalion commander in those days and I had not met him since. He explained the situation to me. I cross-examined him about the Army plans for a withdrawal if Rommel attacked; certain orders had been issued about the withdrawal but they were indefinite. There was an air of uncertainty about everything in the operational line, nor was Army H.Q. in close touch with the H.Q. of the Desert Air Force.

It was clear to me that the situation was quite unreal and, in fact, dangerous. I decided at once to take action. I had been ordered not to take over command of the Eighth Army till the 15th August; it was still only the 13th. I knew it was useless to consult G.H.Q. and that I must take full responsibility myself. I told General Ramsden he was to return at once to his corps; he seemed surprised as he had been placed in acting command of the Army, but he went. I then had lunch, with the flies and in the hot sun. During lunch I did some savage thinking. After lunch I wrote a telegram to G.H.Q. saying that I had assumed command of Eighth Army as from 2 p.m. that day, the 13th August; this was disobedience, but there was no comeback. I then cancelled all previous orders about withdrawal.

I issued orders that in the event of enemy attack there would be *no* withdrawal; we would fight on the ground we now held and if we couldn't stay there alive we would stay there dead. I remembered an inscription I had seen in Greece when touring that country with my wife in 1933. It was carved by the Greeks at Thermopylae to commemorate those who died defending the pass over 2000 years ago, and its English version is well known:

" Go, tell the Spartans, thou that passeth by,
    That here, obedient to their laws, we lie."

We would do the same, if need be.

I thought that was enough for the moment, until I had seen more of the ground and had met some of the subordinate commanders. I decided to leave the H.Q. quickly in case any repercussion came from G.H.Q. about my sudden seizure of command of the Eighth Army. But before going I told de Guingand to assemble the whole staff at 6 p.m. that evening, so that I could speak to them. I had already met Ramsden, Commander 30 Corps, on the northern flank. I now set out to H.Q. 13 Corps, on the southern flank, where I arranged to meet General Freyberg; his substantive command was the New Zealand division, but since the death of Gott he had been acting in command of 13 Corps.

On the way to the H.Q. of 13 Corps I sat in the back of the car and studied the map. My guide, an officer of Army H.Q. whose job it was to know the way always to 13 Corps, sat in front with the driver. After a time the car stopped and I asked my guide if he knew where we were; he said he did not know and was lost.

I then noticed we were inside a large wired-in enclosure and I asked what it was; he said we were in the middle of a minefield.

I wasn't too pleased. I told the driver to back the car along our tracks till we were out of the minefield, by which time my guide had located himself and we started off again.

I had a good talk with Freyberg, and later with Morshead, who commanded the 9th Australian Division. Those two were fine soldiers, and I say this not only because they both approved whole-heartedly of my ideas, which I outlined to them.

I got back to Army H.Q. rather late and found the staff waiting for me. De Guingand had assembled them a few yards from the caravan which was my office; it was now 6.30 p.m., and in the cool of the evening I addressed my new staff.

I introduced myself to them and said I wanted to see them and explain things. Certain orders had already been issued which they knew about, and more would follow. The order " no withdrawal " involved a complete change of policy and they must understand what that policy was, because they would have to do the detailed staff work involved. If we were to fight where we stood the defences must have depth; all transport must be sent back to rear areas; ammunition, water, rations, etc., must be stored in the forward areas. We needed more troops in the Eighth Army in order to make the " no with-drawal " order a possibility. There were plenty of troops back in the Delta, preparing the defence of that area; but the defence of the cities of Egypt must be fought out *here* at Alamein. Two new divisions had arrived from England and were being used to dig positions to defend the Delta; I would get them out here.

Then, from all the bits and pieces in Egypt I was going to form a new corps, the 10th Corps, strong in armour; this would never hold the line but would be to us what the Africa Korps was to Rommel; the formation of this new 10 Corps had already begun.

The policy of fighting the enemy in brigade groups, Jock columns, and with divisions split up into bits and pieces all over the desert was to cease. In future divisions would fight *as* divisions.

I did not like the atmosphere I found at Army H.Q. No one could have a high morale at the headquarters if we stuck ourselves down in a dismal place like this and lived in such discomfort.

We ought to have the headquarters by the sea; where we could work hard, bathe, and be happy.

My orders from Alexander were quite simple; they were to destroy Rommel and his Army. I understood Rommel was expected to attack *us* shortly. If he came soon it would be tricky, if he came in a week, all right, but give us two weeks and Rommel could do what he liked; he would be seen off and then it would be our turn. But I had no intention of launching *our* attack until we were ready; when that time came we would hit Rommel for six right out of Africa.

There was clearly much work to be done and it couldn't be done where we were, in all this discomfort. The H.Q. would move as soon as possible to a site on the sea-shore near the Air Force H.Q.; together with the Air Force we would work out the plan for our offensive. The order forbidding tents was cancelled; let tents and mess furniture be got and let us all be as comfortable as possible.

Finally, I explained my methods of working, and my dislike of paper and details. I appointed de Guingand to be Chief of Staff of the Eighth Army; every order given by him would be regarded as coming from me, and would be obeyed instantly; he had my complete confidence and I gave him authority over the whole headquarters.

My talk was listened to in complete silence. One could have heard a pin drop if such a thing was possible in the sand of the desert! But it certainly had a profound effect and a spirit of hope, anyway of clarity, was born that evening; one thing was very clear to the staff, there was to be no more uncertainty about anything. But the old hands thought that my knees were very white!

My first day in the desert, the 13th August, had been a good one, though long and tiring. Much had been achieved; but much still remained to be done. I knew I must be careful for one more day, until Auchinleck had departed on the 15th August; the existing régime at G.H.Q. regarded me as an unpleasant new broom. So far there had been complete silence from G.H.Q. so far as I was concerned; but they had only been notified of certain orders I had issued and I had made no demands on them for anything. Once Alexander was C.-in-C. on the morning of the 15th August all would be well. He would do all that we sought and would see it was done at once; I had no doubt on that score. On de Guingand's advice I decided to make no demands on G.H.Q. as a result of the change in policy till the evening of the 14th August. He had great wisdom and his advice on these matters was always sound; as time went on he often restrained me from rushing my fences. We wanted a lot, but I also needed to do some reconnaissances before I could make ready my plan.

I had a good talk that night with de Guingand. He now had considerable powers and he wanted to know my views on certain matters. I was going to be out all day on 14th August and a great deal even after that; he was anxious to get hold of me in the evenings. By the time I went to bed that night I was tired. But I knew that we were on the way to success. I'm afraid that it was with an insubordinate smile that I fell asleep: I was issuing orders to an Army which someone else reckoned he commanded!

I was woken up soon after dawn the next morning by an officer with the morning situation report. I was extremely angry and told him no one was ever to come near me with situation reports; I did not want to be bothered with details of patrol actions and things of that sort. He apologised profusely and said that Auchinleck was always woken early and given the dawn reports.

I said I was not Auchinleck and that if anything was wrong the Chief of Staff would tell me; if nothing was wrong I didn't want to be told. The offending officer was very upset; so we had an early morning cup of tea together and a good talk, and he went away comforted. The Chief of Staff issued new orders about situation reports and I was never bothered again.

It was soon pretty clear to me, after talking with de Guingand, that all indications pointed to an early attack by Rommel; he would make a last attempt to get to Cairo and Alexandria, and secure the Delta. It was evident that if so, he would probably make his main effort on the south or inland flank, and would then carry out a right hook in order to get in behind the Eighth Army.

He could not leave the Army intact and pass on towards the flesh-pots of Egypt; he must first destroy the Eighth Army, after which the flesh-pots were all his for the asking.

That being the case, the outline of my plan was at once clear.

The northern flank must be strengthened on the front of 30 Corps and made very strong with minefields and wire, so that it could be held with a minimum of troops; I need not visit that front for the moment. The southern flank demanded careful consideration; it was there I would go. I also wanted a new commander for 13 Corps on the flank; no one had yet been appointed to succeed Gott.

I spent the day examining the ground on the inter-corps boundary and on the southern flank, and at once saw the importance of two dominating areas of ground: the Ruweisat Ridge and the Alam Halfa Ridge. Both were important but the key to the whole Alamein position was the Alam Halfa Ridge. This was several miles in rear of the Alamein Line and south-east from the Ruweisat Ridge; it was undefended, because there were no troops available.

I had pondered deeply over what I had heard about armoured battles in the desert and it seemed to me that what Rommel liked was to get our armour to attack him; he then disposed of his own armour behind a screen of anti-tank guns, knocked out our tanks, and finally had the field to himself. I was determined that would not happen if Rommel decided to attack us before we were ready to launch a full-scale offensive against him. I would not allow our tanks to rush out at him; we would stand firm in the Alamein position, hold the Ruweisat and Alam Halfa Ridges securely, and let him beat up against them. We would fight a static battle and my forces would not move; his tanks would come up against our tanks dug-in in hull-down positions at the western edge of the Alam Halfa Ridge.

During the day I met on the southern flank the general commanding the 7th Armoured Division, the famous Desert Rats. We discussed the expected attack by Rommel and he said there was only one question to be decided: who would loose the armour against Rommel? He thought he himself should give the word for that to happen. I replied that no one would loose the armour; it would not be loosed and we would let Rommel bump into it for a change. This was a new idea to him and he argued about it a good deal.

When I got back to my headquarters that night the outline of my immediate plans for strengthening the Alamein position was clear in my mind. I was determined to make the position so strong that we could begin our preparations for our own great offensive and not become preoccupied by any attack that Rommel might decide to make. All information seemed to suggest that he would attack towards the end of the month in the full moon period; I wanted to begin my preparations for the battle of Alamein before then, and to continue those preparations whatever Rommel might do.

Therefore we must be strong, with our forces so " balanced " that I need never react to his thrusts or moves: strong enough to see him off without disrupting the major preparations. That was my object.

I discussed the problem with de Guingand and we decided to ask G.H.Q. for the 44th Division to be sent to the Eighth Army *at once*, and to position it to hold the Alam Halfa Ridge. Once that ridge was securely held by a complete division, well dug in and properly supported by armour (not to be loosed), I really had not much more to bother about. I asked that another division, the 51st, should be sent to me later; this division was beginning to arrive at Suez. The details of the tactical plan on the southern flank I must leave to 13 Corps. But at the moment I had no Corps Commander. I decided to ask Alexander to get General Horrocks flown out from England at once to command the 13 Corps. Horrocks had been in my 3rd Division as a battalion commander; I had got him a brigade and then a division in my corps in England; I now wanted him to have a corps in my Army. I knew I could not have a better man and so it turned out; he was exactly what was wanted for the job which lay ahead.

We had a little trouble with the staff at G.H.Q. when de Guingand telephoned these requests that night. I then got direct on to Alexander and he agreed to everything; I do not know if he consulted Auchinleck who was due to go the next morning.

And so by the 15th August, the day on which Auchinleck had ordered me to assume command of the Eighth Army, I had already been in command for two days and we had got things moving in the right direction. Above all, by taking grip we had already achieved a definite lift in morale. This was important as the spirit of the warrior is the greatest single factor in war.

We now had to begin planning for what was to be known as the Battle of Alamein. Time was pressing and I already knew that I would be urged to attack in September. But before describing certain aspects of the preparation and conduct of that battle, we must have a quick look at the Battle of Alam Halfa—which was a model defensive battle under the conditions in which it was fought, and which was from my point of view an essential preliminary to the Battle of Alamein. Without Alam Halfa, Alamein might not have been so successful.

The Prime Minister visited the Eighth Army on the 19th August on his way back from Moscow. I took him round the front and explained to him my plans for defeating Rommel's expected attack and also my ideas about our own offensive. He stayed that night with me at our new headquarters on the shore near Burg-el-Arab, to which we had moved. He bathed in the Mediterranean before dinner; he had no bathing costume and I had some difficulty in keeping the Press away as he walked towards the sea in his shirt. He was interested in a group of soldiers in the distance and said how curious it was that they all wore white bathing trunks. I had to explain that no one wore any bathing kit in the Eighth Army. The soldiers wore shorts all day and often not even a shirt; their bodies got very brown from the sun. What in the distance looked like white bathing drawers was actually white flesh, which did not get brown because of the khaki shorts! We had great fun that night in our Mess and de Guingand had arranged suitable wine and old brandy for the Prime Minister.

When he left the next day I asked him to sign my autograph book. He wrote this personal note. I had assumed command of the Eighth Army on the 13th August, the anniversary of the Battle of Blenheim.

" May the anniversary of Blenheim which marks the opening of the new Command bring to the Commander of the Eighth Army and his troops the fame and fortune they will surely deserve.

Winston S. Churchill "

20th August, 1942

CHAPTER 8

THE BATTLE OF ALAM HALFA

31st August to 6th September 1942

IN ADDITION to the general plot which I have just outlined, I had also made it clear to the Eighth Army that " bellyaching " would not be tolerated. By this I meant that type of indiscipline which arises when commanders are active in putting forward unsound reasons for not doing what they are told to do. In the Eighth Army orders had generally been queried by subordinates right down the line; each thought he knew better than his superiors and often it needed firm action to get things done. I was determined to stop this state of affairs at once. Orders no longer formed " the base for discussion," but for action.

What I now needed was a battle which would be fought in accordance with my ideas and not those of former desert commanders; furthermore, it must be a resounding victory and would have to come before our own offensive, so that confidence of officers and men in the high command would be restored and they would enter on the stern struggle which lay further ahead with an enhanced morale. They must come to believe.

I had taken command of truly magnificent material; it did not take me long to see that. The Eighth Army was composed of veteran fighting divisions. But officers and men were bewildered at what had happened and this had led to a loss of confidence. " Brave but baffled " the Prime Minister had called them.

This loss of confidence, combined with the bellyaching which went on and which was partly the cause of it, were becoming dangerous and could only be eradicated by a successful battle: a battle in which Rommel was defeated easily, and must be seen to have been beaten, and with few casualties to the Eighth Army.

I could not myself attack; Rommel must provide that opportunity for me. But in order to reap the full benefit, I must correctly forecast the design of his expected attack and determine in advance how we would defeat it. This was not difficult to do.

My intelligence staff were certain the " break-in " to our positions would be on the southern flank; this would be followed by a left wheel, his armoured forces being directed on the Alam Halfa and Ruweisat ridges. I agreed, and my plans were based on this forecast. We were pretty clear about the timing, the direction, and the strength of his attack. The rest lay on my plate.

I decided to hold the Alam Halfa Ridge strongly with the 44th Division and to locate my tanks just south of its western end. Once I was sure that the enemy main thrust was being directed against the Alam Halfa Ridge, I planned to move the armour to the area between the west of the ridge and the New Zealand positions in the main Alamein line. I was so sure that this movement of my own armour would take place that I ordered it to be actually rehearsed; and when it *did* take place on the morning of the 1st September I had some 400 tanks in position, dug in, and deployed behind a screen of 6-pounder anti-tank guns. The strictest orders were issued that the armour was not to be loosed against Rommel's forces; it was not to move; the enemy was to be allowed to beat up against it and to suffer heavy casualties.

It was obvious to me that Rommel could not just by-pass my forces and go off eastwards to Cairo; if he did so, I could have descended on his rear with 400 tanks and that would have been the end of his Army.

I then decided that my extreme south flank should be mobile; the 7th Armoured Division would hold a wide front and, as the attack came, would give way before it. When the attack swung left-handed towards the Alam Halfa Ridge, the 7th Armoured Division would harry it from the east and south, and generally " shoot it up."

General Horrocks had by now arrived from England to command 13 Corps on my left flank and the details of the plan were placed in his very capable hands. I insisted that in fighting his battle he was not to allow 13 Corps, and particularly 7th Armoured Division, to get mauled. They would have a part to play in our own offensive in October, and I outlined to him the ideas which were forming in my mind about that offensive. He entered into it with his characteristic enthusiasm.

The sketch map will serve to illustrate the battle. The design of Rommel's attack was exactly as had been forecast to officers and men

In the desert, wearing my Australian hat, greeting the Commander of the Greek Brigade in the Eighth Army (Brigadier Katsotas), August 1942. The officer by the car door is John Poston

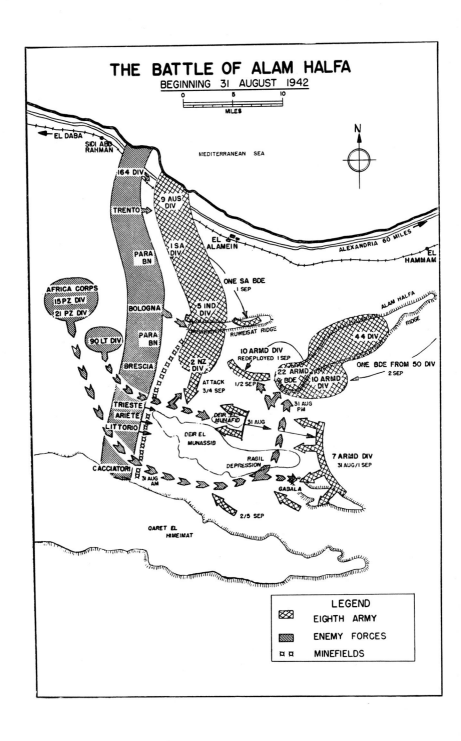

THE BATTLE OF ALAM HALFA
BEGINNING 31 AUGUST 1942

0   5   10
MILES

N

MEDITERRANEAN SEA

EL DABA

SIDI ABD RAHMAN

164 DIV

TRENTO

9 AUS DIV

EL ALAMEIN

ALEXANDRIA 60 MILES

EL HAMMAM

PARA BN

I SA DIV

ONE SA BDE
I SEP

AFRICA CORPS
15 PZ DIV
21 PZ DIV

BOLOGNA

5 IND DIV

ALAM HALFA

PARA BN

RUWEISAT RIDGE

RIDGE

90 LT DIV

44 DIV

BRESCIA

2 NZ DIV

10 ARMD DIV
REDEPLOYED I SEP

22 ARMD BDE

10 ARMD DIV

ONE BDE FROM 50 DIV
2 SEP

ATTACK 3/4 SEP

1/2 SEP

31 AUG PM

TRIESTE
ARIETE
LITTORIO

DEIR MUNAFID

31 AUG

DEIR EL MUNASSIB

RAGIL DEPRESSION

7 ARMD DIV
31 AUG/I SEP

CACCIATORI

31 AUG AM

GABALA

2/3 SEP

QARET EL HIMEIMAT

LEGEND
EIGHTH ARMY
ENEMY FORCES
MINEFIELDS

of the Eighth Army; we fought the battle as I had laid down. Once Rommel's forces had beaten up against our strong positions from the New Zealand Division area eastwards, they became unable to move. We then concentrated on shooting them up from all directions and the Desert Air Force in attacking them from the air. This was very successful and after a few days the enemy losses in tanks and soft-skinned vehicles were so severe that he had to consider a withdrawal.

A most important factor which forced his eventual withdrawal was the action of the Desert Air Force under Air Marshal Coningham. Army and Air Force worked on one plan, closely knitted together, and the two headquarters were side by side. It had seemed to me when I arrived in the desert that the two Services were tending to drift apart and that the true function of air power was not appreciated by com-manders in the Eighth Army. This battle brought us close together again and for the rest of my time in the Eighth Army we remained so.

A major factor in the overall air plan was Tedder's decision to send his Wellingtons to bomb Tobruk behind Rommel's attack, so that his last quick hope of re-supply vanished. This was the operative point in Rommel's decision to call off the attack; he was already beaten, and lack of petrol meant that he couldn't resume the attack. Tedder bit his tail.

Once the plan to deal with the expected attack had been made and preparations begun, I had turned my attention to a consideration of our own offensive.

Rommel's attack came on the night of the 31st August. I had gone to bed at my usual time and was asleep when the attack began soon after midnight. De Guingand tells his own story about that night. He decided he should wake me up and tell me the news; he said I merely replied " Excellent, couldn't be better " and went to sleep again at once, and had breakfast at the usual time in the morning. I don't remember but am prepared to believe him. I was confident that if everyone obeyed orders, we must win this battle; my main preoccupation was to see, in this my first battle with the Eighth Army, that it was fought in complete accord with my master plan.

When I saw that Rommel's forces were in a bad way, I ordered a thrust southwards from the New Zealand Division area to close the gap through which they had entered our positions. The enemy reaction was immediate and violent; they began to pull back quickly to the area of our minefield through which they had originally come.

We left them there and I called off the battle. Moreover, it suited me to have their forces in strength on the southern flank since I was considering making my main blow, later on, on the northern part of the front. I remember Horrocks protesting to me that the enemy remained in possession not only of our original minefields but also of some good view points from which to observe his corps area. I replied that he should get busy and make new minefields for his corps. As regards the observation points, such as Himeimat, it suited me that Rommel should be able to have a good look at all the preparations for attack we were making on our southern flank: they were a feint.

I have sometimes been criticised for not following up Rommel's withdrawal by launching the Eighth Army to the attack. There were two reasons why I did not do so. First, I was not too happy about the standard of training of the Army and also the equipment situation was unsatisfactory; time was needed to put these right. And secondly, I was not anxious to force Rommel to pull out and withdraw " in being " back to the Agheila position. If we were to carry out the mandate, it was essential to get Rommel to stand and fight and then to defeat him decisively. This had never happened to him before; he had often retreated, but it was always for administrative reasons. It was obvious that we would prefer to bring him to battle, when we were ready, at the end of a long and vulnerable line of communications —with ours short. Such would be his situation if he stood to fight at Alamein.

Thus the Battle of Alam Halfa ended in the way we wanted. The action of 13 Corps on the southern flank was all that could be desired. Horrocks fought his battle in full accord with the master plan and he deserves great credit for his action that day. He tells a story of how I congratulated him when it was all over, and then proceeded to tell him what he had done wrong and to give him a talk on how to command a corps in battle.

I was interested to read in 1955 a book called *Panzer Battles* by Von Mellenthin, who was on the operations staff of Rommel at this time. He describes Alam Halfa as: " the turning point of the desert war, and the first of a long series of defeats on every front which foreshadowed the defeat of Germany."

On reflection, certain important lessons emerged from this battle. It was an " army " battle. The power of the Eighth Army was developed on a definite army plan and a firm grip was kept on the battle at all times by Army H.Q. This led to a recognition among officers and men of the necessity for one guiding mind which would control their destinies, and after this battle they accepted me as that one mind.

The Eighth Army consisted in the main of civilians in uniform, not of professional soldiers. And they were, of course, to a man, civilians who read newspapers. It seemed to me that to command such men demanded not only a guiding mind but also a point of focus: or to put it another way, not only a master but a mascot. And I deliberately set about fulfilling this second requirement. It helped, I felt sure, for them to recognise as a person—as an individual—the man who was putting them into battle. To obey an impersonal figure was not enough. They must know who I was. This analysis may sound rather cold-blooded, a decision made in the study. And so, in origin, it was: and I submit, rightly so. One had to reason out the best way to set about commanding these men, to bring out their best, and to weld them into an effective and a contented team which could answer the calls I was going to make on them; and these were going to be increasingly arduous. But I readily admit that the occasion to become the necessary focus of their attention was also personally enjoyable. For if I were able thereby to give something to them—and it was a sense of unity which I was trying to create—I gained myself from the experience by the way it enabled me to get to know them too, to sense their morale and, as time went on, to feel the affection which they generously extended to me. I started in the Alam Halfa battle by wearing an Australian hat—first of all because it was an exceedingly good hat for the desert, but soon because I came to be recognised by it: outside the Australian lines, anyway! Later as readers may know, I took a black beret, again for utilitarian reasons in the first place.

And the twin badges in the beret were, in origin, accidental; but I quickly saw their functional result, and what started as a private joke with the tank regiment which gave it to me became in the end the means by which I came to be recognised throughout the desert. I soon learnt that the arrival of the double-badged beret on the battlefield was a help—they knew that I was about, that I was taking an intense and personal interest in their doings, and that I was not just sitting about somewhere safe in the rear issuing orders. The beret was functional in the way a " brass hat " could never have been. It became, if you like, my signature. It was also very comfortable.

Then again I think the battle is noteworthy as heralding a reversal of the previously accepted doctrine of "loosing" our own tanks at Rommel's armour directly he attacked. With an imperfectly trained army and inferior equipment it is necessary to adjust the tactics accordingly. I refused to exploit our success as such action did not suit my long-term plans.

And finally there was the raising of morale which follows a successful battle, in which the high command has foretold what will happen. It had happened, and we had won with few casualties. In this case the effect on morale was of tremendous importance. In my first few days in the desert we had removed uncertainty by taking a tight grip from Army Headquarters, and announcing a reorganisation which was to hold out prospects of victory in the desert war. All this had caused a feeling of relief. But the general atmosphere was: it looks good, it sounds good, but will it work? There was of course a great willingness to try and make it work, and a growing belief as the days passed. But it was Alam Halfa which produced the final belief in me and my methods, if you like, my prophecies, which was to make Alamein possible.

All in all, the battle had achieved what I wanted. Besides the recovery in morale, the Eighth Army had been given a trial run under its new commander. Commanders, staffs, and troops, from myself downwards, had worked together with the Air Force and had won success.

When the battle was over I wrote to a friend in England, as follows: "My first encounter with Rommel was of great interest. Luckily I had time to tidy up the mess and to get my plans laid, so there was no difficulty in seeing him off. I feel that I have won the first game, when it was his service. Next time it will be my service, the score being one-love."

We resumed our preparations for the Battle of Alamein; but certain matters demanded immediate decision before they got properly under way.

I had decided that in building up the Eighth Army for what lay ahead I would concentrate on three essentials: leadership, equipment, and training. All three were deficient. The equipment situation was well in hand and I knew that Alexander would see that we got all we needed. Training was receiving urgent attention. I soon realised that although the Eighth Army was composed of magnificent material, it was untrained; it had done much fighting, but little training. We had just won a decisive victory, but it had been a static battle; I was not prepared to launch the troops into an all-out offensive without intensive prior training. I remember the shock I received on visiting a certain unit and asking the C.O. if he trained his officers, and how it was done. The C.O. replied without hesitation that he had handed that task over to his second-in-command. I came across the second-in-command later in the day and said: " I understand you are responsible for training the officers in the unit. Tell me how you do it." He replied that he did not do so, and that it was done by the C.O. I ordered that a new C.O. be found for that unit at once; it was clear that nobody trained the officers.

On the higher level I had to have three first-class Corps Commanders. I had one for 13 Corps in Horrocks, and he had proved himself in the Battle of Alam Halfa. I decided it was necessary to replace Ramsden in 30 Corps and I asked for Major-General Sir Oliver Leese who was commanding the Guards Armoured Division in England. He was flown out at once and I never regretted that choice; he was quite first class at Alamein and all through the campaign to Tunis and later in Sicily. After long consultation with Alexander I agreed to give 10 Corps, my *corps d'élite* which was to resemble Rommel's Panzer Army, to Lumsden; he had commanded the 1st Armoured Division in the desert and was highly spoken of in Middle East circles. I hardly knew him and so could not agree with complete confidence; but I accepted him on the advice of others. I had already imported two new Corps Commanders from England and did not want to make the Eighth Army think that none of its senior officers was fit for promotion. I found it necessary to have a new commander for the 7th Armoured Division and asked for Harding from G.H.Q. in Cairo.

If we were to successfully blow a gap in Rommel's defences through which we could debouch, the artillery plan would be all-important. I came to the conclusion that I must have a new head gunner at my headquarters. When I told this to a senior officer at G.H.Q., he remarked that the present man was a delightful person and was also a golf champion. I agreed he was delightful, but added that unfortunately the game we were about to play was not golf. I asked for Brigadier Kirkman from England whom I regarded as the best artilleryman in the British Army. (He is now General

Sir Sidney Kirkman, and in charge of Civil Defence at the Home Office.)

I also wanted a first class senior chaplain. After considerable investigation we found the man I wanted in Hughes, who was the senior chaplain to a division. I never regretted that choice. Hughes remained with me for the rest of the war; he then became Chaplain General of the Army, being the first Territorial Army chaplain to do so. Today he is Dean of Ripon. He was the ideal of what an Army padre should be and became one of my greatest friends; he tells some amusing stories of his first interview with me.

The head of my administration was Brigadier Robertson, now General Sir Brian Robertson, the Chairman of the British Transport Commission. I knew him well as he had been a student under me at the Staff College, Camberley; he was a most able officer and I had no fears on that side of the house. He had under him a highly efficient assistant in Lieut.-Colonel Miles Graham, now Major-General Sir Miles Graham; when Robertson left me on promotion, Graham took over his job and stayed with me to the end of the war.

Another who must be mentioned is Belchem. He was in the Staff Duties and Organisation branch when I arrived in the desert; he was a brilliant officer and after a period away from me, first as a Brigade-Major and then in command of an armoured regiment, he rejoined my headquarters and remained with me for the rest of the war as head of my operations staff.

Finally I cast my eye over the Intelligence organisation at my headquarters. I discovered there a major in the King's Dragoon Guards, by name Williams (now Brigadier E. T. Williams, and Warden of Rhodes House, Oxford). He was an Oxford don and had a brilliant brain; as we shall see later it was a conversation with him which gave me the idea which played a large part in winning the Battle of Alamein. He was not the head of my Intelligence Staff but I was determined that he soon must be. He went right through the rest of the war with me.

Having checked over the leadership problem and made the necessary changes, I was satisfied that I had a team which would collectively handle the task that lay ahead without difficulty. Some of them remained on my staff for the rest of the war: notably de Guingand, Graham, Hughes, Belchem and Williams.

In war-time, when a successful commander has built up a highly efficient staff team, he must take the chief members of the team with him if he is moved to another appointment. The above five went with me to 21 Army Group when I left the Eighth Army; there would not have been time for me to have built up a new team before the landings in Normandy.

Knowing what lay ahead, I pinned up three quotations in my caravan when the Battle of Alam Halfa was over. They remained there during the long journey from Alamein to Berlin and are still there, that caravan now being at my home in Hampshire. The quotations were as follows:

> *Prayer of Sir Francis Drake on the*
> *morning of the attack on Cadiz*
> 1587

> O Lord God, when thou givest to Thy
> servants to endeavour any great matter,
> grant us also to know that it is not the
> beginning, but the continuing of the same,
> until it be thoroughly finished, which
> yieldeth the true glory.

> *James Graham, Marquis of Montrose*
> 1612-1650

> He either fears his fate too much,
> Or his deserts are small,
> Who dare not put it to the touch,
> To win or lose it all.

> *Henry V, Act IV, Scene I*

> O God of battles! steel my soldiers' hearts.

CHAPTER 9

THE BATTLE OF ALAMEIN

23rd October to 4th November 1942

ALAM HALFA had interfered with the preparations for our own offensive, and delayed us. But the dividend in other respects had been tremendous. Before Alam Halfa there was already a willingness from below to do all that was asked, because of the grip from above. And for the same reason there was a rise in morale, which was cumulative. I think officers and men knew in their hearts that if we lost at Alam Halfa we would probably have lost Egypt. They had often been told before that certain things would happen; this time they wanted to be shown, not just to be told. At Alam Halfa the Eighth Army had been told, and then shown; and from the showing came the solid rocklike confidence in the high command, which was never to be lost again.

The basic problem that confronted us after the Battle of Alam Halfa was a difficult one. We were face to face with Rommel's forces between the sea and the Qattara Depression, a distance of about 45 miles. The enemy was strengthening his defences to a degree previously unknown in the desert, and these included deep and extensive mine-fields. There was no open flank. The problem was:

First—   to punch a hole in the enemy positions.
Second—to pass 10 Corps, strong in armour and mobile troops, through this hole into enemy territory.
Third—   then to develop operations so as to destroy Rommel's forces.

This would be an immense undertaking. How could we obtain surprise?

It seemed almost impossible to conceal from the enemy the fact that we intended to launch an attack. I decided to plan for tactical surprise, and to conceal from the enemy the exact places where the blows would fall and the exact times. This would involve a

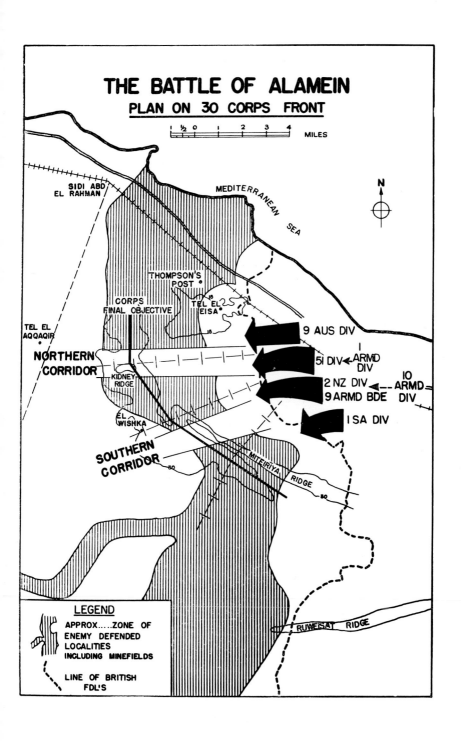

THE BATTLE OF ALAMEIN
PLAN ON 30 CORPS FRONT

MILES

MEDITERRANEAN SEA

N

SIDI ABD
EL RAHMAN

THOMPSON'S
POST

CORPS
FINAL OBJECTIVE

TEL EL
EISA

9 AUS DIV

TEL EL
AQQAQIR

NORTHERN
CORRIDOR

KIDNEY
RIDGE

51 DIV

1 ARMD
DIV

2 NZ DIV

9 ARMD BDE

10 ARMD
DIV

EL
WISHKA

1 SA DIV

SOUTHERN
CORRIDOR

MITEIRIYA RIDGE

RUWEISAT RIDGE

LEGEND

APPROX.....ZONE OF
ENEMY DEFENDED
LOCALITIES
INCLUDING MINEFIELDS

LINE OF BRITISH
FDL'S

great deception plan and I will describe later some of the measures we took.

Next, a full moon was necessary. The minefield problem was such that the troops must be able to see what they were doing. A waning moon was not acceptable since I envisaged a real " dog-fight " for at least a week before we finally broke out; a waxing moon was essential. This limited the choice to one definite period each month. Owing to the delay caused to our preparations by Rommel's attack, we could not be ready for the September moon and be sure of success. There must be no more failures. Officers and men of the Eighth Army had a hard life and few pleasures; and they put up with it. All they asked for was success, and I was determined to see they got it this time in full measure. The British people also wanted real success; for too long they had seen disaster or at best only partial success. But to gain complete success we must have *time*; we had to receive a quantity of new equipment, and we had to get the army trained to use it, and also rehearsed in the tasks which lay ahead. I had promised the Eighth Army on arrival that I would not launch our offensive till we were ready. I could not be ready until October. Full moon was the 24th October. I said I would attack on the night of 23rd October, and notified Alexander accordingly. The come-back from Whitehall was immediate. Alexander received a signal from the Prime Minister to the effect that the attack must be in September, so as to synchronise with certain Russian offensives and with Allied landings which were to take place early in November at the western end of the north African coast (Operation TORCH). Alexander came to see me to discuss the reply to be sent. I said that our preparations could not be completed in time for a September offensive, and an attack then would fail: if we waited until October, I guaranteed complete success. In my view it would be madness to attack in September. Was I to do so? Alexander backed me up whole-heartedly as he always did, and the reply was sent on the lines I wanted. I had told Alexander privately that, in view of my promise to the soldiers, I refused to attack before October; if a September attack was ordered by Whitehall, they would have to get someone else to do it. My stock was rather high after Alam Halfa! We heard no more about a September attack.

THE PLAN

The gossip is, so I am told, that the plans for Alamein, and for the conduct of the war in Africa after that battle, were made by Alexander at G.H.Q. Middle East and that I merely carried them out. This is not true. All the plans for Alamein and afterwards were made at Eighth Army H.Q. I always kept Alexander fully informed; he never commented in detail on my plans or suggested any of his own; he trusted me and my staff absolutely. Once he knew what we wanted he supported us magnificently from behind; he never refused any request; without that generous and unfailing support, we could never have done our part. He was the perfect Commander-in-Chief to have in the Middle East, so far as I was concerned. He trusted me.

The initial plan was made in the first days of September; immediately after the Battle of Alam Halfa was over. This plan was to attack the enemy simultaneously on both flanks. The main attack would be made by 30 Corps (Leese) in the north and here I planned to punch two corridors through the enemy defences and minefields. 10 Corps (Lumsden) would then pass through these corridors and would position itself on important ground astride the enemy supply routes; Rommel's armour would have to attack it, and would, I hoped, be destroyed in the process. The sketch map shows the plan. It will be seen that the defended area, including minefields, through which the northern corridor was to be punched was 5 miles deep.

In the south, 13 Corps (Horrocks) was to break into the enemy positions and operate with 7th Armoured Division with a view to drawing enemy armour in that direction; this would make it easier for 10 Corps to get out into the open in the north. 13 Corps was not to suffer heavy casualties, and in particular 7th Armoured Division was to remain " in being " and available for the mobile operations after the break-out had been achieved. It will be noted that my plan departed from the traditional desert tactics of staging the main offensive on the south or inland flank, and then wheeling towards the sea. I considered that if my main attack was in the south there was only one direction it could take after the break-in—and that was northwards. The fact that a certain tactic had always been employed by all commanders in the desert seemed to me a good reason for doing something else. I planned to attack neither on my left flank nor on my right flank, but somewhere right of centre; having broken in, I could then direct my forces to the right or to the left as seemed most profitable. This decision was not popular with the staff at G.H.Q. and pressure was brought on my Chief of Staff to influence me to change my mind. Alexander never joined in the argument; he understood all my proposals and backed them to the hilt.

I was watching the training carefully and it was becoming apparent to me that the Eighth Army was very untrained. The need for training had never been stressed. Most commanders had come to the fore by skill in fighting and because no better were available; many were above their ceiling, and few were good trainers. By the end of September there were serious doubts in my mind whether the troops would be able to do what was being demanded; the plan was simple but it was too ambitious. If I was not careful, divisions and units would be given tasks which might end in failure because of the inadequate standard of training. The Eighth Army had suffered some 80,000 casualties since it was formed, and little time had been spent in training the replacements.

The moment I saw what might happen I took a quick decision. On the 6th October, just over two weeks before the battle was to begin, I changed the plan. My initial plan had been based on destroying Rommel's armour; the remainder of his army, the un-armoured portion, could then be dealt with at leisure. This was in accordance with the accepted military thinking of the day. I decided to reverse the process and thus alter the whole conception of how the battle was to be fought. My modified plan now was to hold off, or contain, the enemy armour while we carried out a methodical destruction of the infantry divisions holding the defensive system. These un-armoured divisions would be destroyed by means of a " crumbling " process, the enemy being attacked from the flank and rear and cut off from their supplies. These operations would be carefully organised from a series of firm bases and would be within the capabilities of my troops. I did not think it likely that the enemy armour would remain inactive and watch the gradual destruction of all the unarmoured divisions; it would be launched in heavy counter-attacks. This would suit us very well, since the best way to destroy the enemy armour was to entice it to attack *our* armour in position. I aimed to get my armour beyond the area of the " crumbling " operations. I would then turn the enemy minefields to our advantage by using them to prevent the enemy armour from interfering with our operations; this would be done by closing the approaches through the minefields with our tanks, and we would then be able to proceed relentlessly with our plans. The success of the whole operation would depend largely on whether 30 Corps could succeed in the "break-in" battle and establish the corridors through which the armoured divisions of 10 Corps must pass. I was certain that if we could get the leading armoured brigades through the corridors without too great delay, then we would win the battle. Could we do this? In order to make sure, I planned to launch the armoured divisions of 10 Corps into the corridors immediately behind the leading infantry divisions of 30 Corps *and before I knew the corridors were clear.* Furthermore, I ordered that if the corridors were not completely clear on the morning of D+1, the 24th October, the armoured divisions would fight their own way out into the open beyond the western limit of the minefields. This order was not popular with the armoured units but I was determined to see that it was carried out to the letter.

It will be seen later how infirmity of purpose on the part of certain senior commanders in carrying out this order nearly lost us the battle.

I mentioned in Chapter 8 that there was a Major Williams on my intelligence staff who appeared to me to be of outstanding ability. To all who served with me in the war he was known always as Bill Williams. In a conversation one day about this time, he pointed out to me that the enemy German and Italian troops were what he called "corsetted"; that is, Rommel had so deployed his German infantry and parachute troops that they were positioned between, and in some places behind, his Italian troops all along the front, the latter being unreliable when it came to hard fighting. Bill Williams's idea was that if we could separate the two we would be very well placed, as we could smash through a purely Italian front without any great difficulty. This very brilliant analysis and idea was to be a major feature of the master plan for the "crumbling" operations, and it paved the way to final victory at Alamein.

THE DECEPTION PLAN

The object of the deception plan was twofold:

(*a*) To conceal from the enemy as long as possible our intention to take the offensive.

(*b*) When this could no longer be concealed, to mislead him about both the date and the sector in which our main thrust was to be made.

This was done by the concealment of real intentions and real moves in the north, and by advertising false signs of activity in the south.

The whole deception was organised on an "army" basis; tremendous attention to detail was necessary throughout, since carelessness in any one area might have compromised the whole scheme. To carry out such a gigantic bluff in the time available required detailed planning, considerable quantities of labour and transport, mass production of deception devices at the base, a large camouflage store with trained staff, and the co-ordinated movement of many hundreds of vehicles into selected areas. Because all these essentials were provided the scheme was entirely successful, and great credit is due to the camouflage organisation in the Middle East at the time.

A feature of the "visual deception" was the creation and continued preservation of the layout and density of vehicles required for the assault in 30 Corps sector in the north; this was achieved by the 1st October by the placing in position of the necessary dummy lorries, guns, ammunition limbers, etc. During the concentration of attacking divisions just before the day of the attack, the dummies were replaced at night by the actual operational vehicles. The rear areas, whence the attacking divisions and units came, were maintained at their full visual vehicle density by the erection of dummies as the real vehicles moved out. The reason for all this visual deception was that enemy air photographs should continue to reveal the same story. The coordinating brain behind this part of the plan was Charles Richardson, a very able officer in the planning staff of Eighth Army H.Q. (now Major-General C. L. Richardson, recently Commandant of the Military College of Science).

In preparation for the offensive, dumps had to be made in the northern sector. For example, a large dump was created near the station of Alamein. This was to contain 600 tons of supplies, 2000 tons of P.O.L. (petrol, oil, lubricants), and 420 tons of engineer stores. It was of the utmost importance that the existence of these dumps should not become known to the enemy. The site was open and featureless except for occasional pits and trenches. Disguise provided the most satisfactory method of hiding the dumps, and the whole endeavour was a triumph for the camouflage organisation.

Another example I will quote was the dummy pipeline in the south to cause the enemy to believe the main blow would be delivered on that flank. It was started late in September and progress in the work was timed to indicate its completion early in November. The dummy pipeline was laid for a length of about 20 miles, from a point just south of the real water point at Bir Sadi to a point 4 miles east of Samaket Gaballa. The pipe-trench was excavated in the normal way. Five miles of dummy railway track, made from petrol cans, were used for piping. The " piping " was strung out alongside the open trench. When each 5-mile section of the trench was filled in, the " piping " was collected and laid out alongside the next section. Dummy pump houses were erected at three points; water points and overhead storage reservoirs were made at two of these points. Work began on the 26th September and ceased on the 22nd October; it was carried out by one section of 578 Army Troops Company.

There were of course other measures such as the careful planting of false information for the enemy's benefit, but I have confined this outline account to visual deception in which camouflage played the major part. The whole plan was given the code name BERTRAM and those responsible for it deserve the highest praise: for it succeeded.

The R.A.F. was to play a tremendous part in this battle. The AOC aimed to gain gradual ascendancy over the enemy fighters, and to have that ascendancy complete by the 23rd October. On that day the R.A.F. was to carry out blitz attacks against enemy airfields in order to finish off the opposing air forces, and particularly to prevent air reconnaissance. At zero hour the whole bomber effort was to be directed against the enemy artillery, and shortly before daylight on the 24th October I hoped the whole of the air effort would be available to co-operate intimately in the land battle, as our fighter ascendancy by that time would be almost absolute.

I issued very strict orders about morale, fitness, and determined leadership, as follows:

ORDERS ABOUT MORALE: ISSUED ON THE 14TH SEPTEMBER

" This battle for which we are preparing will be a real rough house and will involve a very great deal of hard fighting. If we are successful it will mean the end of the war in North Africa, apart from general ' clearing-up ' operations; it will be the turning point of the whole war. Therefore we can take no chances.

Morale is the big thing in war. We must raise the morale of our soldiery to the highest pitch; they must be made enthusiastic, and must enter this battle with their tails high in the air and with the will to win. There must in fact be no weak links in our mental fitness.

But mental fitness will not stand up to the stress and strain of battle unless troops are also physically fit. This battle may go on for many days and the final issue may well depend on which side can best last out and stand up to the buffeting, the ups and downs, and the continuous strain of hard battle fighting.

I am not convinced that our soldiery are really tough and hard. They are sunburnt and brown, and look very well; but they seldom move anywhere on foot and they have led a static life for many weeks. During the next months, therefore, it is essential to make our officers and men really fit; ordinary fitness is not enough, they must be made tough and hard."

ORDERS ABOUT LEADERSHIP: ISSUED ON THE 6TH OCTOBER

" This battle will involve hard and prolonged fighting. Our troops must not think that, because we have a good tank and very powerful artillery support, the enemy will all surrender. The enemy will *not* surrender, and there will be bitter fighting.

The infantry must be prepared to fight and kill, and to continue doing so over a prolonged period.

It is essential to impress on all officers that determined leadership will be very vital in this battle, as in any battle. There have been far too many unwounded prisoners taken in this war. We must impress on our officers, n.c.o.s and men that when they are cut off or surrounded, and there appears to be no hope of survival, they must organise themselves into a defensive locality and hold out where they are. By doing so they will add enormously to the enemy's difficulties; they will greatly assist the development of our own operations; and they will save themselves from spending the rest of the war in a prison camp.

Nothing is ever hopeless so long as troops have stout hearts, and have weapons and ammunition.

These points must be got across *now at once* to all officers and men, as being applicable to all fighting."

ORDERS REGARDING SECRECY

It was clear to me that we could not inform the troops about our offensive intentions until we stopped all leave and kept them out in the desert. I did not want to create excitement in Alexandria and Cairo by stopping leave with an official announcement. I therefore ordered as outlined below. Officers and men were to be brought fully into the operational picture as follows:

Brigadiers C.O.s of R.E. units }	28 September
Unit commanders	10 October
Company, battery, etc., commander level }	17 October
Remaining officers and the men }	21 October

On the 21st October a definite stop was to be put to all journeys by officers or men to Alexandria, or other towns, for shopping or other reasons.

On the 21st October unit commanders were to stop all leave, quietly and without publishing any written orders. They were to give as the reason that there were signs the enemy might attack in the full-moon period, and that we must have all officers and men present.

What it amounted to was that by the 21st October everyone, including the soldiers, would be fully in the operational picture; no one could leave the desert after that.

There was one exception. I ordered that troops in the foremost positions who might be raided by the enemy and captured, and all troops who might be on patrol in no-man's-land, were not to be told anything about the attack till the morning of the 23rd October: which was D-Day.

GROUPING FOR THE BATTLE

This was the grouping of divisions for the beginning of the battle:

10 *Corps*	13 *Corps*	30 *Corps*
1 Armd Division	7 Armd Division	9 Aust Division
8 Armd Division	44 Division	51 (H) Division
10 Armd Division	50 Division	2 N.Z. Division
		1 S.A. Division
		4 (Indian) Division

Extra Formations

1 Greek Brigade
1 Fighting French Brigade
2 Fighting French Brigade
Fighting French Flying Column
9 Armoured Brigade
23 Armoured Brigade (Valentine tanks)

FINAL ADDRESS TO SENIOR OFFICERS

This was to be an " Army " battle, fought on an Army plan, and controlled carefully from Army H.Q. Therefore every commander down to the Lieut.-Colonel level must know the details of my plan, how I proposed to conduct the fight, and how his part fitted in to the master plan. Only in this way could perfect co-operation be assured. I therefore assembled these commanders and addressed them on the following dates:

13 Corps
30 Corps } 19 October
10 Corps   20 October

I still have the notes I used for the three addresses: written in pencil in my own handwriting. I reproduce them here. I took a risk in saying "Whole affair about 12 days." It will be seen that I originally wrote 10 days, and then erased the 10 and wrote 12. 12 was the better guess. It will also be seen in para. 2 that I couldn't spell "Rommel" properly.

Rough notes used by me for my address to all
senior officers before the Battle of Alamein
(code name "Lightfoot")

ADDRESS TO OFFICERS—"LIGHTFOOT"

1. Back history since August. The Mandate; my plans to carry it out; the creation of 10 Corps.
   Leadership—equipment—training.
2. Interference by Rommell on 31 Aug.
3. The basic framework of the Army plan for Lightfoot as issued on 14 Sep. To destroy enemy armour.
4. Situation in early October. Untrained Army.
   Gradually realised that I must recast the plan so as to be within the capabilities of the troops.
   The new plan; the "crumbling" operations.
   A reversal of accepted methods.
5. *Key points in the Army plan.* Three phases
   30 Corps break-in. ⎫ Fighting for position and the
   10 Corps break-through. ⎬ tactical advantage.
   13 Corps break-in. ⎭
   The dog-fight, and "crumbling" operations.
   The final "break" of the enemy.
6. *The enemy*
   His sickness; low strengths; small stocks of petrol, ammunition, food.
   Morale is good, except possibly Italians.
7. *Ourselves*
   Immense superiority in guns, tanks, men.
   Can fight a prolonged battle, & will do so.
   25 pdr 832
    6 pdr 753   1200 tanks (470 heavy)
    2 pdr 500
   Morale on the top line.

126

8. *General conduct of the battle*
Methodical progress; destroy enemy part by part, slowly and surely.
Shoot tanks and shoot Germans.
He cannot last a long battle; we can.
We must therefore keep at it hard; no unit commander must relax the pressure; Organise ahead for a "dog-fight" of a week. Whole affair about 10 days. (12).
—Don't expect spectacular results too soon.

9. Operate from firm bases.
Quick re-organisation on objectives.
Keep balanced. } If we do all this victory is certain
Maintain offensive eagerness.
Keep up pressure.

10. Morale—measures to get it. Addresses.
Every soldier in the Army a fighting soldier.
No non-fighting man. All trained to kill Germans.
My message to the troops.
11. The issues at stake.
12. The troops to remember what to say if they are captured. Rank, name, & number.

B.L.M.

Finally, I issued the following personal message to the officers and men of the army.

EIGHTH ARMY

PERSONAL MESSAGE FROM THE ARMY COMMANDER

" 1. When I assumed command of the Eighth Army I said that the mandate was to destroy ROMMEL and his Army, and that it would be done as soon as we were ready.
2. We are ready NOW.
   The battle which is now about to begin will be one of the decisive battles of history. It will be the turning point of the war. The eyes of the whole world will be on us, watching anxiously which way the battle will swing.
   We can give them their answer at once, ' It will swing our way.'

3. We have first-class equipment; good tanks; good anti-tank guns; plenty of artillery and plenty of ammunition; and we are backed up by the finest air striking force in the world.

All that is necessary is that each one of us, every officer and man, should enter this battle with the determination to see it through—to fight and to kill—and finally, to win.

If we all do this there can be only one result—together we will hit the enemy for ' six,' right out of North Africa.

4. The sooner we win this battle, which will be the turning point of this war, the sooner we shall all get back home to our families.

5. Therefore, let every officer and man enter the battle with a stout heart, and with the determination to do his duty so long as he has breath in his body.

AND LET NO MAN SURRENDER SO LONG AS HE IS UNWOUNDED AND CAN FIGHT.

Let us all pray that ' the Lord mighty in battle ' will give us the victory.

B. L. Montgomery,
Lieutenant-General, G.O.C.-in-C., Eighth Army"

Middle East Forces,

23-10-42

After briefing the Press on the morning of the 23rd October, I went forward that afternoon to my Tactical H.Q. established near H.Q. 30 Corps. In the evening I read a book and went to bed early. At 9.40 p.m. the barrage of over one thousand guns opened, and the Eighth Army which included some 1200 tanks went into the attack. At that moment I was asleep in my caravan; there was nothing I could do and I knew I would be needed later. There is always a crisis in every battle when the issue hangs in the balance, and I reckoned I would get what rest I could, while I could. As it turned out, I was wise to have done so: my intervention was needed sooner than I expected.

The story of the battle has been told by me in *Alamein to the River Sangro*, and by General de Guingand in his book *Operation Victory*. My purpose now will be to explain the action I took at certain critical moments. Throughout the war I have kept a very precise diary and what follows is taken from notes made each day during the battle.

The deception plan for Alamein. Dummy
petrol station, with soldier filling jerry cans

Battle of Alamein; observing operations
from my tank. In rear, John Poston

Battle of Alamein; having tea with my tank crew. On right, John Poston

<u>Address to Officers — "Lightfoot"</u>   19/20 Oct 1942

1. Back history since August. The Mandate; my plans to carry it out; the creation of 10 Corps. Leadership - equipment - training.

2. Interference by Rommel on 31 Aug.

3. The basic framework of the Army plan for Lightfoot as issued on 14 Sep. To destroy enemy armour.

4. Situation in early October. Untrained Army. Gradually realized that I must recast the plan so as to be within the capabilities of the troops. The new plan; the "crumbling" operations. A reversal of accepted methods.

5. Key points in the Army plan. Three phases.

    30 Corps break-in.
    10 Corps break through. } Fighting for position and
    13 Corps break in.   } the tactical advantage.

    The dog-fight, and "crumbling" operations.

    The final "break" of the enemy.

6. The enemy.
    His sickness, low strengths; small stocks of petrol, ammunition, food.
    Morale is good, except possibly Italians.

Address to officers before

7. Ourselves.

Immense superiority in guns, tanks, men.
Can fight a prolonged battle, & will do so.
25 pdr 832   1200 tanks (470 heavy)
6 pdr 753
2 pdr 500
morale on the top line.

8. General conduct of the battle.

Methodical progress; destroy enemy part by
part, slowly and surely.
shoot tanks and shoot Germans.
He cannot last a long battle; we can.
We must therefore keep at it hard; no
unit commanders must relax the pressure;
Organize ahead for a "dog fight" of a
week. Whole affair about 10 days, (12).
Don't expect spectacular results too soon.
Operate from firm bases.
Quick re-organization on objectives.
Keep balanced.
Maintain offensive eagerness.
Keep up the pressure.

} If we
do all this
victory is
certain.

12. Morale measures to get it. Addresses.
Every soldier in the Army a fighting soldier.
No non-fighting man. All trained to kill Germans.
My message to the troops.

11. The issues at stake.

10 The troops to remember what to say if they are
captured. Rank, name, & number.   B L M.

he Battle of Alamein

SATURDAY 24TH OCTOBER

The attack had gone in on the 23rd October in accordance with the plan I have just described. The whole area was one enormous minefield and the two corridors in the north had not been completely opened for the armoured divisions of 10 Corps by 8 a.m. on the 24th October. In accordance with my orders, I expected the armoured divisions to fight their way out into the open. But there was some reluctance to do so and I gained the impression during the morning that they were pursuing a policy of inactivity. There was not that eagerness on the part of senior commanders to push on and there was a fear of tank casualties; every enemy gun was reported as an 88-mm. (the German A.A. gun used as an anti-tank gun, and very effective). The 10th Corps Commander was not displaying the drive and determination so necessary when things begin to go wrong and there was a general lack of offensive eagerness in the armoured divisions of the corps. This was not the sort of battle they were used to. It was clear to me that I must take instant action to galvanise the armoured divisions into action; determined leadership was lacking. I therefore sent for Lumsden and told him he must " drive " his divisional commanders, and if there was any more hanging back I would remove them from their commands and put in more energetic personalities. This action produced immediate results in one of the armoured divisions; by 6 p.m. that evening the armoured brigade of 1st Armoured Division in the northern corridor was out in the open ; it was then attacked by 15th Panzer Division, which was exactly what I wanted.

Farther south the New Zealand Division began its movement to the south-west as part of the " crumbling " operations. And farther south still, 13 Corps was playing its part according to plan.

SUNDAY 25TH OCTOBER

I have always thought that this was when the real crisis in the battle occurred. At 2.30 a.m. 10 Corps reported that the break-out of 10th Armoured Division in the southern corridor in 30 Corps' sector was not proceeding well and that minefields and other difficulties were delaying progress. The Divisional Commander had said he did not feel happy about the operation, and that even if he did get out he would be in a very unpleasant position on the forward slopes of the Miteriya Ridge. His division was untrained and not fit for such difficult operations; he wanted to stay where he was. Lumsden was inclined to agree. In the northern corridor, 1st Armoured Division was out in the open and was being furiously attacked by the enemy armour; which was exactly what the doctor ordered; so long as I was the doctor in question. De Guingand rightly decided it was necessary for me to see the two corps commanders concerned and grip the situation; he issued orders for a conference at my Tactical H.Q. at 3.30 a.m. and then came and woke me and told me what he had done. I agreed. Leese and Lumsden arrived on time and I asked each to explain his situation. The " atmosphere " at that conference is described most vividly by de Guingand on page 200 of his book, *Operation Victory*.

I discovered that in the 10th Armoured Division, one of the armoured regiments was already out in the open and that it was hoped more would be out by dawn. The divisional commander wanted to withdraw it *all* back behind the minefields and give up the advantages he had gained; his reason was that his situation out in the open would be very unpleasant and his division might suffer heavy casualties. Lumsden agreed with him; he asked if I would personally speak to the divisional commander on the telephone. I did so at once and discovered to my horror that he himself was some 16,000 yards (nearly 10 miles) behind his leading armoured brigades. I spoke to him in no uncertain voice, and ordered him to go forward at once and take charge of his battle; he was to fight his way out, and lead his division from in front and not from behind.

I then told both corps commanders that my orders were unchanged; there would be no departure from my plan. I kept Lumsden behind when the others had left and spoke very plainly to him. I said I was determined that the armoured divisions would get out of the minefield area and into the open where they could manœuvre; any wavering or lack of firmness now would be fatal. If he himself, or the Commander 10th Armoured Division, was not " for it," then I would appoint others who were.

By 8 a.m. all my armour was out in the open and we were in the position I had hoped to have achieved at 8 a.m. the day before.

At noon I had a conference of corps commanders at H.Q., 2nd N.Z. Division. It became clear that the movement south-west of the N.Z. Division would be a very costly operation and I decided to abandon it at once. Instead, I ordered the "crumbling" operations to be switched to the area of the 9th Australian Division, working northwards towards the coast; this new thrust line, or axis of operations, involved a switch of 180 degrees which I hoped might catch the enemy unawares.

WEDNESDAY 28TH OCTOBER

Hard fighting had been going on for the previous three days and I began to realise from the casualty figures that I must be careful. I knew that the final blow must be put in on 30 Corps' front, but at the moment I was not clear exactly where. But I had to get ready for it. So I decided to turn my southern flank (13 Corps) over to the defensive except for patrol activities, to widen divisional fronts, and to pull into reserve the divisions I needed for the final blow. The N.Z. Division I had already got into reserve.

We now had the whole of Rommel's Panzer Army opposite the northern corridor and I knew we would never break out from there. So I made that area a defensive front and pulled 1st Armoured Division into reserve.

I also decided that for the moment I would use only 30 Corps to fight the battle in the north; so I pulled 10 Corps H.Q. into reserve, to get it ready for the break-out.

I ordered that operations by 9th Australian Division towards the coast be intensified, my intention then being to stage the final break-out operation on the axis of the coast road.

THURSDAY 29TH OCTOBER

During the morning it became increasingly evident that the whole of Rommel's German forces were grouped in the northern part of the front. The action of 1st Armoured Division in the northern corridor, and the operations of 9th Australian Division northwards towards the coast, had clearly made him think that we intended to break out in the north along the coast, which was indeed my design at the time.

But we had now achieved what Bill Williams had recommended. The Germans had been pulled against our right and were no longer " corsetting " the Italians. The Germans were in the north, the Italians together in the south; and the dividing line between them appeared to be just to the north of our original northern corridor.

I at once changed my plan and decided to direct the final blow at this point of junction, but overlapping well on to the Italian front. I took this decision at 11 a.m., the 29th October.

When could we stage the blow?

I knew that Operation TORCH, mounted from England, was to land in the Casablanca-Oran area on the 8th November. We must defeat the enemy, and break up his army, in time to be of real help to TORCH. Quite apart from wanting to get to Tripoli first! But more immediately, the timing was affected by the need to get the Martuba airfields so as to assist by giving air cover to the last possible convoy to Malta, which was short of food and almost out of aviation fuel. The convoy was to leave Alexandria about the middle of November.

I decided that on the night 30th-31st October the 9th Australian Division would attack strongly northwards to reach the sea; this would keep the enemy looking northwards. Then on the next night, 31st October/1st November, I would blow a deep hole in the enemy front just to the north of the original corridor; this hole would be made by the 2nd New Zealand Division which would be reinforced by the 9th Armoured Brigade and two infantry brigades; the operation would be under command of 30 Corps. Through the gap, I would pass 10 Corps with its armoured divisions.

The sketch map of the break-out shows the plan very clearly.

We already had the necessary divisions in reserve and they had been resting and refitting.

What, in fact, I proposed to do was to deliver a hard blow with the right, and follow it the next night with a knock-out blow with the left. The operation was christened SUPERCHARGE.

During the morning I was visited at my Tactical H.Q. by Alexander, and by Casey who was Minister of State in the Middle East. It was fairly clear to me that there had been consternation in Whitehall when I began to draw divisions into reserve on the 27th and 28th October, when I was getting ready for the final blow. Casey had been sent up to find out what was going on; Whitehall thought I was giving up, when in point of fact I was just about to win.

I told him all about my plans and that I was certain of success; and de Guingand spoke to him very bluntly and told him to tell Whitehall not to bellyache. I never heard what signal was sent to London after the visit and was too busy with SUPERCHARGE to bother about it. Anyhow, I was certain the C.I.G.S. (Brooke) would know what I was up to.

FRIDAY 30TH OCTOBER

I spent the morning writing out my directive for SUPERCHARGE. I always wrote such orders myself, and never let the staff do it. This was the master plan and only the master could write it. The staff of course has much detailed work to do after such a directive is issued. This procedure was well understood in the Eighth Army (and later, because of the experience in the Mediterranean, in 21 Army Group).

This is what I wrote:

OPERATION SUPERCHARGE

EIGHTH ARMY PLAN

MOST SECRET

20 OCT. 1942

"1. Operation SUPERCHARGE will take place on night 31 Oct/1 Nov. The operation is designed to:

(a) Destroy the enemy armoured forces.

(b) Force the enemy to fight in the open, and thus make him use petrol by constant and continuous movement.

(c) Get astride the enemy supply route, and prevent movement of supply services.

(d) Force the enemy from his forward landing grounds and aerodromes.

(e) Bring about the disintegration of the whole enemy army by a combination of (a), (b), (c) and (d).

30 CORPS TASK

2. To attack by night from the present forward positions between the 297 and 301 Northing grids. Attack to penetrate Westwards to a depth of 4000 yds.

3. On reaching the final objective, armoured and infantry patrols to push out farther to the West so as to cover the debouchment of the armoured divisions and so enable them to get out and deploy the more easily.

4. The flanks of the penetration to be held securely, and their Eastern extremities to be linked up firmly with our existing positions.

5. The whole area of penetration to be cleared, and organised for free movement, and to be held securely as a firm base from which to develop offensive operations.

10 CORPS OPERATIONS

6. 10 Corps will break out into the open through the penetration made by 30 Corps.

7. Armoured cars, at least two regiments initially, will be launched through the bridgehead area before daylight on 1st November and will push out to the N.W., the West, the S.W., and the South.

   The task of the armoured cars will be to operate offensively on the enemy supply routes, destroy everything they meet, and prevent any supplies or reinforcements from coming forward, and prevent any movement from the forward areas to the rear.

   Armoured cars must be prepared to operate on their own for some days, keeping up the strangle-hold and making full use of enemy petrol and supplies.

8. 10 Corps will secure as a first objective the general area Pt 46 in 858299—Tell el Aqqaqir in 860297. Operations will then be developed so as to:

   (a) Destroy the enemy armoured forces.

   (b) Bring about the complete disintegration of the enemy's rear areas.

9. The general axis of operations for 10 Corps, subject to the fulfilment of the task given in para. 8 (a), will be N.W. towards Ghazal Station, so as to get in behind the enemy forces in the Sidi Rahman area and cut them off.

10. The forward movement of 10 Corps will be timed so that the area of the first objective is secured before daylight on 1st November, and operations developed from that area as the sun is rising.

11. It will be clearly understood that should 30 Corps not succeed in reaching the final objective vide paras. 2 and 3, the *armoured divisions of 10 Corps will fight their way to the first objective.*

10 AND 30 CORPS

12. 30 Corps will hold N.Z. Div. in readiness to take over the area of 10 Corps first objective vide para. 8, so as to free 10 Corps for offensive operations against the enemy armoured formations or for a N.W. movement towards Ghazal Station.

13. Very close touch, co-operation, and liaison will be required between 10 Corps and 30 Corps throughout the whole operation.

14. This operation if successful will result in the complete disintegration of the enemy and will lead to his final destruction.

It will therefore be successful.

Determined leadership will be vital; complete faith in the plan, and its success, will be vital; there must be no doubters; risks must be accepted freely; there must be no ' bellyaching.'

I call on every commander to carry through this operation with determination, to fight their formations bravely, and to instil optimism and offensive eagerness into all ranks.

SUPERCHARGE will win for us the victory.

13 CORPS

15. 13 Corps will do what is possible on the Southern flank before or after dark on 31st October to make the enemy think an attack is coming on that flank.

16. The corps will be ready to take immediate action the moment it appears that the enemy is beginning to crack.

ARMY RESERVES

17. 7th Arm. Div. (less 4th Lt. Arm. Brigade).
131st Inf. Bde. (Queens).

These two formations will be held in Army reserve ready for use as the situation develops.

R.A.F. OPERATIONS

18. The R.A.F. are playing a great part in inflicting moral and material damage on the enemy. This is being intensified, from

tomorrow inclusive onwards, and will reach its culminating point as SUPERCHARGE is launched.

FINALLY

19. We know from all sources of intelligence that the enemy is in a bad way, and his situation is critical. The continued offensive operations of Eighth Army and the R.A.F. have reduced him to such a state that a hard blow *now* will complete his overthrow.

The first stage in the blow is the operation being staged by 9th Aus. Div. tonight on the North flank; success in this operation will have excellent repercussions on SUPERCHARGE.

SUPERCHARGE itself, tomorrow night 31st October/1st November, will be the second blow and a staggering one, and one from which I do not consider he will be able to recover."

SATURDAY 31ST OCTOBER

It was clear to me that the stage management problems in connection with SUPERCHARGE were such that if launched on this night it might fail. I therefore decided to postpone it for 24 hours to deliver the blow on the night 1st-2nd November. This delay would help the enemy. To offset this, I extended the depth of penetration for a further 2000 yards, making 6000 yards in all—the whole under a very strong barrage.

I should add that there were doubts in high places about SUPER-CHARGE, and whisperings about what would happen if it failed. These doubts I did not share and I made that quite clear to everyone.

MONDAY 2ND NOVEMBER

At 1 a.m. SUPERCHARGE began and the attack went in on a front of 4000 yards to a depth of 6000 yards. It was a success and we were all but out into the open desert. By dusk we had taken 1500 prisoners.

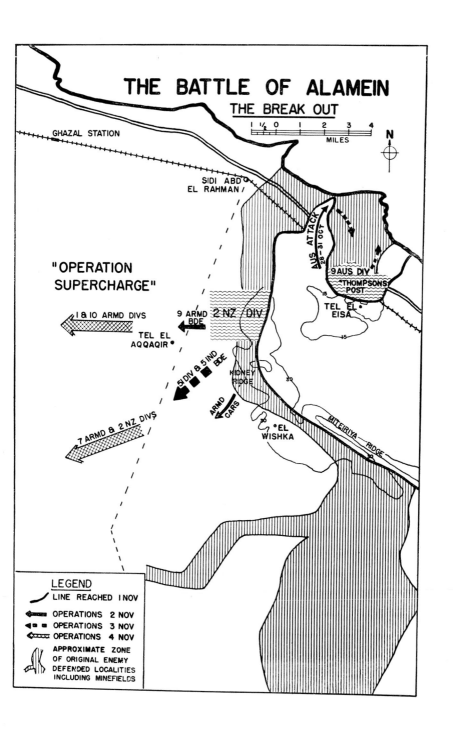

THE BATTLE OF ALAMEIN
THE BREAK OUT

GHAZAL STATION

MILES

N

SIDI ABD
EL RAHMAN

AUS ATTACK
28-31 OCT

9 AUS DIV

"OPERATION
SUPERCHARGE"

"THOMPSONS
POST

1 & 10 ARMD DIVS

9 ARMD
BDE

2 NZ DIV

TEL EL
EISA

15

TEL EL
AQQAQIR

51 DIV & 5 IND BDE

KIDNEY
RIGE

15

30

ARMD
CARS

30

MITEIRIYA RIDGE

7 ARMD & 2 NZ DIVS

•EL
WISHKA

15

LEGEND

LINE REACHED 1 NOV

OPERATIONS 2 NOV

OPERATIONS 3 NOV

OPERATIONS 4 NOV

APPROXIMATE ZONE
OF ORIGINAL ENEMY
DEFENDED LOCALITIES
INCLUDING MINEFIELDS

TUESDAY 3RD NOVEMBER

There were indications the enemy was about to withdraw; he was almost finished.

WEDNESDAY 4TH NOVEMBER

At 2 a.m. I directed two hard punches at the " hinges " of the final break-out area where the enemy was trying to stop us widening the gap which we had blown. That finished the battle.

The armoured car regiments went through as dawn was breaking and soon the armoured divisions got clean away into the open desert; they were now in country clear of minefields, where they could manœuvre and operate against the enemy rear areas and retreating columns.

The armoured cars raced away to the west, being directed far afield on the enemy line of retreat.

The Italian divisions in the south, in front of 13 Corps, had nothing to do except surrender; they could not escape as the Germans had taken all their transport. I directed Horrocks to collect them in, and devoted my attention to the pursuit of Rommel's forces which were streaming westwards.

THE VALUE OF THE " STAFF INFORMATION " SERVICE

This was an organisation for intercepting the signals sent out by our own forward units and relaying them to Army and Corps H.Q. We called the service " J," for short. It was used for the first time in this battle. It was invented by a most able officer on my staff called Hugh Mainwaring; he was unfortunately captured with a reconnaissance party near Mersa Matruh early in November, and I then had to find another officer to operate the " J " Service.

Receiving wireless sets " listened " on division, brigade, and armoured corps forward controls and broadcast the information obtained. This cut down the time-lag between the origination of information by the forward troops and its receipt at Army and Corps H.Q. "J" gives to a higher commander a good indication of the fighting spirit of his troops and, incidentally, although this was not its prime purpose, it could also help by spotting obvious breaches of security. It had the overall effect of tightening the entity of the Army; bringing it all closer together. Wireless links became intimate links between men engaged on the same enterprise. It ended the remoteness of the staff.

It will be remembered that as a GSO 1 in 1918 I had devised a system of getting to Divisional H.Q. quickly the accurate information of the progress of the battle which is so vital. Then I used officers with wireless sets. The "J" Service invented by Hugh Mainwaring was a great improvement on my earlier attempts.

SOME LESSONS

A mass of detailed lessons will always emerge from any battle. In the British Army we are inclined to become immersed in details, and we often lose sight of the fundamentals on which the details are based.

There were three distinct phases in this battle, and operations were developed accordingly.

First: The break-in.

This was the battle for position, or the fight for the tactical advantage. At the end of this phase we had to be so positioned and "balanced" that we could begin immediately the second phase. We must in fact have gained the tactical advantage.

Second: The "dog-fight."

I use this term to describe what I knew must develop after the break-in and that was a hard and bloody killing match. During this we had so to cripple the enemy's strength that the final blow would cause the disintegration of his army.

Third: The break-out.

This was brought about by a terrific blow directed at a selected spot. During the dog-fight the enemy had been led to believe that the break-out would come in the north, on the axis of the coast road. He was sensitive to such a thrust and he concentrated his Germans in the north to meet it, leaving the Italians to hold his southern flank.

We then drove in a hard blow between the Germans and Italians, with a good overlap on the Italian front.

Determined leadership is vital throughout all echelons of command. Nowhere is it more important than in the higher ranks.

Generals who become depressed when things are not going well, who lack the " drive " to get things done, and who lack the resolution, the robust mentality and the moral courage to see their plan through to the end—are useless. They are, in fact, worse than useless—they are a menace—since any sign of wavering or hesitation has immediate repercussions down the scale when the issue hangs in the balance. No battle is ever lost till the general in command thinks it so. If I had not stood firm and insisted that my plan would be carried through, we would not have won at Alamein.

If your enemy stands to fight and is decisively defeated in the ensuing battle, everything is added unto you. Rommel's doom was sounded at Alam Halfa; as Von Mellenthin said, it was the turning point of the desert war. After that, he was smashed in battle at Alamein. He had never been beaten before though he had often had to " nip back to get more petrol." Now he had been decisively defeated. The doom of the Axis forces in Africa was certain—provided we made no more mistakes.

CHAPTER 10

ALAMEIN TO TUNIS

5th November 1942 to 7th May 1943

THE PURSUIT TO AGHEILA

THE PURSUIT proper began on the 5th November with 10 Corps (Lumsden) in the van. I left 30 Corps (Leese) to reorganise to the west of the break-out area. 13 Corps (Horrocks) had the task of cleaning up the battle area of Alamein and of salving all the war material of the enemy and of our own forces. It also had to collect all the Italian prisoners; there were many of them and they surrendered in droves, headed by the generals carrying their suit-cases.

My ultimate objective was Tripoli; this had always been considered the objective of the Eighth Army. But unfortunately the operations to get there had become known as the " Benghazi Handicap ". As one officer expressed it to me: " we used to go up to Benghazi for Christmas and return to Egypt early in the New Year."

I was determined to have done with that sort of thing. Egypt must be made secure for the duration of the war. I had long considered the problem, and when the pursuit began I was clear that the way to achieve this task was as follows:

(a) to capture the Agheila position, and hold securely the approaches to it from the west.

(b) to locate a corps strong in armour in the Jebel about Mekili, trained to operate southwards against any enemy force that managed to break through the Agheila position and make towards Egypt.

(c) to get the A.O.C. to establish the Desert Air Force on the Martuba group of airfields, and also to the south of Benghazi.

The establishment of aircraft on the Martuba group was not just a long-term proposal; it was an immediate requirement since a convoy for Malta was due to leave Alexandria on the 16th November. That island was in dire straits with great shortage of food and fuel; it was vital the convoy should get through and it might fail to do so unless the Desert Air Force could provide fighter cover as it passed in daylight through the narrow area between Crete and Cyrenaica.

By the 15th November the air forces were established in the Martuba airfields, in time to see the convoy safely on its way.

For the development of these operations I agreed the following detailed plan with the A.O.C. Desert Air Force (Coningham). We would use the air arm as the long-range hitting weapon, working in close co-operation with armoured car regiments; fighter squadrons would operate from advanced landing grounds soon after the armoured cars had reported them clear, and well ahead of the main bodies. These tactics would lead to the enemy being shot up and harassed in his withdrawal, while good fighter cover was given to our own forces.

I did not think we would have any serious fighting till we reached Agheila. Rommel would undoubtedly withdraw to that position and would endeavour to stop us there; his supply route would then be shortened while ours would be long, thus reversing the supply situation which had existed at Alamein.

I therefore planned to leave 10 Corps to lead the pursuit as far as the Jebel, and to halt it there with orders to push light forces forward towards Benghazi and Agedabia. I considered Lumsden would handle these operations satisfactorily. I would then pass 30 Corps through to tackle the Agheila position and the movement to Tripoli. I also decided that as soon as 10 Corps was established in the Jebel I would bring Horrocks up to command it and would send Lumsden back to England. I had reached the conclusion that command of a corps in a major battle was above Lumsden's ceiling. On the other hand, he was a good trainer and as such he would be valuable back in England. I decided to ask for Dempsey to be sent out from England to take over 13 Corps from Horrocks. I would then have three reliable Corps Commanders in Leese, Horrocks and Dempsey; they had all served under me before, and Leese and Dempsey had been students under me at the Staff College. All these moves were agreed by Alexander.

The sketch map will serve to illustrate the development of my plans up to the Agheila position.

I gave precise instructions to Lumsden about the development of operations for the pursuit to Agheila, and kept a firm hand on the battle in order to ensure the master plan was not " mucked about " by subordinate commanders having ideas inconsistent with it. I knew well that, in the past, corps and divisional generals had had their own ideas about operations in the desert, and had not liked a firm grip from above; this was one reason why we had nearly lost Egypt. I made it very clear to Lumsden that this time *all* would carry out *my* orders; I had promised the soldiers complete success and I was determined to see they got it.

Soon after the pursuit began I was in danger of capture. A reconnaissance party was sent forward to select a site for my head-quarters in the Mersa Matruh area; two members of this party were Hugh Mainwaring and my stepson Dick Carver. On approaching Mersa Matruh the party took a road leading down to a place on the shore called Smugglers Cove, just to the east of the town. The enemy were still there; they should all have been rounded up by that time but, as will be seen later on, our forces moving across the desert were halted by heavy rain. The reconnaissance party was captured. I myself with a small escort was moving well forward in rear of the leading elements of the army and was about to take the road leading to Smugglers Cove. But at that moment I ran into a sharp engagement which was going on a few hundred yards in front; we had bumped into an enemy rearguard which was trying to hold us off while they cleared Mersa Matruh. If I had gone down the road to Smugglers Cove, it is possible I would have run into the enemy; if so, I'm pretty clear that I wouldn't be writing this book today.

The other—and more important—operations developed success-fully. Twice Rommel's forces were saved from complete disaster by heavy rain. The first occasion was on the 6th and 7th November when we had three divisions " bogged " in the desert, unable to move, and it was not possible even to get petrol to them; this setback saved Rommel's forces from complete encirclement at Mersa Matruh. The second occasion was when very heavy rain on the 15th, 16th and 17th November held up our forces moving across the desert towards Agedabia to cut off the enemy before he could reach the Agheila position.

However, I " drove " the Eighth Army hard and the following figures will show how fast we moved:

5th November	Pursuit began from Alamein.
11th November	Reached Sollum (270 miles).
12th November	Reached Tobruk (360 miles).
17th November	Reached Msus (560 miles).

It was good going to do 560 miles in 13 days; but the administrative situation quickly began to cause me anxiety. To get full value from having established the air forces in the Cyrenaica bulge about Martuba, they must be able to operate at full blast against Rommel's supply routes by sea across the Mediterranean, the port of Tripoli, and the enemy communications between Tripoli and Agheila.

The air force daily requirements for these tasks were given to me as follows:

By 28th November	400 tons.
By 2nd December	800 tons.
By 9th December	1050 tons.
By 16th December	1400 tons (1000 at Tobruk and 400 at Benghazi).

These were big tonnages for the air forces alone. But if Rommel intended to stand and fight at Agheila, we should also have to build up army resources of supplies, petrol, and ammunition before we could attack. However, from the larger angle, it was clear that the air forces had to have all they wanted; they were the long-hitting weapon and their operations if successful would indirectly make the army task much easier.

On the 12th November, when we had driven the enemy forces out of Egypt, I issued the following message to the Eighth Army:

"1. When we began the Battle of Egypt on 23rd October I said that together we would hit the Germans and Italians for six right out of North Africa.

We have made a very good start and today, 12th November, there are no German and Italian soldiers on Egyptian territory except prisoners.

In three weeks we have completely smashed the German and Italian Army, and pushed the fleeing remnants out of Egypt, having advanced ourselves nearly 300 miles up to and beyond the frontier.

2. The following enemy formations have ceased to exist as effective fighting formations:

Panzer Army	20th Italian Corps
15th Panzer Div.	Ariete Arm. Div.
21st Panzer Div.	Littorio Arm. Div.
90th Light Div.	Trieste Div.
164th Light Div.	
10th Italian Corps	21st Italian Corps
Brescia Div.	Trento Div.
Pavia Div.	Bologna Div.
Folgore Div.	

The prisoners captured number 30,000, including nine Generals.

The amount of tanks, artillery, anti-tank guns, transport, aircraft, etc., destroyed or captured is so great that the enemy is completely crippled.

3. This is a very fine performance and I want, first, to thank you all for the way you responded to my call and rallied to the task. I feel that our great victory was brought about by the good fighting qualities of the soldiers of the Empire rather than by anything I may have been able to do myself.

4. Secondly, I know you will all realise how greatly we were helped in our task by the R.A.F. We could not have done it without their splendid help and co-operation. I have thanked the R.A.F. warmly on your behalf.

5. Our task is not finished yet; the Germans are out of Egypt but there are still some left in North Africa. There is some good hunting to be had farther to the West, in Libya; and our leading troops are now in Libya ready to begin. And this time, having reached Benghazi and beyond, we shall not come back.

6. On with the task, and good hunting to you all. As in all pursuits some have to remain behind to start with; but we shall all be in it before the finish.

B. L. Montgomery,
General,
G.O.C.-in-C., Eighth Army "

It will be noticed from the signature of this message that I was now a general, having been a lieutenant-general when I arrived in the desert on the 13th August. I was promoted general for " dis-

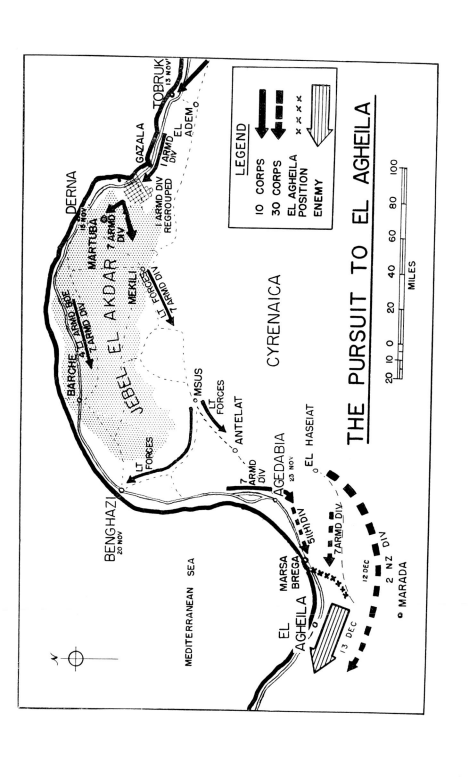

THE PURSUIT TO EL AGHEILA

tinguished services in the field " after the Battle of Alamein, and appointed a K.C.B. at the same time.

A curious incident occurred as our light forces were moving forward south of Benghazi. I was right up behind the leading armoured cars, reconnoitring the area; I had a small escort with me. We had outstripped the fighter cover and from time to time enemy aircraft strafed the road; it was not a healthy place and I suppose that I ought not to have been there.

Suddenly I saw a lorry coming up from behind, and on it a large boat; a naval Petty Officer sat with the driver and some sailors were inside.

I stopped the lorry and said to the Petty Officer: "What are you doing here? Do you realise that you are right up with the most forward elements of the Eighth Army, and you and your boat are leading the advance? This is a very dangerous area just at present, and you are unarmed. You must turn round and go back at once."

He was dreadfully upset. He had been ordered to open up a " petrol point " at a small cove well to the north of Mersa Brega; small naval craft were to land petrol at this point in order that the leading armoured car regiments could refill their tanks; this was the easiest way of getting petrol and oil to them. He explained this to me, looking at me with pleading eyes rather like a spaniel asking to be taken for a walk to hunt rabbits.

He then said: "Don't send me back, sir. If the armoured cars don't get their petrol, they will have to halt and you will lose touch with the Germans. Couldn't I go on with you? I would then be quite safe."

That Petty Officer was clearly a student of psychology! In point of fact I did not know about these small petrol points for the armoured cars; it was a staff plan and a very good one. I took the naval party forward with me and saw them safely to their cove, where I was their first customer for petrol. I have often thought of that Petty Officer; he was from the Merchant Navy and in the R.N.V.R.; his sense of duty was of the highest order, and Britain will never lose her wars so long as the Royal Navy can count on men like him.

THE BATTLE OF AGHEILA: 13TH TO 17TH DECEMBER 1942

As we approached the Agheila position I sensed a feeling of anxiety in the ranks of the Eighth Army. Many had been there twice already; and twice Rommel had debouched when he was ready and had driven them back. I therefore decided that I must get possession of the Agheila position quickly; morale might decline if we hung about looking at it for too long. It was a difficult position to attack.

I therefore decided to attempt bluff and manœuvre, and to bustle Rommel to such an extent that he might think he would lose his whole force if he stood to fight. He would be anxious too about the morale of his own troops; they had been retreating continuously since they were defeated at Alamein, more than 1000 miles away; they had been hustled out of every position on which they had tried to make a stand; they were continuously being " shot up " from the air. All this would tend to make Rommel's forces dispirited and defensively minded, looking over their shoulders for the next position to which to withdraw—as had been the case in the Eighth Army once upon a time.

In view of the awkward country to the south and the difficulty of a frontal attack, it would obviously be preferable to manœuvre Rommel out of the Agheila position and then attack him in the easier country to the west; in view of the probable decline in morale in his forces, I thought this could be done if I did not delay too long.

30 Corps had now taken over the lead from 10 Corps; I reconnoitred the position with Leese in the last week in November and gave him my orders, leaving all the details in his capable hands. The main feature was to be a movement by Freyberg and his New Zealanders round the enemy south flank to a position north of Marada, and from thence to operate against the rear of Rommel's forces; this would be synchronised with a frontal attack by 51st (Highland) Division and 7th Armoured Division. I fixed the 15th December as the date on which the operation would begin. The sketch map illustrates the plan. I then decided that I myself would fly back to Cairo to discuss further plans with Alexander; I also wanted to get some more clothes, and generally get cleaned up after nearly four months in the desert. I spent a very pleasant week-end in Cairo, staying at the British Embassy. I did not realise until I got to Cairo

that I had suddenly become a somewhat " notorious character "; my appearance at St. George's Cathedral for the Sunday evening service, where I read the lessons, created quite a stir. It is a strange experience to find oneself famous and it would be ridiculous to deny that it was rather fun.

When I got back to my headquarters just east of Benghazi, I found preparations for facing up to the Agheila position were well advanced. It seemed clear that the enemy was becoming nervous about our preparations, and had begun to ferry back his immobile Italian troops to the Buerat position—the next good defensive position to the rear. I therefore decided to advance the proposed timing by two days.

Everything went well. The enemy began to withdraw the moment our frontal attack developed; but the New Zealanders had got in behind them by the 15th December, and at one time we had the whole of Rommel's Panzer Army in between the New Zealand Division and 7th Armoured Division, which was advancing strongly. The Germans broke into small groups and burst their way through gaps in the strung-out New Zealand positions; fighting was intense and confused all day on the 16th December, and prisoners were captured and re-captured on both sides. The Panzer Army finally got through to the west, but it was severely mauled by the New Zealanders and also suffered heavily from air attack. I ordered the New Zealand Division to halt and reorganise at Nofilia, and followed up Rommel's army with light forces, making contact with them in the Buerat position which they were holding strongly.

The Battle of Agheila was now over; that position was firmly in our hands.

I had 10 Corps (Horrocks), strong in armour, in the Jebel about Mekili. The Desert Air Force was vigorously supporting our operations from Martuba airfields and from airfields south of Benghazi about Agedabia.

We had in fact achieved our purpose.

I moved my advanced Tactical Headquarters forward to Marble Arch, near the Merduma airfields, close to H.Q. 30 Corps. From this area I was to be well placed to direct the reconnaissance of the Buerat position and to draw up the plan for the advance to Tripoli.

CHRISTMAS 1942 IN THE DESERT

We were now well into Tripolitania, and over 1200 miles from Alamein where we had started. Rommel and his Axis forces had been decisively defeated. Egypt was safe for the duration of the war.

I decided that the Eighth Army needed a halt during which it could pull itself together and get ready for the final "jump" to Tripoli. Indeed, officers and men deserved a rest and I was determined they should have it. I ordered that we would halt where we stood, that no offensive operations would take place until after Christmas, and we would all spend that day in the happiest way that conditions in the desert allowed. It was very cold. Turkeys, plum puddings, beer, were all ordered up from Egypt and the staff concentrated on ensuring that it all arrived in time: and it did.

I issued the following message to the Eighth Army:

" 1. The Eighth Army has turned the enemy out of the famous Agheila position and is now advancing into Tripolitania. It is wonderful what has been achieved since the 23rd October, when we started the Battle of Alamein.

Before the battle began I sent you a message in which I said:

Let us pray that ' the Lord mighty in
battle ' will give us the victory.

He has done so, and I know you will agree with me when I say that we must not forget to thank Him for His great mercies.

2. It is now Christmas time and we are all thinking about our families and friends in the home country.

I want to send you all my very best wishes, and my hope that 1943 will be a very happy year for each one of you.

3. I have received a Christmas Greeting from Hull, in Yorkshire. It is quite the nicest that I have ever received; my only regret is that I cannot answer it, as the writer gave no address. But I shall treasure it all my life. It is intended for you as well as for me, and is as follows:

Dear Sir,

To wish you and our lads of the EIGHTH ARMY a very happy Christmas. Good health. Good luck. And by the Grace of God VICTORY IN 1943.

Keep 'em on the run, Monty. Best wishes from a Yorkshire lass with a lad in the Eighth Army.
4. What better Christmas greeting can I send on to you than the
one from the Yorkshire lass?
I would like to tell her, from us all, that we will do our best
to ' keep 'em on the run.'
5. Good luck to you! And in the words of Tiny Tim, in Dickens's
Christmas Carol: ' God bless us all, each one of us.' "

I realised later that I had misquoted Tiny Tim. But the mis-
quotation did the trick!

I enjoyed that Christmas in the desert; I think we all did. We had
a feeling that we had achieved something. The Agheila bogey had
been laid and we were leaguering as an Army beyond that once-
dreaded position, where hitherto only our advanced patrols had
penetrated. We had made the grade; and morale was high.

De Guingand was not with me. He had borne a tremendous burden
since we had met at the road junction outside Alexandria on the early
morning of the 13th August, and he collapsed during the preparations
for the Battle of Agheila. I sent him back to Cairo for a rest; he had
become engaged to be married and I said he should get married before
he returned—which he did. I borrowed Bobbie Erskine (now General
Sir George Erskine) who was Chief of Staff to Leese in 30 Corps,
and he acted as my Chief of Staff till de Guingand returned.

Duncan Sandys, son-in-law to the Prime Minister, had been visiting
me and when he returned to Cairo he sent us a bottle of port for
Christmas. John Poston, my A.D.C., told the mess corporal to take
the chill off it before putting the bottle on the table. The corporal
wanted to make certain there would be no mistake; so *he boiled the
port*; steam came from the bottle when it was placed before me at
dinner on Christmas night!

I recall particularly one incident about which I heard shortly
afterwards. It took place in the Sergeants' Mess of a certain unit on
Christmas night. Toasts were being drunk. Some of the younger
sergeants reckoned we would soon be in Tripoli and they were drinking
to that day and to the end of our labours. To many who had served
in the desert, Tripoli was the end of the road; once we got there, we
should have done our share and could sit back. An old and seasoned
sergeant-major, a veteran of many battles, watched the fun and the

drinking and then got up to make a speech. He was much respected and there was instant silence when he rose. He spoke very quietly, outlining what had been achieved and what still remained to be done. He finished with these words:

" Some of you think that when we have got to Tripoli, it will be the end of our labours. That is not the case. We went to war in 1939 to defeat Hitler and everything for which he stands. A long struggle lies ahead; when we have cleared the Axis Powers from Africa we shall have to carry the war into Europe, and finally into Germany. Only when we have defeated Germany in Europe, will we be able to return to our families honourable men."

It will be remembered that the First Army (Anderson) had landed in Algeria on the 8th November and was developing operations towards Bizerta and Tunis.

Having secured these places, it was to be directed on Tripoli. There was considerable speculation in high places which Army would get to Tripoli first: the Eighth Army or the First Army. The idea that any army except ourselves should capture Tripoli infuriated officers and men of the Eighth Army. For three years it had been the target; they weren't going to miss it this time.

I wrote the following in my diary on Christmas Eve, the 24th December, 1942.

" And so ends the first phase of this remarkable campaign. We have driven the enemy from Egypt, from Cyrenaica, and across the border into Tripolitania. The next stage may be the most difficult.

The war in Africa is not now so clear cut as it was in October and November; we are away in Tripolitania and are 1200 miles from where we started.

Our war, and the Tunisian war, are now getting close to each other and require co-ordination.

Vested interests are beginning to creep in.

We want some very clear thinking; the object must be defined clearly and pursued ruthlessly; we must not be led away on ventures that do not help in achieving the object. We really want unified command; you cannot conduct operations in a theatre of war with a committee.

My own view is that the surest way of getting to Tripoli quickly is for the Eighth Army, with its accompanying Air Force, to ' drive' forward and that everything should be done to make this possible."

The operations of the First Army made our task easier, without any doubt.

But it was the relentless forward move of the Eighth Army which was eventually to save the First Army from serious disaster.

Shortly after Christmas I received the following letter from a soldier in the Eighth Army. That letter, from an ordinary soldier, made me feel very happy.

> S/13056697, Pte. Glaister G.,
> " A " Branch, Rear H.Q. 8th Army
> 23 Dec. 42

" To: General Sir Bernard L. Montgomery, K.C.B., D.S.O.
General Officer Commanding Eighth Army.

Sir,

For a private soldier to write a personal letter to an Army Commander is perhaps most unusual, even if the Regulations don't wholly forbid it. But this isn't really a personal letter—it is written on behalf of thousands of men in the Eighth Army.

On October 21st 1942, I had been in the Services for $2\frac{1}{2}$ years without feeling very concerned about it. I felt the successful running of the Army was more the business of its officers, not much being expected from its privates.

But on October 21st, the D.A.Q.M.G. gathered us informally together, and read your message to us.

There can never have been such a message read to troops before, with the trust and confidence it placed in them. This message was a bond, and for the first time in my Army life I felt I *belonged* to something—to some live force that had a job to do, a job so hard that even my work as a clerk had a place in a gigantic scheme. I know from talking to men in this and other units, that your speech—a man to man speech, had a tremendous effect on their spirits.

You achieved far more by your human, personal message than any Order of the Day could have done. For myself, thank you,

Sir, for this new feeling. You have made us proud to belong to the 8th Army.

And now you have sent us a Christmas message which, by its friendliness and references to his home, must have gone to the heart of each one of us.

Because circumstances more or less compel troops as a whole to be inarticulate, I again on behalf of thousands of us here in Libya—on behalf of this great brotherhood, thank you sincerely.

In closing, may I wish you a very happy Christmas and a brilliant and successful 1943.

God Bless you, Sir, and guide you at all times.

Yours obediently and humbly,
Geoffrey Glaister.
Pte."

THE ADVANCE ON TRIPOLI: 15TH TO 23RD JANUARY 1943

When the enemy withdrew from the Agheila area he went back to the Buerat position and began to prepare that line for defence. The basis of my plan for dealing with that position was twofold:

(a) I did not want the enemy to withdraw; I wanted him to stand there and fight. If he did this, he could probably be destroyed, since the position could be outflanked to the south. I would therefore hold main bodies of attacking divisions at least 100 miles behind the front, while we built up our administrative arrangements. The opening phases of the advance would then take the form of an encounter battle.

(b) When I attacked the Buerat position my plan must be such that we could go right through to Tripoli, without allowing the enemy to delay us or stop our movement.

The essence of the whole operation must be speed, for the crux of the problem of getting to Tripoli was administration. I calculated that I must have enough petrol, ammunition, supplies, etc., for 10 days' fighting. My forces were based on Benghazi and Tobruk, and it was a long haul by road from them. A pause was now necessary to build up the administrative resources we needed; my staff told me the necessary dumping could be completed by the 14th January. I decided

A picnic lunch on the sea front in Tripoli with General Leese, after the capture of the town, 23rd January 1943

The Prime Minister and General Brooke outside my caravans near Tripoli

The Prime Minister addresses officers and men of Eighth Army H.Q. in Tripoli

The Prime Minister inspecting troops of the Eighth Army in Tripoli. Lt.-Gen. Sir Oliver Leese, 30 Corps, in the back seat with the P.M. John Poston driving

to attack on the 15th January. I well knew that if we did not reach Tripoli in 10 days I might have to withdraw—for lack of supplies. On arrival at Tripoli it would be vital to get the port open and working at full capacity very quickly; the enemy must not be allowed time to damage the port facilities unduly.

My plan then was to complete dumping by the 14th January, to leap on the enemy in strength on the early morning of the 15th January, and to " crash " right through to Tripoli within 10 days. Administratively, it was a considerable risk.

On the 4th January very heavy gales began to rage in the Mediterranean and these created havoc and destruction at Benghazi. Ships broke loose and charged about the harbour; heavy seas broke up the breakwater and smashed into the inner harbour; much damage was done to tugs, lighters and landing places.

The capacity of the port, which had been brought up to 3000 tons a day, dropped at once to 1000 tons a day. The storms looked like continuing and all ships had to leave the harbour; Benghazi was practically " out " as a base port and indeed by the 12th January its capacity had fallen to 400 tons a day.

Here was a " pretty how-de-do "! We were at once thrown back on Tobruk; which place was 1000 miles by road from Tripoli. And having got to Tripoli we would have to build up good dumps there for use in the operations beyond.

G.H.Q. in Cairo got anxious and asked if I would now have to change my dates and thus put everything back.

I decided there was only one thing to do—to " crash " on to Tripoli with *no* change in the timing. To do this I decided to " ground " the three divisions of 10 Corps which were in the Jebel about Mekili, and use all their transport to lift forward from Tobruk and Benghazi the supplies needed by the 14th January. 10 Corps must become Eighth Army's " Carter Paterson."

I sent for Horrocks and put him in charge of the whole business; he entered into it with the greatest enthusiasm and organised a first class transportation service. We kept our dates.

I issued the following message to the Army on the 12th January.

" 1. The leading units of Eighth Army are now only about 200 miles from Tripoli. The enemy is between us and that port, hoping to hold us off.

2. THE EIGHTH ARMY IS GOING TO TRIPOLI.

3. Tripoli is the only town in the Italian Empire overseas still remaining in their possession. Therefore we will take it from them; they will then have no overseas Empire.

The enemy will try to stop us. But if each one of us, whether front-line soldier, or officer or man whose duty is performed in some other sphere, puts his whole heart and soul into this next contest—then nothing can stop us.

Nothing has stopped us since the Battle of Alamein began on 23rd October 1942. Nothing will stop us now.

Some must stay back to begin with, but we will all be in the hunt eventually.

4. ON TO TRIPOLI!

Our families and friends in the home country will be thrilled when they hear we have captured that place."

The advance began on the 15th January. Things went well to begin with and by the 19th January we were up against the Homs-Tarhuna position, which the enemy clearly meant to hold if he could. On the axis of the coast road through Homs the 51st (H) Division seemed to be getting weary, and generally displayed a lack of initiative and ginger. A note in my diary dated the 20th January reads as follows:

" Sent for the G.O.C. 51st (Highland) Division and gave him an imperial ' rocket'; this had an immediate effect."

The leading troops entered Tripoli at 4 a.m. on the 23rd January 1943, three months to a day since the beginning of the Alamein battle.

THE EIGHTH ARMY IN TRIPOLI

We had a good reception from the population; the city was quiet and there was no panic. I myself arrived outside the city at 9 a.m. on the 23rd January and sent for the leading Italian officials to come and report to me. I gave them my orders about the city and requested their co-operation in ensuring the well-being of the population. I appointed Brigadier Lush, Deputy Chief Political Officer for Tripolitania, to take over civil control as soon as he could—working through the Italian authorities. I imposed a strict military control for the first

24 hours, so as to establish a good degree of discipline; shops were shut, curfew was imposed at night, and so on.

I foresaw certain dangers in the proximity of my army to a large city like Tripoli. Palaces, villas, flats, were available for officers. I myself was asked if I intended to live in the Governor's palace. I said " No," and installed my headquarters in the fields some 4 miles outside the city. Much fighting lay ahead and I was not going to have the Eighth Army getting " soft," or deteriorating in any way. I forbade the use of houses, buildings, etc., for headquarters and troops; all would live in the fields and in the desert, as we had done for many months. The army had to retain its toughness and efficiency.

Having given orders about these things, I drove into the city with Leese and we sat in the sun on the sea front and ate our sandwich lunch. We were great friends, and we discussed together the past and the future. Our A.D.C.s and police escort sat not far away, also having their lunch. I asked Leese what he thought they were talking about after many months of monastic life in the desert; he reckoned they were speculating on whether there were any suitable ladies in the city. I had no doubt that he was right. I decided to get the Army away from Tripoli as early as possible.

Two days after we arrived in the city it was reported to me that the food situation was deteriorating among the civil population. I at once issued the following order:

" 1. The food situation in Tripoli is not good; the civil population is likely to be short of food very shortly, and then would have to be fed by the Army. This would be a commitment which would cause us serious embarrassment; it would therefore be exactly what the Germans would like to happen.

2. The British Army, the Allied Air Forces, and the personnel of the Royal Navy in Tripoli, have their own rations and must not eat the food of the civil population. The enemy would make very good propaganda out of the fact that enough food was left by them and a good deal of it was eaten by the British forces.

3. It is therefore my order that no member of the British forces in Tripolitania, whether officer or other rank, shall have any food —breakfast, lunch, dinner or supper—at hotels or restaurants in Tripoli.

4. The only exception to this order will be that tea shops may, if they are able and willing, sell tea and buns to the troops.

5. Officers and other ranks visiting Tripoli must take their rations with them. Arrangements are being made to establish clubs for officers and other ranks in Tripoli which will be run by the N.A.A.F.I., and these will be opened as soon as possible; it will not be possible to provide meals at these clubs, except possibly tea and buns.

6. Commanders will ensure that the terms of my order in para. 3 above are brought to the notice of all officers and other ranks, together with the reasons for it. The D.C.P.O. will ensure that hotel and restaurant managers receive orders not to serve meals to personnel of the British forces."

The Prime Minister and the C.I.G.S. visited Tripoli on the 3rd and 4th February and we organised for them parades of the Highland Division and the New Zealand Division, with certain units of the Royal Armoured Corps and the R.A.S.C.

Winston Churchill was immensely impressed, and was deeply moved when the troops marched past him: looking so fit and well, and with such a fine bearing. I felt a very proud man myself, to be in command of such men.

I asked him to address the officers and men of my headquarters, and it was then that he said:

"Ever since your victory at Alamein, you have nightly pitched your moving tents a day's march nearer home. In days to come when people ask you what you did in the Second World War, it will be enough to say: I marched with the Eighth Army."

After getting to Tripoli on the 23rd January my main pre-occupation was to get the harbour uncorked and ships inside, so as to get a good daily tonnage landed. This was the task of the Royal Navy, and no easy one to do quickly. Speed was vital; my chief engineer went to work with the Navy, and we helped with all our own resources. This made a great difference; the first ship entered the harbour on the 3rd February and the first convoy on the 9th February. I was anxious to do away with the road link from Tobruk and Benghazi as soon as possible, abolish the "Carter Paterson" service, and maintain Eighth Army from the Tripoli base.

The next tough battle would be on the Mareth Line; this was a very strong position and the main feature of the attack upon it would have to be an outflanking movement round its western flank. I envisaged using the New Zealanders on this task and I had launched reconnaissances before Christmas, when we captured the Agheila position, i.e. nearly 3 months before the Battle of Mareth took place.

Meanwhile our first task must be to push the enemy back on to the main position so that we could reconnoitre it. We also needed to secure the necessary road centres of communication at Ben Gardane, Foum Tatahouine and Medenine, and the lateral roads, and the airfields about Medenine. The sketch map makes the picture clear.

Initially I used only 7th Armoured Division for this task. But as our administrative situation eased so I began to build up strength in the forward area, sending up the 51st (H) Division and a further brigade of tanks.

Towards the end of February the port of Tripoli was working well and we were discharging up to 3500 tons a day. My administrative anxieties were over and I could bring 10 Corps forward to Tripoli from the Tobruk-Benghazi area.

I must mention that General Leclerc had joined me, having come up from central Africa with his small French force. He put himself under my command. All he asked in return was that I should give him food, petrol and clothing: which I did, as I was glad to get the help of this remarkable man.

In accordance with decisions taken at the Casablanca Conference, which had assembled in January, the Eighth Army was to come under General Eisenhower for the fighting in Tunisia; Alexander was made Deputy C.-in-C. and was to command the land forces. Tedder became C.-in-C. of all air forces in the Mediterranean theatre. This grouping was good, and if we played our cards properly the successful outcome of the operations in Tunisia was certain. The air power in Tunisia, in Malta, and with the Eighth Army could now be concentrated and the whole of it used to support any one operation.

Coningham went over to join Tedder as commander of the Tactical Air Forces, and Harry Broadhurst took command of the Desert Air Force working with the Eighth Army.

Alexander told me he had found things in a terrible mess when he went over to join General Eisenhower. The First Army was being heavily attacked on the southern part of its front and everything looked like sliding there. Generally, he found stagnation: no policy, no plan, the front all mixed up, no reserves, no training anywhere, no building up for the future, so-called reinforcement camps in a disgraceful state, and so on. He found the American troops disappointing; they were mentally and physically soft, and very " green." It was the old story: lack of proper training allied to no experience of war, and linked with too high a standard of living. They were going through their early days, just as we had had to go through ours. We had been at war a long time and our mistakes lay mostly behind us.

Alexander worked day and night to get things right. But he had some anxious moments and he sent me a very real cry for help on the 20th February, asking if I could do anything to relieve the pressure on the Americans. I replied that I would do all I could—adding that if he and I exerted pressure at the right moments we might get Rommel running about like a " wet hen " between our respective fronts. My staff always used to refer to this message as the " wet hen " signal!

I speeded up events and by the 26th February it was clear that our pressure had caused Rommel to break off his attack against the Americans. This gave Alexander the time he needed, and he wrote to me on the 5th March saying that he reckoned the patient had passed the crisis and was on the way to recovery; but the military body is always left with great weakness after such an illness. When the Americans had learnt their lesson, and had gained in experience, they proved themselves to be first-class troops. It took time; but they did it more quickly than we did.

After Rommel had pulled out from the First Army front I thought it likely it would be my turn to be attacked next: and it was. We got indications of movement down to our front. I brought up the New Zealand Division from Tripoli and got ready to receive the blow which I was sure would come. I was not very strong on the ground at the time because I had taken certain risks in answer to Alexander's cry for help. Any setback we might receive would upset the preparations for our own attack against the Mareth Line, which was timed for about the 19th March. Still, one cannot always get what one wants in war; the great thing is to turn every mischance into an advantage. Perhaps this might prove another Alam Halfa, a defensive battle which would help the offensive one which followed.

On the evening of the 5th March all indications pointed to an attack the next morning.

THE BATTLE OF MEDENINE: 6TH MARCH 1943

As expected, Rommel attacked early in the morning with three Panzer divisions: this attack was beaten off. He attacked again in the afternoon; again he was driven back. Our tank losses were nil; our total casualties in personnel were 130 all ranks. The enemy lost 52 tanks, all knocked out by the anti-tank guns of the infantry, except seven which were destroyed by a squadron of Sherman tanks.

I fought the battle in the same way as I had at Alam Halfa. I made up my mind that Rommel's attack would be made in a certain way and I planned to receive it on ground of my own choosing. I refused to move to counter any of his thrusts.

I refused to follow up when Rommel withdrew. And I proceeded with my plans for our own offensive when the battle was over. It lasted only one day. As Alam Halfa had helped Alamein, so Medenine was to help the Battle of Mareth. The 52 tanks which Rommel lost at Medenine would have been of great value to him at Mareth.

THE BATTLE OF MARETH: 20TH TO 27TH MARCH 1943

The Mareth Line had been constructed by the French in Tunisia as a defensive position in case of Italian aggression from Tripolitania. It was very strong naturally, and had been improved artificially by the French, and later by the Germans. Its eastern flank rested on the sea and its western flank on the mountain massif of Matmata. A switch line ran north-west from Matmata towards El Hamma.

The country to the west of the Matmata hills was reported to be an impassable " sand sea," stretching away to the west for many miles. The French told me that any outflanking movement through this sand sea was impossible. I decided that a frontal attack against such a strong position would be unlikely to succeed by itself, for there was little room for manœuvre between the Matmata hills and the sea. The main feature of my plan must be an outflanking movement to the west of the Matmata hills: to be synchronised with a limited frontal attack.

The problem then was: could a route through the sand sea be found?

It will be remembered that I had launched reconnaissances into this area from the Agheila area before Christmas. A passable route was found by the Long Range Desert Group and the plan then took shape. My plan in outline was as follows:

(a) 30 Corps to attack the eastern flank with three divisions. This would be a relentless pressure, with the right flank on the sea. Its object would be to draw the enemy reserves down to this part of the defensive line.

(b) To launch the New Zealanders, heavily reinforced with other units, round the western flank and to " break-in " behind the Matmata massif.

(c) To hold 10 Corps in reserve with two armoured divisions (1st and 7th), available to fling in on either flank as opportunity offered. This corps was so positioned that it protected all my " vitals," and secured the important ground.

(d) The whole operation to be supported by the concentrated and sustained effort of the air striking forces.

The flank move by the New Zealanders was a force of 27,000 men and 200 tanks. It was assembled on our southern flank, without detection by the enemy, by dawn on the 18th March. On the night of the 17th-18th March we carried out certain preliminary operations on our right flank to mislead the enemy about where the real blow would fall. These operations were successful but during them 201 Guards Brigade ran into very extensive minefields which were defended by Germans: hand-to-hand fighting took place and the 6th Battalion Grenadier Guards lost 24 officers and 300 men. The Guards Brigade fought magnificently that night and made a notable contribution to the final success which was to come our way.

The attack of 30 Corps on the right flank was timed to begin at 10.30 p.m. on the 20th March. It was clear to me on the morning of the 20th March that the enemy had discovered the New Zealand force lying concealed on my southern flank; I therefore ordered it to abandon any further attempt at concealment and to go " like hell " northwards and get on with the job: which it did.

I issued the following message to the Army on the 20th March:

" 1. On 5th March Rommel addressed his troops in the mountains overlooking our positions and said that if they did not take

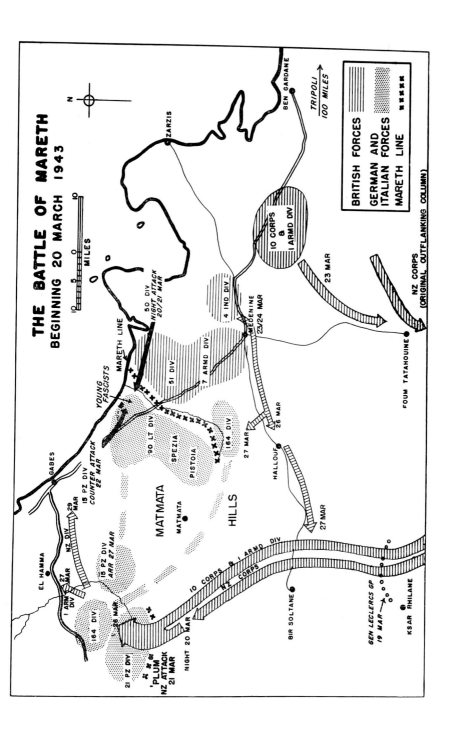

THE BATTLE OF MARETH
BEGINNING 20 MARCH 1943

MILES
10 5 0 10

BRITISH FORCES
GERMAN AND ITALIAN FORCES
MARETH LINE

TRIPOLI
100 MILES

BEN GARDANE

ZARZIS

10 CORPS & 1 ARMD DIV

23 MAR

50 DIV NIGHT ATTACK 20/21 MAR

4 IND DIV

MEDENINE 23/24 MAR

MARETH LINE

YOUNG FASCISTS

51 DIV

7 ARMD DIV

26 MAR

FOUM TATAHOUINE

NZ CORPS (ORIGINAL OUTFLANKING COLUMN)

GABES

15 PZ DIV COUNTER ATTACK 22 MAR

90 LT DIV

SPEZIA

PISTOIA

164 DIV

27 MAR

HALLOUF

27 MAR

MATMATA HILLS

MATMATA

EL HAMMA

29 MAR

NZ DIV

27 MAR

1 ARM DIV

15 PZ DIV ARR 27 MAR

21 PZ DIV

164 DIV

1-26 MAR

'PLUM' NZ ATTACK 21 MAR

NIGHT 20 MAR

10 CORPS & 1 ARMD DIV

NZ CORPS

BIR SOLTANE

GEN LECLERCS GP

19 MAR

KSAR RHILANE

Eisenhower comes to visit me in Tunisia, 31st March 1943. On right, John Poston

Addressing officers of the New Zealand Division on 2nd April 1943, after the Battle of Mareth

Medenine, and force the Eighth Army to withdraw, then the days of the Axis forces in North Africa were numbered.

The next day, 6th March, he attacked the Eighth Army. He should have known that the Eighth Army NEVER WITHDRAWS; therefore his attack could end only in failure—which it did.

2. We will now show Rommel that he was right in the statement he made to his troops.

The days of the Axis forces in North Africa are indeed numbered.

The Eighth Army and the Western Desert Air Force, together constituting one fighting machine, are ready to advance. We all know what that means; and so does the enemy.

3. In the battle that is now to start, the Eighth Army:
   (a) Will destroy the enemy now facing us in the Mareth position.
   (b) Will burst through the Gabes Gap.
   (c) Will then drive northwards on Sfax, Sousse, and finally Tunis.

4. We will not stop, or let up, till Tunis has been captured, and the enemy has either given up the struggle or has been pushed into the sea.

5. The operations now about to begin will mark the close of the campaign in North Africa. Once the battle starts the eyes of the whole world will be on the Eighth Army, and millions of people will listen to the wireless every day—hoping anxiously for good news, and plenty of it, every day.

If each one of us does his duty, and pulls his full weight, then nothing can stop the Eighth Army. And nothing will stop it.

6. With faith in God, and in the justice of our cause, let us go forward to victory.

7. FORWARD TO TUNIS! DRIVE THE ENEMY INTO THE SEA!"

This battle has been described by several writers and it seems unnecessary to tell the detailed story again. The major tactics may be summarised as follows:

(a) The battle opened with a hard blow on our right.
(b) When this blow went in, a strong outflanking movement was set in motion on our left.

M.F.M.   161   F

(c) The blow on the right made good progress at first.
The threat here became so serious to the enemy that the available
German reserves were drawn in to meet it. These reserves
counter-attacked, drove us back, and we lost all our gains.
We were back where we had started two days before. I well
remember the Commander 30 Corps (Leese) coming to tell
me this at 2 a.m. on the morning of the 23rd March. It is
interesting to note that the crisis of the battle of Alamein also
took place at 2 a.m. (on the 25th October). Leese was very
upset. I said: "Never mind, this is where we've got 'em;
but you *must* keep the German reserves tied to your corps
front."

(d) I immediately decided to hold hard on the right, but to maintain
such pressure there that the German reserves would be kept in
that area. I also opened a new thrust line in the centre against
the Matmata hills, using the 4th Indian Division.

(e) I then sent the 1st Armoured Division from my reserve round
to join the New Zealand outflanking movement, which was
gathering momentum.
In short, I decided to reinforce success. I sent H.Q. 10 Corps
(Horrocks) to take charge of this left hook, and while this
reinforcement was moving to the left flank, we tee-ed up the
blitz attack which was to go in when it arrived.

(f) The enemy saw what was happening and tried to move his
reserves from opposite our right to stop our now very powerful
left thrust. They were too late. The blitz attack went in
twenty minutes after the last vehicle of 1st Armoured Division
had arrived, and it swept everything before it.
By 9 a.m. on the 28th March we were in full possession of the
famous Mareth Line, after a battle lasting only one week.
Having received a setback on our right, we recovered quickly
and knocked the enemy out with a " left hook."

We never lost the initiative: without which in war you cannot win.
The enemy was made to commit his reserves in desperation and piece-
meal, as at Alamein; we committed ours in one concentrated blow on
a narrow front.
The outstanding feature of the battle was the blitz attack on the
left flank, in daylight, on the afternoon of the 26th March. It was

delivered at 4 p.m. with the sun behind it and in the enemy's eyes. A dust storm was blowing at the time, the wind also being behind us and blowing the dust on to the enemy. The enemy was making ready for our usual night attack; instead he was assaulted in the afternoon with great ferocity.

The attack was simply conceived; it was dependent on surprise, on complete integration of land and air forces, and on a willingness to take risks and to face casualties.

The air forces played a notable part in the attack, using twenty-two squadrons of Spitfires, Kitty bombers and Hurricane tank-busters, operating in the area beyond the artillery barrage; in that area every vehicle, and anything that appeared or moved, was shot to pieces. Brilliant and brave work by the pilots completely stunned the enemy; our attack burst through the resistance and the battle was won. In this attack we took 2500 prisoners, all Germans; our own casualties were only 600, and we lost only 8 pilots.

This blitz attack was the most complete example of the close integration of land and air power up to that time. It should be noted that there were grave misgivings at the headquarters of the Tactical Air Forces; Coningham considered the risks were too great and an officer was sent over to try and stop the use of air power in this way. But the A.O.C. Desert Air Force (Harry Broadhurst) decided to accept the risks and refused to listen to the emissary. When it was all over and had been proved a great success with very small losses, he received many congratulations from Air Headquarters in Tunisia; and even from the Air Ministry!

THE END OF THE WAR IN AFRICA

It was obvious that the end of the war in Africa would now come quite soon.

The Eighth Army had only to burst through the Gabes gap and join hands with the American forces; the remaining enemy would then be hemmed in, and in an ever diminishing area.

We had a stiff one-day battle on the line of the Wadi Akarit north of Gabes on the 6th April, where we took another 7000 prisoners. On the 8th April, we joined up with the American forces moving eastwards from Gafsa. We were now taking prisoners at the rate of

1000 a day, and no army can lose men at that rate for very long and remain efficient.

On the 10th April we captured Sfax.

General Eisenhower's Chief of Staff, Bedell Smith, had visited me in Tripoli in February and we had discussed the problem of how soon the Eighth Army could join up with the First Army north of Gabes. I had said that I would be in Sfax by the 15th April. Bedell Smith said that if I could do that, General Eisenhower would give me anything I liked to ask for. I said I would do it, and would like an aeroplane for my personal use. Bedell Smith agreed, willingly.

On the morning of the 10th April I sent a message to Eisenhower asking for the aircraft. It arrived on the 16th April, a B17 (a Flying Fortress). It made me a thoroughly mobile general. Later, I got properly ticked off by Brooke, the C.I.G.S., for my action in the matter. He said that it was all a joke on the part of Bedell Smith and that Eisenhower was furious when I demanded the aircraft. I explained that it was very far from a joke on that day at Tripoli when the statement was made. I don't think Bedell Smith had ever told Eisenhower about it, and he was suddenly confronted with having to pay. Brooke added that the R.A.F. could well have provided me with an aircraft; they certainly could, but didn't—in spite of my repeated requests. Eisenhower produced it at once. And, being the great and generous man he is, he arranged that I was provided with an aircraft from American sources for the rest of the war; furthermore, he did this for my Chief of Staff also. He saw the need and acted promptly.

On the 10th April I wrote to Alexander saying a decision was required about which army should make the main effort for the final phase in Tunisia. I recommended that the First Army should do so; the plain west of Tunis was suitable ground for armour whereas my army was likely to be faced with difficult and mountainous country at Enfidaville and Takrouna. Alexander agreed and asked me to send the First Army one armoured division and one armoured car regiment; my task would be to exert pressure all the time, and make the enemy think the main attack would be delivered by the Eighth Army. I made my plans accordingly and attacked the Enfidaville position on the night of the 19th-20th April. It was difficult going in the mountains about Takrouna but we progressed about three miles. I regrouped and made plans to put in another attack after a week. I was not happy about these attacks and considered the main blow should be struck on the First Army front, where the ground was not so mountainous and armour could be used.

But the initial attempt of the First Army to break through to Tunis was not successful. It took place on the 23rd April. 5 Corps attacked on a front of three divisions, each on a front of six miles, and each division with all three infantry brigades up; it was more of a partridge drive than an attack and had no hope of success. 9 Corps with two armoured divisions tried to break through somewhere else. I was in bed at the time with an attack of tonsilitis and influenza, and so I asked Alexander if he would come and see me at my headquarters near Sousse. He arrived on the 30th April. I said it was essential to regroup the two armies, First and Eighth, so that the attack on Tunis could be made with the maximum strength in the most suitable area.

I suggested that I should send First Army the 7th Armoured Division, 4th Indian Division, 201st Guards Brigade, and some extra artillery, together with a very experienced corps commander to handle the attack; I meant Horrocks.

I finally said we really must finish off the war in Africa quickly. We were due to invade Sicily in July and there was much to do before we could tackle that difficult combined operation. Alexander thoroughly agreed.

Horrocks went over to the First Army and staged the corps attack on Tunis on the 6th May; it was made in great strength at the selected point and broke clean through the enemy defences to the west of Tunis. Bizerta and Tunis were captured on the 7th May and the enemy was then hemmed in to the Cap Bon peninsula.

The first troops to enter Tunis were those of our own 7th Armoured Division. They had earned this satisfaction. Organised enemy resistance ended on the 12th May, some 248,000 being taken prisoner.

And so the war in Africa came to a close. It ended in a major disaster for the Germans; all their troops, stores, dumps, heavy weapons, and equipment were captured. From a purely military point of view the holding out in North Africa once the Mareth Line had been broken through, could never be justified. I suppose Hitler ordered it for political reasons. It is dangerous to undertake tasks which are militarily quite unsound, just for political reasons; it may sometimes be necessary, but they will generally end in disaster.

The contribution of the Eighth Army to the final victory in North Africa had been immense. It drove Rommel and his army out of

Egypt, out of Cyrenaica, out of Tripolitania, and then helped the First Army to finish them off in Tunisia. Only first-class troops could have done it and I realised what an honour and what an excitement it was to command such a magnificent army at the time of its greatest triumphs.

Early in June the Prime Minister wrote the following in my autograph book:

" The total destruction or capture of all enemy forces in Tunisia, culminating in the surrender of 248,000 men, marks the triumphant end of the great enterprises set on foot at Alamein and by the invasion of N.W. Africa. May the future reap in the utmost fullness the rewards of past achievements and new exertions.
Winston S. Churchill "

Algiers. June 3, 1943

Before closing this chapter I just want to mention certain matters which, cumulatively, played the major part in this amazing campaign. It is about 2000 miles from Alamein to Tunis, and we had got to Tripoli in three months and to Tunis in six. How was it done?

First, I would say that the soldiery gave of their best. I had told them in August 1942 that I would lead them to victory. There would be no setback, no failures; at all times when we were ready I would tell them what we were going to do, and we would then do it. I gave orders that the Press was to have the fullest facilities for finding out what was going on, and for reporting it. We went from one success to another; the Eighth Army developed a crusading spirit, and the soldiers began to think it was invincible. By the end of the campaign I believe they would have done anything I asked; they felt we were all partners in the battle and that they themselves " belonged," and mattered. They gave me their complete confidence. What more can any commander want? My only fear was that I myself might fail these magnificent men.

Next, I had a superb Chief of Staff. I have already referred to de Guingand. His fertile brain was full of ideas and he was never defeated by the difficulties of any problem. He could take from me an outline conception of a plan, work out the staff details, and let me know quickly if it was possible from the staff point of view: and if not, what changes in substance were desirable. He accepted responsibility readily. I gave him full powers. If he couldn't get hold of me he would give a

major decision himself, and I never once questioned any such decision.
I trusted him completely; he seemed to know instinctively what I
would do in any given situation, and he was always right.

With such a Chief of Staff I could keep clear of detail; I left that
all to him. The first requirement in high command is to have a good
Chief of Staff. Without de Guingand, I doubt if I could have done
my part of the overall task. It was of course a fluke that I found him
in Egypt when I arrived; but I took full advantage of that fluke. It
was, of course, hardly a fluke that he was where he was when I arrived.

Under de Guingand the Eighth Army staff developed into a splendid
team. I have always been a great believer in youth: with its enthusiasm,
its optimism, its original ideas and its willingness to follow a leader.
Our staff was on the young side; many of them were not soldiers by
profession. The only requirement needed for getting on my staff was
ability to do the job; it mattered not whether a man was a regular, or
a temporary soldier for the duration of the war.

I arrived in the desert for the first time on the 13th August 1942.
They were veterans at the game, but they " accepted " me that very
day (or perhaps the day after!) and they laboured unceasingly to carry
out my plans and ideas. And de Guingand welded them into a devoted
unity.

As the campaign developed I learnt the value of Intelligence. Bill
Williams was the main source of inspiration; intellectually he was far
superior to myself or to anyone on my staff, but he never gave one
that impression. He saw the enemy picture whole and true; he could
sift a mass of detailed information and deduce the right answer. As
time went on he got to know how I worked; he would tell me in ten
minutes exactly what I wanted to know, leaving out what he knew I
did *not* want to know. Once a commander and his intelligence chief
have achieved this state of intimate co-operation, it is obvious they
must not be parted; that is why he went right through to Berlin with
me. He was " accepted " and trusted right through the Eighth Army.
In this respect he was possibly helped by the fact that he wore a K.D.G.
badge in his cap and not that of the Intelligence Corps. In the Second
World War the best officers in the Intelligence branch of the staff were
civilians; they seemed to have the best brain for that type of work,
trained in the " rules of evidence," fertile and with great imagination,
and Bill Williams stood out supreme among them all.

Then I must mention my system of personal command from a

Tactical Headquarters, located well forward in the battle area. I divided my headquarters into three echelons:

Tac H.Q.
Main H.Q.
Rear H.Q.

Tac H.Q. was the headquarters from which I exercised personal command and control of the battle. It was small, highly efficient, and completely mobile on its own transport. It consisted chiefly of signals, cipher, liaison staff, defence troops, and a very small operations staff for keeping in touch with the battle situation.

Main H.Q. was the central core of the whole headquarters organisation. I gave verbal orders to my subordinate commanders from Tac H.Q. The staff work consequent on those orders was done at Main and Rear. The Chief of Staff, and the senior administrative officer, both lived at Main. But the chief administrator had to have a good deputy at Rear and this is where Miles Graham began to reveal his capacity. Ultimately as I have said he succeeded Brian Robertson, and then " Rim " Lymer, in his turn, became Graham's deputy.

Rear H.Q. was the administrative echelon of the headquarter organisation. There were located the " A " and " Q " branches, and the services and departments.

We became very experienced in developing and using this type of organisation, and I took it with me to 21 Army Group when I left the Eighth Army. It is applicable from an Army Headquarters upwards; it is not applicable to a Corps H.Q., as a Corps Commander must have the full machinery of his Main H.Q. around him in order to fight the tactical battle.

An Army Commander can only produce the best results by working from a Tac H.Q. If he cannot acquire the Tac H.Q. mentality, he is not and never will be any good in command of an army.

Finally, I must mention the constant advice I was given by all and sundry about how I should fight the battle, what I ought to do next, and so on. I suppose this used to go on with my predecessors in command of the Eighth Army, and possibly they accepted it.

About the middle of November 1942 I wrote to the C.I.G.S. and I quote the following from that letter:

" One of the most interesting points to my mind about this

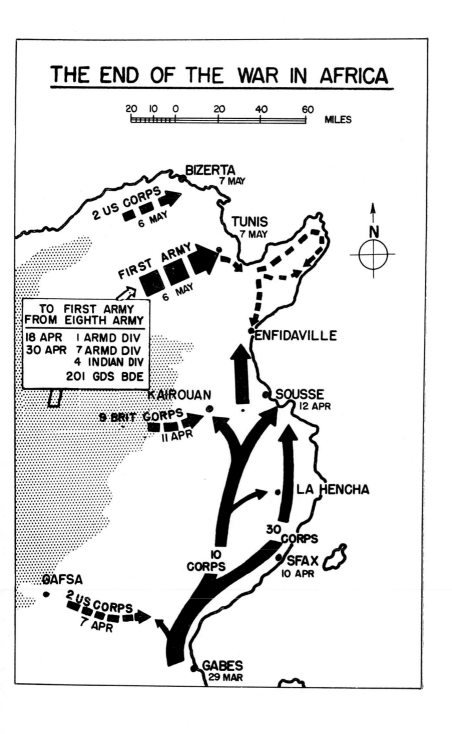

THE END OF THE WAR IN AFRICA

20 10 0   20   40   60   MILES

BIZERTA
7 MAY

2 US CORPS
6 MAY

TUNIS
7 MAY

FIRST ARMY
6 MAY

ENFIDAVILLE

TO FIRST ARMY
FROM EIGHTH ARMY
18 APR 1 ARMD DIV
30 APR 7 ARMD DIV
        4 INDIAN DIV
   201 GDS BDE

KAIROUAN

SOUSSE
12 APR

9 BRIT CORPS
11 APR

LA HENCHA

30 CORPS

10 CORPS

SFAX
10 APR

GAFSA

2 US CORPS
7 APR

GABES
29 MAR

business of making war is the way people try and shake your confidence in what you are doing, and suggest that your plan is not good, and that you ought to do this, or that. If I had done all that was suggested I would still be back in the Alamein area!"

One of the big lessons I learnt from the campaign in Africa was the need to decide what you want to do, and then to *do* it. One must never be drawn off the job in hand by gratuitous advice from those who are not fully in the operational picture, and who have no responsibility.

My great supporter throughout was Alexander. He never bothered me, never fussed me, never suggested what I ought to do, and gave me at once everything I asked for—having listened patiently to my explanation of why I wanted it. But he was too big to require explanations; he gave me his trust.

My upbringing as a child had taught me to have resource within myself. I needed it in the desert campaign. I was also taught to count my blessings, and this I certainly did.

CHAPTER II

THE CAMPAIGN IN SICILY

10th July to 17th August 1943

ORDERS WERE received in North Africa in January 1943 that when the Axis Powers had been turned out of Africa, operations would be developed to knock Italy out of the war. It was decided that the first step was the capture of Sicily; the code name was HUSKY.

On the 18th April, when the Eighth Army was still fighting in Tunisia, I sent a message to Alexander to say that in my opinion the situation regarding the planning for Operation HUSKY was becoming acute. I understood that a plan for the operation had been drawn up in London, which from what little I could learn about it did not sound a good one. It was urgently necessary that we should meet with Eisenhower, and reach decisions on certain vital matters. This was agreed at once and I flew to Algiers in my recently acquired Flying Fortress on the 19th April.

The following were the notes I used at our conference, and I left a copy with Alexander:

" 1. The key dates for the Eighth Army are as follows:

27th April Army admin. plan complete and handed to subordinate formations.

15th May Tonnage allocations for stores in first three convoys passed to G.H.Q.

17th May Subordinate formations submit plans of allocation of troops to ships.

22nd May Consolidated plans, with allocations of troops to ships, sent to G.H.Q.

1st June Start loading ships.

2. The following points need to be understood:

(*a*) I myself, and my Army H.Q. staff, know very little about the operation as a whole, and *nothing whatever* about the detailed planning that is going on.

(b) The following who are to take part in HUSKY are now involved in battle operations in TUNISIA:

Army H.Q.

30 Corps H.Q.

Three complete Divisions.

Various Army and Corps Troops.

(c) The Army staff who are responsible for, and must control, the operation are completely in the dark as to what is going on.

(d) Detailed planning is being carried out by Staff Officers who are not in touch with battle requirements.

(e) There is no responsible senior commander thoroughly versed in what happens in battle who is devoting *his sole attention* to the HUSKY operation.

3. If we go on in this way much longer we may have a disaster. The preparations for the operation must be gripped firmly, and be handled in a sensible way.

4. The crux of the matter is this:

(a) The real and proper answer to the problem is to withdraw from battle operations in Tunisia *now* Eighth Army H.Q. and all troops who are required for HUSKY.

(b) If this is done, can we be certain of finishing the war in Tunisia in time to allow of HUSKY being launched? I do not know the answer to this.

5. Possibly some sort of compromise will be necessary in order to get ourselves out of the mess we are now in.

To compromise is a well-known British habit, and we shall have to adopt it.

6. I consider that the following are the minimum requirements of the compromise, and that these requirements must be implemented at once:

(a) A Chief of Staff to be added to the establishment of H.Q. Eighth Army and to be given the acting rank of Major-General.

(b) By means of this Chief of Staff, who will represent me in Cairo, and whose rank will enable him to carry the necessary weight and to force things through, I will keep my grip on what is going on.

(c) I will, at my discretion, send to Cairo such members of

my staff as I consider must be there, either permanently or temporarily. I will decide to what extent this can be done without affecting adversely the battle of Tunisia.

(d) The following to be withdrawn from the operations in Tunisia at once so that they can get down to HUSKY:

 Comd and H.Q. 30 Corps.

 50th Div. complete.

 51st Div. complete.

(e) I myself to pay an early visit to Cairo to see that all is well. Thereafter I will fluctuate between Cairo and Tunisia at my discretion, as is indicated by the course of events.

(f) The New Zealand Div. to be dropped from the initial operations. It has man-power problems which will take some time to settle.

(g) 56th Div. to go into the battle in Tunisia. I cannot take on HUSKY a division that has never fired a shot in this war.

The Inf. Bde. Group of 56th Div. now in Egypt, to join 50th Div., so as to complete 50th Div. to a three-brigade div.

(h) 78th Division to be allocated as my reserve division. This division to be withdrawn from the battle in Tunisia during May.

7. There will come a time when Eighth Army H.Q. *must* leave the battle in Tunisia. This will come fairly soon, and in any case very early in May.

When that time comes, I suggest that H.Q. 10 Corps should be left in charge of the remaining Eighth Army troops, and come under First Army."

Eisenhower and Alexander gave their full agreement to my proposals, and a telegram was sent to the War Office asking for de Guingand to be given the official appointment of Chief of Staff Eighth Army with the rank of Major-General.

I left for Cairo on the 23rd April. As I flew there I pondered on the future. Private Glaister had referred to the Eighth Army as a "brotherhood." He was right: we were a "brotherhood in arms." We did what we liked. We dressed as we liked. What mattered was success, and to win our battles with a minimum of casualties. I was the head of the brotherhood. I was pretty tough about mistakes and especially mistakes which cost lives; I would allow no departure from the fundamentals of the master plan. But I let subordinate commanders do as they liked about details and didn't fuss about the wrong things. Until we had burst through the Gabes gap and emerged into the plain of Tunisia, it was a private war run by the Eighth Army; we made our own plans and adjusted the time factor to suit the problems. Alexander let me run this private war in my own way and supported me to the hilt; we gave him success all along the road and he was content to leave well alone.

But we were now round the corner and had joined the main body of the forces in North Africa. We had got to learn to adjust our way of doing things, our very behaviour, to a larger canvas—to the war as a whole—and this would often mean, would probably generally mean, compromise. The Eighth Army was now to be taken to sea by the Navy, and then had got to learn to fight in Europe, in close country. The desert which we knew so well, and which we had conquered, was to be left behind. We all knew that the Second Front in Europe, the invasion across the Channel, was looming ahead. Possibly Sicily was to be, in a sense, a rehearsal for the more serious operation which would come in 1944.

Anyhow, the more I thought about it the more I realised that the freedom we had enjoyed in the desert was now over. We had got to learn to work with others, and many of our own ideas and concepts would possibly be brushed aside for the good of the whole. Even so, I was determined to ensure that the Eighth Army was never launched into battle with a bad plan, and that the lives of officers and men were not thrown away in unsound ventures. I had led the Army to victory across two thousand miles of Africa. I had promised officers and men there would be no more failures. And before we went to Sicily I would have to visit all my divisions and tell the soldiers that I was confident of success there.

I knew from what de Guingand had told me that there had been already seven plans for the assault on Sicily.

Plan No. 1 was produced by the Joint Planning Staff in London in January 1943. This plan split the assaulting force up into a large number of landings between Catania on the east coast, southwards round the Pachino peninsula, and thence to a point far away at the western end of the island. To such a dispersion of effort we would never have agreed, but at that time we were fighting our way to Tripoli—and I doubt if I even knew that Sicily was to be the next objective. This plan was apparently accepted *in principle* by Alexander's headquarters in Tunisia in April, and his own staff produced Plan No. 2. This was a *detailed* plan which involved landings between Catania and Palermo, from D-Day to D+5. This was the basis of the plan which, with some modifications, was eventually submitted by General Eisenhower to the Combined Chiefs of Staff in Washington in April 1943, and which I shall call Plan No. 3—since it was the third plan that I knew about.

So far I had not been consulted in any way, although the Eighth Army was to play a major part in the operations.

Further detailed ways of invading Sicily were produced by various planning experts, some of whom came to see me, making a total of seven by the middle of April. This didn't look to me a good way of going about the operation; time was getting short and a firm plan was essential, and quickly.

As I flew towards Cairo I began to see the future more clearly.

Obviously there were rocks ahead and we would have to walk delicately and not force our desert ways down the throats of all and sundry. Also we must try and preserve our sense of humour and— very important—we must not get a name for non-cooperation. We mustn't " bellyache." But I was determined on one thing: I would never agree to compromise over vital issues.

De Guingand met me at Cairo and the next day I was given a presentation of the plan for the invasion of Sicily as finally proposed by Alexander's headquarters. This could be called Plan No. 8. The naval commander responsible for landing the Eighth Army in Sicily was Admiral Ramsay, known as Bertie Ramsay. He was a grand person and I had known him when he was Flag Officer, Dover, and I had been commanding the South-Eastern Army. Later we worked together on the Normandy landings. It was a real tragedy for us all, and to me a great personal loss, when he was killed in an air crash in France early in 1945.

I listened to the presentation of Plan No. 8 and quickly decided that it would not do. The Eighth Army was to land in the south-east of the island in a wide arc stretching from a point just south of Syracuse, southwards round the Pachino peninsula, and then westwards to Gela. The Seventh U.S. Army was to land in the extreme north-west of the island, astride Trapani. Such dispersion was obviously based on meeting only very slight resistance. I had a good talk about it with Bertie Ramsay, and also with Leese and Dempsey who were to be my Corps Commanders for the campaign in Sicily.

I decided to send a signal to Alexander saying I could not accept the proposed plan for the Eighth Army, and to put forward instead a new plan which put the Army ashore in a suitable area between a point just south of Syracuse and the Pachino peninsula inclusive.

This was Plan No. 9 and was called by my staff the "Easter Plan," having been made during the Easter week-end. Plan No. 9 was the one finally agreed for the Eighth Army. I sent the following signal to Alexander on the 24th April:

"1. Am now in Cairo with my Corps Commanders and for the first time am able to investigate the problem confronting the Eighth Army in the invasion of Sicily. I send you the following points.

2. The fact that I have not been able to devote my sole attention to this problem before today has affected all the work here.

3. Planning to date has been on the assumption that resistance will be slight and Sicily will be captured easily. Never was there a greater error. Germans and Italians are fighting well in Tunisia and will repeat the process in Sicily. If we work on the assumption of little resistance, and disperse our effort as is being done in all planning to date, we will merely have a disaster. We must plan for fierce resistance, by the Germans at any rate, and for a real dog fight battle to follow the initial assault.

4. I am prepared to carry the war into Sicily with the Eighth Army but must really ask to be allowed to make my own Army plan. My Army must operate so concentrated that corps and divisions can co-operate. The whole initial effort of the Eighth Army should be made in the area between Syracuse and the Pachino peninsula. Subsequent operations will be developed so as to secure airfields and ports. The first thing to do is to secure a lodgement in a suitable area and then operate from that firm base.

5. Time is pressing. If we delay while the toss is being argued in London and Washington, the operation will never be launched

in July. All planning is suffering because everyone is trying to make something of a plan which they know can never succeed.

6. I have given orders that as far as the Eighth Army is concerned all planning and work will proceed on the lines outlined in para. 4.

7. Admiral Ramsay is in complete agreement with me and together we are prepared to launch the operation and win.

8. It is essential we have close and intimate air support and I must have the Desert Air Force working with me, with Broadhurst and his staff and experienced squadrons.

9. I must make it clear that the above solution is the only possible way to handle the Eighth Army problem with the resources available."

It will be noted that my plan for the Eighth Army separated us still farther from the American landings in the north-west corner of the island, and it involved no troops landing in the Gulf of Gela to secure the airfields about that place. I had my own ideas about the American landings but did not think the moment was yet opportune to put them forward. I expected my signal to produce immediate repercussions in Algiers, and it did!

The next day, the 25th April, Ramsay received a proper " stinker " from Admiral Cunningham, the Naval C.-in-C. working with Alexander. He was rather upset; but we had a good laugh over it and he agreed that I should send the following signal to Alexander.

" I hear that Cunningham and Tedder have told you they disagree completely with our proposed plan for the Eighth Army assault on Sicily. I wish to state emphatically that if we carry out the suggested existing plan it will fail. I state on whatever reputation I may have that the plan put forward by me and Ramsay will succeed. Would you like us both to come over and explain our plan. Meanwhile work is continuing on our plan as time is short."

I then left Cairo on the 26th April and returned to my H.Q. in the field in Tunisia. On arrival, I found I had a high temperature and went to bed in my caravan with influenza and tonsilitis.

Meanwhile Alexander had called a conference at Algiers for the 29th April, which Ramsay and I were to attend. I was in bed so I wired to Cairo that de Guingand was to go in my place. His aircraft had a forced landing at El Adem, and he was removed to hospital with concussion. I then asked Oliver Leese to go and he got there safely, and in time.

The conference produced no result. Tedder said that if the initial bridgehead did not include the airfields at Comiso and Gela, then his air forces could not operate effectively. This led Cunningham to say that unless the air forces could keep the enemy air away, then the convoys could not operate. Alexander was unable to get inter-Service agreement, and the conference broke up without coming to any decision.

It will be remembered that I had previously wired to Alexander saying I was anxious to see him about what could be done to finish off the war in Tunisia quickly, so that we could get on with planning the Sicily campaign. He came to see me on the 30th April. I was still in bed. When we had dealt with the war in Tunisia, he told me about the conference at Algiers the day before: the 29th April. I said something *must* be done, and suggested a full-scale conference at Algiers on the 2nd May; I would be well enough by then to fly over to Algiers and state my case. Alexander agreed.

"THE WRITING ON THE WALL"

I arrived at Algiers on the 2nd May to find that Alexander could not get there; mist and low cloud prevented his flying from his headquarters. I suggested we might hold the conference without him, but Cunningham and Tedder would not agree; they were quite right, since to have done so would not have been fair to Alexander.

I began to wonder what could be done. I went to look for Bedell Smith, Chief of Staff to Eisenhower. He was not in his office and I eventually ran him to ground in the lavatory. So we discussed the problem then and there. He was very upset; he said that for political reasons it was essential to reach a final decision and get on with the job. I said it was far more important to do so for military reasons, and that I could give him the answer to the problem at once; he asked me to do so. I said the American landings up near Palermo should be cancelled and the whole American effort put in on the south coast, astride Gela and west of the Pachino peninsula, with the object of securing the airfields that were considered so essential by our air forces. The Eighth Army and the Seventh U.S. Army would then land side by side, giving cohesion to the whole invasion.

Bedell Smith said there would be no difficulty whatever in doing what I suggested. We then left the lavatory and he went off to consult Eisenhower, who liked the plan but quite rightly refused to discuss it with me unless Alexander was present. The air forces liked it. The navy planners were a bit suspicious, and were doubtful whether the American forces could be supplied over the beaches for any length of time. There was no good port on their front of assault, or anywhere else.

I next persuaded Bedell Smith to assemble a conference. I said it could be a staff conference, and I would sit in with the staff; then when Alexander arrived the next day, the staff could present an agreed plan to him and his brother Commanders-in-Chief.

So this was done.

I presented my case; everyone agreed with it. I had now got Eisenhower and his Chief of Staff on my side. But Eisenhower quite rightly refused to come to a decision until the plan was recommended to him by Alexander and the other Commanders-in-Chief. This is what I said at the conference that day, in the form in which my remarks were taken down in shorthand:

"1. I know well that I am regarded by many people as being a tiresome person. I think this is very probably true. I try hard not to be tiresome; but I have seen so many mistakes made in this war, and so many disasters happen, that I am desperately anxious to try and see that we have no more; and this often means being very tiresome. If we have a disaster in Sicily it would be dreadful.

2. We have now reached a very critical stage in the planning for the attack on Sicily.
Unless some final decision is reached within the next few days, it is very doubtful if we will be able to launch the operation in July.
I would like to put before you the problem as it appears to me, the Commander of an Army which has got to be landed in Sicily and there fight a hard battle.

3. Three outstanding factors are as follows:

(a) The capture of Sicily will depend ultimately on the effective operations of the land forces.

(b) These land forces have to be got there by the Navy, and the Navy has to be able to maintain them once ashore.

(c) The above two things cannot possibly happen unless the air forces can operate effectively and they cannot do so unless suitable airfields are acquired quickly so that fighter squadrons can be stepped forward, and the enemy air is pushed well back and is generally dominated.

4. We next want to be clear that enemy resistance will be very great; it will be a hard and bitter fight; we must go prepared for a real killing match. That is nothing new, and we have had many parties of that sort; but there are certain rules in that sort of game, or killing match, which have to be observed; if you do not observe them then you lose the match.

The outstanding and great rule is that dispersion of effort by the land forces leads to disaster. They must keep collected, with corps and divisions within supporting distance of each other.

5. We next have to consider in what way the land forces must be put on shore by the Navy so that they are then well placed to develop their operations and to maintain themselves.

The area selected must be inside fighter cover; a good port must be seized quickly; good airfields must be secured quickly for the air forces.

The size of the initial bridgehead you can establish is limited by your resources.

With limited resources you will be lucky if this bridgehead includes a good port and *all* the airfields you want; some may have to come later as operations are developed. Therefore it is very important that with limited resources, and against strong resistance you act as follows *in the first instance*:

(a) keep concentrated.

(b) secure a suitable area as a firm base from which to develop your operations.

(c) keep the initial operations within good fighter cover of your own airfields.

6. I have made it clear that the extent of the bridgehead is limited by your resources.

What we must now be clear about is that the initial bridgehead must include the *immediate essentials*, without which the whole combined operation would merely collapse.

7. Let us now apply the above principles to Sicily—the S.E. portion. The best place for the Eighth Army to be put ashore is between Syracuse and Pachino.

This would meet every requirement that I have brought out in the preceding paragraphs, except one.

And *that one is very important*; it does not secure sufficient air-fields for the air forces or deny to the enemy the use of airfields from which he could interfere with our seaborne traffic and operations generally. The airfields in question are those in the general area Comiso-Gela.

These airfields must, according to the air, be included in the initial bridgehead.

In fact they are, as I have already said:

' immediate essentials, without which the whole combined operations would merely collapse.'

8. I must state here very clearly, and beyond any possibility of doubt, that I will never operate my Army ' dispersed ' in this operation. I consider that to do so would mean failure; and Sicily, instead of being a success, would involve the Allied Nations in a first-class disaster; that is exactly what the Germans would like, and would be a shattering blow to Allied morale all over the world.

It is not merely a matter of capturing some beaches, or some airfields, or some ports. It is a matter of the conduct of offensive operations in an enemy country; the objectives include airfields, ports, and so on, and finally we require the whole island.

9. Are there any alternatives?

    (a) You could shift the whole bridgehead layout northwards to include the Catania area and the airfield there.

        This can be discarded *at once*, if only for the reason that it is outside fighter cover of our own air bases.

    (b) You could shift the whole layout westwards to the area of the Gulf of Gela.

        This gets the airfields we require. But you have no port, and the total forces could not be maintained for long only through the beaches.

10. The whole point turns on the size of the initial bridgehead we can secure.

   The factors are as follows:

   (a) The Army won't have dispersion, and we must have a port.

   (b) A bridgehead to satisfy the Army can NOT include, with the resources available, certain airfields to the west which are essential for the air.

   (c) I understand the air point of view to be that these airfields must be denied to the enemy at once, and then quickly secured for our own use. Unless this is done the air forces cannot guarantee air protection beyond the initial stage, i.e. for, say, the first 48 hours.

11. It is therefore quite obvious that these airfields must be taken. But we have not any troops for the purpose. Two divisions, assault loaded, would be necessary, and they would carry out the landings in the Gulf of Gela.

12. We have now reached the stage when we can say quite definitely that we require *two more* divisions, assault loaded and to be landed on D-Day in the Gulf of Gela, if the invasion of Sicily is to be a success.

   Given these two divisions, then all requirements of the Army, Air, and Navy are met and this very difficult and tricky operation will be a complete success.

   Without these two divisions, it would seem—in view of what the air say—that we might well have a disaster.

13. I consider that the answer to the problem is to shift the U.S. effort from the Palermo area, and to use it in the Gulf of Gela, to land on either side of Gela.

   The invasion of Sicily will then be a complete success."

When the conference was over, I returned in the evening to my operational H.Q. in Tunisia to await events.

At midnight the next day, the 3rd May, I received a signal from Alexander saying that Eisenhower had approved. At last we could get on with our work, with a firm plan.

Having been woken up and given the signal, I went to sleep again feeling that fighting the Germans was easy compared with fighting for the vital issues on which everything depended. I wondered if the Germans went on like this in planning their operations.

Two more things were necessary before I could feel happy about the invasion of Sicily. As a result of the acceptance by all concerned of the plan of attack, land operations by British and American forces really became one operation. Each would be dependent on the other for direct support in the battle; our administrative needs would also be interdependent. Time was pressing and it was clear that the co-ordination, direction and control should be undertaken by one Army commander and a joint staff. I put this viewpoint to Alexander and he agreed; his view was that one Army H.Q. should handle the whole operation. Alexander put this to General Eisenhower, who did not agree. The organisation was to be two armies, one American and one British, under Alexander.

Much more important was the second point. We were going to open up a new campaign in a new theatre. The planners, and everyone else, had been concentrating on *where* to land; nobody had considered how the campaign in Sicily should be *developed*. We wanted to secure the island quickly and prevent the escape of its garrison back to Italy. To do this we must work to a master plan, which I suggested should be the following.

The two armies, landing side by side on the south coast, should push quickly northwards and cut the island in half. A defensive flank should then be formed facing west, and the combined efforts of *both* armies be concentrated on getting rapidly to Messina to prevent the get-away across the straits. The navies and air forces must co-operate to see that none of the enemy got away by sea.

Although Alexander then agreed with this conception of how the campaign should be developed by his two armies, and with the role of the naval and air forces, in fact the campaign was not conducted in this way. By the time we had captured the whole island, the Germans had mostly got back to Italy.

I GO TO ENGLAND

All resistance in North Africa ended on the 12th May.

Field-Marshal Messe, the Italian C.-in-C. who succeeded Rommel in the overall command, surrendered to the Eighth Army on the 13th

May; he had dinner with me that night before going off to his prison camp, and we discussed various aspects of the battles we had fought against each other.

I decided then that I would go to England for a short holiday before the Sicily campaign began. I also wanted to see the 1st Canadian Division which was to land direct on the Sicily beaches from the U.K. We should not see them until we were fighting alongside them. This obviously needed buttoning up beforehand.

I left Tripoli in my " Flying Fortress " on the 16th May, arriving in England on the 17th. I enjoyed the visit, and especially my time with David.

One thing made me feel lonely. A Thanksgiving Service for the end of the war in Africa was held in St. Paul's Cathedral on the 19th May; I was in London but was not asked to attend. It was explained to me *after the service* that it was desired to keep my presence in England a secret. Yet to my delighted surprise, wherever I went I was followed by crowds. The incident made me realise that if I were pretty popular with a lot of people, I was not too popular in some circles. Perhaps the one explained the other.

I returned to the Eighth Army via Algiers, and met the Prime Minister and the C.I.G.S. there on the 2nd June; I did the journey from London to Algiers in one day in the " Flying Fortress," in daylight.

I gained the impression that the Prime Minister and the C.I.G.S. had come on to Algiers from Washington in order to ensure that the capture of Sicily should be pushed hard and exploited to the utmost; to do this was somewhat at variance with the decisions taken in Washington, and therefore they had persuaded General Marshall to come with them. The P.M. was determined to knock Italy out of the war. He cross-examined me a good deal about the plan for Sicily. I expressed confidence in our plan and in our ability to carry it out.

This was only natural, since it was my plan! I also emphasised the need for a master plan which would ensure that, once ashore, the operations would be developed in the right way.

While in England I had been told that the King was going to visit the forces in North Africa in June. He arrived in Africa on the 13th June and came to Tripoli on the 17th to see the Eighth Army, or as much of it as was there. He stayed with us in our camp on the sea-shore some miles outside Tripoli, and I think he enjoyed the visit. We certainly enjoyed having him with us; he put us all at our ease and was in splendid form.

I was anxious for his safety at one time as enemy parachutists were still at large, and Tripoli was full of Italians. When the King was actually in that town I confined all civilians to their houses; and on one day fire was opened on suspicious elements trying to break out.

On the day he arrived, the 19th June, he gave me the accolade of Knighthood in the lunch marquee near the airfield.

WE INVADE SICILY

On the 8th July the Prime Minister sent me a telegram: "Every good wish and all our confidence goes with you and your splendid Army."

On the same day I issued my usual personal message to the Eighth Army.

We landed in Sicily two hours before dawn on the 10th July. The story of the campaign in that island has been told frequently and I have already described it myself in *Alamein to the River Sangro*.

I had a difficult decision to make soon after we landed. General McNaughton, the G.O.C.-in-C. First Canadian Army (in England), had arrived in Malta about the middle of July with a party of staff officers and he asked to be sent over to Sicily to see the Canadian troops.

The 1st Canadian Division had not been in action before and officers and men were just beginning to find their feet. Guy Simonds, the Divisional Commander, was young and inexperienced; it was the first time he had commanded a division in battle.

I was determined that the Canadians must be left alone and I wasn't going to have Simonds bothered with visitors when he was heavily engaged with his division in all-out operations against first-rate German troops. However, to make sure I went to see Simonds and asked him if he would like McNaughton to come to Sicily. His reply was immediate—"For God's sake keep him away." On that, I sent a message to Malta asking that the visit be postponed. When the campaign in Sicily was over, I invited General McNaughton to come and see the Canadian troops and he stayed with me at my Tac Headquarters at Taormina. I have not seen him since those days, although I have paid many visits to Canada since the war ended. It seemed to me that he

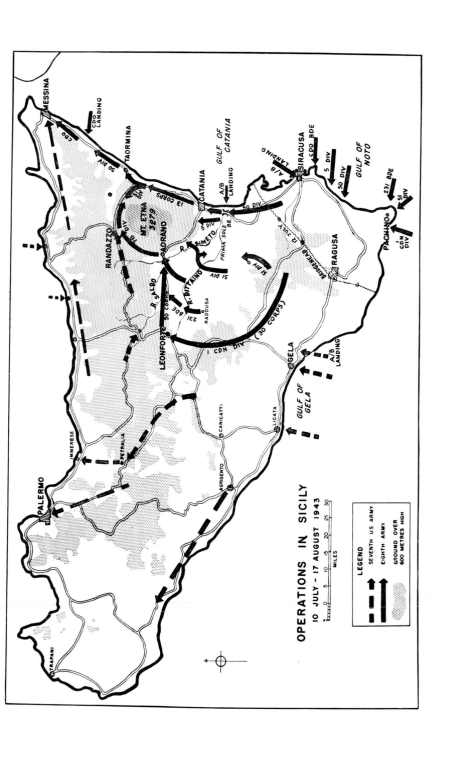

OPERATIONS IN SICILY
10 JULY - 17 AUGUST 1943

LEGEND

SEVENTH US ARMY

EIGHTH ARMY

GROUND OVER
600 METRES HIGH

Speaking to the 11th Canadian Tank Regiment near Lentini, Sicily, 25th July 1943

A lunch party at my Tac H.Q. at Taormina, after the campaign in Sicily was over, 29th August 1943. Seated, left to right: Patton, Eisenhower, the author. Behind Patton is Bradley. On the extreme right, Dempsey

had never forgiven me for denying him entry to Sicily in July 1943.

The Canadians were magnificent in the Sicilian campaign. They had done no fighting before, but they were very well trained and they soon learnt the tricks of the battlefield which count for so much and save so many lives. When I drew them into reserve to prepare for the invasion of the Italian mainland, they had become one of the Eighth Army's veteran divisions.

The men of the Eighth Army enjoyed Sicily after the desert. It was high summer; oranges and lemons were on the trees; wine was plentiful; the Sicilian girls were disposed to be friendly. It was very hot and the mosquitoes were unpleasant; indeed, they were a menace since they were the malarial type. Our medical discipline was not good as regards the regular parades for taking preventive medicines that are so necessary in such conditions; we suffered almost as many casualties from malaria as we did from enemy action. We were all used to the heat; but whereas the desert was dry, Sicily was humid.

The men in back areas discarded all possible clothing and some even took to wearing the wide-brim Sicilian straw hat. I well remember an incident that occurred one day as I was driving in my open car up to the front. I saw a lorry coming towards me with a soldier apparently completely naked in the driver's seat, wearing a silk top hat. As the lorry passed me, the driver leant out from his cab and took off his hat to me with a sweeping and gallant gesture. I just roared with laughter. However, while I was not particular about dress so long as the soldiers fought well and we won our battles, I at once decided that there were limits. When I got back to my headquarters I issued the only order I ever issued about dress in the Eighth Army; it read as follows: " Top hats will not be worn in the Eighth Army."

It was in Sicily that I gave up the " Flying Fortress " I had won at Sfax. We had got away from the large airfields of Africa and there were few in Sicily on which such a large aircraft could land safely. We nearly crashed the day I landed at Palermo to visit General Patton. So I asked Eisenhower if he would kindly change it, and he provided instead a Dakota with a jeep inside it—which was far more useful.

I think everyone admitted that we learnt a great deal in Sicily. In some cases possibly all that was learnt was how *not* to do certain things. But all in all, the experience was invaluable to us all: to the high command at Allied Force H.Q. in the Mediterranean theatre, to my staff and myself, and to every officer and man in the Eighth Army.

But the campaign had an unsatisfactory ending in that most of the German troops on the island got away across the Straits of Messina to Italy, and this when *we* had complete air and naval supremacy. This was to cause us great trouble later on when we ourselves went into Italy. It seems to me worthwhile, therefore, to go back over the ground and try to discover what was wrong.

The operation involved planning a major seaborne assault, incorporating the establishment of a beach-working system of maintenance, without any previous experience of an operation of this magnitude. Simplicity, care, and close co-operation between the Services and Allies, were absolutely vital.

Although orders for the invasion of Sicily were received in North Africa in January 1943, *the plan was not finalised till May, two months before D-Day.* The main reasons for this delay were the following:

(a) The responsible commanders-in-chief, and those who were actually to command in the field, were all engaged in current operations in North Africa.

Planning was undertaken by *ad hoc* planning staffs which went to work without the guidance of commanders.

A series of plans was produced; none of them was good since the planners were inexperienced.

(b) When the field commanders were able to begin work on the plan, major alterations were necessary to make it a practical proposition. Meanwhile much time and effort had been wasted during the "absentee landlord" period.

(c) The headquarters of the responsible C.s-in-C., and of the field commanders, were widely dispersed. For the major planning meetings, Naval and Army Commanders of the Eastern Task Force (the Eighth Army) had to fly from Cairo to Algiers, a distance of over 2000 miles. This led to inevitable delays.

(d) Final decisions had to be made by the Supreme Commander. But he was deeply involved in political matters in North Africa and was not free to devote his entire energies to the campaign ahead.

The responsibilities for the mounting of the operation, and embarkation ports, were most complicated. Troops of the Eighth Army had to be embarked from the following ports:

Haifa, Canal Ports, Alexandria, and some of the follow-up from

Tripoli. G.H.Q. Middle East in Cairo were responsible for all this loading.

Sfax, Sousse, and Kairouan (for airborne troops). Supreme H.Q. at Algiers, and Alexander's H.Q., were responsible.

Canadian Division and certain troops from the U.K. The War Office in London was responsible.

Signals between Cairo, Algiers and London often overlapped or were contradictory.

Above all, there was confusion in the army/air planning, and especially with regard to air photographs. There was a representative of the superior Air H.Q. (North Africa) at Eighth Army H.Q. in Cairo. But he had no executive powers and no experience in army/air operations. He did his best but there was great delay since he had to wait for answers to letters sent from Cairo to Algiers, whence they had to be referred to Malta. The executive air commander, who was supposed to plan the assault and initial stages of the operation with my headquarters, was in Malta—very occupied with current operations. This air commander and his staff were expert in island defence and coastal operations; they had no experience of using air power to assist the tactical battle on land. The expert in working with the Eighth Army was the Commander of the Desert Air Force (Broadhurst) and he sat virtually unemployed in Tripoli; he did not come into the picture until we were firmly on shore and his squadrons could be moved to Sicily.

It will always be a wonder to me how my staff competed with all these dreadful problems, many of which should never have been allowed to occur. It will be remembered that de Guingand was away for much of the time, recovering from his air crash at El Adem; but Belchem was a very able substitute and he handled the exasperating work splendidly.

The intention of the three Commanders-in-Chief under Eisenhower (Alexander, Cunningham, and Tedder) covered only the assault of the island and the immediate seizure of airfields and ports.

The method by which the campaign would be developed once the armies were on shore, and how the island would finally be reduced, was not decided. In fact, there was no master plan. As a result the operations and actions of the two Allied armies were not properly co-ordinated. The army commanders developed their own ideas of how to proceed and then "informed" higher authority. The Seventh U.S. Army, once on shore, was allowed to wheel west towards Palermo. It thereby missed the opportunity to direct its main thrust-line northwards in order to cut the island in two: as a preliminary to the encirclement of the Etna position and the capture of Messina.

During the operations it was difficult to get things decided quickly. The responsible C.s-in-C. had their headquarters widely dispersed; they did not live together. Eisenhower, the Supreme Commander, was in Algiers; Alexander, in command of the land forces, was in Sicily; Cunningham, the Naval C.-in-C., was in Malta; whereas Tedder, the Air C.-in-C., had his headquarters in Tunis. When things went wrong, all they could do was to send telegrams to each other; it took time to gather them together for the purpose of making joint decisions.

I once discussed this campaign with Admiral Morison, the United States naval historian. He holds the same view as myself about the iniquity of letting most of the Germans get away to Italy.

Time was vital if we were to exploit success in Italy before the winter set in. We took some five weeks to complete the capture of Sicily and the Eighth Army suffered 12,000 casualties. With close co-ordination of the land, air and sea effort we would, in my view, have gained control of the island more quickly, and with fewer casualties.

Eisenhower came to stay with me in Sicily when the campaign was over; we always enjoyed his visits and he charmed us all with his friendly personality. He had only one A.D.C. with him, a naval officer called Captain Butcher.

I had established my Tactical Headquarters at Taormina, in a lovely house overlooking the Straits of Messina. At dinner one night, discussion turned on how long the war would last and Eisenhower gave it as his opinion it would all be over before Christmas 1944. It was clear to me that it *ought* to be over by then. But after our experiences in the planning and conduct of the Sicily campaign I felt we had much to learn, and I believed in my heart that the Allies would make such mistakes that the war would go into 1945.

So I asked Eisenhower if he would like to bet on it, as I would bet against it. He said he would and the bet was written out by Captain Butcher for a level £5, being signed on the 11th October in Italy, during his next visit.

A few days before Christmas 1944 when we were fighting on the threshold of Germany, I sent Ike a message saying it looked as if he owed me £5. He replied saying he still had five days left and you never know what can happen in war.

He sent me the £5 on the 26th December.

We had much fun that night at Taormina and I remember asking Ike, to his great amusement, if he had ever been told that the final plan for Sicily had been put forward in an Algerian lavatory!

CHAPTER 12

THE CAMPAIGN IN ITALY

3rd September to 31st December 1943

IF THE planning and conduct of the campaign in Sicily were bad, the preparations for the invasion of Italy, and the subsequent conduct of the campaign in that country, were worse still.

It will be remembered that the next task after clearing the Axis Powers from Africa was to knock Italy out of the war. As a first step we were to capture Sicily but there was no plan for operations beyond. There should have been a master plan which embraced the capture of Sicily and the use of that island as a spring-board for getting quickly across to Italy, and exploiting success.

We proposed to invade the mainland of Europe without any clear idea how operations were to be developed once we got there. The decision precisely where we were to land in Italy was not firm till the 17th August, the day on which the campaign in Sicily ended. So far as the Eighth Army was concerned I was to launch it across the Straits of Messina on the 30th August, but was given no " object." On the 19th August I insisted that I must be told what I was to do in Italy. My object was given me on the 20th August, ten days before we were to land in Italy.

Originally it was intended that the invasion of the mainland was to be carried out by the Eighth Army only, on a two-corps front. Landings were to be made as follows:

Operation BUTTRESS, in the area of Gioia Tauro, on the north coast of the toe.

Operation BAYTOWN, a direct assault across the Straits of Messina.

Towards the end of July a third operation began to be considered in the Salerno area; this would be called Operation AVALANCHE.

In my view, AVALANCHE was a good operation to carry out; everything should have been put into it from the very beginning and all endeavours concentrated on making it a great success. This was not done.

On the 17th August it was decided that BUTTRESS would not take place; my 10 Corps which was to have carried it out was put under the Fifth U.S. Army which was to carry out AVALANCHE.

So by the 17th August it was decided that two armies would invade the mainland of Italy:

Eighth Army, across the Straits of Messina—Operation BAYTOWN.
Fifth U.S. Army, at Salerno—Operation AVALANCHE.

Our troubles now began.

In order to bolster up AVALANCHE, landing-craft began to be taken away from BAYTOWN. I could not proceed with the planning of BAYTOWN because I had no senior naval officer, or any adequate naval planning staff. I protested, and got Alexander to add his protests to mine; but it was without result, and finally the carrying out of BAYTOWN as envisaged became impossible.

On the afternoon of the 19th August, I sent this following signal to Alexander.

"1. I have been ordered to invade the mainland of the continent of Europe on the 30th August. In the absence of information to the contrary, I must assume that some resistance will be offered by the enemy.
2. I have been given no ' object ' for the operation. Is my object to secure the Straits for the Navy and to act as a diversion for AVALANCHE? If not, please define what it is.
3. The landing-craft and naval personnel given me make an invasion of Europe with *any* object *in the face of opposition* quite impossible.
4. The delays that have occurred make it impossible for BAYTOWN to take place on the 30th August.
5. I agree that AVALANCHE must have priority but we do not want to start in Europe with a setback in the toe of Italy.
6. I need definite orders as to the timing and object of any operation you want me to carry out across the Straits of Messina, and the object must be possible with the resources in craft and naval personnel given to me, assuming opposition to the landing.

7. Can you give me any information as to the degree of enemy resistance that is likely? "

This telegram produced immediate results. On the 20th August I received a statement from Alexander laying down the object of Operation BAYTOWN: written in his own handwriting on a half-sheet of notepaper, which I still have.

" Your task is to secure a bridgehead on the toe of Italy, to enable our naval forces to operate through the Straits of Messina.
" In the event of the enemy withdrawing from the toe, you will follow him up with such force as you can make available, bearing in mind that the greater the extent to which you can engage enemy forces in the southern tip of Italy, the more assistance will you be giving to AVALANCHE."

This " object " is worth examining. No attempt was made to co-ordinate my operations with those of the Fifth Army, landing at Salerno on the night 9th-10th September. It was not visualised that the Eighth Army would go farther than the Catanzaro neck, a distance of about 60 miles from Reggio. Our resources were cut accordingly.

What actually happened is well known; the Salerno landings were very soon in difficulties; I was asked to push on and help the Fifth Army, and administrative troubles then built up around my Army.

Eisenhower ordered a conference of his Commanders-in-Chief at Algiers on the 23rd August, and I was summoned to attend. At the conference I was asked to explain in outline my plan for Operation BAYTOWN. This I did. I said that the naval delays had made it impossible for me to do the operation on the night 30th-31st August. I had now got the necessary resources in craft and naval personnel, and could carry it out on the night 2nd-3rd September; the Navy, however, had told me the earliest they could manage was the night 4th-5th September.

Eisenhower suggested to Cunningham that he should go at once to Sicily and sort it out, adding that we must aim to get the operation launched on the night 2nd-3rd September.

Cunningham left the conference at once, and flew to Sicily. As a result of his visit, the Navy agreed to do the operation on the night 2nd-3rd September.

Having settled that matter, Eisenhower told us of the negotiations

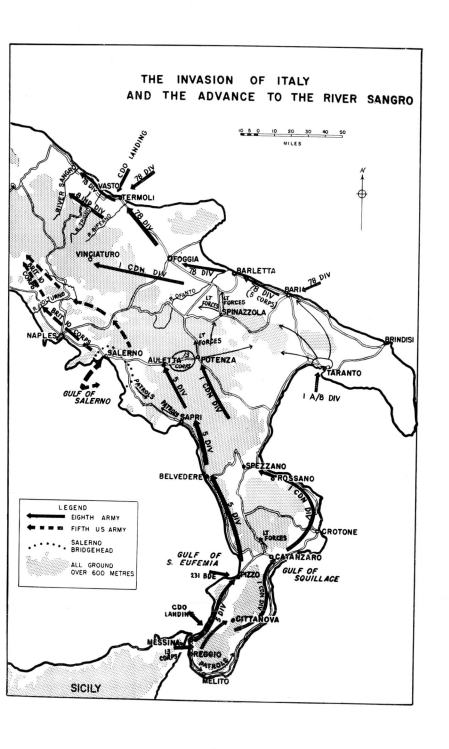

THE INVASION OF ITALY
AND THE ADVANCE TO THE RIVER SANGRO

MILES

CDO LANDING

78 DIV
VASTO
R. SANGRO
78 DIV
8 IND DIV
TERMOLI
R. BIFERNO
78 DIV

VINCIATURO
FOGGIA
1 CDN DIV
78 DIV
BARLETTA
78 DIV
78 DIV
BRIT. 10
CORPS
R. OFANTO
78 DIV
(5 CORPS)
BARI
R. VOLTURNO
BRIT 10 CORPS
LT FORCES
LT FORCES
SPINAZZOLA
NAPLES
LT FORCES
BRINDISI
SALERNO
AULETTA
POTENZA
5 CORPS
5 DIV
1 CDN DIV
TARANTO
GULF OF SALERNO
PATROLS
1 A/B DIV
PATROLS
SAPRI
5 DIV

BELVEDERE
SPEZZANO
ROSSANO
1 CDN DIV
5 DIV
CROTONE
LT FORCES
GULF OF S. EUFEMIA
CATANZARO
GULF OF SQUILLACE
231 BDE
PIZZO
1 CDN DIV
CDO LANDING
5 DIV
CITTANOVA
MESSINA
13 CORPS
REGGIO
PATROLS
MELITO

SICILY

LEGEND
EIGHTH ARMY
FIFTH US ARMY
SALERNO BRIDGEHEAD
ALL GROUND OVER 600 METRES

With General Brooke in Italy, 15th December 1943

At Tac H.Q. after my farewell address to the Eighth Army at Vasto, 30th December 1943. Left to right: de Guingand, Broadhurst, the author, Freyberg, Allfrey, Dempsey

going on with the Italian Government about an armistice. The Italians had said they were fed up with the war. It seemed that at a given moment they were prepared, if we would land on the mainland of Italy, to come in with us and fight the Germans. I remarked that this looked like the biggest double-cross in history. I argued that the Italians would never fight the Germans properly; if they tried to they would be hit for six; the most we could hope for from the Italian Army was assistance in our rear areas, and non-cooperation with the Germans in German-occupied areas.

But if this was to be the general atmosphere, it looked as if the opposition I might expect to receive in BAYTOWN might not be so great after all.

General Mark Clark, Fifth U.S. Army, explained his plan for the landing at Salerno on the night 9th-10th September. The Germans had some twenty divisions in Italy and at least four could be concentrated fairly quickly against the Fifth Army; I mentioned this, but everyone was so pleased about the Italians fighting on our side that it was considered the situation would be good. I was unable to agree.

THE EIGHTH ARMY LANDS IN EUROPE

I issued the following personal message to the Army and it was read to officers and men on the 2nd September:

" 1. Having captured Sicily as our first slice of the Italian home country, the time has now come to carry the battle on to the mainland of Italy.

2. To the Eighth Army has been given the great honour of being the first troops of the Allied Armies to land on the mainland of the continent of Europe.

   We will prove ourselves worthy of this honour.

3. I want to tell all of you, soldiers of the Eighth Army, that I have complete confidence in the successful outcome of the operations we are now going to carry out.

   We have a good plan, and air support on a greater scale than we have ever had before.

   There can only be one end to this next battle, and that is: ANOTHER SUCCESS.

4. Forward to Victory!
   Let us knock Italy out of the war!
5. Good luck. And God bless you all."

I looked forward to landing on the mainland of Europe on the 3rd September, the fourth anniversary of the outbreak of the war. We were about to enter the fifth year of the war and there was still much to avenge. In May 1940 together with many others I had been pushed into the sea at Dunkirk by the Germans. In May 1943 I had the great pleasure of helping to push the Germans into the sea in Tunisia. In August 1943 I had the further pleasure of helping to push the Germans into the sea in Sicily.

Anyhow, Dunkirk was avenged.

I wondered what the attitude of the Italians would be. A curious sight in Sicily was Italian soldiers in uniform, and carrying rifles, policing the embarkation beaches which we were using for the invasion of their mainland. And during the advance in Sicily, Italian civilians accompanied our leading platoons and pointed out the sites of booby traps, mines, etc., thus saving many British lives.

The story of the operations in Italy has been told by many writers and an Official History will doubtless appear in due course. But I have learnt that official histories, and dispatches, almost inevitably miss the " inside story." So let us have a look at it from the inside.

The initial landing went well; there was little opposition and we were quickly on shore. But our troubles soon began once we had got some little distance northwards; the country generally was ideal for delay by the action of small units co-ordinated with skilfully sited demolitions, and the Germans took full advantage of this.

On the 5th September Alexander flew to Reggio and I met him on the airfield. He told me the Italians had signed our armistice terms on the 3rd September, but no announcement was to be made at present. The further plans and arrangements were to be as follows:

(a) At 1800 hours on the 8th September, Badoglio from Rome and Eisenhower from Algiers would broadcast the fact that the Italians had surrendered unconditionally.

(b) At 2100 hours on the 8th September, American airborne troops would land near Rome. At the same time the city would be seized by the Italian divisions in the vicinity.

(c) The Italian Army was to seize Taranto, Brindisi, Bari and Naples.

(d) At 0430 hours on the 9th September the Allies would land as follows:

    Fifth U.S. Army—at Salerno, for Naples.

    5th British Corps—at Taranto.

Alexander was most optimistic and was clearly prepared to base his plans on the Italians doing all they said. I asked him to move away from the other officers who were with us, and then gave him my views. The following is the extract from my diary, written that night:

"I told him my opinion was that when the Germans found out what was going on, they would stamp on the Italians. The Italian Army morale was now very low; that Army would not face up to the Germans. I said he should impress on all senior commanders that we must make our plans so that it would make no difference if the Italians failed us, as they most certainly would. They might possibly do useful guerilla work, sabotage, and generally ensure complete non-cooperation on the part of the local population. But I did not see them fighting the Germans.

"The Germans were in great strength in Italy and we were very weak. We must watch our step carefully and do nothing foolish. I begged him to be careful; not to open up too many fronts and dissipate our resources; and to be certain before we landed anywhere that we could build up good strength in that area. I said the Germans could concentrate against AVALANCHE quicker than we could build up; that operation would need careful watching. Rommel is in charge in Italy and I have fought against him a good deal; he has twenty divisions, of which five are armoured. If the landings at Salerno go against us, we will be in for a hard and long fight. We will have to fight the Germans by ourselves as the Italians will not do so—not yet, at any rate.

"Before we embark on major operations on the mainland of Europe we must have a master plan and know how we propose to develop those operations. I have not been told of any master plan and I must therefore assume there was none."

I also discussed with Alexander the time factor. It was essential to do what we wanted in Italy before the winter set in. Also, we must be certain that our administration in rear was commensurate with what we were trying to achieve in front; but it wasn't. Alexander listened to what I said, but I do not think he agreed.

We all know what happened. The Germans dealt very effectively with the Italian armed forces in their own areas; they were all disarmed.

The Salerno landings soon got into trouble, and a critical situation arose on the night 13th-14th September when the Germans attacked the 36th American Division in strength. That division was new to battle and the enemy thrust got within three miles of the beach and within two miles of Army H.Q. On the 14th September I received a cry for help from Alexander to push on and threaten the German forces opposite the Fifth Army. This I did, and I also sent a staff officer over to see General Clark. On the 16th September the leading troops of the Eighth Army joined hands with the right flank of the Fifth U.S. Army. General Clark wrote me a very nice letter congratulating us: " on the skilful and expeditious manner in which your Eighth Army moved up to the north."

This was good to receive, but I have never thought we had much real influence on the Salerno problem; I reckon General Clark had got it well in hand before we arrived. But we did what we could. We marched and fought 300 miles in 17 days, in good delaying country against an enemy whose use of demolition caused us bridging problems of the first magnitude. The hairpin bends on the roads were such that any distance measured on the map as say 10 miles, was 20 miles on the ground and in some cases 25. But, in my view, Fifth Army did their own trick without our help—willing as we were.

After the first phase was over and the two armies had joined hands, I was ordered to transfer the operations of the Eighth Army to the east or Adriatic side of the main mountain range of the Apennines. This involved switching our administrative axis from Calabria to the ports in south-east Italy, of which the most important were Taranto, Brindisi and Bari. This was a major undertaking and took some considerable time. When it was completed we began a movement northwards which involved capturing Foggia and its airfields, Termoli, and fighting severe battles on the lines of the rivers Trigno and Sangro.

The weather began to break up at the end of October and very heavy rain descended on us. The rains continued and by the 9th November the whole country was completely waterlogged, the mud was frightful, and no vehicles could move off the road, which was covered in " chocolate sauce." The wet season was on us, and on the Adriatic coast it became cold and damp. We now began to pay dearly for the loss of time in Sicily.

I had a little trouble about the middle of September with the G.O.C. 7th Italian Army—General Rizzio. He was the senior Italian officer in my area of operations, and the Italian Army had surrendered to the Allies unconditionally. I was then told that the Italians were now co-belligerents; I asked what was meant by " unconditional surrender " and " co-belligerent " in one and the same case, but could get no clear answer.

The Italian general did not seem to know either; he placed the emphasis on " co-belligerent " and wanted to forget everything else. He was inclined to think that since he was the senior Army general in southern Italy, the Eighth Army should therefore come under his command, as we were now Allies. I decided to go and see him and get the matter cleared up quickly, before trouble arose. I had written out some notes of what I would say to him, through an interpreter since neither of us could speak the other's language. I give these notes below but when I actually met him I decided to leave out para. 3; I saw at once there was no need for it as he was a very decent chap and only too willing to help in any way.

" 1. Delighted to meet him and feel sure he will co-operate whole-heartedly in the defeat of our common enemy—Germany.

2. We do not yet know the exact details of Italian co-operation that have been settled by governments. But in order that our co-operation may be very good it is essential that we should all be quite clear as to our immediate general position. Any misunderstanding would merely tend to prejudice our early defeat of the Germans.

3. The armed forces of Italy have been defeated in battle and have surrendered unconditionally to the Allies.

We do not wish to cause any dishonour to the Italian Army, or to disarm the personnel. But the above basic factor must be remembered.

4. Command in the zone of the armies, and on the lines of communication, must be exercised through British channels— absolutely and completely, and in respect of any situation that may arise.

5. Formations and units of the Italian Army will remain under their own commanders. Orders as to their action, or work, or general routine in garrisons and ports, will be communicated through the British command.

All such orders must be obeyed instantly, and without comment; only in this way will our operations against the Germans be able to develop their maximum power rapidly.

Any representations regarding modifications, etc., will be submitted to the British command; these will always receive sympathetic consideration, and will always be complied with if this can be done without prejudicing the general war effort.

6. In general, the active offensive against the Germans for the present will be conducted by the Allied British and American Forces, pending any other arrangements by governments concerned.

7. The contribution of the Italian Army will be confined to:

   (a) Defence of ports, and of the lines of communication.

   (b) Work on communications, roads, etc.

   (c) Provision of labour as necessary.

It is particularly important that Italian A.A. artillery should be able to play its full part in the defence of ports and of the lines of communications. Detailed orders about this will be issued through the British command."

THE ADMINISTRATIVE MUDDLE

I had built up a most efficient and experienced administrative staff in the Eighth Army, first under Brian Robertson and now under Miles Graham. This staff worked well with G.H.Q. Middle East in Cairo, each having full confidence in the other. When we got to Tunisia we came under Allied Force Headquarters, the administrative staff of which neither had the knowledge themselves, nor the courage and good sense to put their trust in the information they received from the well-tried and veteran administrative staff of the Eighth Army. We first began to be anxious soon after we reached Tripoli; we were very short of many essential needs and when we unloaded the first ship that reached us under the auspices of A.F.H.Q. we found that it contained 10,000 dustbins! We thought, in our arrogant way, that they probably needed them more than we did.

A.F.H.Q. did not understand that an important principle of successful administration during active operations is to put full confidence in the staff of the lower formation and to send up, where possible, without argument what is demanded from the front. If the confidence is found to be misplaced, the only course is to sack the miscreants and put better men in their place. It is useless during battle operations to argue about what the lower formations should or should not have in stock; the time for such discussion is after the battle, and not before or during it. This is the system we worked on in the Eighth Army, and later in 21 Army Group.

I must of course qualify this by saying that the Chief Administrative Officer of the higher formation must know his stuff, and must know the character and foibles of the administrative staffs below him; this can only be done by continual visits and by establishing friendly relations with individuals throughout the administrative chain.

Allied Force H.Q. in Algiers failed in these respects and as a result we had to encounter very great difficulties. At a later stage in the operations in Italy, Robertson became Chief Administrative Officer to Alexander, and he quietly gathered the reins into his very able hands; then we had no more problems which could not be solved.

The basic trouble was that we became involved in a major campaign lacking a predetermined master plan. We had not made in advance the administrative plans and arrangements necessary to sustain the impetus of our operations. The result was the administrative machine became unable to keep pace with the constantly widening scope of our operational commitments. It will be remembered that the " object " given me did not visualise my advancing beyond the neck of the toe of Italy, i.e. about 60 miles. But I drove the Eighth Army forward at great speed beyond this point in order to try to assist the operations of the Fifth U.S. Army at Salerno. In doing so I had been warned by my staff that I was taking big administrative risks. The advice was sound; so was my decision to ignore it. I attempted to relieve the enemy pressure on the Fifth Army at Salerno, but paid the penalty of finding my own reserves were exhausted and that supplies to replenish them were not forthcoming.

I then had to switch my administrative axis to the heel ports of south-east Italy. This should have been foreseen by A.F.H.Q., but it wasn't. Our troubles then became intensified.

On the 4th October we had only 21 tons of petrol in our depots, and my army was in danger of becoming immobilised. We had over five hundred vehicles off the road wanting new engines; instead of having base workshops in Italy with a pool of spare engines, the vehicles had to be sent back to Egypt for repair, and returned later.

A serious medical scandal was narrowly averted; we could not clear our sick and wounded from our hospitals and Casualty Clearing Stations.

Convoys began to arrive in the " heel " ports of Italy loaded in bulk to stock up the depots in Sicily. We had to unload large quantities of stores, useless for the moment, in order to extract vital stores which were needed urgently.

Later, when the Foggia airfields were captured, we had heavy demands for the Strategic Air Force. The question of priorities between the Army and the R.A.F. then became urgent. If the land armies were to maintain the impetus of their operations then they had to be supplied with what they needed for the job. Or the job must be changed. It was essential to get established in Italy a weapon which would be strong enough to get us forward to the line we wanted, if only to cover the strategic airfields. Presumably this was the " Rome Line " but I could get no clear statement on the subject from anyone. The two armies went " slogging " up Italy, with no master plan, and at the risk of a major administrative break-down.

FIRST ANNIVERSARY OF ALAMEIN

The 23rd October was the first anniversary of the Battle of Alamein. I issued an anniversary message to officers and men. Actually, the New Zealand Division was the only division then serving in the Eighth Army which had fought with me at Alamein, and even in that division many officers and men had not been there. So besides issuing the written order to be read out to the troops, I made a record which was broadcast by the B.B.C.

I received two letters on the anniversary which gave me great pleasure, one from my Chief of Staff and one from the Supreme Commander in Yugoslavia—Marshal Tito.

I give them below.

H.Q. Eighth Army
23rd October, 1943

"My dear General,

On this first anniversary of the Battle of El Alamein, I would like, on behalf of your staff at Army H.Q., to send you our warmest good wishes on this great occasion; and to express our gratitude for leading us through the past year with such wisdom, inspiration, and success.

We look forward to the future with solid confidence in your leadership.

(Sgd.) F. W. de Guingand
Major-General
Chief of Staff"

"The Commander of the Eighth British Army:
General Montgomery.

On the first anniversary of the glorious battle and big victory of Alamein, please accept, General, together with your officers and soldiers of the gallant Eighth Army, my very cordial congratulations.

In the name of the National Army of Liberation of Yugoslavia, I express my joy that, as a result of your African victories, we are now within 200 kilometres of each other in our operations against the common enemy.

Thus, with every day, the Allied armies engaged in the fight against the greatest foe humanity has ever had—aggressive German Fascism—are becoming more closely knit into one continuous front.

I am confident that the fraternity in arms, sealed with the blood of the finest sons of Great Britain and Yugoslavia, will not only contribute to a speedy triumph over detested German Fascism, but also foster full comprehension on the part of you personally, your soldiers and the whole British nation of the aspirations which permeate the nations of Yugoslavia.

In the name of these aspirations, a sea of blood of our best sons has been shed. These aspirations are for a new, free and truly democratic federal Yugoslavia, built on the fraternity and equality of all nations in our country.

Kindly accept my respectful regards.

The Supreme Commander N.L.A. and P.G.Y.
(Signed) Tito"

A GIFT FROM HEAVEN

When the winter closed in on us, with the constant rain and appalling mud, I wrote to the War Office and asked the C.I.G.S. if he could send me out a waterproof suit, jacket and trousers, of some mackintosh material. The Bishop of Southwark was to visit the Eighth Army to hold confirmations before Christmas, and he was given the suit to bring out to me. The following signal was sent me from the War Office when the suit had been handed over to the Bishop.

I was told that the poem eventually found its way into an English newspaper, but I am not certain about this; nor do I know who wrote it.

> From: War Office.
> To: Eighth Army.
> Personal for General Montgomery.
> Following to be read as verse.

We've despatched, *pour la guerre*,
A mackintosh pair
Of trousers and jacket, express;
  They are coming by air
  And are sent to you care
Of the Bishop of Southwark, no less.

So wherever you go
From Pescara to Po,
Through mud and morasses and ditches,
  You undoubtedly ought
  To be braced by the thought
That the Church has laid hands on your breeches.

We think they'll suffice
(As they should at the price)
To cover your flanks in the melee,
  And avert the malaise
  (In the Premier's phrase)
Of a chill in the soft underbelly.

According to Moss
(The outfitting Bros.)
'Twon't matter, so stout is their fibre,
If you happen to trip
And go arse over tip,
Like Horatius, into the Tiber.

And you'll find—so we hope—
When you call on the Pope,
That his blessing's more readily given
On learning the news
That your mackintosh trews
Were brought down by a Bishop from Heaven.

I LEAVE THE EIGHTH ARMY

Very early in the morning of the 24th December, I was woken up to be given a signal from the War Office to say I was to return to England to succeed General Paget in command of 21 Army Group, the British Group of Armies preparing to open a " second front " across the Channel. Though sad of course to leave the Eighth Army, I was naturally delighted to have been selected for the great task ahead: the full-scale invasion across the Channel which would truly avenge Dunkirk. It was a relief and an excitement: a relief because I was not too happy about the overall situation in Italy and considered we had only ourselves to blame for the situation which now faced us. No grand design for the opening of a new theatre of operations; no master plan; no grip on the operations; a first class administrative muddle— all these had cumulatively combined to impose such delay on the operations that we failed to exploit the initial advantages which we had gained before the winter closed in upon us.

It was, of course, true that in under six months we had:

(a) Captured Sicily.
(b) Knocked Italy out of the war.
(c) Got the Italian fleet locked up in Malta.
(d) Captured about one-third of Italy, including Naples and the Foggia airfields.

203

These were spectacular results, but they were all at the expense of the Italians. Our real enemy was Germany; we had failed to bring real discomfort to that enemy before the weather broke, because we had not handled the business properly. For these reasons I was not sorry to leave the Italian theatre. I made a quiet resolve that when we opened the second front in North-West Europe we would not make the same mistakes again: so long as I had any influence in the responsible circles concerned.

General Eisenhower had been appointed Supreme Commander for the Second Front some days earlier, and there had been tremendous speculation throughout the Eighth Army about who would go with him as his Commanders-in-Chief, and who would succeed him in the Mediterranean theatre. The favourite for Supreme Commander, Mediterranean theatre, was Jumbo Wilson who was C.-in-C. Middle East.

On the afternoon of the 24th December, Christmas Eve, the new appointments were announced by the B.B.C. and we picked it up in Italy:

Wilson   :   to succeed Eisenhower.
Alexander: to remain in his present job.
Myself   :   C.-in-C. 21 Army Group.

So far I had not mentioned to anyone the signal I had received in the small hours of that morning; I wanted to discuss things first with de Guingand, but he was on leave and was to return to my main H.Q. in the evening. I knew there would at once be great discussion about whom I would take with me to my new staff in England, and I wanted to get it settled.

I was quite clear myself about whom I wanted *at once*:

de Guingand: as Chief of Staff.
Graham   :   as Chief Administrative Officer.
Williams   :   as head of the Intelligence.
Richards   :   as tank adviser.
Hughes   :   as head chaplain.

There were others I would like to come later. I at once signalled the War Office for permission to bring these five home with me. I also wanted Belchem to be head of the operations staff; moreover, he was an excellent man to have handy in case de Guingand went sick, as he sometimes did after too much hard work and strain. For I worked him to the bone; and he would have done that himself even without my pressure. Belchem was quite capable of acting as Chief of Staff at any time. But I couldn't very well remove too many all at once, as this would not have been fair on my successor; I therefore left Belchem out of the first request and decided to rope him in later.

The War Office approved de Guingand, Williams, and Richards without delay. They did not approve Graham and Hughes. I decided to take Graham home with me, and chance the anger in London. I would send for Hughes and Belchem later, when I had sorted things out in London.

I spent Christmas Day quietly at my Tactical H.Q., with the officers and men who had been with me since Alamein. I told de Guingand I wanted to see him and he came up in the afternoon from Main H.Q. After tea I took him to my caravan and told him he was to go back with me to England and be my Chief of Staff in 21 Army Group; I also told him of the others who would go with me. He said he was delighted. I was glad to know that; I could not possibly have handled the gigantic task that lay ahead without the trusted Chief of Staff who had been at my side since Alamein.

He knew me and my ways, and that was all-important.

Oliver Leese had been appointed to succeed me and he was to arrive on the 30th December. I settled to leave myself on the 31st December. Leese knew the Eighth Army well and he would not want a long hand-over.

I flew to Algiers on the 27th December to see Eisenhower and Bedell Smith, who was to go with Eisenhower as his Chief of Staff.

Eisenhower told me that he wanted me to take complete charge of the initial land battle, and that he would place the American armies in England under my command for the landing and subsequent operations. We discussed the type of command set-up I would want and what American officers we would need at the new Army Group H.Q. I got back to Tac H.Q. in Italy on the afternoon of the 28th December.

The problem of a farewell message to my beloved Eighth Army was causing me seriously to think; I had only just issued a Christmas message. I wrote the farewell message in the air on the 28th December during the flight back from Algiers, and arranged that it should be read to officers and men on the 1st January 1944, after I had gone. This is what I said:

" 1. I have to tell you, with great regret, that the time has come for me to leave the Eighth Army. I have been ordered to take command of the British Armies in England that are to operate under General Eisenhower—the Supreme Commander.

2. It is difficult to express to you adequately what this parting means to me. I am leaving officers and men who have been my comrades during months of hard and victorious fighting, and whose courage and devotion to duty always filled me with admiration. I feel I have many friends among the soldiery of this great Army. I do not know if you will miss me; but I will miss you more than I can say, and especially will I miss the personal contacts, and the cheerful greetings we exchanged together when we passed each other on the road.

3. In all the battles we have fought together we have not had one single failure; we have been successful in everything we have undertaken.

   I know that this has been due to the devotion to duty and whole-hearted co-operation of every officer and man, rather than to anything I may have been able to do myself.

   But the result has been a mutual confidence between you and me, and mutual confidence between a commander and his troops is a pearl of very great price.

4. I am also very sad at parting from the Desert Air Force. This magnificent air striking force has fought with the Eighth Army throughout the whole of its victorious progress; every soldier in this Army is proud to acknowledge that the support of this strong and powerful air force has been a battle-winning factor of the first importance. We owe the Allied Air Forces in general, and the Desert Air Force in particular, a very great debt of gratitude.

5. What can I say to you as I go away?

   When the heart is full it is not easy to speak. But I would say this to you:

   You have made this Army what it is. You have made

its name a household word all over the world. Therefore, You must uphold its good name and its traditions.

And I would ask you to give to my successor the same loyal and devoted service that you have never failed to give to me.

6. And so I say GOOD-BYE to you all.

May we meet again soon; and may we serve together again as comrades-in-arms in the final stages of this war.''

The really great hurdle which faced me was to say good-bye to the officers and men of Eighth Army H.Q., so many of whom had been with me since Alamein. I said I would do this on the 30th December at Vasto, in which town was my Main H.Q. De Guingand suggested the Opera House; it had been knocked about somewhat, but he thought it would do for the purpose. I knew it would be a very difficult moment for me when I got on the platform to speak, and it was. I told de Guingand he was to go with me to the hall and take me in; I knew I would need some close and faithful friend to be near me, ready to lend a hand if I faltered.

I had asked my Corps Commanders to attend, Dempsey and Allfrey, and of course Freyberg of the New Zealand Division, and Broadhurst of the Desert Air Force. There was a great gathering in the hall.

I should have difficulty myself in describing the occasion. This is Freddie de Guingand's account of it, taken from *Operation Victory*:

"I drove with him to the hall, feeling as I always do on such occasions, sad and sentimental. My Chief was very quiet and I could see that this was going to be the most difficult operation he had yet attempted. We arrived inside and he said, ' Freddie, show me where to go.' I led him to the stairs leading up to the stage. He mounted at once, and to a hushed audience commenced his last address to the officers of the Army which he loved so well.

He started very quietly, apologising in case his voice might let him down for, as he said, ' this is not going to be easy, but I shall do my best. If I happen to find difficulty in speaking on occasions, I hope you will understand.' I felt a lump coming in my throat, and one could feel every one of his audience was perfectly tuned into his mood. He then very simply and rather slowly explained about his coming departure, and what responsibilities lay ahead. He touched on the past—upon the successes we had gained together, and of the things which he considered important, and which guided him during his command. He summed up the situation, and expressed his thanks to everyone for the support he had received, and for the way they had fought.

He then asked them to follow the new Army Commander, Leese, as they had followed him. There were no great feats of oratory and no false note. It was exactly right and I found it intensely moving. He finished quietly by reading his last of many personal messages to the Army—his message of farewell.

We cheered him and then he walked slowly out to his car. I followed feeling very uncomfortable, for I had tears on my cheeks and we were riding in an open car. We drove back to Main Headquarters, which was only a few hundred yards away, where some of the senior commanders had been asked to come and have a chat. It was a wonderful gathering of old friends. As my Chief talked to this trusted few I could not help thinking of Napoleon and his Marshals, for here surely there was to be found the same relationship, born and tempered by mutual esteem and success in battle. Later Freyberg, Dempsey, Allfrey and the others departed, and I had a feeling that something rather terrible was happening— I was leaving this great family. But then again I remembered that I was leaving in company with the one who had given us that inspiration, and that guidance, and so although sad I felt content with fate."

Oliver Leese arrived that night and I handed over to him.

The next morning, the 31st December, I took off in my Dakota aircraft from the air strip near my Tactical H.Q. We had a heavy load, as besides myself and my A.D.C.s there were de Guingand, Graham, Williams and Richards. We also had with us five soldiers, quite a lot of luggage, and a full load of petrol. The air strip was small and I asked the pilot if we would get off. He said he thought we should just manage it; and we did, but only just.

We headed for Marrakesh. The Prime Minister was there, convalescent from his recent illness, and I was to spend the night with him, and also New Year's Day, and go on to England on the night 1st-2nd January 1944.

As we flew across the Mediterranean I pondered over the past and thought of the future; and especially of my bet with Eisenhower, and his insistence that the war would be over by Christmas 1944. I was certain that it *could* be, but only if we conducted it in the right way; and I was *not* so certain that we would.

At Marrakesh on New Year's Day the Prime Minister wrote this in my autograph book:

"The immortal march of the Eighth Army from the gates of Cairo along the African shore through Tunisia, through Sicily has now carried its ever-victorious soldiers and their world-honoured Commander far into Italy towards the gates of Rome. The scene changes and vastly expands. A great task accomplished gives place to a greater in which the same unfailing spirit will win for all true men a full and glorious reward.

Winston S. Churchill"

CHAPTER 13

IN ENGLAND BEFORE D-DAY

2nd January to 6th June 1944

WHEN I arrived at Marrakesh on the evening of the 31st December, I found the Prime Minister studying a copy of the plan for OVERLORD —the code name given to the invasion of Normandy. He gave it to me to read and said he wanted my opinion on the proposed operation. I replied that I was not his military adviser; OVERLORD was clearly a combined operation of the first magnitude and I had not seen the plan, and had not even discussed the subject with any responsible naval or air authority. He agreed but said he would like me to study the plan nevertheless, and give him my " first impressions." I said I would take it to bed with me and give him some impressions in the morning; he knew that I liked to go to bed early.

Eisenhower had arrived in Marrakesh that afternoon. He was on his way to the United States for talks with the President before taking up his new appointment as Supreme Commander for OVERLORD. I had seen him in Algiers a few days earlier; he had then told me he had only a sketchy idea of the plan and that it did not look too good. He directed me to act as his representative in London until he himself could get there; I was to analyse and revise the plan and have it ready for him on his arrival in England about the middle of January. I replied that I thought his Chief of Staff, Bedell Smith, should be in London with me since he was much more in the general picture than I was. I also asked that he should give Bedell a statement in writing that I was to act for him until he himself arrived. All this had been agreed in Algiers. I had only time for a short talk with Eisenhower in Marrakesh and he took off for the United States at daylight on the 1st January.

That night was New Year's Eve and we had an amusing dinner with the Prime Minister and his staff, and Mrs. Churchill. Lord Beaverbrook was there; I had never met him before and what I had heard had not been very complimentary. After that first meeting I disagreed, for I found him most agreeable. He had at heart the best interests of the Allies in general and of the British peoples in particular; he was all out to win the war as soon as possible.

I knew the dinner-party would go on late and that the Prime Minister would certainly stay up to salute the New Year. So I asked permission to go to bed soon after dinner on the plea that I had to read the OVERLORD plan. I spent some time on this and wrote out my first impressions; these were typed before breakfast and I took them in to the Prime Minister as soon as the paper was ready. He was in bed and read my paper at once. The important paragraphs to my mind were the first four, which ran as follows:

" 1. The following must be clearly understood:
   (a) Today, 1st January, 1944, is the first time I have seen the Appreciation and proposed plan or considered the problem in any way.
   (b) I am not as yet in touch with Admiral Ramsay and have not been able to consult any naval expert.
   (c) I have not been able to consult the Air C.-in-C., or any experienced air officer.
   (d) Therefore these initial comments can have little value. They are merely my first impressions after a brief study of the plan.

2. The initial landing is on too narrow a front and is confined to too small an area.
   By D+12 a total of 16 divisions have been landed on the same beaches as were used for the initial landings. This would lead to the most appalling confusion on the beaches, and the smooth development of the land battle would be made extremely difficult—if not impossible.
   Further divisions come pouring in, all over the same beaches.
   By D+24 a total of 24 divisions have been landed, all over the same beaches; control of the beaches and so on would be very difficult; the confusion, instead of getting better, would get worse.
   My first impression is that the present plan is impracticable.

3. From a purely Army point of view the following points are essential:

(a) The initial landings must be made on the widest possible front.

(b) Corps must be able to develop their operations from their own beaches, and other corps must NOT land *through* those beaches.

(c) British and American areas of landing must be kept separate. The provisions of (a) above must apply in each case.

(d) After the initial landings, the operation must be developed in such a way that a good port is secured quickly for the British and for American forces. Each should have its own port or group of ports.

4. The type of plan required is on the following lines:

(a) One British army to land on a front of two, or possibly three, corps. One American army similarly.

(b) Follow-up divisions to come in to the corps already on shore.

(c) The available assault craft to be used for the landing troops. Successive flights to follow rapidly in any type of unarmoured craft, and to be poured in.

(d) The air battle must be won before the operation is launched. We must then aim at success in the land battle by the speed and violence of our operations."

The Prime Minister was intensely interested. He said he had always known there was something wrong in the proposed plan, but that the Chiefs of Staff had agreed with it and that left him powerless. Now a battlefield commander had analysed it for him and had given him the information he needed—and he was grateful. I asked for my paper back, saying it was written entirely without inter-Service discussion and I did not want to start my new job by troubles with the planners in London. But he kept it, promising to use it himself only as background information. I had the subsequent impression that the background was liable to intrude into the foreground.

Later in the morning we started out for a picnic lunch in the country at Mrs. Churchill's suggestion. I drove with the Prime Minister in his car and he continued to discuss OVERLORD, and my comments. I said one of the lessons I had learnt in the war was the need to get experienced fighting commanders " in on " future operational plans early; if left too late it might be impossible to change the layout of the operation. In all the operations in which I had had a share so far, changes in the plan had been necessary and there had been all too little time, e.g. HUSKY in May 1943, and now OVERLORD which did not look too good.

We had a quiet and refreshing day in the sunshine and warmth of the Moroccan countryside in winter, and much stimulating conversation. I got to know the Prime Minister and Mrs. Churchill well during that short visit to Marrakesh, and it was the beginning of a friendship which developed into my becoming a close friend of them both.

That night after dinner I left Marrakesh for England. Eisenhower had refused to allow me to do the journey in my Dakota two-engine aircraft, although I had had extra fuel tanks fitted. So I transferred to an American four-engine C/54 aircraft. I filled my own plane with oranges and told the pilot to make his way to England. He followed the next night. I reached London on the 2nd January.

Freddie de Guingand, and the other members of my staff whom I was bringing from the Eighth Army, had arrived in London some 24 hours before me. Headquarters 21 Army Group was in St. Paul's School, West Kensington, where I had been as a boy. My office was located in the room of the High Master. Although I had been a school prefect, captain of the 1st XV, in the cricket XI and in the swimming team I had never entered that room before. I had to become a Commander-in-Chief to do so. Many of the people living in that part of London wrote letters asking me to go away. There was a certain amount of enemy bombing going on and we actually suffered some casualties in the Headquarters. The inhabitants considered that our presence there was the cause of the bombing, but there was no evidence to justify that deduction.

Our " A " Mess was established in Latymer Court, a block of flats across the road from the school; I lived in one of them. I asked Admiral Ramsay, the Naval C.-in-C. for OVERLORD, to live in the Mess, and to bring with him Admiral Creasy, his Chief of Staff. We were a most cheerful party and at dinner each evening the conversation roamed over a wide field. Discussion often ended in bets being laid. I suggested we should keep a betting book in which all bets would be entered and signed by both sides. I have the book beside me and it is of considerable historical interest. Some of the bets deal with political and other personalities and will not bear publication—not yet, anyhow. Bets made during our time in the Eighth Army were copied into the book. I never laid any bets myself but was prepared to accept those that looked promising; by this means I made quite a lot of money so that charities in which I was interested benefited. Most of the bets I accepted concerned the ending of the war. I held the view that having now knocked Italy out of the war and got well established in that country, and once a second front was opened in North-West Europe, we should be able to bring the German war to a successful conclusion by the end of 1944. That had been my opinion for some time. But by the autumn of 1943 I had seen a good deal of the higher conduct of the war during the campaigns in Sicily and Italy and the experience did not fill me with confidence. While I considered the Allies *could* win the war by the end of 1944, I was fairly certain we would " muck it up " and would *not* do so.

My Chief of Staff, de Guingand, was the first to be optimistic—unduly so. On the 4th March 1943, when we were still fighting in Africa, he laid bets with me that: " the German Army will not be fighting as a co-ordinated body by the dates stated:

1st January 1944	Even £5.
1st April 1944	Even £5.
1st April 1944	£5 to £15.
1st February 1945	£15 to £5.
20th March 1945	£5 to £10."

General Eisenhower was the next. I have already referred to the bet he laid on the 11th October 1943 in Italy, that: " the war with Germany will end before Christmas 1944—an even £5."

Encouraged by Eisenhower's confidence, General Freyberg laid me an even £10 on the 31st October 1943 in Italy that: " the war will be over by 2400 hrs. October 31, 1944—Japan excluded."

All the above bets were made in my Mess in the Eighth Army. The scene now changes to England, to my Mess in 21 Army Group. Admiral Ramsay, when shown some of the past bets, said he would certainly enter the lists. On the 26th January 1944 he bet me an even £5 that: " the war with Germany will be over by January 1st, 1945."

Not to be outdone by his C.-in-C., Admiral Creasy bet me in April 1944, two months before D-Day, that: " organised German resistance will have ceased by 1200 hrs. on the 1st December 1944."

General Crerar, Canadian Army, was the next victim. I was not able to place the First Canadian Army in command of the left flank of the British front in Normandy till the 23rd July, over six weeks after we had landed in Normandy and just before the break-out from the bridgehead began. Crerar was fearful lest the war should end before he could command the Canadian Army in battle, and he used to press me to let him assume command. On the 24th June he laid me a bet that: "the war with Germany will be over by 1-9-44, i.e. that Germany will have asked for an armistice by that date."

I had some interesting bets with General George Patton, of the Third American Army. On the 1st June 1944, he laid me two bets which I quote in full:

> " General Patton bets General Montgomery a level £100 that the armed forces of Great Britain will be involved in another war in Europe within ten years of the cessation of the present hostilities."
> " General Patton bets General Montgomery that the first Grand National run after the present war will be won by an American-owned horse—an even £10."

One bet involved the Speaker of the House of Commons. Sir Alan Herbert was a personal friend and often visited me; he always arrived dressed as a Naval petty officer. In February 1945 he was staying a night at my Tac Headquarters and an argument about bees developed between A.P.H. and Lieut.-Colonel Dawnay of my personal staff. Dawnay said the drone was sexless and A.P.H. protested it was not. A bet was laid and I said it must be referred for a ruling to the Speaker.

His reply was as follows:

HOUSE OF COMMONS

Speaker's House,
S.W.1.
28-2-45.

" Naturally I am flattered by the faith that you display in Mr. Speaker's impartiality. But at the same time I think that this is the first time since the days of Cromwell that the Speaker has been detailed off for a job by the C.-in-C.! However, I will do my best.

Dawnay versus A.P.H.

1. The drone is surely not without sex—he is a male. When swarming, the mass of bees are males seeking to enjoy the Queen and the lucky one that does so dies at once.

2. Sexless does not mean without sex. Sex may be there but dormant and this condition is then sexless; in short, it is an adjective which applies to a mental state and not to a physical condition.

3. I have forgotten the exact words of the bet but my impression is that under the above (1 and 2) A.P.H. wins."

I know nothing about bees. But I upheld the Speaker's ruling; and Dawnay paid up.

Not all our time was taken up in making bets. It had soon become clear to me on arriving home that we were confronted with a task of great difficulty. I had been appointed to act as Land C.-in-C. for a combined operation of greater magnitude than had ever been attempted in the whole history of warfare. The greater portion of the troops and of the subordinate headquarters, though well trained, lacked battle experience. The operation had to be undertaken just over five months later.

Headquarters 21 Army Group had been formed out of G.H.Q. Home Forces and as such had been in existence for nearly four years. It was a well dug-in static headquarters which had never been overseas and had never had any operational experience. Many of the senior officers had served in the headquarters a long time and had become set in their outlook. Into this somewhat hidebound " staff atmosphere " it was vital to inject new blood, and to bring in senior staff officers with battle experience who knew my methods and would get on with the job without bellyaching. This was done, and the senior officers I had brought back with me from Italy at once took over the top jobs and began work under de Guingand. All this was unpopular and ribald remarks were made in the London clubs, to the effect that " the Gentlemen are out and the Players are just going in to bat."

General Paget had been in command of 21 Army Group until I arrived from Italy. We had been at Sandhurst together and were great friends. It could not have been pleasant for him to be superseded in command of the forces he had trained so well just when they were about to be employed in battle, and to have seen so many changes made so quickly. Although I have never discussed it with him, I have always been under the impression that Paget regarded his replacement by somebody like myself, with recent battle experience, as inevitable in the circumstances. What he did not like was the manner in which it was done, since it was at first proposed to relegate him to the relatively unimportant command of Gibraltar. In the end he was given the command in the Middle East *vice* Wilson.

The army then in England lacked battle experience and had tended to become theoretical rather than practical. Officers did not understand those tricks of the battlefield which mean so much to junior leaders and which save so many lives. In the last resort the battle is won by the initiative and skill of regimental officers and men, and without these assets you fail—however good the higher Command. Some very experienced fighting formations had returned to England however from the Mediterranean theatre at the end of the Sicily campaign. By exchanging officers between these formations and those which had never left the country, I tried to spread such battle experience as was available over the widest possible area. Again, this was unpopular, but was more readily accepted when I had explained the reason.

Another major problem which caused me many initial headaches was the tightness of the control exercised by the War Office over the activities of the army in the United Kingdom—far tighter than that over an army on active service in the field. I held the view that the armies in 21 Army Group were already, in effect, on active service and had to be prepared to challenge the veteran German Army in the very near future. These armies, lacking battle experience, needed firm guidance and quick decisions in order to ensure that they would fight successfully and triumph on the continent of Europe; there was no time for indecision, hesitation, or waiting for approval for essential minor modifications in organisation or doctrine. We had got beyond the text book. I tackled this problem at once. I summoned all the general officers of the armies in England which were under my command, to a conference at St. Paul's School on the 13th January. There I addressed them, gave my views on battle fighting and explained my methods of working; in short, I gave them the " atmosphere " in which, from then onwards, we would all work, and later would fight. During the subsequent discussion it emerged that if divisions were to fight in the way I had outlined, certain minor changes in organisation would be necessary. The need for these changes was agreed by all the generals present; some of them had already been put forward to the War Office, with no result. I at once approved the necessary changes in organisation and ordered them to be implemented immediately.

Some officers from the War Office were present at the conference; they evidently regarded me as a new broom and an unpleasant one at that. My action was at once reported to their superiors. There was quite a storm and I was informed by Brooke that the Secretary of State for War, Sir James Grigg, strongly disapproved of my apparent disregard for War Office authority. I was disturbed at this, since without full War Office support I could not get the armies ready in time. Brooke suggested that Grigg should ask me to lunch so that we could have a good talk; I did not then know Grigg very well, and welcomed the suggestion. At that lunch meeting I explained how much had to be done and how little time there was in which to do it. I apologised for going too fast and asked Grigg to trust my judgment on the operational necessity for what I had done; if I went too fast again I was quite prepared to be sent for by him and " ticked off."

This talk did a great deal to clear the air. It was the beginning of a friendship between Grigg and myself, and he and his wife are today two of my greatest friends. I regard him as the best Secretary of State we have ever had at the War Office within my personal knowledge.

As regards the replacement of unsuitable senior commanders, I asked the War Office for only one change: to bring General Dempsey home from Italy, where he was commanding a corps in the Eighth Army, and give him command of the Second Army. I had the greatest admiration for Dempsey, whom I had known for many years. He took the Second Army right through to the end of the war and amply justified this confidence in his ability and courage.

Concurrently with these worries and changes, I found myself involved in a series of conferences on OVERLORD as soon as I arrived in London. Luckily Bedell Smith was there with me and he proved a tower of strength.

Much has been written about the plan for the invasion of Normandy, and the story of how it was gradually built up has been told by many writers. I do not want to go over all the ground again. I just want to discuss those matters which were my main pre-occupation at that time, and explain certain points which were upper-most in my own mind.

For a considerable time prior to 1944 a planning headquarters in London, organised on an Allied basis and answerable to the Combined Chiefs of Staff in Washington, had been studying the problem of the re-entry of the Allied forces into North-West Europe. The head of this planning staff was General Freddie Morgan, whom I knew well; he had often complained to me how difficult it was to plan properly without a commander. He did a good job nevertheless, and produced an outline plan for OVERLORD which served as a basis for future planning. He had to work on information supplied by the Combined Chiefs of Staff as to the forces which would be available; he had no alternative. And he had no experienced operational commander to guide and help him.

The more I examined the proposed tactical plan of 21 Army Group, based on Morgan's outline plan, the more I disliked it. The front of assault was too narrow; only one Corps H.Q. was being used to control the whole front, and the area of landing would soon become very congested.

No landing was being made on the east side of the Cherbourg peninsula, although the early capture of the port of Cherbourg was vital to our needs. My approach to the problem was based on lessons learnt in the stern school of active battle fighting, of which the following were always to the fore in my mind:

First— It is essential to relate what is strategically desirable to what is tactically possible with the forces at your disposal.

Second—To this end it is necessary to decide the development of operations before the initial blow is delivered. There must be a direct relationship between the two.

Third— If your flanks and rear are secure, you are well placed for battle.

Fourth—Simplicity is vital in the planning of operations. Once complications are allowed to creep in, the outcome is in danger.

There did not seem to be any clear idea how operations would be developed once the armies had been put on shore in Normandy. We were proposing to open up a new theatre of war on the continent of Europe. The campaign would involve the whole problem of the conduct of offensive operations on land in Western Europe with the final object of destroying the enemy's armed forces and occupying Germany.

Therefore, the first need was to decide how the operations on land were to be developed, and then to work backwards from that to ensure that we landed on the beaches in the way best suited to the needs of the master plan. We seemed to be tackling it the other way round. So far as we knew at that time (January 1944) there were over fifty German divisions in France and some of these, probably six, were Panzer type. Bill Williams calculated that we might be fighting hard against six German divisions by the evening of D-Day. We could take no chances; if we failed in Normandy the war might drag on for years.

We would have to blast our way on shore and get a good lodgement before the enemy could bring up sufficient reserves to turn us out. We must gain space rapidly and peg out claims well inland. And while doing this, the air would have to hold the ring, and hinder and make difficult the movement of enemy reserves by train or road towards the lodgement area.

We needed an initial assault by at least five divisions, with additional airborne divisions dropped on the flanks so as to secure us from flank interference while we pushed quickly inland. We would need a build-up which would give us, say eight divisions on shore by the evening of D-Day and twelve by the evening of D+2 (these figures to include the airborne divisions). We should aim to have eighteen divisions on shore by about the end of the first week.

All this would be an immense undertaking and it would be necessary to get additional landing-craft from the Mediterranean theatre; we would also need an air lift for three airborne divisions.

Eisenhower had appointed me to act for him and I had many conferences with the Naval and Air C.s-in-C., and our respective staffs. We were convinced in all our work that full weight must be given to the fact that OVERLORD marked the crisis of the European war. Every obstacle must be overcome, every inconvenience suffered, every priority granted, and every risk taken to ensure our blow was decisive. We could not afford to fail.

We formed a revised plan and it at once became clear that our success was going to depend on whether operation ANVIL could be reduced to a threat and the landing-craft thereby saved transferred to OVERLORD. Operation ANVIL was a proposed landing in the South of France, to the east of Toulon. The Allied forces, American and French, were to come from the Italian theatre. It was an American idea and so far as I was aware it was never liked by any British political or military authority. The American view was that OVERLORD and ANVIL must be viewed as one whole, and that ANVIL would contain enemy forces in the south of France, and thus help OVERLORD. The French liked it since de Gaulle wanted to have a French Army under a French C.-in-C. liberating French soil. Stalin liked it, I imagine, since it would obviously hinder progress on the Italian front by Alexander, and thus enable the Russians to reach Vienna before the Western Allies.

I didn't like it: nor did Winston Churchill.

The discussions about ANVIL went on well into August; indeed, they were still going on when we were finishing off the Germans trapped in the Falaise pocket.

For some reason unknown to me the operation had then been renamed DRAGOON.

I personally had always been opposed to ANVIL from the beginning, and had advocated its complete abandonment for two main reasons. First, we wanted the landing-craft for OVERLORD; and second, it weakened the Italian front at the very time when progress there had a good chance of reaching Vienna before the Russians. (Failure to do this was to have far-reaching effects in the cold war that broke out towards the end of 1945.)

In the end we got the landing-craft we needed for OVERLORD by postponing the target date for Normandy from the 1st May till early in June, and by getting ANVIL postponed till August. But ANVIL (or DRAGOON) went in on the 15th August and in my view was one of the great strategic mistakes of the war. Eisenhower had a tremendous argument about it with the Prime Minister at the end of July and early in August. He thought it would help him with the Prime Minister if he could say that I agreed with him that ANVIL must be launched in August as planned.

By then I was willing to concur since it was already early August, all the forces were assembled ready to go, and it was obviously impossible to stop it and to land usefully anywhere else. It was to have its effect in broadening the front tremendously; it emphasised the drag south, and thus eventually aided a further strategical mistake when we came to advance towards the German frontier. I wish now—as I have often wished—that I hadn't half-heartedly concurred that early August day. But I wanted to show willing to Ike; I had been showing unwilling in other matters, and I sensed then that there were more of these "other matters" to come.

Eisenhower approved our revised plan for OVERLORD at a conference in London on the 21st January. From then onwards, the plan developed steadily as all the details were gradually worked out and fitted into their right places in the grand design. The work involved was terrific and the strain on the staffs was very great. I used to think, in those days, that my experienced staff under de Guingand played a major part in ensuring that the problems which arose were handled in a practical and realistic manner. I doubt if a better and more experienced planning team existed anywhere in those days than de Guingand, Graham, Belchem and Williams: to whom the addition of Herbert (now Lieut.-General Sir Otway Herbert) in the Staff Duties branch was a tower of strength (he had already won a D.S.O. and bar and was a terrific worker). A colossal amount of paper was in circulation and everything was Secret or Top Secret. Hughes, our head chaplain, asked if he should mark his files SACRED and TOP SACRED!!

In order that the reader may understand fully what happened later in Normandy, I want particularly at this stage to draw attention to the fundamental framework of the plan for the development of operations once we were ashore and firmly established, since it was uncertainty on this issue which was to lead to trouble later on.

Our intention was to assault, simultaneously, beaches on the Normandy coast immediately north of the Carentan estuary and between that area and the River Orne, with the object of securing as a base for further operations a lodgement area which was to include airfield sites and the port of Cherbourg. The left or eastern flank of the lodgement area was to include the road centre of Caen.

General Eisenhower had placed me in command of all the land forces for the assault. For this we had two armies—the Second British Army under Dempsey and the First American Army under Bradley. Later, two more armies would come into being—the First Canadian under Crerar and the Third American under Patton. It is important to understand that, once we had secured a good footing in Normandy, my plan was to *threaten* to break out on the eastern flank, that is in the Caen sector. By pursuing this threat relentlessly I intended to draw the main enemy reserves, particularly his armoured divisions, into that sector and to keep them there—using the British and Canadian forces under Dempsey for this purpose. Having got the main enemy strength committed on the *eastern* flank, my plan was to make the break-out on the *western* flank—using for this task the American forces under General Bradley. This break-out attack was to be launched southwards, and then to proceed eastwards in a wide sweep up to the Seine about Paris. I hoped that this gigantic wheel would pivot on

Falaise. It aimed to cut off all the enemy forces south of the Seine, the bridges over that river below Paris having been destroyed by our air forces.

All our work was linked to this basic plot, which I explained at many conferences from February onwards. On the 7th April, I assembled all the general officers of the four Field Armies at my head-quarters in London and gave out my plan in outline, and then in detail. The Naval and Air C.s-in-C. also outlined their plans.

Having got an agreed plan (or so I thought at the time!) I left the details to de Guingand and his staff and devoted my main efforts to ensuring that the weapon we were to use would be fit for battle. I had already outlined to all general officers my views on tactical doctrine, and training was proceeding accordingly. Confidence in the high command by one and all was the next essential, and was vital. I wanted to see the soldiers and, probably more important, I wanted them to see me; I wanted to speak to them and try to gain their trust and confidence.

I had the use of a special train called " Rapier " and in it I toured England, Wales, and Scotland, visiting every formation which was to take part in OVERLORD. My method of inspection was characterised by informality and was, I suppose, unusual; it certainly astonished some of the generals who did not know me well. I inspected two, and often three, parades a day, each of 10,000 men or more. They were drawn up in a hollow square and I first spoke individually to the unit commanders. I then ordered the ranks to be turned inwards and walked slowly between them, in order that every man could see me; the men " stood easy " throughout so that they could lean and twist, and look at me all the time if they wished to—and most did. This inspection of the men by me, and of me by them, took some little time; but it was good value for all of us. It was essential that I gained their confidence. I had to begin with their curiosity. When the appraisal was over I stood on the bonnet of a jeep and spoke to officers and men, quietly and very simply—using a loudspeaker or not, according to the conditions. I explained how necessary it was that we should know each other, what lay ahead and how, together, we would handle the job. I told them what the German soldier was like in battle and how he could be defeated; that if we all had confidence in the plan and in each other, the job could be done. I was their Commander-in-Chief and we had now had a good look at each other. As a result of the meeting between us, I had absolute confidence in them, and I hoped they could feel the same about me.

By the middle of May I had visited every formation in the United Kingdom. I had been seen by practically every officer and soldier who was to take part in the invasion of Normandy, and they had heard me talking to them. I must have inspected, and been inspected by, well over one million men. In this way I strove to gain the confidence of all who were to serve under my command—British, Canadian, American, Belgian, Polish, Free French and Dutch. It was an immense undertaking but I believe that it paid a good dividend. The reaction on the British soldier I could gauge fairly well, as my military life had been spent with him. Of the American soldier I was not so sure. However, I need have had no fear. Shortly after we landed in Normandy, General Bedell Smith wrote me the following letter:

22 June 1944

" Dear General,

I have just received from a most reliable and intelligent source a report on attitude and state of mind of American troops in action. The writer is completely unbiased, and his report contains the following paragraph, which I hope will give you as much pleasure as it has given me:

' Confidence in the high command is absolutely without parallel. Literally dozens of embarking troops talked about General Montgomery with actual hero-worship in every inflection. And unanimously what appealed to them—beyond his friendliness, and genuineness, and lack of pomp—was the story (or, for all I know, the myth) that the General " visited every one of us outfits going over and told us he was more anxious than any of us to get this thing over and get home." This left a warm and indelible impression.'

The above is an exact quotation. Having spent my life with American soldiers, and knowing only too well their innate distrust of everything foreign, I can appreciate far better than you can what a triumph of leadership you accomplished in inspiring such feeling and confidence.

Faithfully

Bedell "

Calling the troops round my jeep for a talk near Dover, 2nd February 1944

The Prime Minister comes to dinner at my Tac H.Q. near Portsmouth, 19th May 1944

The King comes to my Tac H.Q. to say good-bye before we go to Normandy, 22nd May 1944

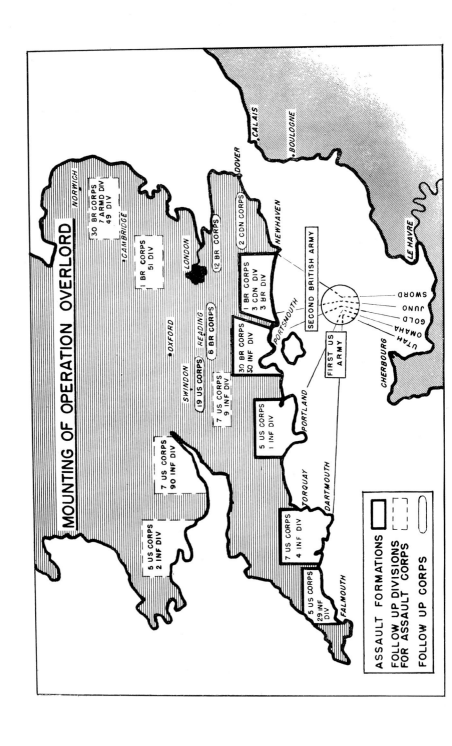

MOUNTING OF OPERATION OVERLORD

5 US CORPS
2 INF DIV

30 BR CORPS
7 ARMD DIV
49 DIV

• CAMBRIDGE

NORWICH

1 BR CORPS
51 DIV

LONDON

12 BR CORPS

• OXFORD

SWINDON

READING

19 US CORPS
7 US CORPS
9 INF DIV

8 BR CORPS

7 US CORPS
90 INF DIV

5 US CORPS
1 INF DIV

1 BR CORPS
3 CDN DIV
3 BR DIV

30 BR CORPS
50 INF DIV

2 CDN CORPS

DOVER

NEWHAVEN

PORTSMOUTH

SECOND BRITISH ARMY

SWORD
JUNO
GOLD
OMAHA
UTAH

PORTLAND

FIRST US ARMY

CHERBOURG

7 US CORPS
4 INF DIV

TORQUAY

DARTMOUTH

5 US CORPS
29 INF DIV

FALMOUTH

CALAIS

BOULOGNE

LE HAVRE

ASSAULT FORMATIONS

FOLLOW UP DIVISIONS
FOR ASSAULT CORPS

FOLLOW UP CORPS

After I had been a few weeks in England, the Ministry of Supply asked me to visit factories in various parts of the country which were engaged in the production of equipment for the armies. In many cases such equipment was urgently required for OVERLORD and men and women were working overtime to produce it for us.

These visits brought me into contact with a large public outside the Army, and I was asked to address the workers at each factory. I used to tell them that we were all one great army, whether soldier on the battle front or worker on the home front; their work was just as important as ours. Our combined task was to weld the workers and soldiers into one team, determined to destroy German domination of Europe and of the world.

On the 22nd February, I addressed at Euston Station a representative gathering of railwaymen from all over England. The Secretaries of the Railway Trades Unions were present, all the men's leaders, and, in fact, a selection from every type of railway official. I spoke for 1½ hours, and told them of our problems in what lay ahead and how they could help. I said we now had the war in a very good grip and the bad days were over; we must all rally to the task and finish off the war. When I had finished speaking the Secretaries of the Trades Union pledged their full support.

On the 3rd March I was asked to go to the London Docks, where I addressed some 16,000 dockers, stevedores and lightermen. My theme was the same as to the railwaymen—there is a job to be done and together we will do it.

As a result of these visits during which I talked to many people, I gained the impression that the mass of the people were jaded and war-weary. The miners, the factory workers, the dockers, the railwaymen, the housewives—all had been working at high pressure for over four years. It was difficult to get away for holidays. The blackout added a dismal tone. It seemed to me more than ever necessary to end the war in Europe in 1944. The people needed it and I made a vow to do all I could to finish the German war by Christmas; I was sure it could be done if we made no mistakes.

In my journeying round the country I was seen by the civil population and received everywhere with great enthusiasm. The people seemed to think I had some magic prescription for victory and that I had been sent to lead them to better things. I sensed danger in this and knew my activities would not be viewed favourably in political circles. Nor were they.

I received an intimation that I should "lay off" these visits—to which I paid no attention, beyond replying that I had been asked to undertake them by certain Ministries in Whitehall.

In point of fact, the working population wanted to have their spirits raised and to be made enthusiastic for the cause. They wanted a new subject of conversation. It was generally considered that the invasion would be a blood bath, with fearful casualties; I assured them it would not be so. All this could only be done by personal contact, and my visits helped in that respect.

The National Savings Committee chose this period to launch a new savings appeal throughout the country on the lines of their "Wings for Victory" and "Navy Week" campaigns. This latest appeal was given the title of " Salute the Soldier."

After years of peace-time neglect by the public, culminating in early disasters in the war, a revival in the Army's prestige was long overdue. Alamein, and the victories in Africa, Sicily and Italy, had restored public confidence in the ability of the Army to achieve results. The British public now saw their Army preparing to go forth to battle from English soil. It was a moment of great psychological importance. The " Salute the Soldier " campaign brought into being in every town and village throughout the country, committees not only to raise money, but also to show the unity of purpose of the country with the Army in the task which lay ahead. The culminating point in the campaign was a luncheon on the 24th March at the Mansion House in London, at which the main speakers were to be the Secretary of State for War (Sir James Grigg) and myself. I decided that my speech would be a call to the Nation to inspire the Army going forth to battle with the greatness of its cause. It was the first public speech I had ever made, except to soldiers. It has been published already but I make no apology for including it here since it shows the way my mind was working in March 1944—when preparing for the great adventure in Normandy.

" I would like to speak to you today about the soldier—about the fighting men who came from all parts of the Empire to answer the call of duty. It has been my great honour and privilege to command a large Imperial Army overseas in Africa, and in the Italian campaign. The men of the British Empire make magnificent soldiers. In the business of war, it is ' the man ' that counts; and it seems to me it must be the same in civil life. The employer must gain the confidence of his men; together they constitute one team, and it is ' team work ' that wins battles and hence wins wars.

THE NEED FOR GOOD WEAPONS

When great forces assemble for battle it is obvious that the armies must be properly equipped, and be supplied with the best possible weapons and equipment. We need not look far back in history to see what happens when this is NOT done. And in this respect it must forever redound to our shame that we sent our soldiers into this most modern war with weapons and equipment that were quite inadequate; we have only ourselves to blame for the disasters that early overtook us in the field. Surely we must never let this happen again; nor will we. And we can show our earnestness in this respect during this ' Salute the Soldier ' Campaign.

THE HUMAN FACTOR

But the key to success in battle is not merely to provide tanks, and guns, and other equipment. Of course we want good tanks, and good guns; but what really matters is the man inside the tank, and the man behind the gun. It is ' the man ' that counts, and not only the machine. The tank, and the men inside it, are a team; the best tank in the world is useless unless the crew inside it are well trained and have stout hearts. One of the chief factors for success in battle is the human factor. A commander has at his disposal certain human material; what he can make of it will depend entirely on himself. If you have got men who are mentally alert, who are tough and hard, who are trained to fight and kill, who are enthusiastic, and who have that infectious optimism and offensive eagerness that comes from physical well-being, and you then give these men the proper weapons and equipment—*there is nothing you cannot do.*
There are two essential conditions.
First— such men must have faith in God and they must think rightly on the moral issues involved.
Second—you must have mutual confidence between the commander and the troops; any steps you take to establish this confidence will pay a very good dividend; and once

you have gained the confidence of your men, you have a pearl of very great price.

A sure method of gaining the confidence of soldiers is success. And I suppose the methods you adopt to obtain success are a life study. I suggest that a study of the military disasters that have overtaken us in our history will reveal that they have been due, basically, to:

faulty command

or

bad staff work

or

neglect of the human factor,

and sometimes possibly to all three.

If you tell the soldier what you want, and you launch him properly into battle, he will always do *his* part—he has never let the side down. The British soldier is easy to lead; he is very willing to be led; and he responds at once to leadership.

Once you gain his confidence he will never fail you.

Amongst races of fighting men he is superb. And when the fighting men of the Empire assemble for the fray, the final result can never be in doubt.

THE ARMY IN ENGLAND

The Army in this country has had a difficult time since the Dunkirk days. It has had none of the excitements, and the interests, of active service overseas. And yet it has retained its keenness and its efficiency. I would like to pay tribute to my predecessor in command, General Paget, who gave of his best in order that the Army in England should stand ready at all times to answer the call of duty.

I find the Army in England in very good trim. I believe that when it goes into battle it will prove to be the best Army we have ever had.

INSPIRATION FOR THE INVASION FORCES

I would like to plead for the help of the whole nation in the task of inspiring the soldiers of our land at this momentous time.

The task of influencing an Army which dwells among an alien population is easy; the thinking and way of life of the people is mainly irrelevant; our own chaplains are the main influence in religious thought.

But an Army which dwells among its own folk is a wholly different proposition. It both regards and understands the people amongst whom it dwells, and they pour their ideas and thoughts into the receptive minds of soldiers all day—from every home, club, church, chapel, restaurant, and so on. Some of these ideas are inimical to battle and to battle morale. The chaplains are not the main influence on men's religious thinking; they are only one element —and not the most powerful.

When overseas I called on my chaplains to help me in my task; and right well did they answer the call. In the Eighth Army the inspiration had its roots in my call to the soldiers before Alamein: 'The Lord mighty in battle' will give us the victory.

But today my devoted brotherhood of chaplains are faced with a different problem; something more is needed—and something far beyond what they can do alone. The inspiration of the Armies requires the inspiration of the Nation—of the whole populace in whose houses and homes it lives, and who are their fathers, mothers, brothers, sisters, friends, and so on.

We must call the whole people to our help, as partners in the battle; only from an inspired Nation can go forth, under these conditions, an inspired Army.

It is absolutely vital that we realise that: 'the tide in the affairs of man which taken at the flood leads on to fortune' will *not* be for this Nation on Armistice Day or on Victory Day.

It will be when our men go forth to battle on this great endeavour. The tide will flow *then*, or not at all. That is the time when there must swell up in the Nation every noble thought, every high ideal, every great purpose which has waited through the weary years. And then, as the sap rises in the Nation, the men will feel themselves to be the instrument of a new-born national vigour.

The special glory of the whole endeavour must be a surge of the whole people's finest qualities, worthy to be the prayer: 'Let God arise and let His enemies be scattered.'

All this is a necessity. A special gallantry is required of our soldiers. The Promised Land is not now so far off; if necessary we have got to hazard all, and give our lives, that others may enjoy it. From a consecrated Nation, such men will abundantly come. And 'The

Lord mighty in battle ' will go forth with our Armies and His special providence will assist our battle.

The substance of the tide which has to turn and flow is quite clear; it is not a personal fad or a one-man doctrine; it is the tide which has borne the Nation through its history.

It is found in the Coronation Service of our King and Queen. The Nation's Church handed to our King from the Altar of Westminster Abbey the Sword of State: 'With this sword do justice, stop the growth of iniquity.'

The task now in hand is the use of His Majesty's consecrated sword in the reawakened spirit of that day.

There is no fear that the spirit which is alive with that resolution will fail, falter, or fade, on the day of victory. All must help, and the Nation's Church must give the lead.

THE TASK OF THE ARMY

I have nearly finished.

The Army is preparing to do its duty, and to play its full part in what may come this year. Every soldier knows that if the Army is to pull its full weight it must have the wholehearted co-operation of the Navy and the R.A.F.; and he also knows that that co-operation will be given in full measure.

I would add to this that the fighting services cannot pull *their* full weight on the battle front without the full co-operation of the home front. We are all one great team and we are preparing to take part in the biggest tug-of-war the world has ever seen. We lost the first few pulls but we are now leading; if we win *this* pull, we win the match.

If any of us should fail, or should let go of the rope, or should fall off the rope, then we lose the match.

Can you imagine this conversation in after years?

'What did you do in the World War?'

'I pulled hard to start with; but after a time I began to lose interest and I let go of the rope. I thought I wanted a rest; and I wanted more pay.'

'And did you win?'

'No, we lost. I let go of the rope, and we lost the match. God forgive me; we lost the match.'

Is it possible that such a conversation could apply to us British?

No. It is impossible; thank God it is impossible.

Then let us all 'stand to' and get on the rope. How long will the pull last? No one can say for certain; it may last a year; it may take longer. But it will be a magnificent 'party'; *and we shall win*. The real burden of this war is borne by the women; the women want us to win this pull; they are all helping already. So we must get right down to it; it will be a proper job for proper men.

The task now in hand is the use of His Majesty's consecrated sword; 'With this sword do justice, stop the growth of iniquity.'

Together the whole Empire team will see this thing through to the end. It is a proper job for proper men."

In February I began sittings for a portrait which I wanted for my son David, in case I did not survive the war. Augustus John was approached and agreement was reached on the financial side. After a time, I found it difficult to give any further sitting, and finally had to say I could not attend his studio any more.

He then asked me to come once more so that he could do a pencil sketch, from which he would complete the portrait—and this I did.

On the 26th February, Bernard Shaw looked in at the studio for a chat with Augustus John and remained there during the remainder of the sitting. I had never met him before and found him most amusing, and with a penetrating brain. That night Shaw wrote the following letter to Augustus John:

26th February 1944

"Dear Augustus John,

This afternoon I had to talk all over the shop to amuse your sitter and keep his mind off the worries of the present actual fighting. And as I could see him with one eye and you with the other: two great men at a glance—I noted the extreme unlikeness between you. You, large, tall, blonde, were almost massive in contrast, with that intensely compact hank of steel wire, who looked as if you might have taken him out of your pocket.

A great portrait painter always puts himself as well as his sitter into his work; and since he cannot see himself as he paints (as I saw you) there is some danger that he may substitute himself for his subject in the finished work. Sure enough, your portrait of B.L.M. immediately reminded me of your portrait of yourself in the Leicester Gallery. It fills the canvas, suggesting a large tall man. It does not look at you, and Monty always does with intense effect. *He* concentrates all space into a small spot like a burning glass; it has practically no space at all: you haven't left room for any.

Now for it. Take that old petrol rag that wiped out so many portraits of me (all masterpieces), and rub out this one till the canvas is blank. Then paint a small figure looking at you straight from above, as he looked at me from the dais. Paint him at full length (some foreground in front of him) leaning forward with his knees bent back gripping the edge of his camp stool, and his expression one of piercing scrutiny, the eyes unforgettable. The background: the vast totality of desert Africa. Result: a picture worth £100,000. The present sketch isn't honestly worth more than the price of your keep while you were painting it. You really weren't interested in the man.

Don't bother to reply. Just take it or leave it as it strikes you. What a nose! And what eyes!

Call the picture INFINITE HORIZONS AND ONE MAN.

Fancy a soldier being intelligent enough to want to be painted by you and to talk to me!

Always yours,

G.B.S."

He obviously gave the matter further thought, and wrote the following letter to Augustus John on the 27th February:

" My dear John,

Having slept on it I perceive that part of my letter of yesterday must be dismissed as an ebullition of senile excitement; for as a matter of business the portrait as it stands will serve as the regulation one which its buyers bargained for and are entitled to have (plenty of paint and the sitter all over the canvas). And between ourselves it has a subtle and lovely Johannine color plan which must not be thrown away.

The moral would seem to be to finish the portrait for your customers and then paint the picture for yourself. Only, as he certainly won't have time to give you a second set of sittings you must steal a drawing or two made from the chair in which I sat.

The worst of being 87-88 is that I never can be quite sure

whether I am talking sense or old man's drivel. I must leave the judgment to you.

As ever, but doddering.

(Sgd) G. Bernard Shaw "

I did not like the portrait when completed since I reckoned it was not like me. I was not sure of the drill on such occasions so I approached Augustus John about whether I need take delivery. This was his reply.

May 19, 1944

" My dear General,

Although I haven't succeeded in pleasing you, I am amply rewarded in having had the privilege of painting you and making your acquaintance. I don't think you are right in rejecting the picture, which some good judges have greatly admired, but I wouldn't dream of insisting on your taking a picture against your will. I have no doubt I have missed some aspect of you which many people might prefer. Another sitting or two would probably have resulted in a more sympathetic likeness. The enclosed letter indicates that you and Colonel Dawnay are not alone in condemning the work. I am deeply grateful to you for giving me so much of your time while being occupied in far more important matters.

Thanks for your letter.

Yours sincerely

Augustus John "

Letter enclosed by Augustus John

May 16th, 1944

" Dear Sir,

It was with great indignation I saw your picture, in The Listener of May 4th of General Montgomery.

I should think you took your copy of Old Gandi or a man of 100 years old.

I call it an insult to The General, he looks like a dead man instead of a living one.

Of course they had to accept your painting or you would have made the fuss like you did a time before when your picture was not hung.

It is also time you took a back place, and gave room for those *younger* ones.

From

Mrs. M. E. Tozer "

The portrait, and the pencil sketch, were both exhibited in the Royal Academy Show in the early summer. Both were sold, and the portrait now hangs in an art gallery in Glasgow.

[*Augustus John writes:* " *G. B. S. didn't come for a chat with him. I got him to come and meet Monty at the latter's request. There was no sitting or painting of course during the interview which lasted an hour. The portrait was acquired by the University of Glasgow (at a good price.)*]

THE TWO MONTHS BEFORE OVERLORD: APRIL AND MAY 1944

By the end of March everything was " set " for OVERLORD and the armies were on the move to concentration areas. These moves were to take some time and had to begin early; they would seriously test the transportation and railway services.

D-Day was fixed for the 5th June.

The whole of April was taken up with exercises, culminating in a very large " grand rehearsal " by all assault forces between the 3rd and 5th May.

I held a two-day exercise at my headquarters in London on the 7th and 8th April, which was attended by all the general officers of the Field Armies. My object was to put all senior commanders and their staffs completely into the whole OVERLORD picture—as affecting the general plan, the naval problem and plan, and the air action. This was done on the first day. On the 8th April we examined certain situations which might arise during the operation—either during the approach by sea or after we had got ashore. The Prime Minister attended on the first day and spoke to all the assembled officers.

On the 28th April my headquarters moved to Southwick House in the Portsmouth area, which was to be our operational headquarters on D-Day. My " A " Mess was established nearby, in Broomfield House.

It was during April that I issued the last tactical instruction to the two Armies which were to land in Normandy. This is what I wrote, dated the 14th April.

" 1. In operation OVERLORD an uncertain factor is the speed at which the enemy will be able to concentrate his mobile and armoured divisions against us for counter-attack.

On our part we must watch the situation carefully, and must not get our main bodies so stretched that they would be unable to hold against determined counter-attack; on the other hand, having seized the initiative by our initial landing, we must ensure that we keep it.

2. The best way to interfere with the enemy concentrations and counter-measures will be to push forward fairly powerful armoured-force thrusts on the afternoon of D-Day.

If two such forces, each consisting of an armd bde group, were pushed forward on each Army front to carefully chosen areas, it would be very difficult for the enemy to interfere with our build-up; from the areas so occupied, patrols and recces would be pushed *further* afield, and this would tend to delay enemy movement towards the lodgement area.

The whole effect of such aggressive tactics would be to retain the initiative ourselves and to cause alarm in the minds of the enemy.

3. To be successful, such tactics must be adopted on D-Day; to wait till D plus 1 would be to lose the opportunity, and also to lose the initiative.

Armoured units and bdes. must be concentrated quickly as soon as ever the situation allows after the initial landing on D-Day; this may not be too easy, but plans to effect such concentrations must be made and every effort made to carry them out; speed and boldness are then required, and the armoured thrusts must force their way inland.

4. The result of such tactics will be the establishment of firm bases well in advance of our main bodies; if their location is carefully thought out, the enemy will be unable to by-pass them. I am prepared to accept almost any risk in order to carry out these tactics. I would risk even the total loss of the armoured brigade groups—which in any event is not really possible; the delay they would cause to the enemy before

they could be destroyed would be quite enough to give us time to get our main bodies well ashore and re-organised for strong offensive action.

And as the main bodies move forward their task will be simplified by the fact that armoured forces are holding firm on important areas in front.

5. Army Commanders will consider the problem in the light of the above remarks, and will inform me of their plans to carry out these tactics."

I sent the Prime Minister a copy. This was his reply:

" For what my opinion is worth, it seems to be exactly the spirit in which the execution should proceed, and I only wish that a similar course had been attempted when the forces landed at Anzio."

During May I had frequent talks with Bill Williams, who was now brigadier and head of my Intelligence staff. In February Rommel had taken command of the coast sectors between Holland and the Loire. After his appearance, obstacles of all types began to appear on the beaches and it was clear he intended to deny any penetration, and to aim at defeating us on the beaches. Williams was very good at sifting the intelligence we got, at discarding what was of little value, and finally giving me a considered enemy picture. His view was that Rommel would aim to defeat us on the beaches and that we must be prepared for stiff resistance in the bocage country as we pushed inland. If Rommel failed to " see us off " on the beaches, he would try to " rope us off " in the bocage. I laid my plans accordingly.

On the 15th May Supreme Headquarters staged a final presentation of our combined plans. It was held in St. Paul's School, and was attended by the King, the Prime Minister, General Smuts, and the British Chiefs of Staff.

Throughout the day Eisenhower was quite excellent; he spoke very little but what he said was on a high level and extremely good. The King spoke before he left; he made a first class impromptu speech, quite short and exactly right. At the end of the day Smuts spoke, and finally the Prime Minister. Altogether, this was a very good day.

Shortly after this final review of plans, Smuts asked me to lunch with him in London. We had a most interesting talk, and this is what I wrote about it in my diary that night.

" Smuts is worried we may lose the peace. Britain, with American aid, won the 1914/18 war. But when it was over we were tired and we stood back, allowing France to take first place in Europe. The result was the present war.

He then went on to say that we cannot allow Europe to disintegrate. Europe requires a structure—a framework on which to rebuild itself. A good structure must have a firm core.

France has failed dismally.

Britain must stand forward as the corner stone of the new structure. Nations that want security must range themselves on the side of Britain; there can be no more neutrals.

It is Britain that stood alone in 1940/41 and then, with American aid, stemmed the tide. Britain is a continental nation. Britain must remain strong and must keep up small, but highly efficient, forces which are capable of rapid expansion. The keynote of the armed force necessary in peace time must be air power; the army can be relatively small.

Smuts said that statesmen cannot always say things like this. He said I had made a great name, and would make a greater one still. I could say practically what I liked; my position with the public in England was secure and they would ' swallow ' whatever I said. He was emphatic that when the war was over, I must speak out and say these things, and give a lead in the matter.

By the end of lunch I was rather startled. I am not convinced it is right for the soldier to lay down the law on such matters; it is more in the sphere of his political masters. However, it certainly gives one seriously to think."

It has been written that I had a row with the Prime Minister shortly before D-Day, and even threatened to resign. This is untrue. I would like to tell the true story. Here it is.

For some time before D-Day the P.M. had not been satisfied that we had the right balance between fighting troops and vehicles for the initial landing on the Normandy beaches. He reckoned there were not enough men with rifles and bayonets, and too many lorries, radio vehicles, and so on. He gave out that he would come to my Headquarters near Portsmouth and investigate the matter with my staff. On that, I invited him to dinner to meet my senior staff officers.

He came on the 19th May 1944. The photograph reproduced

facing page 224 was taken on his arrival. I asked him to come to my study for a short talk before meeting the others. Having got him comfortably seated I said:

" I understand, sir, that you want to discuss with my staff the proportion of soldiers to vehicles landing on the beaches in the first flights. I cannot allow you to do so. My staff advise me and I give the final decision; they then do what I tell them.

" That final decision has been given. In any case I could never allow you to harass my staff at this time and possibly shake their confidence in me. They have had a terrific job preparing the invasion; that work is now almost completed, and all over England the troops are beginning to move towards the assembly areas, prior to em-barkation. You can argue with me but not with my staff. In any case it is too late to change anything. I consider that what we have done is right; that will be proved on D-Day. If you think it is wrong, that can only mean that you have lost confidence in me."

A somewhat awkward silence followed these remarks. The P.M. did not reply at once, and I thought it best to make a move! So I stood up and said that if he would now come into the next room I would like to introduce him to my staff. He was magnificent.

With a twinkle in his eye he said: " I wasn't allowed to have any discussion with you gentlemen."

We had a most amusing dinner and when he left I went to bed feeling what a wonderful man he was—too big to stand on his dignity, or not to see when he was on a bad wicket.

At the end of this chapter will be found the page he wrote in my autograph book after dinner.

King George came to lunch with me at Broomfield House on the 22nd May, to say good-bye. On the next day I was to start on my final tour of the armies to address all senior officers and I gave the King a copy of my notes (which are reproduced below) for those talks.

On the 23rd May I started on that final tour. As I have already said, D-Day was to be on the 5th June and I had to be back in good time. I was determined to address all officers down to the lieut.-colonel level, and to get over to them the main issues involved in the tremendous operation on which we were about to embark.

I visited every corps and divisional area, and spoke to audiences of from 500 to 600 officers at a time. On each occasion it was essential that I should go " all out "; if one does this properly, energy goes out of you and leaves you tired at the end. It took eight days in all and was an exhausting tour.

But I am sure it did good and instilled confidence, and that was vital as the day grew near.

The notes I used for all the addresses ran as follows:

" 1. Before I launch troops into battle I make a point of speaking personally to all senior officers down to the lt.-col. rank inclusive. In this way I can get my ideas across, and ensure a common line of approach to the problem that lies ahead of us; and at a final talk, like this one, I can emphasise certain essential features, and give you some points to pass on to your men. In fact I use these occasions in order to influence the Armies, to instil confidence, and thus to help win the battle.

2. I would like to talk to you today on the following subjects:
     (a) The past—very briefly.
     (b) The present state of the war.
     (c) The future prospects.
     (d) The task immediately confronting us.
     (e) Basic essentials for success.

THE PAST

3. We have been through some very bad times in this war. In our darkest days we stood alone against the combined might of the axis powers; we suffered some great shocks and some bad disasters. But we stood firm—on the defensive, but striking blows where we could.

     Then America joined us; but that great Nation was not immediately ready to strike heavy blows, and required time to develop her strength.

     Then the two of us—America and the British Empire—gradually began to fight back. Slowly, but surely and relentlessly, the lost ground was recovered and we began to pass from the defensive to the offensive.

4. Since that time we have been working throughout on the same strategy. This has been:
     (a) To clear the enemy out of Africa.

(b) To knock Italy out of the war, and open the Mediterranean for our shipping.

(c) To bring Turkey into the war.

(d) To defeat Germany, while containing Japan.

5. That has been the broad strategy of the Allies, and we have stuck to it and never wavered.

We are now about to reap the harvest.

PRESENT STATE OF THE WAR

6. How do we stand today?

Of the four basic points in our strategy (vide para. 4), the first two are achieved.

(a) The Germans are out of Africa.

(b) Italy is out of the war, and the Mediterranean is open for our shipping.

These are great achievements, of which we may well be proud—and we are.

7. We failed in the third point.

Turkey has not reacted in the way we hoped. But the Allies have done so well in other directions that it has not mattered overmuch; and the day may well come when Turkey will regret her present attitude, and will wish she had come in with the Allies—who are now going to win.

8. We are now about to embark on the final phase of the fourth point.

To defeat Germany; that is the crux of the whole matter.

After $4\frac{1}{2}$ years of war the Allies have, by hard fighting on sea, land and in the air, worked themselves into a position where they cannot lose. That is a very good position to reach in any contest; but the good player is never content ' to draw '—he wants to win. And so we must now win, and defeat Germany. And while doing that, we are doing more than contain Japan. That country is now definitely on the defensive and in the S.W. Pacific the American and Australian forces are gradually working their way towards the Philippines and Formosa, and are killing great numbers of Japanese in the process.

FUTURE PROSPECTS

9. Germany is now fighting on three fronts: in Russia, in Italy, and in the Balkans. Soon she will have a fourth front— in Western Europe.

   She cannot do this, successfully.

   She has a large number of divisions, but they are all weak and below strength. Everything is in the shop window; there is nothing ' in the kitty.'

   Her cities and industries are being devastated by bombing; this will continue on an ever increasing tempo all this year; by next winter there will be little left of her more important cities.

   The Allies have the initiative and Germany is ringed round; she is about to be attacked from Russia, from the Mediterranean front, and from England; and all the time the bombing will go on relentlessly.

10. A very great deal depends on the success of our operations. If they succeed, I consider that Germany will then begin to crack. They will succeed; and the bombing will go on, every day and all around the clock. Germany will not be able to stand it.

    If we do our stuff properly and no mistakes are made, then I believe that Germany will be out of the war this year. And Japan will be finished within six months after we have put Germany out.

11. But the essential condition is that the Second Front should be a great success. And that brings me to my next point.

OUR IMMEDIATE TASK

12. When the time comes for us to operate on the Continent, no one will claim that our task will be easy.

    The enemy is in prepared positions; he has protected his beaches with obstacles; we cannot gain close contact and recce his position carefully, so as to examine the problem and ensure we have the right solution. There are, and there are bound to be, many unknown hazards. He has reserves positioned for counter-attack.

13. We have a long sea journey, and at the end of it we will

have to land on an enemy coast in the face of determined opposition.

During all this there is bound to be a certain loss of cohesion in assaulting units; and even reserves coming ashore will require a little time to collect themselves.

The enemy will know every inch of the ground; we shall be operating in a strange country.

14. But we have certain very great assets, and they are the ones that matter.

We have the initiative; the enemy does not know where, or when, we shall land.

We have great fire-power to support our initial landing, from the sea and from the air.

We have a good and simple plan.

We have well-trained troops, who are spoiling for a fight.

15. We have available to see us on shore, the whole of the allied air power in England, and this air power will continue to support our operations and to bomb Germany.

Its strength is terrific.

There are some 4500 fighters and fighter-bombers; and about 6000 bombers of all types.

Nothing has ever been seen like it before.

16. Unknown hazards must have no terrors for us. We have first class engineers, and every kind of mechanical and special equipment.

All we need is a very robust mentality; as difficulties appear, so they must be tackled and stamped on.

17. What we have to do is to blast our way on shore, and gain ground inland quickly so that we secure a good and firm lodgement area before the enemy has time to bring his reserves into action against us.

The violence, speed, and power of our initial assault must carry everything before it.

The enemy reserves will be closely watched from the air; when they sacrifice concealment and begin to move, they will be bombed and shot-up from the air without ceasing, and enemy reserve units will be in poor shape when they reach the battle area.

BASIC ESSENTIALS FOR SUCCESS

18. I would like now to give you a few points which I regard as terribly important. Obviously such points must be few in number, since everything cannot be important. I consider that compliance with the following points is essential for success.

19. *Allied solidarity.*

We are a great team of allies, British and American. There must be throughout this team a friendly spirit; we must have confidence in each other.

As a British general I regard it as an honour to serve under American command; General Eisenhower is captain of the team and I am proud to serve under him. And I regard it as a great honour to have American troops serving under my command.

When we visit each other there should be only one idea; and that is—how can I help the other chap. Let us have no suspicion, and no petty jealousy.

Let us have, throughout, complete mutual confidence and goodwill, all pulling together as one great team.

20. *Offensive eagerness.*

This is vital.

Once on land and the battle starts we must be offensive, and more offensive, and ever more offensive as the hours go by. We must call on the soldiers for an all-out effort.

Every officer and man must have only one idea, and that is to peg out claims inland, and to penetrate quickly and deeply into enemy territory. After a long sea voyage and a landing followed by fighting, a reaction sets in and officers and men are often inclined to let up and relax. This is fatal; senior officers must prevent it at all costs on D-Day and on the following days. The first few days will be the vital ones; it is in those days that the battle will be won, and it is in those days that it could well be lost.

Great energy and 'drive' will be required from all senior officers and commanders.

I consider that once the beaches are in our possession, success will depend largely on our ability to be able to concentrate our armour and push fairly strong armoured columns rapidly inland to secure important ground or communication centres. Such columns will form *firm bases in enemy territory* from which to develop offensive action in all directions. Such action will tend to throw the enemy off his balance, and will enable our build-up through the beaches to proceed undisturbed; it will cut the ground from under the armoured counter-attack.

Offensive eagerness is not only necessary in the soldier; it is essential in the officer, and especially in the senior officer and commander.

Inaction, and a defensive mentality, are criminal in any officer—however senior.

21. *Enthusiasm.*

Every officer and man must be enthusiastic for the fight, and have the light of battle in his eyes. We must send our soldiers into this encounter completely on their toes; they must be imbued with that infectious optimism that comes from physical well-being and absolute conviction in a great and righteous cause.

22. *Confidence.*

I want you, and every soldier, to know that I have complete and absolute confidence in the successful outcome of the operations that will shortly begin.

With stout hearts, and with enthusiasm for the contest, let us go forward, to victory.

23. *An all-out effort.*

Everyone must go all out.

And, as we enter battle, let us recall the words of a famous soldier, spoken many years ago:

> 'He either fears his fate too much,
> Or his deserts are small,
> Who dare not put it to the touch
> To win or lose it all.'

24. Good luck to each one of you.

And good hunting on the mainland of Europe."

It will be noted that in para. 10 I made a definite statement that we could win the German war in 1944 and we would defeat Japan six months later. We did not win the German war till May 1945, and I will have something to say about that later. But we finished the Japanese war three months after the end of the German war.

IST JUNE

As I pondered over all that had taken place since I arrived in England on the 2nd January, I realised how much I owed to the War Office. So I wrote the following letter to Sir James Grigg.

1 June, 1944

" My dear Secretary of State,
    In January last I came home from Italy to take command of the Field Armies in England and to prepare for operations in western Europe. The past 5 months have been a strenuous and a difficult time; but the planning and the preparation are now completed and we are ready for the great adventure.
2. Before we start, I would like to tell you how very grateful I am for all the help and guidance I, and my staff, have received from the War Office. It has not been an easy period for any of us, and I know that at times I have myself been impatient and critical and have frequently upset you all by my methods! Now that we have finished the job, and can look back on it calmly, I would like to say that where friction has occurred, and tempers have run high, it has nearly always been my fault; the War Office, from top to bottom, has been splendid, and every section, both military and civil, has spared no effort to help us to get ready for the battle.
3. The great lesson left in my mind is that the War Office, and the Commanders-in-Chief in the field, are together one team; between them there must be complete mutual confidence and trust. In periods of stress it is all too easy to allow differences of opinion to magnify themselves, and so to drive a wedge between the two branches of the team. You and the War Office have given us a good example of how to work in such a team; on our part, we have done our best and I hope that you have not found us too bad.
4. At this moment, therefore, when our preparations are completed

and before battle is joined, I would like, through you, to express the gratitude of myself and my staff to every member of the War Office—military and civil—for the kindly consideration you have shown us, and for your never failing help and guidance in our difficulties.

   If we gain successes in the field, they will be successes gained by the whole team—as much yours as ours.

5. I felt that I must say this to you—as the head of the War Office. And I hope that you will convey my deep gratitude to all who work under you.

Yours ever,

B. L. Montgomery "

This was his reply:

3rd June, 1944

" My dear Montgomery,

   Thank you for what you have said in your letter of 1st June and for the way in which you have said it. It can seldom have happened that the War Office has received such a generous expression of appreciation from a Commander in the field.

   From top to bottom, soldier and civilian alike, the War Office has one main aim—to see that the needs of the Army are met so that the Army may, with the help of the other Services and our allies, bring the war to a speedy and successful conclusion.

   We are glad to know that you are satisfied that we have been able to give you what you want; we are confident that, if your Army has that, we can safely leave it to you and them to do the rest, and we wish you—every one of you—the best of luck in the doing.

Yours sincerely,

P. J. Grigg "

About this time, the 1st June, we began to scan the weather forecasts anxiously. There were only four days in early June when OVERLORD was possible, for the following reasons:

(a) There were a lot of obstacles on the beaches and we had to be able to tackle them dry, i.e. not under water.

(b) At least 30 minutes had to be available to allow for this.

(c) In order to get full value from the naval and air bombardment, we needed at least one hour of daylight. In certain conditions we could accept less, but we did not want more if it could be avoided.

(*d*) We needed about three hours of rising tide after the leading craft touched down on the beaches.

Allowing for all these factors it was clear that the first dates and times for the operation in June were as follows, civil twilight being 0515 hours.

D-Day	H-Hour	Period after civil twilight
4th	0530	15 minutes
5th	0610	55 minutes
6th	0635	80 minutes
7th	0715	120 minutes

It was my view that the 4th June was unacceptable. That date did not allow us time to get full value from our great air superiority— only about 5 minutes, since bombing by the R.A.F. could not begin till civil twilight plus 10 minutes.

It will be seen that the 5th June was the best date, and that date had been agreed for D-Day some months earlier.

The 6th June was quite acceptable.

The 7th June was not good because it gave two hours of daylight before touch-down on the beaches; but it could be managed.

After that date, the next possible period would not occur for a fortnight. The prospect of having to disembark all the troops after they had been fully briefed, and to wait for two weeks, was full of terrors; we had, however, worked out all details of how it would be done, if the weather forced a long postponement upon us.

2ND JUNE

On the 2nd June, I addressed all officers of my headquarters—Tac and Main at Southwick House near Portsmouth in the morning, and those of Rear H.Q. in London in the afternoon.

That night Eisenhower dined quietly with me at Broomfield House and after dinner we went up to Southwick House for a conference with the Meteorological experts on the weather. The weather looked reasonable, but the experts were worried about a depression over Iceland. It was decided to lay on the operation for the 5th June, without any change, with another Meteorological conference at 9.30 p.m. on the 3rd June.

3RD JUNE

The weather forecast was not good. The depression over Iceland began to spread southwards and the high-pressure system which was coming up our way from the Azores was being pushed back. This meant that the prospect of a good belt of high pressure over the Channel area on the night 4th-5th June, and on the 5th June, was receding.

This was awkward, and I noted in my diary that some big decisions might be necessary. I added:

" My own view is that if the sea is calm enough for the Navy to take us there, then we must go; the air forces have had very good weather for all its preparatory operations and we must accept the fact that it may not be able to do so well on D-Day."

We had our conference at 9.30 p.m. and decided to make no changes. But we knew that a final decision regarding postponement must be taken early on the 4th June, and even then some of the convoys would have sailed.

4TH JUNE

We met at 4 a.m. at Southwick House. Some of the convoys had already sailed, working to a D-Day of the 5th June. The weather reports were discouraging. The Navy reckoned the landing was possible but would be difficult; Admiral Ramsay would not commit himself one way or the other. I was for going. Tedder, Deputy Supreme Commander, was for postponement.

Weighing all the factors, Eisenhower decided to postpone D-Day for 24 hours; it would now be on the 6th June.

We met again at 9.30 p.m. in the evening; the weather reports were still bad and we agreed to assemble again at 4 a.m. the next morning.

5TH JUNE

We met at 4 a.m. A heavy storm was blowing in the Channel and it was clear that if we had persisted with the original D-Day of the 5th June, we might have had a disaster.

But the Met. reports indicated a slackening of the storm, and a period of reasonable weather on the 6th June. Indeed, the experts predicted reasonable weather for some days after the 6th June before the next period of unsettled weather arrived.

On that Eisenhower decided to go. We were all glad. This conference did not last more than 15 minutes. Eisenhower was in good form and made his decision quickly.

I went up to Hindhead that evening to see Major and Mrs. Reynolds and to make final arrangements with them about David. I had not seen him recently and did not want to indicate the nearness of D-Day to all the boys at Winchester by going there to say good-bye to him. Mrs. Reynolds told me afterwards that she knew it was the eve of D-Day—not from anything I said or from the way I behaved, but because I had taken my plain clothes there and had put them away in a wardrobe.

6TH JUNE

I spent the day in the garden at Broomfield House. After breakfast I made a record for the B.B.C. of my personal message to the armies, which had been read to the troops when they were embarked. As the morning wore on, it was clear that we were ashore, and that all was going well as far as we knew. I decided my place was in Normandy; I could do no good just outside Portsmouth. So I sailed at 9.30 that evening in the destroyer H.M.S. *Faulknor* (Captain C. F. H. Churchill, R.N.) which was standing by in the dockyard to take me across. It was nearly six months before I saw England again. I was anxious to make personal contact with the two Army Commanders, Dempsey and Bradley, who were afloat in their command ships with their Naval counterparts.

Discussion with them was the next need.

This is what the Prime Minister wrote in my autograph book when he came to dinner with me at Broomfield House on the 19th May:

> "On the verge of the greatest Adventure with which these pages have dealt, I record my confidence that
> all will be well
> and that the organisation and equipment of the Army will be worthy of the valour of the soldiers and the genius of their chief.
> Winston S. Churchill"

CHAPTER 14

THE BATTLE OF NORMANDY

6th June to 19th August 1944

WE NOW come to events which were to have a marked influence on the future course of the war. Much has been written about the campaign in North-West Europe and it will be a happy hunting ground for historians for many years to come. National feelings on the subject have tended to run high and in particular American writers have launched heavy attacks on the British conduct of operations in general and on myself especially. The seeds of trouble were sown in Normandy so that will be my starting point. My friend Ike has agreed that it is now my turn to put my own point of view. I will try and tell the story truthfully.

On the morning of the 7th June, which was D+1, H.M.S. *Faulknor* arrived off the beaches and then proceeded westwards into the American area. We located U.S.S. *Augusta* in which was General Bradley, and I had a good talk with him about the situation of the First American Army. Bradley was concerned about the operational situation on OMAHA, his eastern beach. We discussed his problem and agreed on how it could be solved. *Faulknor* then returned to the British sector and we located H.M.S. *Scylla* and H.M.S. *Bulolo*, lying close together. From these ships, General Dempsey and Admiral Vian came on board *Faulknor* and I discussed with them their situation and problem; all was going according to plan on the British beaches and there was no cause for anxiety. Just at that time General Eisenhower and Admiral Ramsay arrived off the British sector in the latter's flagship, and I went on board and had a talk with them. I then asked Captain Churchill to return to the American sector so that I could have another talk with General Bradley in *Augusta*. This we did. The news from OMAHA beach was now better and General Bradley had gone ashore; but his Chief of Staff came on board *Faulknor* and gave me the situation. We then returned to the British sector.

The wind and sea had now dropped, the sun was shining, and the "round the Fleet" trips in the destroyer were delightful; there was plenty to look at, ships everywhere, and blockships and artificial harbours starting to arrive. There was no enemy air action and few signs of battle on sea or land. It was difficult to imagine that on shore a battle was being fought which was deciding the fate of Europe. We anchored off the British beaches at about 8.30 p.m. and I asked Captain Churchill if he could put me on shore at 7 a.m. the next morning, the 8th June.

We got under way at 6.30 a.m. and began to move in towards the beach on which I had asked to be landed. It was low water and, as I had asked we should get as close in as possible, the captain began sounding with hand leads and started the echo sounder. All beach-marks were obliterated by smoke-screens. The next thing that happened was that a slight shudder went through the ship; we were aground aft on some outlying sandbank or boulders. I was on the quarter deck with an A.D.C., and I sent him up to the bridge to ask if we were going to get any closer to the shore. This was not well received by the captain. Meanwhile the facts were being explained to me on deck by the first lieutenant. When he told me we were aground I am reported to have said: "Splendid. Then the captain has got as close in as he possibly can. Now, what about a boat to put me on shore?"

I was eventually taken off in a landing craft by some of my staff who were already on shore, and the destroyer was refloated shortly afterwards with the aid of a tug which pulled her stern round. They tell me that this grounding incident, well exaggerated on its journey, no doubt, went round the ward-rooms of the Navy.

Our assault on D-Day had achieved tactical surprise. The weather was bad and the sea rough, but the troops were landed in good heart and at the right places. Slowly and relentlessly we made ground and extended the lodgement area.

On D+1 we were five to six miles inland. By D+4 (10th June) the lodgement area was joined up into one continuous whole; it was sixty miles long and varied in depth from eight to twelve miles; it was firmly held and all anxiety had passed. There had been considerable cause for alarm on OMAHA beach in the early stages; but that situation was put right by the gallantry of the American soldiers, by good supporting naval fire, and by brave work by fighter-bomber aircraft.

The Prime Minister and General Smuts visited me in Normandy on the 12th June. The P.M. was in first class form. For once he was prepared to admit that I was in charge in the battle area and he must do what he was told! Before leaving he again wrote in my autograph book:

" *France*: June 12, 1944
As it was in the beginning so may it continue to the end.
Winston S. Churchill "

Underneath it, Smuts wrote:

" And so it will!
J. C. Smuts
12/6/1944 "

At this time my Tac Headquarters was located in the gardens of the château at Creuilly, a small village a few miles east of Bayeux. The owner of the estate, Madame de Druval, was still living in the château itself. I thought my caravan contained all that I wanted when we left Portsmouth but found that one article was still needed—a jerry, or what the French call a *pot-de-chambre*. So I told my A.D.C. to ask Madame if she could supply the article—on loan. After some discussion it was agreed the situation was delicate, and that he had better ask Madame if she would lend the Commander-in-Chief a vase. Madame said she would be delighted and collected all available flower vases in the château and asked my A.D.C. to select the one he liked best. He looked over them very carefully and said he thought none was really suitable for the general's flowers. Were there any other types? Madame, having great intuition and no small sense of humour, immediately sensed what was wanted—which was of course a *vase-de-nuit*. She told my A.D.C. she thought she could find one more type of vase, rather unusual but which would possibly be suitable for a soldier. She left the room and returned after a few minutes carrying a small white *pot-de-chambre*, ornamented with pink flowers. This she placed proudly in the middle of the now large collection of flower vases and said: " I think that is exactly what the general would like for his flowers." The A.D.C. agreed that it was exactly right and would look very well in the general's caravan!

Madame still lives in the château and I visit her there from time to time. Every visitor is told the story of the general's *vase*, and most people in Normandy know it by now. I expect the story expands considerably in the telling. I should add that Madame insisted I should keep "the vase," and it now occupies a suitable position in my home in Hampshire.

But to return to the campaign.

My master plan for the land battle in Normandy I have described already. Briefly, it was so to stage and conduct operations that we drew the main enemy strength on to the front of the Second British Army on our eastern flank, in order that we might the more easily gain territory in the west and make the ultimate break-out on that flank—using the First American Army for the purpose. If events on the western flank were to proceed rapidly it meant that we must make quick territorial gains there.

On the eastern flank, in the Caen sector, the acquisition of ground was not so pressing; the need *there* was by hard fighting to make the enemy commit his reserves, so that the American forces would meet less opposition in their advances to gain the territory which was vital on the west.

In this master plan we were greatly assisted by the immense strategic importance of Caen. It was a vital road and rail centre through which passed the main routes leading to our lodgement area from the east and south-east. As the bulk of the German mobile reserves were located north of the Seine, they would have to approach our bridgehead from the east and would thus converge on Caen. To the south-east, between Caen and Falaise, was good ground for airfields. I was convinced that strong and persistent offensive action in the Caen sector would achieve our object of drawing the enemy reserves on to our eastern flank: this was my basic conception. From the beginning it formed the basis of all our planning. Once on shore and firmly established, I began to get this strategy working and after the heavy battles in the Caen area, and the overrunning of the Cherbourg peninsula, it began to take shape.

I never once had cause or reason to alter my master plan. Of course we did not keep to the times and phase lines we had envisaged for the benefit of administrative planning, and of course, too, we didn't hesitate to adjust our plans and dispositions to the tactical situation as it developed—as in all battles. Of course we didn't. I never imagined we would. But the fundamental design remained unchanged; it was to that that I pinned my hopes and clung so resolutely, despite increasing opposition from the fainter-hearted. We did not capture Caen, for instance, till the 10th July and we did not finally clear the eastern suburbs till the 20th July. It had been my original intention to secure the high ground between Caen and Falaise as early as possible, as being a suitable area for the construction of airfields; but this was not vital, and when I found it could not be done in accordance with the original plan without suffering unjustified casualties, I did not proceed with that venture. This was not popular with the Air Command.

It was indeed a fundamental object of my strategy on the eastern flank to establish a force strong in armour to the south-east of Caen in the area about Bourguebus; this was the key to ensuring that we kept the bulk of the German armour on the eastern flank, and thus helped the American expansion on the west. We did not get on to this high ground until Second Army launched Operation GOODWOOD on the 18th July, with armoured forces. As soon as the armoured advance came to a standstill because of determined enemy resistance, and also because heavy rain turned the whole area into a sea of mud, I decided to abandon that thrust. Many people thought that when Operation GOODWOOD was staged, it was the beginning of the plan to break out from the eastern flank towards Paris, and that, *because* I did not do so, the battle had been a failure. But let me make the point again at the risk of being wearisome. There was never *at any time* any intention of making the break-out from the bridgehead on the eastern flank. Misunderstandings about this simple and basic conception were responsible for much trouble between British and American personalities. Here, for example, is an extract from page 32 of Eisenhower's report on the campaign, dated the 13th July 1945, to the Combined Chiefs of Staff:

" Nevertheless, in the east we had been unable to break out towards the Seine, and the enemy's concentration of his main power in the Caen sector had prevented us from securing the ground in that area we so badly needed. Our plans were sufficiently flexible that we could take advantage of this enemy reaction by directing that the American forces smash out of the lodgement area in the west while the British and Canadians kept the Germans occupied in the east. Incessant pressure by the Second Army to contain the enemy was therefore continued by Field-Marshal Montgomery during July."

The impression is left that the British and Canadians had failed in the east (in the Caen sector) and that, therefore, the Americans had to take on the job of breaking out in the west. This reflection on Dempsey and the Second Army is a clear indication that Eisenhower failed to comprehend the basic plan to which he had himself cheerfully agreed.

All through the fierce fighting which took place in Normandy, there was never any intention of breaking out on the eastern flank towards the Seine; reference to all the orders and instructions which I issued makes that abundantly clear. This false conception existed only at Supreme Headquarters, and none of the senior officers responsible for the conduct of the actual fighting in Normandy, Bradley included, had any doubt about the true plan. The misconception led to much controversy and those at Supreme Headquarters who were not very fond of me took advantage of it to create trouble as the campaign developed.

One of the reasons for this in my belief was that the original COSSAC plan had been, in fact, to break out from the Caen-Falaise area, on our eastern flank. I had refused to accept this plan and had changed it. General Morgan who had made the COSSAC plan was now at Supreme Headquarters as Deputy Chief of Staff. He considered Eisenhower was a god; since I had discarded many of his plans, he placed me at the other end of the celestial ladder. So here were the seeds of discord. Morgan and those around him (the displaced strategists) lost no opportunity of trying to persuade Eisenhower that I was defensively minded and that we were unlikely to break out anywhere!

In all the " cufuffle " which developed on this issue Morgan was assisted by the airmen, because most understandably, they wanted the airfields on the eastern flank beyond Caen. And some airmen were only too glad to be able to suggest that something had gone wrong. One of the difficulties lay in the command set-up itself. In the desert, " Maori " Coningham and I had been equal partners—he commanding the Desert Air Force and I the Eighth Army. After the capture of Tripoli he went off to work with Alexander in North Africa, and we didn't join forces again until both of us were back in England in 1944. And even then we were not equal partners. Not only did I have two badges in my beret: I was wearing two berets. I was at once C.-in-C. 21 Army Group and the Ground Force Commander for Normandy.

The King lands in Normandy to visit the British and Canadian forces, 16th June 1944

he Prime Minister at my Tac Q. at Blay, to the west of yeux, on a wet day, 21st July 44

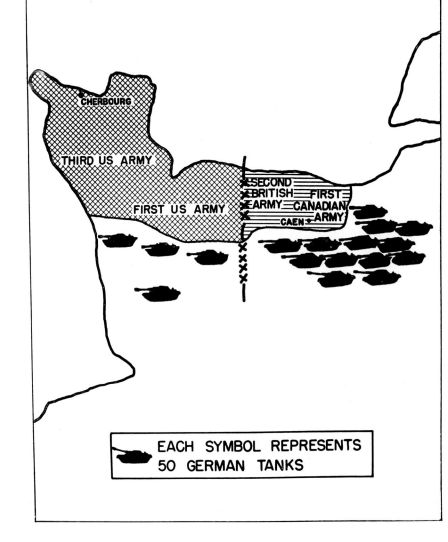

GERMAN TANK DEPLOYMENT
ON EVE OF BREAKOUT
24 JULY 1944

CHERBOURG

THIRD US ARMY

FIRST US ARMY

SECOND
BRITISH
ARMY
FIRST
CANADIAN
ARMY
CAEN

EACH SYMBOL REPRESENTS
50 GERMAN TANKS

So I had two Air Force opposite numbers: Leigh-Mallory, who was Air C.-in-C., and "Maori" Coningham in command of 2nd Tactical Air Force working with 21 Army Group. "Maori" was particularly interested in getting his airfields south-east of Caen. They were mentioned in the plan and to him they were all-important. I don't blame him. But they were not all-important to me. If we won the battle of Normandy, everything else would follow, airfields and all. I wasn't fighting to capture airfields; I was fighting to defeat Rommel in Normandy. This Coningham could scarcely appreciate: and for two reasons. First, we were not seeing each other daily as in the desert days, for at this stage I was working direct to Leigh-Mallory. Secondly, Coningham wanted the airfields in order to defeat Rommel, whereas I wanted to defeat Rommel in order, only incidentally, to capture the airfields. "Maori" and Tedder were old friends. They had spent those crucial years in the Middle East together. So "Maori" had Tedder's ear—they were both good airmen. All this, as I reckon, had its effect on Tedder and thereby provided Morgan at SHAEF with an ally who had an advantage which he himself lacked—experience of war, though not of war on land.

By the middle of July there developed a growing impatience on the part of the Press; it appeared to them that stagnation gripped our lodgement area. Bradley's first attempt at the break-out, made towards Coutances early in July, had failed. Then came Operation GOODWOOD in the Caen section and the Press regarded this as an attempt to break out on the eastern flank; and, as such, that operation, too, appeared to have failed. This was partly my own fault, for I was too exultant at the Press conference I gave during the GOODWOOD battle. I realise that now—in fact, I realised it pretty quickly afterwards. Basically the trouble was this—both Bradley and I agreed that we could not possibly tell the Press the true strategy which formed the basis of all our plans. As Bradley said, " we must grin and bear it." It became increasingly difficult to grin.

By the 18th July Operation COBRA, the final break-out on the American front, was planned and I had approved the scheme.

I should mention at this stage that the weather was generally very much against us. Between the 19th and 22nd June we had a gale of unprecedented violence. Just when we needed fresh divisions to proceed with our plans and retain the initiative, those divisions were in ships anchored off the beaches and unable to land. On the 20th June we had four divisions in that situation, two American and two British. The First American Army suffered particularly badly; the American artificial harbour (the "Mulberry") off OMAHA beach had to be abandoned, American ammunition expenditure had to be rationed, and Bradley became a week behind schedule in his planned build-up.

While our operations were developing according to plan, I kept in close touch with our casualty figures. These were as follows:

22nd June

	Killed	Wounded	Total
British . . .	2,006	8,776	10,782
American . .	3,012	15,362	18,374
			29,156

10th July

	Killed	Wounded	Total
British . . .	3,894	18,314	22,208
American . .	6,898	32,443	39,341
			61,549

19th July

	Killed	Wounded	Total
British . . .	6,010	28,690	34,700
American . .	10,641	51,387	62,028
			96,728

In addition, by the 19th July we had evacuated 11,000 sick from the British sector.

Meanwhile the First American Army was working itself into a position from which it could stage the break-out operation. We had hoped originally to launch the operation from the line St. Lô-Coutances. This concept had to be given up and Bradley finally decided to launch it from the general line of the road St. Lô-Périers. Our hope was to reach this line by D+5 (11th June); it was not finally reached till the 18th July.

All this time the British forces were steadily playing their part on the eastern flank. By hard and continuous fighting they had kept the main enemy strength occupied in the Caen sector. The greater the delay on the American front, the more I ordered the British forces to intensify their operations; and there was never any complaint from Dempsey. The following table serves to show how well the British Second Army performed its task.

		Enemy strength opposite First U.S. Army			Enemy strength opposite Second British Army		
		Panzer Divisions	Tanks	Infantry Battalions	Panzer Divisions	Tanks	Infantry Battalions
15th June	..	—	70	63	4	520	43
20th June	..	1	210	77	4	430	43
25th June	..	1	190	87	5	530	49
30th June	..	$\frac{1}{2}$	140	63	$7\frac{1}{2}$	725	64
5th July	..	$\frac{1}{2}$	215	63	$7\frac{1}{2}$	690	64
10th July	..	2	190	72	6	610	65
15th July	..	2	190	78	6	630	68
20th July	..	3	190	82	5	560	71
25th July	..	2	190	85	6	645	92

The enemy had attempted to " rope us off " in the " bocage " country some 15 to 20 miles inland from the assault area. For a time this policy was successful; but it was only successful by a continuous expenditure of reserves to plug holes in his defences and at a heavy cost in men and materials. These enemy reserves prevented any substantial gain on our part east and south of Caen, but in doing this they were not available to counter the thrusts on the western flank. In short, they were being committed. As at Alamein, we had forced the enemy to commit his reserves on a wide front; we were now ready to commit ours on a narrow front, and so win the battle.

Operation COBRA was due to be launched on the 20th July; this was the day on which I had ordered Operation GOODWOOD on the eastern flank about Caen to be closed down. But again the weather delayed us and COBRA was not actually launched till the 25th July.

It was clear to me that as the American attack gathered momentum there would be severe repercussions all along the enemy front. The enemy line would be bent back and he would try and re-establish a front based on certain strong hinges. I decided those hinges would be three in number:

1. At Caumont.
2. On the River Orne.
3. The high ground between Caen and Falaise.

I therefore planned to knock out in succession the key rivets in the north on which, I reckoned, the enemy would try to "hinge back" his left flank. I gave orders accordingly, and the Second Army began at once to re-group and to transfer its weight from its extreme left south-east of Caen to its extreme right at Caumont. This movement was a major undertaking and Second Army organised it beautifully.

The attack at Caumont (Operation BLUECOAT) was to be delivered by six divisions on the 2nd August. But because of the unexpected speed of the American advance, with Dempsey's agreement I advanced the date to the 30th July.

Thus, on the 25th July, the day on which the American break-out began, we were on the threshold of great events. We were now to reap where we had sown; the strategy of the Battle of Normandy was about to achieve decisive success. And then, without warning, a cloud descended on our affairs.

On the 26th July, Eisenhower had lunch in London with the Prime Minister. Exactly what was said at that lunch party I don't know. But Eisenhower wrote to me that evening and one sentence in his letter caused me misgivings, knowing the feeling that existed against me among his staff at Supreme Headquarters. That sentence read:

"He [the P.M.] repeated over and over again that he knew you understood the necessity for 'keeping the front aflame,' while major attacks were in progress."

It seemed to me that Eisenhower had complained to the Prime Minister that I did not understand what I was doing. Actually, as I heard later, he had told the Prime Minister he was worried at the outlook taken by the American Press that the British were not taking their share of the fighting and of the casualties. He gave the Prime Minister to understand that in his view the British forces on the eastern flank could and should be more offensive; they were not fighting as they should, and he quoted the casualty figures to prove

260

his case. This sparked off quite a lot of trouble. The next night, the 27th July, the Prime Minister summoned a few responsible persons to meet Eisenhower at dinner. I very soon heard what had taken place.

Eisenhower complained that Dempsey was leaving all the fighting to the Americans. His attention was drawn to my basic strategy, i.e. to fight hard on my left and draw Germans on to that flank whilst I pushed with my right. It was pointed out that he had approved this strategy and that it was being carried out; the bulk of the German armour had continuously been kept on the British front. Eisenhower could not refute these arguments. He then asked why it was we could not launch major offensives on each army front simultaneously—as the Russians did. It was pointed out to him that the German density in Normandy was about 2½ times that of the Russian front, and our superiority in strength was only in the nature of some 25 per cent as compared to the 300 per cent Russian superiority on the eastern front. We clearly were not in a position to launch an all-out offensive along the whole front; such a procedure would be exactly what the Germans would like and would not be in accord with our agreed strategy. We had already (on the 25th July) launched the break-out operation on the right flank. It was an all-out offensive; it was gathering momentum rapidly. The British Second Army was fighting to keep the Germans occupied on the left flank. Our strategy was at last about to reap its full reward. What was the trouble?

It was then pointed out to Eisenhower that if he had any feelings that I was not running the battle as he wished, he should most certainly tell me so in no uncertain voice; it was for him to order what he wanted, and to put all his cards on the table and tell me exactly what he thought. Eisenhower clearly was shy of doing this. He was then asked if he would like the C.I.G.S. to help. Would Eisenhower like the C.I.G.S. to tell me what he had said? Would Eisenhower like the C.I.G.S. to accompany him on a visit to me? Eisenhower didn't take to any of these suggestions.

In a few days' time we were to gain a victory which was to be acclaimed as the greatest achievement in military history. The British had had the unspectacular role in the battle, and in the end it would be made to appear in the American Press as an American victory. All that was accepted. But we all knew that if it had not been for the part played by the British Second Army on the eastern flank, the Americans could never have broken out on the western flank. The strategy of the Normandy campaign was British, and it succeeded because of first class team-work on the part of all the forces engaged —British and American. But just when final victory was in sight, whispers went round the British forces that the Supreme Commander had complained that we were not doing our fair share of the fighting. I do not think that great and good man, now one of my greatest friends, had any idea of the trouble he was starting. From that time onwards there were always " feelings " between the British and American forces till the war ended. Patton's remarks from time to time did not help. When stopped by Bradley at Argentan he said: " Let me go on to Falaise and we'll drive the British back into the sea for another Dunkirk."

It was always very clear to me that Ike and I were poles apart when it came to the conduct of war. My military doctrine was based on unbalancing the enemy while keeping well-balanced myself. I planned always to make the enemy commit his reserves on a wide front in order to plug holes in his defences; having forced him to do this, I then committed my own reserves on a narrow front in a hard blow. Once I had used my reserves, I always sought to create fresh reserves quickly. I gained the impression that the senior officers at Supreme Headquarters did not understand the doctrine of " balance " in the conduct of operations. I had learnt it in battle fighting since 1940, and I knew from that experience how it helped to save men's lives.

Eisenhower's creed appeared to me to be that there must be aggressive action on the part of everyone at all times. Everybody must attack all the time. I remember Bedell Smith once likened Eisenhower to a football coach; he was up and down the line all the time, encouraging everyone to get on with the game. This philosophy was expensive in life, as is brought out by the figures I have given earlier in this chapter. On the 11th August, when the Battle of Normandy was nearing its end, the total casualties were:

British and Canadian	68,000
American	102,000
	170,000

We then had thirty-seven divisions in France, as follows:

12 (U.S.) Army Group   .. 21
21 Army Group   16

These differences in military outlook were of course used by my critics at Supreme Headquarters to make trouble, and I always thought it was they who persuaded Eisenhower to complain to the Prime Minister on the 26th July that the Second Army wasn't fighting as it should. Such action was the greatest disservice that could ever have been done to the Allied cause. And the real pity was that there was no need for it—victory was in our grasp, and was achieved in full measure a few days later. The trouble which began in this way in Normandy was to grow and develop into storms which at times threatened to wreck the Allied ship.

The Battle of Normandy can be said to have ended on the 19th August as it was on this day that we finally cleaned up the remnants of the enemy trapped in the " pocket " east of Mortain. The final victory was definite, complete, and decisive. The following table shows the enemy losses in the battle.

Enemy Losses: Battle of Normandy

6th June to 19th August 1944

Army Commanders
Corps Commanders } Killed or captured   20
Divisional Commanders

Army Commanders wounded
(Rommel; Hausser)   2

Supreme Commanders dismissed
(von Rundstedt; von Kluge)   2

Divisions eliminated or savagely mauled   ..   ..   About 40

Total enemy losses: Difficult to estimate accurately. Probably about 300,000 but some German authorities would put the total at under 200,000

Guns captured and destroyed ..   ..   Over 3,000

Tanks destroyed ..   ..   Over 1,000

I do not want to end this chapter on a bitter note. I have been accused of many things in Normandy. Perhaps the most amazing was when I was confronted officially by one of my own staff officers at my Tac Headquarters and accused of not only condoning looting but being concerned in it. Here is the story of how it happened.

At the end of July the Foreign Office wrote to the C.I.G.S. saying it had come to its attention from certain private sources that there had been some rather bad cases of looting by British troops in Normandy. The F.O. asked that the matter be investigated and put right, since the French were complaining about it. I took the matter up at once with M. Coulet, General de Gaulle's representative in the lodgement area, and was informed by him that he had received no complaint and that I could rest assured that the allegations were without foundation. But there is seldom any smoke without a fire and it was clear to me that the rumours were being spread in London by a colonel that I had removed from my Tac Headquarters. Early in July one of my A.D.C.s had rounded up and shot with his revolver a pig belonging to a local farmer which was careering round my camp and could not be caught. The colonel dealt with the matter, the farmer was paid for the pig, and it was eaten by the soldiers.

Later, certain other officers in my team of liaison officers were accused by the colonel of collecting livestock in their journeys round the forward areas; the peasants had left their farms, and rabbits, chickens, etc., were running wild all over the place.

The colonel came to see me about it. I knew nothing of the incidents and asked for details. It was a very worrying moment in the battle and I finally told the colonel he must see the Chief of Staff about it. He then became somewhat argumentative and hinted that I myself obviously condoned this action on the part of my personal staff, and was even quite prepared to take part in it myself. That was too much. I telephoned my Chief of Staff, and said the colonel must be removed from my Tactical Headquarters at once. This was done. On his arrival in London later in July the stories began to circulate and the colonel made a written report to the War Office.

I read the War Office file on the subject when I was C.I.G.S. after the war. It must have been the first time in the history of war that a Commander-in-Chief in the field was accused of looting by one of his own staff officers. But no doubt it kept the War Office busy.

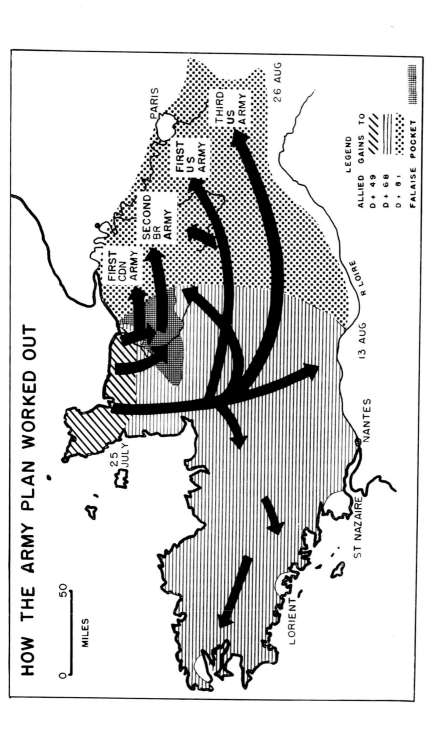

HOW THE ARMY PLAN WORKED OUT

MILES
0   50

FIRST CDN ARMY

SECOND BR ARMY

FIRST US ARMY

THIRD US ARMY

PARIS

25 JULY

LORIENT

ST NAZAIRE

NANTES

R LOIRE

13 AUG

26 AUG

LEGEND

ALLIED GAINS TO

D + 49

D + 68

D + 81

FALAISE POCKET

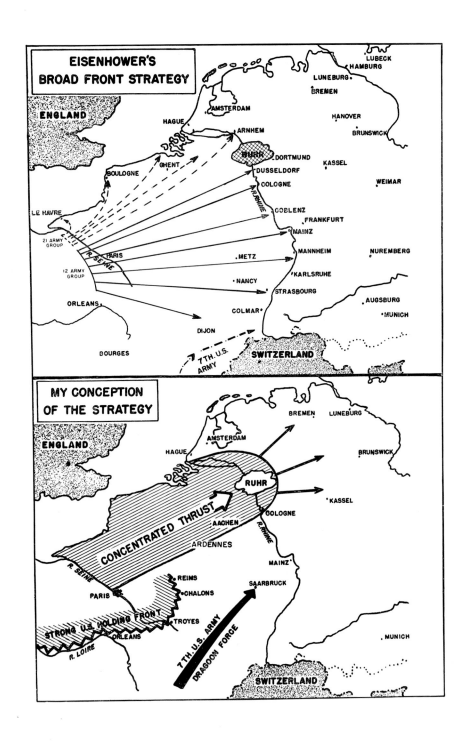

CHAPTER 15

ALLIED STRATEGY NORTH OF
THE SEINE

THE GERMAN situation in France in the middle of August 1944 was desperate.

Paris fell on the 25th August and the next day the Intelligence Summary issued by Supreme Headquarters contained the following sentence:

" Two and a half months of bitter fighting, culminating for the Germans in a blood-bath big enough even for their extravagant tastes, have brought the end of the war in Europe within sight, almost within reach. The strength of the German Armies in the West has been shattered, Paris belongs to France again, and the Allied armies are streaming towards the frontiers of the Reich."

An operational instruction issued by Supreme Headquarters shortly afterwards began with these words:

" Enemy resistance on the entire front shows signs of collapse. The bulk of the remaining enemy forces, estimated as the equivalent of two weak panzer and nine infantry divisions, are north-west of the Ardennes but they are disorganised, in full retreat, and unlikely to offer any appreciable resistance if given no respite. South of the Ardennes the enemy forces are estimated as the equivalent of two panzer grenadier and four poor infantry divisions. A heterogeneous force withdrawing from south-west France may number some one hundred thousand men but its fighting value is estimated as the equivalent of about one division. The equivalent of one-half panzer and two infantry divisions are being driven northwards up the Rhone valley. The only way the enemy can prevent our advance into Germany will be by reinforcing his retreating forces by divisions from Germany and other fronts and manning the more important sectors of the Siegfried Line with these forces. It is doubtful whether he can do this in time and in sufficient strength."

That was the picture. It was my view that the end of the war in Europe was most certainly " within reach." But what was now needed were quick decisions, and above all a plan. And so far as I was aware we had no plan. During the Battle of Normandy we had drawn in nearly every division the Germans had in France; we had enticed our enemy to battle south of the Seine, and there defeated him decisively. The battle decides all; but it must be followed up.

I had a plan ready and, before the final operations of the Normandy fighting were completed, I decided to visit Bradley and try to get his agreement. On the 17th August my Tac Headquarters was at Le Bény Bocage and I flew on that day to see Bradley, who had his headquarters north of Fougères. I put to him the following outline plan:

" 1. After crossing the Seine, 12 and 21 Army Groups should keep together as a solid mass of some forty divisions which would be so strong that it need fear nothing. This force would move north-eastwards.

2. 21 Army Group, on the western flank, to clear the channel coast, the Pas de Calais, West Flanders, and secure Antwerp and South Holland.

3. 12 Army Group to form the eastern flank of the movement and to move with its right flank on the Ardennes—being directed on Aachen and Cologne.

4. The whole movement would pivot on Paris. A strong American force to be positioned in the general area Orleans-Troyes-Châlons-Reims-Laon, with its right flank thrown back along the R. Loire to Nantes.

5. The DRAGOON force coming up from southern France to be directed on Nancy and the Saar. We ourselves must not reach out with our right to join it and thus unbalance our strategy.

6. The basic object of the movement would be to establish a powerful air force in Belgium, to secure bridgeheads over the Rhine before the winter began, and to seize the Ruhr quickly."

In its simplest terms this was the German " Schlieffen Plan " of

1914 in reverse, except that it would be executed against a shattered and disorganised enemy. Its success depended on the concentration of Allied strength, and therefore of maintenance resources, on the left wing. At the same time, Bradley agreed entirely with this outline plan.

On the 20th August Eisenhower held a staff meeting at his Advanced H.Q. in Normandy to collect ideas for the future conduct of the war. My Chief of Staff attended. Certain decisions were reached. Briefly these were:

(a) To change the system of command on the 1st September, Eisenhower taking personal command himself of the Army Groups.

(b) 12 Army Group to be directed towards Metz and the Saar, where it would link up with the Dragoon force.

The staff then began work on a directive to be sent to me. De Guingand suggested it might be as well to consult me before any action was taken; this was agreed, and he came to my Tac Head-quarters that night.

As I did not agree with the decisions which had been reached, I sent de Guingand back to see Eisenhower and gave him some notes on the problem to take with him. He spent two hours with Eisenhower on the 22nd August trying to persuade him on certain points of principle. Eisenhower was given the notes I had written and was told that on the 17th August Bradley had expressed his complete agreement with my suggested plan. These were my notes:

" 1. The quickest way to win this war is for the great mass of the Allied armies to advance northwards, clear the coast as far as Antwerp, establish a powerful air force in Belgium, and advance into the Ruhr.

2. The force must operate as one whole, with great cohesion, and be so strong that it can do the job quickly.

3. Single control and direction of the land operations is vital for success. This is a WHOLE TIME job for one man.

4. The great victory in N.W. France has been won by personal command. Only in this way will future victories be won. If staff control of operations is allowed to creep in, then quick success becomes endangered.

5. To change the system of command now, after having won a great victory, would be to prolong the war."

De Guingand reported to me the result of his talk with Eisenhower, which was negative, and I decided that I must see him myself. So I asked him if he would come to lunch with me at my Tac Head-quarters the next day, the 23rd August, at Condé-sur-Noireau. He accepted gladly.

I was anxious to have a further talk with Bradley before seeing Eisenhower. He had moved his headquarters to Laval and I flew there on the morning of the 23rd August, early. I found to my amazement that Bradley had changed his mind; on the 17th August he had agreed with me, on the 23rd he was a whole-hearted advocate of the main effort of his Army Group being directed eastwards on Metz and the Saar. I returned to my headquarters in time to meet Eisenhower, who had brought Bedell Smith with him; this was the first time I had seen Bedell since I left England on the night of the 6th June.

I asked Eisenhower if I could see him alone as I wanted his decision on certain vital matters of principle; these we must discuss alone, and his Chief of Staff could come in later. He agreed, and we talked alone for one hour. I gave him my views about the immediate need for a firm and sound plan. I said that he must decide where the main effort would be made and we must then be so strong in that area that we could be certain of decisive results quickly. I outlined the administrative situation and said we would soon be very stretched; we must concentrate our petrol and ammunition resources behind his selected thrust line, and if we spread them evenly all along the front we should fail to achieve a decision. I then described to him my own suggested plan, which had originally been agreed by Bradley. I sketched in the details on a map and showed that it offered good prospects of success.

I said that if he adopted a broad front strategy, with the whole line advancing and everyone fighting all the time, the advance would inevitably peter out, the Germans would be given time to recover, and the war would go on all through the winter and well into 1945.

I also said that he, as Supreme Commander, should not descend into the land battle and become a ground C.-in-C. The Supreme Commander must sit on a very lofty perch in order to be able to take a detached view of the whole intricate problem—which involves land, sea, air, civil control, political problems, etc. Someone must run the land battle for him. We had won a great victory in Normandy *because* of unified land control and not *in spite of it*. I said this point was so important that, if public opinion in America was involved, he should let Bradley control the battle and I would gladly serve under him; this suggestion produced an immediate denial of his intention to do anything of the sort.

After further talk, Eisenhower agreed that 21 Army Group was not strong enough to carry out the tasks on the northern thrust, alone and unaided. He agreed that whatever American assistance was necessary must be provided. He agreed that the task of co-ordination and general operational direction on the northern thrust must be exercised by one commander: me.

I said I wanted an American army of at least twelve divisions to advance on the right flank of 21 Army Group. He said that if this were done then 12 Army Group would have only one Army in it, and public opinion in the States would object.

I asked him why public opinion should make us want to take military decisions which were definitely unsound. Possibly I went a bit far in urging on him my own plan, and did not give sufficient weight to the heavy political burden he bore. To adopt my plan he must stop the man with the ball: Patton, and his Third American Army. Looking back on it all I often wonder if I paid sufficient heed to Eisenhower's notions before refuting them. I think I did. Anyhow he listened quietly. Ike is now one of my dearest friends and I never cease to marvel at his patience and forbearance with me on that occasion.

But my arguments were of no avail. The " broad front " strategy was to be adopted and 12 Army Group, while thrusting forward on its left to support 21 Army Group, was to direct its main effort eastwards towards Metz and the Saar. I was to have authority to effect " operational co-ordination " between 21 Army Group and the left wing of 12 Army Group; the term " operational direction " was cut out of the directive. But a later directive issued by Eisenhower when he had assumed direct command of the land armies on the 1st September, laid down that 12 Army Group was to ensure that its troops operating against the Ruhr on my right were " adequately supported " logistically.

And so we all got ready to cross the Seine and go our different ways.

Optimism was in the air, the whips were got out, and the Supreme Commander urged everyone on all along the front. Everyone was to be fighting all the time. But the trouble was we had no fundamental plan which treated the theatre as an entity. Our strategy was now to become " unstitched." I was determined to play my full part in the business; the British forces would show, and did show, that when it came to the mobile battle they were just as good as the next man. But I had great misgivings. All my military training told me we could not get away with it, and then we would be faced with a long winter campaign with all that that entailed for the British people.

In the middle of all these troubles and disappointments I received the following message from the Prime Minister on the evening of the 31st August:

" It gives me great pleasure to tell you that on my submission His Majesty has been graciously pleased to approve your promotion to the rank of Field-Marshal with the date of September 1st, thus recognising your outstanding service in the memorable and possibly decisive battle which you have personally conducted in France."

Later Sir Alan Lascelles, who was then Private Secretary to the King, told me the following story of the circumstances in which the submission appointing me a Field-Marshal was signed. Towards the end of August the Prime Minister had returned from Italy and was ordered to bed by his doctor, since he had a temperature of 103. On the morning of the 31st August the King, accompanied by Sir Alan Lascelles, drove to the annexe in Storey's Gate where the P.M. was lying up and found him in good spirits, robed in a sumptuous pale blue dressing-gown of Oriental design. The P.M. had the submission ready and he asked the King to sign it then and there—which he did, using the pillow as a table. It would be interesting to know if a British general has ever before been promoted to Field-Marshal in the middle of a battle, that appointment being signed by his Sovereign on the Prime Minister's pillow.

This was the second time during the war that I had been promoted on the battlefield. It was announced publicly on the B.B.C. news bulletin the next morning. At once, and characteristically, Eisenhower sent me a telegram of generous and warm-hearted congratulation.

The more I considered what we were setting out to do, the more certain I was that it was wrong. The British economy and man-power situation demanded victory in 1944: no later. Also, the war was bearing hardly on the mass of the people in Britain; it must be brought to a close quickly. Our " must " was different from the American must: a difference in urgency, as well as a difference in doctrine. This the American generals did not understand; the war had never been brought to their home country. Why should we throw everything away for reasons of American public opinion and American electioneering (1944 was the Presidential election year)? The strategy we were now to adopt would mean more casualties in killed and wounded. The armies were not being deployed on a broad front for any reasons of safety; our southern flank was quite secure and could almost be held by air power alone, with a small military backing. If Dragoon had done nothing else, at least it had achieved that. There was no real risk in doing what I suggested. Indeed my plan offered the only possibility of bringing the war to a quick end.

I was beginning to get information from my liaison officer at Bradley's headquarters that the American forces on my right were not getting any priority in maintenance resources. Eisenhower's plan of two thrusts, one to the Ruhr and one to the Saar, meant that everything had to be split—forces, air, maintenance, transport, rolling stock, etc. We were throwing overboard the principle of concentration of effort.

Eisenhower had his headquarters at Granville, on the west side of the Cherbourg peninsula. This was possibly a suitable place for a Supreme Commander; but it was useless for a land force commander who had to keep his finger on the pulse of his armies and give quick decisions in rapidly changing situations. He was over four hundred miles behind the battle front. Furthermore he was laid up with a bad knee. There were no telephone lines, and not even a radio-telephone, between his H.Q. and Bradley and myself. In the early days of September he was, in fact, completely out of touch with the land battle, as far as I could see.

I decided to make one more approach to Eisenhower, in my efforts to get a sound plan adopted. I sent him the following message on the 4th September, the day we captured Antwerp and Louvain:

" I would like to put before you certain aspects of future operations and give you my views.

1. I consider we have now reached a stage where one really power-

ful and full-blooded thrust towards Berlin is likely to get there and thus end the German war.

2. We have not enough maintenance resources for two full-blooded thrusts.

3. The selected thrust must have all the maintenance resources it needs without any qualification and any other operation must do the best it can with what is left over.

4. There are only two possible thrusts: one via the Ruhr and the other via Metz and the Saar.

5. In my opinion the thrust likely to give the best and quickest results is the northern one via the Ruhr.

6. Time is vital and the decision regarding the selected thrust must be made at once and para. 3 above will then apply.

7. If we attempt a compromise solution and split our maintenance resources so that neither thrust is full-blooded we will prolong the war.

8. I consider the problem viewed as above is very simple and clear cut.

9. The matter is of such vital importance that I feel sure you will agree that a decision on the above lines is required at once. If you are coming this way perhaps you would look in and discuss it. If so delighted to see you lunch tomorrow. Do not feel I can leave this battle just at present."

In point of fact, it was now almost too late. The Saar thrust had begun and Patton had been given the necessary resources for his drive on Metz. On my right, the First American Army found itself having to cover Patton's advance and was unable also properly to support my operations as had been ordered. But there was still time to save something from the wreck, if only we could get a decision *at once*.

Eisenhower received my message on the 5th September. At 7.45 p.m. that day he sent me his reply. The signal communications at his Forward H.Q. at Granville were so inadequate that his reply reached me in two parts. Paras. 3 and 4 came first and arrived at 9 a.m. on the 7th September; paras. 1 and 2 reached me at 10.15 a.m. on the morning of the 9th September. Here is his message in full, as it was eventually pieced together.

" *Part* 1 (*Received* 1015 *hrs* 9 *September* 1944)

1. While agreeing with your conception of a powerful and full-

blooded thrust towards Berlin I do not agree that it should be initiated at this moment to the exclusion of all other manœuvres.

2. The bulk of the German Army that was in the West has now been destroyed. Must immediately exploit our success by promptly breaching the Siegfried Line, crossing the Rhine on a wide front, and seizing the Saar and the Ruhr. This I intend to do with all possible speed. This will give us a stranglehold on two of Germany's main industrial areas and largely destroy her capacity to wage war whatever course events may take. It will assist in cutting off forces now retiring from south-west France. Moreover it will give us freedom of action to strike in any direction and will force the enemy to disperse over a wide area such forces as he may be able to assemble for the defence of the West.

Part 2 (Received 0900 hrs 7 September 1944)

3. While we are advancing we will be opening the ports of Havre and Antwerp, which are essential to sustain a powerful thrust deep into Germany. No reallocation of our present resources would be adequate to sustain a thrust to Berlin.

4. Accordingly my intention is initially to occupy the Saar and the Ruhr, and by the time we have done this, Havre and Antwerp should be available to maintain one or both of the thrusts you mention. In this connection I have always given and still give priority to the Ruhr RPT Ruhr, and the northern route of advance, as indicated in my directive of yesterday which crossed your telegram. Locomotives and rolling stock are today being allocated on the basis of this priority to maintain the momentum of the advance of your forces, and those of Bradley north-west of the Ardennes. Please let me know at once your further maintenance requirements for the advance."

On the 7th September I had only received Part 2 of the reply, but it was enough to make me realise that we were unlikely to get the decision needed. I therefore sent him the following.

"Have just received paras. 3 and 4 of your message of 5 September. First part of message has not arrived yet so do not know what it contains. My maintenance is stretched to the limit.

First instalment of 18 locomotives only just released to me and balance still seems uncertain. I require an air lift of 1000 tons a day at Douai or Brussels and in last two days have had only 750 tons total. My transport is based on operating 150 miles from my ports and at present I am over 300 miles from Bayeux. In order to save transport I have cut down my intake into France to 6000 tons a day which is half what I consume and I cannot go on for long like this. It is clear therefore that based as I am at present on Bayeux I cannot capture the Ruhr. As soon as I have a Pas de Calais port working I would then require about 2500 additional 3-ton lorries plus an assured air lift averaging minimum 1000 tons a day to enable me to get to the Ruhr and finally Berlin. I submit with all respect to your para. 3 that a reallocation of our present resources of every description would be adequate to get one thrust to Berlin. It is very difficult to explain things in a message like this. Would it be possible for you to come and see me?"

Meanwhile I had been consulting with Bradley about the parlous state of our logistics and we had agreed that we must cancel all our plans for airborne drops to help the advance, and put all available aircraft on to transport work. This was no great sacrifice because the speed of our advance since crossing the Seine had been so great that we did not need parachute troops to help. Ever since the Battle of Normandy had been won my eyes had been fixed on the Rhine and the Ruhr; I knew that we should require all our airborne resources to ensure we got over the Meuse and the Rhine. I had been allotted the First Allied Airborne Corps and on the 3rd September, the day we liberated Brussels, I had asked its commander (General Browning) to come and see me, so that we might discuss the general axis of the thrust towards the Rhine and the best areas in which to drop the airborne divisions.

On the 9th September I received information from London that on the previous day the first V2 rockets had landed in England; it was suspected that they came from areas near Rotterdam and Amsterdam and I was asked when I could rope off those general areas. So far as I was concerned that settled the direction of the thrust line of my operations to secure crossings over the Meuse and Rhine; it must be towards Arnhem. Dempsey and Browning came to see me again on the morning of the 10th September to discuss the Arnhem operation; but I knew that the maintenance situation would be the limiting factor in deciding when it could be launched.

In response to the request in my signal three days before, Eisenhower flew to Brussels on the afternoon of the 10th September. Tedder was with him and we had a good talk in Eisenhower's aircraft; he could not get out since he was still very lame.

I explained my situation fully. I told him about the V2 rockets which had started to land in England, and from whence they came. He said he had always intended to give priority to the Ruhr thrust and the northern route of advance, and that this was being done. I said that it was *not* being done. He then said that by priority he did not mean " absolute priority," and he could not in any way scale down the Saar thrust. I told him that enemy resistance was stiffening on the line of the Albert Canal; that there was a steady consumption of petrol and ammunition; and that we were outstripping our maintenance. It was becoming clear that I would not be able to launch the large-scale operation towards Arnhem as soon as I had hoped and that this would give the enemy more time to recover. Since crossing the Seine my headquarters had moved northwards, and Bradley's eastwards. The land battle was becoming jerky and disjointed. I said that so long as he continued with two thrusts, with the maintenance split between the two, neither could succeed. I pointed out that Antwerp, and the approaches to the port which we had not yet got, lay behind the thrust on the left flank which I had advocated on the 23rd August—nearly three weeks ago. There were two possible plans—Bradley's and mine. It was essential " to back " one of them. If he tried to back both, we couldn't possibly gain any decisive results quickly. The quickest way to open up Antwerp was to back my plan of concentration on the left —which plan would not only help our logistic and maintenance situation but would also keep up the pressure on the stricken Germans in the area of greatest importance, thus helping to end the war quickly. It was essential for him to know my views; the decision about the action to be taken was then his. It was obvious that he disagreed with my analysis. He repeated that we must first close to the Rhine and cross it on a wide front; then, and only then, could we concentrate on one thrust. We parted without any clear decision, except that, as I understood it, the " broad front " strategy was to remain in operation. But Eisenhower agreed that 21 Army Group should strike northwards towards Arnhem as early as possible, and he admitted that successful operations in that direction would open up wide possibilities for future action.

The next day, the 11th September, I sent Eisenhower the following signal:

" I have investigated my maintenance situation very carefully since our meeting yesterday. Your decision that the northern thrust towards the Ruhr is NOT repeat NOT to have priority over other operations will have certain repercussions which you should know. The large-scale operations by Second Army and the Airborne Corps northwards towards the Meuse and Rhine cannot now take place before 23 Sep. at the earliest and possibly 26 Sep. This delay will give the enemy time to organise better defensive arrangements and we must expect heavier resistance and slower progress. As the winter draws on the weather may be expected to deteriorate and we then get less results from our great weight of air power. It is basically a matter of rail and road and air transport and unless this is concentrated to give impetus to the selected thrust then no one is going to get very far since we are all such a long way from our supply bases. We will do all that is possible to get on with the business but the above facts will show you that if enemy resistance continues to stiffen as at present then no great results can be expected until we have built up stocks of ammunition and other requirements."

This message produced results which were almost electric. Bedell Smith came to see me next day to say that Eisenhower had decided to act as I recommended. The Saar thrust was to be stopped. Three American divisions were to be grounded and their transport used to supply extra maintenance to 21 Army Group. The bulk of the logistic support of 12 Army Group was to be given to the First American Army on my right and I was to be allowed to deal direct with General Hodges (the G.O.C. First American Army).

As a result of these promises I reviewed my plans with Dempsey and then fixed D-Day for the Arnhem operation (MARKET GARDEN) for Sunday 17th September.

I did not know until later (and perhaps it was as well that I didn't) that when General Patton heard of these decisions he decided, with Bradley's agreement, to get the Third American Army so involved beyond the Moselle that Supreme Headquarters would be able neither to reduce its maintenance nor to halt it.

On the 15th September, Eisenhower wrote me as follows:

" Dear Montgomery,

We shall soon, I hope, have achieved the objectives set forth in my last directive (FWD 13765) and shall then be in possession of the Ruhr, the Saar and the Frankfurt area. I have been considering our next move.

As I see it, the Germans will have stood in defence of the Ruhr and Frankfurt and will have had a sharp defeat inflicted on them. Their dwindling forces, reinforced perhaps by material hastily scratched together or dragged from other theatres, will probably try to check our advance on the remaining important objectives in Germany. By attacking such objectives we shall create opportunities of dealing effectively with the last remnants of the German forces in the West. Moreover, we shall be occupying further key centres and increasing our stranglehold on the German peoples.

Clearly, Berlin is the main prize, and the prize in defence of which the enemy is likely to concentrate the bulk of his forces. There is no doubt whatsoever, in my mind, that we should concentrate all our energies and resources on a rapid thrust to Berlin.

Our strategy, however, will have to be co-ordinated with that of the Russians, so we must also consider alternative objectives.

There is the area of the Northern ports, Kiel-Lubeck-Hamburg-Bremen. Its occupation would not only give us control of the German Navy and North Sea bases, of the Kiel Canal, and of a large industrial area, but would enable us to form a barrier against the withdrawal of German forces from Norway and Denmark. Further, this area, or a part of it, might have to be occupied as flank protection to our thrust on Berlin.

There are the areas Hanover-Brunswick and Leipzig-Dresden. They are important industrial and administrative areas and centres of communications on the direct routes from the Ruhr and Frankfurt to Berlin, so the Germans will probably hold them as intermediate positions covering Berlin.

There are the Nurnberg-Regensburg and the Augsburg-Munich areas. Apart from their economical and administrative importance, there is the transcending political importance of

Munich. Moreover, there may be an impelling demand to occupy these areas and cut off enemy forces withdrawing from Italy and the Balkans.

Clearly, therefore, our objectives cannot be precisely determined until nearer the time, so we must be prepared for one or more of the following:

(a) To direct forces of both Army Groups on Berlin astride the axes Ruhr-Hanover-Berlin *or* Frankfurt-Leipzig-Berlin, or both.

(b) Should the Russians beat us to Berlin, the Northern Group of Armies would seize the Hanover area and the Hamburg group of ports. The Central Group of Armies would seize part, or the whole, of Leipzig-Dresden, depending upon the progress of the Russian advance.

(c) In any event, the Southern Group of Armies would seize Augsburg-Munich. The area Nurnberg-Regensburg would be seized by Central or Southern Group of Armies, depending on the situation at the time.

Simply stated, it is my desire to move on Berliu by the most direct and expeditious route, with combined U.S.-British forces supported by other available forces moving through key centres and occupying strategic areas on the flanks, all in one co-ordinated, concerted operation.

It is not possible at this stage to indicate the timing of these thrusts or their strengths, but I shall be glad to have your views on the general questions raised in this letter.

Sincerely,

(Sgd) Dwight D. Eisenhower"

I considered this letter very carefully and sent him the following reply on the 18th September:

" My dear Ike,

I have received your letter dated 15-9-44, and I give below my general views on the questions you raise—as asked for by you.

1. I suggest that the whole matter as to what is possible, and wha is NOT possible, is very closely linked up with the administrative situation. The vital factor is time; what we have to do, we must do quickly.

2. In view of para. 1, it is my opinion that a concerted operation in which all the available land armies move forward into Germany is not possible; the maintenance resources, and the general administrative situation, will not allow of this being done QUICKLY.

3. But forces adequate in strength for the job in hand could be supplied and maintained, provided the general axis of advance was suitable, and provided these forces had complete priority in all respects as regards maintenance.

4. It is my own personal opinion that we shall not achieve what we want by going for objectives such as Nurnberg, Augsburg, Munich, etc., and by establishing our forces in central Germany.

5. I consider that the best objective is the Ruhr, and thence on to Berlin by the northern route. On that route are the ports, and on that route we can use our sea power to the best advantage. On other routes we would merely contain as many German forces as we could.

6. If you agree with para. 5, then I consider that 21 Army Group, plus First U.S. Army of nine divisions, would be adequate. Such a force must have *everything it needed in the maintenance line*; other Armies would do the best they could with what was left over.

7. If you consider that para. 5 is not right, and that the proper axis of advance is by Frankfurt and central Germany, then I suggest that 12 Army Group of three Armies would be used and would have all the maintenance. 21 Army Group would do the best it could with what was left over; or possibly the Second British Army would be wanted in a secondary role on the left flank of the movement.

8. In brief, I consider that as time is so very important, we have got to decide what is necessary to go to Berlin and finish the war; the remainder must play a secondary role. It is my opinion that three Armies are enough, if you select the northern route, and I consider that, from a maintenance point of view, it could be done. I have not studied the southern route.

9. I consider that our plan, and objectives, should be decided NOW, and everything arranged accordingly. I would not myself agree that we can wait until nearer the time, as suggested in your letter.

10. Finally to sum up.
I recommend the northern route of advance via the Ruhr, vide para. 5.
Para. 6 would then apply.
11. I hope the above is clear.
It represents my views on the general questions raised in your letter.
12. The above is actually in accordance with the general views I expressed to you in my telegram M 160 dated 4 Sep.

Yours ever
(Sgd.) B. L. Montgomery"

Eisenhower replied to this letter on the 20th September, as follows:

" Dear Monty,
Generally speaking I find myself so completely in agreement with your letter of 18 September (M-526) that I cannot believe there is any great difference in our concepts.

Never at any time have I implied that I was considering an advance into Germany with all armies moving abreast.

Specifically I agree with you in the following: My choice of routes for making the all-out offensive into Germany is from the Ruhr to Berlin. A prerequisite from the maintenance viewpoint is the early capture of the approaches to Antwerp so that that flank may be adequately supplied.

Incidentally I do not yet have your calculations in the tonnage that will be necessary to support the 21 Army Group on this move. There is one point, however, on which we do not agree, if I interpret your ideas correctly. As I read your letter you imply that all the divisions that we have, except those of the 21st Army Group and approximately nine of the 12th Army Group, can stop in place *where they are* and that we can strip all these additional divisions from their transport and everything else to support one single knife-like drive towards Berlin. This may not be exactly what you mean but it is certainly not possible.

What I do believe is that we must marshal our strength up along the Western borders of Germany, to the Rhine if possible, insure adequate maintenance by getting Antwerp working at full blast at the earliest possible moment and then carry out the drive you suggest. All of Bradley's Army Group, except his left Army, which makes his main effort, will move forward sufficiently so as always to be in supporting position for the main drive and to prevent concentration of German forces against its front and flanks.

I have already directed the Chief of Staff to arrange for the earliest possible meeting with all Army Group commanders and with supply people. I am quite confident that we see this thing almost identically. I merely want to make sure that when you start leading your Army Group in its thrust on to Berlin and Bradley starts driving with his left to support you, our other forces are in position to assure the success of that drive. Otherwise the main thrust itself would have to drop off so much of its strength to protect its rear and its flanks that very soon the drive would peter out.

As you know I have been giving preference to my left all the way through this campaign including attaching the First Airborne Force to you and adopting every possible expedient to assure your maintenance. All other forces have been fighting with a halter around their necks in the way of supplies. You may not know that for four days straight Patton has been receiving serious counter-attacks and during the last seven days, without attempting any real advance himself, has captured about 9000 prisoners and knocked out 270 tanks.

I saw Bradley today and in furtherance of the general plan for building up the left we are moving the Brest divisions up to take over the defensive region east of Luxembourg so that Hodges can concentrate his full strength on his left in his drive forward towards the Rhine. When we get to the Rhine the next concern of Bradley's will be to put a strong fully equipped Army on his left to accompany you to Berlin.

Sincerely,
(Sgd) Dwight D. Eisenhower"

I replied at once (21st September) to this letter by sending Eisenhower the following signal:

"Dear Ike, thank you very much for your letter of 20 Sep sent via Gale. I cannot agree that our concepts are the same and I am sure you would wish me to be quite frank and open in the matter. I have always said stop the right and go on with left, but the right has been allowed to go on so far that it has outstripped its maintenance and we have lost flexibility. In your letter you still want to go on farther with your right and you state in your para. 6 that all of Bradley's Army Group will move forward sufficiently etc. I would say that the right flank of 12 Army Group should be given a very direct order to halt and if this order is not obeyed we shall get into greater difficulties. The net result of the matter in my opinion is that if you want to get the Ruhr you will have to put every single thing into the left hook and stop everything else. It is my opinion that if this is not done then you will not get the Ruhr. Your very great friend Monty."

Eisenhower then summoned a conference at his headquarters at Versailles for the afternoon of the 22nd September, to decide on a plan for the further conduct of the war. The situation at Arnhem was not good on that day, and farther south the Germans had cut the corridor and established themselves on the main road between Veghel and Grave, south of Nijmegen. I decided that I could not leave the battle front and told de Guingand to represent me at the conference. Moreover, I knew I was not popular at either Supreme Headquarters, or with the American generals, because of my arguments about the conduct of the war; I thought it best to keep away while the matter was being further argued.

That night de Guingand sent me a message from Versailles to the effect that Eisenhower had supported my plan one hundred per cent, and that the northern thrust was to be the main effort and get full support. I received this message early on the 23rd September. By that date the Arnhem situation was really bad; the corridor leading to Nijmegen was again cut and it looked as if we would have to withdraw the remnants of the 1st British Airborne Division back over the Neder Rijn. The division was in fact so withdrawn on the 25th September.

I could not help going back in my mind to my meeting with Eisenhower at my Tac Headquarters at Condé on the 23rd August, when I had asked him to take the decision to support my plan. He had refused. Now at last, on the 23rd September, I was told he had agreed and would support my plan. *He had taken the decision exactly one month too late.* Nothing could now prevent events taking the course which I had predicted a month before.

The maintenance situation all along the front got progressively worse. The First American Army on my right was, by the 6th October, unable to develop its operations according to plan because it had not got the necessary ammunition. On the 7th October I reported from Eindhoven the situation on the northern flank very fully to Eisenhower and said I could not continue the planned operations to gain the line of the Rhine unless the maintenance resources allotted to these operations could be stepped up. I said I had asked Bradley to come and see me the next day, the 8th October, to discuss the situation.

Knowing that Bradley would be with me at Eindhoven on the 8th October, Eisenhower sent us both a message giving his views on the problem that confronted us all. His message began with the following sentence (the italics are mine):

" Basic difficulty on northern flank appears to be lack of strength in view of enemy reinforcement. Consequently, the plan for co-ordinated attack to Rhine must be postponed until strength can be gotten up which must come from U.S. divisions on the beach.

Nevertheless, plans of both Army Groups must retain as first mission the gaining of the line of the Rhine north of Bonn as quickly as humanly possible."

Bradley and I were unable to agree with this statement. It was our definite opinion that we must reduce the tempo of our operations towards the Rhine until we could improve the maintenance situation. I reported to Eisenhower accordingly and said I had stopped the operations of the Second Army towards the Ruhr and was now going to concentrate on opening up the approaches to Antwerp—so as to get that port working fully.

The next day, the 9th October, I received a message from Eisenhower in which he stated (again the italics are mine):

" Unless we have Antwerp producing by the middle of November, entire operations will come to a standstill.

I must emphasise that, of all our operations on our entire front from Switzerland to the channel, I consider Antwerp of first importance."

This was a fundamental change from the message of the day before, in which the first mission of both Army Groups was given as " the gaining of the line of the Rhine north of Bonn as quickly as humanly possible." However, we did now all seem agreed on what was to be done.

General Marshall had come with Bradley to my headquarters on the 8th October and I had a long talk with him, alone in my office caravan. I told him that since Eisenhower had himself taken personal command of the land battle, being also Supreme Commander of all the forces (land, sea, and air), the armies had become separated nationally and not geographically. There was a lack of grip, and operational direction and control was lacking. Our operations had, in fact, become ragged and disjointed, and we had now got ourselves into a real mess. Marshall listened, but said little. It was clear that he entirely disagreed.

Later in the month, when I had settled future plans with Dempsey, I moved into Brussels and joined up with my Main H.Q. At Brussels I was better placed to exercise personal direction of the operations to open up the approaches to Antwerp, which was the task of First Canadian Army under Simonds. Crerar had been evacuated sick to England.

On the 3rd November I informed Eisenhower:

" I have to report to you that the approaches to Antwerp and the Scheldt estuary are now completely free from enemy interference. Our troops on Walcheren are now in possession of the coast from Domburg to West Kapelle and round to the east of Flushing the whole of which town is in our hands and we have captured all enemy coastal positions and guns. Our minesweepers are now at work in the estuary and some have reached Terneuzen. We own the whole of North Beveland and South Beveland. There are still some enemy remaining on the northern and north-eastern parts of Walcheren Island but these cannot interfere with shipping in the estuary and they are being mopped up. All enemy resistance on the mainland south of Walcheren and in the Knocke area has now ceased and we have captured 14,000 prisoners in this area since crossing the Leopold Canal. The full and free use of the port of Antwerp is now entirely a naval matter."

The reply came:

" Dear Monty: The capture of the Antwerp approaches will have the utmost significance for us and I am profoundly grateful to you personally for the energy you put into this matter. Will you please convey to the Commanding General of the Canadians my thanks and congratulations. (Signed) Ike."

The proper development of allied strategy north of the Seine will become one of the great controversies of military history. In the end it was the Germans who benefited from the argument. At the time, I was, and I remain, of the opinion that in September 1944 we failed to exploit fully the German disorganisation consequent on their crushing defeat in the Battle of Normandy in August. The quickest way to end the German war was not merely to have the free use of Antwerp, as some have alleged. It was to act quickly in the middle of August, using the success gained in Normandy as a spring-board for a hard blow which would finish off the Germans and at the same time give us the ports we needed on the northern flank. To do these things we had to have a plan and concentration of effort; we had neither. I am still firmly convinced that had we adopted a proper operational plan in the middle of August, and given it a sound administrative and logistic backing, we should have secured bridgeheads over the Rhine and seized the Ruhr before the winter set in. The whole affair if properly handled would not only have shortened the war; it would also have held out possibilities of bringing it to an end in Europe with a political balance very much more favourable to an early and stable peace than that which has actually emerged.

Some have argued that I ignored Eisenhower's orders to give priority to opening up the port of Antwerp, and that I should not have attempted the Arnhem operation until this had been done. This is not true. There were no such orders about Antwerp and Eisenhower had agreed about Arnhem. Indeed, up to the 8th October 1944 inclusive my orders were to gain the line of the Rhine " as quickly as humanly possible." On the 9th October Antwerp was given priority for the first time—as will be seen from the orders quoted above.

The trouble was that Eisenhower wanted the Saar, the Frankfurt area, the Ruhr, Antwerp, and the line of the Rhine. I knew how desperately the Germans had fought in Normandy. To get *all* these in one forward movement was impossible. If Eisenhower had adopted my plan he could at least have got Antwerp and the Ruhr, with bridgeheads over the Rhine in the north, and would then have been very well placed. Or if he had adopted Bradley's plan he could have got the Saar and the Frankfurt area, with bridgeheads over the Rhine in the centre and south. But he was too optimistic. He compromised. He failed to get any of his objectives, and was then faced with a frustrating situation.

I was, of course, greatly disappointed. I had hoped that we might end the German war quickly, save tens of thousands of lives, and bring relief to the people of Britain. But it was not to be.

When I think back I am more and more convinced that the arguments, and difficulties of understanding, about the strategy after crossing the Seine have their origin in terminology. The matter has been argued under the labels "narrow versus broad front." My plan was described by Eisenhower as a " pencil-like thrust," and on another occasion as a "knife-like drive." But a strong thrust by forty divisions can hardly be described as " a narrow front "; it would represent a major *blow*. I was expounding the doctrine of the *single punch* against an enemy who was now weak on his pins. It was on the lines of the " left hook " of the desert battles, leading to the knock-out blow; after all I knew something about that sort of thing. Once we can disabuse ourselves of the word " narrow," all sorts of arguments go by the board, e.g. pencil-like, knife-like and so on.

The dismal and tragic story of events after the successful battle in Normandy may be boiled down to one fundamental criticism. It is this—whatever the decision, it wasn't implemented. In Normandy our strategy for the land battle, and the plan to achieve it, was simple and clear-cut. The pieces were closely " stitched " together. It was never allowed to become unstitched; and it succeeded. After Normandy our strategy became unstitched. There was no plan; and we moved by disconnected jerks.

The rightness or wrongness of the decision taken is, of course, open to argument. But what cannot be disputed is that when a certain strategy, right or wrong, was decided upon, it wasn't directed. We did not advance to the Rhine on a *broad* front; we advanced to the Rhine on *several* fronts, which were un-coordinated. And what was the German answer? A single and concentrated punch in the Ardennes, when we had become unbalanced and unduly extended. So we were caught on the hop.

On the 6th November I left Brussels for a few days' leave in England.

It had been a difficult time for us all since we landed in Normandy on the 6th June, exactly five months earlier. I reckoned that I had earned a short rest.

On arrival in England I went at once to see the Prime Minister, to tell him about our affairs and also that he must now expect the war to go on all through the winter and well into 1945.

This is what my autograph book says:

" The Supreme Battle of Normandy carried with it the Liberation of France. The conquest of Germany remains. Between these two decisive struggles, the Liberation of Belgium and the opening of the Scheldt as the main supply channel of the Allies constitutes a victory of high consequence gained by the 21 Army Group and its Commander.

Winston S. Churchill
6-11-44"

I returned to my headquarters at Brussels on the 10th November.

CHAPTER 16

THE BATTLE OF ARNHEM

17th to 25th September 1944

IN OUR move forward on the northern flank to secure the Ruhr in accordance with Eisenhower's orders, we were confronted with two major river obstacles—the Meuse and the Rhine. Whatever route we took, there would be additional obstacles in the form of large canals.

My plan was to drive hard for the Rhine across all these obstacles, and to seize a bridgehead beyond the Rhine before the enemy could reorganise sufficiently to stop us.

I had been allotted the First Allied Airborne Corps under Lieut.-General Browning. This Corps consisted of: 1st British Airborne Division, 82nd U.S. Airborne Division, 101st U.S. Airborne Division, and the Polish Parachute Brigade. I placed it under the command of Second Army (Dempsey).

I have already explained that the direction of the thrust would be towards Arnhem, and why. The essential feature of the plan was the laying of a " carpet " of airborne forces across the five major water obstacles which existed on the general axis of the main road through Eindhoven to Uden, Grave, Nijmegen, and thence to Arnhem.

30 Corps (Horrocks) was to operate along the axis of the " carpet," link up with the 1st British Airborne Division in the Arnhem area, and establish a bridgehead over the Neder Rijn north of that place.

Second Army was then to establish itself in the general area between Arnhem and the Zuider Zee, facing east, so as to be able to develop operations against the northern flank of the Ruhr.

As 30 corps moved northwards along the axis of the airborne " carpet," two other corps were to widen the axis of advance— 8 Corps (O'Connor) on the east and 12 Corps (Ritchie) on the west.

The whole operation as I have said already was given the code name of MARKET GARDEN. It was certainly a bold plan. Indeed, General Bradley has described it as " one of the most imaginative of the war."

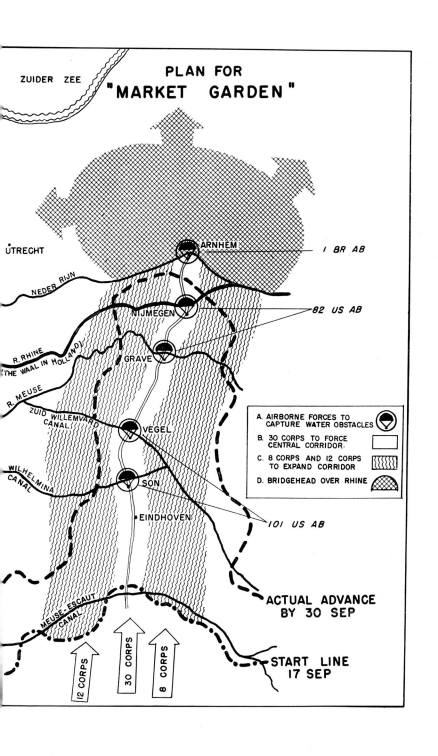

ZUIDER ZEE

PLAN FOR
"MARKET GARDEN"

UTRECHT

NEDER RIJN

ARNHEM — I BR AB

NIJMEGEN — 82 US AB

R. RHINE
THE WAAL IN HOLLAND
GRAVE

R. MEUSE

ZUID WILLEMVARD
CANAL

VEGEL

WILHELMINA
CANAL

SON

EINDHOVEN

A. AIRBORNE FORCES TO
CAPTURE WATER OBSTACLES.

B. 30 CORPS TO FORCE
CENTRAL CORRIDOR.

C. 8 CORPS AND 12 CORPS
TO EXPAND CORRIDOR.

D. BRIDGEHEAD OVER RHINE.

101 US AB

MEUSE-ESCAUT
CANAL

ACTUAL ADVANCE
BY 30 SEP

12 CORPS   30 CORPS   8 CORPS

START LINE
17 SEP

Crossing the Seine at Vernon by a pontoon bridge, 1st September 1944

Leaving the Maastricht Conference with General Bradley, 7th December 1944

But the moment he heard about it he tried to get it cancelled, lest it should open up possibilities on the northern flank and I might then ask for American troops to be placed under my command to exploit them. He was an advocate of the double thrust—the Saar *and* the Ruhr. So was Patton. Whenever Eisenhower appeared to favour the Ruhr thrust, Patton used to say he was the best general the British had.

But Eisenhower believed in Operation MARKET GARDEN. It will be recalled that he had met me in Brussels for a conference on the 10th September, and had agreed my plans for the operation. On page 307 of his book *Crusade in Europe* he has described that conference, and wrote as follows:

> "After completion of the bridgehead operation he [Montgomery] was to turn instantly and with his whole force to the capture of Walcheren Island and the other areas from which the Germans were defending the approaches to Antwerp."

Now this point was not, in fact, ever mentioned at our conference on the 10th September. In my memory his intention was always to occupy the Saar and the Ruhr and, *while advancing to do this*, to be opening the ports of Havre and Antwerp. So far as his orders to me were concerned he never deviated from this intention. Indeed, his orders issued on the 8th October were that the plans of both Army Groups "must retain as first mission the gaining of the line of the Rhine north of Bonn as quickly as humanly possible," and the word Antwerp does not appear in those orders. It was not until the 9th October that for the first time he named the free use of Antwerp as having priority over all other missions.

The orders issued by me on the 14th September are interesting as showing how I was trying to carry out his intentions. I give them in full below. Paras. 2 and 10 seem to be especially important.

OPERATIONAL DIRECTIVE: M 525

"1. Now that Havre has been captured, we are in a better position to be able to proceed with operations designed to lead to the capture of the Ruhr.

2. We have captured the port of Antwerp, but cannot make use of it as the enemy controls the mouth of the Scheldt; operations to put this matter right will be a first priority for Canadian Army.

3. On our right flank, First U.S. Army has entered Germany and is in contact with the defences of the Siegfried Line.
And away to the south, Third U.S. Army has bridgeheads over the Moselle.

4. Together with 12 Army Group, we will now begin operations designed to isolate and surround the Ruhr; we will occupy that area as we may desire.
Our real objective, therefore, is the Ruhr. But on the way to it we want the ports of Antwerp and Rotterdam, since the capture of the Ruhr is merely the first stop on the northern route of advance into Germany.

INTENTION

5. To destroy all enemy west of the general line Zwolle-Deventer-Cleve-Venlo-Maastricht, with a view to advancing eastwards and occupying the Ruhr.

FORWARD BOUNDARY

6. Between 21 Army Group and 12 Army Group.
All inclusive 12 Army Group:
Hasselt-Sittard-Garzweiler-Leverkusen (on the Rhine).
All inclusive 21 Army Group:
Opladen (on the Rhine)-Warburg-Brunswick.

7. This boundary is given only as a general basis on which to work.
The general direction of movement of Second British Army is northwards, and then eastwards round the northern face of the Ruhr; the general direction of movement of First U.S. Army is eastwards round the southern flank of the Ruhr.
The two armies will therefore tend to separate, and they will have to take special measures to watch their inner flanks.

FIRST CANADIAN ARMY

8. Complete the capture first of Boulogne, and then of Calais.

9. Dunkirk will be left to be dealt with later; for the present it will be merely masked.

10. The whole energies of the Army will be directed towards operations designed to enable full use to be made of the port of Antwerp.

Airborne troops are available to co-operate.

Air operations against the island of Walcheren have already commenced and these include:

   (a) the isolation of the island by taking out road and rail bridges.

   (b) attacks on coast defence guns.

   (c) attacks on other artillery, including flak.

11. H.Q. 1 Corps, and 49th Div., will be brought up from the Havre area as early as possible, to the Antwerp area.

   51st Div. will be grounded completely in the Havre peninsula and its transport used to enable the above move to take place; the division will remain grounded as long as its transport is required by Canadian Army for maintenance or movement purposes.

12. Canadian Army will take over the Antwerp area from Second Army beginning on 17th September.

   The boundary between the two armies on completion of this relief will be as decided by Canadian Army; Second Army to conform.

13. Having completed the operation for the opening of Antwerp, vide para. 10, Canadian Army will operate northwards on the general axis Breda-Utrecht-Amsterdam.

   Inter-Army boundary, all inclusive Canadian Army:

   Herenthals-Turnhout-Tilburg- s'Hertogenbosch-Zaltbom-mel- Utrecht-Hilversum.

   Task: To destroy all enemy to the west of the Army boundary, and open up the port of Rotterdam.

14. Subsequently, Canadian Army will be brought up on the left (or northern flank) of Second Army, and will be directed on Bremen and Hamburg.

SECOND BRITISH ARMY

15. The first task of the Army is to operate northwards and secure the crossings over the Rhine and Meuse in the general area Arnhem-Nijmegen-Grave. An airborne corps of three divisions is placed under command Second Army for these operations.

16. The Army will then establish itself in strength on the general line Zwolle-Deventer-Arnhem, facing east, with deep bridge-heads to the east side of the Ijssel river.

From this position it will be prepared to advance eastwards to the general area Rheine-Osnabrück-Hamm-Münster.

In this movement its weight will be on its right and directed towards Hamm, from which place a strong thrust will be made southwards along the eastern face of the Ruhr.

17. The thrust northwards to secure the river crossings, vide para. 15, will be rapid and violent, and without regard to what is happening on the flanks.

Subsequently the Army will take measures to widen the area of the initial thrust, and to create a secure line of supply.

18. D-Day for these operations is Sunday 17th September. Bad weather for airborne operations may possibly cause a post-ponement.

12 ARMY GROUP

19. First U.S. Army is to move eastwards as follows:
    (a) 5 Corps directed on Bonn.
    (b) 7 Corps directed on Cologne.
    (c) 19 Corps carrying out flank protection on the northern flank of the Army, along the inter-Army Group boundary. See para. 7.

20. The Army is to capture Bonn and Cologne, and to establish a deep bridgehead, some 10 miles in depth, on the east side of the Rhine.

21. The Army is then to advance eastwards round the south face of the Ruhr. This operation will be timed so as to be co-ordinated carefully with the move of Second British Army round the north face of the Ruhr.

There will be very close touch between General Bradley and myself during these operations.

GENERAL

22. Attention is drawn to para. 15 of M.523 dated 3-9-44. When we enter Germany, headquarter leaguers, and unit and sub-unit areas, will require to be tighter, and special arrangements will have to be made to prevent spies and gestapo agents getting in. Sniping may be a problem, and senior officers must exercise due care when travelling about their areas.

Once we are in Germany the true form will probably very

quickly be apparent, and we must then adopt measures suitable to the problem."

Eisenhower's reaction to these orders was immediate. He wrote me by return a letter to say how completely he agreed. There was no need for him to have done this. But it shows the wonderful humanity of the man. He obviously thought I would value such a letter, knowing what a lot of argument we had had over the past few weeks—and I did value it. This is what he said:

16 September, 1944

" Dear Monty,

Your M.525 has just arrived here and I must say that it not only is designed to carry out most effectively my basic conception with respect to this campaign but is in exact accordance with all the understandings that we now have.

I sent a senior staff officer to General Bradley yesterday to see that all of his intentions both with respect to application of his forces and distribution of his supplies will co-ordinate completely with this idea. While he had issued a temporary directive on September 10 that on the surface did not conform clearly to this conception of making our principal drive with our left, the actual fact is that everything he is doing will work out exactly as you visualize it.

I believe the enemy is capable of only one more, all-out defensive battle in the West. His major forces will, I feel, try to cover the Ruhr. When our present pushing and thrusting has forced him to his stand we shall close on him rapidly. It is my concern so to shape our operations that we are concentrating for that purpose, and by concentrating I include all troops and supplies that can be efficiently employed in the battle. So Bradley's left is striking hard to support you; Third Army is pushing north to support Hodges; and Sixth Army Group is being pushed up to give right flank support to the whole.

I hear that our frantic efforts to scratch together ad hoc truck companies to deliver you 500 tons a day did not get the supplies flowing on September 15. However, I am assured that the first batch will arrive there tomorrow morning, September 17.

My new headquarters will open at Versailles on Wednesday morning. Personally I will be there only a few days and am going forward wherever I can locate a really good landing ground somewhere in the Compiègne-Reims area. I will give you the exact location later.

Best of luck.

Sincerely

(Signed) Dwight D. Eisenhower

A copy of this will go to Bradley."

It will be noted that I instructed my subordinate commanders to be careful about their security arrangements and personal safety when we entered Germany. A copy of my orders was taken back to the War Office by an officer who had come over to see me. They produced the following telegram, by return:

"*Personal for F.M. Montgomery from V.C.I.G.S.*

Have just read your M.525. Reference para. 22 hope you realise that you yourself have conspicuous appearance and dress and are therefore obvious target for the enemy.

Little doubt that definite and concerted efforts will be made by desperate men to kill you.

It is therefore your duty to put aside your feelings and take most stringent and thorough steps for your personal safety. You can no longer afford to be casual in these matters.

Please regard this message not as a suggestion but as a definite order from C.I.G.S."

Operation MARKET GARDEN was duly launched on the 17th September 1944. It has been described by many writers. Probably the best and most complete account is that by Chester Wilmot in *The Struggle for Europe*. I will not go over it all again. We did not, as everyone knows, capture that final bridgehead north of Arnhem. As a result we could not position the Second Army north of the Neder Rijn at Arnhem, and thus place it in a suitable position to be able to develop operations against the north face of the Ruhr. But the possession of the crossings over the Meuse at Grave, and over the Lower Rhine (or Waal as it is called in Holland) at Nijmegen, were to prove of immense value later on; we had liberated a large part of Holland, we had the stepping stone we needed for the successful battles of the Rhineland that were to follow. Without these successes we would not have been able to cross the Rhine in strength in March 1945—but we did not get our final bridgehead, and that must be admitted.

The following signal was received from the 1st Airborne Division at Arnhem on the night of the 24th September:

"Must warn you unless physical contact is made with us early 25 Sep. consider it unlikely we can hold out long enough. All ranks now exhausted. Lack of rations, water, ammunition, and weapons with high officer casualty rate. . . . Even slight enemy offensive action may cause complete disintegration. If this happens all will be ordered to break towards bridgehead if anything rather than surrender. Any movement at present in face of enemy is not possible. Have attempted our best and will do so as long as possible."

We could not make contact with them in sufficient strength to be of any real help, and I gave orders that the remnants of the division were to be withdrawn back over the Neder Rijn at Arnhem, and into our lines, on the night of the 25th September. Some 2000 wounded who were unable to be moved were left behind with doctors and nursing orderlies, and these were taken prisoner by the Germans.

Of the senior officers in the division we got back only the Divisional Commander (Urquhart), one Brigadier (Hicks) and the C.R.A. (Loder-Symonds). All the battalion commanders were lost, except one.

Of the other officers, and men, we recovered: 125 officers, 400 glider pilots, 1700 N.C.O.s and men. I sent them all back to England at once.

General Urquhart came to stay with me at my Tac Headquarters before returning to England. He asked me to give him a letter which he could read out to the division when it re-assembled in England. I gave him the following, dated the 28th September 1944:

"1. I want to express to you personally, and to every officer and man in your division, my appreciation of what you all did at Arnhem for the Allied cause.
     I also want to express to you my own admiration, and the admiration of us all in 21 Army Group, for the magnificent fighting spirit that your division displayed in battle against great odds on the north bank of the Lower Rhine in Holland.
2.   There is no shadow of doubt that, had you failed, operations

elsewhere would have been gravely compromised. You did
not fail, and all is well elsewhere.

I would like all Britain to know that in your final message
from the Arnhem area you said: ' All will be ordered to
break out rather than surrender. We have attempted our
best, and we will continue to do our best as long as possible.'
And all Britain will say to you: ' You did your best; you
all did your duty; and we are proud of you.'

3. In the annals of the British Army there are many glorious
deeds. In our Army we have always drawn great strength
and inspiration from past traditions, and endeavoured to live
up to the high standards of those who have gone before.
But there can be few episodes more glorious than the epic of
Arnhem, and those that follow after will find it hard to live
up to the standards that you have set.

4. So long as we have in the armies of the British Empire officers
and men who will do as you have done, then we can indeed
look forward with complete confidence to the future.
In years to come it will be a great thing for a man to be able
to say: ' I fought at Arnhem.'

5. Please give my best wishes, and my grateful thanks, to every
officer and man in your division."

There were many reasons why we did not gain complete success
at Arnhem. The following in my view were the main ones.
First. The operation was not regarded at Supreme Headquarters
as the spearhead of a major Allied movement on the northern flank
designed to isolate, and finally to occupy, the Ruhr—the one objective
in the West which the Germans could not afford to lose. There is no
doubt in my mind that Eisenhower always wanted to give priority
to the northern thrust and to scale down the southern one. He ordered
this to be done, and he thought that it was being done. It was not
being done. We now know from Bradley's book (*A Soldier's Story*)
page 412, that in the middle of September, there was parity of logistic
resources between the First and Third American Armies in 12 Army
Group.

Eisenhower is a thoroughly genuine person; he is the very incarnation of sincerity and he trusts others to do as he asks. But in this
instance his intentions were not carried out. The following quotation

from page 531 of *The Struggle for Europe* by Chester Wilmot is of interest:

> " If he [Eisenhower] had kept Patton halted on the Meuse, and had given full logistic support to Hodges and Dempsey after the capture of Brussels, the operations in Holland could have been an overwhelming triumph, for First U.S. Army could have mounted a formidable diversion, if not a successful offensive, at Aachen, and Second British Army could have attacked sooner, on a wider front and in much greater strength."

Second. The airborne forces at Arnhem were dropped too far away from the vital objective—the bridge. It was some hours before they reached it. I take the blame for this mistake. I should have ordered Second Army and 1 Airborne Corps to arrange that at least one complete Parachute Brigade was dropped quite close to the bridge, so that it could have been captured in a matter of minutes and its defence soundly organised with time to spare. I did not do so.

Third. The weather. This turned against us after the first day and we could not carry out much of the later airborne programme. But weather is always an uncertain factor, in war and in peace. This uncertainty we all accepted. It could only have been offset, and the operation made a certainty, by allotting additional resources to the project, so that it became an Allied and not merely a British project.

Fourth. The 2nd S.S. Panzer Corps was refitting in the Arnhem area, having limped up there after its mauling in Normandy. We knew it was there. But we were wrong in supposing that it could not fight effectively; its battle state was far beyond our expectation. It was quickly brought into action against the 1st Airborne Division.

As after Normandy, so again after Arnhem, I was bitterly disappointed. It was my second attempt to try to capture the Ruhr quickly. Bill Williams used to tell me that the Germans could not carry on the war for more than about three months after they lost the Ruhr. But we still hadn't got it.

And here I must admit a bad mistake on my part—I underestimated the difficulties of opening up the approaches to Antwerp so that we could get the free use of that port. I reckoned that the Canadian Army could do it *while* we were going for the Ruhr. I was wrong.

I will close this chapter with a final quotation on the battle from

Chester Wilmot (*The Struggle for Europe*, page 528). This is what he wrote about it:

> " It was most unfortunate that the two major weaknesses of the Allied High Command—the British caution about casualties and the American reluctance to concentrate—should both have exerted their baneful influence on this operation, which should, and could, have been the decisive blow of the campaign in the West. This was no time to count the cost, or to consider the prestige of rival commanders. The prize at issue was no less than the chance of capturing the Ruhr and ending the war quickly with all that meant for the future of Europe."

In my—prejudiced—view, if the operation had been properly backed from its inception, and given the aircraft, ground forces, and administrative resources necessary for the job—it would have succeeded *in spite of* my mistakes, or the adverse weather, or the presence of the 2nd S.S. Panzer Corps in the Arnhem area. I remain MARKET GARDEN's unrepentant advocate.

CHAPTER 17

PRELUDE TO THE ARDENNES

THE BATTLE of the Ardennes, which began on the 16th December 1944 and continued to the 16th January 1945, has aroused such bitter feelings between Britons and Americans that I cannot disregard it. But I think we must first describe the events which led up to it, since this examination will show that the battle could so easily have been avoided.

On the 28th November Eisenhower came to stay a night with me at my Tac Headquarters at Zonhoven. We had long talks that night and the next morning, in the course of which we discussed the situation in which we found ourselves at that time—which, to say the least of it, was far from good.

The war of attrition in the winter months, forced on us by our faulty strategy after the great victory in Normandy, was becoming very expensive in human life. In the American armies there was a grave shortage of ammunition. The rifle platoons in all divisions were under strength and the reinforcement situation was bad. American divisions in the line began to suffer severely from trench-foot as the winter descended on us. In my own Army Group I was concerned about the growing casualties. I give below the cumulative casualties, by divisions, from the 6th June or date of arrival in the theatre, up to the 1st October:

Formation	Casualties
11 Armd Div	3,825
Guards Armd Div	3,385
7 Armd Div	2,801
3 Brit Inf Div	7,342
15 Inf Div	7,601
43 Inf Div	7,605
49 Inf Div	5,894

Formation	Casualties
50 Inf Div	6,701
51 Inf Div	4,799
53 Inf Div	4,984
59 Inf Div	4,911
2 Cdn Inf Div	8,211
3 Cdn Inf Div	9,263
4 Cdn Armd Div	3,135
Polish	1,861

During my talk with Eisenhower I gave it as my opinion that Bradley's 12 Army Group did not look to me to be very well " balanced," tactically. I suggested that to restore tactical balance some of Patton's divisions should be moved up to the north, and that his offensive in the south should be cancelled. These views were passed on to Bradley and on the 3rd December he wrote me a letter to the effect that he could not do this, giving his reasons. This letter is important in view of what was to happen later, and I give below the relevant extracts from it.

EXTRACT OF LETTER FROM GENERAL BRADLEY

" Ike told me of his recent conference with you and I am glad that we are going to have a chance to get together later this week to discuss future operations.

I thought you might like to have a few facts about our present situation and our prospects for the future.

The question of whether I should transfer some of Patton's divisions to the north was given careful consideration prior to our recent jump-off. He had only six infantry divisions and he held a front line of over seventy miles, and this front included the containing of the fortress of Metz. I felt that even though he remained on the defensive I could not take away more than one infantry division, or at the outside two, without too much weakening his front. This would have left him in a position where he would be unable to launch any offensive and thus co-operate with the Sixth Army Group on the south. I therefore decided not to take any divisions away from him so that he could launch an attack in conjunction with Devers, with the hope of cleaning up Lorraine and, if possible, the Saar. As of midnight November 30 he had taken over 25,500 prisoners, and the total losses of the enemy for this period of time must have been much greater.

Because of our inability to receive, equip, and supply troops through our Channel ports, it has been necessary to divert seven divisions to Devers' Army Group. Naturally we wanted to get as much use out of these divisions as possible, and the attack of the Sixth Army Group, in conjunction with Patton's attack, has so far achieved very satisfactory results. I believe that between the Seventh Army and the Third Army this very important attack can be kept up."

I reminded Eisenhower that, overall, we had so far failed to carry out the plan laid down in his directive of the 28th October, i.e. to secure the Ruhr and the Saar. We now needed a new plan.

Before he left me on the 29th November, I suggested to him that what was now indicated was a meeting between himself, Tedder, Bradley, and myself; we could then all give our views and he could give us his plan for the next phase. He agreed; he fixed the conference for the 7th December, at Maastricht. We all four met there at 10.30 a.m. on the 7th December.

The following is the record of the conference I made in my diary that night.

THE MAASTRICHT CONFERENCE
EISENHOWER'S OPENING REMARKS

" He reviewed the past from about early Sept. onwards.

He then made the point that the recent operations had been well worth while, and were going well.

One gained the impression that this part of his statement was not very genuine, and that he was trying hard to put up a good case to off-set what he knew I was going to say.

He finished by saying that the purpose of the meeting was to air our views, and to give him ideas which he could think over. He said he did not propose to issue any definite orders before we dispersed; if any further orders were needed, they were to be issued later.

He then asked me to give my views on the problem confronting us.

THE CASE PUT FORWARD BY ME

I said that in order to win the war quickly there were two main factors which must influence the solution to the problem:

First: The only real worth-while objective on the western front is the Ruhr. If we cut it off from the rest of Germany the enemy capacity to continue the struggle must gradually peter out.

Second: It is essential that we force mobile war on the Germans by the spring or early summer. They have little transport, little petrol, and tanks that cannot compete with ours in the mobile battle. Once the war becomes mobile, that is the end of the Germans.

These two factors are basic and fundamental. It is impossible to argue against them.

It follows:

(*a*) that the Ruhr must be our strategic objective.

(*b*) that our main effort must be made in the north as it is there, and only there, that suitable country exists for a mobile campaign, i.e. to the north of the Ruhr.

Any other routes into Germany will produce no results as the country is difficult and very suited for defensive war; to pursue other routes will merely prolong the war; it is the static defensive battle that suits the enemy.

We must be so strong in the north that we can produce decisive results without any possibility of failure.

We were at present working on the plan contained in his directive of the 28th Oct. That plan had failed to mature.

We require *now* a new plan, and the successive stages in this plan must be objectives towards attainment of the master plan.

The new ' master plan' must cater for continuing the battle all through the winter months so as to wear down the enemy's strength. There will be difficulties caused by mud and by lack of air support, but we must continue throughout the winter to conduct any operations which:

(*a*) gain intermediate objectives towards the Ruhr;

(*b*) wear down the enemy's strength at a greater rate than our own;

(c) place us in a good jumping-off position for a mobile campaign in the spring.

A highly important factor in the winter operations will be to draw into the battle, and to defeat decisively, the enemy 6 Pz. Army. This is his only strategic reserve on the western front, and it contains the only divisions which could make any show at all in a mobile campaign. These divisions must therefore be so mauled during the winter months that they are out-of-action when spring arrives.

The Germans will fight hard to keep us from the Ruhr, and to keep the war static. At all costs they must stop the war from becoming mobile.

So there will be no difficulty in bringing them to battle west of the Rhine.

THE PLAN PUT FORWARD BY ME

12 and 21 Army Groups both to operate north of the Ardennes.

The right flank of 12 Army Group to be about Prum. A strong thrust on the axis Prum-Bonn would have good country for operations and would avoid existing defence lines and obstacles.

12 Army Group to operate towards the Rhine on two main axes: Prum-Bonn, Duren-Cologne.

The left Army of at least ten divisions to operate northwards towards the thrust of 21 Army Group coming southwards between the rivers Meuse and Rhine.

12 Army Group to be made up to a strength of some thirty-five divisions.

21 Army Group to re-group and launch a strong offensive from the Nijmegen area, southwards between the rivers, with the object of securing all ground between the Rhine and Meuse as far south as the line Orsoy-Venlo.

This would be the only offensive action on the front of 21 Army Group; everything would be put into it; it would continue slowly during the winter months. Target date: 1st January.

21 Army Group, reinforced by American divisions as necessary and by airborne divisions, to cross the Rhine at selected places between Wesel and Nijmegen. Then to develop mobile operations north of the Lippe canal and river, designed to outflank the Ruhr

from the north and to penetrate into Germany. This might happen in March 1945.

12 Army Group to cross the Rhine in the Bonn area and develop outflanking operations against the Ruhr from the south.

6 Army Group, based on Marseilles, to continue operations in the Saar as far as its strength and resources will allow.

I said that it was difficult at this stage to say exactly how the operations outlined above would develop.

The two Army Groups north of the Ardennes, 12 and 21, must first advance to battle west of the Rhine, draw in on them all the German strategic reserves and maul them, and then close up to the Rhine. The rest could not be decided in detail at this stage.

But I considered that one commander should be in operational control and direction of all forces north of the Ardennes. That commander must either be myself or Bradley. I would willingly serve under Bradley.

EISENHOWER COMMENTS ON MY REMARKS

He said that we must not put too much stress on the Ruhr; it was merely a geographical objective; our real objective was to kill Germans and it did not matter where we did it.

I disagreed with this and said we would find more Germans to kill if we went for the Ruhr than anywhere else; we should also at the same time be gaining objectives towards the capture or isolation of the Ruhr and towards the attainment of the master plan.

He said he agreed that the left wing of 12 Army Group must certainly be made strong enough to get to the Rhine.

But he did not agree that we should shift the whole of 12 Army Group to the north of Prum.

He said that he considered the right wing of 12 Army Group should be strong, and should advance to the Rhine at about Worms, and should then develop a strong thrust on the axis Frankfurt-Kassel.

This was a new one on me.

He said his general conception of the campaign was as follows:

(a) In the north should be 21 Army Group with Ninth U.S. Army of ten divisions under command.

The southern boundary of 21 Army Group should be on the Rhine about Orsoy, at the N.W. corner of the Ruhr. The task of this force would be to cross the Rhine and outflank the Ruhr from the North.

(b) The left wing of 12 Army Group would be a containing force, not to cross the Rhine in strength, but to make feints and threats in the Cologne-Bonn area and south of it. In other words, no strong thrust here.

(c) On the southern flank, the right wing of 12 Army Group should develop a strong thrust on the axis Frankfurt-Kassel.

(d) The general pattern of this plan is two offensives: one round the north of the Ruhr vide (a), and one away in the south vide (c). In between these two thrusts will be threats and feints.

12 Army Group would stretch from Orsoy—astride the Ardennes—to Worms.

MY COMMENTS ON EISENHOWER'S PLAN

Eisenhower asked me what I thought of his plan, and said he thought it differed from my ideas only very slightly.

I said that we must be clear that we differed, not slightly, *but widely and on fundamental issues.*

I said I was quite unable to agree with his plan. If we split our resources, neither thrust would be strong enough to obtain decisive results; this is what we had done in the past, and we were now paying for our mistakes; I hoped we would not do it again.

I said that we suffered at present from a faulty command set-up; his plan made it no better. In fact it would make it worse.

Bradley would obviously stay at Luxembourg in the south, for the Frankfurt thrust. I had moved my Tac H.Q. to Zonhoven so as to be near Bradley; but he had never come north.

I should now have to move up north of Eindhoven so as to be near my own offensive.

I pleaded again for myself to take charge north of the Ardennes, and Bradley south of the Ardennes. On his plan I would have the northern offensive, and Bradley the southern or Frankfurt offensive.

As things were now going to be, Bradley would be concerned

in both offensives and there would be much waste of time when a quick decision was wanted.

I finished up with a strong plea for the concentration of all available strength in the north, and for making the northern offensive so strong that success was certain.

I also put in a strong plea for a sound set-up for command.

I gave it as my opinion that, unless we did these two things, we would not succeed, and we would arrive at the spring not ready to get on with the business.

Eisenhower did not agree with my views. He considered the way to win the war was to have two strong thrusts:

(*a*)   one round the north of the Ruhr;

(*b*)   one on the axis Frankfurt-Kassel.

In between these two thrusts the plan would be to threaten, and make feints.

It is clear that, although the present plan has failed, we are still to continue to consider it has not failed and are to work on it."

And so we really achieved nothing at the Maastricht conference on the 7th December. I had hoped to get agreement that we would shift our main weight towards the north. I then wanted the activities of 12 and 21 Army Groups to be directed against the Ruhr, and to the task of imposing mobile war on the enemy in the north German plain in the early spring. But no decision was given.

Meanwhile Bradley's 12 Army Group was disposed in two main concentrations, each deployed for attack. In between was a gap of some 100 miles, held by 8 American Corps of four divisions—under Middleton.

CHAPTER 18

THE BATTLE OF THE ARDENNES

16th December 1944 to 16th January 1945

ON THE morning of the 16th December I felt in need of relaxation. So I decided to fly up to Eindhoven in my Miles light aircraft, land on one of the fairways of the golf course, and play a few holes of golf. The H.Q. of the Air Force Group supporting Second Army was in the Club House, and Dai Rees the well-known golf professional was there as driver of the A.O.C.'s car. I knew Rees very well and we were great friends; we had been through the desert together. His civil job was professional at Hindhead Golf Club and he used to give lessons to my son David when the war was over, and before he moved to South Herts. He is a most likeable character. I did not realise then that he was to become the best match player in the U.K.

I asked if Rees could meet me when I landed with a club or two. All was arranged satisfactorily and we began to play. But our game was soon interrupted by a message to say that the Germans had launched a heavy attack that morning on the front of the First American Army, and the situation was obscure. I said good-bye to Rees and flew straight back to my Tac Headquarters at Zonhoven.

The blow had fallen mainly on that part of the First Army front that was thinly held by 8 Corps under Middleton in the Ardennes, and a great "bulge" or salient was being made in the American line.

I think the less one says about this battle the better, for I fancy that whatever I do say will almost certainly be resented. All those with whom I was associated during the battle have now retired—Bradley, Hodges, Simpson, Ridgway, Collins, and Gerow. And Patton is dead. So I will just mention the highlights as they appeared to me at the time.

The situation deteriorated rapidly and finally Bradley's 12 Army Group was split in two. His headquarters were at Luxembourg,

307

whence he could not control the northern half of his Army Group. I kept in close touch with the situation by means of my team of Liaison Officers. And I took steps to ensure that the right flank and right rear of 21 Army Group would be secure, whatever might happen.

At 10.30 a.m. on the 20th December Eisenhower telephoned me from his headquarters and ordered me to take command at once of all American forces on the northern flank of the bulge. That order put two American armies under my command: Ninth Army (Simpson) on my immediate right, First Army (Hodges) to the right of Ninth Army.

The First Army was fighting desperately.

Having given orders to Dempsey and Crerar, who arrived for a conference at 11 a.m., I left at noon for the H.Q. of the First Army, where I had instructed Simpson to meet me. I found the northern flank of the bulge was very disorganised. Ninth Army had two corps and three divisions; First Army had three corps and fifteen divisions. Neither Army Commander had seen Bradley or any senior member of his staff since the battle began, and they had no directive on which to work.

The first thing to do was to see the battle on the northern flank *as one whole*, to ensure the vital areas were held securely, and to create reserves for counter-attack.

I embarked on these measures.

I put British troops under command of the Ninth Army to fight alongside American soldiers, and made that Army take over some of the First Army front. I positioned British troops as reserves behind the First and Ninth Armies until such time as American reserves could be created. Slowly but surely the situation was held, and then finally restored. Similar action was taken on the southern flank of the bulge by Bradley, with the Third Army.

I must mention a joke on my part which was not considered funny in Whitehall. The War Office were very naturally worried and I sent a telegram to the C.I.G.S. giving the whole story of what happened and telling him what I was doing about it. The last sentence read "We cannot come out through Dunkirk this time as the Germans still hold that place."

My telegram was sent on to the Prime Minister but with the last sentence cut out!

The battle may be said to have ended in the middle of January. On the 14th January I sent the following letter to General Bradley.

" My dear Brad,
    It does seem as if the battle of the ' salient' will shortly be drawing to a close, and when it is all clean and tidy I imagine that your armies will be returning to your operational command.
    I would like to say two things:
    First: What a great honour it has been for me to command such fine troops.
    Second: How well they have all done.
2. It has been a great pleasure to work with Hodges and Simpson; both have done very well.
    And the Corps Commanders in the First Army (Gerow, Collins, Ridgway) have been quite magnificent; it must be most exceptional to find such a good lot of Corps Commanders gathered together in one Army.
3. All of us in the northern side of the salient would like to say how much we have admired the operations that have been conducted on the southern side; if you had not held on firmly to Bastogne the whole situation might have become very awkward.
4. My kind regards to you and to George Patton.
                         Yrs very sincerely,
                              (Signed) B. L. Montgomery"

On the 16th January I regarded the battle as over. Eisenhower had ordered me to return the First Army to Bradley on the 17th January, the Ninth Army to remain under my command. I sent the following message to Eisenhower on the 16th January:

" I have great pleasure in reporting to you that the task you gave me in the Ardennes is now concluded. First and Third Armies have joined hands at Houffalize and are advancing eastwards. It can therefore be said that we have now achieved tactical victory within the salient. I am returning First Army to Bradley tomorrow as ordered by you. I would like to say what a great pleasure it has been to have such a splendid army under my command and how very well it has done."

Eisenhower answered this telegram with a letter dated the 17th January in which he said:

" Thank you again for the way you pitched in to help out during the German thrust. Some day I hope I can show my appreciation in a more lasting manner."

There is one characteristic story about General Horrocks and his 30 Corps at this period which I often recall. I had ordered Second Army to position 30 Corps behind the Meuse in the general area between Louvain and Namur. Its role was to prevent any German units crossing the Meuse. I went to see Horrocks in order to make certain he was clear about his orders. He was full of enthusiasm, as always, and had great ideas that he would let the Germans over the river and then win the final battle of the war on the field of Waterloo which was not far away! I told Dempsey that on no account was Horrocks to allow any Germans over the river.

I should also mention that on the 1st January the Germans carried out large-scale attacks on our airfields in Holland and Belgium. My aircraft, the Dakota given me by Eisenhower in Sicily in August 1943 in exchange for the Flying Fortress, was shot to pieces. He replaced it at once and I was so touched that I sent him the following message on the 6th January:

" M 424 Personal for Eisenhower from Montgomery.
My dear Ike, Have received the new C/47 you have so kindly lent me and I understand you have sent me one that was intended for yourself. Such spontaneous kindness touches me deeply and from my heart I send you my grateful thanks. If there is anything I can ever do for you to ease the tremendous burden that you bear you know you have only to command me. And I want you to know that I shall always stand firmly behind you in everything you do."

I will conclude this chapter with an account of the Press conference I held on the 7th January about the battle. I was perturbed at this time about the sniping at Eisenhower which was going on in the British press. So I sent a message to the Prime Minister and said that in my talk to British and American correspondents about the battle I proposed to deal with the story of the battle. I would show how the whole Allied team rallied to the call and how team-work saved a somewhat awkward situation. I suggested I should then put in a strong plea for Allied solidarity. Nothing must be done by anyone that tends to break down the team spirit. It is team-work that pulls you through dangerous times. It is team-work that wins battles. It is victories in battle that win wars.

The Prime Minister agreed and said he thought what I proposed would be invaluable.

I held the conference. Many stories have been told about it, and many quotations have been taken out of their context and published. Nobody has ever published the full text of the notes from which I spoke and which were given to the Press afterwards. Here they are:

" 1. *Object of this talk*

   I have asked you to come here today so that I can give you some information which may be of use to you, and also to ask you to help me in a certain matter.

2. *The story of the present battle*

   Rundstedt attacked on 16 Dec; he obtained tactical surprise. He drove a deep wedge into the centre of the First US Army and split the American forces in two. The situation looked as if it might become awkward; the Germans had broken right through a weak spot, and were heading for the Meuse.

3. As soon as I saw what was happening I took certain steps myself to ensure that *if* the Germans got to the Meuse they would certainly not get over that river. And I carried out certain movements so as to provide balanced dispositions to meet the threatened danger; these were, at the time, merely precautions, i.e., I was thinking ahead.

4. Then the situation began to deteriorate. But the whole allied team rallied to meet the danger; national considerations were thrown overboard; General Eisenhower placed me in command of the whole Northern front.

   I employed the whole available power of the British Group of Armies; this power was brought into play very gradually and in such a way that it would not interfere with the American lines of communication. Finally it was put into battle with a bang, and today British divisions are fighting hard on the right flank of First US Army.

   You have thus the picture of British troops fighting on both sides of American forces who have suffered a hard blow. This is a fine allied picture.

5. The battle has been most interesting; I think possibly one of the most interesting and tricky battles I have ever handled, with great issues at stake. The first thing to be done was to 'head off' the enemy from the tender spots and vital places. Having done that successfully, the next thing was to 'see him off,' i.e. rope him in and make quite certain that he could not get to the places he wanted, *and also* that he was slowly but surely removed away from those places.

He was therefore 'headed off,' and then 'seen off.'

He is now being 'written off,' and heavy toll is being taken of his divisions by ground and air action. You must not imagine that the battle is over yet; it is by no means over and a great deal still remains to be done.

The battle has some similarity to the battle that began on 31 Aug 1942 when Rommel made his last bid to capture Egypt and was 'seen off' by the Eighth Army. But actually all battles are different because the problem is different.

6. What was Rundstedt trying to achieve? No one can tell for certain.

The only guide we have is the message he issued to his soldiers before the battle began; he told them it was the last great effort to try and win the war, that everything depended on it; that they must go 'all out.'

On the map you see his gains; *that* will not win the war; he is likely slowly but surely to lose it all; he must have scraped together every reserve he could lay his hands on for this job, and he has not achieved a great deal.

One must admit that he has dealt us a sharp blow and he sent us reeling back; but we recovered; he has been unable to gain any great advantage from his initial success.

He has therefore failed in his strategic purpose, unless the prize was smaller than his men were told.

He has now turned to the defensive on the ground; and he is faced by forces properly balanced to utilise the initiative which he has lost.

Another reason for his failure is that his air force, although still capable of pulling a fast one, cannot protect his

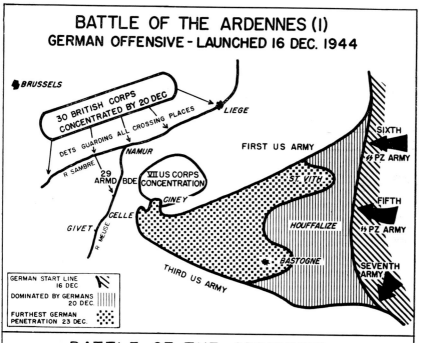

BATTLE OF THE ARDENNES (1)
GERMAN OFFENSIVE – LAUNCHED 16 DEC. 1944

BRUSSELS

30 BRITISH CORPS CONCENTRATED BY 20 DEC

DETS GUARDING ALL CROSSING PLACES

LIEGE

R SAMBRE

NAMUR

FIRST US ARMY

SIXTH

SS PZ ARMY

29 ARMD BDE

VII US CORPS CONCENTRATION

ST. VITH

FIFTH

CINEY

SS PZ ARMY

CELLE

GIVET

R MEUSE

HOUFFALIZE

BASTOGNE

SEVENTH ARMY

THIRD US ARMY

GERMAN START LINE 16 DEC
DOMINATED BY GERMANS 20 DEC.
FURTHEST GERMAN PENETRATION 23 DEC.

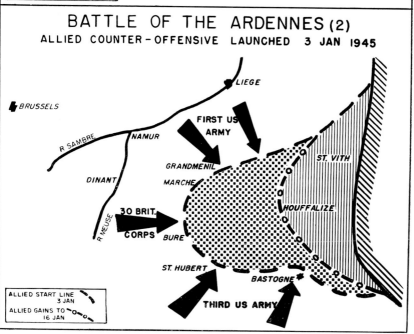

BATTLE OF THE ARDENNES (2)
ALLIED COUNTER – OFFENSIVE LAUNCHED 3 JAN 1945

LIEGE

BRUSSELS

FIRST US ARMY

R SAMBRE

NAMUR

GRANDMENIL

ST. VITH

DINANT

MARCHE

R MEUSE

HOUFFALIZE

30 BRIT. CORPS

BURE

ST. HUBERT

BASTOGNE

THIRD US ARMY

ALLIED START LINE 3 JAN
ALLIED GAINS TO 16 JAN

army; for that army *our* Tactical Air Forces are the greatest terror.

7. But when all is said and done I shall always feel that Rundstedt was really beaten by the good fighting qualities of the American soldier and by the team-work of the Allies.

I would like to say a word about these two points.

8. I first saw the American soldier in battle in Sicily, and I formed then a very high opinion of him. I saw him again in Italy.

And I have seen a very great deal of him in this campaign. I want to take this opportunity to pay a public tribute to him.

He is a brave fighting man, steady under fire, and with that tenacity in battle which stamps the first class soldier; all these qualities have been shown in a marked degree during the present battle.

I have spent my military career with the British soldier and I have come to love him with a great love; and I have now formed a very great affection and admiration for the American soldier. I salute the brave fighting men of America; I never want to fight alongside better soldiers. Just now I am seeing a great deal of the American soldiers; I have tried to feel that I am almost an American soldier myself so that I might take no unsuitable action or offend them in any way.

I have been given an American identity card; I am thus identified in the Army of the United States, my fingerprints have been registered in the War Department at Washington —which is far preferable to having them registered at Scotland Yard!

9. And now I come to the last point.

It is team-work that pulls you through dangerous times; it is team-work that wins battles; it is victories in battle that win wars. I want to put in a strong plea for Allied solidarity at this vital stage of the war; and you can all help in this greatly.

Nothing must be done by anyone that tends to break down the team spirit of our Allied team; if you try and ' get at ' the captain of the team you are liable to induce a loss of confidence, and this may spread and have disastrous results.

I would say that anyone who tries to break up the team spirit of the Allies is definitely helping the enemy.

10. Let me tell you that the captain of our team is Eisenhower. I am absolutely devoted to Ike; we are the greatest of friends. It grieves me when I see uncomplimentary articles about him in the British Press; he bears a great burden, he needs our fullest support, he has a right to expect it, and it is up to all of us to see that he gets it.

And so I would ask all of you to lend a hand to stop that sort of thing; let us all rally round the captain of the team and so help to win the match.

Nobody objects to healthy and constructive criticism; it is good for us.

But let us have done with destructive criticism that aims a blow at Allied solidarity, that tends to break up our team spirit, and that therefore helps the enemy."

Not only was it probably a mistake to have held this conference at all in the sensitive state of feeling at the time, but what I said was skilfully distorted by the enemy. Chester Wilmot (*The Struggle for Europe*, page 611) has explained that his dispatch to the B.B.C. about it was intercepted by the German wireless, " re-written to give it an anti-American bias and then broadcast by Arnhem Radio, which was then in Goebbels' hands. Monitored at Bradley's H.Q., this broadcast was mistaken for a B.B.C. transmission and it was this twisted text that started the uproar."

Distorted or not, I think now that I should never have held that Press conference. So great was the feeling against me on the part of the American generals, that whatever I said was bound to be wrong. I should therefore have said nothing. Secondly, whatever I said (and I was misreported) the general impression I gave was one of tremendous confidence. In contradistinction to the rather crestfallen American command, I appeared, to the sensitive, to be triumphant—not over the Germans but over the Americans. This was a completely false picture. But I had also described the battle as " interesting." Those who did not know me well could hardly be expected to share my professional interest in the art of war and were, not unnaturally, aggrieved by this phraseology; they were too sore to find the battle " interesting " as an objective enterprise. In fact, not only should I not have held the conference, but I should have been even more careful than I was trying to be. All of which shows that I should have held my tongue. The "best-laid" Press conferences of "mice and men gang aft agley."

What I did *not* say was that, in the Battle of the Ardennes, the Allies got a real "bloody nose," the Americans had nearly 80,000 casualties, and that it would never have happened if we had fought the campaign properly after the great victory in Normandy, or had even ensured tactical balance in the dispositions of the land forces as the winter campaign developed. Furthermore, because of this unnecessary battle we lost some six weeks in time—with all that that entailed in political consequences as the end of the war drew nearer.

CHAPTER 19

THE END OF THE WAR IN EUROPE

THE COMMAND PROBLEM

IT WILL be manifest to the reader that from the 1st September 1944 onwards I was not satisfied that we had a satisfactory organisation for command or operational control. I wrote a paper on the subject entitled " Notes on Command in Western Europe " and sent it to Bedell Smith on the 10th October; he showed it to Eisenhower. It will be remembered that I had given my views on the subject to General Marshall in no uncertain voice when he visited me at Eindhoven on the 8th October. My main criticism stemmed from the fact that direct operational command of land armies in war involved close touch with subordinate commanders and therefore was a whole-time job; the commander must be well forward and have a good grip on the battle. In Normandy I had done this job; now nobody was doing it, and we were getting into trouble. Having been shown my paper Eisenhower replied to me direct in a letter dated the 13th October. In this letter he stated that he did not agree that one man could direct the land battle intelligently on the long front from Switzerland to the North Sea. It required an overall commander " to adjust the larger boundaries to tasks commensurate to the several groups operating in the several areas." That overall commander must be the Supreme Commander. The letter also referred to the question of nationalism, as opposed to purely military considerations.

It was a difficult time and Eisenhower was faced with the precise situation which I had outlined to him at our meeting at my Tac Headquarters on the 23rd August; his strategy, and the lack of any plan, had led to our present frustrating situation in October. He was clearly unhappy about the whole affair.

I therefore decided to drop the subject of a single command on land and on the 16th October I sent him the following message:

" Dear Ike, I have received your letter of 13 October. You will hear no more on the subject of command from me. I have given you my views and you have given your answer. That ends the matter and I and all of us up here will weigh in one hundred per cent to do what you want and we will pull it through without a doubt. I have given Antwerp top priority in all operations in 21 Army Group and all energies and efforts will be now devoted towards opening up that place. Your very devoted and loyal subordinate Monty."

Eisenhower's reply was immediate and ran as follows:

" Dear Monty, Thank you for your very fine message. Looking forward very much to seeing you tomorrow. As ever, Ike."

That issue was now closed. What remained was to try and get a ound plan for the winter campaign that lay ahead—the campaign in he Rhineland—and to get proper co-ordination of effort throughout he Allied forces.

During the Battle of the Ardennes the remorseless march of events ad forced Eisenhower to do what I had always suggested; I was placed in operational command of the left flank of the Allies, with two American armies under my command. This could not have been pleasant for my critics at Supreme Headquarters, or for the American generals who opposed my ideas. It had taken a major crisis to do what I had been asking for ever since August.

On the 28th December Eisenhower visited the northern flank and had a long talk with him in his special train at Hasselt. The Ardennes battle was then well in hand and our conversation turned mainly on what was to be done when it was over. I again gave it as my opinion hat the Ruhr was the immediate objective; all available power must be concentrated to secure it; operational control of the forces involved must be exercised by one commander.

The next day, 29th December, I sent Eisenhower the following etter:

" My dear Ike,
    It was very pleasant to see you again yesterday and to have a talk on the battle situation.
2. I would like to refer to the matter of operational control of all

forces engaged in the northern thrust towards the Ruhr, i.e. 12 and 21 Army Groups.

I think we want to be careful, because we have had one very definite failure when we tried to produce a formula that would meet this case; that was the formula produced in SHAEF FWD 15510 dated 23-9-44, which formula very definitely did not work.

3. When you and Bradley and myself met at Maastricht on 7 December, it was very clear to me that Bradley opposed any idea that I should have operational control over his Army Group; so I did not then pursue the subject.

I therefore consider that it will be necessary for you to be very firm on the subject, and any loosely worded statement will be quite useless.

4. I consider that if you merely use the word ' co-ordination,' it will not work. The person designated by you must have powers of operational direction and control of the operations that will follow on your directive.

5. I would say that your directive will assign tasks and objectives to the two Army Groups, allot boundaries, and so on.

Thereafter preparations are made and battle is joined.

It is then that one commander must have powers to direct and control the operations; you cannot possibly do it yourself, and so you would have to nominate someone else.

6. I suggest that your directive should finish with this sentence:

' 12 and 21 Army Groups will develop operations in accordance with the above instructions.

From now onwards full operational direction, control, and co-ordination of these operations is vested in the C.-in-C. 21 Army Group, subject to such instructions as may be issued by the Supreme Commander from time to time.'

7. I put this matter up to you again only because I am so anxious not to have another failure.

I am absolutely convinced that the key to success lies in:

(a) all available offensive power being assigned to the northern line of advance to the Ruhr;

(b) a sound set-up for command, and this implies one man directing and controlling the whole tactical battle on the northern thrust.

I am certain that if we do not comply with these two basic conditions, then we will fail again.

8. I would be grateful if you would not mention to Bradley the point I have referred to in para. 3. I would not like him to think that I remembered that point and had brought it up.

Yours always, and your very
devoted friend
Monty"

When Eisenhower got back to his headquarters and had received my letter, he found waiting for him a telegram from General Marshall saying that he had seen certain statements and articles in the British press which were critical of American command. The telegram went on to say that both the President of the United States and Marshall himself had complete confidence in him (Eisenhower) and that the appointment of a British officer to hold operational command or control over Bradley would be entirely unacceptable in America.

I have always been under the impression that Eisenhower did not know I had been told about Marshall's telegram. That telegram finished the issue of " operational control " as far as I was concerned and I knew it would be useless to open it again.

My Chief of Staff, Freddie de Guingand, was at Supreme Headquarters when Eisenhower returned from his tour and studied my letter which I have quoted above. They discussed the question at length.

De Guingand was impressed by how greatly " het up " Eisenhower was about the whole thing, and he came at once to my Tac Headquarters to tell me all about it. It was from him that I learnt about Marshall's telegram. I decided at once to " pipe down." I sent Eisenhower the following message on the 31st December.

" Dear Ike, I have seen Freddie and understand you are greatly worried by many considerations in these very difficult days. I have given you my frank views because I have felt you like this. I am sure there are many factors which have a bearing quite beyond anything I realise. Whatever your decision may be you can rely on me one hundred per cent to make it work and I know Brad will do the same. Very distressed that my letter may have upset you and I would ask you to tear it up. Your very devoted subordinate Monty."

319

Eisenhower's reply dated the 1st January was as follows:

" Dear Monty, I received your very fine telegram this morning. I truly appreciate the understanding attitude it indicates. With the earnest hope that the year 1945 will be the most successful for you of your entire career, as ever Ike."

Meanwhile, Eisenhower had been working on an outline plan of his own composition. On the 31st December, the day I had sent him my message, he wrote me a personal letter in his own handwriting, which ran as follows:

" Dear Monty,
  Enclosed is my outline plan covering operations as far as they can be foreseen. The immediate thing is to give the enemy in the salient a good beating, destroying everything we can. Following upon that, the plan concentrates everything for the destruction of the enemy north of Prum-Bonn, and gives to you and Bradley each a specific task. The plan also provides for great strength north of the Ruhr when the Rhine is crossed. In these principal features it exactly repeats my intentions as I gave them to you verbally on the train, on the 28th.
  In the matter of command I do not agree that one Army Group Commander should fight his own battle and give orders to another Army Group Commander. My plan places a complete U.S. Army under command of 21 Army Group, something that I consider militarily necessary, and most assuredly reflects my confidence in you personally. If these things were not true this decision would in itself, be a most difficult one.
  You know how greatly I've appreciated and depended upon your frank and friendly counsel, but in your latest letter you disturb me by predictions of 'failure' unless your exact opinions in the matter of giving you command over Bradley are met in detail. I assure you that in this matter I can go no further.
  Please read this document carefully and note how definitely I have planned, after eliminating the salient, to build up the 21 Army Group, give it a major task, and put that task under your command. Moreover, Bradley will be close by your H.Q.
  I know your loyalty as a soldier and your readiness to devote yourself to assigned tasks. For my part I would deplore the develop-

ment of such an unbridgeable group of convictions between us that we would have to present our differences to the Combined Chiefs of Staff. The confusion and debate that would follow would certainly damage the goodwill and devotion to a common cause that have made this Allied Force unique in history.

As ever, your friend,

Ike "

OFFICE OF THE SUPREME COMMANDER

31 December, 1944

OUTLINE PLAN

" My outline plan of operations, based on the current situation and prospects, is as follows:

Basic plan––to destroy enemy forces west of Rhine, north of the Moselle, and to prepare for crossing the Rhine in force with the *main effort north of the Ruhr.* The several tasks are:

(a) To reduce the Ardennes salient by immediate attacks from north and south, with present command arrangements undisturbed until tactical victory within the salient has been assured and the Third Army and Collins' Corps have joined up for a drive to the north-east. Bradley then to resume command of the First U.S. Army. (Enemy action within the salient indicates his determination to make this battle an all-out effort with his mobile forces. *Therefore we must be prepared to use everything consistent with minimum security requirements to accomplish their destruction.*)

(b) Thereafter First and Third Armies to drive to north-east on general line Prum-Bonn, eventually to Rhine.

(c) When *a* is accomplished, 21st Army Group, with Ninth U.S. Army under operational command, to resume preparations for ' VERITABLE.'

(d) All priorities in building up strength of U.S. Armies in personnel, material and units, to go to 12th Army Group.

(e) The front south of Moselle to be strictly defensive for the present.

(f) I will build up a reserve (including re-fitting divisions) which will be available to reinforce success.

(g) As soon as reduction of Ardennes salient permits, H.Q. 12th

Army Group will move north, in close proximity to 21st Army Group H.Q.

(*h*) From now on, any detailed or emergency co-ordination required along Army Group boundaries in the north will be effected by the two Army Group commanders with power of decision vested in C.G., 21 Army Group.

The one thing that must now be prevented is the stabilization of the enemy salient with infantry, permitting him opportunity to use his Panzers at will on any part of the front. We must regain the initiative, and speed and energy are essential.

At conclusion of the battle for the salient, assignment of Divisions to Army Groups and changes in boundaries will be announced.

Dwight D. Eisenhower "

I studied this outline plan. It did all I wanted except in the realm of operational control, and because of Marshall's telegram that subject was closed. It put the weight in the north and gave the Ninth American Army to 21 Army Group. It gave me power of decision in the event of disagreement with Bradley on the boundary between 12 and 21 Army Groups. In fact, I had been given very nearly all that I had been asking for since August. Better late than never. I obviously could not ask for more and I sent Eisenhower the following reply on the 2nd January 1945.

" Thank you for your outline plan dated 31 Dec and letter. I suggest that tactical victory within the salient is going to take some little time to achieve and that there will be heavy fighting. Also it is all bound to get somewhat untidy in that area and I think we want to be very careful to ensure that the moment for changes in command is wisely chosen. I also feel that after we have achieved tactical victory in the salient there may be a considerable interval before other offensive movements begin to develop though I think it is important to try and stage Operation VERITABLE earliest possible. Apart from these few ideas which occur to me I have no comments on the outline plan and details can be worked out later on. You can rely on me and all under my command to go all out one hundred per cent to implement your plan."

I should explain that Operation VERITABLE was the attack south wards of the Canadian Army from the Reichswald Forest, with a view to securing possession of all ground west of the Rhine. The next operation was to be the actual crossing of the Rhine by Second Army, and this was to be planned while Operation VERITABLE was in progress.

All was now agreed in outline.

There were many details to be filled in and a detailed plan to be drawn up; work on those details went on during January. Major-General Whiteley, a British member of the Staff at Supreme Headquarters, was a great help in ensuring that the fundamentals of the plan were not lost sight of in all the detailed staff work that was necessary; he succeeded.

We launched Operation VERITABLE into the Reichswald Forest east of Nijmegen on the 8th February, driving southwards with our left flank on the Rhine.

The Ninth American Army attacked northwards, with its right directed on Dusseldorf, on the 23rd February, in conjunction with the Canadian Army attack.

By the 10th March, the troops of the Ninth American Army and 21 Army Group were lined up along the west bank of the Rhine from Neuss (opposite Dusseldorf) to Nijmegen, all bridges over the river being destroyed. Meanwhile, on the 7th March First American Army had secured intact the railway bridge at Remagen and at once formed a bridgehead on the east bank. The importance of this bridgehead to our subsequent operations was very great. Not only did it lock up a considerable number of surviving enemy divisions in that area, but more important, it loosened up the whole campaign by providing a bridgehead which could be exploited at will. By the third week in March the Allied armies had closed to the Rhine throughout its length from Switzerland to the sea.

In October I had dropped the question of *who* was to command the ground forces; but I did not simultaneously give up the question of *how* to command. The argument about a sound strategy continued. The essential change was to abandon the doctrine of a single ground force commander and to try to get Eisenhower to take a firm grip himself, rather than let his ground armies swarm all over the place without co-ordination. In other words—the purpose remained unchanged but the method of achieving it had, for personal and political reasons, to be argued differently.

Tedder's role as Deputy Supreme Commander was never very

clear to me and, finally, being an airman, he found himself employed
to co-ordinate the air operations.

I never thought that this was what he was originally meant to do.
But it was what he *became* because of the never-ceasing rows between
the lords of the air, each with his own strategic conceptions and with
great jealousies between them.

The generals were little better. So while Tedder dealt with the
air barons, Eisenhower dealt with the warring tribes of generals. The
result was really no strategy at all, and each land army went as far as
it could until it ran out of gas or ammunition, or both.

Insofar, then, as I was concerned the " ground force command "
problem was closed by the end of 1944, as I have already explained.
But to my amazement it was re-opened in February 1945, by the
Prime Minister, who had discussed it I suppose with the British Chief
of Staff.

It was considered in London that Field-Marshal Alexander would
be a better Deputy Supreme Commander than Tedder, since he would
be able to relieve Eisenhower of his preoccupations with the land
battle, which Tedder could not do. I was consulted privately on this
proposal by the Prime Minister and by the C.I.G.S. My answer was
immediate—if Alexander were brought to Supreme Headquarters
there would be storms, both in the Press and with the American
generals. However, the proposal was put to Eisenhower. He asked me
to meet him on the 14th February at some suitable place half-way
between his headquarters and mine, and we met at my old Tac Headquarters at Zonhoven. The British and American delegations to the
Yalta Conference early in February 1945 had been having preliminary
talks in Malta on their way to the Crimea; certain remarks made
in Malta had been reported to Eisenhower, who had not gone
himself to the talks but had sent Bedell Smith. I wrote the following in my diary after Eisenhower had left Zonhoven to return to his
headquarters:

" Eisenhower turned the subject to the question of command.

He said that the P.M. at Malta had told the President (or
Marshall) that he (Ike) did not visit me enough, and implied that
the British side of the party was being neglected.

This hurt him a good deal and he went on to say he was always
being bullied by Marshall and the U.S. Chiefs of Staff for being

too British, or by the P.M. and the British Chiefs of Staff for being too American and for neglecting to visit me.

I am sorry this was said at Malta; it got back to Ike very quickly, and was no doubt attributed to me; he is such an awfully decent chap that I hate to see him upset.

Ike then asked me for my views on the present command set-up; I do not know the reason behind this.

I gave him my views as follows:

(a) I understood that he himself wished to handle the land operations and to command the three Army Groups; he did not want a land force commander between him and the Army Groups.

(b) He had now divided his theatre into ' fronts ' which had a definite relation to strategical and geographical objectives; and he had allotted resources to each ' front ' in accordance with the task.

(c) My ' front ' was to make the main effort. In order that one commander should command all the forces engaged in the main effort, he had placed an American Army under my command. I also had an American Airborne Corps of two U.S. airborne divisions and one British airborne division.

(d) Having in view (a) above, I therefore considered that the command set-up was now satisfactory.

(e) I then said that having arrived at the present command situation I hoped it would remain unchanged till the war was over—which should be in the spring.

Re-grouping might be necessary from time to time, and resources would then be allotted to ' fronts ' in accordance with their tasks. The great point was for one commander always to be responsible for all the forces engaged in the main effort; we should not depart from this principle.

Ike was delighted that I was happy about the present command situation. There is no doubt that he was worried about something when he arrived at Zonhoven, and appeared so during our talk.

I have even now no idea what is at the bottom of his worry. But it was very obvious that as soon as I had said I was very well satisfied with the present situation about command, he became a different man; he drove away beaming all over his face."

Having got me to state that I was satisfied with the existing command set-up, Eisenhower wrote to the C.I.G.S. telling him of this and asking him to consider the following points before advocating the proposed change of the Deputy Supreme Commander:

(a) He (Eisenhower) ran the campaign. The Deputy Supreme Commander handled air problems, since he was an airman. He was responsible also for the administration in rear areas and for planning certain matters such as the Control Commission for Germany; this is all he would ever allow Alexander to do if he came to our theatre.

(b) On no conditions would he agree to have anyone between him and his Army Group Commanders.

(c) If this change was made, there would be great speculations as to the reasons for it. The American generals would quite possibly think that the British were resorting to further pressure in order to get their policy adopted.

On the 1st March Eisenhower visited me again and told me all he knew about the proposal to get Tedder " out " and Alexander " in." He asked me for my views. I gave them as follows:

1. The Allies had been through very difficult and stormy times.

2. We had weathered these storms successfully and the end of the war was in sight.

3. If Alexander were now appointed Deputy Supreme Commander, it would be resented in certain American quarters; a further great storm would arise and all the old disagreements would be revived.

4. For goodness' sake let us stop any further causes of friction at all cost. We are just about to win the German war. Let Alex. remain in Italy. And let Tedder see the thing through to the end as Deputy Supreme Commander.

Eisenhower agreed whole-heartedly with my views.

The Prime Minister visited me on the 2nd March and I told him of my conversation with Eisenhower. He was not very pleased! He went on to see Eisenhower. On the 11th March the Prime Minister wrote to me to say " the matter is now closed."

During March, and before crossing the Rhine, I checked up on our administrative situation. This was good. We had ample supplies of petrol, ammunition and food. The health of the armies was excellent and the sick rate was no more than 6.75 per thousand per week. During the whole winter we had a total of only 201 cases of trench-foot.

Our total battle casualties since D-Day the 6th June 1944 were on the 22nd March 1945 as follows:

Nationality			Casualties
British	..	..	125,045
Canadian	..	..	37,528
Polish	..	..	4,951
Dutch	..	..	125
Belgian	..	..	291
Czech	..	..	438
	TOTAL	..	168,378

The division of this total was:

Killed	Wounded	Missing
35,825	114,563	17,990

The total prisoners captured by 21 Army Group were approximately 250,000.

About 4000 officers and men per day were going to the U.K. on leave. We planned to step this number up to 6000 per day on the 1st April. The following letter of appreciation about leave facilities was received by me from a mother of two of my soldiers:

> 92 Long Street,
> Dordon,
> Nr Tamworth,
> Staffs.
>
> 23/2/45

" Sir,

As a Mother who is lying ill with Cancer and whose two boys are serving overseas, I feel I must write to express my deep appreciation of the splendid arrangements that were made for leave for boys from the B.L.A.

My younger son has just spent seven days at home and now he
has returned to the Western Front. I think you would like to
know that he and his friends were loud in their praise of the
arrangements on his journey. Everything possible was done for
their comfort, even to the issue of new clean battledress to come
home in and refreshments on the journey.

No wonder the armies under your command have proved
invincible in this war. Your men are treated like human beings.

I wish you every possible luck in your campaign and, if it is
not a presumption, may I congratulate you on your brilliant
personal achievements.

With heartfelt gratitude,

I am, Sir,

Your Obedient Servant,

(Mrs.) A. D. Lear"

I issued the following message to the armies on the 23rd March.
That night we began Operation PLUNDER, the crossing of the
Rhine in strength on a wide front between Rheinberg and Rees—
with the Ninth American Army on the right and the Second Army
on the left. The Canadian Army had an important role on the left
flank, north of Rees.

" 1. On the 7th February I told you we were going into the ring
for the final and last round; there would be no time limit;
we would continue fighting until our opponent was knocked
out. The last round is going very well on both sides of the ring
—and overhead.

2. In the West, the enemy has lost the Rhineland, and with it the
flower of at least four armies—the Parachute Army, Fifth
Panzer Army, Fifteenth Army, and Seventh Army; the First
Army, farther to the south, is now being added to the list.
In the Rhineland battles, the enemy has lost about 150,000
prisoners, and there are many more to come; his total casualties
amount to about 250,000 since 8th February.

3. In the East, the enemy has lost all Pomerania east of the Oder,
an area as large as the Rhineland; and three more German
armies have been routed. The Russian armies are within about
35 miles of Berlin.

4. Overhead, the Allied Air Forces are pounding Germany day

328

In the Siegfried Line with General Simpson, Commander of the
Ninth American Army, 3rd March 1945

Lunch on the east bank of the Rhine with the Prime Minister and
Field-Marshal Brooke, 26th March 1945

The Germans come to my Tac H.Q. on Lüneburg Heath to surrender, 3rd May 1945

Reading the terms of surrender to the German delegation—Lüneburg Heath, 4th May 1945. Chester Wilmot is just to the right of the left-hand tent pole

and night. It will be interesting to see how much longer the Germans can stand it.

5. The enemy has in fact been driven into a corner, and he cannot escape.

Events are moving rapidly.

The complete and decisive defeat of the Germans is certain; there is no possibility of doubt on this matter.

6. 21 ARMY GROUP WILL NOW CROSS THE RHINE

The enemy possibly thinks he is safe behind this great river obstacle. We all agree that it is a great obstacle; but we will show the enemy that he is far from safe behind it. This great Allied fighting machine, composed of integrated land and air forces, will deal with the problem in no uncertain manner.

7. And having crossed the Rhine, we will crack about in the plains of Northern Germany, chasing the enemy from pillar to post. The swifter and the more energetic our action, the sooner the war will be over, and that is what we all desire; to get on with the job and finish off the German war as soon as possible.

8. Over the Rhine, then, let us go. And good hunting to you all on the other side.

9. May 'The Lord mighty in battle' give us the victory in this our latest undertaking, as He has done in all our battles since we landed in Normandy on D-Day."

The Prime Minister stayed with me at my Tac Headquarters and watched the airborne divisions land beyond the river on the morning of the 24th March. We were now fighting deep in Germany and I asked the Prime Minister when British troops had last fought on German soil. He told me it was when the Rocket Brigade, now " O " (Rocket) Battery R.H.A., fought in the Battle of Leipzig on the 18th October 1813. The Rocket Brigade was the only British unit in that battle. It was commanded by 2nd Capt. Richard Bogue, who was killed in the battle at a place called Pounsdorff. The Brigade was attached to the Swedish Army and was fighting with Prussians, etc., against French, Saxons, Westphalians, etc. There were thus " Germans " both with us and against us. I consulted the senior artillery officer at my headquarters and told the Prime Minister that " O " Battery (Rocket Troop) R.H.A. was now in the 1st R.H.A. in Italy, under Field-Marshal Alexander. They have always been extremely proud of their title of "The Rocket Troop," and in 1930 were invited by the German Army to send representatives to Leipzig for the unveiling of the Memorial which I believe was supposed to have been a centenary celebration, but was delayed until that year. They took with them Horse Artillery trumpeters who sounded the Last Post and who were dressed in full dress. They were the guests of the Germay Army at Leipzig.

It is interesting to note that gunners once again used rockets on the Continent after a lapse of over 130 years. They were used by the Canadians on the Meuse and were manned by personnel of a Light A.A. Regiment. Second Army also used them at the Rhine crossing.

I asked the Prime Minister if he would send a message to the soldiers of 21 Army Group, who had just crossed the Rhine. He wrote the following:

"I rejoice to be with the Chief of the Imperial General Staff at Field-Marshal Montgomery's Headquarters of 21 Army Group during this memorable battle of forcing the Rhine. British Soldiers —it will long be told how, with our Canadian brothers and valiant United States Allies, this superb task was accomplished. Once the river line is pierced and the crust of German resistance is broken decisive victory in Europe will be near. May God prosper our arms in this noble adventure after our long struggle for King and country, for dear life, and for the freedom of mankind.

(Sgd) Winston S. Churchill,
Prime Minister & Minister of Defence"

When the Prime Minister left me on the 26th March to return to London, he wrote the following in my autograph book:

"The Rhine and all its fortress lines lie behind the 21st Group of Armies. Once again they have been the hinge on which massive gates revolved. Once again they have proved that physical barriers are vain without the means and spirit to hold them.

A beaten army not long ago master of Europe retreats before its pursuers. The goal is not long to be denied to those who have come so far and fought so well under proud and faithful leadership Forward on wings of flame to final Victory.

Winston S. Churchill"

Once over the Rhine I began to discuss future operational plans with Eisenhower. We had several meetings. I had always put Berlin as a priority objective; it was a political centre and if we could beat the Russians to it things would be much easier for us in the post-war years. It will be remembered that in his letter to me dated the 15th September 1944 (Chapter 15) Eisenhower had agreed with me about the great importance of the German capital, and had said:

" *Clearly, Berlin is the main prize*

There is no doubt whatsoever, in my mind, that we should concentrate all our energies and resources on a rapid thrust to Berlin."

But now he did not agree. His latest view was expressed in a message he sent me on the 31st March 1945 which ended with the following sentence:

" You will note that in none of this do I mention Berlin. That place has become, so far as I am concerned, nothing but a geographical location, and I have never been interested in these. My purpose is to destroy the enemy's forces and his powers to resist."

It was useless for me to pursue the matter further. We had had so much argument already on great issues; anyhow, it was now almost too late. But after the victory in Normandy my point was that the final defeat of the German armed forces was imminent—in a few more months.

The important point was therefore to ensure that when that day arrived we would have a political balance in Europe which would help us, the Western nations, to win the peace. That meant getting possession of certain political centres in Europe before the Russians— notably Vienna, Prague and Berlin. If the higher direction of the war had been handled properly by the political leaders of the West, and suitable instructions given to Supreme Commanders, we could have grabbed all three before the Russians. But what happened? The possibility of seizing Vienna disappeared when it was decided to land the DRAGOON force in southern France; the troops for the landing were taken from Field-Marshal Alexander's force in Italy and that put a brake on his operations. It should be noted that Stalin whole-heartedly approved the DRAGOON landing. Of course he did. It made certain that his forces would get to Vienna before ours!

As regards Prague, the Third American Army was halted on the western frontier of Czechoslovakia towards the end of April—for reasons which I have never understood. When finally allowed to cross the frontier early in May, Bradley states in *A Soldier's Story*, page 549, that it was ordered not to advance beyond Pilsen " because Czechoslovakia had already been earmarked for liberation by the Red army." He goes on to say that had SHAEF remanded its order, Patton " could probably have been in Prague within 24 hours."

Berlin was lost to us when we failed to make a sound operational plan in August 1944, after the victory in Normandy.

The Americans could not understand that it was of little avail to win the war strategically if we lost it politically; because of this curious viewpoint we suffered accordingly from VE-Day onwards, and are still so suffering. War is a political instrument; once it is clear that you are going to win, political considerations must influence its further course. It became obvious to me in the autumn of 1944 that the way things were being handled was going to have repercussions far beyond the end of the war; it looked to me then as if we were going to " muck it up." I reckon we did.

There is not much more to tell which has not already been narrated by others. With the Rhine behind us we drove hard for the Baltic. My object was to get there in time to be able to offer a firm front to the Russian endeavours to get up into Denmark, and thus control the entrance to the Baltic. In order to speed up the rate of advance, divisions operated in great depth on narrow thrust lines; enemy areas of resistance were by-passed by armoured spearheads and were later attacked from the flank or rear by other troops coming on behind.

As we moved eastwards, the Prime Minister and Eisenhower both became anxious lest I might not be able to " head off" the Russians from getting into Schleswig-Holstein, and then occupying Denmark. Both sent me messages about it. I fear I got somewhat irritated and my replies possibly showed it! To Eisenhower I replied on the 27th April that I was very well aware what had to be done, but he must understand that when he had removed the Ninth American Army from my command (which he had done on the 3rd April) the tempo of operations slowed down automatically on the northern flank. In the end we beat the Russians to it. We reached the Baltic at Wismar and Lübeck on the 2nd May and thus sealed off the Danish peninsula with about six hours to spare, before the Russians arrived. We established an eastern front from Wismar on the Baltic to the Elbe at Domitz; German troops and civilians were surging against this flank, trying to escape from the Russians. We had a western front from Lübeck, westwards to Bad Oldesloe and thence south to the Elbe. In between these two fronts was great congestion and confusion; the roads were crowded with German soldiers and civilians who had come in from the east. On the 2nd and 3rd May the prisoners taken by Second Army totalled nearly half a million.

It was interesting to consider the difference in the two major catastrophes the Germans had suffered at the hands of the Westesn Allies since June 1944. In August 1944 they had suffered a major defeat in Normandy; but they were allowed to recover and their man-power situation was such that they could form and equip new divisions. Their present defeat in March/April 1945 was not comparable to that suffered in Normandy; they had lost so heavily in personnel and territory that they could not again form and equip new divisions. They would never again have uninterrupted communications and assured mobility. Therefore their cause was lost and the German war had reached its last moments. Hitler's Germany now faced utter disaster.

CHAPTER 20

THE GERMAN SURRENDER

ON THE 27th April I received a report from the War Office that on the 24th Himmler had made an offer of capitulation through the Swedish Red Cross.

Himmler stated that Hitler was desperately ill and that he (Himmler) was in a position of full authority to act. I did not pay much attention to this report. So far as I was concerned the oncoming Russians were more dangerous than the stricken Germans. I knew the German war was practically over. The essential and immediate task was to push on with all speed and get to the Baltic, and then to form a flank facing east; this was the only way to stop the Russians getting into Schleswig-Holstein and thence into Denmark.

Events now began to move rapidly. Late on the 1st May we picked up an announcement on the German wireless that Hitler had died at his command post in Berlin and that he had appointed Admiral Doenitz to succeed him as Führer. No mention was made of Himmler; one of my liaison officers later saw him at Doenitz's headquarters at Flensburg and gathered that he was no longer playing a leading part in the direction of affairs.

On the afternoon of the 2nd May General Blumentritt, who was commanding all the German land forces between the Baltic and the River Weser, sent a message to Second Army headquarters that he proposed to come in the next morning to offer the surrender of his forces. He did not appear but instead sent a message to the effect that negotiations were to be conducted on a higher level.

On the 3rd May Field-Marshal Keitel sent a delegation to my headquarters on Lüneburg Heath, with the consent of Admiral Doenitz, to open negotiations for surrender. This party arrived at 11.30 hrs. and consisted of:

General-Admiral von Friedeburg, C.-in-C. of the German Navy.

General Kinzel, Chief of Staff to Field-Marshal Busch, who was
  commanding the German land forces on my northern and
  western flanks.
Rear-Admiral Wagner.
Major Freidel, a staff officer.

This party of four was later joined by Colonel Pollek, another staff
officer.

They were brought to my caravan site and were drawn up under
the Union Jack, which was flying proudly in the breeze. I kept them
waiting for a few minutes and then came out of my caravan and walked
towards them. They all saluted, under the Union Jack. It was a great
moment; I knew the Germans had come to surrender and that the war
was over. Few of those in the signals and operations caravans at my
Tac Headquarters will forget the thrill experienced when they heard
the faint " tapping " of the Germans trying to pick us up on the
wireless command link—to receive the surrender instructions from
their delegation.

I said to my interpreter, " Who are these men? " He told me.
I then said, " What do they want? "

Admiral Friedeburg then read me a letter from Field-Marshal
Keitel offering to surrender to me the three German armies withdrawing in front of the Russians between Berlin and Rostock. I refused
to consider this, saying that these armies should surrender to the
Russians. I added that, of course, if any German soldiers came towards
my front with their hands up they would automatically be taken
prisoner. Von Friedeburg said it was unthinkable to surrender to the
Russians as they were savages, and the German soldiers would be sent
straight off to work in Russia.

I said the Germans should have thought of all these things before
they began the war, and particularly before they attacked the Russians
in June 1941.

Von Friedeburg next said that they were anxious about the civilian
population in Mecklenburg who were being overrun by the Russians,
and they would like to discuss how these could be saved. I replied
that Mecklenburg was not in my area and that any problems connected
with it must be discussed with the Russians. I said they must understand that I refused to discuss any matter connected with the situation
on my eastern flank between Wismar and Domitz; they must approach

the Russians on such matters. I then asked if they wanted to discuss the surrender of their forces on my western flank. They said they did not. But they were anxious about the civilian population in those areas, and would like to arrange with me some scheme by which their troops could withdraw slowly as my forces advanced. I refused.

I then decided to spring something on them quickly. I said to von Friedeburg:

"Will you surrender to me all German forces on my western and northern flanks, including all forces in Holland, Friesland with the Frisian Islands and Heligoland, Schleswig-Holstein, and Denmark? If you will do this, I will accept it as a tactical battlefield surrender of the enemy forces immediately opposing me, and those in support in Denmark."

He said he could not agree to this. But he was anxious to come to some agreement about the civilian population in those areas; I refused to discuss this. I then said that if the Germans refused to surrender unconditionally the forces in the areas I had named, I would order the fighting to continue; many more German soldiers would then be killed, and possibly some civilians also from artillery fire and air attack. I next showed them on a map the actual battle situation on the whole western front; they had no idea what this situation was and were very upset. By this time I reckoned that I would not have much more difficulty in getting them to accept my demands. But I thought that an interval for lunch might be desirable so that they could reflect on what I had said. I sent them away to have lunch in a tent by themselves, with nobody else present except one of my officers. Von Friedeburg wept during lunch and the others did not say much.

After lunch I sent for them again and this time the meeting was in my conference tent with the map of the battle situation on the table. I began this meeting by delivering an ultimatum. They must surrender unconditionally all their forces in the areas I had named; once they had done this I would discuss with them the best way of occupying the areas and looking after the civilians; if they refused, I would go on with the battle. They saw at once that I meant what I said. They were convinced of the hopelessness of their cause but they said they had no power to agree to my demands. They were, however, now prepared to recommend to Field-Marshal Keitel the unconditional surrender of all the forces on the western and northern flanks of 21 Army Group. Two of them would go back to O.K.W, see Keitel, and bring back his agreement.

I then drew up a document which summarised the decisions reached at our meeting, which I said must be signed by myself and von Friedeburg, and could then be taken to Flensburg, and given to Keitel and Doenitz.

It read as follows:

" 1. All members of the German armed forces who come into the 21 Army Group front from the east desiring to surrender will be made Prisoners of War.

An acceptance by 21 Army Group of the surrender of a complete German Army fighting the Russians is not possible.

2. No discussion about civilians possible.

3. Field-Marshal Montgomery desires that all German forces in Holland, Friesland (including the islands and Heligoland), Schleswig-Holstein and Denmark lay down their arms and surrender unconditionally to him.

He is prepared when the surrender has been agreed to discuss the method of occupying the areas, dealing with civilians, etc.

4. General-Admiral Von Friedeburg is not at present empowered to give the agreement of surrender as in para. 3. He will therefore send two officers (Rear-Admiral Wagner and Major Freidel) to the Oberkommando of the Wehrmacht to obtain and bring back the agreement.

He requests Field-Marshal Montgomery to make available an aircraft for the two officers as transport by road is too slow and requests that Admiral Von Friedeburg and General Kinzel remain at Field-Marshal Montgomery's H.Q. in the meantime."

Actually it was von Friedeburg and Freidel who went back to Flensburg, and they went by car. They were escorted through Hamburg and into the German lines by Lieut.-Colonel Trumbull Warren, my Canadian A.D.C. I said they must be back at my Tac Headquarters by 6 p.m. the next day, 4th May. Kinzel and Wagner remained at my headquarters.

I was certain von Friedeburg would return with full powers to sign. I therefore decided to see the Press at 5 p.m. on the 4th May and to describe to the correspondents all that had happened in the last few days, and to tell them about what I *hoped* was going to happen at 6 p.m. that evening.

It has been said that I was not usually very good at Press conferences. At the end of this one I received the following letter from Alan Moorehead, who was the unofficial spokesman for the Press at my headquarters.

" Dear Field-Marshal,

May I, on behalf of the correspondents, offer our thanks for the admirable conference you gave us today?

We are most grateful for your interest especially at this historic moment, and it only remains to us to offer our heartiest congratulations on the brilliant end of your long journey from the desert.

We have all tonight tried to do justice to the story we have waited so long to write, the best story probably of our lives.

I wonder, as one more kindness, would you sign the enclosed copies of your armistice.

With all good wishes,
(Signed) Alan Moorehead "

Von Friedeburg and Freidel got back to my headquarters while the Press conference was in progress. I saw Colonel Ewart, my staff officer, enter the tent and knew he had the answer. But I finished my talk and then asked Ewart if von Friedeburg was back. He said he was. I told the correspondents they could all go with me to my conference tent and witness the final scene.

The German delegation was paraded again under the Union Jack outside my caravan. I took von Friedeburg into my caravan, to see him alone. I asked him if he would sign the full surrender terms as I had demanded; he said he would do so. He was very dejected and I told him to rejoin the others outside. It was now nearly 6 p.m. I gave orders for the ceremony to take place at once in a tent pitched for the purpose, which had been wired for the recording instruments. The German delegation went across to the tent, watched by groups of soldiers, war correspondents, photographers, and others—all very excited. They knew it was the end of the war.

I had the surrender document all ready. The arrangements in the tent were very simple—a trestle table covered with an army blanket, an inkpot, an ordinary army pen that you could buy in a shop for twopence. There were two B.B.C. microphones on the table. The

Germans stood up as I entered; then we all sat down round the table. The Germans were clearly nervous and one of them took out a cigarette; he wanted to smoke to calm his nerves. I looked at him, and he put the cigarette away.

In that tent on Lüneburg Heath, publicly in the presence of the Press and other spectators, I read out in English the Instrument of Surrender. I said that unless the German delegation signed this document immediately, and without argument on what would follow their capitulation, I would order the fighting to continue. I then called on each member of the German delegation by name to sign the document, which they did without any discussion. I then signed, on behalf of General Eisenhower.

The document was in English, and the delegation could not understand it; but I gave them copies in German. A photograph of the original is facing page 344. It will be noticed that when adding the date I wrote 5 May, then tried to change the 5 to a 4, then crossed it out and initialled it, and wrote 4 alongside. The original is typed on an ordinary sheet of army foolscap. I was asked to forward it to Supreme Headquarters. Instead I sent photostat copies. The original is in my possession and I will never part with it; it is a historic document. I do not know what happened to the pen we all used; I suppose someone pinched it.

INSTRUMENT OF SURRENDER
OF
ALL GERMAN ARMED FORCES IN HOLLAND, IN NORTHWEST GERMANY INCLUDING ALL ISLANDS, AND IN DENMARK

1. The German Command agrees to the surrender of all German armed forces in Holland, in northwest Germany including the Frisian Islands, and Heligoland and all other islands, in Schleswig-Holstein, and in Denmark, to the C.-in-C. 21 Army Group. This to include all naval ships in these areas.
   These forces to lay down their arms and to surrender unconditionally.
2. All hostilities on land, on sea, or in the air by German forces in the above areas to cease at 0800 hrs British Double Summer Time on Saturday 5th May 1945.

3. The German Command to carry out at once, and without argument or comment, all further orders that will be issued by the Allied Powers on any subject.

4. Disobedience of orders, or failure to comply with them, will be regarded as a breach of these surrender terms and will be dealt with by the Allied Powers in accordance with the accepted laws and usages of war.

5. This instrument of surrender is independent of, without prejudice to, and will be superseded by any general instrument of surrender imposed by or on behalf of the Allied Powers and applicable to Germany and the German armed forces as a whole.

6. This instrument of surrender is written in English and in German.
   The English version is the authentic text.

7. The decision of the Allied Powers will be final if any doubt or dispute arises as to the meaning or interpretation of the surrender terms.

B L Montgomery	Friedeburg
Field-Marshal	Kinzel
	Wagner
4 May 1945	Pollek
1830 hours	Freidel

Of the four Germans who arrived at my Tac Headquarters on Lüneburg Heath on the 3rd May, only one is alive today. He is Rear-Admiral Wagner, who is now Deputy Head of the Naval Department of the West German Ministry of Defence. The other three died violent deaths. Von Friedeburg poisoned himself, Kinzel shot himself, and Freidel was killed in a motor accident shortly afterwards.

Following the signing of the Instrument of Surrender there was much to be done. I had ordered all offensive action to cease on the 3rd May when the Germans first came to see me; I knew it was the end and I did not want any more casualties among the troops entrusted to my care. I now sent out a cease fire order to take effect at 8 a.m. on Saturday 5th May 1945.

I felt that I must at once speak to the Commanders and troops under my command who had come so far and fought so well. Victory was far more due to their efforts than to anything I had been able to

do myself. The first message was to my senior commanders, and ran
as follows:

"The German armed forces facing 21 Army Group have surrendered unconditionally to us. At this historic moment I want to
express to Army Commanders and to the Commander L. of C.
my grateful thanks for the way they and their men have carried
out the immense task that was given them. I hope to express myself more adequately later on but I felt that I must at once tell you
all how well you have done and how proud I am to command
21 Army Group. Please tell your commanders and troops that I
thank them from the bottom of my heart."

I then spent some time in drafting a personal message to the officers
and men of 21 Army Group. Many had been with me in the Eighth
Army. It was not an easy message to write and I pondered long over
para. 5. In para. 7 I wrote: "We have won the German war.
Let us now win the peace."

I often wonder if we have won the peace. In fact, I do not think
we have.

MY LAST MESSAGE TO THE ARMIES

"1. On this day of victory in Europe I feel I would like to speak
   to all who have served and fought with me during the last few
   years. What I have to say is very simple, and quite short.
2. I would ask you all to remember those of our comrades who
   fell in the struggle. They gave their lives that others might
   have freedom, and no man can do more than that. I believe
   that He would say to each one of them:
      'Well done, thou good and faithful servant.'
3. And we who remain have seen the thing through to the end;
   we all have a feeling of great joy and thankfulness that we have
   been preserved to see this day.
   We must remember to give the praise and thankfulness where
   it is due:
      'This is the Lord's doing, and it is marvellous in our eyes.'
4. In the early days of this war the British Empire stood alone
   against the combined might of the Axis powers. And during
   those days we suffered some great disasters; but we stood firm;
   on the defensive, but striking blows where we could. Later

we were joined by Russia and America; and from then onwards the end was in no doubt. Let us never forget what we owe to our Russian and American allies; this great allied team has achieved much in war; may it achieve even more in peace.

5. Without doubt, great problems lie ahead; the world will not recover quickly from the upheaval that has taken place; there is much work for each of us.

I would say that we must face up to that work with the same fortitude that we faced up to the worst days of this war. It may be that some difficult times lie ahead for our country, and for each one of us personally. If it happens thus, then our discipline will pull us through; but we must remember that the best discipline implies the subordination of self for the benefit of the community.

6. It has been a privilege and an honour to command this great British Empire team in Western Europe. Few commanders can have had such loyal service as you have given me. I thank each one of you from the bottom of my heart.

7. And so let us embark on what lies ahead full of joy and optimism. We have won the German war. Let us now win the peace.

8. Good luck to you all, wherever you may be."

Then there were the other Services.

No one knew better than I how much we soldiers owed to the Royal Navy and the Royal Air Force since the war began in 1939. My relations with the R.A.F. had been very close throughout; I had not seen so much of the Navy.

I sent each Service a message from us all, which I reproduce below.

MESSAGE TO THE ROYAL NAVY

" *Personal for Admiral of the Fleet Sir Andrew Cunningham from Field-Marshal Montgomery*

1. As C.-in-C. of the armies of the British Empire in Western Europe I would like today to salute you and the Royal Navy.

2. Throughout our long journey from Egypt to the Baltic any success achieved by the British Armies has been made possible only by the magnificent support given us by the Royal Navy. With unfailing precision we have been put ashore, supported, and supplied. Our confidence has been such that the Army ha

never questioned the certainty of a safe landfall nor of the safe arrival of our reinforcements and supplies across the seas.

3. I want to thank you and all those gallant sailors who have supported us with such valour. We soldiers owe the Royal Navy a great debt of gratitude and we will never forget it.

4. Would it be possible for you to convey the gratitude of myself and all those serving under me to all your Flag Officers and Captains and to all ranks and ratings of the Royal Navy. We wish the Royal Navy the best of luck."

THE REPLY OF THE NAVY

" 1. On behalf of all officers and men of the Royal Navy I thank you for your generous message.

2. Ever since the summer of 1940 the Royal Navy has been eagerly looking forward to the day when we could land the Armies of the British Empire once again on the continent of Europe.

3. We sailors never doubted that, when the day came, the soldiers would, however hard the struggle, achieve ultimate victory in battle.

4. We have watched with profound admiration the progress of your operations which have now inflicted on the enemy an overwhelming and decisive defeat.

5. Our warmest congratulations and best wishes to you and all ranks serving under your command."

MESSAGE TO THE ROYAL AIR FORCE

" *Following for Sir Charles Portal from Field-Marshal Montgomery*

1. In 21 Army Group we have no Germans left to fight in Western Europe.

2. At this historic moment I feel I would like to express to you, the head of the Royal Air Force, the deep sense of gratitude that we soldiers owe to you and your splendid Force. The mighty weapon of air power has enabled us firstly to win a great victory quickly and secondly to win that victory with fewer casualties than would otherwise have been the case. We are all deeply conscious of these facts. The brave and brilliant work of your gallant pilots and crews and the devotion to duty of the ground staffs have aroused our profound admiration.

3. I would be grateful if you would convey the gratitude of myself and of all those serving under me to all your commanders both senior and junior and to all ranks throughout the Royal Air Force. And perhaps you would include a special word of greeting and good wishes from myself personally to every officer and man in the Royal Air Force."

REPLY OF THE AIR FORCE

" I am profoundly moved by your most generous message which will be passed to all ranks in the Royal Air Force. From the landing in Normandy until this hour of Victory all of us in the Royal Air Force have felt the highest admiration for the endurance, courage and skill of the officers and men of 21 Army Group and for the wonderful success of the battles they have fought under your brilliant leadership. We count it a high honour to have had the opportunity to speed your advance and the thought that we may have been able to reduce the casualties suffered by your gallant men has given us all the greatest possible satisfaction. Your splendid tribute will be received with deep pride and gratitude by all ranks of the Royal Air Force and of the Dominion and Allied Air Forces who have served with us. May I on their behalf send you and all your men our heartfelt congratulations on the greatest achievements of 21 Army Group."

I would like to quote one of the many messages of congratulation I received—that from the Army Council. I do so because at an earlier stage in my career I had been informed of the displeasure of the Army Council.

This message seemed to cancel the previous one!

" The Army Council congratulate you and all ranks of 21 Army Group on the magnificent success achieved today. The Lüneburg capitulation marks the culmination not only of the brilliant campaign of the last eleven months, but also of the long years of preparation that passed between the withdrawal of our armies from north-west Europe when the British peoples were left to uphold alone the cause of freedom, and the day of your triumphant return. Now, in company with the Forces of great

Instrument of Surrender

of

All German armed forces in HOLLAND, in

northwest Germany including all islands,

and in DENMARK.

1. The German Command agrees to the surrender of all German armed
forces in HOLLAND, in northwest GERMANY including the FRISIAN
ISLANDS and HELIGOLAND and all other islands, in SCHLESWIG-
HOLSTEIN, and in DENMARK, to the C.-in-C. 21 Army Group.
This to include all naval ships in these areas.
These forces to lay down their arms and to surrender unconditionally.

2. All hostilities on land, on sea, or in the air by German forces
in the above areas to cease at 0800 hrs. British Double Summer Time
on Saturday 5 May 1945.

3. The German command to carry out at once, and without argument or
comment, all further orders that will be issued by the Allied
Powers on any subject.

4. Disobedience of orders, or failure to comply with them, will be
regarded as a breach of these surrender terms and will be dealt
with by the Allied Powers in accordance with the accepted laws
and usages of war.

5. This instrument of surrender is independent of, without prejudice
to, and will be superseded by any general instrument of surrender
imposed by or on behalf of the Allied Powers and applicable to Germany
and the German armed forces as a whole.

6. This instrument of surrender is written in English and in German.

   The English version is the authentic text.

7. The decision of the Allied Powers will be final if any doubt or
dispute arises as to the meaning or interpretation of the surrender
terms.

B. L. Montgomery
Field-Marshal

4 May 1945

1830 hrs

*Photo of the original surrender document that was signed by
the Germans at 1830 hrs. on 4th May 1945*

Scene in the Champs Elysées when I visited Paris on the 25th May 1945

Field-Marshal Busch comes to my Tac H.Q. to be " ticked off", 11th May 1945

Allies, you have liberated the territory of our friends, confounded the armed might of the enemy and freed the people of this country from a terrible ordeal and the threat of one still worse.

To your own unerring leadership, and to the skill and courage of your soldiers, the gratitude of the nation is due. Never has Britain had such great need of her Army: never has it served her better."

The immediate problem that now faced us was terrific. We had in our area nearly one and a half million German prisoners of war. There were a further one million German wounded, without medical supplies and in particular with a shortage of bandages and no anaesthetics. In addition, there were about one million civilian refugees who had fled into our area from the advancing Russians; these and " Displaced Persons " were roaming about the country, often looting as they went. Transportation and communication services had ceased to function. Agriculture and industry were largely at a standstill. Food was scarce and there was a serious risk of famine and disease during the coming months. And to crown it all there was no central government in being, and the machinery whereby a central government could function no longer existed.

Here was a pretty pickle!

I was a soldier and I had not been trained to handle anything of this nature.

However, something had to be done, and done quickly.

Meanwhile I will close this chapter by quoting the last entry made in my autograph book by the Prime Minister. It will be noticed that this entry is headed " Chapter X," and the Prime Minister refers to a ' tenth chapter." This is because he wrote, in his own handwriting, ten pages in my autograph book between August 1942 and May 1945. Each one was at a definite milestone in the long journey from Alamein, and was given the title of a chapter. These pages were later photographed and were published by me in a little booklet entitled *Ten Chapters* (Hutchinson and Co.) in June 1946. The autograph book itself is in my possession and very precious it is.

"CHAPTER X

At last the goal is reached.

The terrible enemy has unconditionally surrendered. In loyal

accord with our splendid American Ally, full and friendly contact
has been made with the Russians advancing from the East.

The 21st Group of Armies, wheeling and striking to the north had
the honour of liberating Holland and Denmark and of receiving
and gathering as captive in the space of three or four days upwards
of two millions of the once-renowned German Army. This record
of military glories, predicted or celebrated, now in its tenth
chapter, reaches its conclusion. The fame of the Army Group like
that of the Eighth Army will long shine in history, and other
generations besides our own will honour their deeds and above
all the character, profound strategy and untiring zeal of their
Commander who marched from Egypt through Tripoli, Tunis,
Sicily and southern Italy, and through France, Belgium, Holland
and Germany to the Baltic and the Elbe without losing a battle
or even a serious action.

Winston S. Churchill
May 8, 1945 "

CHAPTER 21

SOME THOUGHTS ON HIGH COMMAND
IN WAR

IT HAS been my unique privilege to have commanded during my career every echelon from a platoon up to and including a Group of Armies. I say " unique " because I doubt if there is any other soldier today still serving on the active list in the free world who has had the same experience.

Times have changed since the campaigns of Marlborough and Wellington; it could almost be said that they won their campaigns single-handed. Certainly they were not bothered with the enormous amount of detailed staff work involved in modern armies. Today a C.-in-C. in the field is the captain of a team, and a large team at that. In the summer of 1945 the question arose whether the nation should make grants of money to the principal commanders in the field in recognition of their services, following the precedent of previous wars. But in modern war, once you start picking out individuals who have really made a first-class contribution to the war effort, great problems arise. What about those responsible for radar, anti-submarine devices, intelligence, medical work, and the many whose devoted work in lower grades made possible the winning of the contest? It was mainly for these reasons that I made it known in September 1945 that, if offered a monetary award, I would not accept it. There were, of course, other reasons.

We were then, financially, almost a bankrupt nation and could hardly afford to spend about a million sterling on such a purpose. The average ex-serviceman, officer or other rank, was going to find life pretty difficult in the immediate post-war years. It would not be good for him to read of individual soldiers, however much he might admire and respect them, being given say £100,000 or £50,000 in addition to their pensions when he (the ex-serviceman) was hard put to it to support his own wife and family. Millions of people were

347

going to starve in various parts of the world. I would not have been able to square my conscience if so large a sum had been given to me simply for doing my duty to the best of my ability as so many others had also done. My view was, and is, that monetary awards, as distinct from honours from the Crown, are out of date.

High Command today is more complicated than formerly and a C.-in-C. has got to have a good staff, and a superb Chief of Staff to co-ordinate its activities. He must also pick his subordinate commanders with the greatest care, matching the generals to the jobs. He must know his soldiers, and be recognised by them. I do not believe the leadership displayed on the Western Front in World War I would have succeeded in World War II. I would remind the reader that in World War I although I served in France, I never once saw French or Haig.

An army today is a self-contained community; it contains everything its members need for war, from bullets to blood banks. I will always remember Churchill's anger when he heard of several dentist' chairs being landed over the beaches in Normandy! But we have learnt since the 1914-18 war that by caring for a man's teeth, we keep him in the battle. The good general must not only win his battles he must win them with a minimum of casualties and loss of life I learnt during the 1939-45 war that four things contributed to the saving of life:

1. Blood transfusion.
2. Surgical teams operating well forward in the battle area, so that a badly wounded man could be dealt with at once without having to be moved by road to a hospital.
3. Air evacuation direct to a Base hospital many hundreds of miles in rear, thus saving bumpy journeys by road or rail.
4. Nursing sisters working well forward in the battle area. When I joined the Eighth Army in 1942, nursing sisters were not allowed in the forward battle area. I cancelled the order. Their presence comforted and calmed the nerves of many seriously wounded men, who then knew they would be properly nursed No male nursing orderly can nurse like a woman, though many think they can.

All these things, and many others like them, have to be in the mind of the modern general.

On the administrative side there must be a clear-cut, long-term relationship established between operational intentions and administrative resources. Successful administrative planning is dependent on anticipation of requirements. A C.-in-C. in the field must, therefore, always keep his staff fully in his mind as regards forward intentions, so that the essential administrative preparations can be completed in time. Many generals have failed in war because they neglected to ensure that what they wanted to achieve operationally was commensurate with their administrative resources; and some have failed because they over-insured in this respect. The lesson is, there must always be a nice balance between the two requirements. The acid test of an officer who aspires to high command is his ability to be able to grasp quickly the essentials of a military problem, to decide rapidly what he will do, to make it quite clear to all concerned what he intends to achieve and how he will do it, and then to see that his subordinate commanders get on with the job. Above all, he has got to rid himself of all irrelevant detail; he must concentrate on the essentials, and on those details and only those details which are necessary to the proper carrying out of his plan—trusting his staff to effect all the necessary co-ordination. When all is said and done the greatest quality required in a commander is " decision "; he must then be able to issue clear orders and have the " drive " to get things done. Indecision and hesitation are fatal in any officer; in a C.-in-C. they are criminal.

No modern C.-in-C. can have any success if he fails to understand the human approach to war. Battles are won primarily in the hearts of men; if he loses the battle for the hearts of his men he will achieve little. This approach, and my general philosophy about command, I have already tried to explain in Chapter 6.

Throughout any force the organisation for command and control must be simple and clear cut. In the desert campaign, in Sicily and in Italy it was so. In the campaign in North-West Europe the organisation worked well at the start, and with it we won one of the greatest battles of modern times—in Normandy. Then it was changed, and smooth and efficient command and control disappeared—as we have seen.

A commander of national forces is always within his rights to make clear his views on operational policies to his superior; indeed, it is his duty to do so. But once his superior commander has given his decision, there can be no further argument. In this connection I repro-

duce below a letter written to me by Eisenhower in February 1946
after I had sent him a copy of a book I had just published. The letter
is noteworthy as making comments on many matters of great interest

"Dear Monty,

I am truly grateful to you for sending me your book, *El Alamein
to the River Sangro*. I will carry it home with me tonight and will
start reading it at once. Naturally I take instant advantage of your
kind offer to send me 100 additional copies. Please send them or
in my care and I will distribute them to various military schools
including West Point, where they will be of the greatest value
and interest.

Your reaction to the book *Soldiers of Democracy* is of course
exactly what I should expect. There is nothing I deplore so much
as the writing of so-called military history by people who are con
cerned mainly with rushing into print so as to catch a market that
is still fresh. It happens that the author of this particular book
dropped in to see me yesterday and I complained about the poor
light in which several very great men were portrayed. He pro
tested that these persons were brought into the book, merely
incidentally, in order to illustrate some particular point and with
no thought of attempting to judge their contributions to the war
effort.

The comments you make with respect to that book are even
more applicable to one that is now being published in serial form
and written by my former Naval Aide, Captain Butcher. It is
called *My Three Years with Eisenhower*. He used the confidential
position he had with me to form his own conclusions about a great
number of things, including personalities and operations, and does
not hesitate to give his judgments with an air of the greatest author
ity. Upon reading a portion of the book in *Saturday Evening Post*
was so embarrassed that I had some correspondence with Mr. Win
ston Churchill about the matter and he understands that I deplore
the whole thing as much as he does. Fortunately he does not hold it
against me, as the statements in the book were made without consultation with me or by my consent. My real error seems to be
that I selected a man to act as my confidential Aide without check
ing up to see whether he wanted to be a " writer " after the war
I am truly sorry that people like yourself, Alex, Tedder

Bradley, Cunningham and so on, cannot, because of holding official positions, undertake now to write the true story about an unparalleled experience in international co-operation and understanding. The fact is that the tremendous accomplishment of the Allied force is, through its handling by narrow-minded people, being made to look small and insignificant; great concessions on the part of two governments in order to establish field unity are lost sight of in the anxiety to put over some pettifogging little idea held in the mind of a writer.

To you personally I can say no more than I have said time and time again: I have always admired you for definitely outstanding characteristics that were of the most tremendous value in whipping the Germans. Moreover, whenever any question or problem came to the point that definite decision by me was necessary, you never once failed to carry out that decision loyally and with 100 per cent of your effort regardless of what your prior opinions and recommendations had been. I have written this to you before and I meant it then just as I mean it now, and if ever you have time to write anything of your experiences you are at liberty to quote me verbatim on the subject.

Entirely aside from the damage to British-American friendly relationship that hundreds of loyal officers labored so hard to advance, I have the personal fear that writers of the kind we are now talking about will succeed in damaging warm friendships that I have formed with men for whom I will always have the highest regard and admiration. The whole thing makes me a trifle ill.

Incidentally, one of the defenses made by one of these authors when I taxed him for bad judgment and inaccuracy, was to pull out a bunch of clippings taken from the British papers about the time of the Bulge battle. He said: ' British writers did not hesitate to criticize you bitterly and unjustly. Why should we be so shy and retiring ? ' My answer of course was that those reporters wrote during the heat of action and were motivated to some extent by fear. Moreover, in later writings they did their utmost to correct what they themselves must have felt to have been hasty judgment. This was an entirely different thing from writing deliberately and from the attitude of ' pure history,' which these books are certainly not.

I suppose there is no use saying anything further on the poin
except that you are free to express my sentiments to anyone who
wants to talk to you about the subject.

Thank you again for sending me the book and I assure you
that I will make excellent use of the additional copies you send
me, when it is convenient for you to do so.

As ever, your friend

Ike "

The point is that honest differences of opinion are almost inevitabl
among experienced commanders, especially if they are also men with
very definite views of their own. But such differences must never b
allowed to overshadow the supreme need of Allied co-operation; thi
co-operation was brought to great heights under Eisenhower. Th
final achievement in the second World War resulted from the good
will of the governments themselves, and from the bigness of the mer
who were selected to act in the critical positions—amongst whom
Eisenhower was a shining example.

In November 1945, I gave a lecture at the University of St. Andrew
entitled *Military Leadership*. I tried to equate the lessons of the pas
with the experience of the present. To illustrate my arguments
chose three great captains of the past and examined briefly why they
were leaders, how they led their men, and how as leaders they suc
ceeded or failed. The three I selected were Moses, Cromwell an
Napoleon. The lecture was subsequently included in *Forward from
Victory*, a book published by me in October 1948 (Hutchinson & Co.)
Each of these three men exercised high command. They had in
common an inner conviction which, though founded (and very closely
on reason, transcended reason. It was this which enabled them at
certain point—the right one—to take a short cut which took then
straight to their objective, more swiftly and surely than equally carefu
but less inspired commanders.

One might put it this way.

There are three types of commanders in the higher grades:
1. Those who have faith and inspiration, but lack the infinit
   capacity for taking pains and preparing for every foreseeabl
   contingency—which is the foundation of all success in wa
   These fail.
2. Those who possess the last-named quality to a degree amountin

to genius. Of this type I would cite Wellington as the perfect example.

3. Those who, possessing this quality, are inspired by a faith and conviction which enables them, when they have done everything possible in the way of preparation and when the situation favours boldness, to throw their bonnet over the moon. There are moments in war when, to win all, one has to do this. I believe such a moment occurred in August 1944 after the Battle of Normandy had been won, and it was missed. Nelson was the perfect example of this—when he broke the line at St. Vincent, when he went straight in to attack at the Nile under the fire of the shore batteries and with night falling, and at the crucial moment at Trafalgar.

No commander ever took greater care than Nelson to prepare against every possible contingency, but no one was ever so well able to recognise the moment when, everything having been done that reason can dictate, something must be left to chance or faith. No commander was ever so careful to ensure that " every captain knew what was in his Admiral's mind."

In my own limited experience certain " moments " come to mind—at Mareth when we switched the main thrust line to the western flank on the 23rd March 1943, in Normandy on the 23rd August 1944 when I advocated a strong thrust on the left flank of the Allied advance to finish the war quickly, and at Arnhem on the 17th September 1944.

Moses and Cromwell believed intensely in a divine mission, which never failed them in battle; Napoleon in a human destiny, which in the end did.

I believe that the one great commander who did not possess this quality of inner conviction was Wellington. One cannot too much admire his foresight, industry, patience and meticulous care. Yet he sometimes lost part of the fruits of victory through an inability to go from the known to seize the unknown. Napoleon never surpassed Wellington's flawless handling of his command at Salamanca and Vittoria, but the defeated French after Vittoria would never have escaped to fight another day had Napoleon—or Cromwell—been in command.

To exercise high command successfully one has to have an infinite capacity for taking pains and for careful preparation; and one has also to have an inner conviction which at times will transcend reason. Having fought, possibly over a prolonged period, for the advantage and gained it, there then comes the moment for boldness. When that moment comes, will you throw your bonnet over the mill and so pass from the known to seize the unknown? In the answer to this question lies the supreme test of generalship in high command.

CHAPTER 22

THE CONTROL OF POST-WAR GERMANY:

THE FIRST STEPS

THE PROBLEM

ᴏɴ ᴛʜᴇ 8th May 1945 the war in Europe ended officially, repre-
ntatives of the German High Command having signed the act of
ilitary surrender. But it must be noted that this surrender was
ade by the high command and not by the German Government of
dmiral Doenitz which, after Hitler's reported death in Berlin, claimed
represent the German nation. Indeed, the Allies refused to recognise
ich a government and it was later arrested at Flensburg. We were
erefore faced with a situation very different from that which had
en envisaged at the meetings between Churchill, Roosevelt and
alin when they had discussed the Allied organisation for the occupa-
on of Germany. They had agreed that a Control Council should be
t up in Berlin consisting of a British, an American, a Russian and a
ench member. Each was to have under him a Deputy and his own
vil and military staff, with a central inter-allied secretariat. The four
embers, meeting together in Berlin, were to dictate to a central
erman government how the country was to be run. Furthermore,
rmany was to be divided into zones; each of the Allies would
cupy a zone within which it would supervise the execution of the
tates of the Control Council, which would come into being on the
conditional surrender of the German government.

However, when the time came the Allies did not recognise any
rman government which *could* surrender and therefore the Control
uncil could not automatically come into operation. No central
vernment machine existed through which the Control Council
uld work. Berlin had been so destroyed that the Russians said it
s not possible to govern Germany from it. Although Eisenhower
1 been appointed a member of the Control Council, no British or

Russian member had yet been nominated. In the area occupied by the Western Allies, therefore, SHAEF continued to function as an operational headquarters, and we had to begin to govern Germany with the Military Government machine.

This was, of course, the direct result of the policy of " unconditional surrender," which policy was, in my opinion, a very great mistake—and was now to be proved so.

In the area occupied by 21 Army Group there were appalling civilian problems to be solved. Over one million civilian refugees had fled into the area before the advancing Russians. About one million German wounded were in hospital in the area, with no medical supplies. Over one and a half million unwounded German fighting men had surrendered to 21 Army Group on the 5th May and were now prisoners of war, with all that that entailed. Food would shortly be exhausted. The transport and communication services had ceased to function, and industry and agriculture were largely at a standstill. The population had to be fed, housed, and kept free of disease. It was going to be a race for time whether this could be achieved before the winter began; if by that time the population was not fed, and housed, famine and disease would run riot through Germany and this would prove a most serious embarrassment to the western Allies.

Finally, there was the impact of the Russians on the Western forces. From their behaviour it soon became clear that the Russians, though a fine fighting race, were in fact barbarous Asiatics who had never enjoyed a civilisation comparable to that of the rest of Europe. Their approach to every problem was utterly different from ours and their behaviour, especially in their treatment of women, was abhorrent to us. In certain sectors of the Russian zone there were practically no Germans left; they had all fled before the onward march of the barbarians, with the result that in the Western zones the crowd of refugees was so great that the problems of food and housing seemed almost insoluble. I wrote the following in my diary at that time:

" Out of the impact of the Asiatics on the European culture, a new Europe has been born. It is too early yet to say what shape it will take. One can only say it will be wholly unlike the old Europe. Its early infancy and growth will be of supreme importance to our civilisation."

It was vital to tackle this vast problem with the greatest boldness and speed. Before the war ended I had foreseen this need, and on the 24th April had informed the War Office that in my opinion the man who was to be C.-in-C. of the British Zone, and British member of the Control Council, must be appointed at once. Meetings and conferences in connection with Control Commission matters were taking place daily at my headquarters in Germany and also in London, and nobody knew who was going to be the boss. We learnt by bitter experience in the war that to work on the principle of the absentee commander is most dangerous and always leads to trouble.

But I could not get Whitehall to take any action in the matter. However, for the time being I was the boss and I decided to get on with the job in my own way. If, later, someone else was appointed, good luck to him. Such procrastination on the part of the British Government at this time was, of course, annoying to me personally; but it could become dangerous to the cause. What was needed was decision, followed by action. I therefore decided to make my own plan for the British Zone and to implement it without further delay.

The first thing was to issue very strict orders about looting and the use of German transport facilities. In the heat of battle certain actions are often overlooked which in peace conditions constitute a most serious offence. Many units had taken German staff cars into use, and one or two generals were driving about in the captured cars of German field-marshals. I decided that one and all must be pulled up with a jerk; if Germany was to recover quickly, she would need transport for communication and distribution purposes.

On the 6th May I therefore issued orders on these matters. Looting by individuals, or bodies of individuals, was of course forbidden at any time and I made it clear that any contravention of this order would be tried by court martial, whatever the rank of the individual concerned. If any commander or unit wanted something for the collective use of officers or men, application would be made to the proper authority and the articles in question would then be requisitioned in a constitutional manner. The same rules would apply to motor cars and other vehicles.

The basis of my plan in the British Zone was to work through the German command organisation in the first instance, and to issue my orders regarding the disposal of the German forces to Field-Marshal

Busch, the German C.-in-C. in N.W. Europe. He was to have his headquarters in Schleswig-Holstein. His Chief of Staff, General Kinzel, with a small staff and a team of liaison officers, would be at my main headquarters.

Busch was to have under him:

General Lindemann—commanding the German forces in Denmark, who would work under the SHAEF mission in Copenhagen (in charge of General Dewing).

General Blumentritt—commanding the German forces between the Baltic and the Weser, who would be under Second British Army (General Dempsey).

General Blaskowitz—commanding the German forces between the Weser and Western Holland, who would be under First Canadian Army (General Crerar).

German army boundaries were to be altered to coincide with British boundaries. All German troops were to be moved into peninsulas along the coastline, and then sealed off in those peninsulas with their backs against the sea. There was no other way of dealing with a million and a half prisoners; we could not put such a number into camps or P.O.W. cages. The selected peninsulas were on the east and west coastlines of Schleswig-Holstein, in the Cuxhaven area, and about Wilhelmshaven and Emden.

Once in these areas, prisoners were to be documented and checked over. They were then to be demobilised and directed back to their civil vocations, as and when they were needed and work became available—the farmers, the miners, the post office workers, the civil servants, etc., etc. When they left the P.O.W. areas to go back to civil work, they were to be dressed in plain clothes.

I then organised the British Zone into Corps Districts for occupational duties, as follows:

Berlin District (General Lyne)	Certain troops to be held ready to go to Berlin when Russian agreement was obtained.
Schleswig-Holstein (General E. H. Barker)	8 Corps, with two divisions, and one armoured brigade.
Hanover (General Horrocks)	30 Corps, with three divisions and one armoured brigade.

Westphalia	I Corps, with four divisions and one
(General Crocker)	armoured brigade.

Certain other formations were kept by me as reserve in case trouble developed. I had also been given a " stand still " order regarding the destruction of German weapons and equipment, in case they might be needed by the Western Allies for any reason, and all these had to be guarded.

My purpose was to re-establish orderly local government in the British Zone by using my military command organisation of corps, division, brigade and regimental headquarters. These would have areas corresponding to the local civil counties, boroughs, rural districts, etc., and in all cases would work through the appropriate civil organisations. I laid it down that the requirements of the civilian population were to be met in the following order: food, housing, and the prevention of disease. Thereafter, transportation and many other problems would have to be tackled.

The greatest problem was food and much would depend on the coming harvest. I ordered that the armed forces were not to purchase or requisition any foodstuffs from the civil population; the latter would need it all themselves.

It seemed to me that only by working on these lines could we establish quickly some form of orderly control and get a grip on the chaotic situation that existed in the British Zone. I had suddenly become responsible for the government and well-being of about twenty million Germans. Tremendous problems would be required to be handled and if they were not solved before the winter began, many Germans would die of starvation, exposure and disease.

EXCHANGE OF VISITS WITH THE RUSSIANS

The Russian forces in contact with 21 Army Group belonged to the White Russian Army Group commanded by Marshal Rokossovsky, who later became Minister of Defence in Poland. On the 7th May he had visited me at Wismar, where I entertained him and some of his officers to lunch. Rokossovsky was an imposing figure, tall, very good-looking, and well dressed; I understand he was a bachelor and was much admired by ladies. He invited me to visit him at his H.Q.

about twenty miles inside the Russian area, and I accepted for the 10th May. The Russians were clearly anxious to make a good impression and they sent a special envoy to the H.Q. of the 6th Airborne Division in Wismar to find out what sort of entertainment I liked, and what were my tastes and habits. The envoy began by asking what sort of wine I preferred; he was told that I disliked wine, never drank any alcohol, and preferred water. He then said they proposed to produce some very fine cigars at lunch. Did I like cigars? He was told I did not smoke. By this time he was somewhat shaken; but he had one more suggestion to make. They had some very fine women and dancing girls and they would produce these for the Field-Marshal. He was told that the Field-Marshal did not like women. That finished him and he exclaimed: " He doesn't drink, doesn't smoke, and doesn't like women. What the devil does he do all day?"

However, an agreed programme was drawn up without difficulty and I motored into the Russian Zone to visit Rokossovsky at the H.Q. of the White Russian Army Group.

Two things interested me during that drive—I did not see one single German civilian as they had all fled into the British area; and secondly, I was impressed by the Russian women police, whose traffic control was most efficient. The visit was a great success, and after an enormous feast the Russians produced a concert party which entertained us for about an hour with songs and dancing.

Among the staff that accompanied me was a young gunner major who had recently joined the team of liaison officers at my Tac Headquarters. He was a delightful person, very popular with everyone and the Russians set out to make him drunk—and they succeeded. This was concealed from me and when it was time to leave he was taken ahead and put on board my aircraft before I arrived, being deposited in the lavatory at the rear end of the cabin. When I arrived and boarded the aircraft I asked if we were all present, and was told we were. As I did not see the young major I asked where he was, and was told he was in the lavatory; I then gave the order to take off. As we taxied to the end of the runway the Russians fired a salute of 21 guns. The major in the lavatory considered he must take part, so he drew his revolver and fired it through the window, round for round with the Russian artillery. When he had finished his six rounds he continued to operate his revolver and " clicking " noises were heard coming from the lavatory for some time. I understand that an A.D.C. finally persuaded him to discontinue and to go to sleep in the lavatory. When he arrived at our own airfield and disembarked, I was somewhat suspicious and asked to see the young major. I was told he was not well and he would be taken back to Tac Headquarters in an ambulance.

There are occasions in this life when it is advisable to leave things alone and say nothing. But on arrival back at Tac Headquarters I demanded to be told the truth. I then said I would see the officer concerned but was asked if I would delay the interview for forty-eight hours; he had consumed so much vodka, and had mixed his drinks to such an extent, that it was considered by experts that it would be two days before he " surfaced." That delay was good for all of us. The interview duly took place and he was very upset. I explained that I could not have officers on my staff at Tac Headquarters who were not able to go anywhere with me and be able to carry out their duties at all times; he had failed to measure up to this standard, and would have to go. But as I looked at him my heart warmed towards him; he was the very best type of young British officer who might well rise to the highest ranks in the Army, and I could not let one indiscretion ruin a promising career. On leaving me he would lose his temporary rank of major and revert to his substantive rank. I told him I would send him back to regimental duty with orders that he was to be given the command of a battery as early as possible, which would thus make him a major again, and that no official report would be made of the incident. He was, of course, delighted, and we parted good friends. The next time I met him he was an instructor at the Royal Military Academy, Sandhurst: conspicuously sober and with no revolver!

I had one further experience of ceremonial Russian visits; this took place on the 10th June at Supreme Headquarters at Frankfurt. A few days earlier, on the 5th June, the Allied Commanders-in-Chief had met in Berlin to sign a declaration regarding the defeat of Germany and the assumption of joint responsibility with regard to that country by the Governments of the United Kingdom, U.S.A., U.S.S.R., and France. At that meeting Zhukov informed Eisenhower and myself that Stalin had conferred on each of us the Order of Victory, a Soviet decoration which had never been given previously to any foreigner. Apart from the honour, the decoration is of great intrinsic value, being in the form of a five-pointed star beautifully set with rubies and diamonds. After some discussion Eisenhower invited Zhukov to visit his headquarters at Frankfurt for the presentation ceremony. I said that as I had served throughout the campaign in Europe under Eisenhower's command, I would like to receive the decoration at the same time, and this was agreed.

Eisenhower had his headquarters at the I.G. Farben building in Frankfurt, a magnificent modern building on high ground overlooking the desolate and bombed city; the building itself had received practically no damage. On arrival there early on the 10th I had a short private talk with Eisenhower, during which he gave me the Distinguished Service Medal, the highest American decoration which can be conferred on a soldier of another nation. I had already been made a Chief Commander of the American Legion of Merit, Eisenhower having pinned that Presidential order on me in Sicily in 1943. Later in the morning Zhukov arrived with a large entourage, composed mostly of photographers and pressmen. The decoration ceremony took place in Eisenhower's office. Then on a large balcony outside Zhukov presented medals to twenty-four British and American officers of Supreme Headquarters; this was a most disorganised and undignified spectacle, the photographers all jockeying for position. However, the decorations were in the end conferred without mishap although it seemed to me that some may easily have got handed medals who were not meant to get them!

Before lunch some 1700 American and British aircraft flew past in formation giving an impressive display of Western air power—which was not lost on the Russians. During lunch the Americans produced a coloured cabaret show, with swing music and elaborate dancing by negro women who were naked above the waist line. The Russians had never seen or heard anything like this before and their eyes almost popped out of their heads! Nonetheless they enjoyed it thoroughly and encored every time. The whole organisation of the day was on a most elaborate scale, so was the lavishness of the welcome extended by the Americans. It was a day which revealed undeniably the wealth and power of the United States.

SIC TRANSIT ...

On the 7th June I flew to Antwerp to receive the freedom of the city. After the ceremony there was a civic luncheon at the *Hôtel de Ville*; this was a tremendous affair, with very rich food and many courses. Rich food always upsets me and it certainly did so on this occasion; I began to feel ill soon after lunch and asked that the remainder of the programme should be cut short, so that I could return to the airfield and fly back to my headquarters in Germany. This was at once arranged, my car was summoned, and I drove through streets lined by cheering citizens—with myself sitting on the floor of the car being violently sick. That sickness was exactly what was needed, and once it had taken place I felt well again. But the floor of the car was not in a good state and I apologised very humbly to the driver, who belonged to the local military headquarters and who had never driven me before. When I apologised for the mess in his car, he drew himself up, looked me in the face, and said: " Sir, it's an honour." And he meant it.

BRITISH MEMBER OF THE ALLIED CONTROL COUNCIL IN GERMANY

As the days passed after the end of the German war I became increasingly worried at the lack of any proper organisation to govern Germany.

I had been informed privately in April that I would probably be made responsible for the long-term government of the British Zone; but the proposed appointment was delayed, with the result that there was a serious lack of co-ordination between the British section of the Control Commission in London and the Military Government staff working under me in Germany. I therefore flew to London on the 14th May to impress on the Prime Minister the urgent need for a decision in the matter, so that the man appointed could co-ordinate the planning of the Control Commission with the practical activities of Military Government. I arrived in England at a politically unfavourable moment. The Coalition Government was coming to its expected end and the prospects of an early general election discouraged Cabinet Ministers from taking any but the most vital decisions. My task was to persuade the Prime Minister that the problems of government in Germany were of such importance that an immediate decision was vital. I succeeded. The Prime Minister decided to appoint me Commander-in-Chief of the British Forces of Occupation and British Member of the Allied Control Council in Germany. I asked that Lieut.-General Sir Ronald Weeks, D.C.I.G.S. at the War Office (now Lord Weeks), should be appointed as my Deputy, and this was agreed. The announcement of these appointments was made on the 22nd May.

The next day I assembled in London the heads of the British civil divisions of the Control Commission and spoke to them of the existing problem in Germany. We did not know each other and it was essential that they should hear from me personally, in broad outline, how I proposed to tackle these problems.

I explained that having conquered Germany, all we could do immediately was to impose Military Government on it, and that that was being done—through the Army. But that must not be allowed to last too long; we must get civil control re-established and that would mean the civil divisions of the Control Commission dealing with the Germans themselves. It was therefore essential that the short-term planning of the Military Government régime should have a definite relation to the long-term planning of the civil divisions. To achieve this object, we must all be together. We would make little progress so long as the civil divisions remained in London; my object was to get them deployed in Germany as quickly as possible. They could not go to Berlin yet; that could come later. But they could come to the British Zone at once and, after all, that was where the problem lay. I then explained my own methods of working, and how I used the Chief of Staff system.

This talk did good. It showed the civilian element in the Control Commission that we wanted them to join us in Germany as soon as possible, because without them we couldn't do the job.

MY VISIT TO PARIS

Having given orders about the deployment in Germany of the British element of the Control Commission, so that we could all be

ogether, I returned to my headquarters *via* Paris. I had been asked
to open the British Military Exhibition in that city on the 25th. Paris
turned out *en masse* and the reception I received was stupendous. I was
decorated by General de Gaulle with the Grand Croix of the Legion
of Honour at a colourful parade in the courtyard of the *Invalides*, and
later in the day I opened the exhibition. I decided to speak mainly in
English but occasionally to turn over to French, as I thought this
would please the audience. I had some difficulty composing the
French sentences as my knowledge of that language was still of the
English schoolboy type; however, with the assistance of certain
members of my staff who professed to be fluent in the language, the
French sentences were drafted. This is what I said:

" 1. It is my privilege and a great pleasure to speak to you today in
your famous capital—this fair city which, better than any other,
exemplifies the spirit of our long European history. To my
shame I have to confess that I have not visited Paris for ten
years.

2. Today I come here to open this British Military Exhibition.
In it we seek to show you something of the part played by the
armies of the British Empire in this war—which now happily
is ended in Europe.

   In the early days of the war the British and French Empires
suffered some grievous wounds, and to many of our enemies
those wounds looked mortal. The British Empire reeled from
these blows, but in due course managed to fight back.

   France was struck a heavy blow, and for a while the home
country lay prostrate under the heel of the invader. But though
you can occupy a country you cannot quell the spirit of a
fighting race. Elsewhere the fight went on, and it grew in
volume as the years passed.

   L'esprit français vivait toujours. Cette flamme sacrée n'a
jamais été éteinte. On nourrissait la flamme. Cette flamme a
jailli finalement des abîmes lorsque vous et vos alliés avez chassé
l'ennemi du sol ensanglanté de la France: magnifique épisode
dont la France a bien le droit d'être fière.

   Je salue les soldats de la France, mes compagnons d'armes
de tant de batailles.

3. I have many friends among the soldiers of France. And of the

ones I have known best in this war I would mention General
Leclerc. This gallant man fought his way with a small force
from Central Africa and joined the Eighth Army in Tripoli in
January 1943. With no obligation to do so, he freely placed
himself under my command; he played a notable part in the
Mareth battle and in the advance to Tunis, and was ' in at
the kill ' in Africa. A fine story and typical of a soldier of
France.

4. But it is not only of your fighting men that I would speak
today. The liberation of France has restored to us that inex-
haustible well of literature, art, and science from which we have
drawn so freely in the past. The achievements of the French
genius, of Racine, Cézanne, Berlioz and Pasteur, are part of
the heritage of our civilization: above all for the compatriot
of Shakespeare and Newton.

At this moment Europe needs France. We need not only
your soldiers, your writers, your scientists, but also the simple
but enduring virtues of French family life.

It is not surprising that France has played such a notable
part in these fields. Great arts flourish only among fighting
peoples, and the people of France are a fighting race.

5. Dès ces jours qui suivent la défaite totale de l'Allemagne vous
reprenez votre destin historique. Pendant les siècles passés les
Anglais et les Français se sont souvent regardés en adversaires.
Aujourd'hui nous marchons ensemble.
Vive La France! "

Later in the day large crowds assembled outside the British Embassy
where I was staying, and kept calling for me. Finally I went out on
a balcony to thank them. I made a very short speech in English; but
the crowd still kept cheering and showed no signs of dispersing; so
I made a second appearance on the balcony and said: " Allez-vous en."
That finished it! There were shouts of laughter and they all went away,
seemingly quite happy.

THE GERMANS BECOME RESTIVE

I got back to Germany on the 26th May and learnt that there was
disquiet in the German prisoner-of-war camps and among the German

opulation of the British Zone; they did not know how they were
be treated in the future. I should explain that I had already
xperienced trouble with the German military command organisation,
hich I had kept " in being " in order to implement the surrender and
deal with the enormous numbers of prisoners.

The German military leaders, having been saved from the Russians,
ere only too willing to be friends with the British and to do what-
ver was wanted. But in return for this co-operative attitude they
xpected to be treated as allies of the British against the Russians, and
some cases my orders had been queried and delay had occurred in
rrying them out. On the 11th May I had sent for Field-Marshal
usch, the German C.-in-C. in North-West Europe, and told him that
is attitude was entirely unacceptable. I explained that I was making
se of him and his headquarters so long as the job of implementing
e surrender could be more efficiently carried out by that method.
he did not carry out his orders promptly and efficiently, I would
move him from his command and find some other senior German
fficer to do the job. In the last resort the British Army would do the
b themselves; but this method would result in delay which could
nly cause further hardship to the German civil population, and this
was anxious to avoid. He was to understand that the German Army
d been utterly defeated in the field and must now accept the con-
quences of that defeat.

After this I had no more trouble with Busch or with any other
erman commander. When therefore I discovered at the end of May
at the Germans generally in the British Zone were becoming restive,
d anxious about their future, I decided to issue them a message
hich would tell them what I proposed to do—in exactly the same
ay that I had issued personal messages to the soldiers in the armies
der my command during the war. The war messages called forth
political comment so far as I was aware. But these messages to
e twenty million civilian Germans in the British Zone were viewed
ith some mistrust in Whitehall. Was I becoming a military
ctator who would seize power? And so on. Later, the need for them
as queried by the Labour Government. But I stuck to my guns and
fused to be " seen off" by my political masters; so long as I was
sponsible I was determined to use my own methods. I give the first
essage in full below.

TO THE POPULATION OF THE BRITISH AREA IN GERMANY
30TH MAY 1945

" 1. I have been appointed by the British Government to comman
and control the area occupied by the British Army.

This area will be governed for the present by Militar
Government under my orders.

2. My immediate object is to establish a simple and orderly life fo
the whole community.

The first step will be to see that the population has:
(a) food
(b) housing
(c) freedom from disease

The harvest must be gathered in.

The means of transportation must be re-established.

The postal services must be restarted.

Certain industries must be got going again.

All this will mean much hard work for everyone.

2. Those who have committed war crimes according to inte
national law will be dealt with in proper fashion.

The German people will work under my orders to provi
the necessities of life for the community, and to restore th
economic life of the country.

4. There are in the British Area a very large number of Germa
soldiers, sailors and airmen, and all these are now being assemble
in certain localities.

The German Wehrmacht, and other armed forces, will
disarmed and disbanded.

All German soldiers, sailors, and airmen, are being sort
out by trades and occupations. In a few days they will sta
to be discharged from the armed forces so that they can get o
with the work. The most urgent need is the harvest; therefo
workers on the land are going first; men of other occupatio
and trades will be discharged to work as soon as it can
arranged.

5. I will see to it that all German soldiers and civilians are ke
informed by radio and newspapers of how the work is going o
The population will be told what to do. I shall expect it to
done willingly and efficiently."

THE PROBLEM OF FRATERNISATION WITH THE GERMANS

In March 1945, prior to the assault across the Rhine and when it was clear that the German war was coming to an end, I began to consider the problems which would arise when our soldiers were living amidst the German population under peace conditions. To what degree should we fraternise with our former enemies? I decided that one and all must be given guidance in this very difficult matter. We should be firm to begin with, and later could relax our rules; a reverse procedure would be unsound. And so I decided to issue a personal letter to officers and men under my command. It was printed in card form so that it was easily carried in the pocket of the battle-dress tunic. The object of the letter was to explain the problem to officers and men before it became a serious issue, and to give them a doctrine on which to base their actions.

I told them that if we mixed freely with the Germans, went to their houses, danced with their girls, and so on, it would be resented by our own families in England and by millions of people who had suffered under the Gestapo. When we entered Germany it would be too soon to distinguish between good and bad Germans; we must hold back and not fraternise until we could see our way clear.

The soldiers accepted the basic doctrine laid down in the letter, and we started well. But when fighting ceased and the peace-time occupation of Germany was becoming established, it was clear to me that we must review our orders about fraternisation. While the soldier was fighting his opportunities for friendly intercourse with the civil population were in any event restricted; but when the fighting ended, and the soldier had some leisure for recreation, it became necessary to " let-up " by degrees on the rule of complete non-fraternisation. Such an order would simply not be obeyed. We must be sensible about it. Furthermore, if we were ever to re-educate the German population it would be a good thing to mix freely with them and teach them our standards of freedom and individual responsibility. I had already given the Germans " the form " in my first message. It was now necessary to tell them *why* we did not fraternise with them. And so I decided to issue a message on this subject to the German people and it ran as follows:

TO THE POPULATION OF THE BRITISH AREA IN GERMANY
10TH JUNE 1945

" You have wondered, no doubt, why our soldiers do not smile when you wave your hands, or say ' Good morning ' in the streets, or play with the children. It is because our soldiers are obeying orders. You do not like it. Nor do our soldiers. We are naturally friendly and forgiving people. But the orders were necessary; and I will tell you why.

In the last war of 1914, which your rulers began, your Army was defeated; your generals surrendered; and in the Peace Treaty of Versailles your rulers admitted that the guilt of beginning the war was Germany's. But the surrender was made in France. The war never came to your country; your cities were not damaged, like the cities of France and Belgium; and your armies marched home in good order. Then your rulers began to spread the story (legend) that your armies were never really defeated, and later they denied the war guilt clauses of the Peace Treaty. They told you that Germany was neither guilty nor defeated; and because the war had not come to your country many of you believed it, and you cheered when your rulers began another war.

Again, after years of waste and slaughter and misery, your armies have been defeated. This time the Allies were determined that you should learn your lesson—not only that you have been defeated, which you must know by now, but that you, your nation, were again guilty of beginning the war. For if that is not made clear to you, and your children, you may again allow yourselves to be deceived by your rulers, and led into another war.

During the war your rulers would not let you know what the world was thinking of you. Many of you seemed to think that when our soldiers arrived you could be friends with them at once, as if nothing much had happened. But too much has happened for that. Our soldiers have seen their comrades shot down, their homes in ruins, their wives and children hungry. They have seen terrible things in many countries where your rulers took the war. For those things, you will say you are not responsible—it was your rulers. But they were found by the German nation; every

370

nation is responsible for its rulers, and while they were successful you cheered and laughed. That is why our soldiers do not smile at you. This we have ordered, this we have done, to save yourselves, to save your children, to save the world from another war. It will not always be so. For we are Christian forgiving people, and we like to smile and be friendly. Our object is to destroy the evil of the Nazi system; it is too soon to be sure that this has been done.

You are to read this to your children, if they are old enough, and see that they understand. Tell them why it is that the British soldier does not smile."

My next object was to relax by stages the complete non-fraternisation order and, while doing so, to keep in the closest agreement with Eisenhower's policy in the American Zone. The British soldier has always been fond of children and on the 12th June I relaxed the order to the extent that soldiers might speak to, and play with, children. They were, of course, doing it anyway.

In July I relaxed the rules still further, allowing conversation with Germans in the streets and public places but forbidding troops to enter German homes. Finally in September 1945 I raised the subject in the Control Council and got it agreed that the ban on fraternisation should be lifted, the rules to be the same in each zone.

We were then left with only two rules—no members of the armed forces were to be billeted with Germans, nor were they allowed to marry them.

It was a great relief to get this matter settled. I had never liked the orders which we had had to issue; but it was the Allied policy. After the German war had been over for some weeks it became practically impossible to enforce the non-fraternisation orders. The British soldier is an intensely friendly person; he is kind and gentle in victory, and is chivalrous to his enemies. He is usually liked by the inhabitants of other countries because of his knack, despite his ignorance of the local language, of fitting in with the people and making himself at home: which is sometimes called " getting his feet under the table." That is why he is such a good representative of his country abroad. It was almost hopeless to stop him talking to the Germans.

THE GENERAL ATTITUDE OF THE GERMANS
DURING THIS PERIOD

In the days that followed the surrender, the general attitude of the Germans, both civilians and soldiers, was on the whole correct. They were willing to carry out whatever orders were issued to them, their chief fear being that they might be handed over to the Russians. The arrest and interrogation of Himmler is of interest in this connection. He left Flensburg on the 9th May under an assumed name, intending to roam the country for some weeks until the tumult of victory had died down. He then hoped to obtain an interview with me so that he could expound his views on the situation. He was, however, arrested by a British patrol on the 21st May and taken to an internment camp where he eventually disclosed his identity. He needed no encouragement to speak. He said that before leaving Flensburg he had called off all German resistance movements and that for some time before then he had been urging the conclusion of peace with the Western Allies. His purpose in seeking an interview with me was to stress that sooner or later there would be another war to stop the march of the Asiatic hordes into Western Europe, led by Russia. Now that Germany was beaten, Britain was left alone to face the Asiatic onslaught. It was essential to save the fighting man-power of Germany from falling into Russian hands, since it would be needed to fight with the British against the Russians in the near future—such war, in his view, being inevitable. This attitude of mind as expounded by Himmler was general throughout the civilians in the British Zone. Subsequently, while being searched to ascertain if he carried poison, Himmler bit on a concealed phial and committed suicide.

At the end of 1945 the following conversation between a British officer and a German boy was published, in translation, in the Rhine Army Intelligence Review. It shows the type of young chap we had to deal with.

THE BOY FROM THE WAFFEN SS

" He is 19 years old, fair haired, well built, good-looking. An officer saw him in an internment camp and the following conversation ensued:

O: Why are you here?

SS: Waffen SS, sir.

O: Did you volunteer or were you put into it?

SS: Volunteered.

O: Why?

SS: Most of my friends were already in it, so I joined too.

O: Did you see any atrocities?

SS: I never saw any myself, but I know they have happened.

O: Did you believe in National Socialism?

SS: Of course I did. What else do you expect? My father was an admiral. Both my parents were convinced Nazis. At school I was taught National Socialism; in the Hitler Youth I was taught National Socialism; in the SS I was taught National Socialism.

O: How were you arrested?

SS: I was wounded and in hospital near our home. As an SS man I was under arrest there. My parents came to see me. My father said SS men would be imprisoned for twenty years; he heard it over the wireless. There was no alternative for me, I should escape, he said; and my mother agreed. Then they went away and committed suicide. I have always obeyed my parents and it was their last wish that I should escape, and I did not want to be imprisoned for twenty years. I fled. I tried to get a job as a forestry apprentice. It didn't work—eventually I was arrested again.

O: Do you still believe in Nazism?

SS: No, but I am trying to sort it out. You see, for the first time in my life I hear the other side. I am 19. I only knew one thing—National Socialism; now I begin to see other things. For the first time in my life I am going to church. My parents had not allowed it. Now I think I can find something there. I don't know yet. But, for God's sake, give me a chance.

O: But has it never occurred to you that there was something inherently bad in National Socialism?

SS: No, I did not know about the concentration camps and of the atrocities. I only heard at the very end.

O: What about the injustice of the racial theory?

SS: Why injustice?

O: Well, why should a man be treated differently just because he belongs to another race?

SS: But if it's an inferior race?

O: This is quite a wrong term; we are all human beings.

SS: No, I don't agree. You cannot tell me that you believe negro is not inferior to us—to you and me.

O: He might be in some ways, but not because he is a negro He may perhaps be less civilised, or less intelligent or of lowe moral character, but he is still a human being and has to be treate as such.

SS: But surely you cannot treat all men alike.

O: No, but it is not a question of race, but, as I have tried t explain, a question of individual value. I prefer a decent negro t a criminal Englishman. I treat everybody according to his mor; value. It may be that there are more valuable people among th English who have the benefit of an old culture and education tha among the negroes. Even so, I respect the uncivilised negro as human being, perhaps more than the uncivilised Englishman.

SS: I see what you mean. In effect by treating them ; individuals it sorts itself out anyhow that more Englishmen deserv recognition as ' valuable ' than negroes, but the principle remair you do not go by race but by an ethical conception of the individua I think you are right.

O: You only need to think and you will see the gross injustice and immorality of Nazism.

SS: But how could it ever occur to me? The only time I cam into conflict with the Nazi organisation was over something quit plain that I could see.

O: What was it?

SS: I am very keen on tennis. But, whenever I wanted t play, there was always duty in the Hitler Youth. The duty w; silly and I did not go. There was a lot of fuss over it, but in th end I won.

O: You should now think and have the courage to come t decisions just in the same way.

SS: Yes, that is what I am trying to do. But what have I t look forward to? My parents are dead and I am a prisoner. Ge: many is destroyed. Do you think I'll ever get out?

O: Yes.

SS: But don't you think my attempted escape will be hel against me? It was very silly, but I told you how it came abou

O: I certainly think it will be held against you. However, if you have not committed any crime I am certain that you will eventually be released. In the meantime you have leisure to think and to continue on the lines you told me about. The main thing is not to lose courage. You have been misled, now find your own way out, keep trying and help to rebuild from the debris.

SS: I have every intention of doing so. But you must understand, most of us here, especially the younger ones, are in the same fix as I am. We cannot teach each other much, we have no books or things to read and no lectures from outside. I wish you could do something about this. So far my mind has been made up for me; now I want to make it up myself."

CHAPTER 23

DIFFICULTIES WITH THE RUSSIANS

BEGIN

ON THE 23rd May 1945, the King signed a declaration giving me fu
powers under the Great Seal to sign the Allied declaration regardi
the defeat and unconditional surrender of Germany, and to negotia
with other Powers and States about all matters relative to that surrend
I was later directed to ensure that the provisions of the declaration we
strictly carried out. The actual signing ceremony, and the inaugu
meeting of the Control Council, were to take place in Berlin on t
5th June, so I arrived at the Templehof airfield at 1 p.m. on that da
having flown up from the British Zone. I was met by a number
senior Russian officers in the midst of a jostling crowd of pressmen
every nationality. After inspecting a guard of honour of toug
looking young soldiers, the British delegation was driven to a gro
of small villas in a suburb which had been placed at our dispos
We were then left to ourselves, with one Russian officer as our ho
I asked to see Marshal Zhukov but was told he was busy. I then becat
very insistent and said that if I was not taken to see the Marsha
would leave Berlin and return to the British Zone—which, of cour
I could hardly have done!

However, this did the trick and I was taken to Marshal Zhuko
residence, which was in fact quite close to our group of villas. I w
delighted to meet the man about whom I had heard so much and
had an interesting conversation. He suggested that the declarati
should be signed by the four Allies at 4 p.m. The ceremony wou
be followed by an official dinner after which General Eisenhow
proposed to leave Berlin. I said this would suit me and that I also m
leave Berlin that evening.

I then began to discuss with Zhukov the stages by which the mach
ery of the Control Council could be built up, and how the Coun
would operate. I suggested that the first need was for a Secretariat

erlin, and that the Deputies should meet at once to examine the
many pressing problems awaiting attention and to prepare the ground
rior to the meeting of the four members of the Council. Zhukov
isagreed. His view was that no useful work could begin until the
Western Allies had handed over to the Russians those portions of the
Russian Zone which they still occupied; in other words, we must
withdraw at once within the Zonal boundaries that had been agreed
t the Yalta Conference. During the fighting of the last few weeks of
he war the British and American forces had advanced far beyond
hem. I pointed out that there were many problems of disentangle-
ment which would have to be solved before the withdrawal to our
wn zones could take place, and that the date of handing over would
ave to be decided by our Governments. Zhukov agreed with this.
But he counter-attacked by saying that Berlin would not be in a fit
tate to receive any part of the Allied Control Council for some
weeks. This sounded ominous to me.

When I left Zhukov I went at once to visit Eisenhower at his villa;
wanted to discuss with him the result of my talk with Zhukov and
he trouble which seemed to be looming ahead. It was obvious that
we would not be able to do any business with the Russians until we
ad withdrawn back within our own zones.

The boundaries of these zones had been agreed by the European
advisory Commission in London on the 12th September 1944, and
s findings had been approved by the three Governments.

At the Yalta Conference the following statement had been issued
y the Prime Minister, President Roosevelt and Marshal Stalin on the
1th February 1945:

" Under the agreed plans the forces of the Three Powers will each
occupy a separate zone of Germany. Co-ordinated administration
and control has been provided for under the plan through a Central
Control Commission consisting of the Supreme Commanders of
the Three Powers with Headquarters in Berlin.

It has been agreed that France should be invited by the Three
Powers, if she should so desire, to take a zone of occupation, and
to participate as a fourth member of the Council Commission.
The limits of the French Zone will be agreed by the Four Govern-
ments concerned through their representatives on the European
Advisory Commission."

The agreement regarding the boundaries of the French Zone we
not decided by the European Advisory Committee until the 26th Ju
1945, i.e. until after the Potsdam Conference had assembled on t
16th July.

But in spite of these international agreements the British Gover
ment considered, and instructed me accordingly on the day before
went to Berlin, that the *de facto* occupation by British and Americ
armies of large parts of the Russian Zone was an important bargainir
counter for obtaining satisfaction from the Soviet Government on
number of outstanding questions, such as our policy towards Germai
and its treatment as one whole economic unit, the problems of Polan
the Balkans, and Austria, and other related matters.

I knew that the Prime Minister (Churchill) attached the utmo
importance to the British and American armies standing firm on t
existing tactical boundary line reached by VE-Day; he reckoned th
they should not withdraw until the impending meeting of the thr
Heads of Governments in Berlin (the Potsdam Conference), whe
these and other questions could be discussed and settled.

I also knew that the attitude of the American Government w
different. While they would have liked to reach a settlement of t
German and Austrian problems before withdrawing the America
armies, they were not prepared to link any outside question such
Poland or the Balkans with the question of withdrawal; nor woul
they give an assurance to stand firm until the Heads of Governmen
had met. Indeed, the American Government had said that if t
Russians insisted on an immediate execution of the zones agreemer
they would not delay their own withdrawal.

All this looked a bit awkward to me. I discussed with Eisenhow
the divergent views of our two Governments. His view was that w
could not challenge the pledged word of our respective Government
to do so would wreck any possibility there might be of working i
friendly co-operation with the Russians. I agreed with him, especiall
after my talk with Zhukov. But I was of course bound by t
instructions I had received from my Government; if the question w
raised I was to say it was a matter for inter-governmental decisior
Eisenhower agreed to adopt the same line.

Meanwhile Eisenhower and I were waiting impatiently at his vill
for information about the signing of the declaration. He was gettin
very angry at the delay; so was I. Finally we sent a combined ultimatur

Zhukov that we would both return to our own zones unless the four
Commanders-in-Chief met at once. That produced quick results and
we were summoned to the conference, which was held in a clubhouse
nearby. But, on arrival, there was further delay owing to a Russian
objection to one word in the English text which disagreed with the
Russian version. I had no idea what the word was, or what effect it
had on the general problem. But I was so fed up with the whole
affair that I suggested the offending word be deleted from the text;
this suggestion was at once agreed by the Russians and by everyone
else, and to this day I do not know what difference it made.

The declaration was then signed at 4.30 p.m. in a blaze of arc lamps
and before a milling crowd of pressmen and photographers.

Following the formal signing, the four members of the Control
Council and their advisers withdrew for a private meeting. Eisenhower
began the discussion by saying that the Four Power Declaration we
had just signed made the four Commanders-in-Chief, in effect, a
governmental autonomy. We must now decide on the machinery
which would make that governmental autonomy work. He suggested
that our staffs should at once begin the study of Control Council
problems and, upon approval by the Council, the results would be
submitted to Governments.

But Zhukov made it very clear that the setting up of the Control
Council machinery could not begin until the British and American
forces had withdrawn to their own zones; until this was done there
could not even be any joint exploratory work by the Deputies or
staffs. I explained that all our troops had arrived in their present
positions as a result of the war, and that it would take some time to
sort them out and get them back into their proper areas. Zhukov
asked how long this would take. I said at least three weeks. He
accepted this at once, and added that during those weeks the four
Commanders-in-Chief could gather together their staffs for the
Control Council. He indicated that in due course he would have no
objection to the Control Council being in Berlin.

Eisenhower then made a very good speech which brought the
meeting to a close. He said that he had come to the meeting with
the definite view that the setting up of the machinery of the Control
Council, and the withdrawal of the Western forces from the Soviet
zone, could be done simultaneously. It was now clear from
Zhukov's remarks that this was not so, and that the Russians were

not prepared "to play" on Control Council matters until th
British and American forces withdrew to their proper zones. Ther
was therefore nothing further that could be done at the momen
other than to report to our respective Governments what had take
place and to ask for new instructions.

We were then taken to a room nearby to partake of a large banque
It was now 6 p.m. There were many speeches and we developed int
a sort of mutual congratulation society. Soon after 7 p.m. Eisenhowe
insisted on leaving for the airfield and we left the banquet, which b
that time was beginning to get lively. Eisenhower, Zhukov and I a
crowded into one car and drove at high speed through Berlin to th
Templehof airfield; there we had very friendly farewell greeting
with Zhukov and took off for our respective headquarters.

The direct result of the meeting in Berlin on the 5th June was t
make the Russian position crystal clear. They were not prepared t
operate the machinery of the Control Council, or even to begin sta
discussions on the many problems that lay ahead in Germany, unt
the Western Allies had handed over those portions of the Russia
Zone they still occupied. No central organisation for the control c
Germany was therefore possible for the time being. I reporte
accordingly to the British Government and gave it as my view tha
because of the Russian attitude, we should get back into our agree
zones at once. If we had captured Vienna, Prague and Berlin befor
the Russians, as we could have done (see Chapter 19), the positio
would possibly have been different. We now had to begin to pay th
price for that failure. There were no military reasons for stayin
where we were; there were many political reasons for withdrawing
and unless we did so we couldn't even begin to control the German
we had conquered.

The Prime Minister did not agree with this view; indeed, as I hav
already indicated, his opinion was that we should stay where we wer
until the Russians had become more amenable. I remember discussin
the subject with Eisenhower when I was staying with him i
Washington in 1946; he was then Chief of Staff of the America
Army, and I was C.I.G.S. On reflection he reckoned that if we ha
stood firm the Russians would eventually have given in, and if the
had used force to make us go back, we would have fought them.
could not agree. The British people were completely fed up with wa
and would never have been persuaded to fight the Russians in 194

The Russians had been built up as heroes during the German war, and any British Government that wanted to fight them in 1945 would have been in for trouble at home. Furthermore, Britain had reached the limit of her man-power resources and could not have sustained further active operations in Europe; the American armies in Europe were being rapidly re-deployed for the intensifying of the war against Japan. And whatever I may have said in Paris, on the 26th May, France was still down and out.

PROBLEMS ARISE IN THE BRITISH ZONE

As we have seen, the first meeting of the Allied Commanders-in-Chief had not achieved results. The Russian attitude, though outwardly friendly, was very uncertain and difficult to fathom. There were definite indications of Russian communist propaganda in certain areas of the British Zone, and " cells " were being formed in all the areas occupied by the Western Allies. This needed most careful watching since communist cells would " turn the heat on " whenever there were signs of dissension in the Western camp. Communist propaganda was particularly active in our Displaced Persons' camps.

The food position was causing me concern and, unless it could be improved, we were to be faced with serious famine in the winter. The British Zone could not at any time produce even half the food needed for its twenty million inhabitants. The present ration was only 1200 calories a day; if we were to step this up to about 1800 calories a day we would require two million tons of imports of wheat equivalent during the next twelve months. Furthermore, much would depend on transportation and distribution, and facilities for these were lacking.

The great and crying need everywhere was going to be coal. We had 140 mines working, producing 40,000 tons a day; not nearly enough. If we wanted more coal, we would have to feed the miners properly.

Then we had two and a half million German prisoners of war; these were being discharged to work at the rate of 12,000 a day. My policy regarding these prisoners was to discharge the harmless ones to work, to keep the S.S. in camps, and to disperse those of the General Staff in camps on the lines of communication.

In addition to these prisoners, we had over one million Displaced

381

Persons, nearly all from the East. Some 400,000 of these were Russian and we could reasonably hope that Zhukov would take these off our hands. But the remaining 600,000 would probably remain with us for all time.

It was obvious to me that we must get the Germans down to hard work; only in this way could we get things right. The Russians were encouraging Trade Unions; I decided not to do so. I was anxious the Unions should grow slowly and naturally, and not be " forced "; this policy would, I hoped, ensure that the right leaders would be thrown up gradually as time went on; if we proceeded too quickly the Unions might get into the wrong hands and we would then be in for trouble.

If we were to get the Germans all working to resuscitate their country, we had to stop cursing them. The German war was over. We must give them definite orders and see they were obeyed; we must be very firm, but just. It would be important to get our propaganda across to the Germans by the use of newspapers and cinemas, keeping at all times a tight control over editors and cinema managers. It would be useless to try to make the Germans like unto ourselves, as some people wanted to do; our aim should be rather to turn them into good and right-thinking Germans.

I then had to turn my mind to our own army. We must not let the soldiers become fed up with occupational duties, or weary them with too many guard duties. We could not watch everything, and I decided that we would only guard food, explosives and certain weapons, and dangerous prisoners. The British soldier was to have at least three nights in bed out of four.

I explained to the troops that Germany was in a bad way; great privations, and probably actual starvation, would be undergone by many of the people. There would be much hardship all over Europe, and definitely so in the British Isles. Our own living standards and habits must be simple and not extravagant. We ourselves were well off in Germany; we must not flaunt our well-being in the sight of the impoverished and hungry inhabitants.

Britain was still at war in the Far East. In order to prosecute that war, and to accelerate reconstruction at home, economy was essential. Sports and games would be on a wartime, and not peacetime, basis. There would be no hunting or racing for the time being.

Then there was the problem of wives. I decided that for the time being no wives or families would be allowed in Germany, or anywhere else in North-West Europe. This order was to be 100 per cent, and to apply to Navy, Army, Air Force, and civilians; it would obviously be reviewed should conditions change. Military wives would of course be allowed, i.e. those who were in the Services and worked in uniform; but these were not to be in the same area as their husbands, i.e. they must not set up house together. I may say that this order was not popular!

As regards leave to the U.K., I ordered that there must be a fair deal to everyone. Our figures early in June were 7500 daily, which gave each officer and man leave about once every 5 months. It would be necessary to step up the leave facilities in the Italian theatre, and the overall problem for both theatres would be affected by the rolling stock situation.

The release scheme was beginning to operate. I did not feel I could let those who had fought so well go away without some word of thanks for what they had done. I decided to give to each officer and man a personal message, which was printed on a card and ran as follows:

" I feel I cannot let you leave 21 Army Group on your return to civil life without a message of thanks and farewell. Together we have carried through one of the most successful campaigns in history, and it has been our good fortune to be members of this great team.
God bless you and God speed."

Finally I decided that, as the atmosphere in Germany was highly charged with electricity and politicians were eyeing us with suspicion now the war was over, all Press conferences by commanders were forbidden. The background would be given to the Press by my Chief of Staff and by no one else.

Immediately after our conference in Berlin on the 5th June, I had decided to deploy the Main Headquarters of the Control Commission (Military and Civil Divisions) in the British Zone between Hanover and Osnabrück. Berlin was clearly impossible at present. I decided to have a Tac Headquarters with the Americans at Frankfurt, and Eisenhower welcomed this move. By this means I hoped to get orderly government working in the British Zone as quickly as possible and at the same time to keep in step with the Americans. When we were allowed into Berlin, I would move there the Tac Headquarters from Frankfurt. In fact, I proposed to keep the main body of the Control Commission " built-in " in the British Zone, since there was where the problems lay. What we kept in Berlin was entirely our own affair and I was not going to submit to Russian dictation on that score.

WE WITHDRAW TO THE AGREED ZONES

Having given orders on all these, and many other, matters I went to London on the 16th June to try and get decisions on certain matters of policy. The major problems I raised were the following three:

(a) The Russians would not co-operate with us on Control Commission matters, or allow reconnaissance parties into Berlin, until all the Allies withdrew into their proper zones. There was no military reason for staying where we were, and the man-power situation made it disadvantageous to do so. It was essential to begin discussions on Control Commission matters as soon as possible; much valuable time had already been lost, and many decisions were being held up pending discussion by the Control Commission. I therefore strongly recommended the agreement of an early date by which the withdrawal to agreed zones should be completed.

(b) The intended operation of the release scheme was such that, unless a large number of officers were retained under the military necessity clause, certain branches of the staff would lose the majority of their trained officers, and their quick replacement would be a matter of the greatest difficulty.

(c) Immense quantities of German arms and equipment were being collected, and, in addition to all his other commitments, the British soldier was now having to guard these dumps of arms. Owing to the number and size of these dumps, adequate guards were difficult to arrange, and there was a serious danger that a number of the weapons would find their way back into enemy hands. I had been told that these weapons were to be kept intact. I pressed that this order be cancelled so that I could destroy the weapons.

While in London I made clear to the British Government the

oblems with which we were faced, and the impossibility of making
uch progress in the government of Germany until the machinery of
e Central Commission could be got going. I learnt that discussions
ere then in progress between the Prime Minister, President Truman
d Marshal Stalin, on the occupation of agreed zones both in Germany
d also in Austria—where the Russians had to hand over a considerable
ea to the Western Allies. On the 19th June, I was informed that
arshal Stalin had agreed to the simultaneous withdrawal into agreed
nes in Germany and in Austria, and to the move of Anglo-French-
nerican garrisons into Berlin, such moves to begin about the 1st July.
onsiderable importance was attached to this agreement, since the
g Three Conference had been arranged for the middle of July in
rlin, and it was considered that the Allies should all have occupied
eir agreed zones by that date.

Following this agreement by Governments to the simultaneous
thdrawal to agreed zones, General Weeks and General Clay, the
itish and American Deputies on the Control Commission, flew to
rlin on the 29th June, for a conference with Marshal Zhukov to
tle how the withdrawal should be carried out. At this conference
was agreed that withdrawals should commence on the 1st July; the
itish would evacuate the Wismar "cushion" in one day, and the
agdeburg "bulge" in two days; the Americans would evacuate
eir portion of the Russian Zone in six to nine days. British and
nerican advance parties would take over their sectors in Berlin on
e 1st July, and main bodies to occupy Berlin would follow on the
n July. There was considerable discussion about communications
om the British and American zones to their sectors in Berlin. The
cessity for free and unhampered access was emphasised, and the
ussians agreed to the allotment of a road and a railway over which
e British and Americans would have full running rights, the Russians
aining responsibility for maintenance and control. The allotment
an airfield for the period of the Big Three Conference was also
reed, but the subsequent allotment of airfields was reserved for
ther discussion. An air corridor to Berlin twenty miles wide was
be established, and the free use of this corridor was permitted subject
one hour's notice being given to the Russians of an aircraft entering
eir zone.

As a result of this conference, withdrawals to agreed zones began
the 1st July and on the same day advance parties started for Berlin.

Arrangements for the Big Three Conference in Berlin were also agree and work on the British sector in Berlin for the conference was push ahead. The hand-over of the Wismar and Magdeburg areas to t Russians went smoothly and was completed on the 4th July. At t same time, a force drawn mainly from 7th Armoured Division went occupy the British Sector in Berlin. This force took over the sect from the Russians, who withdrew the majority of their troops; b they refused to withdraw their troops carrying out Military Gover ment there unless the British would take over the responsibility f feeding the 900,000 Germans living in the sector. The Americans we faced with a similar request in their sector. Berlin as a whole h normally drawn its food from the area within 50 miles of the capit all of which was now occupied by the Russians; this therefore seem an unreasonable request. After considerable discussion and seve conferences, it was finally agreed that the British and the America would provide food for one month for the population in their sect of Berlin, without prejudice to any future decision on the question principle—which would be discussed at the Big Three Conference.

MY GENERAL POLICY IN THE BRITISH ZONE

Meanwhile the future of Germany and the function of the Cont Council was left to be decided at the Big Three Conference, due open in Berlin on the 16th July. It was already clear to me that Russians were not going to agree to the reconstitution of Germa as one economic whole. In their zone the Russian armies were livi off the country, which they had systematically sacked. I wrote following in my diary at the end of June 1945:

" The immensity of the problem of the future of Germany, a of Europe, to be settled at the Big Three Conference is becomi clear. So is the divergence between the views of the West Allies and the Russians as regards the solution. It remains to seen whether a workable solution can be achieved. It is far m likely that eastern Europe up to the line from Lübeck to Trie will fall under solely Russian domination, and will remain so many years."

Following my nomination as British Member of the Allied Cont

DIFFICULTIES WITH THE RUSSIANS BEGIN

ouncil, I had received a wide and loosely worded directive to cover
e course of action I was to pursue. This directive assumed that
e Control Council would be functioning and would by unanimous
cision settle all problems which arose. The situation however was,
fact, other than that which the politicians had envisaged. The
ussians were not prepared for the Control Council to begin to
erate; furthermore, no central authority existed in Germany through
hich the Control Council could function. To meet this situation I
quired further guidance from Whitehall on the course of action
hich I should pursue. Eventually I received authority from the
cretary of State for War to act on my own initiative but to endeavour
work in line with the Americans as far as possible. I subsequently
ued a series of memoranda to my staff giving them my general
licy for the government of the British Zone of Germany. These
emoranda showed at once how different from the problems of war
ere those with which I now had to deal. It was brought home to me
ery day that I had much to learn. But I had some first-class civilian
visers. My Chief of Staff, General Weeks, was a tower of strength.
en the heads of the civil divisions of the Control Commission were
e best that Whitehall could produce for me. The ones with whom
ealt the most were:

Political Adviser	..	Sir William (now Lord) Strang.
Political Division	..	Christopher Steel (now Sir Christopher).
Finance	..	S. P. Chambers.
Industry	..	Sir Percy (now Lord) Mills.
Transport	..	Robert Inglis (now Sir Robert).
Labour	..	R.W. Luce.

I could not have had a better team; each was an expert in his own
ticular sphere.

As the summer of 1945 wore on it became clear that things were
: going to work out in the way we had hoped. This was due to
able with the Russians and also to somewhat divergent viewpoints
ong the Western Allies. We were committed to the Potsdam
tocol which entailed, among other things, the provision of repara-
as from the British Zone to Russia, the settlement of refugees in the
tish Zone, and the treatment of Germany as an economic whole
er a central German administration. Because the British Zone
er had been economically self-sufficing and because, owing to the

past bombing and future reparations, it would become eventually eve
further from that desirable state, we obviously wanted Germany treate
as one economic entity. For us, the battle of the winter lay ahead

A further trouble was the fact that if Germany was to pay for th
cost of the British occupation, she must be made capable of doing s
But her industrial capacity was to be immensely reduced, her shippir
removed and her foreign assets frozen. There was to be an influx
refugees into Western Germany; this would entail a larger populatic
to feed, a greater population for which to find employment, and a
inability to export. Unless Germany could rebuild her foreig
exchange position, she could not pay.

The Russians did not mind that. For them Germany must pay b
immediate reparations in machinery and labour; a dismembered ar
discontented Germany would help the spread of Communism. Th
French saw the British point of view but were suspicious of ar
attempt to rebuild Germany, their ancient foe. The Americans wer
not sympathetic to a viewpoint which might put Germany on its fe
with American aid, merely to provide a market for Britain or to sa
the British taxpayer.

Failing Quadripartite control, we would presumably run our zor
like a colony, and the French would act the same way in their zor
But the difference in our colonial theories was considerable; th
French would run their zone by holding it down and we would t
to hold ours up.

The job of the Control Council was to evolve a new Europe, ar
one in which seventy million Germans would live peaceably as o
entity. We could achieve this only by Quadripartite control of
central German Government. Upon our ability to succeed rest
more futures than Germany's alone.

What would happen if we failed?

That is how it appeared to me in the summer of 1945. Possib
my impressions were painted with too broad a brush, and possibly t
colours used were too obviously red, white and blue. Anyhow, it w
becoming obvious that we were going to fail in our aim of Qua
ripartite government of Germany. However, my immediate conce
was with the British Zone, in trying to establish there some order c
of the existing chaos, and in getting our twenty million Germa
through the winter which lay ahead. I did not propose to be dra
away from that purpose because of difficulties with the Russians.

CHAPTER 24

THE STRUGGLE TO REHABILITATE

GERMANY

N THE middle of July 1945, SHAEF was disbanded, but Eisenhower remained as C.-in-C. and Military Governor of the American Zone. I have always considered this to have been a major error on the part of the Western Allies. The whole of eastern Germany was one zone controlled by one man (Zhukov); we split western Germany into three separate zones, each controlled by a separate Military Governor. I hold the view that Eisenhower should have been left in overall control of the western half of Germany; we would then have confronted the Russians with a united front. We were to pay the penalty for this nationalistic self-importance.

When Supreme Headquarters was disbanded, Eisenhower wrote me the following letter:

"Dear Monty,

Combined Command terminates at midnight tonight, 13 July 1945, and brings to a close one of the greatest and most successful campaigns ever fought.

History alone will judge the Allied Expeditionary Force in its true perspective, but we, who have worked and struggled together, can feel nothing but pride in the achievements of the men we have been honoured to command, and sadness at having to be parted now.

Whatever history may relate about the exploits of this Allied Force, and the memory of man is short and fickle, it is only we, at this time, who can fully appreciate the merit and due worth of the accomplishments of this great Allied team.

These accomplishments are not limited to the defeat of the Nazi hordes in battle—a continent has been liberated from all that is an antipathy to the ideal of democracy which is our common heritage.

389

Above all, we have proved to the whole world that the British and American peoples can for ever be united in purpose, in deed and in death for the cause of liberty.

This great experiment of integrated command, whose venture was cavilled at by some and doubted by many, has achieved unqualified success, and this has only been made possible by the sympathetic, unselfish and unwavering support which you and all other commanders have wholeheartedly given me. Your own brilliant performance is already a matter of history.

My gratitude to you is a small token for the magnificent service which you have rendered, and my simple expression of thanks sounds totally inadequate. Time and opportunity prohibit the chance I should like to shake you and your men by the hand, and thank each one of you personally for all you have done. I can do nothing more than assure you of my lasting appreciation, which I would ask you to convey to all those under your command for their exemplary devotion to duty and for the most magnificent loyalty which has ever been shown to a commander.

As ever

Ike "

I had always had a tremendous admiration for Eisenhower and his intensely human qualities; now, in the middle of 1945, that admiration was turning to a personal devotion that was to grow as the years passed, and today I count him one of my closest friends. In November 1945 he left Germany to return to Washington as Chief of Staff, U.S. Army. I then lost his wise counsel and willing assistance and it was brought home to me very forcibly what—to use Mary Martin's words in *South Pacific*—" a wonderful guy " he was.

THE GENERAL SITUATION IN JULY 1945

By the time SHAEF had ceased to exercise control, each of the four occupying Powers had already taken over its zone in Germany and Military Government was becoming well established. Free movement within and between the zones of the Western Allies was permitted, but access to the Russian Zone was still not allowed. In order to reach their sectors in Berlin, the Russians had allotted a road, railway and air route for the use of the Western Allies, but no deviation off this route could be made. Only within Berlin was circulation between all Allied sectors allowed.

In the zones of the Western Allies close liaison on all matters of high policy was being maintained. The British section of the Control Commission kept a strong liaison detachment with the American Headquarters at Frankfurt, and General Weeks paid frequent visits there for meetings to co-ordinate British, American and French policy. No liaison on similar lines had as yet been arranged with the Russians.

In the British Zone the disbandment of the German Army was proceeding well, and sufficient men had been discharged for work on the land to ensure adequate labour for the harvest. But to offset this, large numbers of fresh prisoners were arriving from Norway, and the total number of German prisoners held in the British Zone now amounted to 1,850,000. Coal production was slowly being raised as more food was given to the miners, and the services of transportation and distribution were being restarted as the supply of vehicles and the repair of roads and railways permitted. The fishing industry had been revived all round the coast and stocks of food were being supplemented from this source. The problem of Displaced Persons, of which some 1,300,000 remained for disposal, was still a very difficult one; the Russians were most irregular in their acceptance of Russian D.P.s, and in any event refused to accept Polish D.P.s until all their own had been repatriated.

Furthermore, it was now becoming clearer how the Russians were governing their zone in Germany. On the cessation of hostilities the Russians had systematically plundered it, removing and sending eastwards all machinery and stocks on which they could lay their hands. They regarded this action as partial reparation for what they had suffered at German hands, and for what the Germans had looted in Russia. In addition, the Russian Army was living off the country and thus eating up food supplies in their zone. Finally, all territory east of the Oder-Neisse line had been given by the Russians to Poland. Many of the Germans in this region, which before the war supported about ten million people, were being evicted by the Poles into the Russian Zone in Germany, and the small remaining population in this rich food-producing area was now unlikely to be sufficient to cultivate the area to anywhere near its previous productivity. From this it was clear that far from having a surplus of food, as in the past, to feed western Germany, the Russian Zone in Germany was likely to go very hungry and might well starve. Furthermore, the industrial capacity of eastern Germany in the future would be negligible.

THE BIG THREE CONFERENCE AT POTSDAM

The Prime Minister, President Truman and Marshal Stalin arrived in Berlin for the conference at Potsdam on the 15th July. I went up to Berlin to receive the Prime Minister on his arrival, and took the opportunity then, and on the following day before the conference began, to inform him, Anthony Eden, and the C.I.G.S. of the problems of government in the British Zone in Germany, and of the questions which urgently required a decision at the forthcoming conference. The main question was whether there was in future to be one Germany or two. I gave it as my opinion that if Germany was to be treated as one administrative and economic whole, then the following implications of this decision would have to be accepted:

(*a*) Free circulation of Allied nationals between all zones.

(*b*) A central German administrative machine, to deal in particular with finance, transportation and communications.

(*c*) A common policy regarding the reconstruction of industries, wage rates, and price controls.

(*d*) The exchange of resources and services, including food, between zones so as to preserve a balanced economy throughout Germany.

(*e*) Consequential on (*d*), global demands on outside sources to make up deficits.

Just when the conference looked like reaching some decisions on these matters, the British delegation had to return to England for the opening on the 26th July of the ballot boxes in order to discover the results of the General Election. All arrangements were however made for the return of Mr. Churchill and his delegation on the morning of the 27th July. But it was not to be.

The decisive defeat of the Churchill government came as a great surprise to all, and the formation of a new government caused a slight delay in the return of a British delegation to Potsdam. There was not unnaturally some uncertainty about the effect that the change of government would have on the deliberations of the conference. All doubts were, however, set at rest when Mr. Attlee and Mr. Bevin arrived in Potsdam; these two grasped the problems with both hands and created a very good impression on everyone.

The results of the conference appeared on the surface to be gratifying. The main results as far as they affected Germany were as follows:

(a) The establishment of a Council of Foreign Ministers to prepare peace treaties with Italy and with the Axis satellites; to prepare a peace settlement with Germany, for use when a German Government was ultimately set up; and to consider certain European territorial questions.

(b) Three-Power agreement to treat the German population uniformly throughout Germany, as far as practicable; to remove all Nazis from office; to permit freedom of speech, of the Press and of religion, and the formation of free trades unions, subject to military security; and to decentralise the political structure—no central German government being contemplated for the time being.

(c) Agreement that Germany should be treated as an economic unit; that the German economy should be decentralised and that the first charge on the proceeds of exports from current production and stocks should be the payment for essential imports approved by the Control Council.

(d) A settlement was reached whereby the occupying authorities should take reparations from Germany in the form of capital goods to the extent of Germany's ability to surrender industrial equipment.

(e) Agreement to transfer to Germany the populations remaining in Poland, Czechoslovakia, and Hungary; this to be effected in an orderly and humane manner.

THE CONTROL COUNCIL BEGINS TO FUNCTION

All this looked good—to me too good, and I could not see much of happening. However, the great point now was to push ahead and relied very much on Eisenhower to give a lead in the matter. He played up well and insisted that the Control Council should now meet and get on with the job. The Council held its first executive meeting in Berlin on the 30th July.

No central machinery for governing Germany any longer existed. But, largely due to the great energy of General Weeks, Chief of Staff British Zone, various boards on a Tripartite basis had been set up to ensure that at least in the British, American and French Zones, the Military Governments of each zone were marching in step and that the economic problems within these zones were being considered as a whole. However, these boards now ended with the setting up of the Quadripartite machinery.

The Quadripartite machinery began to function after our meeting on the 30th July, the whole organisation being called the "Allied Control Authority." This was divided into three bodies:

The Council —The heads of the British, American, Russian and French zones.

The Co-ordinating
Committee—Their four deputies.

The Control Staff —Divided into twelve divisions, and working frequently together to evolve an agreed policy.

At the end of July, General Weeks was forced by ill-health to resign his post as my Deputy, and Chief of Staff of the British Zone. His departure was a great blow to me. Apart from our friendship, I was to lose his wise counsel. It is not too much to say that without his effort we would not have progressed so far as we had in the organisation of government in the British Zone, and in the initial arrangements for getting the Control Commission organised in Berlin. I was lucky to secure as his successor General Sir Brian Robertson, who had served with me in the Eighth Army.

Meanwhile I was pondering deeply over the problem of the rehabilitation of the mentality of the German people on the right lines. There must be a plan for this, and at present we had none. I therefore decided on the following outline plan:

(i) To allow the people to discuss their problems amongst themselves, and generally to set on foot measures for self-help.

(ii) To eradicate the best allies of Nazism—idleness, boredom, and fear of the future—and to replace them by good ideas and by hope.

(iii) To work particularly on the youth of the German nation.

The next thing was to tell the Germans about this plan. While the Potsdam Conference was in session I had written a third message to the German people in the British Zone. It was dated the 25th July, 1945, but I held it up until the results of that conference were published and it was finally issued on the 6th August. It ran as follows:

TO THE POPULATION OF THE BRITISH ZONE IN GERMANY

" 1. Three months have now passed since Germany surrendered and your country passed to the control of the Allied Nations. The Allies are proceeding to the complete disarmament and demilitarisation of Germany and to the final destruction of the Nazi Party and its affiliated organisations. These aims will be carried through to the end.

2. During this time the British Zone has been under Military Government.

Members of the German armed forces have been sorted out by trades and occupations; many thousands have been discharged to work on the land and in other spheres, and this will continue.

There is every prospect of a good harvest, and you must see that it is all gathered in.

My officers have been active in their endeavours to arrange that the German population have adequate food and housing and are kept free from disease.

The first stage in the rehabilitation of Germany is under way.

3. I am now going to proceed with the second stage of the Allied policy.

In this stage it is my intention that you shall have freedom to get down to your own way of life: subject only to the provisions of military security and necessity.

I will help you to eradicate idleness, boredom, and fear of the future. Instead, I want to give you an objective, and hope for the future.

4. I will relax by stages the present restrictions on the freedom of the Press.

It is Allied policy, subject to the necessity for maintaining military security, to encourage the formation of free trade unions in Germany.

It is also Allied policy to encourage the formation in Germany of democratic political parties, which may form the basis of an ordered and peaceful German society in the future.

We aim at the restoration of local self-government throughout Germany on democratic principles. And it is our intention that Nazis removed from office shall be replaced by persons who, by their political and moral qualities, can assist in developing genuinely democratic institutions in Germany. It is our purpose also to reorganise the judicial system in accordance with the principles of democracy, of justice under law and equal rights for all citizens without distinction of race, nationality or religion.

You may hold public meetings and discussions; I am anxious that you should talk over your problems among yourselves, and generally set on foot measures to help yourselves.

5.   Your children are at present lacking juvenile organisations and facilities for education.

I intend to encourage the forming of such organisations, on a voluntary basis, for the purpose of religious, cultural, health or recreational activities. Educational facilities will be provided at a relatively early date.

6.   I have relaxed the rules about fraternisation. Members of the British Forces are now allowed to engage in conversation with the German people in streets and in public places; this will enable us to have contact with you and to understand your problems the more easily.

7.   The coming winter will be a difficult time; there is much to mend and put right and time is short. We are faced with the probability of a shortage of food, a shortage of coal, insufficient accommodation, and inadequate services of transportation and distribution. It is well that you should realise this now.

I will do all I can to get the population of the British Zone through the coming winter. But you, the German people, must plan for these contingencies now; you must work to help yourselves.

8. I will continue to see that you are all kept informed by radio, and by the newspapers, of how we are progressing; I will give you German news as well as foreign news.
9. I expect the co-operation of you all in the second stage of the Allied policy."

I then began to consider German education. We were opening schools and universities as soon as possible. New school books must be printed which were not tainted with Nazi ideologies, and all Nazi teaching and ideas must be eradicated from educational establishments. There would be a shortage of suitable teachers and that matter must be tackled energetically.

MY AEROPLANE CRASH

On the 22nd August I flew in my light aircraft, a Miles Messenger, to visit the 3rd Canadian Division (General Vokes). As we were circling the airfield preparatory to landing, the engine cut out; we had the flaps down and so lost speed rapidly. My pilot could not make the airfield and we crash-landed nearby; the plane was completely written off, but the pilot, and an A.D.C. who was with me, were unhurt. I was not so lucky, being severely shaken and bruised and breaking two lumbar vertebrae. It was a lucky escape but, with a less skilful pilot, the results might have been much more serious.

I managed to begin my address to the officers of the 3rd Canadian Division but had to break off in the middle as I felt too ill. It was suggested that I should return to my headquarters (about 100 miles) by car. I refused, as I could not face a car journey of that distance with a damaged back; I said I would fly back in another light aircraft. This upset the Canadians who said I might have another crash. I replied that no one had ever crashed twice in the same day and the flight back to my headquarters would, therefore, be the safest I would ever make.

It took me some time to recover and during the winter of 1945-46 I got frequent attacks of influenza and finally contracted pleurisy. I suppose my resistance to illness had become weakened during five years of war, and the aeroplane crash was the last straw. Finally, in February 1946, I had to go to Switzerland for a month to recover my

397

health. My back continued to give trouble and some years later began to get arthritis. An X-ray examination then showed that m spine had been left somewhat out of shape; this was dealt with, b it was some years before I fully recovered.

DEADLOCK IN THE CONTROL COUNCIL

Early in October 1945 the London Conference of Foreign Ministe ended in disagreement. It had been assembled to prepare the way f the peace treaties with ex-enemy States, as agreed at the Potsda Conference. It was now fairly clear that we were heading for troub in a big way.

About the same time the Control Council machine in Berlin can up against serious obstacles and a position near deadlock had bee reached. The immediate cause of this was the opposition of France the creation of central German administrations; having been attacke three times in a century France wanted security above all else, and dismembered Germany was held to be less dangerous. Furthermoi the French wished the Ruhr area, which contained a very substanti part of Germany's war potential, to be separated from Germany an internationalised, and they considered that the setting up of centr German administrations while the Ruhr remained within German would prejudge its fate.

All the really important work in progress within the Quadriparti machine had been based upon the idea of establishing central Germa administrations. The effect of putting this idea into cold storage wou virtually bring the Quadripartite machine to a standstill. The resul of the last meetings of the Control Council and Co-ordinatin Committee had proved this. Every measure of consequence at tho: meetings was blocked either by French opposition to central a ministrations or by Russian intransigence, for the Russians took fu advantage of the fact that they were no longer the only or even th chief obstruction to progress and agreement. A continuation of th state of affairs would put a strain on this delicate machine from whic it might never recover. The importance of this consideration wou depend upon the value which was attached to Quadripartite workin in Germany as a prelude to inter-Allied co-operation in wider fields

The Russians were creating a desert in their zone; anything in

value was being sent to Russia, and conditions were already
palling in the area. Our reconnaissance parties in search of routes
d camps for Poles returning to Poland reported that the Germans in
e area were living like beasts on whatever they could get, and that
rvation was already evident.

As a result of the terrible conditions in the Russian Zone, and
cause of the eviction of Germans from the territory given by the
ussians to Poland, from Czechoslovakia, and from elsewhere, 40,000
erman refugees were infiltrating into the British Zone weekly; and
is movement looked likely to continue.

The Russians had altered the gauge of the German railways in their
ne to the Russian gauge. This was an ominous step. The only
lway as yet unaltered was that leading from the western zones to
erlin, which was being used for the transport of supplies to Berlin.

When the Foreign Ministers failed to reach agreement about
ermany, I went to London to see the Prime Minister (Attlee). I saw
m early in October 1945 and gave him my views as follows:

(*a*) I had once thought Four-Power government of Germany was
possible. I now considered that it could never be made to work.
Agreement could not be reached in the Council, and the
Americans in particular were becoming restless. They had now
tabled a motion that, when unanimous agreement in the Council
was not possible, each zone might act as it thought best. This
was the first rift in the lute. It was clear to me that the Western
Powers must now prepare for a continuous struggle with the
communist East, which would last for many years. Basically,
this struggle would be for " the soul " of Germany. We had
got half of Germany and we must hang on to it.

(*b*) It seemed to me, as a soldier, that it was not really a practicable
proposition to de-industrialise the Rhur, when Germany and
all the Allied States on her frontiers were suffering great
privations due to the destruction of industrial potential. Provided
the industry of the Ruhr was properly controlled it would fulfil
a very useful function in supplying the needs of the Western
Allies, and thereby indirectly in providing food for starving
Germans.

(*c*) Having in view the troubles that were descending on us, did
Britain really want a unified Germany *just at present*? If

Germany was unified too quickly, the British Zone would hav
to supply the desert in the Russian Zone, and those living in th
Russian Zone would all want to come into the British Zone—
which we hoped eventually would become a thriving place

(d) The Russians were very difficult people to deal with, and w
must be very sure about what points in our strategy matter
and what points did not matter. In my opinion, Wester
Germany, the Mediterranean, especially the eastern part, an
Libya mattered; for the present the Balkans did not matt
since Russia had too firm a grip on that area for us to c
anything about it.

(e) Finally it was vital at the present time to maintain adequa
strength in the fighting services. If we did not do this, we shou
cut no ice with anyone, particularly the Russians. It was ther
fore most important to reach a decision about National Servi
in peace-time as soon as possible.

I made it clear to the Prime Minister that the immediate bar
Quadripartite progress was the French opposition to central Germ
administrations. The Russian "iron curtain" policy, if it was co
tinued indefinitely, would later be the real obstacle, since witho
freedom of movement of Allied and German officials, Press and aircra
central German administrations could not work. If the Russia
insisted on keeping the "iron curtain" drawn over their zone, the
was no hope for the continuance of Quadripartite control.

A quick solution had to be found to our problems, as Germa
was drifting towards economic chaos. This could only be avoided
important decisions were quickly taken on currency, taxes, loans, et
establishing for the purpose either a central financial administration
zonal administrations. The choice must be made soon; once taken
could not easily be reversed.

EVENTS IN THE BRITISH ZONE

With the approach of winter all my apprehensions about epidemi
of disease appeared likely to be fulfilled. Food was very short; owi
to bad weather the harvest had been poor, contrary to my earlier hop
and no coal would be available for the heating of private houses. T

German people had not the resistance to withstand any serious epidemic. In addition, reports from the Russian Zone indicated that many Germans, especially children, were already slowly starving in parts of Eastern Germany; epidemics starting in that area would be likely to spread rapidly among people seriously weakened by hunger and without adequate housing, clothes or fuel.

From the point of view of our own organisation, things were going smoothly. A gradual transition was taking place from the completely military machine set up by 21 Army Group to an eventual civilian organisation in which there would be a German administration with British control at the top. Two important steps had been taken: the Control Commission and Military Government had been integrated, and civilians had been brought out from England. The future development of the organisation would be gradual and would continue slowly until completed. It would start at the bottom and work up, and eventually the Corps Commanders would have to be withdrawn from the administrative machine and become exclusively commanders of troops. It was unlikely that this would happen until the " Battle of the Winter " was over; or before the problems of Displaced Persons and prisoners of war were more manageable; or before the German administrative machine was capable of functioning without large-scale assistance from Corps Districts.

Meanwhile I had issued a directive on the evolution of Government in the British Zone. It was based on the principle that Military Government of Germany must be succeeded as soon as possible by a system of control on a civilian basis. The speed with which this change took place would depend on the progress made in demilitarisation, denazification, and the foundation of a democratic system of administration. In order to enable the process of change to proceed smoothly, a phased programme was to begin at once. In the first phase Corps District Commanders were already dealing with their Military Government responsibilities through their own Military Government staffs. In the second phase Regional Commissioners would be trained to replace Corps District Commanders as Military Governors. In the third phase Corps District Commanders would cease to be Military Governors. And in the fourth phase personnel of Military Government detachments would gradually be transferred to a civilian status and their strengths much reduced. On the completion of Phase Four, the Germans would be governing themselves, subject to a general supervision by us, and the head of the administration would be a civilian and not a soldier. Phases three and four were very important and this is how I described them.

PHASE III

" At this stage Corps District Commanders cease to be the Military Governors of their Corps Districts. They will have no responsibility for civil administrations other than as Commanders of troops which may be required to act in support of the civil power or to assist the civil administrations with the administrative resources at their disposal. This question of assistance is important. At present Military Government relies a great deal on the assistance which it obtains from the troops. This is one of the reasons why Phase III cannot take place immediately. The degree of assistance which will be required when the change does take place will be considerably less than it is now, but the need for some assistance will remain and Corps District Commanders will have a responsibility to furnish it so far as their resources permit.

A Regional Commissioner will be appointed at each Provincial Headquarters, including Hamburg.

I am not prepared at this moment to fix the date on which Phase III will take place, but I shall aim at putting it into force in April 1946.

PHASE IV

This involves the gradual transference of the personnel of Military Government Detachments from a military to a civilian status, and a reduction in the size of these Detachments at lower levels. The reason for such reduction is that the principle of civil control implies an exercise of control over German administrations at higher levels, while at the lower levels no control will eventually be exercised other than such inspection as may be necessary to ensure that instructions given to the higher echelons of administration are being faithfully executed by the lower.

It is not necessary to fix any time for this Phase at present. It will be carried out by the Regional Commissioners after they have assumed their responsibilities.

I am holding a Corps District Commanders' Conference on the 14th December. An opportunity will then be provided for discussing the detailed implications of the plan which I have set out above. It must, however, be clearly understood that the general framework of this plan is a matter on which I have already made my decision.

Finally I want to emphasise that the essence of the change from Military Government to civil control does not lie in the substitution of civilians for soldiers in administrative appointments. It is desirable that the principal appointments should be handed over to civilians because this emphasises the fact of the change and has a psychological importance.

The real essence of the change, however, is that under Military Government we govern our zone through the Germans. Our government depends on the Commander-in-Chief and his Corps District Commanders and it is supported immediately by our military forces. Civil control, on the other hand, means that the Germans govern themselves, subject to control and supervision by us, that our administration is headed by someone other than the Commander of the troops and that military forces are regarded as a reserve to be used in support of our administration in emergency only.

I have thought it important to emphasise this point because it is not my intention that officers who are doing a competent job in Military Government now should automatically be replaced merely because they are not civilians."

ZHUKOV ACCUSES THE BRITISH

In November, just when I was thinking we were beginning to get our affairs in the British Zone into good working order, Zhukov circulated a memorandum to the Control Council in which he accused me of retaining organised units of the former German Army in the British Zone.

The presence of organised disarmed units of the German Army in the British Zone had first been discussed in the Co-ordinating Committee on the 17th September; had again been brought up on the 3rd October; and had been the subject of two letters by General Robertson to Marshal Zhukov and General Sokolovsky.

The question had originally been discussed in relation to the " Law for the Elimination and Limitation of Military Training," but it had become apparent that the Soviet authorities were suspicious of the intentions of the British Government in retaining in their zone large numbers of ex-Wehrmacht personnel, and Marshal Zhukov's memorandum was, in effect, a direct attack upon us. It was based on the Potsdam Declaration which laid down that all German units and headquarters must be immediately disarmed and disbanded. The memorandum alleged that organised German headquarters with full "operations" staffs existed from army group level down to the military and air districts into which the British Zone was divided. It also claimed that two corps groups existed, each 100,000 strong; that tank detachments were in being; and that we were maintaining considerable numbers of Balts and Hungarians in organised units. In conclusion, the memorandum stated that it considered it imperative that a commission of the Control Council should visit the British Zone to examine the situation on the spot.

This meeting was the first occasion on which one Ally had criticised the conduct of another in the Control Council. It was important to allay at once all Russian suspicions of our good faith, but at the same time the Russian method of approach and the direct challenge thrown out called for a blunt reply. I decided that a heavy counter-attack must be launched against the Soviet delegation.

There were two main reasons for the presence of the 700,000 ex-Wehrmacht personnel in concentration areas awaiting disbandment First, we had nowhere to put them if they were disbanded, and we could not guard them if they were dispersed in prison camps over our area. Second, the British Government required 225,000 Germans a reparations labour for the United Kingdom. All had been disarmed and their headquarters only had sufficient staffs to enable them to administer their troops. I cabled my views to London, and at the Control Council meeting on the 30th November I read out a statemen in which, after expressing my astonishment that Marshal Zhukov should have ignored General Robertson's letters and chosen to directly challenge British policy, the following main points were made:

(a) Ex-Wehrmacht personnel were not described as Prisoners o War because we did not wish to apply the Geneva Conventio to them.

(b) German headquarters were retained for administrative purposes since it was ridiculous to employ British to administer Germans.

(c) The numbers contained in the Soviet memorandum were grossly exaggerated: there was only one corps with 99,000 personnel in it.

(d) There was no army group headquarters in the British Zone; none of the staffs had operational branches; and none of them was capable of doing anything but administrative work.

(e) The military and air districts only administered labour gangs, and the tank detachments were all completely disarmed and waiting in concentration areas to be discharged.

(f) The presence of Hungarians and Balts was extremely unwelcome to the British, and in the case of the Hungarians the only reason for their continued presence in the British Zone was the refusal of the Soviet authorities to afford them transport facilities through the Russian Zone.

(g) The proposal to send a Commission was accepted on two conditions: first, that it visit all zones, and, secondly, that it be the forerunner of similar commissions which would investigate other matters within the scope of the Control Council.

Marshal Zhukov in his reply to this statement accepted the idea of Commission to visit all zones but rejected the second condition. He e-affirmed that in his opinion the British were not fulfilling the terms f the Potsdam Agreement. It was finally agreed, on my proposal, 1at the matter should be referred to the Co-ordinating Committee for onsideration, and that the British Delegation should submit to the :o-ordinating Committee full facts and figures.

The meeting was throughout very friendly. But it was undeniable 1at, in spite of the excellent personal relationship existing between Marshal Zhukov and myself, the Soviet authorities were deeply uspicious of our holding of 700,000 German troops. The Control :ouncil meeting had not gone badly for us, but it was now essential) disband the German headquarters and to discharge all German isarmed personnel held in concentration areas. I therefore urgently equested permission to be relieved of the order which made me hold 25,000 Germans as reparations labour for the United Kingdom.

Without waiting for authority from London, I gave out orders to 1y Chief of Staff to organise the disbandment of all ex-Wehrmacht ersonnel held in concentration areas. Conferences were immediately held at H.Q. British Army of the Rhine, and on the 10th December Operation CLOBBER began. The object of the operation was to disban the German headquarters and to discharge the personnel by th 30th January. After that date the only Germans held by us would b those required by the three services and certain categories that coul not be discharged without trial. It was hoped to persuade our Allie to accept Austrians, and to induce the Russians to grant transpor facilities for Hungarians and Rumanians. The matter was the brought to a successful conclusion, and it had been done withou upsetting friendly personal relations on the Control Council—whic had always been good.

THE WINTER OF 1945-46

Towards the end of the year I pondered deeply over the progres or lack of progress, we were making in the British Zone. The " Battl of the Winter " was proceeding and I reckoned that we would win i The Control Commission was well established, and was working. W seemed to be marching forward. Our danger now was complacency we had made a good beginning but there was still much to be don I saw stormy weather ahead.

While we had been proceeding methodically with our plans t rehabilitate Germany, the British Zone had remained quiet; th Germans were busy with their own immediate troubles, chiefly con cerned with getting food and keeping warm. But I considered that ou conflicts with them lay ahead. If we could get them safely throug the winter, they would be feeling better in 1946. They would the see their factories and coal being removed, and would realise that the themselves were not to be allowed to benefit from the recovery of the country. Our industrial and economic policy was such that there wa bound to be widespread unemployment in Germany as time went on We had removed from positions of responsibility large numbers o Nazi Germans, many of them immensely capable people and first-cla organisers; these people were now idle and might well cause unres We had demobilised into the zone about two million fighting men an another half million remained to be added to the figure. Clearly the was much fertile ground in which evil persons could sow the seeds o discontent and trouble.

As these thoughts passed through my mind I came to the conclusion at we must not let the strength of our armed forces in Germany run wn too quickly. We must keep sufficient troops to back up the lice in maintaining law and order, and to aid the civil power should ings show signs of getting out of hand.

There were so many possibilities of trouble, and so many things at could go wrong, that I decided we must be sure of our ground we went along. The tendency in Whitehall was to push things along ickly. My view was that to go too quickly might involve us in pleasant repercussions.

For instance, to me it was clear that political and trades union tivities should be allowed to grow from below, steadily and pro- essively. We had planted the seeds; if they were "watered" unduly ey might grow too quickly and become unpleasant weeds. If they aintained a sturdy growth from below, throwing up the right type leader, then all would be well. But if we tried to hasten the crop imposing a top dressing from above, we might well land ourselves trouble. But my Socialist political masters in Whitehall did not together agree, saying they knew more about politics and trades ions than I did—which was of course true. But I was responsible r what might happen. So I stuck to my guns and refused to change y policy, though I understand things were pushed along a bit more ickly after I left Germany in May 1946.

CHAPTER 25

LAST DAYS IN GERMANY

ON THE 26th January 1946, I received official intimation that I h
been selected for the appointment of Chief of the Imperial Gene
Staff, and was to take over the post on the 26th June. It was of cou
an immense honour to become professional head of the British Arm
I little thought in my Sandhurst days that I would ever rise to th
position. Nor did anyone else. I wondered how I would get on wi
my new political masters. I had already had dealings with Attlee a
Bevin which had given me much confidence. But I was not so su
about other personalities in the Socialist hierarchy. In August 194
very soon after the new government assumed office, two Social
M.P.s (one a junior Minister) visited the British forces in Germa
and stayed a night with me at my Tac Headquarters. The next d
they left on a tour of army units and I had agreed that they cou
address gatherings of officers and men if they wished. I was inform
the next day that, at the first unit, they had asked the officers to lea
the hall so that they could speak to the soldiers alone, and that had be
done. I was extremely angry and at once issued an order to all Briti
forces in Germany forbidding such action. I was responsible f
discipline in the armed forces in Germany and I was not going to ha
it undermined by wandering Members of Parliament. I had these vie
conveyed to the two M.P.s concerned, explaining that I had
objection to their addressing the troops, but it must be in the presen
of their officers. I also heard that one of the M.P.s had asked the batm
to the general with whom he was staying the night, what he thoug
of the general. The batman rightly reported the conversation. The
incidents had disturbed me. I well knew that good and friend
relations between Service chiefs and their political masters we
essential. My dealings with members of the Conservative Governme
had always been most friendly. In January 1946 I had sent Church
a copy of my book *Alamein to the River Sangro* and had written in

408

tribute to him; I wanted him to realise how much we all owed to
m, even though he was no longer our political master. I give below
the reply he had sent me. The book he refers to (in his second paragraph) was my autograph book which I have quoted in earlier chapters.

28, Hyde Park Gate,
London, S.W.7.
January 8, 1946.

" My dear Monty,

I am most deeply obliged to you for sending me a copy of
the story of your Campaign from Alamein to the Sangro River,
and particularly touched by the all too kind and complimentary
inscription which you have written in it. This is indeed a most
generous tribute from a great Commander to his Political Chief.
Certainly the relations which I had with you, with Alexander, and
with the High Command of the three Services generally, were of a
most friendly and intimate character in spite of the great stresses
through which we went. How different from the rows of the
' frocks ' and ' Brass hats ' which characterised the last War ! I am
proud that you feel that contribution of the Minister of Defence
made your great task easier of accomplishment.

I hope one day that your book, in which I wrote so many
entries, will be published in facsimile to a wide public. There is set
out, milestone by milestone, the glorious advance of the Eighth
Army and of the British Army of the Rhine, and almost all the
forecasts of the Political Chief were vindicated superbly by the
sword of the Commander.

I am so glad we had that day on the Rhine together and saw a
few shells playing about.

With every good wish,
Believe me,
Yours very sincerely,
(Signed) Winston S. Churchill "

THE PROBLEM IN GERMANY: FEBRUARY 1946

As I was to leave Germany in a few months, I turned my attention
the two matters which in my opinion were the root of the whole
matter—the problem of the German people, and the evolution of

government in the British Zone in order to cope with that problem

In my opinion one of our most important objects in Germany wa to change the heart, and the way of life, of the German people. Fo the past thirteen years the Germans had had nationalistic and dictatori ideas forced into their minds; the authority of the family had bee minimised, the influence of the Church reduced, and the power of th State had increased. This period had been one of full employment an a high standard of living for the German people. Now there w nothing but misery. There was a danger that the people would soc begin to look back with longing on the old régime; my informatio was that a large percentage, probably 60 per cent, were out-and-o Nazis. Opinion in the zone was hardening against the British and subversive organisation had recently been uncovered. The fact w that we had some twenty million Germans in the British Zone wh due to the shortage of food, were going to experience a hard tim Without doubt conflicts with these people lay ahead; in some wa they must be influenced for good so that they would not cause troub in the future. How was this to be done?

It seemed to me that we could divide this mass of human materi into three categories for the purpose I wanted to achieve.

First, there were the children. These should not be difficult handle, though of course there was always the danger of a bad hon influence if the elder members of the family were Nazis. Then can the young men, and young women too, between the ages of say to 25. Here was a much more difficult problem and this age gro was probably the crux of the problem; they had been brought up an atmosphere of National Socialism—having been taught it at scho in the Hitler Youth, and many of them in the S.S. also. And last there were the older people; amongst these were many who cou probably be got on our side.

I decided that the best way to begin influencing all these grou was through economics; this was probably the foundation of t overall solution. We must give the German people hope for the futu they must be made to realise that they could reach a worthwhile futu only by their own work. That meant fixing the level of industry that there would be a decent standard of living with the minimu of unemployment. If this were not done the Germans would mere look to the past and be ready to follow any evil leader who mig arise.

With this foundation, and having got the Germans down to work,
e must then tackle the political problem. On the practical side, this
eant the decentralisation of the Government and the Civil Service.
also reckoned that we should encourage contacts with the outside
orld so that the Germans could study a new ideology to replace that
f the Nazis. On the psychological side, we must tell the Germans
hen the process of de-nazification would be completed.

And then there was the educational problem. For children still at
hool we must ensure a good supply of books, reliable and trust-
orthy teachers, and decent buildings. The troops were living in many
 the school buildings; they must hand them back to the Germans
once. Of the age group 18 to 25, a small minority were being
ucated in universities. But the vast majority of this group were un-
uched by such advantages; for them the important things were good
nemas, the Press, books, and so on, all controlled and run by the
ermans themselves. I thought selected members of this age group
ight well be sent to England to learn a new way of life, and one
hich they had never known; they had been children when Hitler
me to power and National Socialism was the creed in which they
d been brought up.

THE EVOLUTION OF GOVERNMENT IN THE BRITISH ZONE

I had already ordered that on the 15th April 1946, Corps Com-
anders were finally to hand over their responsibilities for civil
ministration. Phase Three of my instructions issued in December
45 would then be complete. It was now necessary to issue in-
uctions to initiate the execution of Phase Four, and on the 25th
arch 1946 I circulated a memorandum which was intended to do so.
 the memorandum I pointed out that the " Battle of the Winter "
d been won. No epidemics had broken out and the general health
the German people had been maintained. But the outlook for the
ture was now worse than ever before. The food situation over-
dowed everything else, and other factors would soon aggravate the
uation. The future level of German economy would cause distress
d unemployment; the influx of refugees was just beginning; all
cks of consumer goods had now been used up. The next battle was
ing to be more serious than the " Battle of the Winter " just con-

cluded. It could not be tackled by Military Government because of the drastic cuts in establishment and the speed of demobilisation. It must be tackled by the Germans themselves, but with our aid, especially by the import of food. Moreover, we must give them clear orders on such questions as de-nazification. In order to make my scheme possible we should have to build up German administrations, staffed by vigorous men who must be supported by us. The most important of these administrations was the Zonal Advisory Council which I had had formed. All domestic matters should be put to it for advice, should be encouraged to discuss as many matters as possible, and its advice accepted whenever we could do so. These principles also applied to the other functional bodies which were being gradually set up in the zone. All these administrations should eventually be given executive power. What it really amounted to was that the Germans must now be entrusted with the responsibility for their own problems. We would have to help them, but also continue to supervise and control their activities indirectly.

MY MEMORANDUM FOR THE BRITISH GOVERNMENT

I was to leave Germany on the 2nd May 1946, being due to take up my new duties at the War Office in June. After prolonged thought I decided it was my duty to prepare a memorandum for the British Government on the situation in Germany as I believed it to be.

My time in Germany since the war ended had convinced me that a united Germany was at present not possible. I doubted if it would ever be possible without fighting. But the Western Allies had half Germany, and they would have to continue to strive for a united Germany.

Our object must now be to bring the Western Germans into the community of Western nations, and to make their territory so attractive and prosperous that the Eastern Germans would regard it envious when comparing it with their own miserable lot. But if we were to do this, we would have to grasp the nettle firmly with both hands. Courageous decisions would be necessary—and without delay.

I devoted my last day in Germany to writing the memorandum. I took it to England with me on the 2nd May and handed it personally to the Prime Minister. This is what it said:

" 1. I leave Germany tomorrow. I have set out below a concise statement of the situation as I believe it to be. I am not happy about it. I consider the general overall picture is sombre, if not black.

For the present the food crisis overshadows all else, but it is not by any means the only serious factor in the situation.

2. We have a sick economy.

Coal is short; only the basic industries can be developed; the others lie idle, and there are few consumer goods being produced, and nothing in the shops for people to buy.

We have reached agreement on the future level of the German economy; there will soon begin the removal and destruction of a large part of German industry; this will cause distress to the German people and may produce unemployment on a large scale in the British Zone.

The present level of production is such that our exports do not pay for our imports.

3. A sick economy means that we cannot have a sound currency. There is little to buy with marks and the people are tending to use a system of barter to get food. Marks are gradually becoming of no value to people. Under such a system industry cannot be got going, since there is no incentive; this is the beginning of inflation, i.e. the phase when money begins to lose its value.

4. In my Memorandum entitled "The Problem in Germany: February 1946," I dealt with the subject of how we should handle the great mass of human material we have in Germany. I said we must work on a definite and concrete plan designed to bring about a change of heart in the German people.

I stated that the foundation of the plan must be the economic line of attack.

I said that the Germans must know what is to be the future of their country; they must be given a reasonable standard of living; they must be given some hope for a worthwhile future.

I gave it as my opinion that if we did not do this, we would fail in Germany.

We have not done it and I would say that at the moment there is a definite danger that we may fail. By that I mean there is a danger that if things do not improve the Germans in the British Zone will begin to look East. When that happens we shall have failed, and there will exist a definite menace to the British Empire. In this connection, much communist propaganda is coming westwards over the iron curtain.

5. If we are to progress at all we must have:
   a sound economy,
   a balanced budget,
   central financial control.

We must produce more consumer goods.

The essential financing of the cost of reparations must be borne by Germany as a whole; at present it falls heavily on the British Zone, which has most of the industries.

I still consider that the real answer to the problem is contained in my memorandum of 1st Feb. 1946 (*See page 409 The problem in Germany: February* 1946). But adequate economic conditions must be established before we can make any progress with the plan set out in that memorandum; at present these conditions do not exist.

6. While we are in this sorry economic condition, good progress is being made with the formation of political parties and trades unions. But we want to be clear that herein lies a possible danger.

There is no doubt that in a contented Germany, a strong Social Democratic party would be a great asset and one making for peace and security in Western Europe.

But, if the Germans become discontented and we get organised hostility of the people against the occupying Power, then they have machinery in the political and trades union spheres which could be used to implement their nefarious purposes. This aspect of the problem needs to be carefully watched during the next few years; close touch must be kept with propaganda coming from the Russian Zone.

BASIC FUNDAMENTALS IN THE SOLUTION TO THE PROBLEM

7. We must decide what is to constitute " Germany." The eastern frontier of Germany was agreed at Potsdam. The western frontier is not yet agreed; it is wrapped up in the

whole problem of the future of the Saar, the Ruhr and the Rhineland.

We must tell the German people what Germany is to consist of.

8. The people living inside that Germany must be given a reasonable standard of living, and hope for a worthwhile future. A reasonable standard of living can be set up in Germany on the basis of the level of industry which has been agreed, but only under certain conditions. These conditions were emphasised in our acceptance of the level of industry agreement. The principal one is that Germany should be treated as one economic whole. This is not happening at present, firstly on account of French opposition and, secondly, because of the attitude of the Russians. I do not feel confident that the Russians ever intend to treat Germany as an economic whole as we understand that phrase. I am certain that they will not do it unless we join with the other Allies in exerting strong pressure upon them.

9. The whole country is in such a mess that the only way to put it right is to get the Germans " in on it " themselves. This is being done by Zonal Advisory Councils; but this is not enough.

It means Central Administrations; we do not have these; we must have them. We must secure French agreement to their establishment. We must then take great care to ensure that they are set up under genuine Quadripartite control, and that neither their constitution nor their functions shall be such as to make them susceptible to the influence of one Power more than of others.

10. We must decide whether we are going to feed the Germans, or let them starve. Basically, we must not let them starve; if we do, then everything else we do is of no avail.

It does not look at present as if we can increase the ration beyond the present rate of 1042 calories; this means we are going to let them starve: gradually.

In spite of the difficulties of the world food situation, we must get back to a reasonable ration standard in the British Zone as quickly as possible. The discrepancies which exist between the standard of feeding in our zone and that in other zones must be removed by agreement on a common standard.

CONCLUSION

11. I regard the four points outlined in paras. 7 to 10 as the four pillars on which we must build the new Germany out of the ruins of the old. The master pillar is the fourth, or food pillar; if that breaks, the other pillars fall down.

12. So far, the four pillars do not exist. Therefore we cannot progress.

13. We must start to build the four pillars. And above all, we must tell the German people what is going to happen to them and to their country. If we do not do those things, we shall drift towards possible failure. That " drift " will take the form of an increasingly hostile population, which will eventually begin to look East.

Such a Germany would be a menace to the security of the British Empire.

14. On the other hand, a contented Germany with a sound political framework, could be a great asset to the security of the Empire and the peace of the world."

CHAPTER 26

PRELUDE TO WHITEHALL

MY farewell address to the officers of the British Army of the Rhine referred to the fact that I had reached a stage in my career when I ould not again exercise direct command of British soldiers. This ade me sad. On the other hand, as C.I.G.S. I would be responsible r the organisation of the Army and the welfare of everyone in it. ere were some seven weeks before I was to begin work at the ar Office and I decided to use that period as a time for thinking out how I would tackle the job, and for trying to fit myself for y new task.

While in Germany I had been observing the political and military ne in Britain. Political minds seemed to be concentrated on the ation of a welfare state, on a complete re-organisation of industry ving towards nationalisation, and on the raising of the school ving age—all these to be carried out simultaneously and as quickly possible. The state of the world, British commitments overseas, l a long-term plan for the armed forces all seemed to have been shed into the background; I had been chafing at the way the ssure of home events had forced delay in the consideration of these blems. It seemed to me important to clear my own mind, to mulate a policy and prepare the way so that no time would be lost en I took office as Chief of the Imperial General Staff on the 26th e 1946. The British Army must not, as after World War I, be wed to drift aimlessly without a policy or a doctrine.

Looking back, I reckon that the seeds of anything I was able to ieve during my two and a half years at the War Office were sown ing the first six months: in 1946. These were months of terrific k and during them we made definite progress—and, because of direct methods of tackling problems, I made many enemies. I pose to deal, very fully, with those first six months, and thereafter elect for mention only certain important subjects which require

to be followed up in order to present a balanced picture of th
whole period up to the end of October 1948—when I left the Wa
Office.

On my return from Germany I went to live at Hindhead, in th
house of my friends Major and Mrs. Reynolds. That had been m
home all through the war and they had looked after David for m
who was now seventeen and still at Winchester. I had no other pla
to go to, and they allowed me to continue on there until I could mal
a home for David and myself somewhere else. I had brought m
caravans back from Germany and parked them in the grounds. I w
supposed to be on leave; but I soon realised that no rest was possibl
there was too much to be done. I worked all day and every day,
my office caravan.

Certain matters were essential and urgent and, so far as I kno
no action was being taken about them. There was a grave danger th
the Army would drift along, shaping itself to events as they occurre
this was not at all what I had in mind. Therefore, the first point
tackle was the organisation of the post-war British Army, in order
design it on a sound basis which would last for the next ten to fifte
years. It was vital to have a long-term plan. And so I began work
a paper called *The Problem of the Post-War Army* and decided to produ
it for Army Council approval the day I became C.I.G.S. In this pap
I also described how we must modernise the way of life of officers a
men, and create an efficient army with a high morale to which
would be proud to belong. I planned to do this not only by acti
within the War Office, but also by enlisting the aid of the Press a
by taking advantage of official occasions when I had to speak.

Then it would be necessary to evolve a broad tactical doctrine
the Army, which would be capable of application in all theatres, w
variation in detail according to local topographical and clima
conditions. This would obviously take time. I decided to tackle t
problem by holding a series of exercises at the Staff College, Camberl
which would be attended by all general officers in the Army at ho
and overseas, and to which Chiefs of Staff of Dominion armies wo
be invited. The first thing was obviously to get inter-Service agreem
to the fundamental principles of modern war, and I drafted out th
principles as I saw them, and got them agreed by the First Sea L
(John Cunningham) and the Chief of the Air Staff (Tedder). I t
began work on the first War Office Exercise, which I planned to h

1 August, six weeks after I had become C.I.G.S. The object of this xercise was:

" To take the basic principles of modern war and, with that background, to study the stage-management and conduct of offensive land operations, and to enunciate in broad outline a tactical doctrine for the Army."

Finally, it was my aim to obtain a personal grip on the Army; must be the commander to whom all C.s-in-C. looked for orders. his would have to wait until I became C.I.G.S. But I decided to hold onferences of home Army Commanders every three months, at the /ar Office. At these conferences I would give a general survey of orld affairs, and my main plans and orders for the future. The ommanders would produce their problems and the War Office would ve decisions where they were needed. In general, I decided that I ould spend two months in the United Kingdom followed by one onth on tour overseas, and on this basis I planned tours up to the d of 1947. These tours took in every part of the British Empire, me of which had never before been visited by a C.I.G.S. when in fice.

All the foregoing concerned me in my capacity as professional ad of the British Army but not in my capacity as a member of the iefs of Staff Committee. In this latter respect I realised that I would required immediately on taking up my duties in Whitehall to give y views and assist in making decisions about problems in all parts of roubled world. Without visiting the countries concerned, it would arly be impossible to speak with the authority which was essential. ame to the conclusion that I ought to visit at least the Mediterranean untries where British troops were stationed—Malta, Egypt, Palestine, eece and Italy, and also look in on Trans-Jordan—and that I should so before beginning work in Whitehall. This would enable me to sorb the atmosphere in which the problems were evolving in those untries, and meet the men who were grappling with them; I would n be better able to advise about the problems on a Chiefs of Staff d Cabinet level after I had become C.I.G.S. And so I intensified work in my caravan at Hindhead, and completed it in time to set on this tour on the 9th June. The tour was planned to end on the d June. But when I arrived in Cairo a signal was received from the eroy of India, my old friend Archie Wavell, asking me to visit him

419

in Delhi and discuss urgent matters with him and Auchinleck (who wa C.-in-C., India). I accepted the invitation and did not arrive back i London till the evening of the 26th June—having become C.I.G.S that morning. The tour was absolutely invaluable as a preparation fc meeting the many difficult problems looming ahead. But it was tirin and I was not exactly fresh when I entered the War Office on th 27th June.

EGYPT

At the time of my visit, June 1946, the Treaty negotiations had bee going on for some time and had reached a temporary standstill. knew enough about the Middle East to realise that in war, or thre of war, we would require similar facilities to those which we ha enjoyed under the existing Anglo-Egyptian Treaty. In peace it w necessary to have the use of the Suez Canal and such other facilities we needed for our imperial communications to India, Australasia an the Far East; we must also be able to maintain our base installatio for use by our forces in war, and have the right to station forces strategic areas and to move them in and through the Middle East.

But the British Delegation, then in Egypt, had reported that an attempt to insist upon our full requirements would lead to gra disorders, to the necessity to use force and, ultimately, to reference the Security Council of the United Nations. As the (seemingly) on possible alternative, they had suggested that we should propose withdraw all British armed forces from Egyptian soil, and th negotiate with the object of making satisfactory alternative arrang ments. It was considered that this alternative would be the les of two evils. An announcement to this effect was accordingly mac but it did not achieve the desired results; the Egyptians display no sense of gratitude nor did they show any intention of meeting half-way.

By the time I was due to leave England on the 9th June t negotiations had reached a standstill. The Foreign Secretary (Bev wanted to start the ball rolling again and he saw me in London on 8th June. He said we must stand firm on our basic requirements, l asked me to investigate and if possible " ginger up " the evacuation the Delta cities; he hoped by this demonstration of the sincerity of c intentions to get the Egyptians to advance some way towards meeting our requirements.

With this background I arrived in Egypt on the 10th June, having spent the previous night in Malta. I had long talks with the British Ambassador (Sir Ronald Campbell), with the C.-in-C. Middle East (General Sir Bernard Paget), and also with the King of Egypt and his Prime Minister (Sidky Pasha). To the two latter I spoke very plainly. I said that what was wanted in Egypt was a clear understanding that, in the event of world war, it was to the best interests of Egypt that British forces should co-operate with Egyptian forces in maintaining the integrity of Egypt and of the Arab States in the Middle East. It followed that there must be maintained in peace-time adequate base facilities for the British forces, and that these must be maintained on a scale commensurate with war needs; if this was not done, both countries would start the war with a series of disasters from which they might not recover. The base must be in Egypt. The details about exactly what base facilities were required for the British forces was a matter for careful examination by the Service Chiefs of the two delegations, and discussions to this end should be going on with great intensity. But nothing was happening because the Egyptian Service Chiefs had no clear terms of reference from their political chiefs.

I rubbed into the King and to Sidky that both sides must approach the problem in an atmosphere of mutual confidence; the Egyptians should realise that the British desire for a base to be maintained in Egypt in peace-time was exactly what they themselves should most desire, and that the more such a base could be on a regional basis, with other Arab States showing interest and approval, the better for all concerned. The natural custodians of the base would be the Egyptians, since it was in their country; but we would like to have representatives in touch with it so that when an emergency appeared on the horizon we could all get busy and thus be well prepared should war break out later.

The King didn't seem interested in all this; he kept on saying that what Egypt was suffering from was forty years of British misrule! So I did not waste any more time on him. Sidky displayed much more understanding. He agreed with my presentation of the problem and promised to co-operate. I said that we would evacuate the Delta cities as soon as possible; a plan to do so would be begun at once, and we might hope to be out in two to three months. The rapidity of this move would possibly lead to a longish time being required to evacuate from the Canal Zone, and this might take anything up to five years—depending on how the international situation was developing.

I made it clear to the British commanders in Egypt that the business of evacuation from the Delta cities to the Canal Zone was a live and pressing question; it was to be tackled earnestly and at once, and that when I became C.I.G.S. on the 26th June I would want to see definite progress.

I reported to Whitehall the result of my talks in Egypt.

As a result of my visits to Malta and Egypt I came to the conclusion that, without occupying Egypt, we could still dominate the eastern Mediterranean and be in a position to protect our vital interests in war, provided that we could ensure the following minimum requirements:

(a) Some agreement by which we had full rights to station such forces as we wished in Libya. This was a good base for air forces. With Malta in our possession, and with air and ground forces in Libya, we would be well placed to protect our vital interests in the Mediterranean and in North Africa.

(b) Advanced forces, air and ground, in Cyprus—and air forces in Trans-Jordan, by agreement.

(c) The retention of full military rights in Palestine.

(d) The right to return to Egypt on the threat of war, a nucleus of our base requirements being maintained for us in peace-time by the Egyptians.

(e) It was vital to remain strong in the Sudan, in case of difficulties with the Egyptians. The weaker our position in Egypt the greater our need for strength in the Sudan—so as to be able to control the Nile, the life-blood of Egypt.

My last engagement in Cairo was to address a gathering of about one thousand British officers of the Middle East Command. I outlined the steps I proposed to take to try and make the Army more attractive for officers and men in peace-time, and how I was going to work to shape it into an efficient fighting machine for a generation ahead.

PALESTINE

My next port of call was Palestine. For many months the situation here had been deteriorating and acts of terrorism were being perpetrated by illegal Jewish armed organisations, such as the Irgun and the Stern Gang. Shortly before my visit the Anglo-American Committee had issued its report, advocating amongst other things the immediate admission of 100,000 Jews, and the report was still under consideration. Its issue had caused a temporary lull in terrorism; but there were signs that the Jews were becoming impatient at the delay in an announcement in their favour, and it seemed that the quietness would not continue much longer.

I was much perturbed by what I heard and saw. A political decision was, of course, needed in Palestine but the terms of it were not at the moment my concern. What was very definitely my concern was the action of the Army in aiding the civil power to maintain law and order, and in this respect the outlook was dismal. The High Commissioner seemed to me to be unable to make up his mind what to do. Indecision and hesitation were in evidence all down the line, beginning in Whitehall; a policy was required, and then decisions. The Palestine Police Force was 50 per cent below strength, and this at a time when the situation was clearly about to boil over; its morale was low and it was considered as a force to be no more than 25 per cent effective—through no fault of its own. All this had led to a state of affairs in which British rule existed only in name; the true rulers seemed to me to be the Jews, whose unspoken slogan was—" You dare not touch us."

I made it very clear to the G.O.C. in Palestine (Lieut.-General Sir Evelyn Barker) that this was no way to carry on. The decision to re-establish effective British authority was a political one; we must press for that decision. If this led to war with the Jews, from the Army's point of view it would be a war against a fanatical and cunning enemy who would use the weapons of kidnap, murder and sabotage; women would fight against us as well as men, and no one would know who was friend or foe. All this demanded a drastic revision of the way of life of the serviceman in Palestine; social activities would have to cease, the fullest precautions must be taken and, generally, everyone must

be given a proper understanding of the task that lay ahead. I would
insist that the Police and the Army be given a firm and very clear
directive, and I would then give the troops the fullest support in
their difficult job. Before leaving Palestine I expressed my views
very forcibly by cable to Whitehall. As I had done in Cairo, my last
act was to address a large gathering of officers in Sarafand Camp,
at which I told them what was going on and my ideas about the
future.

TRANS-JORDAN

Before leaving for India, I flew to Amman and had lunch with
King Abdullah, who was an old friend. We had a tremendous
reception in Amman, which was a welcome experience after the somewhat chilly atmosphere of Cairo and Jerusalem. The King said he
would use all his influence to support the British cause among the
Arab States. He added that a decision on Palestine in favour of the
Arabs was essential to British interests in the Middle East. I said this
was a matter for politicians and that I would pass on his remarks to the
British Prime Minister—which I did.

BASRA

I stopped for one night in Basra on the way to India. The main
preoccupation here was the alarming way in which events were
developing in Persia, and, in particular, in the south Persian oilfields.
The Tudeh party, through Russian influence and support, had set up
its own Government in the newly declared autonomous province of
Azerbaijan and was engaged in furthering Russian policy throughout
the rest of Persia; this included attempts to embarrass British interests
in the oilfields. I discussed the problem with the O.C. British Troops
in Iraq; he had the task of protecting British and Indian lives and
interests in Abadan, and in the five main oilfields about 150 miles to
the north-east and east of Abadan. He had insufficient troops for these
two tasks and needed an additional infantry brigade. I agreed and
reported accordingly to London, recommending that the brigade
should be located at Shuaiba, with an air lift for one battalion

The climate in this part of the world was not suitable for young British soldiers for any length of time and I decided to ask the Viceroy and the C.-in-C. India if they would send an Indian brigade, as the importance of these oilfields was as great for India as for Britain. (This was later agreed, and the brigade sailed from India early in August 1946.)

INDIA

The major military problem in India was dependent on future political decisions. Wavell told me that he was convinced the British would have to hand over the country to the Indians; there had been no recruitment into the civil service and we could not continue to govern it much longer. He wanted to do it gradually, beginning in the south; the British Government wanted it done quickly. The Cabinet Mission was in Delhi at the time. I was concerned with the military repercussions of whatever plan was finally adopted. If developments resulted in civil disturbances, then the military would be faced with the task of safeguarding British lives and interests; in this connection the attitude of the Indian Army would be a factor of the greatest importance.

In addition to long talks with the Viceroy and Auchinleck, I had discussions with the late Maulana Azad, leader of the Congress Party, and with Mr. Jinnah of the Muslim League. Mr. Gandhi sent his regrets that he could not get to Delhi to see me as he was attending a meeting of the Congress Higher Committee.

While talking with Maulana Azad I overheard him say something to his interpreter about British troops; the Maulana did not know I could speak Urdu. (I had passed an examination in that language in Peshawar in 1910.) I at once asked him if he supported the popular demand for the withdrawal of British troops from India, and he said he did. At this I expressed delight and, referring to the extensive demands on British man-power in other parts of the world, I asked him if he would agree to their immediate withdrawal; if so, I would begin at once to get them away. Azad was horrified and said: " No, no; not for a long time." He replied in the same terms to my request that he should agree to release British officers from the Indian Army.

Jinnah, in his talk, made it very clear that he would never tolerate

Hindu rule over Moslems. He gave it as his opinion that collaboration between the two was impossible. When I asked why this must be so he said: " How can the two lie down together; the Hindu worships the cow, I eat it." Jinnah also said that civil war was inevitable if British troops were withdrawn.

These talks were of great value to me, not only as background to what might come but also because they revealed that, whatever they said in public, the political leaders of both parties were equally desirous for the continued presence of British troops in India.

I myself was uneasy in my mind at the treatment British troops would receive in India if and when a purely Indian Government took over the reins. It seemed to me that Auchinleck was wrapped up entirely in the Indian Army and appeared to be paying little heed to the welfare of the British soldiers in India. I therefore decided, with the full approval of Wavell, to arrange for the appointment of a " Major-General, British Troops " at G.H.Q. in Delhi, and to get him sent to India at once. This was agreed in London and I nominated Major-General Whistler for the job; he was a first-rate infantry soldier who had served under me during the war, and he proved to be the right man.

All these talks in Delhi were crammed into two days. But they gave me a good picture of the general situation in India, and the extension of my tour had been shown to be well worth while.

HALTS IN PALESTINE AND CYPRUS

My return journey to England lay by way of Athens and Naples. But I decided to halt for an hour at Lydda, in Palestine, for a further talk with General Barker. I had also asked General Paget to meet me there. I re-emphasised that there must be no weakening towards the maintenance of law and order as regards terrorist outrages. I said that General Barker, as the confirming authority for death sentences on Jews convicted by military tribunals, must not be deterred from his duty by threats of the murder of five British officers who had been kidnapped since my visit a few days earlier. This did a good deal to strengthen his resolve. Barker was suffering from a lack of support by the Government authorities; I promised him my full support in his difficult task.

And so on to Athens, with a halt for refuelling in Cyprus. I wrote in my diary:

" The atmosphere in Cyprus was indeed one of peace and quiet; there were no problems (as yet) to disturb the even tenor of the daily round."

GREECE

The situation in Greece was explained to me by the British Ambassador, Sir Clifford Norton, and by General Crawford. the G.O.C. There was a great lack of faith in paper money.

The struggle between " Right " and " Left " was becoming a serious problem, and the atrocities committed by left-wing elements during the recent elections had given rise to deep bitterness against the Communists on the part of the majority of the Greek people. But for the presence of British troops, the Communist minority, supported by Russian influence, might have succeeded in seizing power by terrorism and force of arms. At this time the Greek police, even with the support of the Greek Army, were not capable of keeping law and order. British civil and military authorities in Greece considered that there was a real danger of external interference in Greek affairs by Yugoslavs, Bulgarians, or Russians. I was told that the size of the British Army in Greece must depend, amongst other things, on the need to prevent a *coup d'état* backed by foreign arms. But I pointed out that our policy in Greece must be based on the fact that it was the task of the Greeks to maintain law and order in their country, and that this was their first responsibility. Man-power would not permit of British forces remaining in Greece indefinitely; the most pressing task of the British Army in Greece was to assist in the training of the Greek Army, with a view to fitting it in the shortest possible time to control the internal situation in the country. External aggression was unlikely to materialise unless grave and uncontrollable internal disorders broke out.

Before leaving Greece, after only two days, I inspected a parade of the Greek Army. The smartness, fitness and enthusiasm of the soldiers contrasted sharply with the adiposity and lethargy of many of the senior officers; at dinner that night I commented jokingly on this to the Greek C.-in-C., and recommended that physical training should be made compulsory for the senior ranks in the Army.

After the parade, at which I was decorated with the Gold Medal for Gallantry by the War Minister, I addressed the assembled senior officers. I stressed the need for high morale, discipline and the production of the basic qualities of leadership. I also laid it down as an axiom that an army must be above politics and must be loyal to the Government of the day; a soldier's allegiance is given to the State and it was not open to him to change his allegiance because of his political views. I did not say in my address that this quality of loyalty to the Government of the day had not been much in evidence among Greek armies of the past.

Finally, I addressed in Athens a large gathering of British officers, my talk being on the same lines as those given in Cairo and Palestine. I had been greatly impressed by the high standard of smartness and turn-out of the British forces in Greece, and this was a striking testimony to their high morale and also a good example to the Greeks.

ITALY

The alteration in the tour to include a visit to India had resulted in reducing the time in Italy to eighteen hours, in order that I could arrive back in England on the 26th June—the day I was to take up my new appointment. After landing at Naples we drove to Caserta and began work at once. The great fear in Italy was of a Yugoslav invasion into Venezia Giulia; this was emphasised by Allied army, navy and air force speakers, who all emphasised the weakness of their forces. Just as in Greece, a far more serious view was taken of the local picture than was justified; the Russian war of nerves, or battle of wits, was looked on not as a bluff but as an indication that hostilities would break out at any moment.

I said that there could be no minor war with Yugoslavia which would not entail a major world war; and that the other side knew that very well. If we were forced to fight for Venezia Giulia it would be the duty of the Western Allies to ensure that our forces were in a position to meet the enemy on advantageous terms; this was not at present the case. I promised to keep the matter under continual review and to get agreement for the evacuation of Pola, a commitment which was unacceptable from a military point of view. It seemed to me that the commitments in Austria and Italy were closely connected, and I agreed to reduce the British troops in Austria and thus provide extra strength in Venezia Giulia. Finally, I gave it as my opinion that, apart from minor incidents and terrorist activities designed to work to the disadvantage of the West, I did not believe that Tito would receive sufficient Russian backing to allow him to pull off or even attempt a *coup* in Venezia Giulia. In my view there was no danger of open war at present.

Later, after Tito had " broken " with Russia, he invited me to visit him in Yugoslavia as his personal guest; the visit was repeated every year and we became—and remain—very good friends.

I left Italy on the morning of the 26th June and arrived back in London later that day—tired, but feeling that I was now far better equipped to advise on the handling of our external problems than I had been when I left Germany in May. I had learnt that our senior commanders overseas were grappling with many difficult problems and generally with totally inadequate forces. Everywhere I endeavoured to instil confidence, and I promised my help in solving the problems and my support in facing up to unpleasant situations.

CHAPTER 27

BEGINNINGS IN WHITEHALL

I HAD never before served in the War Office and knew little about its organisation or how it conducted its business. I was soon to learn about the great work it had done during the war, and before I left it in 1948 I had come to the conclusion it was easily the best Ministry in Whitehall. I was once asked which was the worst, and replied without any hesitation: the Colonial Office.

I should begin by saying that I served under three Secretaries of State in succession. The first was Jack Lawson, now Lord Lawson and Lord Lieutenant of Durham. One could not have had a nicer boss; he had been a miner in his early days and his book about it, called *A Man's Life*, is one of the best of its type that I have read. In the autumn of 1946, Lawson was obliged to resign owing to ill health and was succeeded by Fred Bellenger. He also was easy to work with and had possibly a better brain than Lawson. I often used to think he was not very popular with the Cabinet; he got rough-housed by the Prime Minister quite a bit and this had its repercussions on the War Office. But we liked him and he fought our battles in Parliament with considerable success, at any rate, to begin with.

The third one was Emanuel Shinwell. I would describe him as the best of the three, and this is no reflection on the other two. Shinwell had a quick and clear brain and his heart was in the right place; he could understand and decide, quickly. Once we had satisfied him that some line of action was essential, he would fight for it in the Cabinet and in Parliament. He and I became great friends. I used to tell him that when he was in his chair in the War Office from Monday to Friday he was excellent, and just what we wanted as our political chief; I added that he slipped back when he went to his constituency in the week-ends and made political speeches. He would retaliate by saying that I was much the same, my reply being that I never made political speeches.

430

Overall, therefore, I was lucky in my political masters at the War Office. The same was generally true of the Junior Ministers, except in one case. This one had planned an overseas tour, and he took it on himself to issue an order to the Adjutant General telling the latter to lay on the tour and giving the most amazing instructions about how he was to be treated. The following are some extracts:

" I give advance warning that from time to time I shall see troops without officers being present.
My working day will be from 9 a.m. to 6 p.m.
I should like to lunch sometimes with officers, sometimes with other ranks.
I want no guards of honour, special parades, special meals. This is to be treated as an order which I expect to be obeyed.
It will generally be desirable for me to meet as early as possible . . . the C.-in-C.
I shall listen to complaints on any military subject from any rank. I wish Commands to be prepared to answer detailed questions."

This order caused the father-and-mother of a row. The Adjutant General went to see the Secretary of State and tendered his resignation unless the letter was withdrawn; he then blew in to my office. My reactions were a mixture of anger and amusement. The letter was too silly to cause anger; it could only have been written in colossal ignorance or colossal conceit, and it seemed more charitable to accept the former. I saw the Secretary of State myself and made it clear to him that, quite apart from the other considerations of this case, on no account would any outside agent ever be allowed to address bodies of troops in the enforced absence of their officers. The letter was cancelled. The Junior Minister then requested me to detail a General Staff officer to accompany him, and asked for an operational brief covering the theatres he proposed to visit. I refused both requests. Finally, in order to clarify his position I informed C.s-in-C. overseas that the Junior Minister's job was to look into all matters connected with the living conditions and general welfare of the troops. He was in no sense the " superior officer " of any C.-in-C. He was a civilian and was only empowered to tour in his capacity as a civilian member of the Army Council. He was in no way a proper person with whom to discuss operational or strategic matters. I think the real trouble was that the Junior Minister had once been brigade major to one of the generals

in the War Office, and he reckoned the time had now arrived when h
would give orders to generals.

But in spite of all this I was determined there should be no rif
between the civil and military sides of the War Office. Being well awar
that those on the civil side were apprehensive of what I might do,
took great trouble to put them at their ease. In particular, I mad
friends with the Permanent Under-Secretary (Sir Eric Speed) and h
lunched with me every Monday at my flat, when we would discus
our problems and agree on plans to solve them. This human approac
I carried a stage further. If the policy was to promote high moral
throughout the Army, the War Office must itself set the tone. For thi
reason I started the custom of addressing gatherings of staff officers an
civilians in a nearby cinema hired for the purpose. I outlined th
steps which were being taken to improve conditions and my genera
plans for the Army, calling for a great effort from the team as a whole
I said it should be regarded as an honour to serve in the War Offic
and proposed the introduction of a formation sign to be worn by a
military personnel, and by those civilians who wished to do so; thi
sign has been worn ever since.

At one of these addresses I described the unsatisfactory state o
affairs by which unmarried officers posted to the War Office were lef
to their own devices to find accommodation. Apart from the difficulty
of finding anywhere to live, these officers had a lonely life once thei
day's work was over. We tackled this problem energetically an
arranged that the former Royal Military Academy at Woolwich shoul
be organised as a mess for 250 officers.

These talks to War Office audiences had never been given before
they produced a good dividend as they ensured that everyone knew
what was going on. All agreed that my proposals were excellent
but there were some who said: " it sounds good, but we must wai
and see." The quick arrangements for the unmarried officers were a
good tonic for the doubters.

I used to address the War Office audience whenever I returned from
an overseas tour, and would tell them of the local problems, of the
decisions I had given, and what further action was necessary in the
War Office.

Turning to the wider sphere outside the War Office, I appointed
a special committee under Major-General Macmillan to examine
the way of life in barracks of the British soldier, and to recommend

in what respects it could be made more in keeping with the times; the committee was also to bear in mind the needs of the young officer.

I regarded all these human problems as immensely important and they were the first to be tackled by me when I went to the War Office.

At the first meeting of the Army Council which I attended, I presented my paper on " *The Problem of the Post-war Army* " which I had prepared at Hindhead immediately on my return from Germany in May 1946. In introducing it I said that I had attempted to include in one document the main problems that would affect the post-war Army; some such document was necessary for planning purposes, so that everyone might work to a common target. I realised that action was already being taken on a number of points, and that other points would require considerable investigation and discussion. But meanwhile I asked the Army Council to give general approval to the paper so that it could be used as a basis for planning within the War Office, and this was agreed. Among the points covered in the paper were the following:

(*a*) The need for agreement on the shape of the Army for the next ten to fifteen years.

(*b*) The importance of a contented Army and the factors necessary to this end.

(*c*) The regular and citizen Armies together to form one balanced whole, capable of the necessary action quickly on the outbreak of war. Specialised units which could not be economically maintained within the man-power ceiling of the regular Army to be provided by the citizen Army.

(*d*) The need for good liaison with Dominion armies.

(*e*) The shape and size of the regular Army; garrison and internal security troops throughout the Empire, with strategic reserves in the U.K. and Middle East.

(*f*) The shape, size, and role of the citizen Army.

(*g*) The importance of scientific research and development; the Army must be able to take the field with confidence against any enemy.

(*h*) The conception of modern war; a clear doctrine to be evolved from the lessons of the past and to be taught throughout the Army.

(j) Collective training to be imaginative, realistic, in keeping with modern battle conditions, and to be carried out in all seasons of the year—and not only in the summer, as had been the pre-war custom.

(k) Army schools to cover the over-all education of the officer, not only in his own army but also in a wider sphere embracing the co-operation of all arms, organisation, and administration.

(l) Training in command for senior officers, and the training of higher commanders.

(m) Morale: the need to study this subject, and to teach how to create high morale.

(n) The importance of developing close co-operation with the Royal Air Force.

Attached to the document were notes on the fundamental principles of war. There was also a memorandum on staff organisation in which I urged the introduction of the Chief of Staff system in the Army. The existing British system placed on the commander the responsibility for co-ordinating the work of his staff; the experiences of World War I had convinced me that this system was out of date. A commander has got to be left free to tackle the essentials of the problems which confront him, together with those details, and only those details, which are vital. It is only in these conditions that the plan can be made by the commander himself; nobody else can make it and it must not be forced on him by his staff, or by circumstances, or by the enemy. I stated that our existing staff system did not produce the best results, senior commanders becoming involved in far too much detail and thus being liable to neglect the major considerations; details were the province of the staff, and a Chief of Staff was essential in order to free the commander for quiet thought and reflection. There was much opposition in the War Office to this change in the staff system, both on the military and civil sides. Believing as I did that it was vital for successful administration in peace and command in war, I finally said that if the Chief of Staff system was not introduced into the British Army, I would resign and the Prime Minister could get another C.I.G.S. That finished the argument and the change was introduced, but it took me some few months to get it.

After a few weeks in the War Office I reached the conclusion that there was no clear policy between scientific research and the need to go into production at some date; a never-ending tug-of-war seemed to be going on. I realised it was useless to ask the politicians for guidance on this subject. After studying all relevant reports, and thinking the matter over, I laid it down that the Regular Army must within five years (by 1951) be adequately equipped to handle any small troubles which might arise. I further said that the balanced whole, Regular and Territorial Armies, must be ready within fifteen years (by 1961) as regards equipment, man-power, ammunition, reserves, etc., to fight a major war, and thereafter must be kept so ready. To get a firm decision on this matter was a great relief to all in the War Office. I naturally informed the Prime Minister, the Secretary of State for War, and the Chiefs of Staff Committee of the ruling I had given. There was no comment. Later, I informed General Eisenhower, and the Chiefs of Staff of the Dominion Armies, of my action; they all agreed. So much for the shaping of the Army; the biggest step had been taken.

I next came to the conclusion that there was in ministerial and military circles in Whitehall no clear conception about how we would fight a major war. In a paper on Imperial Defence written prior to my becoming a member of the Chiefs of Staff Committee, the Middle East had been classified as one of our vital " main support areas." The Prime Minister (Attlee) had not accepted this contention, and had argued against it at the first meeting I had with him. After that meeting I told my two colleagues that the Chiefs of Staff should write a paper on western strategy in a major war, and submit it to the Prime Minister. They did not agree, pleading lack of sufficient evidence of the power of future weapons and lack of time for their staffs; I then said I would produce the paper in the War Office within a week. In accordance with my usual practice I gave my staff the framework of the paper on the following lines:

(a) We must plan to build up the strength of our potential allies in Europe and establish a strong western bloc, so as to protect the peoples, territories and civilisation of the western world against any invasion from the east. We ourselves must be prepared to fight on the mainland of Europe, alongside our Allies, with all that that entailed.

(b) We must ensure our freedom to use the major oceans and seas. In particular we must fight for the North African coast line and

435

thus enable our communications through the Mediterranean to be kept open.

(c) We must fight for the Middle East, which, with the United Kingdom and North Africa, would provide the bases for the launching of a tremendous air offensive against the territory of any aggressor from the east. The Army must maintain a Corps H.Q. in the Middle East, available to go off anywhere to handle an emergency.

The paper was written in a week and I sent copies to the First Sea Lord and the Chief of the Air Staff; although these two disagreed with me only on the first of the points set out in the paper, they were unwilling to adopt it as a Chiefs of Staff memorandum for submission to the Prime Minister. Such was the beginning of my struggle in Whitehall to get an agreed British strategy on which all would work; it was also the beginning of much friction in the Chiefs of Staff Committee.

I continued unceasingly to advocate the need for a Chiefs of Staff memorandum on the lines outlined above. But my colleagues did not agree with me about the need to be prepared to fight in the mainland of Europe alongside our Allies. They agreed with the second and third points. Indeed, in January 1947, when the Prime Minister challenged the Chiefs of Staff about the necessity to hold the Middle East, I asked them if they were prepared, with me, to resign rather than give way over that area. I added that I would do so, with or without them. They both agreed whole-heartedly and this information was conveyed privately to Attlee. We heard no more about it. In the end the strategy advocated by the War Office in July 1946 was the one eventually adopted.

A major point of disagreement in the Chiefs of Staff Committee was on the subject of how to handle future planning. I maintained that the Chiefs of Staff should provide broad outline guidance to the Joint Planners when the latter were asked to examine problems, and particularly when the problems involved strategy and the conduct of war. My two colleagues considered it was preferable to let the planners tackle the problems with an open mind. I argued that when it came to consideration of problems involving the handling of vast armies, air forces and navies, it was preposterous to ask junior officers to begin work without some guidance; it was our duty to lay down in broad

utline the general direction in which the answer lay. My arguments
iled to influence the other Chiefs of Staff and, consequently, no
fficial guidance was ever given to the Joint Planners. However, I
nformed my colleagues that, whilst I was C.I.G.S., the Army repre-
ntatives on all joint planning endeavours would always be given my
iews on the subjects under consideration. As the planners from the
ther Services were not given the opinion of their own Chiefs, the
War Office views generally swung the discussion in the way we
anted !

One further point of disagreement must be mentioned. There was
neasiness on both sides of the Atlantic about where our troubles with
he Russians might eventually lead us, and it became clear early in
ugust 1946 that the British and Americans ought to engage in some
ombined thinking. Discussion about this had been going on with the
mericans but on a low level; the top level had not yet been brought
n and nothing definite had emerged. My colleagues on the Chiefs of
taff Committee considered that we must first make a short-term
eview of world problems, and use that as an introduction to a long-
erm review which might follow later. This was also the American
iew, as disclosed by the low-level talks that had been going on. I
isagreed. I argued that it was unsound to consider local operations
n Venezia Giulia, or Germany, or elsewhere except within the framework of our strategy for a possible third World War; local fighting
night spark off a major war, and our local plans must fit into the wider
icture. After much argument I got the First Sea Lord to agree with
he War Office view, and the Chief of the Air Force then withdrew
is opposition.

The points covered so far in this chapter will be sufficient to
xplain my activities both inside the War Office and in the Chiefs of
taff Committee up to the 19th August 1946, on which date I sailed
om Liverpool for Canada to pay visits to that country and to the
U.S.A.

My visits to these two countries resulted from invitations extended
espectively by Mr. Mackenzie King, on behalf of the Government of
Canada, and by General Eisenhower. The original intention was to
nable me to see these two countries, which I had never yet visited
nd whose armies had at varying times served under my command
uring the war; naturally there were, in both cases, more important
ubjects with which I proposed to deal. In the event, circumstances

provided me with the opportunity to go far beyond the field originall
envisaged and to initiate action which at the outset of the tour wa
thought to be quite out of the question.

The Canadian tour embraced visits to the capitals of each Province
and to Ottawa the Canadian capital. I met all the Lieutenant-Governors
civic officials and Veteran organisations, and many prominent Canadian
who did not figure in official civic circles. I met so many people, an
learnt so much from them about Canadian thinking, that I had littl
time to consider it all quietly and make up my mind about what shoul
be the next steps. However, the programme allowed for two days
rest at Jasper National Park in the Rockies, and we arrived there o
the 5th September. That gave me the time I needed to consider th
future. In Ottawa I had discussed the standardisation of weapon
equipment, and operational procedures between Britain, Canada an
the U.S.A. I had reported to the Chiefs of Staff in London, suggestin
that the top level should now be brought in so as to thrash out th
whole business, and asking if there was any Whitehall objection to m
discussing the matter in Washington. On arrival at Jasper I receive
a cable giving permission for me to go ahead on the lines I had proposed
But my thoughts at Jasper went well beyond standardisation. The ide
matured in my brain that the time had come for Britain, Canada, an
the U.S.A. to co-operate closely in all defence matters; discussion
should deal not only with standardisation but should cover the whol
field of co-operation and combined action in the event of wa
Obviously it would save time, and help me when I got to Washingto
if I could get the agreement of the Canadian Prime Minister before
left Canada. I therefore asked if I could stop for a couple of hours a
Ottawa on my journey to the U.S.A. and see Mr. Mackenzie King
and this was arranged. He agreed in all respects with my suggestio
and authorised me to inform the President of the United Stat
accordingly. I reported the result of this meeting to the Chiefs of Sta
in London, and wondered how my activities would be viewed i
Whitehall circles.

On leaving Canada, I was asked if I would make a nation-wid
broadcast. I agreed and wrote it at Jasper in the Rocky Mountain
Since that first tour I have paid many visits to Canada, and I ofte
recall my broadcast message to the people of Canada made in Septembe
1946. This is what I said:

438

" It is difficult for me to express adequately my feelings on leaving Canada.

I have travelled your country from coast to coast, from the Maritimes to British Columbia. My object was clearly stated at Halifax: to see in their home surroundings the men who fought with me on the battlefields of Europe, to see something of the life of the people, to capture something of the ' Spirit of Canada.'

I like to feel that I have succeeded in part. I have met a very large number of my old comrades in arms; I have talked with many people in every Province and have gained an impression, possibly a small one, of the life of the people. I could not have done more in the time.

Always during my travels I have searched for the spirit of Canada. And while resting for a day in your Rocky Mountains of superlative beauty, I reflected on all I had seen and I feel that I caught a fleeting glimpse of the spirit I sought.

I saw a great and wonderful country; a land containing in its soil everything that man desires; a proper land, fit for proper men to live in and to prosper exceedingly.

And I saw that this country produced a people of sturdy independence, of enterprising versatility, of robust mentality—a people of great courage and character.

The former Canadian son of two good bloods, French and British, has grown to full manhood; a worthy son has now become a full partner, whose advice and counsel is eagerly sought in the old home and whose strong right arm is ever ready to be raised in the cause of freedom. But how few are the people living in this country: this country with such limitless possibilities!

In the distance I seem to catch a glimpse of a great nation of 50 million people, and more; a virile people, ideally located, who through its strength enjoy peace and security. This great Nation, joined by close ties of blood and battle to the Old World and the New World, seems to me to form a hinge between the two.

You may say that all this is but a vision, the daydream of a soldier resting for a day in the Rockies of Canada.

But we soldiers try to reduce every problem to its simplest form and to avoid all complications.

Twice in a generation we have taken part in a great World War. In each case we entered it with high resolve and determined

439

resolution, and we fought through to victory with great devotion to the cause; in each case the youth of our Nations have willingly given their lives that our countries might survive; in each case the harvest of victory has been difficult to gather in.

We do not want it all to happen again. Our young men died on the battlefields in World Wars I and II in order that the present youth of our Nations might grow up as citizens of free countries in a peaceful world.

We want peace.

There could be no stronger factor for peace than the working together of the English speaking peoples; all bound together by common language, the same common law, the same religious tolerance, the same love of democracy and the freedom of men. Such a partnership would be a strong shield against the evil things we have fought to overcome. These evil things might well rise up again and spread: unless faced by a union of free and freedom-loving peoples, which could be linked to any peace-loving Nation within the framework of the United Nations Organisation.

And in such a conception there seems to stand poised the ' Spirit of Canada,' a hinge between the Old World and the New: a priceless hinge of pure gold.

On my departure from Canada I want to thank the Prime Minister and the Government for having invited me, and the people of Canada for the wonderful welcome I have received wherever I have been.

I shall never forget my first visit to Canada."

I arrived in the United States on the 10th September. My tour was to include visits to the major military installations, and time was allowed for talks in Washington with the President and the American Chiefs of Staff. Whilst in the U.S.A. I was the guest of General Eisenhower and the American Army.

On arrival in Washington I received a reply to my message to the British Chiefs of Staff, in which I had reported my discussions with Mr. Mackenzie King. I was urged to confine my talks to the American Chiefs of Staff, and on no account to make any reference of my ideas to the President of the United States; it was stated that no Ministers knew what was going on. This reply was in the nature of a damper on my activities, but it did not deter me in any way. I discussed the whole matter with Eisenhower as soon as we were alone in his house, where I was going to stay, and told him of my talk in Canada with Mackenzie King. Eisenhower agreed that the time had come to get down to the study and planning of combined action, not only in standardisation but in all aspects of defence and preparedness. He said that, contrary to the information available to the British Chiefs of Staff, in Washington the Secretaries of the Army and Navy were fully in the picture about what had already been going on below the surface, and he thought it was high time the Heads of State were brought in. He did not wish to approach the President himself, but urged me to do so when I saw him at the White House the next day. And this I was determined to do, in spite of the rebuff from London.

I saw the President the next morning; we were alone. I opened the conversation by saying that Eisenhower and I considered the time had come to begin discussions covering the whole field of defence. Seeing at once that I was on very receptive ground, I went on to tell the President of Mackenzie King's approval. I finally said that if the Heads of State would merely give their approval, the military staffs would get on with the job at once. The President replied without hesitation : " That's O.K. by me, go right ahead."

I had met Mr. Truman before at the Potsdam Conference but had not talked with him; I was much impressed. He seemed to me to be alert and vigorous, and had the great quality of decision. After our talk we went out to the rose garden where the photographers were waiting. He told me about the White House, saying it was in bad repair and needing rebuilding. I said that perhaps I should apologise for the burning of the house by British troops many years ago, and he replied: " No need for that; as far as I am concerned you can burn it again."

After leaving the White House I went back to Eisenhower and told him of my talk with the President. He was delighted and at once began to arrange for me to meet the American Chiefs of Staff. He had to be careful and so the meeting was to be represented as a social gathering on board the S.S. *Sequoia*, during which we were to cruise down the Potomac and have a look at George Washington's house at Mount Vernon. I reported all these happenings to the British Chiefs of Staff and asked them to tackle the Prime Minister. I received in reply a second " cold breeze," which showed apprehension and a lack of a full appreciation of the earnestness of the Americans to sit round the table with us and discuss these matters. This telegram was followed by one from the Prime Minister; he stated that he fully realised the importance and potential value of the issues being raised, and that while there was no objection to further exchanges of information and of methods of procedure, he asked me to avoid entering into any specific commitments. I replied saying that I fully understood the situation and that, being on a private visit, I had no power to negotiate.

The next day, the 16th September, we boarded the *Sequoia* for our " social gathering " on the Potomac. The American Chiefs of Staff were represented by Admiral Leahy who was present in his capacity as Chief of Staff to the President, General Eisenhower, Admiral Nimitz, and General Spaatz. We reached agreement that discussion should begin as soon as possible and should cover the whole strategic concept of the West in a third World War, together with the best way of handling the business of standardisation and combined action. It was agreed that the first meeting might well be held in Washington and that a planning staff from Canada should be included.

I asked the American Chiefs of Staff what value, if any, they attached to Middle East oil; the reply was immediate and unanimous —vital.

A most interesting feature of the meeting was the immediate and favourable reaction of the American Chiefs of Staff, and their appreciation of a direct approach on this subject; they said with one voice that they had been hoping and waiting for such an approach for a long time.

That evening I reported the results of the meeting to the British Chiefs of Staff and asked that the Prime Minister be informed. In the telegram I said that all further action should now be handled by them; I reckoned I had done my bit, in spite of cold showers from Whitehall. I added that our team of planners from London must not arrive in the U.S.A. without the clear and definite views of the British Chiefs of Staff about the grand strategy of the West in the event of war. For them to arrive with an open or blank mind would be useless and would create a bad impression. I thought it wise to make this point at once since I knew the other two members of the Chiefs of Staff did not agree with my views on this point.

And so ended a remarkably successful visit—successful beyond my wildest dreams. It had been established that the continued functioning of the machinery of the Combined Chiefs of Staff was accepted without

question by the President and the American Chiefs of Staff. Although
I had to represent myself as being engaged on nothing but a private
visit, I had managed to do an enormous amount for the British Chiefs
of Staff. It was obvious to me from the many telegrams which had
passed, that I had stepped into the middle of the political stage, and
there was apprehension in the Chiefs of Staff Committee, in the War
Office, in the Foreign Office, and at No. 10 Downing Street, about
what I was doing and what I would do next. The truth was that they,
sitting in England, could not catch the same spirit of enthusiastic
realism which was to be found in Canada and the U.S.A. They had
had to deal with the American politicians for so long on a sticky wicket,
that they were mentally unprepared to find that it was the Americans
who were now wondering when on earth the British would face
realities and frankly broach the question of co-operation in all spheres
of defence.

The fact remained that within a matter of a few days I had managed
to obtain the approval of the Heads of State and the Chiefs of Staffs of
Canada, America and the United Kingdom to the opening of military
discussions on a wide basis, and this should now lead to the unification
of the defence policy and plans of the British Empire and the United
States *before* another war was thrust on us. Indeed, such unity might
well prevent the outbreak of just such a war.

I left Washington by air for London on the afternoon of the 19th
September. As we flew eastwards, I wondered what my reception
would be in Whitehall. I didn't fancy that the red carpet would be
out; some form of mat, perhaps.

CHAPTER 28

OVERSEAS TOURS IN 1947

DURING THE war I had commanded military contingents from Canada
Australia, New Zealand, South Africa, Southern Rhodesia, India
and many of the Colonies. When the war ended I received invitation:
from the Governments of these countries to visit them. I was delighted
since this would enable me to meet in their home surroundings my
former comrades-in-arms and also to discuss future problems on ;
Chiefs of Staff level. I am not so certain that my colleagues on the
British Chiefs of Staff were equally pleased—they were apprehensive
of what I might be up to. However, I got Governmental agreemen
to the visits and made my plans.

But first there was an urgent matter that had to be settled quickly
and that was the problem of a home for myself and David. We could
not continue to live with the Reynolds much longer; it would no
be fair to them.

For the period of my time at the War Office I had taken a flat ir
Westminster Gardens. But although I am a Londoner by birth, I like
the country and everything that goes with it. And so, after due
reconnaissance, I found what I wanted in Hampshire—an old mill or
the River Wey, Isington Mill. Once I had established that the main
structure was sound, I bought the mill, the meadow in which it stood
and a field or two on either side. The mill itself was full of machinery
and nobody had ever lived in it. " Main " supplies of water, gas, and
electricity would have to be brought some distance, the electric " grid '
being a mile away; whereas the outer shell of the building was intac
it needed repair, and the inside would have to be turned into a residence
I decided to go ahead. One of my friends said—" You are mad.'
And when one surveyed the scene, there was some justification for hi
remark. But I had a good architect (Robert Bostock) and a good
builder (Mardon Ball of Farnham) and we agreed I was not mad—yet
But how to get a licence for the work? That was the immediate

444

problem, since in the first few years after the war ended there was a scarcity of materials and labour, and all building was strictly controlled by the Minister of Health (Mr. Aneurin Bevan).

I applied for a licence to the Alton Rural District Council, in whose area the mill was; my application was referred to the Regional Headquarters at Reading, and was refused. I then wrote direct to Aneurin Bevan and asked him to intervene on my behalf. He was very sympathetic but said I placed him in a constitutional difficulty; if he took the initiative and asked the local authority to grant a licence in my particular case, it would stimulate the liveliest curiosity and publicity and neither he nor I would benefit from the result; he advised me to wait until the edge had been taken off the housing shortage a little further. Finally I appealed to the Prime Minister and explained that all I wanted was to be allowed to spend my personal savings on making a home for myself and my son, and that the licenceable portion of the work was small. My only alternative would be to live in my war caravans in the meadow by the mill stream. I was given the licence.

The photographs of Isington Mill and meadow before and after, show what we were able to achieve. The interior owes much of its character to the timber presented to me by various organisations in Australia and Tasmania, all handled by the late Mr. Chifley—the then Commonwealth Prime Minister. The whole of the flooring is Tasmanian oak, and the stairs, doors, and built-in cupboards are mountain ash from Victoria. The Australian Government also gave me the barn in which my war caravans are housed, except the roof which is of cedar shingles given by the Canadian Government. Australia and New Zealand, knowing that I had no furniture for my home, both gave me various articles. So while I had some difficulty in getting the British Government of the day even to let me spend some of my own savings on a home, all my worldly possessions having been destroyed by German bombing during the war, the Dominion Governments did their best to help me as soon as they heard of my plight.

It will be convenient to describe my main overseas tours in the order in which they were carried out—excluding that in Canada and the U.S.A., which has already been dealt with in an earlier chapter.

445

MOSCOW: 6TH TO 10TH JANUARY 1947

At the Potsdam Conference in July 1945 I had got to know Marshal Stalin, and he had invited me to visit him in Moscow at some future date. The Prime Minister (Churchill) had agreed. Later, when I left Germany in May 1946, General Sokolovsky said that Stalin had been enquiring when I was going to visit him. I informed the Foreign Office; they replied on the 25th September 1946 to the effect that Anglo-Soviet relations had so deteriorated that they doubted whether the invitation was still valid.

However, I decided, with the approval of the Prime Minister and the Foreign Secretary (Mr. Ernest Bevin), that I might possibly be able to improve this state of affairs if I could get myself invited to Moscow. I planted the "birdseed," curiously enough, when I was in New York. I also sent a copy of my book *Normandy to the Baltic* to Marshal Vassilievsky, Chief of Staff of the armed forces of Russia. In due course the invitation was received and the Prime Minister agreed it should be accepted; he thought that I " might be able to do much to dissipate the cloud of suspicion with which the Russians were involved." I also obtained Government approval to invite the Soviet Marshals to pay a return visit to England.

I arrived in Moscow on the 6th January 1947 in a R.A.F. York aircraft. Marshal Vassilievsky headed an ugly rush of Marshals, photographers and newspaper correspondents towards the aircraft and with some difficulty I made my way to the Guard of Honour. The airfield was decorated with Union Jacks and the Red Flag, and the whole atmosphere was most friendly. That evening I had a long talk with Vassilievsky during which we discussed the programme for my stay in Moscow. I asked particularly that I might visit the following: the Voroshilov Military Academy, the Stalin Academy for Mechanised Troops, and the Frunze Military Academy. This was agreed.

Every day there was a lunch party, and a banquet at night; these were tremendous affairs of never less than twelve courses, with speeches between every course. On one night we were the guests of the Red Army at the Bolshoi Theatre, where we witnessed a magnificently staged ballet, *Romeo and Juliet*; the prima ballerina of Russia, Ulanova, gave a wonderful exhibition of graceful movement and dancing, and the whole evening was most enjoyable.

I found the long meals and rich food rather trying. But I soon discovered that there was no need to eat any of the food unless you wished. On the other hand, it was necessary to be served with every course, since to refuse would be regarded as an insult; after an interval your plate would be removed whether you had eaten what was on it, or not. Similarly with your glass, whether or not you had drunk the wine. Each guest had an array of glasses, all of which were filled with different coloured drinks; but there was no need to drink any of them. I noticed that the senior Russian officers never mixed their drinks; they would stick to red wine throughout, or vodka, or white wine. Personally, I always asked for mineral water and this caused no comment.

In my speeches at these meals, I used to praise the Russian Army for their great feats and the people for their stoical endurance of many hardships. I said that nations which had fought together for so many years against aggression should not become irritated with each other if there were misunderstandings and delays in framing the conditions for a long period of peace. I added that the soldiers of our two nations, by themselves fostering the bonds of mutual confidence built up on the field of battle, could help the statesmen to overcome suspicion and so contribute to the development of friendly relations.

On one morning we were taken to see the Kremlin. We began with an outside tour to see the great mortar which had never fired its two-ton cannon balls, and the biggest bell in the world which broke in manufacture and was never rung. It was a bitterly cold day with driving snow and I asked if we could see the inside of the ancient cathedrals; the guide explained that they were being repaired, an excuse which was always made to visitors. I said that my great passion in life was to see things being repaired as this was so much more interesting than seeing them whole! There were embarrassed looks between the various Russian officials and eventually my request was granted; we visited the three cathedrals, the old and new palaces, and the museum—altogether a most interesting morning.

The highlight of my visit was the talk I had with Stalin, which took place in his office in the Kremlin at 5 p.m. on the 10th January, the last day of my stay in Moscow.

I began by presenting to Stalin a case of whisky, and a copy of each of my two books: *Alamein to the River Sangro* (Eighth Army) and *Normandy to the Baltic* (21 Army Group). He thanked me with great warmth and said, with a twinkle in his eye: "You bring me these presents; what do you want of me?" I replied that I wanted nothing tangible but would like his help in a matter which I would explain. We were alone, except for two interpreters—his and mine.

I said that in order to get the best results from the British and American armies during the war, we had become very closely linked together; we had used each other's schools and equipment; we had integrated our two armies to a great degree and a close comradeship had grown up between us. Stalin said he quite understood this and he realised that such an integration and comradeship was very natural because as soldiers we spoke the same language.

When peace came, I continued, we had automatically continued our close relations with the American Army; some warm friendships had grown up between our officers during the war, from Eisenhower and myself right down the chain of command to the individual man in the ranks. I felt that this was good.

When the war ended, we soldiers were somewhat inclined to sit back and let the politicians struggle *alone* with the problem of winning a good peace; and indeed we were apt to laugh at the politicians for not making quicker progress at the various peace conferences. It seemed that this was not right. We fighting men did not win the war; our swords were drawn and wielded in accordance with the orders of our political chiefs; the war was won by great national teams, civil and military, directed by Heads of States. We fighting men might well be able to help in the matter of getting a good peace. Our contribution must not be a political one. But I felt that we could help our politicians greatly by establishing friendly relations between our respective armies; this would help to produce mutual confidence and good will, and thus would tend to eliminate suspicion and mistrust. Stalin said he agreed completely.

For this reason I had come to Russia to establish friendly contact with the Soviet Army. I had been received with the greatest warmth and cordiality. We had had free and frank talks on all military subjects; we had discussed the whole subject of the organisation of armies and the conduct of war on land.

I had been told everything I wanted to know and I had seen everything I wanted to see—including the new Russian tank (which no foreigner had ever been allowed to examine before). And above all, I had met all the Marshals of the Soviet Union, and had made many

Isington Mill, when purchased in February 1947

Isington Mill in 1955, *having been converted to a residence*

In the Kremlin with Stalin, after dinner on 10th January 1947

A joke with Ernie Bevin at the Bertram Mills Circus lunch, 17th December 1948

iends. I wanted him to know this; and I wanted to thank him.
talin said he already knew all this as it had been reported to him;
or his part, he wanted to thank me.

I then said that this was only the beginning of what I wanted to
chieve. A close link and real comradeship between our Armies would
ot be easy, as we lived so many miles away from each other and we
poke different languages. Both sides would have to make a real
fort. We British would make the effort; the Russian Army must
o the same, and this was where I wanted his help. The Russian Army
ust now visit the British Army in England. I had invited Marshal
assilievsky to come to England in June and to bring with him
Iarshal Koniev (C.-in-C. Land Armies) and Marshal Rybaltko
.in-C. Armoured Forces). I would show them our schools and
tablishments in the U.K. Stalin said he had given his approval to
is visit.

I added that the next step would be to have an exchange of officers
our various military schools; the language difficulty would be a
oblem and would probably dictate the numbers to be exchanged.
ut we must make a start, even with only one or two officers; the
heme would grow and develop *gradually* as confidence was established
d interest awakened, and it was better so.

What had he to say to this?

Stalin said he was much interested in my scheme. But he considered
at the time had not yet come for an interchange of officers; such
tion might be misunderstood in political circles and he might be
ackguarded in the world Press for being a warmonger. What did
hink of that?

I replied that I understood his point of view but did not agree. I
d that I personally always did what I thought was right and did not
e in the least what anybody thought or said about it. We British
ere so used to being blackguarded in the Press of various countries
at we now regarded it as normal and did not bother about it; the
eat point was to be open and frank in all matters, to have nothing
hide from anybody, and to go quietly forward with a clear
nscience.

Stalin said he realised we had a close tie-up with the Americans in
matter of military talks about the conduct of war and of training;
also understood that we had a definite plan for standardisation of
apons and equipment. He did not see how we could do these things

unless we had a definite military alliance or agreement with the United States. He added that he wished to make it quite clear that he did not in the least object to any such alliance, provided it was not directed against the Soviet Union. He assumed that there was such an alliance or agreement. Would I care to say anything on the matter?

I said he had mentioned " standardisation " and I would deal with that first.

During the war our officers had attended each others' schools and had got to know and like certain types of weapons and equipment; this had led to a demand for certain types of equipment, each from the other. Indeed, in the very early days of the war, while Russia was neutral, we had had to borrow a good deal of American equipment; we had lost so much ourselves at Dunkirk. As the war progressed we often used each other's equipment. For the landing in Normandy three of my divisions had their artillery completely equipped with American guns; during the Ardennes battle in December 1944, the Americans lost a good deal of equipment and I lent them British equipment, including a number of 25-pounder field guns. We had thus got to know and like certain types of American equipment, weapons, W/T sets and so on. When the war ended we began to consider the equipment of our post-war Army and we decided we would adopt certain American weapons that we liked—making them in our own factories in England and altering them as necessary to suit our British ways and methods. That was all there was in this matter of standardisation. But it had been taken up by the Press of certain nations and tossed about the world as if there was something sinister about it; there was nothing sinister about it; it was all just a natural outcome of a very close integration in war. I said I would be delighted to have a similar arrangement with the Soviet Army, each examining each other's equipment and each adopting in his own Army anything he liked. Was this now clear? And did he now understand *that there existed no plan of any sort* for a sinister standardisation of equipment?

Stalin said it was now clear and he was glad I had explained it to him.

Next I dealt with alliances.

Any military alliance between two countries was a political matter and could not be concluded by soldiers. I was the professional head

e British Army and it would be *quite impossible* for any military
liance to be made between Britain and America without my know-
dge. I wished to assure him that there existed between Britain and
merica, or between Britain and any other country, *no* military
liance, *no* military agreement, and *no* sinister plan for the standardisa-
on of weapons and equipment. I hoped he would believe me.

Stalin looked me straight in the face and said with great earnest-
ess: "I do believe you, absolutely." He turned to his interpreter,
d said: "Tell the Field-Marshal again that I believe him."

I said that he had talked a good deal about military alliances, and
d said he had no objection to an alliance between Britain and
merica provided it was not directed against Russia. I would now like
ask him a question:

"Did he think there should be a military alliance between Britain
d Russia?"

He said at once:

"That is what I would like, and I think it is essential."

I then said that I thought we already had a treaty or agreement
tween our two nations which had been signed in 1942, and I was
der the impression that it was still in operation. He asked if I would
: him explain his view about that treaty, and he gave the following
planation.

The Treaty was in two parts. Part I provided for mutual co-
eration and combined action in the war against Germany; the war
ainst Germany was now over and therefore Part I of the Treaty
ased to apply.

Part II provided for mutual assistance and non-aggression for a
riod of 20 years after the end of the German war, or until some
orld Organisation or League of Nations had been formed and was
working order. The United Nations had been formed and was
orking, and therefore Part II was, in theory, what he described as
uspended in the air." Therefore it could be said that the whole
eaty was now inoperative and in suspense. But on the other hand it
d been provided that the Treaty was not "washed out" until an
reement to that effect had been signed; such an agreement had not
en signed; therefore the situation was not clear.

I said that his explanation was quite clear. Was I to understand
t he wished me to tell the British Prime Minister that he (Stalin)
uld like a new Treaty and a definite military alliance with Britain?

He said he would hesitate *to give me* such a commission as he felt I would merely be accused of some sinister move and would be black guarded accordingly. I replied that I would hesitate *to accept* such commission as I was not an accredited agent of my Government. had come to Russia as a soldier, and I imagined that the proper perso to be given such a commission would be the British Ambassador Moscow. Stalin agreed. He added that he had no objection whatev to my telling anyone I liked, as a matter of interest, that he (Stalin would welcome a military alliance with Britain and considered was very necessary; he repeated this statement twice, and seeme anxious that I should understand his views.

I told him that Marshal Vassilievsky had asked me the reasons f the continued existence of the Combined Chiefs of Staff organisatio I had explained the reasons, and he had said he was satisfied. T reasons were obvious. During the war, the combined effort of Brita and America had required the closest integration and handling; v had established Allied H.Q. in S.E. Asia, in the Mediterranean, and N.W. Europe. The international problems were so great that Combined Chiefs of Staff organisation to handle them had grown naturally. Even in 1947, we still had an Allied H.Q. in Italy ar British forces under American command in Japan. There were tremendous number of problems still to be handled which remain as a hang-over from the war; there were a very great many Angl American matters still to be cleaned up. All that was done through t Combined Chiefs of Staff organisation.

We had now been talking for well over one hour and Stalin look at the clock. I was to return at 8 p.m. to have dinner with him. I sa I would like to raise one more question. During the war certa British service and civilian personnel had married Russian wives; th wanted their Russian wives to join them in the U.K. but could r get permission. There were now only seven such service peop If I gave him a list or nominal roll of these seven, would he look ir the matter and see if he could help? Stalin said " Certainly," and gave me his assurance that he would personally look into the mat and give his help. I gave him the list.

I then got up to leave. We parted with great friendliness. Sta was in good health; his brain was very clear; he gave me the i pression that if you did not know your subject you would quicl get tangled up in argument with him.

I returned to the Kremlin at 8 p.m. for dinner. Among the thirty or so at dinner were:

Generalissimo Stalin.

Molotov and Vyshinsky.

Bulganin
Voroshilov } of the Politburo.

Marshal Vassilievsky and some seven other Marshals of the Soviet Union.

A number of Russian generals.

The British Ambassador and Mr. (now Sir) Frank Roberts.

The three Service Attachés of the British Embassy.

Conversation was very restrained to begin with and it was clear that the Marshals, Ministers (including Molotov and Vyshinsky), and Generals were all in the greatest awe of Stalin and shut up like an oyster in his presence.

I sat on Stalin's right; Molotov sat opposite Stalin, with the British Ambassador on his right. Bulganin sat on the left of Molotov and next to Vyshinsky. In the somewhat frigid atmosphere that existed at the table, I felt I would have to make a real effort to open up the battle and get some *joie de vivre* going; it was obvious that everyone was frightened of Stalin, and nervous; something must be done. So I decided to rag Molotov. I asked him about his life in New York, and made him describe a typical day. I said it was obvious that he spent the mornings planning how to outflank his opponents in the afternoons; he spent the afternoons in developing his outflanking movements; and he spent the evenings in dancing and drinking. Obviously the politicians did no work.

This promised very badly for the Moscow Conference in March 1947; nothing would be accomplished, except to decide to have some more conferences; would he give me the programme of conferences for the next two years.

Stalin enjoyed all this hugely. He joined in with great keenness, taking my side; he talked about " we soldiers " as against " you politicians," and obviously liked to be considered a soldier. He ragged the politicians with great enjoyment. I urged him on and said some dreadful things about politicians, for which I hope I may be forgiven. Stalin said I ought to join with him; between us we would defeat any combination of civilian politicians. I said I was a soldier only. He said that he welcomed the present world tendency for soldiers to take over the direction of affairs and become Ambassadors, etc., etc. He was delighted that General Marshall had become the American Secretary of State. He said that soldiers of experience made very good soldier-politicians, because they were much more sensible than civilian-politicians. I said I would give him my views on this matter privately; when no one else was about!

In this way we passed a very pleasant evening. There were no formal speeches. Molotov proposed all the toasts, about seven, including The King. He made no speech with any toast; he merely got up and said we would now drink a certain toast.

After dinner we retired to an ante-room where we sat at small tables for coffee. I now asked Stalin if I could make a speech, and he called for silence. In my speech I referred to the great war effort of Russia. Britain had gone through some bad times in 1940, 1941 and 1942, and for a long time we fought alone against the combined might of Germany and Italy. But we were lucky in that the German armies failed to carry the land war into England, and we were saved from having our homeland destroyed by the Fascist hordes. Not so with Russia. While Britain and America were gathering their strength the German armies overran and ravished the homelands of Russia, causing terrific destruction and great loss of life. Britain and America in those early days could do little to help, except to supply equipment by sea; Russia had to bear, almost unaided, the full onslaught of Germany on land. We British would never forget what Russia went through; she had suffered more severely than any other nation. And then came peace. I referred to the need for happy relations in peace between armies, and thanked the Generalissimo and his Marshals for the very friendly reception I had been given in Moscow. As professional head of the British Army I extended the right hand of friendship to the Soviet Army and to its great Generalissimo. I then advanced with outstretched hand to Stalin and we shook hands warmly.

Earlier in the day I had been presented by Marshal Vassilievsky and the Soviet Army with the full dress overcoat and hat of a Marshal of the Soviet Union. After my speech I told Stalin that I would like to put on my coat and hat and, dressed as a Russian Marshal, salute the Generalissimo. He was delighted and said we must both be photographed. So I dressed as a Russian Marshal and was photographed with him. Stalin then asked what I would like to do next. Would I like to have some music, or see a film in his private cinema, or go out in the city to a theatre? I replied that I would like to go home to bed. It was 10 p.m. and I had an early start the next day for my flight back to London. Stalin said: "Certainly, let's all go to bed." And I suppose for the first time in the history of Russia an official banquet in the Kremlin broke up soon after 10 p.m.

Stalin was an interesting personality. He had a keen sense of humour, was a good host, and was courteous to his guests. I noticed that he was abstemious both with food and drink, and gave the impression that he was dieting; he was a chain cigarette smoker. He showed his age, about 68 or 70, I thought; he seemed to have shrunk in size and was thinner since I had last seen him in Potsdam in July 1945, and was not so firm on his legs. At dinner he talked little; but he opened up readily if you made the running.

The difficulty of language was overcome by each of us having his own interpreter; Stalin could not speak French nor any other European language. He asked me once, rather quickly, what I thought about a certain thing; without thinking I replied that it was the "cat's whiskers." Stalin and I had to sit and wait while the two interpreters argued about how to put that expression into Russian. They finally decided that it was impossible, and we passed on to the next subject.

From what I saw and heard I gained the definite impression that Russia was in a poor state. Very great destruction had been caused by the German invasion of Russia. In White Russia (Minsk, Smolensk, and the north-west generally) the towns and villages had been destroyed. In the Ukraine (Odessa, Kief, Karkov, Don Basin, Dnieper) the fighting had been fierce and the destruction terrific. This area contained about 60 per cent of the Russian industrial potential and it was knocked out. Food was scarce; the 1947 harvest had been poor. Housing conditions were appalling. Moscow was a drab city; it had been built for a population of 800,000 and the total inhabitants in January 1947 numbered seven million; the people looked depressed and miserable. I was left with the impression that the Russians were worn out; it was not just war weariness; I was told that the whole nation was tired. All-in-all, I reckoned that Russia was quite unfit to take part in a world war against a strong combination of allied nations, and that she knew this very well. She needed a long period of peace in which to recover. I came to the conclusion that she would watch the situation carefully and ensure that she did not "overstep the mark" anywhere by careless diplomacy and thus start another war,

which she could not cope with. I reckoned then that it would b
fifteen to twenty years before Russia would be in a position to fight a
major war with a good chance of success. She would go as far as sh
could to get what she wanted, and if opposed only by weakness woul
be prepared to go a long way—short of actual war. If always oppose
by strength, or by apparent strength with robust methods, she woul
pull in her horns very quickly—owing to her fear of war and he
knowledge that she was not fit for it. After some fifteen to twent
years, if Russia had recovered by that time, then matters would b
different; she would be in a position to " thump the table," and t
fight for what she wanted—if she wished to do so.

I reported accordingly to the British Government and the Chief
of Staff.

VISIT TO AUSTRALIA AND NEW ZEALAND

On the 21st June 1947 I left London by air to visit Australia an
New Zealand at the invitation of the Governments of those countrie
At the conference of Dominion Prime Ministers in 1946, both countrie
had declared that they wished to take on more responsibility fo
defence matters in the Pacific. My " standing " whilst on this tou
therefore became a matter of some moment in Whitehall, and
considered that I must be prepared to discuss the problem with th
respective Dominion Governments. I knew very well that bot
Tedder and Cunningham disliked my overseas tours, in which
discussed major problems with Governments and, in their view, acte
as a sort of Ambassador Extraordinary. They never allowed me t
" represent " the British Chiefs of Staff. They made it very clear tha
I travelled only as professional head of the British Army and
" member " of the Chiefs of Staff Committee. This suited me ver
well. Indeed, I preferred it that way, since it left me free to give m
personal views on a wide range of subjects, often to the extrem
annoyance of my two colleagues in London, especially when the
found that my personal views, with which they mostly disagree
often carried the day in the end.

DELHI: 23RD TO 25TH JUNE 1947

I had arranged to visit India on the way to Australia for two reasons —first, to settle the programme for the withdrawal of British troops from that sub-continent and, secondly, to get agreement in principle for the continued use of Gurkha troops in the British Army after India had gained its independence.

I arrived in Delhi at noon on the 23rd June and began discussions with Nehru and Jinnah that afternoon. By that time the Partition Plan had been accepted.

There was no difficulty about the first point; both Nehru and Jinnah agreed that the withdrawal of the British troops should begin on the 15th August 1947 (the date of the transfer of power) and be completed by the end of February 1948.

The second point was discussed with Nehru alone. He raised many objections and I did not get his final agreement till the evening of the next day, the 24th June.

I was intensely interested in the personalities of the leaders of the two parties, Hindus and Moslems. Nehru I had not met before. He was calm and self-confident, had a marked sense of humour, and was easy to deal with. We became very good friends; it was impossible not to like him. Jinnah was totally different. He was keyed up to a high state of tension; he openly expressed his deadly hatred of the Hindus, saying he would have nothing to do with them. He was deeply suspicious of being asked to share anything with the Indian Union and was determined that Pakistan should stand alone. He expressed his intense distrust of Auchinleck, and his hatred of Mountbatten (the Viceroy) who, he said, was " in the pocket " of Nehru. I wrote the following in my diary on the 24th June 1947:

" The division of India into Pakistan and the Indian Union at such speed raises terrific problems. These can only be settled satisfactorily by the closest co-operation between the two new Dominions. Failing this, there will be the most awful chaos and much bloodshed."

There was to be a terrible fulfilment of this prophecy.

SINGAPORE: 26TH TO 29TH JUNE 1947

I left Delhi on the 15th June and flew, via Ceylon where I spent that night, to Singapore. I sparked off quite a lot of trouble here when I gave it as my opinion that the Naval Commander-in-Chief in the Far East should have his headquarters in Singapore with his colleague of the Army and Air, and should not sit by himself in Hong Kong. I reported my views officially to the Chiefs of Staff in London and simultaneously, the local sailors reported me to the Admiralty. The First Sea Lord was intensely angry and I was informed that in the London clubs the sailors would hardly speak to the soldiers. In Singapore, on the quarter-deck of the flag ship, the staff officer who was accompanying me (Lieut.-Colonel George Cole) got ticked off in no uncertain voice by the wife of the Naval C.-in-C. I rode the storm, though somewhat uneasily, and demanded that the question as to where the Naval Headquarters should be located be referred to the Prime Minister for decision. Eventually I won my point, and the Naval H.Q. in the Far East was moved to Singapore. All-in-all, I was glad to get away from Singapore on the 30th June. As my aircraft took off the Naval C.-in-C. was heard to remark: " I hope that chap won't come back here again; the trouble he has caused will last us for some time."

AUSTRALIA: 30TH JUNE TO 16TH JULY 1947

I reached Darwin on the 30th June and went on to Canberra the next day, the 1st July. I was simply delighted to see the home country of the magnificent Australian soldiers who had fought so well at Alamein. My tour included visits to every State, and of course to Tasmania where I had spent my boyhood. In Hobart I was presented to a group of oldish ladies, each of whom claimed to have been my nannie when a baby and remembered how difficult I was in the bath. I did not know I had had so many nurses: or so many baths.

In replying to an address of welcome in Hobart, I said how nice it was to see the place again and even the railway station looked just the same. This caused a tremendous laugh and was taken up at once by the local Press; the station *was* the same one I had known fifty years earlier, in spite of repeated representations for it to be modernised.

Everywhere I went in Australia there were assembled to meet me the local branches of the Returned Servicemen's League; this was a great joy to me since so many of them were my former comrades-in-arms.

I had prolonged discussions with members of the Australian Government and made many friends; I liked particularly Sir William McKell (the Governor General) and Mr. Chifley (the Prime Minister). Our talks were concerned with two main subjects. First was the degree of responsibility which Australia was prepared to accept in the development of defence problems relating to security in the Pacific region. In London it had been assumed that Australia was willing to undertake primary responsibility for Commonwealth strategic interests in the Pacific at once. But I very soon found out that this assumption was not correct. What Australia wanted in the first instance was the creation of some suitable machinery, and then to use that machinery to develop gradually the final scope of responsibility. Personally, I agreed with the Australian view and reported accordingly to Whitehall.

The second point concerned the question of British Service representation in Australia. Here I disagreed acutely with my two colleagues on the British Chiefs of Staff, and the continued argument provoked much ill-feeling. Under the existing system the British Chiefs of Staff were represented in Australia by a trinity—one from each of the Services. Each of these three received separate guidance and instructions from his own Service Ministry in Whitehall; for instance, the Admiralty and Air Ministry, through their representatives, had briefed the Australian sailors and airmen with opposite points of view regarding the control of the Australian Fleet Air Arm. The Australians were determined that this system must cease, and instead, that the British Chiefs of Staff should be represented by one single joint-Service representative, with an integrated inter-Service staff working under him. Furthermore, this one representative should not be a member of the Australian Chiefs of Staff Committee, as were the existing three representatives; he should attend their meetings only when matters affecting British interests were to be discussed. I agreed whole-heartedly with this viewpoint and told the Australians so; I reported accordingly to London, and urged that the Australian view be accepted. The reply came that the First Sea Lord and the Chief of the Air Staff did not agree and that the Minister of Defence (A. V. Alexander, now Lord

Alexander of Hillsborough) had been asked to give a decision. To cut short a long story, the matter was finally settled in accordance with the Australian view—as of course it had to be.

NEW ZEALAND: 16TH TO 31ST JULY 1947

On the 16th July 1947 I left Australia by air and arrived in New Zealand later the same day. My tour embraced visits to all the chief cities of the Dominion, in both the north and south islands. As had happened in Australia, so in New Zealand I met again many of my comrades-in-arms who had fought with me in the Desert and in Italy. It was a real joy to see so many of them again, and splendid soldiers they were.

Military discussions turned chiefly on the method of the representation of New Zealand in the Commonwealth defence machinery in that part of the world. The Prime Minister (Mr. Peter Fraser) wished to have the closest co-operation with Australia and said he would accept one integrated defence organisation; but he added that the New Zealand Government must be allowed an effective voice in the execution of policy, and their integration with Australia must be on a basis of equality. There was no difficulty about this and an agreed integrated organisation was eventually established.

IMPRESSIONS GAINED IN AUSTRALIA AND NEW ZEALAND

It would be difficult to find words to describe my feelings during my visit to these two Dominions, whose soldiers had fought under my command in the war. I was received everywhere with a depth of affection which seemed at all times to be genuine, warm and sincere. I knew that the warmth of the greeting was not meant for me personally but for that which I represented; it was an expression of appreciation for the bravery and devotion to duty of the men I had commanded.

Everywhere we saw the intense loyalty of both Dominions to the Mother Country, and their desire to help her in the economic difficulties which she was then experiencing. Coupled with this was the desire for closer understanding and closer bonds in the future. The devotion to the Crown was absolute. In the face of these feelings

was embarrassing to reflect on the almost complete lack of apprecia-
on, knowledge, and understanding of these Dominions and their
roblems back in Whitehall.

The broad picture of the tour was one of a hurried rush from one
own to another, and from one reception to another. I made some
ighty speeches in four weeks, most of them impromptu and all fully
eported. As I said once in Sydney: " There are more speeches per
quare meal in Australia than there are people per square mile." I was
den with gifts, ranging from 126,000 square feet of Tasmanian oak
or the floors of Isington Mill given by Kilndried Ltd., of Tasmania,
o a beautiful hand-carved lampstand presented by the Maoris of New
ealand. There were boomerangs, badges, inkstands, walking-sticks,
lankets, travelling-rugs, writing-desks, dining-room furniture, tall-
oys, Maori tikis, food parcels, shoes, socks, and even pink woollen
nderwear. But, above all, there was that incredible good will and
armth of affection. I had met and made friends with the Prime
Ministers, Cabinet Ministers, State Premiers, big industrialists, Chiefs
f Staffs, and with the man in the street. So far as I was aware, no
iscordant note marred my stay in either country. Indeed, Mr. Chifley
ongratulated me on having not expressed any criticism of Australian
leas and methods, as some Service visitors had done previously. I will
ever forget those two visits.

I had accepted an invitation to go to Japan on my way home, in
rder to meet General MacArthur and hear his views on that part of
te world. But while in New Zealand I became increasingly worried
y serious news from London about the man-power and economic
isis, the run-down of the armed forces, wobbling by the Government
ver the Middle East in general and Palestine in particular, and the fact
at my V.C.I.G.S. (Simpson) was having to bear unaided the full
rath of the First Sea Lord and the Chief of the Air Staff on matters
ised by me in Singapore and Australia. I feared that all these things
ight have adverse effects on the Army if I was not there to fight its
ttles. I therefore decided regretfully that it was necessary for me to
turn to England with all speed and I cancelled my visit to Japan.
e left New Zealand on the 31st July, spent two days in Sydney
earing up certain doubtful points, had conferences in Singapore and
Egypt with the respective Commanders-in-Chief, and arrived back
London on the evening of the 8th August.

AFRICA: 13TH NOVEMBER TO 18TH DECEMBER 1947

In the middle of November 1947 I left London to carry out a tou of Africa, which embraced the following territories: French Morocc the Gambia, Gold Coast, Nigeria, Belgian Congo, Union of Sout Africa, Southern Rhodesia, Kenya, Ethiopia, Sudan, Egypt.

I talked with many people in every walk of life. During the tou an immense number of Army matters came to my notice and reques were received for decisions or for rulings on policy. It is impossib to tour Africa without being impressed with the enormous possibiliti that exist for development in British Africa, and the use to which suc development could be put to enable Great Britain to maintain h standard of living and to compete successfully in an increasing competitive world. But there appeared to be no " grand design " fc the development of British Africa and consequently no master pla in any Colony. The number of authorities involved was so great th the effort was patchy and disjointed. There were too many conferenc and committees, and not enough policy laid down by a centr authority. Because of the lack of a grand design or master plan, r real progress in development was being made. British Africa containe most things that we needed:

Minerals
Raw materials } in unlimited quantities.
Labour
Food: could be grown to any extent desired.
Power: could be developed economically, since co seemed to be unlimited and could be obtaine cheaply; there was also water power.
Communications: given raw materials, power, labour, and foo it was then essential to have good communic tions—and these ought to be developed so as be suitable for economic and strategical requir ments.

The two primary essentials seemed to be, first, to develop tl resources with the necessary capital, capital goods, brains, and mai power as rapidly as possible; and secondly, to effect such a groupir of British (or Commonwealth) Africa as would break down the mai

xisting barriers. Economic necessity and sound common sense should
e the yardstick. Africa was a sphere of influence of the Western
'owers; no potentially hostile foreign Power had a footing in that
ontinent. If ever there was a " show down " between East and West,
\frica would go with the West; its development was therefore an
nportant and urgent matter.

In my report to the Government I pointed out all these things. I
aid that long-term planning was necessary, based on the grand design;
 would be useless to adopt a short-sighted policy of expansion and
evelopment only where an immediate dividend was likely.

I finally gave it as my opinion that British Africa must be developed
s a definite part of our economic progress. I said that the difficulties
vould be immense and many would say that what I advocated was
ardly possible; I added that I could easily have written a paper
roving the theoretical impossibility of a landing in Normandy in 1944.

In the first instance I sent copies of my report only to the Prime
Minister and the Foreign Secretary, and I asked the former what
istribution, if any, he would like given to it. The Prime Minister very
uickly replied that he wished me to send copies to the Colonial
ecretary (Mr. Arthur Creech Jones) and certain other Cabinet
Ministers. It was obvious to me that the Colonial Secretary would
ake the strongest objection to the document, that he would resent the
ttack on the (lack of) energy and drive of Colonial administrators, and
hat he would raise all sorts of difficulties to the development of a
' Grand Design " for British Africa.

I had anticipated this and had inserted a special paragraph to meet
he situation. An extract from this paragraph ran as follows:

" Immense ' drive ' will be required to formulate the Grand Design
and, in fact, to get a move on at all. Many people will say it can't
be done; such people should be eliminated ruthlessly. Bellyaching will assume colossal proportions; it must be stamped on."

The bellyache from the Colonial Secretary came all right! It took
he form of an eighteen-page memorandum in which he disagreed
vith nearly all my points; he affirmed that there was no lack of a
lan nor of "drive" in the Colonial administration, and that there was
 good plan already in existence; he ended by saying that I had
xaggerated the potential resources of Africa. My reply to the Colonial
ecretary began and ended with expressions of thanks for all the

trouble he had taken; but I doubt if these disguised the " castor oil '
in the middle, which ran as follows:

"I have read your Memorandum with immense interest. I am
delighted to hear that there is a clear and well-understood policy
and regional plans, for the development of Africa; I went all round
that continent and failed to discover anything of that sort myself
Perhaps I am very stupid! I have nothing to add, except to refer
to the conclusions on page 10 of my report; I adhere to those
conclusions.
It is obvious that we disagree fundamentally on the whole
subject; time will show which of us is right."

I enjoyed particularly my time in South Africa, as the guest of
Field-Marshal Smuts and his Government. I had a great admiration
for that remarkable man and I had many talks with him about defence
matters. Before I left I drafted some principles which seemed to me to
define the position of South Africa in a global war, and got his agreement to them. They ran as follows:

"1. A threat by a hostile power to any part of the African
Continent contains a potential threat to the security of the
Union of South Africa.
2. Therefore South Africa is directly interested in preventing
domination in Africa by any potentially hostile power. If
such domination was attempted and it led to war, South
Africa would inevitably be forced to take such action as was
necessary to keep the threat at a distance.
3. In such circumstances:
(a) The Union would be actively concerned in opening
up and keeping open essential communications for its
security and in dealing with submarine threats to
shipping round its coasts, and generally in lending a
hand to keep open the sea routes in the Southern
Atlantic and in the Indian Ocean.
(b) The country would become a great supply area in the
struggle and would develop a powerful munition
industry.
4. The development of peace-time forces should be carefully
balanced with the general economy of the nation and be such

as will be best suited to the development in war-time of the strategy outlined above."

I finished my tour of Africa with a visit to the British troops in the Canal Zone of Egypt. While there I received a message to say that David had passed out of the Royal Armoured Corps O.C.T.U. at Bovington top of his batch, and had been awarded the "Belt of Honour." I at once decided to speed up my business in Egypt and get back to England in time to take the Passing Out Parade myself, so that I could fasten the Belt of Honour on my son. David was receiving a National Service Commission; he never had any desire to make the Army his profession, so far as I am aware. On completing his period of National Service he was to go to Cambridge in October 1948, and was to read for an engineering degree. I arrived back in England on the 18th December 1947 and had the immense pleasure of giving David the Belt of Honour at the Passing Out Parade on the 20th December.

Our tour had involved a complete circuit of Africa, and the experience gained was of tremendous value to me. Wherever we went —whether it was French Morocco, British Africa, the Belgian Congo, Ethiopia—the local inhabitants were enthusiastic in their welcome. They seemed anxious to see someone whose name they knew well, but whom they had previously seen only in pictures or possibly in the cinema. Now they saw him in the flesh. I used to hope they were not disappointed.

I was told in Nigeria that it was the first time a C.I.G.S., or even a member of the Army Council, had ever visited British or African troops in British West Africa.

As in previous tours I returned laden with gifts, the more so as I had celebrated my birthday, the 17th November, in the Gold Coast (now Ghana).

CHAPTER 29

STORM CLOUDS OVER PALESTINE

No ACCOUNT of my time as C.I.G.S. would be complete without mention of the troubles in which I became involved over the Palestine problem. I explained in Chapter 26 how I had visited that country in June 1946, before beginning my duties in Whitehall, and had been disturbed by what I saw and heard. In telling the story from that time up to the final evacuation of the British forces in the summer of 1948, I will deal only with the military side of the problem—the use of the Army in aid of the civil power. A political decision was needed in Palestine. What that decision should have been was not my business. But infirmity of purpose in Whitehall, and the lack of a clear political policy, resulted in the death of many young British soldiers; it was against these things that I fought. There is much to be learnt from a study of how the problem was handled by the Labour Government of that day—chiefly how *not* to handle such matters.

Since my visit to the Eastern Mediterranean in June 1946, Dempsey had succeeded Paget as C.-in-C. Middle East; Barker was still in command of the troops in Palestine. The general situation in that country had deteriorated. Following various outrages the Army had swooped on the Haganah and the Jewish Agency at the end of June 1946, and a number of the leaders of both organisations had been arrested and detained. Later, after the blowing up of the King David Hotel in Jerusalem, in July 1946, another swoop had been made in Tel Aviv directed against the Irgun, and more suspects had been arrested. This had led to a tense situation; troops were going about armed, and stringent precautions were being taken to protect men and buildings against terrorist attacks.

Towards the end of October 1946 the Colonial Secretary (Creech Jones) came to the conclusion that if we released from detention the leaders of the terrorist campaign whom we had arrested, and "laid off" further searches for arms, a better atmosphere would be created indeed, it was even stated that if we acted thus the Jewish Agency would denounce terrorism and call upon all right-minded Jews to fight it. Accordingly the detained terrorist leaders were all released early in November, and searches for arms were suspended except after actual terrorist incidents. As a result of this concession by the Labour Government, more and more restrictions were placed upon the troops in Palestine regarding their activities in the maintenance of law and order. Meanwhile, British soldiers and British members of the Palestine Police continued to be killed and wounded.

I became exasperated at this state of affairs. I had arranged to fly to Palestine on the 28th November 1946 and I "faced up" to the Prime Minister on the subject before my departure. I said that since the 1st October, 76 soldiers and 23 police had been killed or wounded. Murder and sabotage was on the increase; rail communication was at a standstill. The Palestine Police Force was 50 per cent below strength and it needed 3000 recruits quickly. Since the recent release of detained terrorist leaders, the general incidence of terrorist activity had increased —not decreased, as the Colonial Secretary had said would happen. I challenged the existing policy in Palestine, from the point of view of the right use of the Army. The whole situation was rapidly deteriorating. A large army of 100,000 men was being maintained in Palestine; it was suffering casualties at the average rate of two per day and was not allowed to take appropriate action against its assailants. The Army was being misused, a great portion of it being employed on purely defensive tasks. The only way the Army could stamp out terrorism was to take the offensive against it, and this was not allowed. We had, in fact, surrendered the initiative to the terrorists. The Colonial Secretary seemed to think that this did not matter. He kept saying there was a real desire on the part of the Jewish Agency to stamp out terrorism. I finally said that if we were not prepared to maintain law and order in Palestine, it would be better to get out. I could not agree to a lot of young British lads being killed needlessly. This statement sparked off the devil of a row, and the Prime Minister called for an early report on the matter. I then left for Palestine.

The High Commissioner in Palestine at that time was General Sir Alan Cunningham, who had at one time commanded the Eighth Army in the desert campaign and had been removed from that command by Auchinleck in 1941. On the 29th November Cunningham, Dempsey and myself had a conference in Jerusalem about the general situation. The many political factors involved in the use of the Army were not discussed. But from the military angle even Cunningham had to agree that proper military action was not being taken in Palestine, and that the Army was not able to assist the Police Force to maintain law and order because of the restrictions placed upon it.

The more I examined the situation in Palestine during that visit, the less I liked it. The High Commissioner had at his disposal certain forces with which to keep law and order—the Police and the Army. Neither was being used properly, with the result that the total effort was ineffective. The Police in no way resembled my conception of a Police Force. Instead of the tolerant, good-natured, British policeman in whom the whole community had complete confidence, and who carried out his duties unarmed, the Palestine Police Force was armed to the teeth and a large part of it was organised in the form of mobile columns with armoured cars. In other words, it was a bad imitation of the Army—and in that role its personnel could never be any better than third-class soldiers. It was able to carry out the duties neither of a normal Police Force nor of a normal Army. In consequence it commanded neither the respect nor the confidence of the population, many of whom were prejudiced against any Police Force anyhow— owing to their experiences in central Europe.

Then again, the High Commissioner seemed to think that provided we took no executive action against lawlessness, the Jewish Agency and the Haganah would suppress it. He also reckoned that we could not stop lawlessness by offensive action, and that if we tried to do so we would merely annoy the Jews and make matters worse; in other words, we could no longer govern Palestine except by sufferance of the Jews. In that case, I said, let's get out.

A good example of what was going on occurred when I was actually in Jerusalem during my visit. At 6.30 p.m. one night a police station was attacked by armed Jews, who had laid mines in certain streets to cordon off the area. The attack was repulsed; troops arrived and picked up the mines; normal life was then resumed. A conference was held *the next morning* to decide whether to search the area in which the outrage had taken place. If the matter had been properly handled, mobile columns of troops would have been on the scene within ten minutes and few of the terrorists would have escaped. The only firm and quick decision taken in Jerusalem that night was to cancel a dinner-

arty at Government House because the mines in the streets prevented
1e guests from getting there!

I reported my views on the situation by cable to Whitehall, saying
1at:

" the whole business of dealing with illegal armed organisations
in Palestine is being tackled in a way which is completely gutless,
thoroughly unsound, and which will not produce any good
results."

The gloves were now off and all got ready for a showdown between
1e War Office and the Colonial Office. The Prime Minister decided
) referee the contest and ordered (in Whitehall parlance " invited ")
oth Ministries to prepare a joint paper expressing their views on the
tuation, with particular reference to the use of the armed forces.

A joint paper was, in fact, impossible, since the two Ministries did
ot agree on anything. The paper finally produced expressed in Part 1
1e views of the Colonial Office and in Part 2 those of the War Office
-the two views being in direct conflict. The paper was to be discussed
. a meeting on the 1st January 1947. But on the 29th December 1946,
British officer and three N.C.O.s were kidnapped and flogged by the
ws in retaliation for our whipping of a Jewish terrorist youth. This
1cident incensed public opinion in England, and it was reflected
. the meeting on the 1st January. The Prime Minister came
own heavily on my side, and the Colonial Secretary was routed. The
pshot was that the Colonial Office was instructed, in consultation
ith the War Office, to draw up a new directive to the High
ommissioner. To my intense surprise, as we left the meeting the
olonial Secretary asked me to draft the new directive—which I did.
ran as follows:

" 1. His Majesty's Government have decided that further efforts
    will be made to stop lawlessness and terrorism.
  2. They have also decided that all possible steps will be taken at
    once to establish and maintain law and order in Palestine,
    using the police and military forces at your disposal as may
    be necessary.
  3. There can of course be no question of taking reprisals which
    would merely bear hardly on innocent people. Apart from
    this, the efforts of police and troops should be designed to take

the offensive against breakers of the law and to ensure tha
the initiative lies with the forces of the Crown.

4. Such action as you take to implement the policy outlined i
paragraphs 2 and 3 above will receive the full support (
His Majesty's Government."

The directive was accepted and was sent to the High Commissione
The next event of note was the kidnapping on the 26th Januar
1947 of an ex-Army officer and a British judge. The High Commi
sioner immediately announced that if these two citizens were n(
returned within forty-eight hours, military administration would l
established in certain areas. This fairly got my goat, and I wrote (
the Colonial Secretary pointing out that to give such notice to tl
enemy would merely enable him to make his plans. I repeated th
it was action of this sort which had led us into the existing un
pleasantness.

On the 30th January I sent a hot telegram to Dempsey in the san
vein, emphasising in particular that the new directive by itself w
useless; success depended on the way in which it was carried ou
I added that what was needed in Palestine was a firm policy but that
had not seen one since I had been C.I.G.S. I ended the telegram l
saying that we must try and inculcate a strong will-power in Palesti
and in Whitehall, and firm determination that we would not tolera
insults to the British rule from a lot of gangsters; I would do my be
in London and he must do what he could his end.

I now committed a grave tactical error—I sent a copy of the tel
gram to the Colonial Secretary, and it very soon reached the Prin
Minister. It was not well received and I expected a kick in the pant
but, in fact, Mr. Attlee was very decent about it. I was summoned
No. 10 the next morning and told that if my views became general
known considerable embarrassment would be caused to the Gover:
ment; this might lead to a critical situation in the debate on Palesti
in the House of Commons which was to take place shortly. The Prin
Minister then said he would be obliged if I would withdraw the tel
gram in case it was seen by eyes other than those of Dempsey. I,
course, complied at once and told Dempsey to cancel the telegram, a:
destroy all copies. But, no doubt, it had been seen by many ey
already!

As I did not know where the Government policy might lead

ordered that no more Army families were to be allowed to go to Palestine. A day later the High Commissioner adopted an even more drastic policy, ordering that all British women and children, and all non-essential British male civilians, were to be evacuated from Palestine at once. The decks were now cleared for action.

When the struggle in Palestine was at its height, attacks on persons and buildings were made by various illegal organisations. One organisation, called the Stern Gang, even sent a party to Europe and it had succeeded in blowing up the British Embassy in Rome.

Since it was considered that I might be a target for Jewish attack, a policeman was posted outside my flat in No. 7 Westminster Gardens; and whenever I went to Hindhead for a week-end with the Reynolds family, a policeman from Haslemere was sent to watch the house. Personally, I did not think police protection was necessary. However, one day my A.D.C. answering the telephone in my office heard a voice at the other end say: "Is that the War Office? This is the Stern Gang speaking."

He replied: "Good. What can I do for you?"

The voice said: "Tonight, for the Field-Marshal, a bomb."

My A.D.C. said: "Thank you. I will let him know."

The voice: "Are you trying to be funny?"

The A.D.C. said: "No. I thought you were."

The voice: "Did you? Then there will be a bomb for you too." After which parting shot it rang off.

No bombs arrived that night, or later. Perhaps it was because of the policeman.

In February 1947 the Government decided to place the Palestine case before the United Nations, without any British recommendation about what the answer should be. That organisation appointed a fact-finding committee to report to the General Assembly by the 1st September, not only factual information relevant to the Palestinian problem but also suggestions for its solution. At the same time Russia championed the cause of the Jews and urged the ending of the British Mandate. It might have been expected that reference of the case to the United Nations would have brought about a temporary lull in terrorist activities, but this did not happen. However, the Government was now committed to a firm policy and for the moment showed no wish to withdraw from that attitude.

The problem then became how to preserve law and order during the next six months, and in this connection it was suggested that i might be necessary to impose martial law over the whole country I was against this. Such action would tend to paralyse economic lif and to cause unemployment; it would bear hardly on Jew and Ara alike, and, overall, would be damaging to the country. The Hig Commissioner already possessed very great powers under the Defenc Regulations, and these were adequate—if he had the courage to us them. It was therefore decided in March 1947 not to impose martia law on the country.

We had a difficult time in Palestine during the summer of 194 and it gradually became clear that, whatever the United Nations migh say, the Government was determined to lay down the Mandate an withdraw all British forces from Palestine by the 1st August 1948 But, in fact, at the end of November 1947 the General Assembly vote in favour of the partition of Palestine as between Jews and Arabs, an arranged that a Commission should decide the frontiers. Consequen on this decision, the Government decided in December to terminat the Mandate on the 15th May 1948 and to complete the withdrawa of the British forces by the following 1st August; this latter date wa eventually changed to the 1st July.

Beginning in December 1947, the situation in Palestine begai rapidly to deteriorate. The Jews started to secure all the tactica advantages that they could during the period before the Mandate wa ended. The Arabs on the other hand, with the exception of their Aral Liberation Army, did not advance to battle immediately; they spen the time in collecting their regular forces, trying without much success to agree on a system of command for the coming contest, an in issuing threats to the Jews as to what would happen to them afte the 15th May 1948. By mid-March fighting was in progress betweei Arabs and Jews on a considerable scale; the High Commissioner go " windy " and asked that the termination of the Mandate should be advanced to the end of April. There was some wobbling in Whitehal but eventually we managed to persuade the Government to stand firm on the date originally agreed (the 15th May).

The fighting in Palestine between Jew and Arab had, curiously enough, brought relief to the British troops since they were no longer the target for attack by the Jews—as they had been for so long. We ceased to suffer casualties. Instead, the troops were chiefly engaged ir holding the ring and trying to ensure a fair deal for both sides. A good instance of this occurred in Jaffa towards the end of April 1948. Heavy fighting was taking place in the town and reports indicated that the Arabs were getting the worst of it. Jaffa was the only Arab port in Palestine and I was asked by the Government to take all necessary steps to ensure that it did not change hands before the 15th May. I gave orders accordingly, and said that if the Jews captured Jaffa, our troops must retake it and hand it back to the Arabs. The C.-in-C. sent troops and tanks in to Jaffa on the 28th April and these, supported by Spitfire aircraft, pushed the Jews out and brought about a truce in the town. We had one British soldier killed.

The three main areas which we decided to hold until the 15th May were Jerusalem, Jaffa and Haifa. The final evacuation was to take place from Haifa.

I must now relate the story of my row with Ernie Bevin. I had an enormous respect, admiration, and liking for that very great man, but we had a proper showdown as the Palestine situation moved to a close.

On the 22nd April 1948 a flood of Press reports came during the day describing heavy fighting in Haifa where, it was said, a massacre of Arabs was taking place. At 7.30 p.m. that night, just as I was leaving my flat for the Mansion House to deliver a speech in support of the Army Cadet Force, I was sent for by the Prime Minister. At No. 10 were also Ernie Bevin and the Minister of Defence (Mr. A. V. Alexander). The P.M. opened the ball by asking if I had read the newspaper reports about the fighting in Haifa. I replied that I had, but that I did not believe all I read in the papers; I relied on reports from the generals, and I had received none. At this Ernie became very worked up; he said 23,000 Arabs had been killed, and the situation was catastrophic; he demanded to know what I was going to do about it. I said that as the War Office had received no reports, it was clear to me that he must be greatly exaggerating the situation in Haifa. I added that the first thing to do was to get an accurate report, and that until we had it it was useless discussing the matter further. I then went to the War Office and set in motion the machinery to obtain the report that was needed. I was, of course, somewhat late at the Mansion House.

At 9 a.m. the next morning I went again to No. 10. Ernie Bevin was even more agitated than he had been the night before. He said that the Army should have stopped any nonsense in Haifa and that the massacre of the Arabs had put him in an impossible position with all the Arab States. I replied that all reports received up to date went to show that the whole affair was grossly exaggerated, and at no time had the situation got out of hand. Ernie then blew up, and concluded his outburst by saying that he had been " let down by the Army." I got very angry and said that he would have to withdraw the insult.

I at once reported the incident to my colleagues on the Chiefs of Staff Committee, informed the Secretary of State for War, and cabled the C.-in-C. Middle East. A few days later I went to see the Minister of Defence and asked if the Foreign Secretary had withdrawn his insult to the Army; I did not ask an apology; I merely wanted to know if he stood by the remark. Mr. Alexander pooh-poohed the whole thing; he said there was no need to worry as the remark had not been made in public. I replied that the whole Army now knew about it. This shook him badly and he angrily said that I should not have passed it on. I then went right off the deep end. I said that the Army had not forgotten Mr. Bevin's previous statement that he staked his political reputation on the successful solution of the Palestine problem. He had consistently refused to listen to the Army's views, he had been led down the garden path by the Colonial Secretary and the High Commissioner, he had made a proper mess of the whole business, and that now he was trying to make the Army the scapegoat. I was not going to put up with this. Either the Foreign Secretary stood by his remark, or he did not. He (Alexander) must find out. If they wanted to sack me it would be O.K. by me; I could say a jug-full in the House of Lords about the Government's handling of the Palestine situation since I had been C.I.G.S.—and would be delighted to have the opportunity to do so.

This fairly put the cat among the pigeons. No more was said. I decided to maintain the pressure. The next morning, the 3rd May, I wrote Mr. Alexander the following note:

" On the 23rd April last Mr. Bevin, the Foreign Secretary, stated that he had been ' let down by the Army in Palestine.' You will doubtless remember the incident since you were present at the time, though you did not intervene to refute the statement.
Will you please ascertain from Mr. Bevin, and let me know if this statement still stands, or not? "

I was invited to attend a meeting at No. 10, at 5.15 p.m. on the

th May, with the Prime Minister, Foreign Secretary and Minister of
Defence. I duly arrived at the meeting and found a fourth person
here—Sir Norman Brook, Secretary to the Cabinet, complete with
pencil and pad.

Attlee began by asking Ernie Bevin to make a speech. He was his
old self again by now, full of fun, and we had always been very
good friends. He said it was a new experience to be hauled over the
coals in the Cabinet room; he had nothing against the soldiers, who
were all doing their best in difficult situations. Attlee then intervened
to say that many things were said in the Cabinet room compared with
which the matter then under discussion was insignificant. He was sure
that my anger, roused in the heat of the moment by an unfortunate
remark, would be forgotten just as soon as the remark itself. Ernie
said, " 'Ear, 'ear." We all then laughed. Attlee handled the situation
beautifully; and it was impossible to be angry with Ernie Bevin for
long.

But all was not yet finished. Mr. Alexander piped up and produced
from his pocket the letter I had sent him on the 3rd May; he read it
out in a threatening tone and asked what I meant by the phrase " you
did not intervene to refute the statement." I replied that I meant
exactly what I had written.

But the Prime Minister had had enough; he intervened and
changed the subject. I have often wondered what Sir Norman Brook
wrote on his pad about that meeting!

We handed over the Mandate to the United Nations on the 15th
May 1948 and got the troops all safely away by the 1st July.

The result of being driven out of Palestine was to weaken our
overall strategic position in the Middle East, and that of the Western
world generally in the struggle between East and West. By this time
we had lost India, that sub-continent having been partitioned, and we
were on the way to being driven out of Egypt. A firm position in both
the Sudan and Libya was now more than ever important, and this I
emphasised continuously to Ministers.

CHAPTER 30

I MAKE MYSELF A NUISANCE IN

WHITEHALL

OF ALL the troublesome matters that came my way during my time as C.I.G.S., I would place in the forefront the struggle with the Government to save the Army from decline. The two factors that influenced all decisions were man-power and money.

THE FIGHT FOR NATIONAL SERVICE

By September 1946 it had become clear that drastic measures would be necessary if we were to meet the increasingly serious man power situation, brought about by the rapid rate of release from the Army at the end of the war. The introduction of National Service in peace-time was essential.

It had been hoped by the Government that our commitments would decrease when the war ended; but they did not, nor did they show any signs of doing so. We were likely to be in Venezia Giulia and Greece for some time. Palestine was in a state of grave unrest. Egypt was on the boil due to the delay in the Treaty negotiations. Trouble threatened in the Persian Gulf oilfields. Internal strife loomed ahead in India. In fact, an uneasy peace brooded over the world. Voluntary recruitment was not producing the number of men we wanted; service in the Army is never popular, especially directly after a war.

On my return from America in September 1946 I reached the conclusion that a showdown with the Government over the whole man power question was imperative—to include National Service, reserve liability, and the future rate of release. My colleagues on the Chiefs of Staff Committee were not too keen to face this issue. The Navy had little use for National Service, the First Sea Lord saying it would merely be a " millstone round the neck of the armed forces." This did not deter me and in October 1946 I submitted a comprehensive paper to the Chiefs of Staff Committee proving the need for National Service in peace-time for the Army. After much argument my paper was forwarded to the Government with a note pointing out that, while it dealt only with the Army, the principle of conscription applied equally to all three Services.

There were some stormy meetings before the need for National Service in peace-time was agreed by the Government. Sir Stafford Cripps led the opposition. He said at one meeting that the War Office paper was sketchy and that sufficient thought had not been given to the matter. I attacked and routed him, with the help of the Prime Minister with whom I had had several private talks on the subject. Later, the Secretary of State for War (Mr. Bellenger) advised me to leave the handling of Ministers to him, saying that he knew how to deal with them and that it was unwise to make enemies. I said that I would never let anybody get away with an unjustified accusation against the War Office.

The general feeling in Governmental circles at that time was that compulsory National Service in peace-time was inevitable if we were to meet our commitments. But nobody liked the idea very much and the majority of Ministers, always excepting Attlee and Bevin, would have been glad to find some excuse for postponing a decision. No such act of God was forthcoming. The Cabinet approved, and on the 6th November 1946 the proposals were announced in the King's Speech on the Prorogation of Parliament. It had taken us six weeks of hard fighting to get Governmental agreement that we needed National Service in peace-time. But we were by no means out of the wood even then, as we will now see.

Early in March 1947 the Government introduced in Parliament the National Service Act which embodied all the War Office proposals.

The whole idea of conscription in peace-time being repugnant to British traditions, it was not surprising to find that the Bill received considerable opposition—particularly from the Labour benches. When, therefore, the Bill came up for a second reading at the end of March the stage was set for a first class row—which duly materialised. Many Labour M.P.s opposed the Bill and the Government found itself faced with a crisis arising from differences within its own party. The Minister of Defence (Mr. Alexander) got the wind up and asked the

477

Chiefs of Staff, at a hurriedly summoned meeting in the House of Commons on the 2nd April, if they would agree to reduce the period of active National Service from eighteen to twelve months. If this could be agreed, all opposition to the Bill would fade away. I said that I couldn't understand why the Government was windy about a few rebels; they would still be left with a large majority, and anyhow the Conservative M.P.s would see the Bill through for them. This last remark was not popular.

All three Chiefs of Staff made it clear that eighteen months was the period needed. I said that if the period was reduced to one year, we would have to re-deploy the Army. This re-deployment would be possible only on condition that our commitments overseas were all liquidated at the latest by January 1949. I gave it as my opinion that the reduced period of one year could be accepted by the Army *provided* the commitments were so liquidated and that no further ones materialised. If this did *not* happen, we would have to come back to the Government and ask for the period of wholetime National Service to be stepped-up again to eighteen months, or even two years. Mr. Alexander agreed with this condition. To make sure, I wrote him a letter in which I asked for his written agreement that the conditions for twelve months' National Service as expounded by me were clearly understood by the Government. I got his written agreement. The fact of the matter was that the Government, to meet a crisis in its own ranks, made a sudden change of face. As I pointed out to Mr. Alexander, the reduction in the period of whole-time service from eighteen to twelve months was made solely for political considerations; there were no military considerations existing at the time which could justify such a reduction. Because of the shortage of regulars, we would have to send the National Service men overseas to Austria, Greece, Palestine, Egypt, Gibraltar, Malta, and to the Far East; we could not do this if we were only to have them for twelve months in the Army.

The National Service Act, 1947, was passed by Parliament and received the Royal Assent in July. It was to come into operation on the 1st January 1949. From that date all men called up were to do one year's full-time service, and thereafter six years in the Reserve or Auxiliary Forces with a liability for part-time training. Men who were called up between the 1st January 1948 and the 1st January 1949 were to have periods of service laid down which would decrease progressively from two years to one. All this had been agreed by the

War Office on the basis that our overseas commitments would be liquidated, that no more would arise, that there was no enemy to fight, and that there was no need for any unit of our field force to be kept immediately operational—in other words, full peace-time conditions.

But the winter of 1947-1948 unfortunately witnessed grave developments in the international field, culminating in the Russian blockade of West Berlin which began on the 24th June 1948. It was now clear that "full peace-time conditions" could not be expected for many years; at the least, a struggle for power was likely during the next year. What about our man-power situation?

The Government answer to this question was to propose that all releases from the Services should be stopped for six months. I said that this would lead to an impossible situation. It would be illogical to impose this ban and at the same time begin the operation of the National Service Act on the 1st January 1949. The legal position would then be that a man called up on the 31st December 1948 would be liable for up to two years' service, whereas a man called up one day later (1st January 1949) would only be liable for one year.

The only practical way to solve the Army problem would be to link releases to a two-year cycle of National Service with the Colours, until we could see our way more clearly. I told the Prime Minister that what the Army wanted above all was stability. The Army manpower requirement could be satisfied *fully* only by the institution of two years' National Service from the 1st January 1949, and the Government should amend the National Service Act accordingly.

The remainder of the story about National Service can be quickly told. I came to the conclusion that we would not get the Government to agree to a period of two years' National Service with the Colours. We could present a case for eighteen months which was unassailable. We would fight for that.

I assembled the Military Members of the Army Council on the 19th October 1948 and asked them if they were all prepared to resign in a body, led by me, if anything less than eighteen months' National Service with the Colours was decided upon by the Government. They all agreed. I notified the Secretary of State for War (Mr. Emanuel Shinwell). He was a bit startled; he obviously had to inform the Prime Minister that he was about to lose his Army Council. The matter was urgent, since the National Service Act (giving only one year with the Colours) was due to come into operation in a little over two months (on the 1st January 1949). A member of my staff rashly bet me 2s. 6d. that a Governmental decision would be given by the 1st November. I was due to leave the War Office on that date to become Chairman of the Commanders-in-Chief Committee of the Western Union. I reckoned that the Cabinet would wait till I had departed, and would then settle for one year—knowing that the Admiralty and Air Ministry would raise little objection. I won my half-crown. The decision was not taken until late in November. But in the interim I had put my successor (Bill Slim) in possession of all the facts, and he got the eighteen months. I don't know whether he had threatened to resign.

When all is said and done, one must pay tribute to the courage of the Labour Government in introducing National Service in peacetime, in the face of great opposition within its own party. Attlee and Bevin pushed it through for us.

THE PARLOUS STATE OF THE ARMED FORCES

Discussions on the overall strength of the Armed Forces began to have serious repercussions in the summer of 1947. It was because of them that I cancelled my visit to Japan and hurried home from New Zealand, as was explained in Chapter 28. Early in August 1947 the Minister of Defence (Mr. Alexander) announced that the Prime Minister wished an immediate examination to be made of the possibility of reducing the total strength of the fighting Services. He said that the total defence expenditure must be reduced to £600 million. No headway was made on this proposal. Then came a threat of arbitrary cuts to reduce the Navy to £160 million, Army to £270 million, R.A.F. to £170 million. The War Office strongly deprecated this method of arbitrary cuts; I said we in no way accepted that way of reaching a reduced total. However, the Minister of Defence instructed us to work on the assumption that £600 million would be the maximum annual expenditure of the Armed Forces, and that it must be accepted that this financial limit would entail taking serious risks. On this the Chiefs of Staff submitted their recommendations, under strong protest. These gave the Army ceiling as follows:

ceives the Belt of Honour from his
ving passed out top from the OCTU

David when at Trinity College Cambridge in
1950. Laying " the smell " for the Varsity Drag

valk in Hyde Park with Mary Connell, who married David on the 27th February 1953

The garden and mill stream at Isington Mill

The author enjoying the evening of life at Isington Mill

1 *April* 1948   1 *April* 1949
527,000   339,000

This entailed drastic reductions, e.g.:

> a heavy cut in all Arms (infantry battalions cut from 113
> to 72, of which only 24 would be operational);
> heavy cuts for new production, maintenance, and so on,
> and leaving us with no Regular armoured division.

Try as we would, the War Office was unable to prevent the Government from approving these figures—which was done early in October 1947.

An interesting debate took place in the House of Commons on the 27th October 1947. At the end of it, Mr. Alexander gave his priorities for the development of the Armed Forces. I did not hear the debate but I read it in Hansard the next day, and found his views were contained in Column 652 as follows (the italics are mine):

" In the light of the circumstances with which we are faced, my own view is that the first priority, which must not be interfered with, is defence research. The second, in the light of the present developing situation, must be to maintain the structure of the Royal Air Force, and its initial striking power. The third priority is for the maintenance of our sea communications, and, therefore, for the most efficient Navy we can get in the circumstances, *and then we will do the best we can for the Army*."

I was now thoroughly alarmed. The cold war was " hotting up " and the main load had to be carried by the Army; the Navy and the R.A.F. were essentially " hot war " Services. If we won the cold war, there would be no hot war. But Mr. Alexander put the Army as last in the order of priority—"We will do the best we can for the Army."

The situation was now so serious that I decided it was necessary to remodel the British Army and work towards a conception of one national Army. The Regular and Territorial Armies would each have to be composed of regulars and National Servicemen, with a volunteer element in the Territorial Army. What was lacking in the Active Army would have to be provided on mobilisation by the Territorial Army. The two Armies must be re-designed to form together a balanced national Army.

Mr. Shinwell had come to the War Office in the Governmen re-shuffle in October 1947 and the recommendation for this " new model Army " was almost the first I made to him. He accepted it

Early in January 1948 the Minister of Defence circulated a pape in which he asked for a decision that the total Defence Budget in 1949-50 should be £600 million (less terminal charges) and that h should be empowered to divide this up in accordance with th priorities he had already laid down in Parliament on the 27th Octobe 1947.

I protested vigorously against these priorities and demanded tha the word " priority " should not be used when assessing inter-Servic roles; I won my point about this.

However on the 14th January I was informed by the Ministry c Defence that the Army share of the £600 million was to be:

Money:	£222 million
Regulars:	185,000 (including women)
National Servicemen:	105,000

This involved further most drastic cuts in the organisation of Arm units. We refused to accept the total of 185,000 Regulars and said th total must be 200,000; this was agreed. A Defence White Paper wa issued in February 1948 and we then had to plan the Army for 1949 1950 and subsequent years on the basis of the above figures.

During the period between August 1947 and February 1948 I ha continuously protested about the impossibility of producing a decer Army on the money and manpower allotted, having in view our com mitments. We were moving towards a situation in which we woul be unable to produce an effective fighting force of any appreciabl size, should events demand it. The Army would progressivel deteriorate until by the 1st January 1950 more than one-third of th men in the active Army would be only eighteen years old, and hav less than one year's service. The fighting units would be heavil diluted with immature soldiers. This was quite unacceptable.

During the early months of 1948 the international situation becan gradually and steadily worse, and the blockade of West Berlin by tl Russians began on the 24th June—as I have already said. At a meetin with the Minister of Defence on the 7th July I suddenly shot at hii the question:

" Is the Government prepared to go to war for Berlin? "

This was a real " yorker." I gained the impression that in Mr. Alexander's view I had committed the unpardonable offence of asking him to give a decision. I pointed out that if the answer to the question was " Yes," the Government must realise that the Army was not ready for war in any way. If war was contemplated, then certain steps were essential at once; without such action, we would merely suffer a series of appalling disasters when fighting began. I received no answer to my question, neither then nor later.

During all this wrangling I was becoming more and more " fed-up " with the Minister of Defence. It was my view that he always sat on the fence, never committed himself, and never gave a decision. I am sure he disliked me intensely; but he couldn't say that I sat on the fence, or never committed myself to a definite course of action.

After a particularly exasperating conference on the 15th July 1948, I put it to the First Sea Lord and the Chief of the Air Staff that Mr. Alexander was a " passenger "; I asked them to form up with me in a combined approach to the Prime Minister and ask for his removal, on the plea that we had no confidence in him. To my immense astonishment they both agreed! It was duly arranged that we would all three meet in the Air Ministry (since Tedder was our chairman) at noon on Tuesday the 20th July to decide the tactics of our approach to the Prime Minister.

I had learnt over the years that on such matters the important things are timing and tactics—as, in fact, they are in war. All seemed set, and each day passed without any signs of cold feet on the part of my colleagues. Came Tuesday the 20th July. The hours passed—10 a.m., 11 a.m., 11.30, all seemed good. But at 11.40 a.m. Tedder came through on the telephone. He said that he had been talking the matter over with the First Sea Lord; they agreed that none of us had any confidence whatsoever in the Minister of Defence, but they both thought that the action I proposed was unconstitutional and would undermine the future position of the Chiefs of Staff Committee. They could not associate themselves with it. Since I found myself alone on the battle front, the matter had to be dropped. I have often wondered if Mr. Alexander knew what was going on.

My next step was to produce a paper on the situation in Western Europe and the British Army problem arising therefrom. This paper made it clear that the Army was in a parlous condition, and was in a complete state of unreadiness and unpreparedness for war. The other

Services were little better. The situation was, in my view, very serious. I therefore suggested to the Chiefs of Staff that we should, collectively, inform the Government that the state of the defence Services of Britain gave cause for "grave concern," and that unless steps were taken to put the matter right we could look forward only to great disasters if we became involved in war. This was agreed and the Prime Minister was informed accordingly on the 29th July 1948. This caused the very devil of a stir. But it soon became clear that Ministers were not prepared to take any steps that might be considered provocative. It was however agreed that steps could be taken to place the Armed Forces in the best possible position to fight in the event of war, provided such steps could be taken without publicity and without serious impact on the economy of the country. This did not help; practically nothing could be done without publicity, or without cost in terms of money or materials.

I continued to push things along and tried to infuse a sense of urgency into defence matters. All this nettled the Minister of Defence and one day he spoke disparagingly about me to Mr. Shinwell, saying I was a very difficult person and asking whether he had started thinking about my successor!

We now come to momentous days.

On the 10th September 1948 the Chiefs of Staff had a first-class row with the Minister of Defence. Curiously enough the battle was started by Tedder, who was usually not at all bellicose on such occasions. I quickly rallied to his support and, between us, A.V.A. was utterly routed. It happened in this way.

Mr. Alexander wanted to discuss a statement about release from the Services which was to be made in Parliament on the 14th September. Tedder at once asked that reference should be made in the statement to the need for giving every possible encouragement to regular recruiting, as it was the "regular content" of the Services which was the hard core of our fighting efficiency; we depended on the regular for our technical efficiency, tradesmen, and so on. But Mr. Alexander informed him that he was not prepared, for political reasons, to do this.

Tedder then got very angry and said that the Government had never given the Services any help in this very difficult matter, and had given no lead to the nation about the importance of a good response for regular enlistment in the fighting Services. This upset the Minister of Defence. He said that no Government in British history had ever done so much for the Services as had the present Labour Government, and he instanced particularly two points:

(a) The Pay Code for the Services, which had been acclaimed as a major achievement.
(b) National Service.

I then chipped in and said that in the Army whenever the Pay Code was mentioned everyone began to curse. Married officers had used up their war gratuities and were now getting into debt. The statement in Parliament that married personnel received quarters, or an allowance in lieu, had caused intense irritation in the Army because it was untrue—the allowance in lieu being inadequate to get any reasonable accommodation. The pay of the Services had not increased with the increased cost of living, as had been the case in civilian professions. I concluded by saying that far from being a major achievement, the Army regarded the Pay Code as first-class nonsense. As regards National Service, everyone knew that we had had the hell of a fight to get it, and the Government had " wobbled " badly at the last moment. I then said that I agreed entirely with the views of the Chief of the Air Staff about the need to encourage regular enlistment and to give the reasons. I said I could not understand the refusal to include this in the statement to be made in Parliament. Was the Government frightened to do so?

Mr. Alexander was now getting really angry. He said the Government were frightened of nothing. The real trouble was we were making a mountain out of a molehill. To this Tedder made a very neat *riposte*, saying that the Minister was using the molehill in his statement and was refusing to recognise the mountain; the crying need today was a better " regular content " in each Service, and this was not going to be mentioned in the statement. I chuckled (audibly I fear!) at this *riposte* and chipped in again, saying that I agreed entirely with Tedder. I then said that I had been forty years in the Army and I had *never* known the Services reduced to such a parlous condition in relation to their commitments. I said we had sunk to the lowest depths.

This fairly put the cat among the canaries. Mr. Alexander was so angry he could not speak for several seconds. He then said that statements had been made which would have to be taken up again in another place. I said I would gladly repeat my statement in *any* place and in *any* society—in the House of Lords if he liked.

The First Sea Lord (Lord Fraser) said practically nothing. He had only just taken over at the Admiralty and this was, I think, his first attendance at the Chiefs of Staff Committee. The proceedings seemed to astonish him—as well they might!

It was commonly said in Whitehall that the Minister complained to his friends that he had been " stabbed in the back " by the Chiefs of Staff. I warned the War Office to get ready to deal with snipers, and possibly to repel boarders. If I had learnt anything at all in Whitehall, it was that after such a squall the Chiefs of Staff must at once justify their attitude; this could only be done by submitting statements giving the condition of the Royal Navy, Army, and Royal Air Force and the principal factors which affected them. We did this on the 21st September. Certain adverse factors were common to all the Services, and all of them had to be remedied in some degree if the state of the Armed Forces was to be brought to a position commensurate with all their commitments—present and foreseeable.

These common factors were :

(a) The lack of regular recruits, particularly in the Army and R.A.F.

(b) The adverse effect of the length of service under the National Service Act, 1947.

(c) The pay and conditions of servicemen, which did not provide sufficient to meet the existing cost of living. This reacted against the morale of the Forces and against any improvement in recruiting.

(d) A complete lack of balance, and practically no reserves of fighting equipment.

The War Office statement proved that the Army could not meet its commitments with the man-power, and financial and material resources allotted to it.

The Chiefs of Staff paper ended with a statement that the present state of the forces gave cause for the " gravest alarm." I doubt if any British Government had ever before been told by its professional Service advisers, twice within the space of two months, that the state of the Armed Forces gave cause for "grave concern" (29th July), and the " gravest alarm " (21st September).

When the Minister of Defence discussed our paper with us, I told him in very clear terms that we could not make proposals to him for three balanced Services within the limits of £600 million. I said that " it simply was not on." I added that the Government seemed to think that the problem was merely one of what could be bought for £600 million. But the problem was not so simple as that. We needed " security." That meant preparedness, and in modern times real preparedness was necessary as never before. To obtain this it would be necessary to get our man-power, our production, and our mobilisation plans so organised that the nation could take the strain efficiently and quickly in an emergency. This would cost money. It was useless trying to buy security on the cheap. There is no doubt that all this plain speaking was having some effect; we had definitely worked up considerable alarm in Government circles.

Mr. Alexander made a speech in the House of Commons on the 23rd September 1948 in which he announced that, in view of the international situation, steps were being taken to review " the whole of the problems of man-power and equipment of the Services in the light of the changing circumstances." At long last it did seem that we might get a dividend from the uphill fight we had been waging with the Government for the past two years. But it was not to be. There now began a series of meetings, wrangles would be a better word, about virtually everything affecting the shape and size of the Armed Forces. The wrangles went on all through October (my last month as C.I.G.S.) and by the time I left the War Office on the 31st October 1948 they were still raging with rather more vigour than previously—and no decision had been reached.

DEFENCE ORGANISATION IN WHITEHALL

When I went to the War Office in June 1946 I soon discovered that the Chiefs of Staff Committee as a body was not the efficient machine that it had been in the past. The departure of General Ismay, Sir Ian Jacob, and some prominent members of their staff, had severely weakened the Secretariat. At one time I even considered asking my colleagues to agree that Sir Ian Jacob should be asked to return and take over the reins; I did not do so since I knew that they would not agree and would attribute to me some *arrière pensée*. This inefficiency of the machine did not make for ease of working in other directions.

First, Mr. Alexander, although he had had a long term of office as First Lord of the Admiralty, for some reason proved quite incapable of getting a grip on his job as Minister of Defence. We considered that he had " risen above his ceiling "—to use an Army expression. He made a very poor showing in Parliament during the debate on the National Service Act, and at no time did he give any sign that he understood the problems of Imperial Defence and how to set about tackling them.

Secondly, there was not harmony and mutual confidence among the Chiefs of Staff themselves. This was largely my fault. Before and during my period of office I toured extensively, visited the seats of trouble, investigated the fundamental problems, exposed all wrong action, and telegraphed instructions to my Vice-Chief at the War Office to take the matter up at once in Whitehall. This was not my colleagues' method. They were content to let things go along quietly and to deal only with problems put before them by the Secretariat in the Ministry of Defence, and then to refer such problems to the Joint Planning Staff for investigation and report. Since the Joint Planners consisted of the Directors of Plans from the three Service Ministries, the resulting reports always contained a compromise recommendation. The result of this procedure was to give the Joint Planning Staff a competence it did not, and never could, possess. Sometimes the Joint Planners were asked to resolve problems about which the Chiefs of Staff themselves were unable to agree!

My soul revolted against this way of doing business, and I fear made that very plain. My colleagues seldom produced any original ideas; they expected these to be given them by the Secretariat. They therefore resented those put forward by me, and their resentment was not lessened by the fact that my proposals were, in the end, often accepted. I used to insist that any matter which I considered really important should be referred to the Prime Minister for final decision, and on more than one occasion the decision was in accordance with my recommendation. Good examples were the arguments that developed about the location of headquarters in the Far East, and the problem of British Service representation in Australia (both referred to in Chapter 28); in each case Mr. Attlee decided in favour of my recommendation, much to the annoyance of my colleagues.

I can recall only one case of real unanimous agreement in the Chiefs of Staff Committee and that was when I put forward a proposal in July 1948 that we should ask the Prime Minister for a new Minister of Defence. But that agreement came to nothing, since my two colleagues declined to face the music on the day of battle. In all other cases agreement was reached only by compromise. I suppose this was not surprising; money and man-power were in short supply after the war, and the tendency of each Service Ministry was to fight for its own interests.

Looking back on those days, I would therefore cite four main reasons for the lack of efficiency and harmony in the machinery of the Chiefs of Staff Committee:

1. A poor Minister of Defence.
2. An inferior Secretariat in the Ministry.
3. Incompatibility of temperament among the three Chiefs of Staff.
4. The tendency of each Service Ministry to fight for its own corner when money and men are scarce.

All these considerations forced me to the conclusion that the system of compromise inherent in any form of committee system of management was not the best way to conduct our defence affairs. It worked in the war partly because Winston Churchill was Minister of Defence, and partly because from 1942 onwards the Chiefs of Staff had as Chairman a man of outstanding character in Alanbrooke. But Churchill had gone, and so had Alanbrooke. And the next Minister of Defence after Churchill was incapable of ever coming down firmly on one side or the other. We would always have had to accept a decision eventually, but we never got one. But one must be fair to Mr. Alexander. He very seldom got clear and unanimous advice from the Chiefs of Staff. A Minister of Defence in peace-time must be a skilled politician, and able to handle the political side of Service affairs. But it was unlikely that such a man would understand defence problems sufficiently well to guide, direct, co-ordinate, and settle the great issues of policy with which his Chiefs of Staff would have to grapple. Some of the problems were too serious for a compromise solution. The Minister needed to know the right answer from the larger and national angle; compromise solutions might be dangerous. And he would get that right answer only from an independent military adviser of great experience. At least that is how I saw it in peace-time, when money and men are in short supply.

In March 1948 I came to the conclusion that the situation was too serious to permit of further delay and I drafted a memorandum in which I recommended that a Ministerial committee should examine our defence organisation in Whitehall. I sent copies privately to the Prime Minister and to the Minister of Defence, and asked for their agreement that I should submit the memorandum to the Chiefs of Staff Committee; it would be bound to create a stir in Whitehall and I did not want it to come as a surprise to the Government. Mr. Attlee replied the same day, agreeing that I should do so.

The memorandum (dated the 16th March 1948) ran as follows:

" 1. I submit the following views on the Chiefs of Staff Committee and the organisation of our defence system.

2. The Chiefs of Staff Sub-Committee of the Committee of Imperial Defence was set up in 1924 for the purpose of advising the Cabinet jointly and individually.

Ten years or so later it had shown itself to be a useful instrument for high-level inter-service consultation in times of emergency, and also in day-to-day matters of a minor role. But it had conspicuously disappointed the main hopes which had been centred in it.

As Lord Trenchard pointed out in 1935:

' it has done very little to explore, and still less to settle, larger problems of defence policy. Lord Hailsham, speaking for the Government, claimed it as a merit of the Chiefs of Staff Sub-Committee that the Government " in almost every case gets a unanimous report from the three professional heads " and that any great question of difference about strategic questions was " very unlikely to arise." I fear that, under pressure of work and from other causes, unanimity has been too often reached by tacit agreement to exclude vital differences of opinion, to avoid issues on which such differences might arise, and to restrict the scope of the Committee's reports to matters on which agreement can be reached by " give and take." What is wanted in the higher examination of defence policy is not that the

490

Government should get unanimous reports but that means
should exist for the examination of defence requirements
untrammelled by Departmental compromises. We want to
promote free discussion and not drive differences of opinion
underground.'

3. The remedy which Lord Trenchard proposed in 1935 was that
there should be a whole-time Ministerial chairman of the Committee of Imperial Defence who would preside regularly at
meetings of the Chiefs of Staff Sub-Committee. This Minister
should have a 'Permanent Secretary' for the C.I.D., and a
separate staff consisting largely of promising officers from all
three Services. These suggestions were not, so far as I am
aware, adopted even though it was later found necessary to
appoint a special Minister for the Co-ordination of Defence—
who was entitled to summon the Chiefs of Staff Sub-Committee for consultation from time to time.

4. The system of a Minister for Co-ordination of Defence continued into the war period up till April 1940, when a special
responsibility was assigned to Mr. Churchill, First Lord of the
Admiralty, with power to give guidance and directions to the
Chiefs of Staff Committee and for this purpose to summon
them for consultation at any time. This arrangement was
transformed after Mr. Churchill became Prime Minister, for
he became also Minister of Defence: in which capacity he
presided over a Defence Committee at which both the Service
Ministers and the Chiefs of Staff regularly attended. The
Minister of Defence also presided in war-time at meetings of
the Chiefs of Staff Committee and he had his own special
representative on that Committee.

5. There is no doubt that the arrangements adopted in war-time
by Mr. Churchill worked well, and that high-level matters of
strategy and operational policy were dealt with expeditiously
without there being any inclination on the part of the Chiefs
of Staff to suppress fundamental divergencies.
The White Paper of October 1946 clearly recognises this,
though it equally clearly points out the shortcomings of the
system which had prevailed in peace-time and up to April
1940. The aim of the White Paper of 1946 was to produce a

system in peace-time which would ensure a unified defence policy and in pursuance of this end it recommended the creation of a separate Minister of Defence: whose relations with the Chiefs of Staff were to be very much like those laid down by Mr. Churchill in April 1940.

6. The question now arises whether the arrangements recommended in 1946, and adopted, have succeeded in their main object of securing a unified defence policy. I have no hesitation whatever in saying that they have not.

   I examine below why they have failed.

7. I start by the obvious platitude that war and peace are very different, even though the peace may be in fact a ' cold war.' In peace-time the demands of the Services for men and money and materials are certain to be severely limited. Though it may be a truism that a certain minimum of defence expenditure ought to be a first charge on a nation's resources, it will very rarely happen that the three Services will get all, or even the bulk, of what taken separately they regard as the indispensable minimum. And this will be especially the case when the nation has not sufficient materials and labour and external resources to maintain its existing standard of living. This restriction operates very much less in time of war because the needs of defence must and do take priority over all other requirements: save the provision of the minimum food and clothing which will serve to preserve the life, health and efficiency of the civilian population.

   It may well be that Britain's unaided resources, especially those of foreign exchange, will never suffice to enable her to wage war as vehemently and ruthlessly as we should like. But in the last two Great Wars we were abundantly helped by the vast good will and productive power of the U.S.A. and, as a consequence, it could be said that few if any military demands were neglected at the outset as not being justifiable: though in practice no doubt it became necessary for some to be given a higher priority than others. In these circumstances the Chiefs of Staff could easily achieve unanimity by conceding the justice of the demands of their colleagues; their disputes could in the main be confined to the question of who came first.

8. In a time of limitation from the start, quite different considerations prevail.

The three Chiefs of Staff are the professional heads of their own Services. They are not only the advisers of the Cabinet on policy and strategy; each is also the guardian of the present and future interests of his own Service and in some ways the custodian of the prospects of every member of it. Naturally each fights for his own cause and will compromise on nothing. One of the three is Chairman of the Committee; this is a most invidious position for a Chief of Staff to be in; he is asked to be an impartial Chairman; this is humanly impossible as he naturally has his own strong views to press on everybody.

9. And so in the end we arrive at the state of affairs described by Lord Trenchard in 1935 and to which I have referred in para. 2 above.

I consider that his description applies almost word for word to the present day.

10. I do not however think that the remedy is to be found in Lord Trenchard's proposal for a whole-time Ministerial Chairman of the Chiefs of Staff Committee.

I consider that what we now need is to adopt the device of a Chief of Staff—not, be it noted, a Chief Staff Officer—to the Minister of Defence.

Such an appointment would be a great step forward towards our final aim.

This Chief of Staff to the Minister of Defence should be ex-officio the permanent Chairman of the Chiefs of Staff Committee.

11. What the Minister for Defence wants is for the Chiefs of Staff organisation to produce for his consideration and for subsequent recommendation to the Cabinet a coherent defence policy which shall:

(a) be within the compass of the resources which the Cabinet is prepared to allot for defence;

(b) lay down clearly and unequivocally the parts in it allotted to the three Services and to the relevant civilian organisations, and

(c) be mutually compatible as to its various elements.

At present what he tends to get is nothing at all on the wider aspects of defence policy—for the reason that the three Chiefs of Staff are so divergent that they take refuge in not reporting at all, or in furnishing wishy-washy recommendations which lead nowhere.

Something would be gained if the Chiefs of Staff furnished the Minister of Defence with an agreed statement of their differences, but more is really needed.

The Minister of Defence needs to get out of the discussions of the Chiefs of Staff Committee a plan which hangs together, which is workable, and which is easily explainable to the laymen who have to decide it.

If he has a Chief of Staff who is also Chairman of the Chiefs of Staff Committee, he can at all events get two things:

(i) a dispassionate statement of all the conflicting views, and

(ii) a viable plan which takes account of the limitation of resources, which is reasonable and balanced, and which does the least violence to the recommendations of the three individual Services.

12. I realise that the perfect Chief of Staff to the Minister of Defence will not be easy to find. But that in no way affects the principle; we should first decide whether we will accept the principle and need the appointment; the man can be found later. To perform the present task he must be a man with a wide practical experience of modern war, he must have held high command, and he must be receptive to new ideas.

13. I am convinced that we must begin to make some progress towards balanced national Defence Forces. It is now nearly three years since World War II ended; we have made no progress, in fact we have tended to drift backwards.

14. Each Service has developed within itself a system which provides for specialisation where it is wanted, and yet ensures overall unity in direction.

But the fact remains that we have not achieved for the three Services in combination a system which is comparable to that which each Service has evolved for itself. The specialization is there, it is true; but there is not that junction in the higher ranks that alone can give the strategical skill we seek. We had glimpses of the possibilities during World War II when

Supreme Commanders were appointed; but these have faded out, and we are back with our triumvirates of specialists wherever inter-service affairs have to be dealt with. It is rather as if a ship was commanded by a committee consisting of the Gunnery Officer, the Major of Marines, and the Engineer Officer, each of whom had under him one third of the crew, and each wearing a different uniform.

15. There are several reasons why we should not allow this situation to persist.

In the first place, the tasks of the three Services are not nearly so differentiated as they used to be; the Navy flies, the Air Force devotes much of its efforts to crippling the enemy's army and transporting our own; all three Services are equally committed in an invasion.

Secondly, the advance of scientific discovery has produced ideas and weapons which do not fit neatly into the picture of three separate Services; they tend to unify warlike operations, and it is more important than ever before that objective minds should examine the application of science to war.

And thirdly, our nation is very hard up and we can no longer afford the luxury of duplication and the waste which comes from adding together the demands of three Services.

CONCLUSIONS

16. We need a unified defence policy.
We have not got one, and we have no hope of getting one under our present system.

17. We need to make some progress towards balanced national forces; we have made no such progress.

18. We need an efficient system of command and control in the various theatres in peace-time which will enable us to take the strain and develop our full potential without the dislocation caused by changes in that system when the threat develops. We have no such system.

19. I recommend that the whole subject be considered by a Ministerial Committee without delay."

I discussed the memorandum with my colleagues at several meetings.

In order to support my contention that the Chiefs of Staff Committee had achieved little on the vital issues, I prepared a statement showing the major points of fundamental divergence or lack of progress by the Chiefs of Staff. I used this as evidence to support the points I had made. The statement gave, in each case, the reference to the official document which proved my case. I confined my arguments to the following four major points:

National strategy.
Long-term plans for balanced national forces in peace.
Plans for balanced national forces on the outbreak of war.
Organisation for command and control in peace and war in overseas theatres.

I proved that we had been unable to reach any agreement on these subjects.

I then waited for the counter-blasts that my memorandum would inevitably produce—which came quickly enough.

It at once became obvious that no amount of discussion within the Chiefs of Staff Committee would help to resolve the divergency of views that existed on this subject. I was alone in wanting the defence organisation examined; the other two Chiefs of Staff, and the Chief Staff Officer to the Minister of Defence (General Hollis, a Royal Marine) were strongly opposed to any such examination or any change in the system. It was finally agreed that the Chief of the Air Staff, as our Chairman, should submit the matter to the Minister of Defence for a decision. This was done on the 14th April 1948.

Five days later came the Minister's reply. He took refuge behind the majority view expressed by the First Sea Lord and the Chief of the Air Staff. At least he had given a decision! I said no more. And so ended my attempt to get a sound defence organisation in Whitehall. But I had at least caused the subject to be aired, and forced the decision to be officially recorded.

The existing system was to stay. Most people in Whitehall believed it could be made to work provided we had a good Minister of Defence. But no one pretended that we had. All we could do was to pray for a really good replacement. It has already been recorded how, three months later (in July 1948), I made an unsuccessful attempt to unseat him, with the agreement (initially) of my two colleagues.

In 1955 a beginning was made by the Eden Government to get

ome improvement in the machinery of the defence organisation. But the Minister of Defence was not then given the power of decision hat is essential, nor had he a Chief of Staff. It was not until 1957 that he matter was tackled energetically. In January of that year the Macmillan Government gave a clear directive to the new Minister of Defence (Duncan Sandys), telling him what he must do and giving him full powers to do it. His first task was to formulate, in the light of strategic needs, a new defence policy which would ensure a substantial reduction in expenditure and in man-power, and to prepare a plan for re-shaping and re-organising the Armed Forces in accordance with that policy. He was given authority to give decisions on all matters of policy affecting the size, shape, organisation and disposition of the Armed Forces, their equipment and supply (including defence research and development) and their pay and conditions of service. He was also given powers of decision on matters of Service administration or appointments which in his opinion were of special importance. Furthermore, when a Service Minister or the Minister of Supply wished to make proposals to the Prime Minister, the Defence Committee or the Cabinet on any matter within the scope of the new powers of the Minister of Defence, the approach was to be made through the latter. And finally, the Minister of Defence was to have Chief of Staff responsible to him direct; this Chief of Staff was to be the Chairman of the Chiefs of Staff Committee.

CHAPTER 31

BEGINNINGS OF

DEFENCE CO-OPERATION IN EUROPE

WHEN I went to the War Office in July 1946 I discovered that ther
was no clear conception of British strategy in a major war, nor di
my colleagues on the Chiefs of Staff Committee consider that w
should produce a paper on the subject just at present. I did not agree
and we had some discussion about it. In the end the War Office pro
duced a paper defining the strategy, and on the 25th July I submitte
it to the Chiefs of Staff (see Chapter 27). The main feature of the pape
was that we must build up the strength of our potential allies i
Europe, and thus establish a strong Western bloc which would protec
us all against another invasion from the East. We ourselves must b
prepared and organised to fight on the mainland of Europe alongsid
our allies, with all that that entailed.

So far as I am aware this was the first attempt in British circles t
get agreement that we must fight in Continental Europe in the even
of war. I was unable to get my two colleagues to agree and, as I wa
then a " new boy " in Whitehall, I did not force the issue at that tim
(July 1946)—being much occupied with other matters.

The scene now changes to December 1947. The Foreign Ministe
of the occupying Powers in Germany had been engaged in a cor
ference in London on the subject of that country, and it became obviou
that no agreement with Russia could be reached. When I arrive
back from my African tour, Ernie Bevin sent for me (on the 23r
December 1947) and said that he had suggested to the Foreign Minist
of France (M. Bidault) that the time had come to begin the formatic
of a Federation or Union in Western Europe, and if possible to brin
the Americans into it. He added that Britain and France must fir
agree on the military strategy, and staff talks to that end should ther
fore take place. He had in mind to initiate staff talks with the America
on a unilateral basis, but not until we had cleared our own mind

nd discussed the problem of Western European defence with the rench.

On the initiative of the Foreign Office, General Revers, Chief f Staff of the French Army, was invited to London and I had long lks with him on the whole problem. Meanwhile Bevin pushed 1ead with the project of a "Western Union." His plan was as ollows:

(a) To begin by concerting an Anglo-French Treaty with the Benelux nations (Belgium, Holland, Luxembourg). In fact, to build up the Western Union by bringing in Britain and France.

(b) Having done that, to consider how best to associate it in a wider alliance with the other non-Communist States, notably Scandinavia and Italy.

He then approached General Marshall Secretary of State in resident Truman's Administration, who warmly welcomed the idea f a political and economic union of the Western European and lediterranean countries on the lines suggested. Encouraged by this, lr. Bevin suggested that we should now begin private talks with the mericans, with a view that they might eventually join a wider liance. This was not agreed by the Americans. They were not pre-ured to face up to Congress at that time on the question of a military immitment to fight in Europe.

My view on all these matters was that, before we ourselves began lking with other people, we must first formulate our own ideas on e overall strategy of the United Kingdom in the event of war in 1rope, leading to global war. I said that the Chiefs of Staff should oduce an agreed paper on the subject; I was willing to start the ball lling by submitting at once a paper giving the War Office views. 1is was not agreed; the Joint Planners were already producing a per for the Chiefs of Staff and we must wait for that. It duly arrived. 1ey had considered three courses of action in Europe:

1. An air strategy.
2. A Continental strategy.
3. A semi-Continental strategy, involving holding Spain and Portugal and liberating Europe by an offensive through the Pyrenees.

The paper dismissed the Continental strategy in a few lines and th
choice was left between the air strategy and the Pyrenees strategy.

I blew right up, saying that I disagreed completely with the cor
clusions of the report. What was meant by the expression " the be
strategy appears to be the air strategy "? We must defend Wester
Europe, not liberate it; if we allowed it to be overrun from the Eas
there would be all too little to liberate.

I said the paper demonstrated once more the futility of letting th
Joint Planners write papers on vitally important subjects witho
proper guidance from the Chiefs of Staff. I then said I would subm
a paper containing my own views by the next day. My paper w
dated the 30th January 1948 and in it I said:

> "We must agree that, if attacked, the nations of the Wester
> Union will hold the attack as far to the east as possible. We mu
> make it very clear that Britain will play her full part in this strateg
> and will support the battle with the fullest possible weight of o
> land, air and naval power.
>
> Unless this basic point in our strategy is agreed, and is accept
> whole-heartedly by Britain, the Western Union can have no ho
> of survival, and Britain would then be in the gravest danger."

I discussed the paper with my two colleagues on the 2nd Februar
They disagreed, as I had expected. The Chief of the Air Staff and t
First Sea Lord both lined up firmly against embarking on a land car
paign in Continental Europe. They argued that it was militarily a
economically impossible to do this, and further that it was useless
discuss our own European strategy until we knew what the America
would do. I replied that in the past we had twice gone to war witho
knowing " what the Americans would do," and on both occasic
they had finally followed our lead. Maybe they would do so aga
In any case we must do our duty, whatever the Americans did. T
meeting broke up in disorder! But not before I had forced a decisi
that my paper should go up to the Prime Minister.

The conference with him took place on the 4th February 19.
I said it would be mighty difficult to achieve an effective Weste
Union if we could not promise support on land in the event of w
The Prime Minister then weighed in strongly against a commitme
to send our Army to the Continent. I replied that we already h
an Army there, the British Army of the Rhine. Did he propose

ould withdraw it (through Dunkirk!) if the Russians attacked? uch action was unthinkable. Attlee was then counter-attacked by rnie Bevin, and curiously enough also by A. V. Alexander, each of hom supported me in his own way. It was finally agreed to consider ie implications of the strategy I advocated, including the effect on ie shape and size of our armed forces consequent on the adoption of uch a strategy. At any rate I had routed the Pyrenean strategists!

Much planning activity then began and continued during March id April 1948. I continued to "put over" my views to all and undry and to build up belief in the Western Union. I was convinced f the essential need to fight a campaign in Western Europe, whether ie emergency came in 1948, or ten or even twenty years later. The eed was therefore to examine the method by which such a campaign uld be fought.

I argued on the following lines. France and the Benelux countries id little military value at that time; their forces, and particularly ieir land forces, must be reorganised on the right lines and imbued ith the spirit to resist aggression. This would happen only if the overnments of the Western Union gave a clear lead by ordering iat, whatever situation might arise, any Russian aggression would be et and resisted with all the strength and means available. All must ght with whatever was available. As time went on, the military ipabilities of the Western Powers would increase. Unless the doctrine f full and active resistance to any Russian threat to Western Europe as adopted, then the Western Union might just as well close down. said that of course we needed American help; but unless that country as convinced that all would fight whatever the situation, we would ot get her help—nor would we deserve it.

My great point was that if France or the Benelux countries suspected iat the British troops then in Germany were to be withdrawn in the ent of war, there would be no hope of our bolstering them up to ay their part. The nations of Continental Europe had been occupied y the Germans in the war and were now struggling to recover. What ey needed most was inspired leadership. Britain must put her foot Europe and provide that leadership. If we held back, France and e Benelux countries and Western Germany would all collapse ainst the growing Communist pressure from the east—and we ould then lose the peace.

I was, of course, doing exactly what Smuts had told me I should

do when I lunched with him in London in May 1944 (see Chapter 13
But I do not think I had his remarks in mind. I was doing it becaus
it was so obviously the only right and proper course of action. It a
bore good fruit. At a conference with the Minister of Defence on th
10th May 1948 I got agreement " on the essential need of fighting
campaign in Western Europe," with all that that decision entaile
This was a great triumph.

The situation in Europe deteriorated rapidly during the first ha
of 1948. I had won agreement that we would fight in Europe if tl
need arose; it had been a hard fight which had lasted over four month
Now something more was needed—a proper set-up for effectiv
command and control of all the forces involved. The hard facts
war were that without such an organisation, you merely suffere
disasters. A proper set-up in the realm of command would also p
us in the way of solving other problems, such as the infusion of
fighting spirit, the national organisations which were to produce tl
forces required, and so on. Many questions remained to be answere
e.g.:

Who would take command of the land armies in Europe?

Who would decide how the armies should be grouped with regar
to the geographical features of the ground?

Who would decide where the left flank should rest, or the rigl
flank, or where the line must be strong and where a chance can l
taken?

Who would decide what strength must be held in reserve fc
counter-attack?

Who would weld the armies of the West into an effective fightin
machine?

The answer to all these questions was the same—there was no on

On the 1st June 1948 I put these points to my colleagues but g
little response. The First Sea Lord did not think the matter was ve
urgent and reckoned that possibly something analogous to the o
COSSAC organisation might do the trick. I asked how an inte
national committee of staff officers sitting in London could be of tl
slightest use in solving the problems I had raised. In the end tl
matter was referred to the Joint Planners for investigation! Tin
went on and by the 23rd June we were still arguing the toss, tl
majority view inclining towards a planning authority in Lond
similar to the old COSSAC. I gave my opinion on this point of vie

no uncertain voice, saying that there must be a clear-cut and simple
t-up for effective command and control of the forces of the
'estern Union, and that we must create the organisation at once.

On the 24th June 1948 the Russians began the blockade of West
erlin. The effect in London was immediate. On the 28th June the
hiefs of Staff recommended to the Government that the most
fective way to convince both the Russians and the nations of Western
rope of our determination would be to appoint a Supreme Allied
ommander for the forces of the Western Union. But at a conference
ter that day the First Sea Lord insisted that the proposal to create a
preme Allied Commander was merely a political gesture in con-
ction with the Berlin crisis—which, he said, already showed signs
easing. He again stood out for a form of COSSAC. The *bonhomie*
as not very good when the conference ended!

However, after the meeting I got hold of the Chief of the Air
aff (Tedder). We had seen a lot of hard fighting together in the
ar, and he agreed with me that the establishment of a proper com-
and organisation had now become a serious and urgent matter.
me further conferences took place and on the 9th July the Govern-
ent agreed that we needed to establish:

(*a*)   A Western Union Defence Committee, composed of Ministers
of Defence.
(*b*)   A Western Union Chiefs of Staff Committee.
(*c*)   A command organisation; the actual form of the command
authority to be decided later.

So yet another " Battle of Whitehall " had been won, but only
ter the direct intervention of the Russians in Berlin.

Moreover, there were still some " mopping up " operations to
undertaken. On the 1st September 1948 I told the other two Chiefs
Staff that there was an urgent need for some *one man* to give a firm
ad in military matters to the Continental nations of the Western
nion. It was necessary to agree on what was needed, to get them
do something about it, and to co-ordinate their actions. The two
tal points were, first the fighting spirit and the determination to
ght for the defence of their home lands, and, secondly, the organisa-
on to produce the necessary forces for the purpose. To my astonish-
ent the Chief of the Air Staff raised difficulties. He thought that all
e needed was a Land C.-in-C. and an Air C.-in-C.; they would take

all the action required, and the need for some one man to direct the activities was not established. However on this occasion the First S‹ Lord (Sir John Cunningham), who had in the past always oppos‹ practically everything I had suggested, agreed with me on all count he weighed anchor and rammed Tedder—sinking him! It w Cunningham's last appearance, since he was to leave the Admiralty ‹ retirement. I was grateful to him.

Events were now reaching a climax.

On the 20th September 1948 I was summoned to see the Minist of Defence at 12.45 p.m. The hour was unusual and there w speculation in the War Office about the reason for the summon Some thought I was to be ticked off for my behaviour at the meetin on the 10th September, at which I had referred to the parlous con dition of the Army. Others thought that the Minister had heard abo my attempt on the 15th July to unseat him, as described in Chapter 3 But all prophets were confounded. Mr. Alexander offered me th appointment of Chairman of the Western Union Commanders-i‹ Chief Committee.

The next day the Minister met the Chiefs of Staff in Committe He told us that with the concurrence of the Prime Minister, th Foreign Secretary, the Chancellor of the Exchequer, and the Lo President of the Council, he intended to propose the appointment a Chairman of the Western Union Commanders-in-Chief. F intended to nominate me for that appointment.

I replied that if it was the unanimous wish of the Government, my colleagues on the Chiefs of Staff Committee, and the other Gover‹ ments of the Western Union that I should take up the appointmer then I accepted—indeed I could not refuse. I made, however, o stipulation. That was that I must remain a British officer and on th books of the War Office; I had been looked after by the War Offi for forty years, and I was not prepared to have my personal affai transferred to some international organisation. This stipulation w agreed. In subsequent discussion, the question was mentioned of Supreme Commander if war broke out. I said that if this happen‹ during my tenure of office of Chairman, I would at once step dow In the event of another World War the Supreme Commander Europe must be an American officer, and it would make things easi for me if it could be agreed that I would never be considered for t top post. This was agreed.

On the 27th September 1948 my appointment was unanimously
proved by the Defence Ministers of the Five Powers of the Western
nion, meeting in Paris. It was announced in the Press on the 3rd
ctober.

At last we had achieved that for which I had been fighting—
decision that in the event of war the British Army would fight on
e Continent of Europe, and something concrete in the way of a
ommand organisation. But it had taken months of intense effort,
d I then found myself given the task of organising the details.

I often think that A. V. Alexander "took his coat off" to ensure
at I got the job. I must have been an awful nuisance to him during
y time as C.I.G.S. Socially—off parade as it were—we were very
od friends. But in defence matters I just couldn't get on with him.
was probably my fault.

I have made it more than clear that by now there were plenty of
ople anxious to see the back of me. When I recall those days I often
ink that Whitehall was my least happy theatre of war. It did not
ovide "my sort of battle." I have never minded making myself an
fernal nuisance if it produced the desired result. I don't know in
is case whether it did—sufficiently. It is true that I managed to force
reement on certain fundamental issues, but only after terrific
ttles. And as a result of it all I was pretty unpopular when I left
hitehall to become an international soldier.

CHAPTER 32

THE UNITY OF THE WEST

BEFORE CLOSING this book of memoirs I must make clear my poi
of view about the future—a sort of final testament. In fact, I want
take this opportunity to state categorically—as I pull out from acti
employment—how I think the land should be made to lie. Th
may involve a change of " tone " from the rest of the book, but th
will not matter—provided that I explain clearly what is in my min
The title of this chapter indicates very simply the goal which has
be reached if the Western Alliance is to flourish; we have a long roa
to travel before we reach it.

To understand the attempts to achieve unity and co-operation
Western Europe in the post-war years we must go back to 194
When the German war ended in May of that year, the nations
Europe began to drift apart. Later, however, a number of treati
were made as the beginning of collective security in Europe. The fir
was the Treaty of Dunkirk in March 1947 between France and Britai
this was aimed expressly against renewed German aggression. Tl
last and most important was the North Atlantic Treaty of 1949.

By the spring of 1945 many of the nations of Europe were in a ba
way economically. It soon became clear that outside help would l
needed. And speed was necessary too, since Russian Communis
was beginning to spread westwards—where fertile soil existed for th
insidious disease.

This was realised in the United States and on the 5th June 1947,
Harvard University, General Marshall made his famous speech abo
aid for Europe—known thenceforward as Marshall Aid. This off
was seized by Ernest Bevin with both hands, and he organised a coi
ference in Paris the next month, July, to work out the details. At th
conference the Russians said that they did not want Marshall Aid f
themselves or for any of their satellite countries, although Gener
Marshall had made it clear that it could be given to *all* the countri

f Europe and some of the satellites had started by welcoming it.
his was a clear indication that the Russians did not want Europe to
cover. They preferred a disrupted and dismembered Europe;
covery might impede the spread of Communism. I regard that date,
ily 1947, as an important one in the post-war era, since it was then
iat the Russians definitely showed their true hand—beyond any
oubt.

However, notwithstanding the Russian refusal, Marshall Aid was
iade legal in the United States on the 3rd April 1948, and the Mission
o implement the scheme was set up in June 1948 under Averell
larriman. The free nations of Europe owe a very great debt of
ratitude to the U.S.A. for that aid—which was freely given and
hich has contributed so much to their recovery. The plan was
itended to provide aid for economic reconstruction and was visualised
; being operative only for a limited number of years. Marshall Aid
nder that name has now ceased, but the plan still continues under
ie title of Foreign Aid.

When the Russians refused Marshall Aid in 1947 the cold war,
hich had been going on for some time, took a turn for the worse.
. group of nations in Western Europe then began to get anxious
oout the growing threat from the East, and the need for unity was
alised in order to be able to stand up to the threat. Benelux (Belgium,
letherlands, Luxembourg) was the first organisation to be formed,
ie treaty being limited initially to economic measures. Then the
eed for some wider organisation became apparent and the United
ingdom and France joined with Benelux to form the Western Union
-which was brought into being by the Treaty of Brussels, signed on
ie 17th March 1948. This treaty was at first also limited to economic
iatters, to the furtherance of democratic principles, and so on.

Soon after the Treaty of Brussels was signed the Russians began,
i June 1948, the blockade of West Berlin which was finally defeated
y the tremendous feat of the air-lift. This created great tension in the
Vestern world, and considerable alarm; plans for the defence of the
Vest were considered necessary and Defence Ministers and Service
hiefs of the five Brussels Treaty nations met to consider man-power
nd equipment problems. Then in September 1948 it was decided to
reate a Western Union Defence Organisation which would prepare
lans for combined action in case of attack. I was appointed per-
ianent Chairman of the Land, Naval, and Air Commanders-in-Chief

Committee of the Western Union. We set up our headquarters Fontainebleau, the short name for our combined headquarters bein UNIFORCE.

Meanwhile, on the other side of the Atlantic talks had been goin on about the need for a single mutual defence system, which wou. include and supersede the Brussels Treaty. It was realised in the U.S./ and in Canada that, if real security was the aim, they themselves ar certain other nations must be brought in—in order that the Atlant Ocean could be made secure for getting help to Europe. Preliminar talks had begun in Washington in July 1948, shortly after the start the blockade of West Berlin, and they continued throughout the yea

Finally on the 4th April 1949 the North Atlantic Treaty was signe by which twelve nations joined together in a defensive alliance maintain international peace and security and to promote stability ar well-being in the North Atlantic area. It was called the North Atlant Treaty Organisation, known for short as NATO.

As planning proceeded it became obvious that the Western Unic military organisation must be absorbed into the NATO set-up and this was done. Then on the 2nd April 1951 General Eisenhow assumed operational control of the military forces of the defensiv alliance. Later, on the 18th February 1952 Greece and Turkey joine NATO and we became fourteen nations. The last to join NAT was the Federal Republic of Germany, in May 1955, and we the became, as we remain today, fifteen nations.

We must now return to the early days of the Western Union ar see what happened when the nations of Western Europe were require to co-operate closely together in defence matters. They soon four it was going to be difficult; I sometimes wondered if it would ev be possible.

When I was appointed Chairman of the Commanders-in-Chi Committee, I went to live in France—near Fontainebleau. M colleagues and I travelled all over Western Europe examining t problem. We made plans to defend the West against aggression. B none of the plans could be carried out because the nations were unwil ing to produce the necessary forces—properly trained, with a soun command structure and a reliable communication system. It was t more difficult as there was no true unity, and no nation was willing t make any sacrifice of sovereignty for the common good.

The emphasis was on economic recovery. It was not understoo

at economic strength without military strength is useless; both are
necessary, with a proper balance between the two. Military strength
necessary in order to have power behind the politics; power is
essential when dealing with the Communist bloc. I quickly saw how
difficult it was to obtain economic fusion and to build up military
strength until the political association between the group of nations
concerned had first been clearly defined and agreed. It was one thing
for a number of Foreign Ministers to sit round a table and sign a Treaty,
followed by luncheons and dinners at which sentiments of friendship
and unity were exchanged. It was quite another thing to get Governments to do anything about it, as the Ministers very soon found when
they got back to their own countries.

An intense national feeling existed among the nations of Continental Europe; one had to live over there, as I did, to appreciate it.
Their countries had all been occupied by the Germans and their armed
forces disbanded. When the war ended they had to begin to build
up their forces again from scratch; in many cases their senior officers
had spent the war either in London or in German prison camps.
There was a tremendous lack of knowledge about the kind of organisation needed to produce the armed forces suitable for modern war.
Few of the generals had seen modern war. We were asking the
nations to get their affairs so organised as regards man-power, production, and mobilisation that they could take the strain easily and
quickly if a war crisis should arise.

This involved clear thinking on the subject of armed forces, and
these had to be organised within the limits of financial possibilities.
To do this economically, joint defence within the alliance would be
necessary. But each nation wanted everything. It was not understood, and is not today, that if every nation wants self-sufficiency there
is little value to be got from the alliance. Then again, money was
tight. The nations wanted peace above all. I used to tell the Governments that peace in the modern world cannot be assured without
military power, and this costs money. That fact might be sad, but it
is true. Peace was, in fact, a by-product. The real need was for freedom and justice—freedom within the law—with a right of every man
to live his own life. A nation which worked for these things, and was
prepared to risk a war to defend the Western way of life, would have
peace. What was the use of peace if you lost your soul to Communism?
I reckon the Prime Ministers of Western Europe got pretty fed up

with me in those days. They were never allowed to escape from the
practical realities of the problem that faced them about the defence of
their peoples and territories against aggression. It was a very frustrating
time. It was necessary to become international, and few could. I used
to say that though I was of course British by birth, it was my duty
to draw my sword and die for France, and for the other nations in
Continental Europe, just as much as for Britain.

After a few months I came to the conclusion that drastic steps
would have to be taken if we were to organise any sort of defence at
all in Western Europe. Our defensive lay-out must include Western
Germany. But the forces available made this impossible; it was
doubtful if we could even hold the line of the Rhine. I therefore went
to see Ernest Bevin in January 1949 and I asked him to set in motion
measures which would aim at bringing Western Germany into the
Western Union, and ultimately into the wider North Atlantic Organisation which was then under discussion. Bevin was somewhat startled.
I pointed out to him that the Western Union countries had neither
the man-power nor the resources to build up the necessary military
forces without " busting " themselves economically and financially.
Our plans were based on conventional weapons and we would need
strong forces if we were to match those which could be deployed
against us by Russia. Without the Germans, we could not hope to
produce those forces. In November 1949 I went to the United States
and preached the same doctrine to the national Chiefs of Staff, to
President Truman, and to General Eisenhower—who was the
President of Columbia University. My argument was that existing
forces, or those which could be foreseen, were wholly inadequate to
give effect to a " forward strategy "—one which would aim at defending the whole of Western Germany as a necessary part of Western
Europe.

The long struggle to get Western Germany (now the Federal
German Republic) integrated politically and militarily into the
Western camp is well known. The pace quickened in June 1950 when
the Korean war began. I reported that month to the governments of
the Western Union, in writing, that:

" As things stand today and in the foreseeable future, there would
be scenes of appalling and indescribable confusion in Western
Europe if ever we were attacked by the Russians."

Following on this statement, the problem of German partici-
ation in Western defence was discussed in the NATO Council in
eptember 1950, and met with heavy opposition from the French.
'here will be no need to remind readers of the proposal of the Pleven
Government in October 1950 for the formation of a European Army
n which there would be " a complete fusion of all the human and
naterial elements " of the proposed force. Such a conception was,
f course, utterly impracticable. The NATO nations argued the
oss continuously for nearly four years, and the arguments finally
eased only with the rejection of the plan by the French National
Assembly on the 30th August 1954. In the end, Federal Germany
oined NATO as a full member for all purposes on the 9th May
955—over six years after I had made the approach to Mr. Bevin in
anuary 1949. It had been a long up-hill struggle.

Then there was another problem, involving the United Kingdom.

After I had been on the job for a few months I realised that there
vas deep suspicion of the British in political and military circles in
Continental Europe. There were three main causes:

First. The United Kingdom would not state firmly the contribution
proposed to make on land in Continental Europe in the event of war.
Ministers would talk about the main contribution of Britain as being
ir and sea power. This cut no ice at all in Europe.

Secondly. In defence discussions, British delegations referred continually
o the vital importance of the " security of the U.K. Base " if ever
var broke out again in Europe.

Thirdly. British delegations continually stressed the importance of the
Middle East, and never the importance of Western Europe. Nobody
new the relative priority they proposed as between the two areas.
My view was that you could lose the Middle East and still win the
var, although you might have to re-conquer it before you finally
von. The same could not be said in the case of Western Europe.

These three factors gave the impression on the Continent that the
British were concerned with a battle in Western Europe only in so
ar as it would provide a cushion for the defence of Britain. Hence
Continental nations were deeply suspicious of British intentions. This
uspicion was greatest in France, where it was commonly hinted that
he British would stage another " Dunkirk " for any forces they had
n Europe.

I became so alarmed at this attitude that I had a meeting with the

British Chiefs of Staff on the 2nd December 1948. I told them tha
French morale would not recover unless that nation could be con
vinced that Britain would contribute a fair quota of land forces to th
defence of Western Europe. There was already the British Army c
the Rhine in Germany but it was not battle-worthy and all units wer
under strength. Would the British Chiefs of Staff recommend t
the Government that in the event of war the British Rhine Arm
would at once be reinforced? Only if this were done would there b
effective resistance. Without it, the battle would be lost befor
it ever began.

The British Chiefs of Staff would not play. They considered tha
if war broke out in the near future, before the Continental nations ha
built up their forces, any additional forces would be lost. I could nc
but agree. But the factor of morale demanded some reinforcemen
I would not insult them by asking for a reinforcement of on
battalion. Would they recommend a reinforcement of one in
fantry brigade group? They would not.

I then wrote a paper on the subject and discussed it with the Britis
Chiefs of Staff on the 5th January 1949. I pointed out the suspicion i
France about British intentions. I agreed that the reinforcement c
the British Rhine Army by one infantry brigade group would nc
affect the battle to any degree; but the promise of such reinforcemen
was the only way to convince our continental allies of our determina
tion to fight alongside them. The C.I.G.S. (Field-Marshal Slim
swayed opinion to my viewpoint, and the Chiefs of Staff agreed t
recommend to the Government that a reinforcement of one infantr
brigade group should be sent to the British Rhine Army in the even
of war. But the recommendation contained so many argument
against the proposal that the Government had no difficulty in turnin
it down—which it did on the 10th January 1949. This very quickl
became known to the nations in Western Europe; it resulted i
immense harm to the cause of Western unity, and I doubt if we hav
ever properly recovered from it.

We cannot wonder at the Continental attitude. The suspicion i
directed against the Americans just as much as against the British. I
two world wars Europe has seen the United States watching from th
touchline during the first two years of the war; the European nation
do not want this to happen again.

In spite of all the troubles and frustrations which I have outlined

General Eisenhower, on arrival in Europe, found that the Western Union Command Organisation had already studied the European problem, and had prepared plans which could serve as a basis for future work. We had done our best in the face of every conceivable difficulty and obstruction. But the forces available were still totally inadequate for our purpose. However, all-in-all we had laid solid foundations on the military side.

Supreme Headquarters, Allied Powers Europe (SHAPE), the direct descendant of UNIFORCE, was opened in Paris on the 2nd April 1951, with General Eisenhower as Supreme Commander. I joined him as Deputy Supreme Commander.

He had given me the following directive on the 12th March 1951:

"I trust that you realize how delighted I am that the British Government has agreed to make you available for duty in SHAPE, in which you are hereby designated as the Deputy Supreme Allied Commander. In this capacity, you will have a most important role to play in the development of an integrated force for the defence of Europe, which is our objective.

You will act, during any temporary incapacity of mine, as Supreme Allied Commander, Europe, under the authority invested in me by the North Atlantic Council. Your principal normal duty will be to further the organisation, equipping, training, and readiness of National Forces contemplated for later allocation to this command, and through and in co-operation with subordinate commanders, to perform a similar function for troops already allocated to SHAPE.

These duties will require your direct contact, in my name, with the several governments, military staffs and agencies of NATO nations, and with principal subordinate headquarters established by competent orders of SHAPE. I suggest that you acquaint yourself with the terms of the directive issued to me by the Standing Group, particularly those provisions that authorise direct communication between this headquarters and the several governments of NATO. For assisting you in this work, the entire SHAPE staff, through its Chief of Staff, will be at your disposal. Any executive instructions to subordinate commanders are, of course, to be issued through the staff."

I should explain that the Standing Group is a small executive sub-

committee of the Military Committee of NATO. It is in permane
session in Washington.

From the start Eisenhower was determined that all staff officers
SHAPE must forget they belonged to a particular nation or Servic
All were to be international and inter-Service. The headquarters w
to be bi-lingual, all work being done in English and French. I
never quite succeeded in the second objective; SHAPE is still ve
much an English-speaking headquarters and an officer who cann
speak English (or understand American) does not achieve much.

In peace-time SHAPE is occupied mainly with the problem
readiness for war. This subject embraces the organisation of the acti
and reserve forces of the NATO nations, their mobilisation, provisic
of equipment, training, logistic support, communications, and A
Defence system.

In war SHAPE would leave the handling of tactical battles to tl
subordinate commanders-in-chief, devoting itself mainly to strategic
direction, forward planning, intelligence, logistics, and the control
the air and missile arm.

Conferences are held in English and in French. Papers and signa
are in both languages; which are taught to all ranks in the hea
quarters. All work is on a strictly international basis. For instance,
is possible to find a Turkish Air Force officer working on a proble
concerning the lines of communication between England and Scanc
navia for the support of the Norwegian Army.

I have served at SHAPE under four Supreme Commanders
possibly the only officer who has done so.

Eisenhower was the first of them. As time went on he became ve
fully occupied with the Presidential campaign which loomed ahead
1952, and he left a good deal to General Gruenther—his Chief
Staff. He had no qualms about this, nor had anyone else. Al Gruenth
was a Chief of Staff *par excellence*, most able, with a quick and cle
brain, and very approachable. At that time there was a crusadir
spirit in the atmosphere at SHAPE, which took much of its inspiratic
from Eisenhower. Under him and Gruenther, SHAPE soon develop
into a very happy headquarters. Then Eisenhower retired from t
United States Army and left us; he had decided to run for Presider
I knew that he was being pressed by the Republican Party to ru
and we used to have long talks on the subject. He tells a story of ho
I changed my mind about it—which, he says, is not my habit.

appened this way. I had told him he must not go; we needed him
SHAPE, and Europe needed him too. Later, European defence and
-operation began to run into difficulties; we seemed to be in the
doldrums," becalmed in an area where nothing much happened
cept an occasional squall. I of course was well used to this,
ving by now been in the game since 1948. Then one day
walked into Ike's office and said, "Ike, I've changed my mind. You
ust go back and run for President. European co-operation is in the
oldrums and the only man who can get things moving is the Pre-
dent of the United States. You can do more good to us in the White
ouse than you can here." He went. But we had to pay the price.

General Ridgway arrived in Paris on the 27th May 1952, and
ok over from Eisenhower on the 30th May. He was a fine battle-
ld general and had done magnificently with the U.S. Eighth Army
Korea at a most critical time. I knew him well; he had served
der me as a Divisional and Corps Commander in the campaign in
orth-West Europe from Normandy to Berlin. I knew he was not
e right man to succeed Eisenhower and I opposed the appointment,
th to members of the NATO Council and to the British Chiefs of
aff.

I wanted Al Gruenther to succeed Eisenhower; so did most others.
ut the British Chiefs of Staff said Gruenther had never commanded
ything in his life, and they asked for Ridgway. The United States
hiefs of Staff agreed. Ridgway didn't fit into the set-up; his merits
a fine battlefield commander were wasted in a role which didn't
it his temperament. He surrounded himself with an all-American
rsonal staff; we got the feeling that there was too much "United
ates Eyes Only" in the headquarters. Morale began to decline.
he crusading spirit disappeared. There was the sensation, difficult
describe, of a machine which was running down.

Ridgway left Europe on the 11th July 1953 and Al Gruenther became
ir new Supreme Commander. He is a most human and sympathetic
rson, very popular, and a quick worker. He soon eliminated the
ver-Americanisation which had tended to distort the atmosphere of
e headquarters. Under him and his brilliant Chief of Staff (General
huyler) SHAPE regained its former morale and prestige. Al
ruenther did a terrific job in Europe and at SHAPE, first as Chief
Staff to Eisenhower and Ridgway, and finally as Supreme Com-
ander himself—a total period of nearly six years. I became devoted

to him and to his wife. The letter he wrote me when he left SHAP
is one which I shall treasure all my life. Here it is, dated the 19
November 1956.

"Dear Monty,
It has been a tremendous comfort to me to have you he
during the period I have been the Supreme Commander. Y
have never failed me. Your loyalty and your integrity of charact
have always been unchallengeable. The contribution you ha
made to our unity has been a major one.
For all of these things I am deeply grateful to you. Your ro
in the NATO cause has placed the entire Free World in your del
I wish you all possible success for the future. May you ev
climb higher—although how that can take place, I cannot imagin
A thousand thanks for everything, Monty. My service wi
you will always be one of my fondest memories.
With warm regard—as ever—Al."

Gruenther was succeeded in November 1956 by General Norsta
a brilliant officer of the United States Air Force—a very firm frien
and I gladly served on under him.

Under Eisenhower's guidance, and that of his successors, o
military strength gradually increased; furthermore, the progress
science gave us nuclear weapons in ever-increasing quantity, makir
us all the stronger. Two developments then began to influence o
strategy.

First, the nuclear weapon gave us the power to destroy to an exte
never before envisaged. That power could be developed into such
powerful offensive weapon that it was clear that no profit from w
could come to any nation; an aggressor nation might inflict tremendo
destruction on Western civilisation but would itself suffer equal
even greater damage. Here then was a new key to our strategy, t
nuclear deterrent—an offensive nuclear capability which could l
launched by aircraft and missiles from air, sea and land, and which
would be almost impossible to knock out by a surprise attack provid
it was suitably dispersed.

Secondly, the NATO nations had been building up convention
forces with which to defeat an enemy attack. It became clear to n
that if we relied only on such forces, then we could never match t
strength which could be brought against us; to do that would ne

reatly increased forces, and this would "step up" defence budgets
o a degree which nations were not prepared to face. The only alter-
ative was to state publicly that if we were attacked we would use
ll the resources at our disposal against the aggressor, including the
uclear weapon—even if that weapon was not used against us in the
irst instance. After some discussion with General Gruenther, I said
his at a talk I gave in Paris on the 24th May 1954, and repeated the
tatement at a lecture which I gave at the Royal United Service
nstitution in London on the 21st October 1954. There were the
sual questions about me in the House of Commons. But in the end
he NATO Council had to agree that all our operational plans could
e based on doing what I had said—it being laid down that the final
ecision to use the nuclear weapon was to be kept in political hands.
'his may not seem altogether satisfactory to Service Chiefs. But there
re many other types of conflict in which we might become involved,
anging right down the scale to so-called police actions in undeveloped
ountries. A commander should use whatever strength is necessary
o deal with the problem that confronts him, and no more. World
pinion today is such that before using the nuclear weapon he must
ecide whether to do so is strategically desirable, tactically profitable,
nd politically acceptable. Political leaders in their turn must realise
lat if they retain in their own hands the power to use the nuclear
veapon, the slightest delay in agreeing to the military demands for its
se in an all-out global war could result in much of the NATO
rritory being overrun by enemy land forces.

As time went on our strategy therefore gradually became to use
le nuclear weapon at once if we are attacked; and that is how we
and today, in 1958. It was a big change to go over to basing our
efence organisation on nuclear weapons; but it had to be, and I
uppose I played some part in bringing it about. I have always thought
lat the Russians made up their minds from the very beginning they
vould only fight a "cheap" war. Our tactics will now make a war
ery expensive for them, since they would suffer great damage and
luch loss of life—equally as great as we would. Therefore they will
ot attack us, so long as we remain strong and retain the ability to
eact instantly with nuclear weapons.

There was no alternative to this deterrent strategy except an
greement on disarmament, and this we could not get. We now have
le deterrent and it is a good one; it has prevented a major war. But

it is doubtful whether the deterrent is also a good defence. One thin
cannot be denied—we have no sure defence in a major war in whic
nuclear weapons are *not* used. A third major war need not necessaril
be a nuclear war (gas was not used in the second World War, althoug
both sides had large stocks). The crux of this matter can be expresse
very shortly—we have a good deterrent against war, but no sure defen
if the deterrent fails and we are attacked.

There is one further point about the deterrent which should b
mentioned. Over the years confidence has been restored in Cor
tinental Europe and there is slowly growing up a determination t
resist aggression with all the means at our disposal, even if this shoul
lead to nuclear attack against Western cities.

The overall deterrent against attack includes this sturdy determin.
tion. There is also a growing consciousness that a nation must n
recoil from any sacrifice—however great it may be. This is right. Fo
the nation which sets itself a limit beyond which it will not go wi
abandon the struggle when that limit is reached, and will the
inevitably succumb.

All these things have happened during the past ten years, sin
1948, in spite of the frustrations and obstructions which we experienc
in the early days. The sacrifices which have been made, financial a
otherwise, to build up military strength have prevented a third Wor
War; they have therefore been well worth while. But what are w
to do during the next ten years? And where are we going? This
the problem we face in 1958 and certain beacon lights seem to me t
point the direction in which we should seek for the solution.

First, we must understand that Russia is just as frightened of attac
by the Western Alliance as we are of attack by her. She therefore h
her deterrent. Part of her overall security is the belt of satellite natio
in eastern Europe. Any move by the Western nations which suggest
that they might help the satellite countries to regain their freedo
would meet with instant counter-action by Russia. Similarly on o
part, if Russia should bring pressure to bear on any part of the NAT
area. It is a curious situation and fascinating to study—the deterre
versus the deterrent.

Secondly, it is clear that the launching of war by Russia agair
the Western Alliance can be considered unlikely in any future th
we can foresee, provided we do not reduce the overall deterre
against attack which we have created. This qualification is importar

Ve have reached the stage where Russia has counted the cost of rmed aggression against the Western Alliance and has found it likely) be too expensive for her—for the time being at any rate. She has ierefore re-aligned her policy. Her new policy aims to stir up the ountries of Asia against their former "imperialist" masters; it icludes the fomenting of Arab hatred for the Jews in the oil-producing ıd oil-transit areas of the Middle East and of directing it " at one move " against the Powers which were dominant in that area before litler's war. In this way Russia aims to outflank the NATO area and) threaten its oil supplies in the Middle East. The new Russian policy iade considerable headway in 1956—succeeding in damaging the ood relations which existed between Britain and France and the Jnited States, not only on the immediate measures to be taken to ounter Russia's outflanking action but also over the appropriate long-rm policy to be pursued towards the Arab world. This Russian iccess will go much farther unless the Western Alliance realises what going on and adjusts its policy and plans accordingly.

And thirdly, Service Chiefs must realise the general trend of Vestern political thought in 1958. Although confidence in our ability) deter armed aggression, and determination to resist if we are attacked, ave been restored in the NATO area in Europe, there is nevertheless feeling that we should now examine the NATO military structure ıd see whether we cannot get an equally good defence far more ieaply—which, in my opinion, is definitely possible.

Then there is another point. When the war ended in 1945 the eographical and strategical position of the West *vis-à-vis* the Eastern loc was good; today, 1958, it can only be described as bad. We ave lost our former positions in Indo-China, India, Palestine, Egypt, ıe Sudan, and in much of North Africa. The Middle East is in a isturbed state. Nationalism is in the ascendancy. It is true that we ave a United Nations Organisation to handle world problems, but is not united and not organised; perhaps it needs a new name. The iture of world civilisation really depends on the Western Alliance; ' that is neither united nor properly organised the future will indeed e grim.

For these reasons, those NATO nations with world-wide commit-ients and responsibilities must consider carefully the strategical osition of the entire free world, agreeing amongst themselves those :eas which must be retained in the Western camp at all costs, and giving political backing to the nations responsible for such areas. All the NATO nations must widen their horizon and cease to take a major interest only in their own affairs. They must understand the possible repercussions of events outside the NATO area—being prepared, and ready for instant action, when such events threaten their own security.

Now that the main object, the prevention of war, has been achieved, the time has come for a thorough overhaul of the whole NATO organisation. We should begin by stating without any qualification that the contribution made by NATO to the security of the free world has been tremendous. There are two other regional organisations, the Baghdad Pact and the South-East Asia Treaty Organisation.

Of the three, NATO is by far the most important; indeed, it is the only answer to the political and military problems of the free world. But we must not be complacent and think that the organisation cannot be improved; there are many improvements which could be made, making for greater efficiency, greater security, less waste and far greater overall economy. At present (1958) NATO is in the doldrums. It needs a roll of drums and a clarion call—to put its house in order while the going is good. If it neglects to do so, NATO will become ineffective in a few more years—like the United Nations Organisation has become—and it could disintegrate.

The conference of Heads of Governments in Paris in December 1957 was assembled for the purpose of putting a new sense of unity and determination into a hesitant NATO. It achieved only moderate success and much still remains to be done. It is particularly necessary that member nations should learn to look outwards at what is going on in the world beyond the NATO area—and not just inwards at their own parish pumps.

Let me indicate some of the more positive measures which, if taken, would tend to make NATO more effective.

I have already stated that a major war can now be considered unlikely—in fact, the " test match " (in American " the World Series " is postponed indefinitely because of the deterrent strength of the Western Alliance. But limited and cold war activities outside the NATO area are likely to increase—what might be called " village cricket" (in American " sand lot baseball "). These local matches on overseas fields must be handled firmly so that they do not become the forerunner of a test match; the major contribution of certain selected nations to NATO defence could well be to produce forces which are organised and equipped for these contests. In fact, national contributions to NATO must now be balanced. First, direct contributions to the deterrent in the NATO area to prevent a test match; secondly, indirect contributions to handle local matches and preserve peace outside the NATO area. We have reached the stage when, provided the NATO machinery is reorganised and made more effective, and the deterrent forces are properly organised and deployed, the indirect contributions to NATO are becoming increasingly important. No European nation could be expected to make both direct *and* indirect contributions of any significant size.

The politico-military structure of NATO needs a searching examination; at present it is top-heavy, expensive, and does not work well. The NATO Council is in permanent session in Paris, each nation being represented by an ambassador; its military advisers, the Standing Group (the executive body of the Military Committee of NATO), are in Washington. How can two organisations co-operate closely and efficiently if they are 3000 miles apart? If the Standing Group is required at all it should be in Paris, alongside the permanent Council.

There is no organisation for the higher direction of any war in which we might become engaged.

National organisations for producing the forces we need in peace and war are unsound in the case of many Continental nations; they are mostly based on the *levée-en-masse* system, which is out of date.

Simplicity and decision, two absolute essentials in war, have disappeared from the NATO military organisation. We are producing commanders trained in the art of compromise.

The staffs of the major headquarters have grown beyond all possible peace-time needs; they should be ruthlessly pruned.

The output of paper is tremendous; so much time is taken with reading it, that few officers have enough time to think; all work suffers accordingly.

The high cost of defence is not being seriously tackled, except in the United Kingdom—where the Defence White Papers of April 1957 (Outline of Future Policy) and of February 1958 (Britain's Contribution to Peace and Security) are steps in the right direction.

There are many ways in which the overall cost to the NATO nations can be reduced. One is that when the German contribution is complete we should aim to get a proportion of the armed forces of

the other Continental nations back into their own countries, thu
saving expenditure on foreign currency. It is always expensive t
keep your forces in another country. I exclude from this plan th
forces of the U.S.A., Britain and Canada; these nations must cor
tinue to maintain some forces in Germany for the time being in orde
to give confidence, but the size of their contingents is not now so im
portant as formerly.

Then we must think sensibly about surprise. Total readiness t
meet a surprise attack at any time would mean very high defenc
budgets; furthermore it is unnecessary. Surprise could of course b
obtained by air and missile attack only, but this means unlimited wa
—with the certainty of devastating retaliation. Victory in war ca
come only as a result of the maximum efforts of all land, sea, air an
civilian forces in truly joint operations; a nation which plans aggres
sion must know that unless it is ready for these operations before th
first strike, it may never be ready. The steps Russia would have t
take before launching unlimited war might not be mobilisation as w
have known it in the past; but she would have to take certai
measures which could not be hidden. Furthermore, no nation woul
risk general war in a missile age unless it had an adequate defenc
against such weapons; and today (1958) there is no known defenc
against the ballistic missile.

Linked to this is the problem of mobilisation. Mobilisation a
known to us during the last two world wars looks archaic against th
background of nuclear war. The word brings to mind an entirel
erroneous picture—a picture portraying an effort spread over day
weeks, and even months before completion. A new word is perhaj
required for mobilisation in a nuclear age. We need a system whic
is effective in a matter of hours—following national radio warning
It must not be dependent on vulnerable communication systems. It mu
be based on a decentralised method of call up and dispersed equij
ment depots. It must be founded on a body of men and women a
of whom know in peace time exactly where they go in war, an
what they do.

It is clear that the whole question of mobilisation requires a ne
look. We are not paying sufficient attention to this vitally impor
ant part of national and allied defence.

A very efficient way to reduce defence expenditure would be t
have collective balanced forces for NATO as a whole, rather than on

national or regional basis as at present. Indeed, only by so doing can NATO develop integrated and effective armed forces which are within our means in peace-time but which at the same time are adequate to meet our requirements. It is an obvious necessity if we are to eradicate waste, inefficiency and duplication. Another advantage of balanced forces for NATO as a whole is that such a system would tend to bind the nations more closely together, since they would be dependent on each other; it would be joint defence in the true sense of the word. Under such a scheme, each nation would be asked to produce those forces most suited to its geographical location, its national character, its economic situation, and so on—all working towards a balanced whole. I first drew attention to this need in 1949, in the Western Union, but practically no progress has been made since then. National sensitivity is the trouble, and this is a great bar to progress. A further trouble in the realm of defence is that nations don't trust each other; no nation is willing to be dependent on another nation in the Alliance. There is no doubt that when the threat of war lessened and fear began to disappear, Western unity began to weaken.

It will be clear from what I have said that NATO is an organisation in which there is a tremendous waste of money and effort, and a great deal of unnecessary duplication. Much of the thinking is muddled and confused. The global aspect of defence is disregarded. Defence problems have got into the hands of the Foreign Ministers; these know little about the subject, and, furthermore, they are not responsible for defence. There should be a NATO Defence Committee, on which sit a few selected Defence Ministers; this committee would deal with all defence problems and make recommendations to the full Council.

In 1956 the NATO nations spent over twenty thousand million pounds on their defence budgets—a vast sum. If we can design a simple and effective structure for NATO, and eradicate waste and duplication, we could have an equally good defence for far less cost. We now have the time to do this—to re-organise, re-group, re-design where necessary, regain the flexibility we have lost, and so on. The object will be to achieve an organisation which is less complicated than the present set-up, is less costly, which works better, and is equally effective. And the result—more money available for hospitals, education, roads, industrial development, and to reduce taxation. Also, and very important—more money available for fighting the cold war and for dealing with incidents outside the NATO area. There cannot be a major war which is confined to the NATO area. If war comes it will be global, and it could have its beginnings in some incident elsewhere. We must therefore ensure that we have force available, and mobile, as a strategic reserve—ready for instant use anywhere in the world. In this re-organisation, it will be vital to ensure that the launching of war will always be expensive to the aggressor— equally expensive as it would be today (1958).

Then there is the question of disarmament. Basically, the real answer to the international arms race is to work for some future form of disarmament. But we have a long way to go before we get general agreement on how this is to be done. No nation will agree to any plan which makes it give up something. Russia has much to hide; the West little. I do not see Russia agreeing that mobile inspection teams from Western nations should have the freedom of her country!

We cannot see into the future accurately. But we can at least ensure that we do not disregard the lessons of the past: only a madman would do that. Twice in my own lifetime an enemy has attempted to exert his will by force, and has plunged the world into war. We now have a powerful weapon, the nuclear weapon, which will make this form of activity very expensive for similarly minded rulers in the future. It has been suggested that as a first step towards general disarmament European nations, including the United Kingdom, should not manufacture nuclear material or possess the weapon. Surely this is tantamount to allowing the United States and Russia to divide the world between them, with Europe as a cushion in the middle? In my view it is vital that *one* of the Western European nations should have the nuclear weapon, with all the means of using it; as things stand today that nation must be the British. On no account can we allow our nation, and Western Europe, to become a sort of " hedgehog " between two great giants who alone have the latest weapons. The British nuclear capability can be small; but we must have one.

It is so important to understand the tremendous change that has taken place in the realm of defence in the NATO area during the past ten years that, at the risk of repeating myself, I will summarise the main features of the progress.

In 1948 my colleagues and I in the Western Union defence organisation pleaded for a strong British contribution in Continental Europe and devoted all our energies to building up strong forces to defeat attack. We had no nuclear weapons to stiffen our defence, and no nuclear delivery capability to deter an aggressor. Western Germany was unarmed.

By 1958 we had nuclear weapons integrated into our defensive system and had built up a strong nuclear deterrent against attack; also, Federal Germany had become a member of NATO (in 1955) and had begun to re-arm. A direct attack on NATO Europe had now become the most unlikely thing that could happen; the dangers lay elsewhere.

I would sum up in this way. Having averted war, in the NATO area, we must now examine the strategical and political situation *throughout the world*—since our present plans are based to a large extent on unreality. So long as we are reluctant to face the facts, thus long will we not achieve a more effective NATO or a more economical overall defence organisation.

It is essential to understand the global problem. Western Europe, including the United Kingdom, is the centre of a world-wide economic system. It has no large supplies of raw materials, except possibly coal, and large imports of food are necessary to support the populations. The sources of raw materials, particularly of oil and food, are sensitive to threats of a " cold war " nature; these sources must be protected, together with the bases and communications from which they are controlled. Failure would lead to the collapse of the whole economic system, and ultimately to the loss of NATO Europe to international Communism. Russia will strive for success in this direction rather than by armed aggression against the NATO front in Europe, since the latter action would lead to her own destruction. Nonetheless, the front in Europe must be guarded in peace, and plans made for its security in war—but not to the exclusion of all else. Here, then, is a nice problem—to determine within the limits of man-power and finance the level of armed forces necessary for the two conflicting tasks, remembering that the problem is further bedevilled by the rival economic demands of modern socialism, welfare states, and a hotly competitive world market.

The war we shall have to fight for the next ten years will not include a shooting war in Europe; we have managed to postpone that for the time being by what we have achieved during the past ten years. We now face an economic and financial war, directed at the very foundations of our civilisation and standard of living; if we lose it, international Communism will gain a bloodless victory. What is the use of " busting " ourselves financially in preparing for a major war in Europe which is unlikely to take place, and neglecting the real dangers which lie elsewhere? Preparations for the two must be carefully balanced in proportion to the risks.

Obviously we must do some new thinking if we are to have a sure defence against the changed threat—and for less cost. We will *not* get the right answer by keeping our eyes fixed on every tree in NATO; we must be sure we never lose sight of the global wood.

Our new thinking should be based on the following principles. From the earliest days, the great lesson of history is that an enemy who is confined to a land strategy is, in the end, defeated. The Second World War was fundamentally a struggle for control of the major oceans and seas—the control of sea communications—and until we had won that struggle we could not proceed with our plans to win the war. Therefore, in the event of war between the Communist bloc (led by Russia) and the Free World, our strategy must be based on confining Russia to a land strategy and ensuring for ourselves the free use of the sea and air flanks. Any other strategy will be of no avail.

This entails a global approach to the problem. We now have ballistic missiles with ranges up to 5000 miles and more, with nuclear warheads; man-made satellites circle the earth. The nuclear offensive and all defensive problems, need to be viewed globally. We must have a global early warning system and centralised global planning for air defence. The need is vital for some central organisation to plan and direct all these activities, and to control the satellites, which is above the level of the present Supreme Commander. Every day which passes without such a higher organisation merely decreases the value of our deterrent.

To achieve these ends there must be a greater effort in the political field, and a more sensible and practical approach to the problem of defence. The geographical limits of NATO as laid down by the Treaty of Washington have become too narrow today. The common policies of the NATO countries must be practised on a world-wide scale. The 1949 concept must be broadened. It is ridiculous to suppose that we can be allies to the north of a certain parallel, and at the same time pursue our contradictory national policies to the south of the same line.

It has become a question of striking the right balance in taking risks. The risk in NATO Europe is small—so long as we maintain our nuclear deterrent and make it very clear that we will use it to destroy the country of an aggressor. The risk outside the NATO area is tremendous. We need a strategy which will give us a sure defence in any type of war.

This is merely the outline of a very big problem. But the solution to our difficulties lies in the general direction I have indicated, and only in that direction are we likely to find reality.

And here I will leave the subject of collective defence in Europe and in NATO. We are too close to events to be able to comment further on them; indeed, the events are still unfolding as I write these words. But what I can say is this, and it cannot be stated too clearly nor too often.

The Western Alliance was brought into being because of fear of aggression from the East; fear is the basic component of the cement which holds the Alliance together. No alliance based on fear alone has ever lasted, or ever will—because whenever fear recedes the cement begins to crumble.

The nations of the free world would be well advised to close their ranks, and co-operate whole-heartedly and unreservedly. If they want to survive against the relentless pressure of international Communism, they must cease to pay lip service to Allied co-operation and must instead embark on a policy of mutual discussion and unselfish solidarity. Allied co-operation must become something more than the political phrase it is today. There is too little political unity among the nations of the Western Alliance in the true sense of that word, and too much national sensitivity. True unity involves a willingness to make sacrifices for the common cause. Yet what nation is willing to do this, or even to submit its sensitive problems to international discussion? We need a better cement than fear to bind us all together. An economic cement would be more permanent than one of fear. In any case, an important component of the new cement must be the solidarity of the English-speaking peoples and their determination to help the nations of Continental Europe to defend their freedom and maintain their way of life. The hard core of that solidarity must be Anglo-American friendship; if that link breaks, that is the end for each one of us—including the U.S.A.

Political leaders must understand the differences of outlook in the three main areas that surround the Communist bloc. In Western

Europe, and generally throughout the NATO area, the enemy is Russia with her aim of world domination to be achieved by international Communism. Among the Arab nations in the Middle East the immediate enemy is not Russia, but Israel; the Arabs will not combine to fight Communism, but only to fight Israel and to prevent expansion of the Jewish State. In the Far East, if the nations fear an external menace it is China—not Russia. The overall problem has to be viewed against this general background, and a sound and consistent policy pursued.

World leadership in all these matters has now passed to the United States of America. That nation has not always been in this position. For many years the British supplied the leadership and they have been dealing with great world problems for centuries. The U.S.A. has only the experience of decades. But the Western world must understand that without the United States of America the Western Alliance would collapse. This statement may be unpalatable—truth often is. For its part the United States must exercise convincing powers of political, economic and military leadership in the free world. Some Americans are apt to think that the success of their leadership will depend on the quantity of dollars which is made available for other nations; this is a false doctrine. History will measure United States leadership not so much by the quantity of dollars as by the quality, understanding and sympathy of the leadership provided and by the consistency of the foreign policy. I often think that the United States foreign policy is inconsistent. She appears to have one policy in the Assembly of the United Nations, and another and different one when her own national interests are involved. She supports the ex-" Colonial " powers in Western Europe, but works to destroy their influence and strength in Asia and Africa. These inconsistent policies of the U.S.A. have played a large part in the weakening of the general strategic position of the West, to which I have referred already. If continued they could lead to the break-up of the Western Alliance.

My experience as an international soldier has taught me that if the West is to survive it must evolve a far greater degree of common purpose and common responsibility than exists today. It needs close co-operation in wider fields than the mere defence of national territories. The Western Alliance must be based on unity, hope and courage—cemented together by the joint strength of some four hundred and fifty million people.

"Only be thou strong and very courageous," said God to
oshua, when appointing him to high command in the field *vice*
Moses.

The Hungarians have reminded the world what can be achieved
by courage alone. If the Western Alliance can have strength *and*
courage, there is no limit to what it could achieve—provided that its
members also have unity in the true sense.

Western unity is the only thing the Russians fear and all their
plans are linked to one fundamental object—to prevent it.

At all costs the unity of the West must be restored.

CHAPTER 33

SECOND THOUGHTS

I HAVE come to the end of my tale. I have certainly enjoyed writing it. As a schoolboy, and possibly also as a young man, I realise now that I saw little straight and nothing whole, and generally failed to detect the difference between what is important and what is trivial. But as I grew older I began to learn these things. Possibly the factor of the greatest use to me in later life has been the ability to be able to simplify a problem and expose the fundamentals on which all action must be based—to concentrate on essentials and to leave the details to my staff. I also learnt to regulate my life, not to overdo social activities and never to worry. Then again it took me some time to learn that personal matters count for a great deal in this life. Individual happiness, cheerful loyal service, giving a helping hand to others, gaining the trust and confidence of those you deal with—it is these things that matter most, to mention only a few.

In the first chapter I explained how I had learnt before I left school that of the many attributes necessary for success two are vital—hard work and absolute integrity. To these two I would now add a third —courage. I mean moral courage—not afraid to say or do what you believe to be right.

When you bear tremendous responsibilities it is not always easy to live up to these ideals and I fear I have often lagged behind. I also had the mental unrest of seeing certain aspects of the tactical conduct of the Second World War mishandled, and the British people thereby made to endure its horrors longer than should have been the case, with the loss of life which that entailed.

Under these sorts of strains it is difficult to appear always cheerful; one generally has to work off one's irritation on somebody. That "somebody" was my personal staff and I fear that at times they suffered. I am referring to my A.D.C.s, and those who lived at my

Tac H.Q. with me, and not to the staff headed by Freddie de Guingand. There were of course other occasions when they themselves were intensely irritating! But all in all, my personal staff were magnificent; they were all young and few were soldiers by profession; I cannot adequately express my gratitude for the part they so thoroughly and loyally played in such success as we achieved together.

Reference has been made to the team of liaison officers which I organised to keep me in touch with events on the battle front. These were young officers of character, initiative and courage; they had been much fighting and were able to report accurately on battle situations. I selected each one personally, and my standard was high. It was dangerous work and some were wounded, and some killed. They were a gallant band of knights; they had their own Mess at my Tac H.Q. and were well known throughout the Armies I commanded.

Sir Winston Churchill knew them intimately and one of his greatest delights was to sit in my map caravan after dinner at night and hear these young officers tell me the story of what was happening on the battle front. One day towards the end of the war, in April 1945, one was killed (John Poston) and another wounded (Peter Earle); both had been engaged on the same task, given them by me. The Prime Minister heard about it and he sent me a message which ended with the following words:

"I share your grief. Will you kindly convey to their gallant comrades the sympathy which I feel for them and you. This marvellous service of Liaison Officers, whose eyes you know and whose judgments you can exactly measure, will be one of the characteristic features of the manner in which you exercise your superb command of great Armies."

I suppose that by the time I withdrew from active soldiering I had achieved a certain fame—notoriety, anyway! But I had definitely learnt that the road which leads you there is hard and strewn with rocks, and the route to the summit is difficult. He who reaches the top will often be misunderstood and the target for much criticism; this will produce at times a feeling of loneliness, which is accentuated by the fact that those with whom he would most like to talk will often avoid him because of his position. The only policy in high positions is an intense devotion to duty and the unswerving pursuit of the target, in spite of criticism—whispered or in the open. This is what I sought to do.

Much of my life has been concerned with the problem of leadership, and I have already tried to explain how military leadership today needs a somewhat different approach. Two thousand years ago men obeyed automatically because of the " authority " vested in the superior. The centurion in St. Matthew's Gospel clearly thought that because he had authority his soldiers would obey, and he was right. But today the authority has got to be exercised wisely and sensibly, and, if it is *not*, soldiers get restless. The first thing a young officer must do when he joins the Army is to fight a battle, and that battle is for the hearts of his men. If he wins that battle and subsequent similar ones, his men will follow him anywhere; if he loses it, he will never do any real good. The centurion was dealing with regular soldiers who had made the Army their profession; with such disciplined men, the habit of obedience is strong. But in practically all armies today the bulk of the soldiers are National Servicemen. These men do not serve for long and have to be disciplined and taught obedience; some do not take too kindly to it. My experience of the British soldier, Regular or National Service, is that once you have gained his trust and confidence and won his heart, he is easy to lead. In fact, he responds at once to good leadership and likes it.

I got into trouble in March 1947 when I was asked to speak on leadership at the Anniversary Festival Dinner of the London Association of Engineers. The people of Britain had been through a most unpleasant winter, with shortages of everything; we even had to work by candlelight in offices by day because of power cuts, and everyone was getting thoroughly fed up with the Government. In my speech I examined the problem that faced us in Britain at that time, and said that the solution depended on leadership, on the need to pull together as a team, and on hard work. I had the following to say about leadership:

" How do you define leadership?
I would define it as:
' the capacity to rally men and women to a common purpose, and the character which inspires confidence.'
There must be truth in the purpose and will-power in the character.
It is vital today that we should have leaders at all levels in every

walk of life who are able to dominate the events that surround us, and who will never let those events get the better of us or of the Nation.

A leader who cannot do this, but who lets ' events ' dominate him, is useless. The good leader will first study the problem and will then grapple with it."

The Tory Press which was looking for an opportunity to beat up the Labour Government found it in my speech. In point of fact, Government leadership was proving itself unable to dominate the events which encompassed the nation, and we were in a bad way; but I had not that matter in my mind when I wrote my speech.

There was a terrific row, in the Press and in Parliament, and in due course I was summoned to No. 10 and expected the usual ticking off. But Attlee was very decent about it when I had explained my point of view. Not so A. V. Alexander; he accused me of wanting to take over the political leadership of the country—which was nonsense.

Shortly after this excitement I received an invitation from the Wool Textile Industry to deliver the annual address to the Bradford Textile Society, the subject being " leadership." In view of the hullabaloo which followed my remarks on leadership to the London Association of Engineers, I thought I would have some quiet fun. So I wrote to Attlee and asked if he thought it would be of value if I gave the address. He replied that while he thought my address would be most inspiring, he advised me to decline the invitation!

I would like here to make the point that from the time I first met Clement Attlee (now Earl Attlee) in 1943 I have developed a growing respect for his integrity, loyalty and courage. He must have found me an awful nuisance when he was Prime Minister and I was Chief of the Imperial General Staff. But he was very approachable and would always find time to discuss a problem when I sought his advice. He gave decisions readily. And he was absolutely fair; if he administered a rebuke it was deserved.

I have several times had to resist invitations to enter the political field. I do not think that I would make a good politician. War is a pretty rough and dirty game. But politics!

When the war began to near its end, I received one day a letter from Margot Asquith (Lady Oxford) asking me to join the Liberal Party and lead it to better days. I politely declined. About the same

time I received a letter from the Editor of a well-known Sunday
newspaper asking me to write a series of articles for his paper about
what we should all do when the war ended. I replied regretting that
I could not do as he asked and gave the following reason:

> "That subject is nothing whatever to do with me and if I were
> to write about such things it might convey the impression that
> intended to seek a political career. *I have no intention whatsoever
> of doing anything of the sort* and it would be very foolish to get
> mixed up in matters about which I know nothing."

The late Lord Addison, who was Lord Privy Seal in 1948, once
tried to drag me into politics. He wrote to me on the 2nd June 1948
and asked me to go into the division lobby on the side of the Government at the second reading of the Parliament Bill. This was virtually
an invitation by H.M.G. to the C.I.G.S. to participate actively in
politics. I sent the letter at once to Mr. Attlee; he saw the matter
in the proper light and asked me to take no action on the request
had received.

It will be seen that while there were strong currents of opinion
which tried to drag me into politics, I resisted and kept clear—which
I consider was essential while I was serving the Government. The
soldier's allegiance is given to the State and it is not open to him to
change that allegiance because of his political views. When he has
retired, the matter is different; he can then do as he likes in the matter

Most books have their "acknowledgments" at the beginning—
and so has this. But I have still some acknowledgments to pay, and
these are they. As I look back over the years I am constantly
reminded of the extent to which my life has been influenced by four
men—my father in my early life, Field-Marshal Alanbrooke in much
of my military life, and Sir Winston Churchill and General Eisenhower
in the later years. My father's influence has been dealt with in Chapter
1; I must now say something about the other three.

I first got to know Alanbrooke ("Brookie" as he has always been
to me) in 1926 when I went as an instructor to the Staff College
Camberley; he was already there, as instructor in artillery. I quickly
spotted that he was a man of outstanding character and ability, and
my liking and respect for him can be said to have begun then. He
left the Staff College before me and I did not see much of him until
I was commanding the 9th Infantry Brigade at Portsmouth in 1937

he was then Director of Military Training at the War Office. Our really close association began in 1939, when I commanded the 3rd Division in his 2nd Corps, and from that time onwards we were in constant touch until I finally succeeded him as Chief of the Imperial General Staff in June 1946. He was well tuned to my short-comings and often administered a back-hander, sometimes verbally and sometimes in writing ; in neither case could they ever be misunderstood! But I suppose he reckoned I had certain good qualities, otherwise he would not have pushed me along the road in the way he did. He always stood firmly by me when I was in trouble, and his advice was the best I knew. After the war I discovered from my staff that he was their strategic reserve. If I was " hell-bent " on some particular course which they thought ill-advised, the last card they would play was—" Have you consulted the C.I.G.S., sir? " If that ultimate censor had concurred, they knew that the game was up and opposition crumpled.

Brookie is not an easy person to get to know. But once you have managed to penetrate his quiet reserve, you find there the splendid qualities that one is so conscious of lacking oneself.

I remember how angry I was when Eisenhower described him as a person who lacked the ability to weigh up conflicting factors in a problem and, like General Marshall, reach a rock-like decision. My feeling was that in strategic matters Brookie was generally right and Marshall wrong. However, any anger which developed in me against Eisenhower during the war years has long since evaporated; I now have a deep devotion for that great man.

It is my opinion that Alanbrooke and Winston Churchill together did more to ensure that we won the Second World War than any other two men. They were a great pair. And in spite of all that he is and all that he has done, Brookie is the most retiring and modest man I have ever met.

Then there was Winston Churchill. I have described how we first met in the Brighton area in the summer of 1940, after Dunkirk. It has been my privilege and honour to be associated closely with this very great man from that time onwards. We did not always see eye to eye; I doubt if any soldier ever has done with his political chief, and certainly not with that one. But we did not have in the Second World War the rows that developed between soldiers and politicians in the First; that was due to Churchill. It was also due to the fact that we had in existence the British Chiefs of Staff Committee, a constitutional body responsible direct to, and effectively tied-in with the War Cabinet. In the 1914-1918 War we had no such body and one has only to read Lord Beaverbrook's book *Men and Power* to learn of the appalling rows and intrigues which went on between the " Frocks " and the " Brass-hats " in those days.

Whatever may have been his private views, I personally know of no case in which Churchill insisted on his own ideas being carried out once he was opposed by the united British Chiefs of Staff—provided they stood firm and did not retreat when bullied. And they did not retreat.

It has always seemed to me that Winston Churchill combined within himself—within one man—almost all the qualities which we humans can possess, and, as with all humans, they were not by any means all good. Of all his remarkable traits I would put " domination" as the most prominent. He must dominate. He certainly dominated the events and persons surrounding him in the war years, as should all good leaders; you could look out for squalls if he was prevented from doing so. As time went on I ceased to regard him as my political chief. He became my friend. We were " Winston " and " Monty," and so it is today and will be ever after. When he was presented with his portrait by the Cinque Ports, he being the Lord Warden, I was asked to attend the ceremony and propose his health—I being Freeman of Hastings (where the ceremony took place) and also of Dover. The speech I then made explains better than anything else can say what I feel about Winston Churchill. It went as follows:

" I have been given the great honour of proposing the toast of the Lord Warden, and nothing could be a greater pleasure. During the late war Sir Winston Churchill was my Chief; as we got to know each other, he became my friend; today he is chief among all my friends.

As Lord Warden he holds the Office of Admiralty within the Cinque Ports.

I would like to remind him that I once served as his shipmate in an operation of war, when we crossed the Rhine together in a naval craft in March 1945 and later got heavily shelled for our misdeeds. It was he who suggested we should make the crossing!

The association between the Cinque Ports and Sir Winston

Churchill, which has reached so charming a climax today, is singularly appropriate. For what could be more suitable than that the towns which once provided most of the men and ships for the King's Navy should know and harbour a ' Former Naval Person ' ? In far off but still memorable days the Ports and their Lord Warden were the active practitioners of that eternal vigilance which is the price of freedom.

In much more recent and even more memorable days, the present Lord Warden showed himself to be the incarnation of the traditional spirit and duty of the Ports. To him more than to any other man we owe the fact that the citadel of freedom was kept inviolate.

This is one of the occasions, I think, on which it is right and proper to break through the reserve of the English heart, and to say in that tongue of which he is so unquestioned a master why it is that his portrait exists not only on canvas but also in the souls of free men throughout the world, and in the souls of many not so free.

First, because he is a Man.

There is not one of us who has had the privilege of sharing his work and his thoughts who cannot say with Mark Antony:

'He was my friend, faithful and just to me.'

He has seen, undismayed, truth ' twisted by knaves to make a trap for fools.'

He has met ' with Triumph and Disaster ' with equal serenity.

He has filled every ' unforgiving minute ' with ' sixty seconds' worth of distance run.'

The capacity to do these things was Kipling's definition of a Man. He qualifies.

Let me remind you of his own prescription for conduct in the great adventure of life:

      In War: Resolution.
      In Defeat: Defiance.
      In Victory: Magnanimity.
      In Peace: Goodwill.

Surely he has practised what he thus preached.

It may seem strange to some of you to hear a soldier praising a politician! The two professions have not always hit it off. Indeed, this politician deliberately abandoned my profession at an early age. I am grateful, because if he had not it might have been he who won at Alamein.

But whatever the soldier may sometimes in his wrath say about the politician, I would exempt this particular one. For he redeemed himself by being often and for long periods the politician who was best hated by other politicians. I am told that some of them called him ' turn-coat,' ' untrustworthy,' even ' lacking in judgment.'

How small, how shame-faced, they must feel today?

We soldiers think of him as Wordsworth's happy warrior, ' that every man in arms should wish to be.' I would like to repeat to you some of the lines.

> ' 'Tis, finally, the Man, who, lifted high,
> Conspicuous object in a nation's eye,
> Or left unthought of in obscurity—
> Who, with a toward or untoward lot,
> Prosperous or adverse, to his wish or not—
> Plays, in the many games of life, that one
> Where what he most doth value must be won.'

It seems to me that these words exactly fit Sir Winston.

And what is it that the Lord Warden

> ' most doth value '?

Here again a soldier finds a kindred spirit in the definition which he himself has given of the aims and purposes of his career:

> ' The maintenance of the enduring greatness of Britain, and the historical continuity of our island life.'

But we are met to commemorate not only what he did to win wars, but also what he did to prevent them. And therefore I would add what he said only a few years ago:

> ' Peace is the last prize I seek to win.'

Nobody knows better than a soldier the overwhelming value of that prize—because nobody knows better than a soldier the monster called War.

Nobody knows better than a British soldier how a strong Britain and an untarnished British spirit are the prime ingredients of peace.

A few final words about the Lord Warden in one other capacity— that of a national leader in times of crisis.

Our British leaders are not ' Fuhrers,' ' Duces,' or Cæsars. They are potent, but not potentates; guides, not dictators; too human to pretend to be super-human. They do not put themselves above the rules. Power does not go to their heads. They receive it with

modesty; they lose it with resignation, if not with exhilaration.
But when weighed in the balance they are not found wanting.
Never has any land found any leader who so matched the hour as
did Sir Winston Churchill.
When he spoke—in words that rang and thundered like the Psalms
—we all said:

'That is how *we* feel'
and
'That is how we shall bear ourselves.'

He gave us the sense of being a dedicated people with a high
purpose and an invincible destiny. There was—there is—a moral
magnificence about him which transforms the lead of lesser men
into gold; he inspired us all.
He was once good enough to refer to me as a Cromwellian figure
no doubt because I have always tried both to praise the Lord and
to pass the ammunition. Let me therefore conclude with the words
which Cromwell used about the men whom the State chooses to
serve her:

'So that they render good service, that satisfies.'

Sir, you have rendered good service.
Sir, we are satisfied.
I give you the toast of:

Sir Winston Churchill

Knight of the Most Noble Order of the Garter, Lord Warden of
the Cinque Ports, the greatest Englishman of all time."

And last is Eisenhower, a remarkable and most lovable man. I
first met Ike in the spring of 1942, in England, but only for a few
minutes and he made no great impression on me at that time. The next
occasion was in Tunisia in April 1943. The Eighth Army, having
fought its way from Alamein, was about to join hands with his forces
which had landed in North Africa in November 1942. I was now
under his command. This time he stayed a night with me and made
a very definite impression. He had never seen a shot fired in war till
the landings in North Africa on the 8th November 1942, and he had
never before commanded troops in battle. We talked much and I
was greatly impressed by his quick grasp of a problem and by the way
he radiated confidence and kindness. He was a very heavy smoker
in those days and at breakfast in our mess tent he lit a cigarette before

I had begun the meal. We were sitting together and I at once moved my seat to the other side of the table. He quickly sensed that I did not like smoke circulating around me at meal times and apologised, throwing away his cigarette!

I remained under his command from those days until the end of the German war in May 1945. The reader will have noted that we did not always agree about the strategy and major tactics of the war in which we were engaged. But history will do no harm in talking about honest differences of opinion between us, provided, as in our case was the fact, it does so under the shadow of the great truth that Allied co-operation in Europe during the Second World War was brought to the greatest heights it has ever attained. Although it may be true to say that no one man could have been responsible for such an achievement, the major share of the credit goes to Eisenhower —without any doubt.

I would not class Ike as a great soldier in the true sense of the word. He might have become one if he had ever had the experience of exercising direct command of a division, corps, and army—which unfortunately for him did not come his way. But he was a great Supreme Commander—a military statesman. I know of no other person who could have welded the Allied forces into such a fine fighting machine in the way he did, and kept a balance among the many conflicting and disturbing elements which threatened at times to wreck the ship.

It was not until the war was over that I began to know him really well, and also his charming wife Mamie. He was then Chief of Staff, United States Army, and I was C.I.G.S. I stayed with him in Washington in October 1946 and we had long talks about the post-war world. Later, in 1951 and 1952, we served together in Europe again—he as Supreme Commander of the NATO forces and I as his Deputy. Then he went away to become President of the United States of America. I have visited him regularly since he has been in office, always staying with him and Mamie—either in the White House or in his home at Gettysburg. Our friendship has grown and developed, and today I have the very greatest admiration and affection for him. I have read a good deal of American history and it is my belief that historians will record that Ike reached his greatest heights as President of the U.S.A. Where does his strength lie? He has a good brain and is very intelligent. But his real strength lies in hi human qualities; he is a very great human being. He has the power of drawing the hearts of men towards him as a magnet attracts the bits of metal. He merely has to smile at you, and you trust him at once. He is the very incarnation of sincerity. He has great common sense. People and nations give him their confidence. Whenever I go to Washington I visit the Lincoln Memorial, where Abraham Lincoln sits in an imposing setting looking out over the city. I never visit that Memorial without gaining inspiration; it is the same when I visit Ike. He has tried to be the President of *all* Americans, irrespective of party or politics. I am devoted to him, and would do anything for him. He is a truly great man, and it is a tremendous honour to have his friendship. He has done a great deal for me, in difficult times and in good, and I can never adequately express what I owe to his personal kindness and forbearance.

During my life abroad since the autumn of 1948 it was my privilege to get to know intimately the Prime Ministers and Cabinets of the Western Powers. I was constantly on the move between Norway and Turkey, and crossed the Atlantic every year to visit the United States and Canada. When I returned to England from the Eighth Army in January 1944, an accurate log book began to be kept of my air travels. The log shows that from January 1944 to September 1958 I have flown over 400,000 miles, and my flying hours have been over 2200. It has been hard work, but possibly my contribution to the cause of peace has been of some value.

I count among my friends such differing personalities as His Holiness the Pope and Marshal Tito, both of whom I have visited often. I value greatly my friendship with Dr. Salazar, Prime Minister of Portugal. With such friends all over the Western world, it is obvious that I must have led a very full life and learnt much that I did not know before. My contacts with so many nations have led me to certain conclusions.

Each nation has its own views on certain matters, which must be understood and respected by the others. You can't sell refrigerators to the Eskimos. Again, American boys are brought up to believe certain things; they grow up in the shadow of those beliefs, and nothing will ever change them. The British people will never follow a dominant personality, or leader, unless they are frightened; at other times they are frightened about where he may lead them. Winston Churchill is a good example.

Over all, the true and ultimate strength of a nation does not li
in its armed forces. It lies in the national character, in its people, i
their capacity to work, in their virility.

Surveying then the international field, it seems to me that a natio
needs two things if it is to survive and not become engulfed i
centralised control and mediocrity. Those two things, which are basi
and fundamental, are:

(a) A religion.
(b) An educated *élite*, who are not afraid to take an independen
line of thought and action and who will not merely follow th
" popular cry."

Perhaps I had better explain what I mean by a religion. The out
standing influence in my life has been a deep sense of religious truth
It can best be expressed by quoting the last sentences of my address a
the unveiling of the Alamein Memorial in the desert on the 24t
October 1954:

" And let us remember when all these things are said and done
that one great fact, the greatest fact, remains supreme and un
assailable. It is this. There are in this world things that are tru
and things that are false; there are ways that are right and way
that are wrong; there are men good, and men bad. And on on
side or the other we must take our stand; one or the other w
must serve.

A great Commander once dismissed his troops after a long campaig
with these words:

' *Choose you this day whom ye will serve; as for me and my hous
we will serve the Lord.*' Joshua 24, 1

These words seem to me to be the foundation of the whole matte
and it is my belief that they ought to be impressed on every youn
person from the earliest days. We can only secure a better world
and abolish war, by having better men and women; there is n
other way and no short cut."

The last word in the Foreword to this book is " truth." I hav
tried to write the truth. I suppose everyone claims that about h
memoirs! Most official accounts of past wars are deceptively we
written, and seem to omit many important matters—in particula

anything which might indicate that any of our commanders ever made the slightest mistake. They are therefore useless as a source of instruction. They remind me of the French general's reply to a British protest in 1918, when the former directed the British to take over a sector from the French which had already been overrun by the Germans forty-eight hours previously. The French General said: " *Mais, mon ami, ça c'est pour l'histoire.*"

This book is not written " *pour l'histoire,*" in that sense.

I withdrew from active employment in the Army in September 1958, after fifty years of continuous duty in the service of my Sovereign, without a break of any sort. This is a long time. Since 1855, when the War Office came into existence and the Board of Ordnance was abolished, no officer has served longer. Lord Roberts had a span of 52 years between the date of his commission and his laying down of the office of Commander-in-Chief in 1904; but there was a period in the '90s when he was not employed and, what is more, his early service was not with the forces of the Crown but with the East India Company. I understand that in the eighteenth century there are one or two examples of service longer than mine from the Board of Ordnance. But they were in a rather special position and, in general, commissions in the seventeenth and eighteenth centuries could be held by officers at most unseasonable ages!

However, I am informed that despite the conditions of those times my service still exceeds that of Wellington, Marlborough and Monck.

I will conclude my military service by paying homage to the British soldier, my friend and comrade-in-arms during all those years.

The British soldier is second to none in the communities of fighting men. Some may possess more *élan*, others may be better disciplined; but none excels him in all-round character. We require no training in bravery in Britain; we can trust to our own native manliness to see us through. So it is with the soldier. It is his natural pride which gives him his fighting qualities. How often he has stood firm before tyranny and oppression, the last hope of the free world! In the midst of the noise and confusion of the battlefield, the simple homely figure of the British soldier stands out calm and resolute—dominating all around him with his quiet courage, his humour and his cheerfulness, his unflinching acceptance of the situation. May the ideals for which he has struggled never vanish from the world! May he never be forgotten by the nation for which he has fought so nobly! I know better than most to what heights the British soldier can aspire. His greatness is a measure of the greatness of the British character, and I have seen the quality of our race proved again and again on the battlefield.

I shall take away many impressions into the evening of life. But the one which I shall treasure above all is the picture of the British soldier—staunch and tenacious in adversity, kind and gentle in victory —the man to whom the nation has again and again, in the hour of adversity, owed its safety and its honour.

INDEX

INDEX

Aachen, 266, 297

Abadan, 424

Abdullah, King of Trans-Jordan, 424

Addison, Lord, 534

Africa, Montgomery's tour of, 462-465

Africa, North: plans for landing in, 77, 177; topography of, 91-92; campaign in, 107-169, 170-172, 182; prisoners in, 140, 144, 163-164, 165; as an air base, 436

Africa, South, 462, 464

Agedabia, 141, 142

Agheila, 91-92, 110, 160; pursuit to, 140-145; Battle of, 146-147, 157

Air battle, essential before landings in OVERLORD, 212, 247

AIR FORCE, GERMAN: attacks Allied airfields, 310; failure to support army, 312

AIR FORCE, ROYAL: component with B.E.F., 53; Advanced Air Striking Force, 53-54; Battle of Normandy, 242, 247, 248, 255, 256-257; Ardennes, 313; Montgomery's message to, on German surrender, 343-344; close army co-operation with, 434; threatened reductions in, 480

DESERT AIR FORCE, 109, 122, 135-136, 140-141, 143, 144, 147, 157, 161, 162-163, 176, 181, 187, 206, 207, 256

STRATEGIC AIR FORCE, 200

TACTICAL AIR FORCES, 157, 163, 257, 313

Air lift, in Ruhr advance, 274

Air power: in Eighth Army, 109, 140-141, 143, 144, 147, 157, 161, 162-163, 176, 179-181; long-range killing

weapon, 141, 143; integration with land power at Mareth, 163; in Sicily, 176, 179, 180-181; in peace-time, 237

Air support: Eighth Army, 206; Italian campaign, 193, 200; OVERLORD, 220, 242, 247

Airborne forces: American near Rome, 194; in Normandy landings, 220; in advance to Rhine, 274, 276, 281, 303; at Arnhem, 282, 288, 291-292, 295-298; under 21 Army Group, 325, 329; PLUNDER, 329

Airfields: in North Africa, 122, 140-141, 147; Italy, 196, 200, 203; Sicily, 175, 177-178, 179, 180-181, 185, 187; Normandy, 222, 254, 255, 256-257; Holland and Belgium, 310; occupied Germany, 385

Alam Halfa, 104-105; Battle of, 105, 107-115, 116, 117, 158, 159; "turning point" in desert war, 110, 139

Alamein, 101, 103, 104-105

Alamein, Battle of, 116-139, 162; plan for, 118-120; "crumbling" process in, 119, 129-131; deception plan, 121-122; Royal Air Force in, 122, 135; secrecy in, 124; grouping of divisions for, 125; Operation SUPERCHARGE in, 132-137; "staff information" service in, 137-138; lessons of, 138-139; first anniversary of, 200-201; memorial unveiled, 542

Alamein to the River Sangro (Montgomery), 128, 184, 350, 408, 447

Alanbrooke, Viscount—*see* Brooke, Field-Marshal Sir Alan

Albert Canal, 60, 275

Aldershot, 51

DIVISIONS, INFANTRY, *continued*

4th Indian: Battle of Alamein, 125; Tunisia, 162, 165

5th: Battle of France, 61

8th: Arab rebellion, 46-47, 48, 99

9th Australian: Battle of Alamein, 125, 131, 132, 136

44th: Egypt, 104; Battle of Alamein, 125

47th (London): First World War, 36

49th: 291

50th: Battle of France, 61; Battle of Alamein, 125; Sicily, 172

51st Highland: Battle of Alamein, 125; advance to Tripoli, 146, 154, 156, 157; Sicily, 172; Havre, 291

56th: Sicily, 172

78th: Sicily, 172

BRIGADES, ARMOURED

7th: 135

9th: 125, 132

23rd: 125

201st Guards: 160, 165

BRIGADES, INFANTRY

9th: 43, 44, 45, 47

10th: 32-34

17th: 39-40

131st (Queen's): 135

Rocket: 329

REGIMENTS

11TH HUSSARS, 96

ROYAL HORSE ARTILLERY: Rocket Troop in, 329-330

GRENADIER GUARDS, 160

ROYAL WARWICKSHIRE, 26, 27-35, 42-43

ROYAL NORFOLK, 96

ROYAL HAMPSHIRE, 99

ROYAL ULSTER RIFLES, 69

COMMANDOS: raid on Dieppe, 75-77

ARMY, CANADIAN: raid on Dieppe, 75-77; standardisation of weapons with U.S. and Britain, 438, 449-450

ARMY, FIRST: in Normandy, 214-215, 222, 262; at Antwerp, 284, 290-291, 297; Scheldt estuary, 289; Channel ports, 290-291; Reichswald Offensive, 323; PLUNDER, 328; use of rockets, 330

DIVISIONS, INFANTRY

1st: Sicily, 183, 184-185

2nd: Dieppe, 75-77

3rd: 397

ARMY, FRENCH: B.E.F. under (1939), 52-54; chain of command, 54-58; breakdown of communications, 56-57; Montgomery's fears about, 59; collapse of, 62, 65-66

ARMY GROUP

No. 1: 54, 57

ARMIES

FIRST, 54, 56, 57

SECOND, 54

SEVENTH, 54-56

NORTH, 54, 57

ARMY, GERMAN: advance (May 1940), 57, 60-62; in Desert, 92 *et seq.*; Italians in, 92, 120, 132, 137, 138-139, 140, 144, 147; Rommel's "corsetting" of, 120, 132; defeated in North Africa, 116-169, 240; prisoners taken in, 144, 163-164, 165, 166, 284, 301, 328, 333, 345; in Sicily, 175, 182, 186, 188; in Italy, 193, 195-196; bets concerning, 214; in France, 220, 235-236, 241-242, 252-264, 265 *et seq.*; strength in Normandy, 259; losses in Battle of Normandy, 263; shows signs of collapse, 265; defence of Berlin approaches, 277; disorganisation not fully exploited, 285; loss of mobility, 302, 303; regains initiative in Ardennes, 307; casualties

organisation from Tactical H.Q. in Eighth Army, 167-168; Montgomery and Eisenhower differ over system of, 267-269, 316-320, 324-326; nationalism in, 316, 319; and operational control, 317-320, 322, 324-326; overall commander needed, 316, 317-319; High Command in war, 347-354; administration, 349; Chief of Staff system, 434

Commanders: and decision, 81-82, 349; and conference, 82; selection of, 85-86, 348; and immersion in detail, 86-87, 349; and master plan, 87-88; and religious truth, 90, 542; monetary grants to, 347-348; and inner conviction, 352-354

Communications: inadequate in B.E.F., 50, 56-57; inadequate at Eisenhower's H.Q., 271, 272; in occupied Germany, 356, 357, 368

Communism: propaganda in British Zone, 381, 414; spread to West, 506

Condé-sur-Noireau, 268, 282

Conference, during active operations, 82

Congress Party, India, 425

Coningham, Air Marshal Sir Arthur, 109, 141, 157, 163, 256-257

Copenhagen, 358

Corbett, Lieut.-Gen. T. W., 93

Cork, 39, 70

Corps Districts, in British Zone oₗ Germany, 358, 401-3

"Corsetting" of German troops, 120, 132

Cossac, Operation, 256, 502-503

Coulet, M., 264

Coutances, 257, 258

Crawford, General Sir Kenneth, 427

Creasy, Admiral (now Admiral of the Fleet Sir George), G .E., 213, 214

Creech Jones, Rt. Hon. Arthur, 463, 466-467, 469, 470

Crerar, Gen. H. D. G., 214-215, 284, 308, 358

Crete, 141

Creuilly, 253

Cripps, Sir Stafford, 477

Crocker, Lieut.-Gen. J. T., 359

Cromwell, Oliver, 352, 353

Crowe, Sir Edward, 42

"Crumbling" operations, 119, 126, 129-131

Crusade in Europe (Eisenhower), 289

Cunningham, General Sir Alan, 467-468, 470, 472

Cunningham, Admiral of the Fleet Sir Andrew (now Viscount Cunningham of Hyndhope), 176, 177, 187, 188, 192, 342

Cunningham, Admiral of the Fleet Sir John, 418, 504

Cuxhaven, 358

Cyprus, 422, 427

Cyrenaica, 141, 143

Czechoslovakia, 332, 393, 399

D-Day (Normandy): selection of, 234, 238, 246-247, 248-249; postponed 24 hours, 248

Dakota aircraft, Montgomery's, 185, 208, 213, 310

Dawnay, Lieut.-Col., 215, 216, 233

Deception plans, Alamein, 117, 121-122

Defence: British-Canadian-U.S. co-operation, 438, 440, 441-443; beginning of European co-operation, 498-505 (see also Western Union); high costs of, 521, 523; means of reducing cost, 522, 523-524; and surprise, 522; and mobilisation, 522

Defence, Minister for Co-ordination of, 491

Defence, Ministry of: and Joint Planning Staff, 488; and Chiefs of Staff, 491-497; Chief of Staff for Minister, 493, 494, 497; Sandys at, 497
Defence in depth, 74-75
Defence organisation: Chiefs of Staff and, 487-497; weakness of committee system, 489-490; Montgomery's suggested improvements in, 493-497
Delhi, 425-426, 457
Dempsey, Gen. Sir M. C., 207, 208, 284; takes over 13 Corps, 141; Sicily campaign, 175; commands Second Army, 218, 358; Battle of Normandy, 222, 249, 256, 259, 260, 261; and Arnhem, 274, 276, 288, 297; Ardennes, 308; Palestine, 467, 470
Denmark, 332, 334; German forces surrender, 336, 337, 339, 358
Details, danger of immersion in, 86-87
Deventer, 290, 291
Deverell, General Sir Cyril, 39
Devers, General J. L., 300, 301
Dewing, Major-Gen. R. H., 358
Dieppe, raid on, 75-77
Dill, General (now Field-Marshal) Sir John, 38, 51, 52, 64, 67
Displaced Persons, 345, 318-382, 391
Doenitz, Admiral, 334, 355
Domburg, 284
Dominion Prime Ministers, Conference of (1946), 456
Domitz, 333, 335
Douai, 274
DRAGOON, Operation, 221, 266, 267, 271, 331
Dresden, 277, 278
Druval, Madame de, 253-254
Dunkirk: evacuation from, 62-66, 194, 290, 308, 450; Treaty of, 506
Duren, 303
Dusseldorf, 323

Dyle, River, 58, 60

Earle, Peter, 531
Eden, Rt. Hon. Sir Anthony, 392
Egypt, 465; Alexander in, 77, 78; Montgomery ordered to, 78, 93; defence of, 101, 140; Germans driven from, 129-143, 148; Treaty negotiations, 420-422, 476
Eindhoven, 307, 316
Eisenhower, General Dwight D. (now President), 77, 172, 188, 205, 270, 299, 383, 435, 442; Montgomery's first meeting with, 74; C.-in-C. North Africa, 157; and gift of aircraft to Montgomery, 164, 185, 310; and plans for Sicily, 174, 178, 181, 182, 188-189; bets on end of war, 188, 214; and Italian campaign, 192-193, 194; Supreme Commander for Second Front, 204; and OVERLORD plan, 210, 220, 236, 247-249; and ANVIL, 221; postpones D-Day for 24 hours, 248; in Normandy, 251; his report on campaign,255; persuadedof Montgomery's defensive-mindedness, 256, 260-261, 263; belief in constant aggressive action, 262; differs from Montgomery in conduct of war, 262; insists on "broad front" strategy, 267-269, 271-274, 277-286; and Saar thrust, 275-276; and Berlin thrust, 277-282, 331; plans for Rhineland campaign, 280-284, 304-306, 321-323; and MARKET GARDEN, 289, 296-297; and Ruhr campaign, 293-294, 296; his humanity, 293; Maastricht Conference, 301, 304-306; and Ardennes offensive, 308, 309-310; British Press criticism of, 310, 314, 319; Montgomery's tribute to, 314; and command problem, 316-320, 324-326; changed opinion on importance of

in Europe, 499-500; and command in Western Union, 502

Kairouan, 187
Kassel, 304, 305, 306
Keitel, Field-Marshal W., 334, 335, 337
Kenya, 462
Kiel, 277
King, Rt. Hon. W. L. Mackenzie, 437, 438, 440-441
Kinzel, General, 335, 337, 340
Kipling, Rudyard, 71, 537
Kirkman, General Sir Sidney, 113-114
Kluge, Field-Marshal Günther von, 263
Knocke, 284
Koniev, Marshal T., 449

La Panne, 62-64
Lancing College, 69
Landing-craft: for AVALANCHE, 191; for BAYTOWN, 192; for OVERLORD, 212, 220, 221
Laon, 266
Lascelles, Rt. Hon. Sir Alan, 270
Laval, 268
Lawson, Rt. Hon. John (now Lord), 430
Le Bény Bocage, 266
Le Cateau, 32
Leadership, Montgomery's doctrine of, 80-90, 123, 348, 531-533
Lear, Mrs. A. D., 327-328
Leclerc, Major-Gen. P. E., 157, 366
Leese, Lieut.-Gen. Sir Oliver, 155, 177; commands 30 Corps, 113, 141; Battle of Alamein, 118, 130, 140; Sicily, 175; takes over Eighth Army, 205, 208
Lefroy, Captain, 31
Leigh-Mallory, Air Chief Marshal Sir Trafford, 257
Leipzig, 277, 278, 329, 330
Lenk, 42

Leopold II, ex-King of Belgians, 54; surrenders Army, 61
Leopold Canal, 284
Leverkusen, 290
Liaison officers, system of, 36, 89, 138, 308, 531
LIGHTFOOT, Operation, 126-128. See also Alamein
Lille, 58
Lindemann, General, 358
Lindsay, Major-Gen. Sir George, 39
Lippe Canal, 303
Locomotives, for Ruhr advance, 273, 274
Loire, River, 266
London, passim; 21 Army Group H.Q. in, 213, 217, 223, 234; bombing of, 213; OVERLORD planning H.Q. in, 218, 221, 247; Docks, Montgomery visits, 225
Long Range Desert Group, 160
Longwy, 54
Looting: Montgomery accused of, 264; in occupied Germany, 357
Lorraine, 300
Louvain, 58, 60-61, 271, 310
Lübeck, 277, 332, 333
Luce, R. W., 387
Lumsden, Lieut.-Gen. Herbert, 113, 118, 129, 130, 141-142
Lüneburg Heath, German surrender at, 334-340
Lush, Brigadier, 154
Luxembourg, 305, 307, 499, 507
Lydda, 426
Lyne, Major-Gen. L. O., 358

Maastricht, 290; conference at, 301-306, 318
MacArthur, General Douglas, 461
Macdonald, Colonel C. R., 26
McKell, Rt. Hon. Sir William, 459

Norstad, General Lauris, 516
North Atlantic Treaty, 506, 508; Organisation—*see* NATO
Norton, Sir Clifford, 427
" Notes on Command in Western Europe" (Montgomery), 316
Nuclear deterrents, 516-518, 526
Nurnberg, 277, 278, 279
Nursing sisters, 348

O'Connor, Lieut.-Gen. Sir Richard, 288
Officers: and tradition, 27-28; German general's classification of, 38; effect of Geddes axe on, 40; "dead wood" among, 72; wives and families of, not to accompany units, 72-73; selection of, 85-86; liaison, 89, 138, 308, 531
OMAHA Beach, 251, 252, 258
Operation Victory (de Guingand), 128, 130
Opladen, 290
Oran, 132
Orleans, 266
Orne, River, 222, 260
Orsoy, 303, 305
Osnabrück, 292
Ottawa, 438
OVERLORD, Operation: planning of, 210-213, 218-250; crisis of European war, 220; plan for development after landing, 222-223, 254-255; fixing of D-Day, 234, 238, 246-249; exercises for, 234; tactical instructions for, 234-236; weather conditions, 246-249, 257; execution of, 251-264; misunderstandings about, 255-257, 260-263

Pachino Peninsula, 173, 174, 175, 177, 180
Pacific Ocean, 459; South-West, 240
Paget, General Sir Bernard, 41, 71, 76, 77, 228, 426; Montgomery succeeds in 21

Army Group, 203, 216-217; C.-in-C. Middle East, 217, 421
Pakistan, 457
Palermo, 174, 177, 181, 185, 188
Palestine, 42-43, 421, 466-475; Arab rebellion (1938), 46-48; possible. Eighth Army withdrawal to, 94; terrorism in, 423-424, 426, 466-473; United Nations and, 471-472; Britain ends Mandate, 471-475
Palestine Police Force, 423, 467, 468
Panzer Battles (Von Mellenthin), 110
Paratroops: eliminated from Dieppe raid, 76; German, at Alamein, 120; Allied, in MARKET GARDEN, 288, 291-292, 295-298
Paris, 222, 223; liberated, 265; British Military Exhibition in, 365; SHAPE in, 513-517; NATO Council in, 521
Pas de Calais, 266, 274
Passchendaele, 35-36
Patton, General George, 185, 276, 289, 332; bets with Montgomery, 215; Battle of Normandy, 223; comments on British, 262; advance to Metz, 269, 272, 281, 297; favours double thrust, 289; and advance into Germany, 300-301
Périers, 258
Persia, 93, 424-425, 476
Peshawar, 26, 27-30
Philippines, 240
Pilsen, 332
Pipeline, dummy, 122
Pius XII, Pope, 541
Plumer, Viscount, 35
PLUNDER, Operation, 328-330
Pola, 428
Poland, 378; invaded, 49, 58; partition of, 391; population transfer, 393, 399
Polish Parachute Brigade, 288
Pollek, Colonel, 335, 340

Taormina, 184, 188-189

Taranto, 195, 196

Tarhuna, 154

Tasmania: Montgomery family in, 18, 19; Montgomery revisits, 458

Tedder, Air Chief Marshal Sir Arthur (later Marshal of the Royal Air Force Lord), 248, 275, 418, 503; and air support at Alam Halfa, 109; C.-in-C. all air forces in Mediterranean, 157; and Sicily, 176, 177, 187, 188; and Battle of Normandy, 257; and co-ordination of air operations, 323-324, 326; dispute with Minister of Defence, 483, 484-485

Tel Aviv, 466

Tell el Aqqaqir, 134

Templer, Lieut.-Col. (now Field-Marshal Sir) Gerald, 57

Ten Chapters (Montgomery), 345

Termoli, 196

Terneuzen, 284

Territorial Army, 481

Thermopylae, 100

TIGER, Exercise, 74

Tilburg, 291

Tito, Marshal, 201, 429, 541

Tobruk, 91, 92, 109, 143, 152, 153, 156

TORCH, Operation, 77, 117, 132

Tozer, Mrs. M. E., 233-234

Trade unions, in occupied Germany, 382, 396, 407, 414

Trafalgar, Battle of, 353

Trans-Jordan, 422, 424

Transport: inadequate in Field Army, 50; aircraft for, in Ruhr advance, 274; concentration of, 276; in occupied Germany, 356, 357, 368

Trapani, 175

Trench-foot disease, 299, 327

Trenchard, Marshal of the Royal Air Force, Viscount, 490-491, 493

Trigno, River, 196

Tripoli, 91, 92, 132, 140, 141, 143, 148, 187, 198; plans for advance on, 149-150, 152-154; Eighth Army in, 154-158; Churchill visits, 156; King George VI visits, 183-184

Triumph and Tragedy (Churchill), 36

Troyes, 266

Truman, Harry S., 80, 385, 442-443; at Potsdam, 392, 441

Tunis, 150, 161, 188; capture of, 165

Tunisia, 157-169; Eighth Army in, 159-169, 170-172, 173, 175

Turkey, 240, 508

Turnhout, 291

Uden, 288

Ukraine, 455

" Unconditional surrender," mistake of, 356

UNIFORCE, 508, 513

United Nations Organisation, 451, 519, 520, 528; and Palestine, 471, 472, 475

United States: Press criticism of British forces, 260-261; and zoning of Germany, 377-381, 385; and rebuilding of Germany, 388; Montgomery visits, 437, 440-443; defence co-operation with Britain and Canada, 438, 440, 441-443; and Western Union, 499; and Marshall Aid, 506-507; European suspicion of, 512; and world leadership, 528

Urquhart, Major-Gen. R. E., 295

Utrecht, 291

V2 rockets, 274, 275

Vassilievsky, Marshal, 446, 449, 452, 453, 454